PELICAN BOOKS

THE NEW FRANCE

John Ardagh was born in Malawi, East Africa, in 1928, the son of a colonial civil servant. He was educated at Sherborne School and at Worcester College, Oxford, where he took an honours degree in classics and philosophy. After a year as a reporter in the provinces he joined *The Times* in 1953, and from 1955 to 1959 was a staff correspondent in Paris and in Algeria. It was during this time that he began his love-hate relationship with the French, and formed the idea of writing a book about changes in France that could not easily be summed up in newspaper articles. Back in England, he worked for a while in television news, then spent five years on the *Observer*, writing mainly about the arts. He was managing editor of *The Good Food Guide* from 1966 to 1968, and now devotes himself to free-lancing and writing books. Besides working for the BBC and French radio, he is a frequent contributor to such papers as *The Times*, *Sunday Times*, *Sunday Telegraph Magazine*, *Spectator*, *New Society*, *Washington Post* and *Le Point*. He is about to publish a book on five European provincial cities, and is now working on a definitive study of France during the German Occupation, in collaboration with the University of Sussex.

His special interests include the cinema and gastronomy, and he is devoted to almost every aspect of French life. He lives in Kensington, is married to a publisher, and has one son, Nicholas, born in 1957.

John Ardagh

THE NEW FRANCE

THIRD EDITION

Penguin Books
in association with Martin Secker & Warburg

Penguin Books Ltd, Harmondsworth, Middlesex, England
Penguin Books, 625 Madison Avenue,
New York, New York 10022, U.S.A.
Penguin Books Australia Ltd, Ringwood, Victoria, Australia
Penguin Books Canada Ltd, 2801 John Street,
Markham, Ontario, Canada L3R 1B4
Penguin Books (N.Z.) Ltd, 182–190 Wairau Road,
Auckland 10, New Zealand

—

First published as *The New French Revolution* by Martin Secker & Warburg 1968
Revised edition published in Pelican Books 1970
Second edition 1973
Reprinted 1974
Third edition 1977
Reprinted 1978

—

Copyright © John Ardagh, 1968, 1970, 1973, 1977
All rights reserved

—

Made and printed in Great Britain by
Cox & Wyman Ltd, London Reading and Fakenham
Set in Monotype Times Roman

CONTENTS

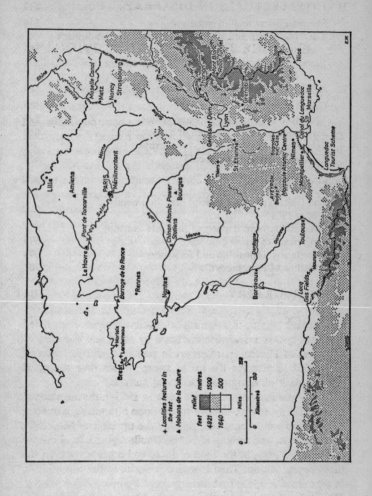

Rhine
Moselle Canal
Meuse
Nancy
Metz
Strasbourg
Nice
Lille
Amiens
PARIS
Ménilmontant
Seine
Pont de Tancarville
Le Havre
Loire
Bourges
Chinon Atomic Power Stations
Vienne
St. Etienne
Tarn
Lyon
Rhône
Grenoble
Mont Blanc
Durance
Nîmes
Montpellier
Marcoule Atomic Centre
Canal du Languedoc
Marseille
Languedoc Tourist Scheme
Barrage de la Rance
Rennes
Nantes
Toulouse
Garonne
Dordogne
Lacq Gas Fields
Bordeaux
Brest
Morlaix
Landerneau

+ Localities featured in the text
▲ Maisons de la Culture

relief
feet   metres
4921   1500
1640   500

Miles
0   150
Kilometres
0   250

PREFACE TO THE THIRD EDITION

THIS is not a book about politics, nor about de Gaulle and Giscard d'Estaing. It is a book about French society in transition. In other countries, and especially in Britain, public opinion during the 1960s so often identified France with de Gaulle and his foreign policies that the rest of the complex French scene tended to pass unnoticed. But de Gaulle was not typical of modern France. He was not greatly interested in domestic affairs and had little direct influence on them save to provide continuity of government. Only in a rare moment of crisis, like that which forced itself upon him in May 1968, would he descend from the heights to pay much attention to the desires and frustrations of the mass French public.

Therefore I have given de Gaulle little space in a book that is essentially about the lives of ordinary Frenchmen. I have also largely ignored French party politics and constitutional affairs – not because I think them unimportant, but because this ground has already been covered many times by other Anglo-American observers of France, more expert in politics than me. Instead I have tried to describe the broad sweep of post-war change at grass-roots level, economic, social and cultural.

I wrote the first edition of this book in 1966–7, during a period of great calm and stability in France. Soon afterwards, a number of dramatic events occurred, notably the uprising of May 1968, and the defeat and resignation of de Gaulle a year later. I revised this book in 1969, in the light of these and other events, for the first Pelican edition. Then I revised it again, at the end of 1972, to take account of the first three years of Pompidou's presidency. The book may help to explain why the May uprising took place, and how it has intensified the real problems that still lie beneath the surface of France's growing prosperity and renewed stability.

For this third Pelican edition, I have now extensively revised the book yet again, in the summer and autumn of 1976, to take account of the first two-and-a-bit years of Giscard's regime. This edition assesses the reforms that Giscard has been able to carry through, as well as the impact on France of the post-1973 world economic crisis, and the subtle change of climate in France now that 'environment' and 'quality of life' are beginning to mean as much to the French as the emphasis they have placed on modernization and material progress since the 1950s.

I first lived in Paris from 1955 to 1959 as a correspondent of *The Times* and have returned to France regularly ever since. During these twenty or so years I have seen the style and mood of the nation alter radically, though some of the changes were obscured on the surface, till the early 1960s, by the tensions of the Algerian crisis. Like other francophiles, I have developed an acute love–hate relationship with this stimulating and exasperating race: finally, love has triumphed over hate, and today I feel as emotionally committed to France as to my own country, and as much at home with French as with English people. I say this, in order to explain the spirit in which this book has been written. I have been severely critical of many things in France, but in much the way that a progress-minded Frenchman might himself be critical. The book tries to look at France from within, more from a French than an English point of view; and it takes for granted all that is great and unique and lovable about French civilization. As the French say, *qui aime bien, châtie bien.*

In order to research and revise this book, I have travelled to almost every corner of France between 1960 and 1976, interviewing literally thousands of people: technocrats and schoolgirls, prefects and peasants, grocers and film-directors. Everywhere, except sometimes in Paris, I met with courtesy, readiness to help, and the highest degree of Gallic communicativeness; though France is a complex and difficult country to understand, and often a trying country to live in, she is ideal terrain for the note-taker. And if you meet the French on their own terms, rather than patronizing them in English, they can be as charming as any people on earth. The many hundreds of people, high and low, who gave up their time to help me are too numerous to mention, but among them I should especially like to thank:

Jean Monnet, Michel Debré, Pierre Sudreau, Edgard Pisani, Simon Nora, Jacques Delors, Jean Sérisé, Jacques Mallet, René Foch, Bernard Cazes, Pierre Saulière, Alain Lancelot, Georges Buis, Paul-Marie de la Gorce; Michel Rocard, Claude Estier, Christian Goux, René Andrieu, Dominique Frélaut; José Bidegain, Jean Saint-Geours, Gérard Pikatty, Martine Aubry, Gilles Guérithault; Michel Debatisse, François Clerc, Bernard Lambert, Jean Desouches; Alexis Gourvennec and his staff (in Brittany); Jean Caville and Raymond Lacombe (in the Aveyron); Jean-Marie Crochet; Edouard Leclerc, Denis Defforey; Philippe Lamour, François Essig, Robert de Caumont; Henri Fréville (mayor of Rennes) and Charles Lecotteley, Victor Janton and the Pilpré family (all in Rennes); Jean Voisard (Nantes), M. Dussarat (Bordeaux), Paul Barrière (Biarritz); Michel Valdiguié, André Brouat, Jean Krynen, Paul Ourliac, Michel Augier, John Prince, Bernard Kayser (all in Toulouse); Jean Servier (Montpellier); Hubert Dubedout (mayor of Grenoble), Raymond de Robert; Leon Chadé and P. Sadoul (Nancy); Pierre Madaule, Olivier Sérard; Gilles Anouil; Michel Crozier, Roland Sadoun, Serge Antoine, Alain de Vulpian, Roger Boisramé, Marie-Thérèse Guichard, Dr Simon; Jacques Ozouf, Henri Appiah, Monica and Jean Charlot, Marcel Bonvalet, Marc Mortimer; Jean-François Revel, John Weightman, Christine Brooke-Rose, Jean-Marie Benoist, Alain Robbe-Grillet, Michel Butor, Jean-Marie Domenach, François Bédarida; Jean-Luc Godard, Jean de Baroncelli, Robert Benayoun, Yvonne Baby, Jérôme Brierre, Claude Degand, Cynthia Grenier, Jean Genet; Pierre Desgraupes, Pierre and Françoise Dumayet, Edouard Sablier, Max-Pol Fouchet, Elaine Victor, Jacques-Olivier Chattard, Olivier Todd, Jacques Thibau, Pascal Michel, Jean-Pierre Joulin.

I should also like to thank all those friends and acquaintances who gave me special help with advice, contacts or hospitality, or by reading part of this book: in Paris, Gill and Peter Prescott, Robert Mauthner, Peter Taylor, Susan Taylor, William Farr (alas, now dead) and his wife Joy, Bill and Sheila Harding, Dick and Jeannine Langridge, John and Jenny de Courcy Ling, George and Sarah Walden, Robert and Judith Cottave, Francis Cassavetti, Jean-Louis Gergorin, Alain Duhamel, Bruno Delaye,

Jérôme and Françoise Monod, Jean-Pierre and Odile Angremy, Claude and Christine Benoît, Louis Le Cunff, Peter Simpson-Jones, François Nourissier, Marc Ullmann, as well as Georges Suffert and all his colleagues at *Le Point*, my French publisher, Robert Laffont, and his colleague, Jean Rosenthal, my agent, Marie Schébéko and her late husband, Jean Biche, and above all my translator, Bernard Willerval and his wife; in the provinces, Pierre-Yves and Catherine Péchoux, and Claude Bonfils; in London, Yvette Wiener, John Haycraft, Christopher Johnson, Jean Wahl, Daniel Contenay, Philippe Girbal and his colleagues in the DATAR office, Richard Mayne and his staff in the EEC office, as well of course as the directors and staff of Martin Secker & Warburg and Penguin Books who have been unfailingly kind, and my long-suffering wife Jenny, and our cats who generously refrained from chewing up too much of the manuscript or from sitting on my typewriter *all* the time.

Chapter 1

INTRODUCTION

UNTIL quite recently the French were often accused, with reason, of living with their eyes fixed on the past. Now they have suddenly opened them to the fact of living in the world of the 1970s; and it thrills and scares them, like a convalescent emerging into harsh daylight from a shuttered room. Few other nations in the West are so schizophrenic about modernism: the British, by contrast, take it placidly in their stride, perhaps too placidly. With one part of themselves, the French are adapting eagerly to a new world of glamour, speed and technical efficiency, and they show some creative flair in lending it a French flavour of its own; in other ways, they still cling for security to old habits and rituals, wary of altering the inner fabric of their lives and society. Thus, though many of the outward traits of modernism, from computers to 'pop' songs, are the same as in any Western country, the special conflicts and contrasts between old and new are sharper than almost anywhere else; and it is not always easy to tell whether France is transforming fundamentally, or only in style and mood.

Anyone returning to France today, after a long absence, will quickly be struck by the outward changes. In Paris, where almost nothing had been built for the first half of this century, the suburbs are now ringed by endless white megaliths of new apartment blocks, while nearer the city centre famous historic buildings are being dwarfed by much-disputed skyscrapers, and the old grey house façades along the boulevards have been scoured clean; down every street and alley, picturesque Parisian squalor is yielding to glitter. The Seine valley with its ruined abbeys and castles is filling up with big new factories. In the countryside, the peasants have brought tractors and Citroëns, and village girls in the garb of Chelsea walk beside their beshawled, black-smocked grandmothers. In the cafés, people are less inclined to swill litres of wine and get excited about politics; instead, they sit in the dark watching television over soft drinks. Clochemerle no longer gets worked up about a *pissotière*, but over a hypermarket, or slip road for a motorway. French advertisements, which used to concentrate on food, drink and underwear, now devote themselves to the latest luxury gadgets, and the *lingua franca* of their snob-appeal is English. France, in short, is becoming less quaint and, maybe, less French.

Some changes go deep. Under the spontaneous momentum of economic advance, society is shifting its equilibrium. More than four million people have migrated from the farms since the war to new jobs in the towns, and the old-style peasant is slowly dying out. An artisanal economy is turning to mass consumption. A score of provincial cities, such as Rennes or Tours, quiet back-waters till a few years ago, are strident with new energy and activity. And a society hitherto dominated by older people and the prerogatives of age is now invaded by youth and a new cult of youth. The national mood has changed remarkably since I first knew France in the years after the war. Then, I used to think of the typical middle-class Frenchman as, say, a local lawyer or shopkeeper, sedentary and cautious, his roots deep in the town where his family had lived for generations; a man passionate in his ideological attachment to Church or Left, fond of big family reunions, heavy lunches, and ceremonial public occasions where he would make rhetorical speeches full of references to the French classics and history. Today this Third Republic flavour of life has turned fusty and is fading out, or at least is being overlaid with a different spirit. The prototype today might be, say, a salesman for an American-owned computer firm, quite ready to move across France if it means a bigger salary and a smarter flat, more likely to quote Galbraith than Victor Hugo, passionate about 'modern-ization' and the enjoyment of slick new possessions and exotic holidays.

Yet dig deeper still, and many of the changes appear curiously uneven, sometimes illogical. A firm may install a costly computer, yet fail to educate its junior staff away from archaic methods of book-keeping. Small farmers eagerly buy tractors, yet shy from regrouping their farms in a way that would make those tractors effective. Everyone wants fast cars and seaside holidays, yet they cling to the tradition of going away only in high summer, thus jamming the roads and resorts. Glossy new flats with glass portals stand beside crumbling slums, protected by out-of-date property laws. France has built some of the world's finest hydro-electric and nuclear centres, but many local post offices and domestic electricity services are still crudely antiquated.

Basically, what is happening is this: an economic and technical revolution has suddenly rendered out of date the age-old social and administrative structures of France, and only slowly and painfully have these been adapting to meet the new conditions. The French may have changed their ambitions and material interests, but their basic character-traits, built round individualism, social mistrust and desire for formalism and routine, are inevitably slower to change, and so is the legal and official framework of France which derives from the French character. The result is a fascinating turmoil and transition, rich terrain for the sociologist. This turmoil found its most dramatic expression in the uprising of May 1968.

It is in the essentially economic field that the new France appears most positive and encouraging. Here the French have recovered a vitality, and a faith in their future, that many people thought impossible twenty years ago. This economic renaissance began just after the war, but for years was obscured by sloth and political crises, and did not gather real momentum until the late 1950s. Writing in 1953, the great Swiss expert Herbert Lüthy was still highly sceptical about France's prospects of recovery.* 'The true face of France,' he suggested, appeared to foreigners and Frenchmen alike as 'that of a farmcart stuck in the mud', and he compared the French economy to a rock of Sisyphus, ever hauled up the hill by ardent technocrats only to fall down again each time, beneath the weight of petty vested interests and general apathy. Since then, as Lüthy himself foresaw might happen one day, that rock has been pulled over the crest, and the farmcart is partly out of the mud. Industry and commerce have been forced to stir from their artisanal slumber and are fast modernizing, even

* *The State of France* (Secker & Warburg, 1955).

though they still have some way to go before they can meet American or German competition on equal terms.

France is in the throes of a belated industrial revolution. And so urgent and absorbing does the nation find this process that its whole energies seem to be given over to material progress and reform, and to private money-making and the enjoyment of new wealth – and the traditional French creative involvement in ideas, literature and painting appears, for the moment, to be taking second place. Paris is no longer the powerhouse of European culture. Our old image of the French, fecund and original in the arts and philosophy, but financially weak and politically unstable, today needs a certain revision.

In order to trace the origins of the French recovery, we must look back to the war and even earlier: it sprang from the shock and humiliation of the 1940 defeat and the Occupation, and from the upturn in the birth-rate, which began modestly just before the war. In the 1930s France was an extreme example of a general Western malaise: industrial production was actually on the decline during that decade, and the mood of the nation was sullen, protectionist and defeatist, with many of the classic symptoms of decadence. The population, too, was declining – a phenomenon rare in the modern world in time of peace – and experts today see this as a key factor in the pre-war malaise. After 1946 the French birth-rate was one of the highest in Europe; again, the experts trace intimate links between this and the national dynamism of the post-war era.

Nowadays, when the population explosion in Asia and elsewhere is the world's gravest problem, it may seem odd to regard a stagnant or declining birth-rate as a national calamity. But although for a backward country a high birth-rate is a menace, for a developed nation like France the opposite is true: a falling population usually limits investment and self-confidence. And France is still under-populated in relation to her neighbours and to her own territory and resources. As early as 1800 she began to fall behind her European rivals in her rate of population growth, due to mysterious factors arising from her social and political structure. In 1800 France was the most populous country in

Western Europe, with 28·3 million against Britain's 16 million and 22 million in what is now Germany; by 1910 France had risen to only 41·5 million, overtaken both by Britain (45·4 million) and Germany (63 million). The French middle classes were seriously inhibited by the Napoleonic laws of equal inheritance, which provided an incentive against large families. And added to this were the ravages of alcoholism among the peasantry, and then the losses of the Great War, when France in proportion suffered more heavily than Germany or Britain. After 1918 the decline continued: by 1935 the birth-rate had fallen to 87 per cent, or seven births to eight deaths, and in the 1930s the global excess of deaths over births in France was 125,000. In 1939 Germany was able to put nearly twice as many men of military age into the field as France – and the results were inevitable.

During the 1930s French politicians grew increasingly worried about the low birth-rate. In 1932 a first attempt was made to remedy it, with the institution of family allowances: this was under the impulsion of the great demographer Adolphe Landry, then Minister of Labour, who is sometimes described today as 'a saviour of modern France'. The allowances were later extended, and in 1939 they were formalized in the famous Code de la Famille, basis of all post-war social legislation. By the outbreak of war they were already beginning to show results: between 1935 and 1939 the birth-rate crept up from 87 to 93 per cent, though it was still below par. Then came the war-time Pétain Government which at once promoted a strong pro-family policy, not perhaps with the noblest of democratic motives, but at least it meant that the allowances were continued; and so, in the darkest years of the Occupation, denatality was not as great as might have been expected. Directly after the war the child allowances were further extended and are now among the highest in Europe, often accounting for 30 per cent or more of a worker's income. They were certainly a major cause of the demographic boom of the post-war years, but not the only one. That boom must be attributed also to more spontaneous psychological factors: a regaining of faith in the future, and what the demographer Alfred Sauvy has called 'a collective national conscience', a survival instinct forced into action by the shock of war-time defeat. In the middle and upper classes, where children used to be fewest, families increased in size relatively more than in the working classes, and this may have been due partly to the decline of bourgeois reliance on inherited property under the new economic conditions.

In 1945–6 the birth-rate rose suddenly from 93 to 126 per cent and then stayed at more or less that level until the 1960s. In most European countries the rate fell back in the 1950s after an early post-war spurt, but in France it held steady for longer. The annual net increase of births over deaths has stood at between 250,000 and 350,000 right up until 1974, and thanks to this and to immigration (notably of settlers from Algeria in 1962–3), the population increased from 41 million in 1946 to reach 52 million in 1974. This has given industry an important impulse for expansion; and the economy has proved sufficiently buoyant, at least until very recently, to be able to absorb the extra numbers that have poured on to the labour market since about 1962. France, happily for her, is still an under-populated and under-exploited territory compared with nearly all her neighbours, and could easily contain twice her present numbers without strain or over-crowding, so long as the economy stays sound. De Gaulle and his Ministers several times proclaimed their dream of a powerful France of one hundred millions in the next century. It is true that in the past few years the birth-rate has tended to drop, as elsewhere in the West. The number of births in 1975 was 115,000 less than in 1973, and in West Germany that year there were more deaths than births. Yet France's birth-rate is still higher than that of nearly all West European countries, except Italy.

'Le bébé-boom' has also brought with it a new cult of youth, and of young motherhood, in a nation hitherto addicted to patri-archal values. Baby-making is a prestige industry, and the ideal of nearly every young couple is to settle down in a new flat and breed. As for teenagers, they used to be ignored as a group in France, or treated as small-scale adults and expected to keep quiet: now they are indulged, courted, endlessly scrutinized, and are beginning to find a voice of their own. *La jeunesse* has become a national slogan: every Frenchman, old or young, professes his faith in it, as a symbol of France's rejuvenated vitality. Frequently this is no more than lip-service; the barriers of age, as of class, remain, and young people, despite the eruption of 1968, have not yet really achieved the same power breakthrough as in Britain. But at least they have far more freedom and status than before the war; and younger people are now finding it easier to gain promotion through merit into key posts, in a land previously devoted to nepotism, hierarchic respect for age, and waiting for dead men's shoes.

The second fundamental factor behind the French recovery has been, paradoxically, the defeat of 1940 and the Occupation. These humiliations, coming after the decadence of the 1930s, provided the French with a much-needed traumatic shock: it opened their eyes to the root causes of French decline, and forced a number of the more thoughtful and forceful ones to prepare action to stop it happening again. Maybe it is because Britain was spared this kind of shock that we have not developed the same post-war economic dynamism as the French, the Germans or others; we have not had to take stock of ourselves in the same way, and we have continued into peace-time with the illusion of self-sufficient invincibility.

Even the Vichy régime itself, though odious in many respects, was not without one or two incidental elements which helped pave the way for later recovery. I have mentioned the family allowances. In agriculture, too, and in regional development, Vichy's corporatist policies, though fascist in inspiration, may have helped to generate a certain local awareness and self-dependence that was to prove useful later.

But much more important than this was the fact that the war gave the French a breathing-space in which to re-think the future. Under the enforced paralysis and inactivity of the Occupation, they had time to ponder, plan and regroup, while the British were far too busy fighting. Many of the French post-war achievements and reforms can be traced back in inspiration to those years. On the land, young peasants of the Christian farming movement began to form little groups that later took the offensive to modernize French agriculture; in the Church, priests and laymen were preparing the way for a new social activism that has since transformed the spirit of Catholicism in France. Even Sartrian existentialism, one of the most fertile intellectual movements in France since the war, had its roots in the Occupation. Elsewhere, little groups of *Résistants* and Free French were plotting how to renovate the nation's economy and structures: the most important of these groups was formed around Jean Monnet in Washington, and out of it grew the 'Plan', which has played such a vital role in the French revival.

The Plan's greatest achievement, as the next chapter will describe, is that it has helped to instil in industry and the civil service a belief in expansion and progress that was absent before the war. The innovating technocrat began to come to the fore, in place of the conserving bureaucrat. At first, the new ethos of reform and modernization was confined to a few pioneers in key posts, like Monnet and his team, and to local élites that sprang up sporadically around the country, like the Young Farmers. The rest of the nation stayed with its eyes on the past, protecting its *positions acquises*. Gradually, however, over the past thirty years, the new spirit has spread more widely to infect public opinion as a whole. This is the greatest change between modern and pre-war France: ordinary people now believe in progress, and accept the need for change – however much, when change actually presents itself, many of them still fight hard to defend their vested interests!

Steadily, a number of diverse movements have developed, some of them stage-managed by the State technocrats, others led by private crusaders, or growing spontaneously from local grassroots. The painful but ineluctable modernization of factories, farms and small shops; the remarkable rebirth of the provinces; the dawn of modern town-planning in Paris; the fiercely contested reforms in education, birth-control and land ownership – this book will tell the story of these and other changes, and of their uneven pattern of success.

It is often assumed abroad that the French recovery was due essentially to de Gaulle and his decade of political stability. But I doubt whether this is really so. Though the Gaullists achieved a great deal in the years 1958–69, they also hindered much, or simply continued a process that was already in motion. In nearly every sector the changes were under way by the time de Gaulle returned to power in 1958, though overshadowed by the crises of colonial wars and by weak, shifting Governments. Soon after the Liberation the Plan had laid the first foundations of industrial recovery, and then a strong and stable civil service helped to provide continuity of policies despite fluctuating Ministries. And it was the Fourth Republic, not the Fifth, that prepared French opinion for the Common Market and signed the Treaty of Rome, which has done so much to stir French industry forward and to open French eyes to a wider international outlook. But, inevitably, many of the post-war improvements in France have taken years to reach fruition, and so the Gaullists have managed to steal the credit.

This is not to say that Gaullism's own record has been negative. In the first years after his return, de Gaulle was able to restore French self-confidence, and foreign confidence in France, notably by his handling of the Algerian problem and his bold financial measures of December 1958.* And in scores of instances de Gaulle's strong Government succeeded in applying vital and difficult reforms, where its weak predecessors had failed. For these various reasons, I feel that de Gaulle's final credit with French history is favourable, on balance, and I still do not regret the Treize Mai revolt that returned him to power in 1958. But in the last years of his reign that balance grew steadily finer. Even leaving aside his foreign policies, in domestic affairs too the same high-handedness that he showed abroad finally alienated from him a number of the ablest and most liberal of the men who originally consented to work with his régime. Pierre Sudreau and Edgard Pisani, two ex-prefects who were perhaps the best of all de Gaulle's Ministers, both resigned in the mid-1960s in protest at his treatment of Parliament and public. At the same time, the régime lost a part of its earlier reformist energy and idealism and veered towards classic conservatism, in closer alliance with big business. This is one reason why the fruits of the new prosperity have not been shared more evenly in France: the peasant and working classes are still noticeably poorer and less emancipated than in Britain, and the upper classes tend to be richer. To an

* See p. 36.

extent this extreme inequality is hard to avoid, as in Italy, so long
as some sectors of the economic structure, such as small farms,
remain so archaic. But partly it has been due to the Gaullists'
failure to devote more money and attention to social progress.
And this helps to explain the reasons for the uprising that rocked
France in 1968. Under de Gaulle, national prestige won the
highest priorities, as any visitor will notice. The liner *France*, the
Concorde, the Mont Blanc tunnel, the new Orly airport: these
maybe were valuable achievements in themselves, but that is not
the only reason why they attracted public funds more easily than
less eye-catching but more urgent matters such as housing,
schools, roads and telephones. And the same applied, *a fortiori*,
to de Gaulle's costly nuclear ambitions. Georges Pompidou,
when he took over from de Gaulle in 1969, back-pedalled on the
prestige policy: but, as we shall see, he remained too much in
alliance with big business and high finance to pay adequate attention to social needs. His successor since 1974, Valéry Giscard
d'Estaing, is a genuine social reformer and liberal for whom I
have the highest admiration, while recognizing his weaknesses.
Despite a climate of world economic crisis, and a tricky domestic
political situation, he has managed to carry through some important social reforms, which these pages will describe. He is putting
a new emphasis on environment and on the human need for a
better 'quality of life', as well as on the continuing process of
material modernization.

In France there are two economies that uneasily co-exist: a
modern one, most of it implanted since the war by the technocrats
and a few big State and private firms; and below it, an old, creak-
ing infrastructure, based on artisanship, low turnover with high
profits, and the ideal of the small family business. The modern
sector has expanded considerably since Lüthy in 1953 described it
as 'an isolated enclave inside old France', and today it clearly
predominates. But it has not yet absorbed the old system, which
is strongly rooted in the traditional framework of French law and
society. This society has been built up of a honeycomb of little
sectional interests, each with its clearly defined rights and privileges, all mutually suspicious but carefully balancing each other
in order to avoid conflict. It is a system that served France not

too badly in the past: it ensured a certain stability and helped to protect the individual. But modern conditions now necessitate a different framework, more open and flexible.

Some features of the old system are gradually disappearing of their own accord, under the natural weight of economic change: many small firms and farms, for instance, find they can no longer subsist unless they merge or modernize. But other features are so powerfully sanctioned by law or custom that they cannot be altered except by legislation or other official action – this is true of the restrictive privileges of a number of professions. Until changes of this kind are made, the modernization of the economy can go so far but no further: improved techniques of production lose half their value if archaic and inefficient cartels and marketing methods cause waste and keep up prices. De Gaulle's Government did, in fact, put through a number of needed reforms: but there is much else it failed to do, despite its power. It saw its popularity slump in later elections, and dared not offend too many group interests. De Gaulle was not normally a man who cared for such tactical considerations: if he wanted a thing, he got it done. But in his last years he seemed to have lost interest in domestic affairs, save to ensure that he stayed in power. Some of his Ministers knew precisely what needed to be done, but they were not always given the authority or the money to do it. And the same was true under Pompidou. Giscard has been rather more successful and far-sighted; but he too has not always had the courage, or the political room for manoeuvre, that reforms demand. Yet, as the French economy becomes steadily less protected, many of the problems grow more pressing each year.

It is because of the special strength of her past, and the weathered wholeness of her traditions, that France, like Britain, finds many of the structural changes so difficult, more so than a newer and more malleable nation like Germany. As the brilliant sociologist Michel Crozier* has pointed out, French society throughout its history has shown a tendency to resist change until the last possible moment, to allow an intolerable situation

---

* *The Bureaucratic Phenomenon* (Tavistock Publications, 1964).

to build up and then, when the strain and inconvenience are too great, to change together in a vast reshuffle, usually under the impulse of a few pioneering individuals. This is happening today, probably on a grander scale than ever before, or at least since 1789. And this attachment to the past also helps to explain the fascination for the future. Even for the most dedicated French modernist and reformer, the wrench from the womb of safe tradition has been traumatic at some stage or other, and so he flings himself at tomorrow with all the more force, in over-compensation, as a man breaking an old habit discovers a new passion. If France, in de Gaulle's own phrase, is at last 'marrying her century', it is on the rebound.

The French have been suddenly dazzled by new material prospects they had hardly dared trust in during their decades of archaism. Ordinary public interest in what life will be like in twenty or thirty years' time is noticeably greater than in Britain, and papers and magazines are full of optimistic articles about '*Le Paris de l'an 2000*' or '*La Vie française de demain*'. Some of this, in the pro-Government Press, may be an astute move to distract public attention from the fact that much of France has not yet reached 1960, let alone 2000. But it does correspond to what people want to believe – that tomorrow their tenements will be skyscraper garden cities, that aerotrains and freeways will banish the rush-hour tedium of Paris, and that there will be smart cars, long leisure and free opportunity for all, in a new California – *à la française*. When the sober experts of the Plan produced an objective report on the France of 1985, it was eagerly read and discussed on all sides; and there may be some relevance, too, in the spectacular post-war popularity in France of Teilhard de Chardin, whose books relate older Christian humanist values to a radiant faith in the scientific future.

The French can also enjoy the feeling that their land, though ancient, is in huge areas still virgin and under-exploited, rich in untapped resources – 'Europe's Texas', as someone said. They have that rare commodity in this corner of the old continent: *Lebensraum*. It is this, as much as anything, that makes planning and expansion a heady business for today's young technocrats, as new factories are implanted on the silent plains of the Béarn,

or new power-dams in the lost mountain valleys of Savoy. In
Britain, we look at the material future with cautious apprehen-
sion: it means the Buchanan Report, the dangers of pollution and
overcrowding, the difficulties of replanning old industrial eyesores on a narrow island. France too is not without her pollution
problems: but not only does she have more space, she was spared
the full horrors of Victorian industrial growth. In many things,
in architecture, décor, town-planning, industry, as well as in
aspects of her economic and social structures, France is in a sense
making a leap straight from the late eighteenth into the twentieth
century – and though the leap is a harder one than the more
continuous British process has been, there may in the longer term
be practical advantages.

There is something impressive about the enthusiasm of quite
a number of the French, especially the younger ones, for an
efficient, technology-based future. But not all of them are looking
at the future quite squarely; there is a tendency to theorize about
ideal solutions rather than grapple with immediate unsolved problems ahead. The Press will more readily project the millennium
than criticize schemes in hand; and even the planners, though
much more pragmatic than the French ever used to be, still show
an over-fondness for perfect blueprints and generalizations. Some
of this is simply an aspect of the French love of theorizing and
formalism, derived from the way they are taught to think at
school; and some of it may have been due to the limitations on
free discussion under the Gaullist régime. But I think it shows
also that French society, in its present crisis period of mutation,
does not quite dare look at itself in the mirror, for fear of not
recognizing the old familiar features. And this is one reason why
so few contemporary novels, films or plays deal squarely and
frankly with current social themes – the changes in the working
class and peasantry, for instance. Material change, the buying
of cars and computers, is much less frightening than change
of personality. And thus, while many thinking Frenchmen
are sanguine about France's socio-economic future, others are
worried at what might be happening to French civilization.

They are aware that France, in modernizing, faces two dilemmas. The first is whether the present revolution will bring a more

egalitarian and trustful spirit into French society, or whether the old barriers will simply go up again in a different form. More is at stake than solely economic efficiency: it is also a question of social justice and freedom in the widest sense. French society has always practised a certain tolerance and has based itself on respect for individual privacy and on legal *égalité* between all citizens. But in order to uphold these very virtues it has made itself into a closed and segmented rather than an open society: *égalité* has not equalled egalitarianism. So stubbornly has change been resisted that class barriers remain more rigid than in Britain today; professional advance still depends too often on having the right diplomas and contacts; and high respect is still paid to formal titles, hierarchies and privileges. The individual's loyalties are traditionally towards family rather than community, and civic co-operation in the Anglo-Saxon sense is not highly developed. Public initiatives are expected to come from the State and the authorities, rather than from *ad hoc* citizen groups; and, even discounting the influence of Gaullist paternalism, public opinion does not have the same open force as in some countries.

Today the old groupings and loyalties are beginning to break up, under new conditions. Family ties which count for so much in France are weakening, society is becoming more exposed, and the French are having to re-assess their social attitudes. Individualist peasants are discovering the need to share their resources; on the vast modern housing estates, a new un-French neighbourliness is perforce emerging; a rigorous élitist system of education is being modified and democratized to meet modern needs; and the rigidly stratified and impersonal French pattern of bureaucracy is under agonizing reappraisal in firms and public offices. Under the impulse of the reformers and modernists with their eyes on foreign models, a more open and egalitarian ethos appears to be emerging, though the process is slower than in Britain and is still heavily opposed by old reflexes of habit and suspicion. The question is whether, when the reshuffle is completed, the barriers will remain down; or whether a cycle familiar to France in the past will recur, and society will simply reclose its ranks on new ground.

The next dilemma goes even deeper, and I think it is a fundamental question to pose about France today. French and foreigner alike are aware that much of the best in France, perhaps more than in other countries, is intimately bound up with a certain traditional way of thought and civilization, which risks being lost beyond recall in the inexorable process of modernization. Is France fated to undergo a kind of lobotomy, which will cure many of the old economic and social weaknesses, but also kill the old turbulent creativeness and individuality? Some of the current signs are not too encouraging. While the tradition of individual craftsmanship is inevitably declining, few of the new mass-consumer industries are yet showing the same French genius for style and quality. Less time and care is spent nowadays on *cuisine* and Paris is filling up with cafeterias and hamburger bars. The Ville Lumière is no longer the world's art capital; her theatres are full of foreign plays or revivals, her literature has lost its human universality, her intellectual brilliance has grown stale. Above all, the French seem to have lost some of their old originality, and to have become oddly imitative, especially of their sworn rivals, the Anglo-Saxons. Their national pride cries out against the process but seems unable to stop it. While French words and phrases have for centuries been *à la mode*, even *de rigueur* in British polite society, today in France *c'est O.K., même snob*, in many circles, to speak the new hybrid language known as *franglais*; and few outward changes in the France of the 1960s and 1970s are more startling than the massive incursions of English, mainly into the vocabulary of advertising but also into some daily speech. In central Paris there is now a charcuterie called *The Little Pig* and a boutique called *Le Sweater Shop*. Anglo-American gadgets, techniques and mannerisms are all the rage. *L'Express* magazine has remodelled its format on *Time*, and pop singers have adopted Anglo-Saxon names like Johnny Hallyday. To be fair, the French do frequently add an authentic national flavour of their own to the things they borrow (for example, *un drugstore* is now something typically Parisian, quite unlike a drugstore). And on a more serious level, the copying of American business and industrial techniques may be healthy, if it helps towards efficient modernization. But where will it all lead? Will the French, after their present difficult transition period, recover their old creative zest for ideas and style? Or is France fated to become a more prosperous, efficient and contented country, maybe, but also a duller and much less French one?

Such, in brief, and politics apart, are the main problems and opportunities facing the French in the late 1970s. In the following chapters they will be examined in detail.

Chapter 2

THE ECONOMY:
PRECARIOUS MIRACLE

WHEN Britain, in recent years, came to borrow money from France and her other allies in her moment of need, many Frenchmen from de Gaulle downwards could hardly resist a twinge of *Schadenfreude*. For decades the British and others had looked down on France as the 'sick man of Europe', politically and economically. But now the picture was reversed. Britain's economy looked the sicker of the two, and so it still does today.

France's recovery during the 1950s and 1960s had come as something of a surprise to many people abroad, since for the first years after the war it was camouflaged by recurrent financial crises and political upheavals. It was not until the early 1960s that we really became aware of a change in France more profound than the change of régime under de Gaulle. Exports and gold reserves were rising fast, industry was modernizing, Caravelle and Dauphine became familiar words in many parts of the world.

Today France's economy is relatively strong, despite sporadic crises and a number of structural defects yet to be cured. Statistics may give some idea of the post-war progress. Industrial production, actually declining in the 1930s, had regained its pre-war peak by 1951 and then *tripled* between 1952 and 1972. In the 1950s it rose 44 per cent, against 26 per cent in Britain. Confronted with figures of this kind, Englishmen often reply, 'Yes, but France started from so much lower a level.' Yes, she did; but what they find harder to accept is that, starting from this lower level, France has now gone on to overtake Britain both in total production and in average standard of living, and looks set fair to forge far ahead of her in the next few years. Some American experts have predicted that, at the present rate, France by 1985 or so may even overtake Germany, to become the number one industrial power in Europe.

Exports more than doubled in 1956–62, while gold and foreign exchange reserves, down to 10m francs in 1959, rose steadily in the 1960s and by early 1968 had reached 35,000m francs. The franc grew able to look the dollar in the face, and de Gaulle with arrogant self-confidence could even suggest a return to the gold standard. This arrogance was wiped off his face by the 1968 crises which cut France's huge reserves by nearly 50 per cent in six months. But the resilience which industry showed in recovering from these crises gave evidence of how much the basic strength and stability of the economy had improved in the previous two decades. More recently, industry has again shown resilience in its reactions to the much more serious and prolonged economic crisis that followed the Yom Kippur war. The French economy has weathered the storm less easily than West Germany's, but a great deal better than Britain's or Italy's. Even at the worst period of the crisis, in March 1976, exchange reserves stood at the high figure of 95,600m francs: growth in 1975 was –2 per cent, the first negative year since the war, but so strong was the ensuing recovery that a 5 or 6 per cent growth was forecast for 1976.

It is true that the German economy is stronger still, and the figures for German post-war growth even more striking. But the French growth rate has recently been higher on average than Germany's. And the Germans, as we know, are organized and methodical, and their economic structure makes sense. The French so-called 'miracle', in its French context, has been the more remarkable of the two, for it has been achieved in the face of France's fundamental ailments. Some of these are now on the way to being cured: industry, for instance, has given up most of its pre-war neglect of exports and productivity. But many structural weaknesses, rooted in old French traditions, are inevitably slower to change. Over-centralized State bureaucracy, lack of a vigorous capital market, clumsy systems of distribution, too many small family firms, a fiscal and unemployment system that encourage inflation: these are some of the burdens that the economy still has to carry with it, and they were added to by de Gaulle's policy of costly prestige projects and by the shoring-up of out-of-date industries with huge subsidies. Because these have been such heavy burdens, France, throughout the 1950s and again in the late 1960s, seemed balanced on a knife-edge between collapse and recovery, and many experts repeatedly predicted her downfall. Yet, with many ups and downs, she seems to be winning through. And she is even reaching the point where, as in some other advanced countries, the virtues of expansion as an end in itself are beginning to be questioned.

Undoubtedly the Plan and then the Common Market have played a large part in the post-war revival. But the original causes of it would seem to lie deeper, and to be psychological as much as economic. As I have already suggested, they spring from the shock defeat in 1940 and retrospective shame and dismay at the decadence of the 1930s. Had it not been for this basic change in outlook and in will-power, the French could never have made a success either of their planning or of their entry into the Common Market.

POST-1945: THE IMPETUS FOR RENEWAL

In the eighteenth century France was the strongest and richest power in the world. But soon after 1800 the first signs of backwardness began to appear, and, as the next century wore on, France increasingly failed to keep pace with the rapid industrialization of Britain and Germany. During the late nineteenth and early twentieth centuries she spent huge sums on her colonial empire, but neglected her home development. The 1920s, it is true, saw a certain revival, prompted by the need to repair the ravages of war, and helped by the return to France of Alsace and Lorraine with their heavy industries. But France survived the 1929 recession with less success than most countries, and the 1930s were a decade of serious economic decline. Over-cautious Governments put all the emphasis on financial stability, rather than expansion, and protected agriculture with price-supports at the expense of industry.

The Second World War brought less loss of life than the first, but more severe physical damage. By 1944, France's railways were shattered and their rolling-stock depleted; her ports, her northern towns and many of her factories were devastated. And yet, as in the case of Germany, the very scale of this destruction

T—TNF—B

was a blessing in disguise; it brought a chance to make a new start on modern lines. That is one reason why, for instance, continental railways today tend to be more efficient than British ones.

These opportunities might have been muffed, had not a number of Frenchmen emerged from the war with a new determination. Some, especially the younger ones, had used the enforced inactivity of the war years to think seriously about the future and to explore new ideas and techniques. That is how the Plan was born. Then, many of the older, deadbeat generation came out of the war publicly discredited by their part in the Vichy régime or the Occupation. This helped new, younger men to push them aside and to fill some of the key posts of industry and the civil service, in defiance of the pre-war French *penchant* for gerontocracy.

Economists mostly agree on this view of the French revival, though sometimes with bewilderment. Professor Charles P. Kindleberger, of the Massachusetts Institute of Technology, has written 'to conclude that the basic change in the French economy is one of people and attitudes is frustrating to the economist' but, after examining and discounting a number of purely economic explanations of the French recovery, he has declared it to be 'due to the restaffing of the economy with new men and to new French attitudes'.*

Civil servants began to move from a static to a more dynamic concept of their role. Whereas before the war they had been the faceless executives of a smooth, unchanging routine, now some of them came to see themselves as animators, reformers, leaders. Together with some industrialists, they steadily discarded the pre-war notion that *regular* economic progress was impossible. This shuffling of the economic pessimism of the 1930s has, of course, been fairly general in the West since the war: in France it has stood out most sharply, just because of the gravity of the earlier decline.

In 1946 Jean Monnet launched the First Plan, under the slogan 'modernization or downfall'. This was a long-sighted austerity plan that gave the immediate housing crisis a much lower priority than the reconstruction of basic industries, such as steel, coal and

* *France: Change and Tradition* (Gollancz, 1964), p. 157.

electricity, as the necessary basis for a lasting recovery. Then in 1947 Marshall Aid from the United States began to arrive in Europe, and in France this provided the investment funds that were needed for the success of the First Plan. In fact it was largely because of her planning that France was able to make better constructive use of Marshall Aid than most of her neighbours. At the same time, the innate French flair for technology and engineering was given a new lease of life: scientists and technicians were provided with the funds and the encouragement to put France in the front rank once more in the creation of new cars and aircraft, railway engines, hydro-electric works and computers.

By 1949 some signs of reborn prosperity were already apparent in the streets and shops. But the next years were difficult ones. Parallel with the steady, long-term rebuilding of key industries went a succession of financial crises due to the archaic structure of much of the rest of the economy. For the euphoric post-war resurgence of new ideas and new men was confined at first to a minority of planners and pioneers: the rest of France, *la vieille France*, stayed attached to its old ways with its vested interests, its petty bureaucracy, its dislike of change. Writing in 1953, Herbert Lüthy described the new industries, most of them State-controlled, as 'an isolated enclave of modernism inside old France'.* The clash between the two structures produced imbalance and was one cause of inflation: it was like giving a sick man too strong a medicine, or putting too powerful an engine in a rickety car. Every year the budget was in deficit and the balance of payments position grew worse. Costly colonial wars, in Indo-China and later in Algeria, did not help matters.

The Fourth Republic Governments patched over the budgetary cracks, but were too weak and too short-lived to apply the basic remedies that would have meant upsetting countless vested interests and sinecures. Yet, to their credit, these Governments did pursue two basic lines of policy that were to safeguard the future. They allowed the Plan to continue its work; and in the mid-1950s they took the courageous political decision to go into the Common Market, in face of the doubts or open opposition of most private industry.

* *The State of France.*

When de Gaulle returned to power in 1958, the recovery of industry was well advanced and output was rising rapidly. But inflation and rising costs made it increasingly hard for France to export competitively, and the drain on reserves was greater than ever. The franc was trailing along as almost the weakest currency in Europe. With the first of the Common Market tariff cuts due to be made in January 1959, it looked as though France would have to suffer the ignominy of being the only one of the Six to invoke the 'escape clauses' protecting her from the shock of competition.

Such prospects were intolerable for de Gaulle. He and his finance minister, Antoine Pinay, instructed Jacques Rueff, an orthodox 'liberal' finance expert, to prepare drastic remedies. Rueff did so. On 27 December 1958 the franc was devalued by 17.5 per cent to the level it was to hold for the next ten years (then 13.65 to the £). As a psychological boost for French morale, the decimal point was shifted and a New Franc born, equalling one hundred old ones. The scheduled Common Market tariff cut was respected without recourse to the escape clauses; and, most daring of all for this land of protectionism, trade liberalization with other OEEC countries was pushed up to the unprecedented level of 90 per cent, after having been suspended altogether in the black year of 1957.

These reforms were the greatest economic achievement of de Gaulle's eleven-year régime – a bold start which it never equalled later. The results were immediate. Thanks to devaluation, imports were rapidly balanced by exports. Gold and other reserves, down almost to nil by 1958, began to climb again and went on doing so, at intervals, for the next ten years. Large sums of capital, much of it French, began to return home from Swiss and other foreign banks, encouraged by the prospect of political stability and no more inflation. In ripping open the cocoon around her economy, France had indeed taken a big risk: but she was now far better prepared to face the test of the Common Market, and she was able at last to behave like a financially independent nation.

The years 1959 to 1962 were fat ones for the economy, although for the nation as a whole they were also the years of grave moral crisis over Algeria. Industry faced and survived the first shocks of German competition, and its self-confidence swelled. France began to show the outward signs of a nation suddenly growing rich. Sleek new cars, like the Renault Floride and the Citroën DS 19, were filling the streets; new luxury flats, luxury shops and holidays found a ready market. The Algerian war, whatever its other unpleasant effects, had not in itself done too much damage to the economy; and as soon as it ended, the return to France of nearly a million *colons* brought a powerful new contribution of skill, energy and much-needed manpower.

But inflation had once again been merely curbed, not cured. Wages had been rising much faster in private industry than in the public sector, provoking, in March 1963, a large-scale strike of miners and other public servants. The Government emerged from this strike with its prestige jolted, but with a determination that the upward spiral of wages and prices must stop. In September de Gaulle's young finance minister, a certain Valéry Giscard d'Estaing, launched an austerity plan that involved a credit squeeze, a wage and price freeze and severe curbs on public spending. Immediate results were satisfactory: the balance of payments again improved, and prices were held steady without any serious growth in unemployment. But by late 1964 the inherent drawbacks of this policy were also making themselves felt. Over-all expansion slumped from a rate of about 5 per cent to less than 3 per cent. France had a year of malaise in 1965, reflected in the slump in de Gaulle's vote in the presidential election. Once re-elected, he dismissed Giscard and replaced him with the ex-premier Michel Debré. After 1969 Giscard was again finance minister and the economy did extremely well, despite difficult world conditions in 1970–71 and continued structural weaknesses in France which were only slowly being cured. Before we look at these in detail, and at the economic record since 1974 and the future outlook for France, we should examine the influence of the Plan; of the Common Market; and of the capital/labour conflict which reached an initial climax in the general strike of 1968.

TECHNOCRATS AND THE PLAN

Throughout the first two post-war decades with their ups and downs and shifts of policy, the principal motor of continuity was the Plan. And though today its role has become far less crucial, it is still valuable. This voluntary and pragmatic association between State and industry seems, at first sight, most untypical of the formal and legalistic French. Yet its success has devolved from two other factors, both typically French: the large role of the State in the French economy, unusual for an advanced Western country, and the special position of the 'technocrat' in France. In this context, a national Plan is not such an innovation as it might be in Britain or the United States.

For several centuries, so much of the wealth of France has belonged to the State, whether monarchy or republic, that large-scale private industry has always had to rely on State funds and has therefore accepted a measure of State direction. The oldest French nationalization, that of the tobacco industry, dates from Louis XIV. In the nineteenth century, the mines, the railways, the banks and heavy industry were all built up with the help of public capital, although remaining themselves in private hands. Even the idea of State planning is not new in France: Colbert made attempts under Louis XIV, and so did Bonaparte.

Therefore when large-scale formal nationalization came, in 1936 and in 1944-6, it did not mark such a turning-point as in Britain. The Left-wing Popular Front Government had made a start before the war: it took over most armaments, the railways, and to an extent the Bank of France, and set up State aeronautical firms. The immediate post-war Governments then made a much more sweeping movement – a task eased by capitalism's taint of Nazi collaboration: they swiftly nationalized the Renault car firm (whose private owners had allegedly helped the Germans) as well as Air France, the coal-mines, electricity and gas, and the larger insurance companies and clearing banks, while the Bank of France came fully under public ownership. Most of these moves were made in an anti-capitalist spirit. However, since 1946 there have been no more major changes, save that the Government has been building up the State oil concerns so as to depend less on the Seven Sisters.

The list of public concerns may look impressive. But in fact only about 7 per cent of manufacturing industry, in terms of turnover, is in State hands – no more than the figure in Britain now that British Leyland is publicly owned. As for the service industries such as railways and electricity, the pattern of State control is much the same in France as in Britain. If the French bodies tend to work more efficiently, one factor could be the high calibre of their top administrators, technocrats of intense zeal and loyalty who come mostly from the élite worlds of the Grandes Ecoles and the Grands Corps. Another factor is that the State, while subjecting these industries to its long-term planning, and keeping a watch over their finances, has also increasingly encouraged them to operate on commercial lines like private firms, with all the risks involved. This is even more true of Renault, which is run just like a private company; the State has never interfered in its commercial policy even though it owns all the capital and appoints the management.

In the manufacturing field, Renault is a rare case, for nearly all industry is in private hands. Here the State's influence is strong, but this is more a matter of tradition and personal contacts than of organic structure or rules; if firms lean heavily upon the State, it is often because they choose to. This said, it is true that the State does have much more control over the financial markets than in Britain, as there is little equivalent to the City. The State controls most of the big credit bodies, so that a firm depends on it for financing of loans. And the Ministry of Finance has much formal power; over many matters a firm must seek its authorization where this would not be necessary in Britain. Many firms also rely on State purchases, and the State controls many leading financial institutions, not only the larger insurance companies but credit bodies such as the powerful Caisse des Dépôts, and the three biggest banks which account for 70 per cent of French banking.

The position of these banks is equivocal. On the one hand, the Government has recently been encouraging them to behave just like private banks, and tries not to interfere in their daily running.

Yet, if they step out of line, they may get slapped down; in 1975 the chairman of Crédit Lyonnais, François Bloch-Lainé, was dismissed on Giscard's orders, partly because he had not followed the credit-squeeze guidelines. So it is not easy to tell how far these banks truly have their own policies, or how far they are tools of Government policies, and there are many different views on this. One clue is that at the top level of the economy there is such an intermesh of personal relationships and pressures that it is hard to tell which are the State's initiatives or interests and which are private ones.

Private industry resents this *étatisme* much less than you might expect. Perhaps it has grown to accept it; or else it sees the advantages of State guidance and protection. At the Patronat (the employers' federation) the line recently put to me was: 'It is not true that the State tells us what to do. The association is a voluntary one, of mutual confidence, and generally we trust the Administration whose economic policies tend to be far-sighted.' And at the Ministry of Finance I was told, 'The problem is not so much State interference as the converse, that most firms, like most Frenchmen, expect too much from the State. They come running to us to solve their problems. They have an exaggerated faith in what we can do for them, and should learn to help themselves more.' This is a common view.

But it is the State that provides a dynamic leadership for economic development, more markedly than in most Western countries. The effect, though controversial, is almost certainly beneficial – you have only to look at France's progress since the war. There is a continuing tradition of the State as entrepreneur and originator of bold schemes, especially regional ones, of a kind that in Britain might be undertaken more locally or haphazardly. Often the State will take the initiative by setting up *sociétés mixtes*, development bodies associating public, local and private interests. Recent ventures include the creation of a 'scientific park' near Cannes; the running down of the Lorraine steel-mills and building of a huge steel-based complex at Fos in the Rhône delta; the new modernistic resorts on the Languedoc coast; and the decision to endow Toulouse and Brittany with what is termed 'an electronics vocation'. And private industry follows along. This kind of State leadership may sometimes put a damper on private initiative, but it continues to serve France well. The secret is that the State manages to attract into its service – via the Grandes Ecoles and the Grands Corps – men of the right quality and imagination to operate it.

Without this tradition of State initiative, and this network of technocrats, the Plan could never have played such an effective role in rebuilding France's post-war economy. It has been staffed by men with the same ideas and background as many of the key people in industry and the civil service, who have thus been able to win each other's trust and find a common language.

Yet Jean Monnet himself, who inspired and founded the Plan, is not a typical technocrat at all. His origins were modest: he was born in Cognac in 1888, where his family were vine-growers and brandy distillers. He never went through the technocrat's usual educational mill, but was brought up partly in the United States, and much of his first knowledge of the world was gained in the humble role of overseas salesman for the Monnet cognac firm. Yet he is a man of the most sophisticated international vision and sympathy; he has great personal charm, speaks perfect English and is the kind of warm idealist who inspires high devotion in his followers.

After leaving the family firm, he spent more than twenty years in public service before and during the Second World War, working for the League of Nations, the French Government and then the Allies in many parts of the world. He came to know the United States well, and to admire American efficiency; and during the war he and a number of friends began to plot how to pull France up to American standards – by novel, non-American methods. In 1945 he met de Gaulle in Washington, and won him over to the idea of the Plan. The following year the five-year First Plan was approved, and its secretariat, with Monnet as Commissioner-General, moved into an elegant little private house, most unlike a formal Government office, in the shadow of the Ste Clothilde church on the Left Bank. And there the secretariat still lives today, though Monnet himself has long since left, and in his old age has been devoting himself to promoting the cause of a united Europe.

As soon as the Plan was in action Monnet, never a conformist, broke at once with many of the taboos and formalities of French administration. Unlikely groups of people, Communist union-leaders and old-style financiers, were shoved together at short notice without form or ceremony. Instead of long, formal memoranda, there were often little notes scribbled by Monnet on sheets of pink or yellow paper while walking in the woods near his quiet home west of Versailles. Instead of long, elaborate business lunches, there were working meals of un-French simplicity in the Plan's headquarters. Life there was in some ways more monastic than bureaucratic, with working sessions taking little account of office hours, week-ends or even holidays. There was even a faint air of revivalism, according to some accounts, about the inter-industry meetings of those early years, where the planners communicated their faith.

This may help to explain why a certain mystique has grown up around the Plan, both at home and abroad. In France, many otherwise unexplained achievements were credited by public opinion to the Plan; there's been an element of faith-healing about it. Economists, in fact, are often dubious about how valuable it has been in strictly *economic* terms. Some of them argue that much of the French recovery would have happened anyway, and they point to Germany's even greater progress with no planning at all. Yet few of them disagree about the value of the Plan's psychological influence on industry. It has torn some of the barriers of secrecy from private firms, helped to create a new climate of competition and productivity, and induced different classes of people to think and work together as in France they had rarely done before.

The two main facts about the Plan are, first, that it has always been 'voluntary' and 'indicative' rather than formally binding; and secondly, that although it is run as a Government department, it is simply a forum for drawing up blueprints and exchanging ideas, without the executive powers of a Ministry. It constantly seeks to guide the economy in a certain expansionist direction, and successive Governments have tended to use its forecasts and advice as the basis of their policy; but neither they, nor even private firms, are under any constitutional obligation to do so, and only the Government can turn the Plan's projections into decisions. It has been so effective simply because both parties, State and private industry, have most of the time agreed to collaborate with it.

Its small full-time secretariat, never more than forty strong, is an informal brains trust of clever, mainly youngish men, drawn from the civil service, universities or industry. After a number of years at the Plan, they may well return to these fields; few are academic economists. Today they are still the same kind of team that Monnet first drew round him in 1946, many of whom are now well known: Robert Marjolin, a former vice-president of the European Economic Commission in Brussels; Etienne Hirsch, who took Monnet's place at the Plan; and Paul Delouvrier, who later took charge of planning the future of the Paris region and now presides over Electricité de France.

The Plan's basic task is to set targets for growth, in all the different sectors of the economy, over five-year periods. First, the staff of the Plan discuss with the Government the best over-all expansion rate to aim at, basing their verdict on estimations of natural growth rather than of needs. For each industry they set three possible targets, high, low and medium. Then, having decided on the most realistic target in each case, the Plan convenes its twenty-five 'modernization commissions', to work out and apportion the details of growth within each sector. These commissions were Monnet's principal innovation, and their system of direct round-table confrontation marked a sharp break with French administrative practice. Within each commission the heads of private firms large and small, some union leaders, and civil servants, sit round the same table with the planners over a period of months, thrashing out in detail how to achieve their growth and their investment targets, say, in textiles, pig-breeding or aluminium. Then the sum of the commissions, reports – a vast dossier – is submitted for approval to Parliament.

This system is flexible and strictly empirical – in defiance of French tradition. It is what the French call *une économie concertée*, operating a kind of working compromise between economic liberalism and *dirigisme*. Professor Kindleberger even describes it as 'in some important respects the opposite of planning', and comments: 'The roles have been reversed from the nineteenth century when the British were the pragmatists and the French were doctrinaire.'*

Yet it may still seem puzzling that French private industry, often so individualistic and suspicious of the State, should have co-operated so readily with the Plan. One reason I have already suggested: the common background of the planners and the technocrats in some key firms. Another factor has been that the big State industries obviously gave a lead in supporting the Plan, and their smaller competitors felt obliged to follow suit. Some of them were spurred by memories of pre-war stagnation; or, emerging near-bankrupt from the war, they were obliged to turn to the State for funds, and accepted a measure of planning and supervision in return. Once inside the Plan, each larger firm was encouraged to feel itself an integral part of the operation, with a democratic voice in the outcome. But of course there have been less democratic pressures, too, especially under de Gaulle. Firms' collaboration has been secured by an elaborate system of Government rewards and incentives – tax relief, tariff concessions, loans for investment, or valuable State contracts, sometimes amounting to bribery.

As the planners and the industrialists are on an equal footing within the commissions, the larger firms tend to give at least as much advice to the Plan as they get from it. 'We, and bodies like us, *are* the Plan,' I was told imperiously at the State-run Electricité de France; 'we make our own long-term forecasts, and submit them to the Plan for approval.'

It is true that the many thousands of very small firms tend to get left out of this process, and their spokesmen have often criticized the Plan as being too *dirigiste*. Inevitably it is of less value to them, individually. But its influence on larger and medium-sized firms has been considerable: simply by getting them round a table together, the planners have been able gradually to coax many industrialists out of their ingrained secretiveness and mistrust. In a France of so many family firms this mistrust extended as

* *France: Change and Tradition*, p. 155.

much to a firm's colleagues and its own professional confederation as to the State and its tax inspectors: many companies, in fact, have habitually indulged in treble book-keeping – one set of figures for the public auditors and inland revenue, one for shareholders, and a third, the real figures, to be kept a close secret among directors! But today many of the larger firms, at least, have grown readier to share details of their plans, techniques and costs. By some Anglo-Saxon standards there is still a distance to go. For instance, one of France's giants, the Michelin family tyre-making firm, still makes a virtual fetish of its old-fashioned secretiveness. But on the whole the new atmosphere has facilitated joint planning, as well as the preparation of mergers and the sharing of research or export services. The Plan has done much to encourage productivity and the mergers of small firms, as well as investment, which in pre-war days was often regarded as a luxurious frill. All this helped to prepare French industry for the Common Market. And over the years the Plan has also been steadily building up something that France always badly lacked: a bank of economic information and industrial statistics.

In accepting the Plan as the basis of their economic policies, Gaullist and pre-Gaullist Governments alike came to rely less than in the past on the cautious orthodoxy that has generally held sway at the Ministry of Finance. The powerful experts there were penetrated by new ideas and influences: no longer were they dedicated solely to budget-balancing and careful economies. In periods of credit squeeze the existence of the Plan certainly acted as a brake on cuts in vital investments; and at other times, the Plan spurred the Government to give loans to the right industries. Of course there have been failures, as well. Sometimes the Plan has led to unbalanced growth, and it has rarely succeeded in checking inflation. But at least its forecasts have largely prevented the kind of shortages so frequent in post-war Britain. When, in 1965, a sudden early cold spell caused power cuts in Britain but not in France, an Electricité de France technocrat told me, smugly, 'Ah, if you had a Plan . . .'

One important early success of the Plan lay in securing the co-operation of the trade unions. At first, even the Communists' union leaders took part in its round-table meetings and seemed

prepared to help. But this success was short-lived. It gradually
became clear that most of the complex technical work of the Plan
was above the union leaders' heads: they had neither the economic
training nor the inside information to be able to contribute effective ideas. The largest and most powerful union, the Communist-
led Confédération Générale du Travail, virtually opted out of the
Plan after about 1950; and its leaders were not alone in suspecting
that the invitation to the unions was a sly move to silence their
opposition to capitalist expansion. Of the three main unions, only
the more-or-less Catholic CFDT* (formerly the CFTC) has
taken a sincere part in the Plan's committee-working, but has
made no bones about its dilemma of approving of planning while
disapproving of the capitalist framework. It is probably not even
true that the relative infrequency of strikes in French industry
from 1948 to 1968 was due to the presence of the unions in the
Plan: other factors played a larger part, such as the weakness
and division of the unions, and the steady wage-increases.

In a number of aspects the Plan's role and position have been
changing over the years. While the First Plan (1946–52) concentrated on reconstruction of basic industries, the Second (1953–7)
switched the emphasis to target-setting for the whole of industry
and agriculture, still its main concern. The Third (1958–61) and
Fourth (1962–5) Plans widened the range to include social needs,
such as welfare and housing, and regional development. Sections
of the Plan are now regionalized, and each small town is proud
to have its own little plan as a segment of the national one. In
fact the Plan, long accepted by Government and big business, has
finally become part of the ordinary coinage of local public
opinion. It is part of the landscape, like elections or the budget.
Everyone wants to plan – farmer, grocer, tinker, clerk. Yet this
has been happening just at a time when, nationally, the role of
the Plan has been declining. There are two main reasons for this
decline. First, political stability under de Gaulle and his successors has not only made the Plan less necessary as a factor of
continuity; it has also, as we shall see, caused it to be identified
with the Government as it never was under the quick-changing

* Confédération Française Démocratique du Travail.

Prime Ministers of the Fourth Republic. Secondly, due to the Common Market and other world influences, the French economy has become much less enclosed and therefore less amenable to purely domestic planning: in fact, certain features of the Plan have been incorporated into the wider planning mechanisms of the EEC. But though the Plan's role is now more modest, that does not detract from the crucial part it did play in the earlier French post-war revival.

The influence of the Plan itself may have waned; but the power of those who are loosely known as 'the technocrats' has been greatly increasing. It took a step forward under de Gaulle, who despised the old-style career politicians and put civil servants such as Maurice Couve de Murville and Edgard Pisani into many key Ministerial posts. And it has made a further advance under Giscard, who, unlike his predecessors, de Gaulle the soldier and Pompidou the former *lycée* teacher, is himself a supreme product of that uniquely French élitist system, whereby public life both political and economic is dominated by the upper stratum of the civil service known as *les grands corps de l'Etat*, recruited from two all-powerful colleges. Some of these brilliant public servants then become career politicians, as Giscard himself did at an early age. He wears *all three* of the system's proudest badges, 'X', ENA, IF – that is, he is one of the very few men in France to have passed through *both* the Ecole Polytechnique *and* its younger rival, the Ecole Nationale d'Administration, *and* then to have joined the Inspection des Finances, the most influential and exclusive of the Grands Corps. Many of his chief *aides* at the Elysée as well as his senior Ministers since 1974 – Chirac, Poniatowski, Fourcade, although not Barre – are fellow-*énarques* (the nickname for ENA old-boys), pragmatists very different in outlook and background from the old demagogues of the Fourth Republic. So, the new régime at the Elysée has been regarded in France as an apotheosis of the gradual take-over of political power since 1958 by the new civil-service mandarins and technocrats with their tight old-boy networks.

It is all highly controversial. Is this system one of the main factors behind France's envied economic dynamism? Or, as many people believe, has it become a dangerous obstacle to the growth of a more open society? The public looks on the technocrats sometimes with awe and admiration, but often with suspicion. They can be seen as benevolent sages, sweeping away past inefficiencies; but to some people, notably on the Left, they are more sinister and inhuman figures, like the technocrat rulers of *Alphaville*, Jean-Luc Godard's film of a nightmarish computer-city of the future. A different but even more widespread criticism is that the system is perpetuating power in the hands of a tiny section of society.

The concept of technocracy, always stronger in France than in Britain, applies properly to rulers with a technical training or outlook, but has come to apply loosely also to civil servants in political roles. In any case, the species is very different either from the old wheeling-and-dealing politician, or from the traditional businessman, or from the more passive kind of bureaucrat. The emphasis is less on party intrigue or ideology than on practical progress and modern efficiency, which itself becomes a kind of ideology.

If asked to name the archetypal technocrat, many Frenchmen might mention the late Louis Armand, a stocky, unpretentious-looking *polytechnicien* engineer who reorganized France's railways after the war, led the Government's search for mineral wealth in the Sahara in the 1950s, pioneered Euratom, produced with Jacques Rueff in 1960 the key report on French structural reform, and then rounded off a fabulous career by heading the Channel Tunnel study group. Armand, who died in 1971, was typical of idealistic technocrats, a man of ideas as well as action, as alarmed at France's archaic structures as he was proud of what he described to me as her 'ideal link between *dirigisme* and capitalism'. It is hard to conceive of a mere engineer in Britain enjoying the same kind of status as public sage and Grand Old Man. Besides Giscard, other examples of *polytechniciens* in top public posts include Pierre Guillaumat, overlord of the State oil concerns, and Pierre Massé, head of the Plan in 1962–6. Pierre Dreyfus, chairman and managing director of Renault during the great years of its expansion and right up till 1975, came from the non-technical stream: he studied law and then went into business before switching to public service, first in electricity and mines.

But his detailed interest in technical innovation, coupled with advanced social welfare projects for his workers, were typical of the more enlightened kind of technocrat; and he seemed the very opposite of the popular image of a car tycoon. Slight, reserved, very intellectual, he hated the world of Paris society, and devoted himself off-duty to books, music and family life, or to long evenings with fellow-technocrats discussing, for instance, how technology can help developing countries. Many other technocrats, at least in the heady period of post-war renewal, have shared the same idealistic faith in technical progress, the same belief in a planned economy insulated as far as possible from the pressures of party leaders, trade unionists or mere capitalists. Some have elevated this into a philosophy: technology is a key to human happiness, and an élite possessed of this secret will guide and save the world. Most of these technocrats are also men of personal culture – this as much as anything distinguishes them from their Anglo-Saxon managerial counterparts. Since 1958 they have been moving into Government, too. De Gaulle appointed a number of prefects and other civil servants with a technocratic outlook to senior Ministerial posts – Pierre Sudreau, Edgard Pisani, Olivier Guichard and others – and Pompidou and Giscard continued the process.

The specific élitist structure in France that nurtures the technocrat is not in itself new; some Grands Corps date back long before Napoleon. The corps' mechanism is highly complex and subtle, and there is nothing like them in Britain. They consist of a dozen or so State collegiate bodies that operate parallel to the Ministries; each has a specific technical role – for instance, the Inspection des Finances audits State accounts – but their more significant function, by tradition, is to keep State and industry supplied with a pool of top-level talent, mobile and polyvalent. The corps are in two camps, in constant rivalry: 'technical' ones (such as the Corps des Mines), led by engineers recruited essentially from the mighty Polytechnique, a Napoleonic creation; and 'administrative' ones (such as the IF) whose members today are drawn mainly from ENA, the post-graduate civil-service college set up in 1946.

Each school and corps has its active old-boy loyalties, especially strong among *les X,* as *polytechniciens* are nicknamed. This may bear some relation to the days when the British Cabinet and Whitehall were dominated by Etonians, Wykehamists and Balliol men; but whereas in Britain these old-school-tie networks are today weakening and becoming largely social, in France they are stronger than ever and more specifically professional. Moreover, the prestige of the two great Schools and the grander Corps, and the golden careers they offer, may explain why so much of France's finest young talent is tempted in that direction. Conversely, fields such as broadcasting or journalism, the universities or merchant banks, offer lower prestige and fewer outlets than in Britain, so that the kind of brilliant graduate who might aim for the BBC or the City is more likely in France to go into public service – not only into the *cabinets ministériels* but into a wide range of State industrial bodies that recruit their leaders from the Grands Corps. All this may have various advantages for the economy. And so, as the British look a little enviously at France's superior record in recent years, it might be right to attribute some of this success to the élitist system. And yet, the system is always under criticism in France. Polemical books have appeared recently with names like *La Mafia polytechnicienne* or *L'Enarchie, ou les mandarins de la société bourgeoise* – usually written by ex-alumni. J.-A. Kosciusko-Morizet, the young 'X' who wrote *La Mafla,* accuses men such as Giscard of '*un terrorisme de la rationalité mis au service de l'ambition personnelle*', of ignoring or despising all popular feeling. Yet this is exactly the image that Giscard has been striving, since 1974, to shake off. Other common criticisms of the system are: that its recruitment is too narrowly bourgeois; that a technocracy increasingly cut off from the people is undemocratic and may lead to new explosions of which May 1968 was just a warning; that within the civil service, the gulf between the pre-selected upper strata and those condemned to the middle ranks leads the latter into frustration, apathy and incompetence; and that, even within the élite, the constant feuding in defence of vested interests is really the enemy of modern efficiency, whatever the brilliance of individuals.

Let us look first at the ENA stream, which is steadily gaining ground today over the *polytechniciens,* as the early post-war *énarques* now aged around fifty move into the top posts. The school, a few metres from St-Germain-des-Prés, recruits mainly from the smarter bourgeois Paris *lycées*, via 'Sciences-Po'. During their twenty-nine months with ENA, students spend part of their time on practical attachment to prefectures, *mairies*, or embassies abroad, and the rest acquiring the techniques and correct attitudes of the civil service. The final exam then classifies them in order of merit, enabling the top ones to choose – in that order – the thirty or so places offered each year by the Grands Corps. The rest of the annual output of about a hundred must settle for ordinary jobs in Ministries or other public bodies; but even this, such is the prestige of ENA, ensures them a safe if less glorious career for life.

Of the five corps served by ENA, the most sought-after by those high on the list is the Inspection des Finances, followed in order by Conseil d'Etat, Cour des Comptes, Corps Préfectoral, and lastly Corps Diplomatique. This may seem odd: why should the prospect of becoming an ambassador or prefect have less appeal than joining one of the other corps whose work seems relatively dull and anonymous? – the Cour des Comptes, like the IF, has the job of verifying public accounts, while the Conseil d'Etat advises on legal disputes between State and citizen. But there is more to it than this. The Quai d'Orsay, as much as the Foreign Office, has seen its appeal decline in an age when the exciting diplomatic work is done by jet-setting Kissingers, and ambassadors are 'mere post-boxes'. The prefectoral corps, it is true, has raised its prestige, as the new *super-préfets de région* win increasing economic powers. But even this cannot compete, in the eyes of ambitious young *énarques*, with the advantages of those three corps that offer unrivalled freedom and scope, and are often the best springboards for a political career – Michel Debré is a member of the Conseil d'Etat, and Chirac and Jobert of the Cour des Comptes, while Couve de Murville and Chaban-Delmas as well as Giscard are *inspecteurs des Finances*. Consider the Conseil d'Etat: with its elegant premises in the Palais Royal, it is almost a political club, and to join it is a little like becoming a Prize Fellow of All Souls – with the significant difference that one is *far* closer to the seats of power. The young *conseiller* is expected to work there for his first four years after ENA, but with a bit of initiative he can in practice combine this with more exciting work too. He may, to quote a specific case, spend his morning at the Conseil on some typical routine work – adjudicating on whether parents of children born in adultery can claim family allowances – and his afternoon at the Quai, advising the Minister on East–West strategy. The pay, too, is no disincentive: a 26-year-old told me in 1975 that his annual salary from the Conseil was 65,000 francs, and on top of this he was picking up 35,000 from various public jobs. After his four years, his path might be open to a regular post of some power in a Minister's *cabinet* (whose more brilliant staff are often recruited from the Grands Corps), with a basic salary of some 80,000 francs at 32.

Once a member of a corps, you remain so for life and are salaried by it. So, if your political or business career comes unstuck for a while, you can always make a tactical retreat to safe obscurity. Thus Michel Jobert, having fallen out with Giscard in 1974 and failed to rally the UDR, can potter away at the Cour des Comptes while preparing some political come-back. Many less ambitious souls do in fact prefer to stay inside their corps all their lives, not attempting the rat-race. The system can be accused of offering excessive privilege to a pampered few, but it does also provide a flexibility that, arguably, enables a brilliant and energetic man to make the fullest use of his talents in the State's service. On the ordinary staff of a Ministry, you are strait-jacketed by hierarchy; as a *corpsard*, you can take endless sabbaticals.

It is the *inspecteurs des Finances* who have most successfully exploited this system. Their corps is attached to the Ministry of Finance, and its junior members spend their time – as under the Monarchy – touring France to check that State funds are not being misspent. But the more senior ones have manoeuvred their way into every corner of real power. The head of French Railways is an *inspecteur*; so is F.-X. Ortoli, President of the EEC Commission until the end of 1976; so even is Michel Rocard, ablest of Socialist leaders around Mitterrand. By unwritten custom, every Minister is expected to have in his *cabinet* at least one *inspecteur*,

chosen by the corps and acting almost as a spy for *les Finances*.
The Inspection is a real mafia, maintaining its hold over public
life not only through intellectual superiority but also by fostering
a calculated mystique: 'Do not allow the politicians you serve to
understand you too well,' the secretary-general of the corps
recently advised a batch of new members; 'preserve the mystery
of your economic intuition and they will respect you the more.'

The *inspecteurs* are often resented by the *polytechniciens* in the
rival camp whose fiefs – such as French Railways – they have been
invading. *Les X* form a much larger mafia than the *énarques*, with
a stronger solidarity; they are also much more conservative, and
their qualities are less evident. After a two-year general technical
course at their famous military college (formerly beside the
Panthéon, now in the southern suburbs), they mostly go on to
more specialized *écoles d'application* of which the most superior
are the Ecole des Mines and the Ecole des Ponts et Chaussées –
although a very few 'X', such as Giscard, opt for ENA. The old-
boys of each of these colleges constitute a corps. They are less
closely involved in the political scene than the various ENA
corps, but they do play a part; men of the Corps des Mines have
held key posts under Giscard both at the Elysée and the Quai.
And whereas the engineers from the other Grandes Ecoles (such
as Centrale) remain in technical jobs, *les X* will often become
senior administrators. In ministries such as Equipment or Industry, and in the big State bodies running electricity, oil supplies,
postal services and so on, they have a near monopoly of power.
Rivalries are intense even between different clans of the mafia,
notably *les Mines* and *les Ponts*, each with its own fiefs; in some
administrations where both clans are present, they fight 'frontier
battles' with all the savage pettiness of a demarcation dispute
between British unions. But they will always drop the feud and
close ranks in face of their common adversary, the non-'X'.
Any 'X' will always try to fill a vacancy on his staff with another
'X', and will prefer to do business with another 'X' or help out
another 'X', whether he knows him or not.

This virtual closed-shop has some negative aspects and can
lead to the opposite of dynamism. Another common criticism of
les X is that many of them have a *rentier* spirit; protected by their

status which ensures them a cushy job for life, they feel little concern for new ideas and methods – for example, blame for the well-known inadequacies of the French telephone system has sometimes been laid at the door of the 'X' who run it. The drama of the *polytechniciens* is that, trained as engineers and not executives, they find themselves in a competitive world of modern management for which they are seldom suited. It is true that a new wind has been blowing in recent years: a number of younger 'X' and others have been on graduate courses in the United States to places such as the Harvard Business School, and have come back with new techniques that have hugely benefited the French economy. But they are still a minority. Meanwhile, a growing number of 'X' are today buying themselves out of State service and moving into private industry or commerce, where many firms welcome them with open arms – less, very often, for their actual abilities than for their precious contacts. If you have an 'X' on your staff, he will be able to ring up just the right pal in the ministry that is blocking the crucial permit you need. Recently the French branch of Sony was in dispute with the Ministry of Finance on some vital issue and found itself getting nowhere – until Sony in Tokyo astutely appointed an 'X' as its director for France; he quietly settled the problem with an 'X' in the Minister's *cabinet*. This kind of thing happens all the time.

So this network and other lesser ones have created an intricate mesh of close personal links between public and private sector – banks, ministries, industrial firms and so on. This has some advantages in a France notorious for its rigid compartmentalization: a few men at the top, speaking the same language, have been able to short-circuit the bureaucratic *lenteurs* of contact between administrations, and get things moving. The Plan, as we have seen, benefited hugely from these links. They can even bestride political barriers too – potentially useful in a nation of political extremes. Though the Communists are outside the system, the Socialists are not; some of their leaders belong to the Grands Corps and one of them, Michel Rocard, was able to use his friendship with fellow-*inspecteurs* at the Elysée to mediate behind the scenes in some recent crises with the unions.

And yet, though the élites are a means of bypassing some of

the blockages in French society, they in turn create others. This is the paradox. One critic of the system, J.-C. Thoenig, writes in his book *L'Ere des technocrates*:* 'The existence of groups so enclosed, with practices so monopolistic, may be one of the principal obstacles to the adaptation of the administration to modern management.' His criticisms are directed mainly against the technical corps, where these faults are in general more evident than in the ENA corps. How far is he right?

It is not easy to draw up a balance-sheet. On the positive side, one of the virtues of the system is integrity. The State, by paying its senior servants so highly and treating them well, has over the centuries built up a body of men who – with far fewer exceptions than in other Latin countries! – are honest and unbribeable. They are largely free, too, from party political pressures, even if, in turn, they may influence or enter politics. And most of them, for all their rivalries and intrigues, do have a real sense of vocation and public service. Yet, time and again in France, one is struck by the contrast between the energy and inspiration of some individuals and the rigidity of the system enclosing them; it is as if the two are connected, and the very rigidity is a necessary challenge to initiative.

There are three main aspects to this rigidity:

– A degree of competition between the corps may be healthy, but some, especially the technical ones, carry it too far; like medieval barons, they spend much of their energies on conducting sallies into each others' territories, trying to extend their influence or alternatively to protect their interests.

– A more serious problem is the gulf that exists, in any public body, between the élite stream and the rest. Promotion on merit from the middle ranks is almost impossible: if by ill chance you failed to acquire the right diplomas from some Grande Ecole in your youth, you have little means of moving far up the hierarchy, however able and intelligent you may prove yourself. The closed-shops prevent it. This is especially true in technical bodies and also in the Ministry of Finance, where by custom the key posts are reserved for *inspecteurs*, and if you join an ordinary department you tend to stay there for life. Inevitably this leads to apathy,

* *Les Editions d'Organisation* (Paris 1973).

lack of initiative and even incompetence in the middle ranks where so much of the regular work is done. Able people, if they are barred from the élite, have little incentive to enter public service. This may explain why French bureaucracy is such an odd mixture of torpor and dynamism.

– A third kind of barrier is the one between the public service and other professions. People rarely move from one career to another. The university world is a proud ghetto and its professors would rarely deign, or be invited, to take up public duties. Raymond Barre, who for some years has alternated between university and civil-service duties, is a rare exception. Similarly, a brilliant businessman or industrialist would rarely be co-opted into State service as often happens in the United States or even Britain. He would just not be accepted without the right pedigree. It is true that a reverse process happens often enough, especially under the Fifth Republic: State technocrats become managers of private firms or Ministers, often with valuable results. But the corps will not allow the process to be two-way. It is partly a matter of pedigree but also of family custom, in a country where the bourgeoisie has its own internal barriers: some leading families are traditionally producers of civil servants, others of academics, while others own factories – and that is the way it stays. Many Frenchmen today think that this lack of cross-fertilization has become a drawback.

Simon Nora, a distinguished *inspecteur des Finances*, told me in 1975: 'Our élite system was a great asset until a few years ago – that is, in the post-war decades when our politics were unstable and France was fast modernizing and industrializing. The technocrats then were a dedicated *clergé*, the secular priests of progress, pulling France forward with autocratic zeal. But that phase is over. Today France is largely modernized and what is needed is something else, the emergence of a more open and egalitarian society where ordinary people can participate more. The system is now an obstacle to that.'

Of course, on paper, Polytechnique and ENA are perfectly democratic; anyone can go there, the entry and passing-out exams are impartial, and there is no nepotism at this stage – that comes later, inside the corps system. But in practice the intake is overwhelmingly bourgeois and – in the case of ENA – Parisian to boot. This is partly a matter of social convention, partly of teaching; only a few smart Paris *lycées* are properly geared to provide the specialized teaching that the ultra-competitive entry exams demand. Undoubtedly ENA has succeeded superbly in the role given it: to turn out, within a certain conformist mould, a certain kind of able administrator. The average *énarque* is markedly more confident, articulate and enthusiastic than his British counterpart. But he goes straight into a privileged desk job and rarely has contact with 'the people'. There is a growing feeling today that he should at least start in the ranks in some way. Polytechnique's intake is a little more varied and provincial than ENA's; but from the moment he enters, the 'X' is every bit as secluded as the *énarque*. Thus the system may be a major factor behind the French citizen's regular sense of grievance against the State, and the sense of alienation felt by the working-class, peasantry and others.

This is not new. Read Balzac, and you will find the same criticisms of *les X* as are made of *énarques* today. And since the war the system has changed little; while the teaching at Polytechnique has been modernized a little, the creation of ENA has simply strengthened the grip of *its* Grands Corps. The most important of recent trends has been the growth of a new inner mafia, made up of those of the élite who are also old-boys of the Harvard Business School or the Massachusetts Institute of Technology. These new mandarins have played a positive and crucial role in the recent modernization of French management. But they are also using their new prestige to carve out new vested interests.

Visit ENA or Polytechnique today, and you will find plenty of students ferociously critical of the system they are entering. Yet they stand to gain too much from it to be prepared, except in a few quixotic cases, to try to transform it by calling its bluff. In 1972 a whole 'year' of *énarques* decided bravely, on passing out, to boycott the three grander corps in favour of ministries or prefectures. But their gesture has had no sequel. It seems that effective reform of the system can come only through *either* basic reforms of higher education – such as integration of ENA and the Grandes Ecoles into the general university structure – *or*

through a new Government staffing policy for the upper administration, willingly bringing in outsiders and thus breaking up the
closed-shops of the corps. Either move would let all hell loose.
It is hard to see Giscard, not only a legatee of the system but a
believer in it, fouling his nest in this way. So, would a Left-wing
Government attempt reform? Even this is not certain. The unions
and parties of the Left are all outspokenly critical of the system;
but, in power, they might need to lean on it, at least in the shorter
term. Mitterrand and his colleagues know well that, for France
to be kept on the rails both politically and economically, they
would need the power and stability of the existing structure. And
while Communists are virtually debarred from the corps, there
are plenty of talented Socialists and Radicals sitting quietly inside
bodies such as the Conseil d'Etat, forming a kind of 'shadow'
administration and ready to take active office when called. The
Left might well seek to modify the system, but not to dispense
with it.

I suggest that, on balance, the virtues of the system outweigh
its defects, in terms of stability and economic progress. The
weightiest charge against it is not ineffectiveness but unfairness.
It is perpetuating the role of State as nanny, and a situation where
all citizens enjoy *égalité* but some enjoy more *égalité* than others.
The French people are becoming less ready to leave their destiny
in the hands of technocrats who claim to know best. If there is
ever another and worse 1968-style explosion, the tumbrils will be
full of short-haired, tidy-suited 'X' and *énarques*, clutching their
confident slide-rules and eloquently argued dossiers. This is a
theme I will return to at the end of this book. But now, let us
look at some other aspects of the economy today.

INDUSTRY AND THE COMMON MARKET

French industry has not yet fully completed the painful process of
adapting itself to the Common Market and to wider competition
after its long years of protectionism. But it has been managing the
process rather better than most people expected, and has found to
its own surprise that its earlier fears of the German juggernaut
were exaggerated. It has been helped by a few incidental factors,

notably the Rueff financial reforms of 1958: but much has been due also to the skill and energy of industrialists themselves, when they finally faced up to the choice between extinction and rapid and drastic renewal. The Common Market provided the shock they so badly needed.

The Plan had earlier helped to prepare the ground: by the time the Treaty of Rome was signed on 25 March 1957 several industries were modernized and reasonably competitive. One of the largest of these, steel, had already learned to face German competition under that valuable dress-rehearsal for the Common Market, the European Coal and Steel Community.* Jean Monnet, who played a leading role in founding CECA in 1951, told me: 'Back in 1946, we tried to persuade the Loire steel industry to modernize, but they refused. They began to do so only in 1953, under pressure from CECA and through fear of competition from Lorraine steel. If it hadn't been for CECA, the Loire industry would still be in the dumps today.'

The Patronat Français, the principal federation of big employers, had strongly opposed the creation of CECA, and later found to their surprise that French steel *was* able to compete! It was partly this discovery that modified the Patronat's subsequent hostility to the Common Market preparations. Yet they *were* still afraid, and it was not hard to understand their fears, seeing how backward and cloistered much of French industry still was in the mid-1950s. The Germans easily led the field in chemicals, machinery and metallurgy; their global production was 45 per cent higher; and they were not lumbered with the same high percentage of small artisan firms.

The Common Market was pushed through Parliament, more for political than economic reasons, by a handful of politicians on the Left and Centre, led by the far-sighted Robert Schuman. They resisted counter-pressure from the Patronat; but in order to ease French industry's problems, they did manage to extract important treaty concessions from the Germans to cover the ten transitional years. The Patronat were also being coaxed along by a few enlightened leaders within their own ranks, notably Georges Villiers, the president, who realized at an early stage how much

* CECA in French: Communauté Européenne du Charbon et de l'Acier.

France might benefit in the long run. So, when the treaty was finally signed, the Patronat boldly faced up to reality and switched their official policy, while many individual firms set about adapting to the new circumstances. For the Plan this was a signal victory: 'What we like best about the Common Market,' one planner told me, 'is that it helped shock our industry into modernizing.' Once again, as in 1940–44 – and this time, *before* defeat, and without bloodshed – the German menace had provided a catalyst.

Today nearly every executive – in industry, commerce or the civil service – accepts the EEC as a matter of course, even though he may be sceptical about its achievements to date and its prospects in the future. '*Moi, je suis très européen*' is a stock phrase. The relative ease with which the Common Market has been accepted, and the general shift in business attitudes that this has involved over the past twenty years, are remarkable in this land of protectionism.

French trade with the rest of the Six began to increase rapidly even before the first 10 per cent all-round tariff cut in 1959. After this date tariffs came down by an average 10 per cent each year, while trade grew at a much faster rate. In 1958–62 France doubled her over-all exports and trebled her exports to the rest of the Six: a record exceeded only by Italy. In chemicals and automobiles, French exports to Germany alone rose more than eightfold in those years. French imports from her partners rose as well, of course, but not so fast because of the effects of the 1958 devaluation. Of course much of this growth of trade would have happened anyway, as a result of the European boom: the Common Market simply speeded it up and gave it a framework.

The sectors of French industry that have fared best under the Common Market have been those already well organized – cars, heavy engineering and chemicals – as well as a few traditional luxury industries such as wines, perfume and glass. Consumer durables and machinery have had a more difficult time, largely because firms were too small or ill-equipped. But in every field, the average French firm's attitude to exports and productivity has changed strikingly in the past ten years. Today the share of French national production that goes for export is as high (16·9 per cent) as Britain's or Germany's. Yet in 1957 France, along with Italy, had the highest tariffs of the Six, backed by a long history of protectionism dating from Louis XI in the fifteenth century. Until 1939 France concentrated on high craftsmanship and deliberately low production, leaving the big world markets to her rivals except in a few 'quality' fields. The change began after the war, led by a few pioneers. Teams of young industrialists known as *missions de productivité*, several hundred in all, went to study in the United States, encouraged by the Plan and the Government, and came back convinced at last of the need to make more, and to sell more abroad. Renault then led the car industry into the export field.* Even today the export drive is by no means general: two-thirds of all exports come from the four hundred largest firms. But with the coming of the Common Market many smaller firms, too, have hurriedly joined forces to create new export subsidiaries, and for the first time are stirring outside their frontiers.

At the Plan I was told: 'We try to urge firms to feel that Germany or Britain are now part of their home market.' Exports are the first stage, but the next is to form structural links between firms in different countries: Monnet himself set a remarkable lead some years ago when he allowed a German wine importer to buy a large share in his own family cognac business. Many French firms now conduct regular exchanges of technicians or information with their counterparts in the rest of the Nine, and oblige their own executives to learn English and German. Robert Valentini, owner of a small metallurgical firm in Lyon, told me, 'Four years ago, at the Cologne Fair, I met the head of a similar firm in Hamburg, and we decided to work together. His firm used to be stronger on exports, but we were stronger internally, with better production. Now, by pooling our research and marketing, and standardizing our products, we've both of us pushed our sales up everywhere.'

In order to meet foreign competition the French have been grappling with what they regard as one of their industry's biggest problems: the small size of the average firm and the shortage of really large ones. This has proved a damaging legacy of

* See pp. 107–10.

protectionism, and puts a strain on French competitiveness now that trade barriers are down. A much-quoted article in *Fortune* magazine in 1964 made the point that of the sixty-four firms in the world with a turnover of more than $1,000m, forty-nine were American, five German, four British and *none* French. According to other statistics, 36 per cent of German workers and only 21 per cent of French ones are in firms with more than 1,000 employees, while over half of all French workers are in firms with less than 200.

This pattern is beginning to change. Four French firms including Renault and the Péchiney metal combine have now moved into *Fortune*'s league of the world's sixty largest. And Government encouragement of mergers has yielded some good results among larger firms in the past few years, notably in steel, chemicals, automobiles and heavy electrical equipment. Now the pressure is on medium-sized firms to follow suit, and many of them have at least come to accept intellectually the need to do so, even though for human reasons they are often slow to take any action. The Government has been trying out various carrot-and-stick incentives.

In addition to mergers, other forms of 'concentration' or 'rationalization' have been taking place too: the regrouping of small, scattered factories belonging to the same firm, conversion away from uneconomic products, and the setting up of joint subsidiaries for research or sales, of which a star example has been the Peugeot-Citroën tie-up of 1974. In 1966 more than two thousand mergers and associations of one kind or another took place in French industry, against 450 nine years earlier. Certainly this process is a useful and necessary one, but in some cases it seems to have been happening too casually and hastily. A merger between two small inefficient firms does not of itself produce one dynamic firm, and now that the vogue has caught on there has been rather too much merging for merging's sake. Sheer size is not the only consideration, and it is pointed out that in some sectors even a tiny firm can be well suited to its market if it is intelligently run. I was quoted the case of a specialized clothing concern in Savoy with only six workers yet with 60 per cent of the European market in its field.

This however is a rare example compared with the thousands of little firms that are quite uneconomic. Some goods, that in other countries are made in big factories, in France are still produced almost on a cottage-industry basis. This system may ensure high craftsmanship in certain fields, but in marketing and other modern techniques it is often so inefficient as to make competition difficult. Many hundreds, perhaps thousands, of such firms (figures are hard to come by) have been pushed out of business in the past twenty years, or have sold out or merged of their own accord, and this process has intensified under the post-1973 economic crisis. But other firms often succeed in hanging on with remarkable tenacity, frequently operating a kind of cartel arrangement with shops and wholesalers that makes it hard to squeeze them out. It is just the kind of structural defect that holds up economic progress, and yet its reform requires a more ruthless attack on vested interests than the Government has yet dared apply.

MANAGEMENT AND UNIONS IN CRISIS

Under the impact of these and other changes, the world of the *Patronat* – employers and managers – is today in a phase of uneasy transition. On the one hand, new ideas of management are gaining ground fast and many firms are modernizing; but thousands of others, especially the family-based ones, are resisting change or proving unable to adapt. The gap between the modern and the backward sectors of French industry remains huge.

The resilience of small firms to the changes of the past twenty years has surprised many observers. Some 600,000 manufacturing firms in France employ less than twenty employees, and they form a powerful lobby. In the 1950s their national leaders were showing a 'Poujadist' resistance to change, but today these men are urging the small firms to adapt rapidly if they want to survive. The monarch of this world is Léon Gingembre, a handsome and eloquent needle manufacturer from Normandy, who just after the war founded the Confédération Générale des Petites et Moyennes Entreprises (PME) or union of small and medium-sized firms. He has been its president and evangelist ever since. Lüthy, writing in 1953, made Gingembre the scapegoat of all that he disliked most about the old France of selfish small interests, and several times he contrasted 'the France of M. Gingembre' with 'the France of M. Monnet'. Lüthy was right, then. But around 1958 Gingembre sloughed off his negative Poujadism (he had been a leading ally of the reactionary grocer-demagogue, Pierre Poujade), gave up his open hostility to the Common Market, accepted the inevitable, and used his immense influence for persuading his million members in commerce and industry to modernize and group together, or perish. The PME now provides numerous services to help its members to export or make use of modern technology. It is true that Gingembre makes an ideology out of the small family business *per se*, regardless of whether a modern economy really needs it; and basically he is still acting in cunning defence of PME vested interests. But at least he now accepts that, if a small firm is to have any *right* to survive, it must be able to compete openly on its own feet; and this is a big change from Poujade's view that State and society have a kind of duty to support and subsidize helpless little businesses. Gingembre once told me: 'The Common Market has forced us to make as much progress in the past six years as in the preceding sixty, and this is fine.'

Following this lead, a number of small firms have begun to group together. In Normandy, for instance, seven manufacturers of hand agricultural tools formed a joint service for sales and buying of materials, and were thus able to break into the German and American markets; in Marseille eight coppersmiths set up a joint technical research service which led to a contract from the Atomic Energy Commission. Such examples represent signs of a change of heart in the traditional France of a myriad self-centred little firms, suspicious alike of each other and of progress.

This world still powerfully exists. It could even be argued that Gingembre's campaign, though sincere and valuable, has acted as an alibi or cover to protect a vast number of firms far more reluctant to change. Gingembre in effect says to the Government: 'Keep your hands off the PME! Don't worry: we *are* adapting ourselves. Give us time.' But how much time can be afforded?

Some industries are still antiquated: textiles, furniture, cutlery and watch-making are often quoted as examples. There are over 15,000 furniture firms in France, all but 1,000 of them employing less than ten workers each and happy within their home market. Here, as in textiles, firms have so far been spared the full shock of the Common Market by a kind of 'protectionism of national taste': the French consumer is conservative, and will often stick to a national product that he or she is used to, even if imports are cheaper or superior. Thus German furniture, generally better designed than French, has not yet made much headway into the French market. But this may not last indefinitely, as modern taste creeps forward.

The pleasant little country town of Thiers (population 20,000), in the green hills of Auvergne, calls itself 'the French Sheffield'. But it has no large factories: its side-streets are lined with literally hundreds of little cutlery workshops, producing 21,000 different models. They have failed to increase exports, and some firms survive only by underpaying wages and allowances: in this one-industry town they can control the labour market. A few more dynamic firms have diversified into, for instance, car accessories; but most of them cling sentimentally to Thiers' long traditions of cutlery, established here in the thirteenth century. To judge by some of the dark and dingy little workshops I visited, it is still in that century. I met old men who had spent all their working lives lying on their bellies on wooden planks, polishing knives; many suffered from chronic rheumatism because electricity was introduced only ten years ago and till then the polishing-wheels were turned by water from a stream directly below where the men lay. This kind of artisan work is slowly dying out, destroyed by competition from elsewhere: nearly half the firms in Thiers have closed since 1964. The problem is largely a human and social one – and the same is true in the watch industry. Some two hundred separate French firms make watch parts and two hundred others put them together, while only seven firms do the combined operation. Some 3,000 different brands of watches are then sold by 11,000 little independent watch-shops, who control all repairs and dictate the market. It is the shops' restrictive attitude, rather than the makers', that holds up modernization. Short of more drastic

Government intervention, the solution will depend on long-term professional education and a change of generation.

Many small firms in industries such as these continue deliberately to limit production rather than risk capital on expansion. Or else they suffer from a fault common enough in Britain too: failure to study the overseas market. These are some of the typical failings of the old-style family firm, once the dominant feature of industry in this bourgeois land. Not all such firms, however, are small or out of date: some are both large and efficient, such as Peugeot and Michelin. But though it still holds a larger place in France than in most Western countries, the numbers and influence of the family firm are declining. Many an owner, worried by modern competition, has retired to a chairman's desk and handed over the reins of daily management to a hired executive, the technocrat. Or else, growing more conscious today of the need for profit and investment, he has put his shares on the market rather than go on running the firm as a private money-bag. Nepotism, hitherto rife in France, is likewise on the wane. Many French owners habitually used to regard the family firm as a nice way of giving sinecures to doltish cousins or nephews. This, they realize, they can no longer so easily afford.

The new salaried managers and executives have been bringing a new spirit and approach into many older firms. In fact, there are now two totally distinct styles of management and business in France today. Since the war, and especially in the past decade or so, many younger French executives have been to the United States on business courses, sometimes of a year or more; or they have been learning modern methods at new American-influenced business schools in France. Such men are now trying to marry French habits and psychology to the best of American methods. Several major firms have allowed themselves to be reorganized by American management consultants such as McKinsey. And so American notions of group responsibility and decentralized decision-taking are permeating a number of firms, and modern marketing methods, hitherto neglected in France, are now all the rage with younger executives. Not that these changes are always a total success. The French have a habit of falling in love intellectually with new ideas and theories, and then not bothering too much with their actual application. In some firms, new American jargon and gadgetry barely conceal the persistence of old French systems of hierarchy and routine. But at least the awareness of the *need* for change is now widespread. And though French firms, as compared with British ones, may tend to be weak in financial expertise, they have moved well ahead in such matters as productivity, the need for expansion, modernization of plant and rational use of resources.

However, the pattern is still very uneven. The world of French management has been in a state of crisis for more than two decades and has not yet emerged. It has been much more successful in switching to modern technology, production and sales methods than in solving its more human problems, notably in establishing less rigid hierarchies and accepting a modern style of labour relations. Here there is still a profound division between a minority of liberal firms and employers, and the majority who remain suspicious of worker participation. This crisis was marked throughout the 1960s by a doctrinal dispute between the old guard, represented by the powerful but cautious Patronat, and the new wave, led by its smaller and more radical rival of those days, the Centre des Jeunes Patrons (CJP).

The Conseil National du Patronat Français represents not only the big employers but also, through their federations, some 80 per cent of PME members. Though some of its leaders have been liberal and far-sighted men, and though it showed in the case of Common Market entry in the 1950s that it is capable of adjusting to change, it remained – at least until 1968 – an incarnation of the more stolid aspects of French management. Its huge, gloomy Paris headquarters near the Etoile, with their heavy marble pillars and uniformed elderly *huissiers*, seemed an accurate reflection of the Patronat's bureaucracy and narrowness of outlook. Notably it upheld the authoritarian tradition of French industry and stressed unity of command. The CJP on the other hand always laid its own very special stress on social progress. Founded just after the war, by the 1960s it included some 3,500 owners and *cadres* under the age of forty-five, representing about 10 per cent of medium-sized industry. It was stronger in the provinces than in Paris, and helped to break down the intellectual isolation of the provincial entrepreneur. Its inspiration, as with so many of the really dynamic forces in post-war France, was rooted in Leftish, new-style Catholicism. And it held the creed that a manager has a duty to his workers, he should be their moral leader, he must associate them with his policies, and he should regard profit as a means for the wealth of all, not just of his family and shareholders.

In the post-war years this doctrine appeared very radical, in a country that has lagged behind many of its Western neighbours in effectively developing modern labour relations. But the doctrine gained sympathy in the 1960s and was known to be not far from de Gaulle's own thinking. The CJP has had an influence out of proportion to its numbers, and it worried the Patronat so much that in 1965 the latter expelled the CJP leaders from their seats on its own governing board, and a year later published a doctrinal manifesto that reaffirmed the authoritarian ideal: 'In the management of a firm, authority cannot be shared. Any other formula leads to impotence.'

Up until the 1968 crisis, labour relations in France had little solid democratic basis. Directly after the war, the CJP ideal had at least found some incarnation in a reform prompted by de Gaulle that set up obligatory *comités d'entreprise* (works councils) in firms with a staff of over 50. These still exist today. Each council is chosen by the staff from candidates generally put forward by the unions, and has monthly meetings with management. The council supervises welfare and social activities, and is also supposed to act as a forum where managers can keep staff informed of their policies and even seek their advice. But this latter role has never worked too well. The unions have tended to look on the councils as irrelevant to their main objectives, while many managements too have been unco-operative, and in many cases have complained that the staff delegates lack the right background and knowledge for any economic consultation to be feasible. 'All that the *comités* do is arrange the Christmas parties,' is a jibe one hears frequently. And in fact, in 40 per cent of those firms large enough for it to be compulsory, there is no *comité* at all – simply because there is no demand for it from the staff or, in a few cases, because of pressure from management. Firms also have what are called *délégués du personnel*, whose job it is to channel grievances about working conditions to the management; these generally work much better than the *comités*, perhaps because their role is more precise and less loftily ambitious. De Gaulle, after his return to power, made it clear that he saw these two minor institutions as merely the first embryo of a much grander utopia of 'participation'; and in 1967, as a further step in that direction, he decreed a law obliging all firms over a certain size to distribute a small portion of their profits to their employees. The Patronat were hostile, and were pacified only when Pompidou managed to secure them some tax concessions in return. The unions too were at best lukewarm, mostly regarding profit-sharing as '*une tarte à la crème*', a capitalist lure to buy off the workers and weaken their solidarity. But the scheme has since gone quietly ahead, though hit inevitably by the economic crisis which has reduced firms' profits. In 1974, French employees received an average of 700 francs per head, equal to 3·2 per cent of their salary.

Unions in France have always been relatively weak. Out of a salaried working population of 17·3 million, only some 25 per cent are unionized; the largest union, the Communist-led Confédération Générale du Travail, claims some 2·4 million members, the CFDT (liberal-Catholic in inspiration, and formerly called the CFTC) and the Force Ouvrière (Socialist) each claim about 800,000. The real figures may be lower. The numerical weakness is partly due to the fact that the French worker, like his boss, is an individualist and not a club-joiner. But more than this, the unions are divided on lines of politics and ideology, rather than by craft or trade as in Britain, and this often makes it hard for them to unite for joint action. Another handicap, before 1968, was that the unions did not enjoy the same legal status within a firm as in many other countries, including Britain. A shop steward had no right to offices on the premises, nor to do union work in the firm's time. It may be true that one great national advantage of this union weakness has been that France has not been plagued by the same kind of demarcation disputes, wildcat strikes and workers' closed-shops that result from union strength and intransigence in Britain. But if the French worker felt until 1968 –

and still feels – a bit of a second-class citizen it has been due partly to managerial attitudes and to the unions' failures. Progress in labour relations before 1968 was left largely to individual firms' initiatives. In the public sector Renault set the pace; in private industry, a few Jeunes Patrons succeeded in carrying out their own ideals.

But such initiatives were few. And when in May 1968 the students seized the Sorbonne, millions of workers spontaneously joined in the strike without waiting for their unions' orders. Workers occupied their own factories, hoisting red flags on the roof and in some cases locking up the managing-director or proprietor in his office. Nine million took part in the strike, the largest in Europe since the war. Motives for it were very mixed.* Some aspirations were the usual material ones: workers wanted shorter hours, and many were dismayed at a recent lag in real wages and at growing unemployment in certain sectors. But the strike was also the explosion of years of frustration – an outburst against employers' aloofness and secretiveness, against the boring repetitiveness of much modern factory work, against the rigid and bureaucratic chains of command, the fear of delegating authority and the lack of group discussion, which have characterized French industry at all levels, on the shop floor as well as between *cadres* and managers. In some firms, the *cadres* themselves led the revolt against a system of which they, too, were the victims. This was novel in modern France; rarely before in this stratified society had two social classes, *cadres* and workers, taken action together. Slogans like *dignité du travail* and *contre l'aliénation* were hurled about, while some young militants went further and demanded *co-gestion*, by which workers' councils would take part in managing the firms. But the union leaders and the mass of the rank and file were not really interested in anything as revolutionary as *co-gestion*; they simply wanted better conditions, and better human treatment. And so the Government and Patronat were ultimately able to bring the strikes to an end by offering massive wage increases and a fairer deal in labour relations.

But what kind of fairer deal? This seemed to demand a change of heart, more than a change of texts: 'You can't turn France

* See also pp. 657–61.

into a Scandinavian-type society simply by a Minister waving a wand,' a young official at the Plan told me. De Gaulle's own solution was what he called '*participation*', the ideal of some kind of management/labour partnership which he had nursed over the years and saw as France's historic answer to the old dilemma between capitalism and communism. De Gaulle talked a lot about *participation* in the months after May. He also appointed René Capitant, the most Left-wing of all Gaullists, as Minister of Justice, charged with preparing a new labour charter. Capitant's ideas were known to be very radical: he had once even suggested that the managing-director of a firm should be elected by the workers and staff in a kind of parliament. The Patronat fought hard against this dangerous stuff; and the CGT too were hostile to what they regarded as 'camouflage'. In face of various press- ures, the proposed charter was quietly shelved in the autumn and nothing more had been heard of it by the time de Gaulle resigned. But at least the legal status of unions inside the firms was finally recognized, by a law passed in December. Shop stewards now had the right, as in other countries, to do union work in the firm's time, to have their own offices inside the factories, and to do canvassing and other such activities on the premises. This was welcomed by all the unions, and was seen as the most important concrete achievement of the strike.

Another immediate result of the crisis was a flood of new union membership, as after the 1936 strikes. Many non-unionized workers saw that united action had brought results, and so they took out cards. And the unions' 'responsible' behaviour during the strikes – in containing the revolutionary ardour of the *gauchistes* – gave them new credit in the eyes of the Patronat, the Government and the public. Thus the French trade union move- ment, as a result of May 1968, not only won a stronger legal basis but also more respectability and influence – and this today appears as having been no bad thing for labour relations as a whole and for French society. But the unions' effectiveness is still hampered by the divergences between them. Since 1968 the most important of them, CGT and CFDT, have significantly shifted their respective roles but remain at loggerheads. Before May, the CGT used to be the more militant and intransigent, while the CFDT with its vague Catholic leanings was the readier to accept the premises of capitalist society. This is no longer so. The CFDT played a more dynamic and less cautious role during the strikes than the CGT, and in the process discovered a new sense of purpose; it has since developed some highly radical ideas and has shown itself much readier than the CGT to combine traditional union thinking with the new notions of *autogestion* and *participation*. It favours workers' control of factories, an idea still anathema to the CGT. It tries to run its union democratically from the base up, while the CGT remains centralist in good Muscovite style. A CFDT leader, Albert Detraz, even told me in 1972: 'We want to revolutionize society, while the CGT simply want a transformation of capitalism – it's almost a reversal of our former positions.' The CGT concentrates its efforts on practical immediate objectives such as higher wages and other material benefits – hence its high membership. Though it continues to pay lip-service to the ideal of revolution, in practice – obedient to higher Communist policy – it has become more docile and readier to compromise with employers and State.

Since the CGT is much the most powerful union, the relative calm on the labour scene since 1968 is not so surprising. There have been the usual sporadic strikes in the public services, none of them very successful or prolonged. In industry, strikes have tended to be local affairs, not always officially supported by the unions; workers have come out for better conditions – as in the Renault plant at Le Mans in 1971 – or else they have struck mainly in the declining industries in depressed areas, where wages are below average and jobs are insecure. There have been very few nationally-led strikes in the large, better paid industries. One reason for this relative calm, at least until 1974, was that the buoyant state of the economy kept wages rising steadily; another, that the Government had some success in wooing the unions into accepting long-term wage agreements in public services.* But the main factor was that the unions – and not only the CGT – were anxious, in pre-electoral periods, to avoid the kind of widespread unrest that might panic voters into a conservative reaction, just as happened in the summer of 1968.

* See p. 87.

The Patronat, too, became rather more conciliatory after May 1968, readier to talk to the unions and to take labour relations seriously. The trend had been noticeable even before May, as the ideas of the Jeunes Patrons steadily percolated the higher echelons of industry. And then the May events did teach the Patronat a certain lesson: the next year it hugely expanded its departments dealing with labour relations, and put at their head a liberal-minded and diplomatic figure, François Ceyrac, who conducted a series of successful talks with the unions in a relatively easy climate. In 1973 he became President of the Patronat. And around this period a number of new national agreements were worked out, giving greater security of employment and granting every employee the right to further education. France now has one of the most advanced vocational training systems in Europe: a firm is obliged to spend a sum equivalent to at least 1 per cent of its wage bill on this training, and as a result since 1972 large numbers of executives and technicians at all levels, as well as shop-floor workers, have attended courses that are intended to lead to job-enrichment and greater prospects of promotion. The scheme is far from perfect, but is working better than many sceptics had expected, and is doing something to reduce inequalities of opportunity within industry.

As a result of May 1968 the Patronat also repaired its schism with the CJP, whose leaders, now men in their middle years, have been re-absorbed inside the parent body where today they form a new group called Entreprise et Progrès. This keeps up reformist pressure on the Patronat from within. The old CJP itself still exists, however, as a forum for younger executives. In sum, there is plenty of evidence that the Patronat has not only become more tactful since 1968; it has also developed a better awareness of workers' aspirations and needs. This is an advance of no small importance. But it is an advance on a formal national level, concerning Patronat and unions as institutions. What is harder to assess is how far the May crisis has led to an improvement of direct daily relations *inside* firms. Certainly there has been no revolution, nothing even to compare with the sweeping changes taking place in universities. When the red flags were hauled down after May, the pattern of command returned much as before – though with a few sporadic signs of improvement. In factories where *cadres* took part in the strike, contacts across the hierarchic barriers are now a little easier and less formal in some cases, and white-collar and blue-collar workers have emerged with a clearer sympathy for each other's problems. 'I had no idea, before May,' an engineer told me in Toulouse, 'of the bitterness of the workers' sense of isolation from the executive life of the factory.' In other cases, the barriers have gone up much as before. The same pattern applies to relations with management. In some older family firms there has been a hardening of positions, a last-ditch attempt by *patrons* to hold on to authority. But a majority of employers seem to have accepted that some change, at least of style, is necessary. The wiser among them did not fail to note that the strike was bitterest and lasted longest in the autocratic old-style firms like Citroën, whereas those with a more enlightened labour policy had little trouble and in some such cases the strikes lasted only two or three days. Many firms take personnel relations much more seriously: their personnel manager, previously a junior and ignored executive, is now a man with a big desk and a large staff, equal in status to the sales director. And most employers are now giving their workers more information about their projects and finances, as directed by the new law. In some cases, it is the workers who have been liberated by the strikes from a certain class inhibition and are coming forward to make direct contact with employers. The owner of a small firm near Montpellier told me: 'My workers are readier now to come and talk to me about their work and its problems. Previously they seemed far too shy. I'm all in favour of this progress.' According to an opinion survey published in February 1976 by the business magazine *Expansion*, as many as 74 per cent of employees (including 71 per cent of shop-floor workers) said they felt their firm had changed for the better in the past five years.

It is difficult to generalize about a situation that is still highly confused. Though the unions may appear to have matters in control, when local unofficial strikes take place there is evidence of considerable violence of feeling especially among younger workers. These revolutionary elements were born of the May revolt; it is hard to assess their strength today, for they have no formal movement, they are mostly disavowed by the unions, and since 1968 they have not taken to action except locally. But they remain a powder-keg, capable of being ignited.* It would therefore be unwise to be too optimistic about the progress that has been made towards social justice and consensus in labour relations. But at least a previously static situation has been turned into a more open one where new ideas and experiments are less likely to be blocked by inertia and routine.

When Giscard came to power in 1974, he immediately revived de Gaulle's grand design for *participation* that had aborted after May 1968. Giscard promised that reforms in the direction of worker co-management would be a major element in his quest for an 'advanced liberal society', and he appointed Pierre Sudreau, one of the most progressive of de Gaulle's former Ministers, to draw up proposals. Early in 1975 the Sudreau commission duly produced a bulky report, recommending various steps to improve working conditions and to ensure closer contact between staff and management, and suggesting notably that larger firms should be invited on a voluntary basis to experiment with a system of 'supervisory councils' including worker delegates. The proposal was not as radical as the German *Mitbestimmung* reforms that were voted about the same time; but it immediately drew hostile reactions from both Patronat and unions. Many of the more powerful Patronat leaders voiced fears that this would be the thin end of the wedge towards real co-management where the authority of the head of the firm would be undermined. The unions too, at least the CGT and CFDT, were suspicious of any such 'capitalist collaboration'. And even ordinary workers, as far as it was possible to tell, felt little enthusiasm for this kind of sharing in top-level decision-making; what they wanted was a fuller say in routine decisions, at shop-floor level, affecting their daily working lives.

In face of these reactions, the Government prevaricated. It was a full year before Giscard came out with his own official project in April 1976, based on the Sudreau report. This project included a number of measures for improving working conditions

* See pp. 657–68.

and encouraging a fuller flow of information on company policy from management to staff. There was also now to be a legal framework for staff representatives to sit with management on 'supervisory councils' with limited powers, in firms with more than 2,000 employees. But this would apply only in firms where both sides wanted it; clearly it was not politically feasible to impose forcibly on industry even such a very tentative form of co-management. And the Government continued to drag its feet. By the autumn of 1976, there were still no very precise plans for bringing this project before Parliament. Giscard was clearly afraid of the furore it would cause. Yet his credibility as a social reformer risked suffering a heavy blow if he delayed much longer.

Two events since his access to power in May 1974 had in fact produced a new climate that made the introduction of a new labour charter much harder. The first was the economic crisis, and the second the growing political polarization as the 1978 elections loomed closer and the Left began to scent victory. All this had a strange and contradictory effect on the unions and on workers. On the one hand, major industrial strikes continued to be extremely few, as in the whole period since 1968. It was not only that the unions were now more reluctant than ever to provoke disorders that might spoil the Left's electoral chances; but the rank-and-file workers, however discontented, were also hesitant to jeopardize their jobs by striking in a period of mounting unemployment. Besides, the Government also partially succeeded in buying their acquiescence with generous unemployment benefits and strict measures against mass redundancies. Yet the wave of bankruptcies in smaller firms, and the growing confidence of the Left, led at the same time to worker tactics of a new kind. Whenever a factory threatened to close, or to make large-scale dismissals for economy reasons, the unions organized sit-ins which often lasted for months and in some cases did achieve their aim of forcing the Government to take steps to save the firm. These sit-ins became routine, and in 1974–6 there were several hundreds of them. In some cases the gesture was carried a stage further, and managers or other executives were briefly kidnapped or shut up in their offices – a tactic inherited from May 1968. But pranks of this kind were only a superficial aspect of a much more serious politicization that began to spread through many firms, especially larger ones, in 1975–6. The two main parties of the Left both intensified their rival efforts to create new political cells in firms. The unions, though supposedly their allies, often resented what they saw as an intrusion into their own domain that might detract from the central battle for better wages and working conditions. There were even, so it was reported, angry exchanges about this between Georges Marchais, the Communist Party leader, and Georges Séguy, head of the CGT and also a Communist. The unions in their turn set about politicizing the *comités d'entreprise* and *délégués du personnel*, in a number of firms; and bodies that were supposed to deal with welfare matters thus found themselves the scenes of stormy political confrontations. Many industrialists were furious at what they saw as attempts by politically motivated shop stewards to use these works councils as a forum for carrying on the crusade against capitalism, thus distorting them from their proper non-political function.

This whole confusing situation may give the impression that today the French labour scene is in turmoil and that the post-1968 spirit of conciliation has been lost. In practice this is not quite so. The pattern varies greatly from firm to firm: in many, daily relations between management, foremen and workers remain much smoother and closer than before 1968 and have not been eroded by the national sharpening of knives or the agitation of political activists. There are even some enlightened industrialists who have quietly set about applying their own version of the Sudreau charter. For example, the manager of the Guilliet machine-tool firm in Auxerre, Jean-Albert Mary, embarked on a revolutionary course eight years ago by inviting the 800 workers to vote to endorse his own appointment and that of other senior executives. Workers also take part in decisions on what the firm should produce and what new equipment it should buy. This does sometimes lead to problems, but the general results are effective: the firm has expanded steadily and sailed through the recession unscathed.

For the moment this is a rare case, and its example cannot easily spread in a period when, at national level, the gulf between

Patronat and unions has again been widening. The Patronat, even under Ceyrac, has again moved back to a more intransigent defence of the creed of capitalism. Many of its leaders are disturbed, not only by the prospect of a Left-wing Government committed to nationalizations, but also by what they see as Giscard's current softness towards the unions and woolly crypto-socialism. Late in 1975 Léon Gingembre himself wrote an open letter to Giscard with the warning: 'Instead of advancing against those who seek to destroy our society, we are simply making their task easier.' In this climate, with workers and employers alike preoccupied with present economic crisis and future electoral uncertainties, the short-term prospects for a radical new labour charter are not bright. But the Sudreau report, which sold 150,000 copies, has made a big impact and its ideas will not be forgotten. The best hope is that some of the proposals will be copied voluntarily over the next ten years or so by a number of more liberal companies, will be found to succeed, and so will take root.

THE FUTURE

In the years between the 1968 upheaval and the post-1973 world crisis, the French economy seemed to be more firmly based than ever. Its growth rate was about the highest in Europe, and its balance of payments was healthy. The built-in weaknesses of the economic structure at last seemed to be under control, and in some cases on the way to cure. One sign of the strength and resilience was the relative ease with which the economy was able to recover from the May crisis and its after-effects. One result of May was a huge drain on gold and foreign exchange reserves which over the next twelve months fell by nearly 50 per cent from their previous high level of some 35,000m francs. Speculation against the franc became so intense that during the world monetary crisis, in November, France was forced to take severe austerity measures, including tight new exchange controls. Even so, production made up lost ground so fast after the strikes that the final growth rate for 1968 was 4 per cent, less than average but creditable in the circumstances. When Pompidou became President in 1969, he promptly took the wise step of devaluing the franc by 12·5 per cent and brought Giscard d'Estaing back to the Finance Ministry. After this the economy bounded ahead again, despite some difficult world conditions and domestic tensions. Giscard managed to keep expansion so finely tuned that inflation did not gallop. Thanks largely to his policies, gold and foreign currency reserves were by 1972 back to a new peak of 39,334m francs; exports were growing in volume at about 10 per cent a year; and economic growth was averaging 5 to 6 per cent a year in 1970–73. Then came the world economic crisis, which hit France harder than her main competitor, Germany, if less badly than Italy or Britain. Growth was – 2 per cent in 1975, the first minus figure since the war, and unemployment rose to well over a million. And, although the world recovery and domestic reflation policies then enabled France to resume a rapid expansion in 1976, there was no curing of inflation, which that year was running at twice the German or American figures. At the end of this chapter I shall look at the effects of the crisis more closely, but at this stage two seemingly contradictory points need to be made. The crisis, much more than that of 1968, showed how vulnerable the French economy can still be, owing to its unsolved structural defects, and the danger this presents to the social fabric. At the same time, as in the aftermath of 1968, the crisis again proved the resilience of the economy in terms of productive capacity.

This is especially remarkable after a period of growing exposure to world competition. Each year, France's economy becomes more open to the world, more enmeshed with those of her EEC partners; each year, French manufacturers and financiers are forced to think less in a purely French context and more in a European or even a world-wide one. But far from being pushed under by this challenge, they seem to flourish on it. Perhaps this is because the modernized sector of the economy has proved even stronger than was thought and has carried the rest with it. Yet so long as the weaknesses subsist, France's fine performance must remain something of a tour de force.

Some of her problems are drearily familiar. Inflation has become more than ever a chronic threat to stability – it was running at over 11 per cent in 1976 – and it can be small consolation to France that this is now a world problem rather than a

French domestic one and that some countries, notably Britain, have become worse sufferers than she is. Even before 1974 inflation was the price being paid for the high expansion rate, yet this expansion did not even provide in return the benefit of full employment; in the past few years serious unemployment has arisen in France for the first time since the war. At the same time, doubts have been growing in France as in some other countries about the validity of a philosophy of unlimited expansion.

For the economy to become fully efficient and balanced, what needs to be done? Some of the problems are structural and psychological: how to modernize those sectors that are still rooted in the past, in their organization, equipment, methods and attitudes. Some are due simply to a shortage of funds, and could be solved with more generous State help. Some are a matter of political or social priorities – what level of American investment is desirable? Is money for housing and hospitals more or less important than higher investment loans to help France's competitiveness on foreign markets? In nearly every case, the solution requires a strong Government lead, for it is the State that operates the levers of power. In many cases basic reforms are needed – but reforms that even Giscard with his good intentions has rarely had the courage or strength to carry out.

One obstacle to development in recent years has been the lack of capital for investment, due less to the effects of austerity than to the innate weaknesses of the French financial market. Industry is still under-capitalized and under-equipped; firms sometimes feel obliged to seek capital from the United States, though this in turn may create other difficulties. Investment drives by the Government after 1969 yielded some results, while the increased confidence in the franc during that period led to large inflows of capital. Thanks to these and other factors, the level of self-financing by firms rose in the early 1970s, after falling badly during the 1960s. Then the crisis wiped out these gains, and today productive investment is well below the German level. Much of the necessary capital still has to come from State loans rather than from the Paris stock exchange (the Bourse) which has been quietly stagnating: its index fell from 800 to 550 between 1962 and 1972.

There are several reasons for the weakness and narrowness of the French stock market. One is the depreciation caused by steady inflation. Another, the incompetence of French stockbrokers and their lack of tradition. A third, the preference of the French public for short-term liquid assets rather than long-term savings, and the paucity of insurance – many Frenchmen, with their roots in an agricultural past, still think in terms of gold rather than paper money, and are only now beginning to learn about savings. The celebrated St Gobain/BSN affair in January 1969, when the dynamic BSN glass firm failed in a take-over bid for its more orthodox rival, showed up the conservatism of the average French shareholder. Most important, the State's control of the big banks and savings institutions serves to inhibit private finance.

The Government, aware of the dangers of this situation, recently began to make serious efforts to enlarge the French capital market and to stimulate banking. In 1967 two of the largest State banks were merged and the private merchant banks were given important new incentives to increase their reserves and adopt a more dynamic policy. Symptomatically, the venerable house of Rothschild extended itself from its traditional merchant role into that of deposit-taking in order to find more money. But though the efficiency of banking has increased, the Bourse remains antiquated in its methods and weak in its resources. It is ill-equipped to meet the competition from the Stock Exchange in London. While such a large part of French banking and financing remains in the hands of the State, the Paris market is not finding it easy to achieve the wealth and flexibility that French industry needs if it is to attract enough capital for investment. This is one of the drawbacks of the *étatiste* tradition which in some other respects has given so much strength to the French economy.

One of the results of the shortage of industrial investment has been the lag in scientific research. Although the State spends a fair amount in this field, notably for military purposes, few private firms are conducting nearly enough research to keep them abreast of their world rivals. The 'balance of payments', as it is sometimes called, is severely adverse; that is, France sells only one patent to the US for every five she buys from there, two-thirds of all new patents registered in France are of foreign origin, and

France comes only eighth in the world 'league table' of origina-
tors of patents. Even that proud French achievement, the Caravelle, lost the chance of a large sales order from China because its
electronics and pressurization system were American patents and
were forbidden under contract to be sold to Peking.

The situation is especially disturbing to French pride, as science
in the past was always something she could boast about. Photography, cinematography, many early aspects of electricity and
aeronautics, Pasteur, de Lesseps and the Curies: the roll-call of
French inventions and inventors has been a fine one. But for a
long time French public opinion has tended to rest complacently
on its scientific laurels, its attitude summed up by a remark I once
heard a Frenchman make to an American: 'No, we don't have
pasteurized milk in France, but we *do* have Pasteur!' This, in
fact, has often been part of the trouble; French science has shown
itself better at pure invention than at application, and one reason
why French industry fell behind that of Britain and Germany in
the nineteenth century was the failure of French firms to make
proper use of the inventions of the period although many of them
were French.

Yet there is clearly no lack of potential grey matter; and today,
as ever, when scientists do get the right lead from the State or
private firms, they can still produce brilliant results. After the
war, the State-led aeronautical industry pulled itself up by its
own bootstraps to produce the Caravelle (or most of it); Renault
pioneered automation in France and created a new machine-tool
industry; the State railways commissioned some of the world's
best electric locomotives, made by French firms; Electricité de
France built the world's first tidal power dam, at St-Malo, using
a new type of turbine; the steel industry invented a special new
non-corrosive tube for pumping the sulphurous natural gas at
Lacq. Today, in several branches of atomic energy, telecommuni-
cations and chemicals, France has been able to move ahead
without relying too much on foreign expertise. She even invented
her own colour television system, SECAM, which Russia and
some other countries found worth supporting.

But today, as advanced research grows more specialized and
more expensive, France is faced not only with shortage of equip-

ment but with shortage of top-level scientists. This is even more acute than in Britain, despite the fact that France does not suffer the same brain-drain across the Atlantic. One trouble is that the manager or engineer has higher prestige in the middle class than the pure boffin, and so the most brilliant brains turned out by the élite colleges such as the Ecole Polytechnique generally prefer to sit behind a big desk with a fleet of secretaries rather than don white coats in laboratories. And in another way too, intellectual resources are often misused: of the 1,298 million franc State budget for research in 1966, more than two-thirds was for atomic and military purposes, and though this stimulates a few key industries, such as electronics, it does not necessarily meet the needs of industry as a whole. Most of the rest of the State research budget is channelled to the universities, which till now have been generally too conservative and academic to apply it to practical needs. So there is little rapport between universities and industry for research; and in their ivory towers too many scientists are encouraged to pursue theoretical lines. The lack of expensive equipment favours mathematics rather than physics or chemistry; and so it may be no surprise that no post-war French scientist won a Nobel prize until 1965.

While one need is for a reform of university science, another is to encourage more private firms to do their own research. This is something that, in France, few of them are used to doing. But there has recently been some progress, under Government pressure, and a few big firms, such as the Rhône-Poulenc chemicals giant, are producing successful results. A few companies, notably at Grenoble, have even begun to commission universities to help them with the kind of joint work that is still much commoner in Britain or America. But few French firms are large enough to be able to compete adequately on a world scale; according to one statistic, the Bell Telephone Company in America has half as many research workers (8,000) as there are in the whole of French private industry. The Government has now become more aware of this problem, and under the Seventh Plan the huge sum of over 10,000m francs of public money is earmarked for stimulating research.

Inevitably, lack of modern techniques as much as lack of

capital has been driving French firms to seek American help. And so the whole research issue has become a matter of national pride as much as an economic one. There are people who argue that France must swallow more of her pride and accept the need to buy techniques and know-how from abroad, rather than pursue them herself so expensively.

Another direct result of the shortage of French investment capital has been the large-scale entry of American business into France. Here, as in the case of science, national pride is involved. From 1959 onwards the invasion of France by American firms increased sharply, and by 1964 was causing quite a scare. Understandably, the Americans were looking for footholds inside the Common Market, or in some cases for escapes from their own anti-trust laws; and a number of French firms, desperate for financial or technical help, were ready to accept their offers of partnership. These individual firms therefore benefited, economically; but de Gaulle began to see threats to national independence. The issue became far more explosive than ever it has in Britain, although the level of US investment in Britain is more than three times as high. In France, it still accounts for no more than 5 per cent of total assets.

In the summer of 1964 the notorious *affaire Bull* hit the headlines. Les Machines Bull were the largest makers of electronic calculators in Europe, and fully French. From 1935 to 1960 the firm's record of technical pioneering had been remarkable; it was a showpiece of modern French industry. But then its progress mysteriously stopped and it began to lose money, for reasons apparently connected with its family management. General Electric, the fourth largest firm in the world, then made a bid to help Bull. Anxious to stave this off, the Government produced a counter-bid which amounted virtually to nationalization, since little French private capital could be found. But Bull found GE's offer more commercially interesting, and the Government finally felt they could not resist.

Many Frenchmen saw this take-over as a humiliation, and not the only one they had to face. The Simca car firm is now largely controlled by Chrysler, and l'Alsacienne, the largest French biscuit firm, by General Mills. Other American companies, such as

IBM, Caterpillar and United Carbon, have formed their own French subsidiaries without resorting to partnership or take-over, and are extending their hold on the French market. It is a pattern common throughout Western Europe, but in France the trend for a while was fastest: 616 new American investments there from 1958 to 1965, against 489 in Germany in the same period.

While Americans in the 1960s seemed to regard France as the most attractive growth area in Europe, de Gaulle's Government reacted erratically to this doubtful compliment. In some cases it encouraged American entry as a stimulant. In other cases it adopted a *laissez-faire* policy until, in 1965, it suddenly clamped down on all US investment for several months. Remington Rand were even pressured into abandoning their new factory near Lyon, and had to switch their European typewriter production to Holland and Italy. From then on, all dossiers were studied much more carefully and many were refused. Since de Gaulle's departure, however, the doctrinaire hostility has disappeared and policy has become much more pragmatic: the official aim is to keep certain industries in French or at least European hands while allowing selected American investment in other sectors, especially when it can bring new jobs to a backward region, or new techniques to an industry where France needs expertise. Thus, in electronics, France now accepts that a measure of American help is inevitable. Motorola's new transistor plant at Toulouse provides a fascinating example, for here it is not just American technical know-how that is being imported, but American-style work relations. The factory's local management are entirely French, but most of them were sent for a year's training at head office in Phoenix, Arizona, and came back suitably indoctrinated. These French scientists and executives now take lunch in their shirt-sleeves in the canteen with their secretaries whom they call by their Christian names – all very un-French. They claim that young French workers, given the right environment, will adapt quite easily to American team methods and shared responsibility, so different from the rigid French chains of command. It is an experiment that could have some influence on the labour problems described a few pages back.

American investment poses another major question: what can

be the place of French industries in a world increasingly dominated by the giant international corporations? How are they to
survive? This has now become the dominant issue, more than
that of German competition within the EEC. Even the larger
French firms are usually too small to compete on a world level
by themselves, and they will have to form outside links. The
answer could be to create 'European' firms of American size; but
one of the disappointments of the Common Market has been its
slowness in achieving just this. German investment in France is
little more than a tenth that of the United States. In the first
decade of the Common Market, the only successful inter-EEC
merger of any size was between two non-French photographic
firms, Agfa of Germany and Gevaert of Belgium. Since then,
several ventures involving French firms have come to nothing: the
abortive tie-up between Fiat and Citroën, the attempt to build a
European computer consortium based on Siemens and CII, and so
on. Most firms find that it is more advantageous to form links
with American expertise than to co-operate with each other. And
though tariffs have come down, there are still barriers to the flow of
capital between the Nine, while national systems of taxation and
company law still differ so widely as to make mergers difficult.

In the past few years the focus of French planning and decision-
making has so much shifted into an EEC context that the old
national Plan worked out in Paris has lost much of its *raison
d'être*. It is true that the EEC has taken over some of the features
of the Plan, so that the Common Market has meant more of a
change for the non-planning Germans than for the French. But
it was also the advent of the Fifth Republic, as much as of the
EEC, that altered the role of the Plan. De Gaulle tended to
exploit it, either as a scapegoat for unpopular measures, or as
window-dressing; and anti-Gaullists, whether big business, unions
or Left-wing parties, grew less ready than in the past to collaborate with the Plan, because they saw it as a Gaullist tool. The
basis of Monnet's sacred non-party rendezvous was undermined.
And neither Pompidou nor Giscard have been great believers in
planning. Today the Plan still goes on, but in a much more
modest way. The Government still uses it for long-term pro-

gramming in its own public sector, but the Plan has far less influence on private industry than in the old days. It has become more political, in the sense that it sets social rather than strictly economic objectives; thus the Seventh Plan, for 1976–80, is an ambitious blueprint for all kinds of improvements to be made in the quality of French life, but is not to be taken too literally as a working document. For one thing, the uncertainty provoked by the economic crisis since 1973 now makes forecasting and contingency planning much less feasible.

Yet the French recognize that a measure of domestic planning is still needed, not only for regional or social development but for coping with the wage-price spiral. Attempts in the mid-1960s to found an incomes policy in France never got very far, for the Patronat was suspicious both of contractual agreements with the unions and of further State interference in firms' affairs; the Government, likewise, feared committing itself to bargains that might limit budgetary freedom; and the unions were mistrustful all round. Then, around 1967, the threat of unemployment began to grow. Before this, steady economic growth since the war had led to regular near-to-full employment and even a shortage of labour in many sectors. But when the 'baby-boom' began to flood the market, at a time of slow-down in growth, industry found itself for the first time since the war unable to offer jobs to all the new young recruits. The jobless total rose to 480,000 by May 1968 – a high figure for a country always very sensitive to unemployment.

After the May 1968 crisis, which at last brought a prospect of a break in the stalemate between employers and unions, Jacques Chaban-Delmas launched his 'new society' programme. He charged Jacques Delors, a progressive and brilliant young man on his staff, with elaborating and negotiating the famous '*Contrats du progrès*', which were a kind of embryonic incomes policy. They were to cover a large number of public services and national industries, including the railways, and gas and electricity. In each case the unions, in return for their promises to use strikes only as a last resort, were guaranteed regular wage increases in excess, by about 2 per cent a year, of the likely rise in prices. It was a bid to proof pay rises against inflation. The unions at first showed characteristic suspicion of what they denounced as a political manoeuvre, an attempt to ensnare them in 'the system'; but finally most of them did sign in most industries, in 1970–71. Over the next three years, until sabotaged by the economic crisis, the *contrats* operated with a certain success. They helped to avoid major strikes or the kind of excessive wage claims that have been so damaging in Britain. They were paralleled too by a number of new agreements in private industry, covering wages and other benefits: in the period 1969–72 nearly all lower-paid workers went over from hourly to monthly payment, thus gaining greater status and security. And so, thanks in part to the *contrats du progrès*, inflation and unemployment remained more or less under control until 1974. Since then, the rapidity of inflation has rendered the *contrats* obsolete. And union attitudes have hardened again: even before the crisis, the big unions in some key industries were refusing to sign prolongations of the agreements, which firms thus had to continue unilaterally. Even so, today, the final legacy of the *contrats* has not been negative. They have left behind them a more intelligent and realistic attitude to wage bargaining than existed before.

One running cause of union discontent over the years has been the Government's choice of priorities for public spending – and especially de Gaulle's costly nuclear and military policies, which coincided in the mid-1960s with bitterly resented cuts in social welfare. Once emotion and prejudice have been cast aside, it is hard to answer objectively this long and vexed question: how far have France's military efforts since 1946, the wars in Indo-China and Algeria, and then the nuclear weapons programme, *really* affected economic growth and social progress? On the Right, there are people who point out that the Algerian war (1954–62) overlapped precisely with the years of fastest economic growth. But this was no more than a coincidence; 1954 happened to be the year when the post-war recovery began to gather pace. Although the active use of a large army in Algeria helped the expansion of some industries, it also promoted inflation; similarly, today, the costly nuclear policy is a boon for the electronics industry but has also added to inflation. After an analysis of the statistics it is hard to argue that the *force de frappe* (as the nuclear policy is called) has *in itself* been holding back French development, any more than the Algerian war did. And yet that money has been badly needed for more valuable things. The *force de frappe* is eating up funds that could better be spent on schools, houses, roads, hospitals.

France today presents the spectacle of a nation trying to live beyond its means, where individual wealth has been allowed to outstrip public services to a painful degree. Most people can afford a car, but they get caught in traffic jams through lack of modern roads; most people can afford a telephone, but the waiting lists are long; most people can afford theatre-tickets or sports gear, but the promised new local cultural and sports centres lag behind schedule through lack of State funds. Some of the trouble has been due to the Government's reluctance to levy higher taxes in pre-electoral periods when its popularity has been waning. But the *force de frappe* has also been to blame – and so maybe is the fact that France cannot really afford to spend as much as she does on overseas aid. This is certainly not money wasted, but it may be beyond her means. In 1972 French aid to developing countries stood at $1,873m, proportionately much more than Britain or the United States spends. Yet France too is in some ways a developing country – look at the squalid farms of the Massif Central or the tenements of eastern Paris. It is this kind of social progress that was sacrificed to de Gaulle's *politique de grandeur*, and this was certainly one factor behind the May 1968 explosion.

Pompidou then proved more realistic, to the extent that he spent much less money than de Gaulle on expensive new prestige projects. He did not really share de Gaulle's particular ideals of *grandeur*. And though initially the financial crises of 1968–9 forced him to make severe cuts in public spending, he later allowed the budgets for equipment and social services to jump ahead again, much faster than the defence budget. Giscard then showed himself even more hostile than Pompidou to costly prestige projects; and as far as was possible in a period of belt-tightening he continued the policy of greater social spending.

Another questionable aspect of public spending under de Gaulle was the sharp rise in subsidies to meet the deficits of declining industries. Grants to the nationalized coal-mines went up forty-four-fold from 1960 to 1969, to reach 2,200m francs. The State railways too were shored up to the tune of 5,600m francs in 1969. All this put a strain on the State budget: total subsidies to the mines, railways and farmers came to more in 1969 than the entire State revenue from income tax! This held up expansion and improvements in other fields. Government officials and the Patronat were growing anxious, and finally de Gaulle in 1968 authorized the brilliant civil servant, Simon Nora, to prepare a plan for reorganizing the mines, railways, and some other nationalized concerns. This problem of subsidies is very complex. On the one hand, they can be regarded as humanitarian: to alleviate hardship in declining areas. But modern-minded economists like Nora have argued that the way the money was spent was short-sighted. To bolster up activities that could never pay their way was simply a waste; those activities should be cut back severely, and the money spent on pensioning older workers and expanding new, competitive industries. The only trouble is that miners, farmers and others are notoriously resistant to change; and for political reasons the Government did not want to face their combined grievances. It was easier simply to pay them to keep quiet. Finally, however, early in 1969 de Gaulle accepted the findings of the Nora report, and Pompidou began to apply them. The railways, the mines, the electricity and gas services, even to an extent the Post Office, were reorganized on more commercial lines, like public firms; their civil service administration was pruned; and their personnel and other costs were reduced. In this way it became possible in some cases to reduce their subsidies too, since much of the wasted money was due simply to over-heavy administration.

It is clear that many of the troubles of France in the past years have been due simply to misdirection of public money – and happily there are signs today of a new approach here. Less money spent on prestige, and on useless subsidies; more attention to efficiency, and a little more for social services. But many remaining troubles are due to outmoded structures, and these are harder to cure. The rapid economic progress of recent years is now coming up against out-of-date systems and practices that make it hard to advance farther. The engine, as it were, has been revved up to a fair speed, thanks to the Plan, the EEC, and other factors; now it cannot go faster without a de-coke and a change of plugs. Nearly everyone in high positions has become acutely aware of this; *la réforme des structures* is now a parrot-cry. Later chapters of this book will look at this problem, sector by sector.

True, de Gaulle's record of reform was better than that of the Fourth Republic; but it was poor compared with the power he enjoyed. And many problems have grown more pressing each year. In 1960, at de Gaulle's own request, a team of experts headed by Rueff and Armand drew up a dossier of needed reform in many fields, including such matters as the closed-shop among Paris taxi-drivers. The Government tacitly accepted most of their ideas – but applied very few. Louis Armand, when I saw him soon before his death, said, 'Politicians aren't interested in invidious structural reforms. They prefer spectacular new projects, like the liner *France*, or the Mont Blanc tunnel. Basic structures will probably not be reformed without a new shock from outside – that is why, in my view, the answer is effective European unity. And that was always my quarrel with de Gaulle.'

The administration must also put its own house in order. The Napoleonic legacy of a strong civil service and strong State economy has many advantages; but in the complex world of today its over-centralized system leads to growing inefficiencies and delays. State control was useful for rebuilding France after the war, and is still needed for running the big supply industries and co-ordinating research. But in the American and Japanese-dominated world of mammoth private enterprise, to which France is now wedded, it could be argued that French private firms would fare better if the State allowed them more freedom and helped the capital market to develop.

The crisis years, 1974–6, have put the French economy to a severe test, but one that it seems to be narrowly surviving as it might never have done two decades earlier. As in other countries, the crisis first began to bite after the rise in oil prices at the end of 1973. But France then had a dying President, Georges Pompidou, who took no action. When Giscard came to power in May 1974, the signs of recession and high inflation were ominous, and he and his Finance Minister, Jean-Pierre Fourcade, quickly took their first austerity steps to check price rises. For the next two years or so, Giscard tackled the crisis with a succession of stop-go measures that somewhat resembled, in quicker tempo, the policies he had helped to carry out as Finance Minister under de Gaulle a decade or so earlier. His measures were frequently criticized for being too little and too late, or for compromising uncertainly between true economic liberalism, on the German model, and true *dirigisme*. But they did produce results, in purely economic terms at least. Thus the minus growth trend that France shared with many other countries during the recession's worst year, 1975, was converted by skilful reflation in the nick of time into an expected 5 to 6 per cent growth for 1976. And a highly dynamic exports policy, led by the foreign trade Minister, Norbert Segard, helped to turn a 14,000m franc deficit in 1974 into a 5,000m franc surplus the next year.

But at home the successive austerity measures made enemies for Giscard, not only among the workers but also in the ranks of his own supposed supporters, the middle classes and business people. Industrial firms were obliged to bear the brunt of the first squeeze, in 1974, through a new tax on company profits. This infuriated the Patronat, and so did the new measures introduced to limit rising unemployment by making it much harder for firms to carry out mass redundancies. It was reckoned that by early 1976 there were some 300,000 surplus workers on pay-rolls who in economic terms should have been out of work. With their dwindling profits thus eaten away by taxation and excessive wage-bills, many firms had no money left for investment in new plant. Investment fell by 9 per cent in 1975, at a time when the German rate was again rising, and the Patronat feared for the long-term consequences.

Some 32,000 businesses of all kinds, mostly small ones, went bankrupt during 1974–6. In a very real sense this has been salutary for the economy, for there are far too many small firms in France, and the process of natural selection in time of crisis has eliminated the least efficient. But in the shorter term it has also caused unrest. Despite the Government's measures, unemployment by 1976 was running at well over a million, about the same rate as in Germany though lower than that in Britain. In order to pacify the Left, the Government introduced exceptionally high unemployment benefits, amounting in some cases to 90 per cent of previous salary. But only those already in work and paying social insurance were eligible for these benefits, which thus did not cover young people entering the labour market. And as firms found it hard to dismiss employees, they in most cases stopped recruiting new young ones. So it was school and university leavers who bore the brunt of the employment crisis: in 1976, 38 per cent of those seeking work were under 25, and there were fears that this might fuel a new May 1968.

The Government further sought to pacify the Left and the unions by allowing wage increases to outpace inflation. The inflation rate had initially been reduced from 15·2 per cent in 1974 to 9·6 in 1975, but in 1976, with wages rising at an average rate of 16 per cent a year, it increased again to over 11 per cent. In Germany, a policy of greater restraint was keeping wage increases down to 4·5 per cent, even lower than the inflation rate of 5·3 per cent; and the French viewed this with disquiet, for Germany is not only their main trading rival but also – unlike Britain – their main yardstick of economic health and sanity. Giscards' reflationary measures in September 1975, permitting a 40,000 million franc budget deficit for 1976, also helped to refuel inflation. The franc again grew weaker, and Giscard was soon forced to abandon his ill-judged re-entry into the Mark-dominated currency 'snake'. The franc fell some 12 per cent against the Mark during this period. Foreign exchange reserves were still standing comfortably high, at over 80,000m francs, but uncertainties over the franc put them repeatedly under pressure.

It was thus a delicate economic situation that Raymond Barre inherited when he became Prime Minister in August 1976. He came to the job with a reputation as a pragmatic and experienced economist, and he at once told the French nation that they were living above their means and that it must stop. Incomes were rising faster than production, and the summer drought had added to the difficulties by cutting farmers' export earnings and so further weakening the franc. Barre's much-trumpeted austerity plan, introduced on 22 September, included a three-month price freeze on higher incomes, new taxation for the rich, a huge rise in motoring taxes, and some new steps to encourage firms' investment. The unions at once denounced the plan on principle; but some more detached observers criticized it for not being astringent enough, and for merely tinkering superficially with finance rather than trying to cure the structural defects that were the root of France's problems. Barre and Giscard were really trying to do two near-contradictory things at once: firstly, to restore the economy, by imposing some unpopular austerity; and secondly, to prepare the ground for the elections, through popular social reforms that might steal the thunder of the Left. But such reforms usually cost money and are incompatible with austerity. The only way to square this difficult equation seemed to be to reduce the incomes of the rich and thus redistribute wealth, and this Barre tentatively began to do. But in economic terms his measures hardly seemed enough to check inflation; and as the dust settled after September, it became clearer than ever before that what France needed most was some kind of regular incomes policy – if not a statutory policy, then at least the kind of *de facto* social contract that was saving Britain – hopefully – from total collapse. But the main French unions continued to reject any such idea. With the two major unions committed formally to Marxism and scenting the prospect of a Government of the Left by 1978, neither was prepared to do anything to shore up what they saw as a 'dying' capitalist system.

If the world recovery is maintained, then France will recover too, but with her economy possibly in a more vulnerable state than at any time since before 1958. The crisis has shown, once again, that major sectors of French industry are now sufficiently modern to be highly resourceful, even under harsh conditions. It has also shown that unsolved imbalances lead to growing social tensions. It may well be possible to achieve something near to the 6 per cent annual growth target set by the Seventh Plan; but this Plan also admits, as do many other experts, that by 1980 unemployment could still be running at around a million. This is because the modern sector of the economy cannot possibly grow fast enough to absorb labour from the dying sector, and from the new generation. The crisis has brought home more sharply than ever before the lesson that growth of itself does not cure all social ills. And as in some other countries, the crisis has obliged politicians, economists and others to reappraise their attitudes to the credo of growth. The crisis, you could say, has affected men's minds more than their wallets.

France's economy has come a long way since 1945 and has surprised everyone with its resilience. But it is still unbalanced, and therefore vulnerable. Along with Italy, France is one of the very few advanced countries to be facing simultaneously the problems of pre-industrial *and* post-industrial society. While the technocrats struggle to pull some areas of the economy out of the nineteenth century, in the case of others they are already scenting what may be the hazards of the twenty-first. And as the dangers of pollution grow, as cities spread and the quality of urban life faces new threats, so the golden philosophy of expansion that has guided France ever since 1945 begins for the first time to come under question. But the technocrats remain certain where their first priorities still lie. Lionel Stoleru, one of the most influential of Giscard's advisers, told me: 'The anti-expansion argument may have some validity for the United States, but not yet for France. We have still a lot to catch up, before we reach America's level of affluence and America's kind of problems. And it is only by *first* completing our modernization and making industry thoroughly efficient that we can produce enough wealth for the whole community. Therefore expansion remains our priority – and it is a human priority. Of course I agree that at the same time we must spread the wealth more fairly, we must spend more on public services so as to improve quality of life, we must do more to protect the environment. But none of these things need be incompatible with expansion; in fact, most of them would be impossible without it. Only when the whole of France is modern and prosperous – maybe in another ten to twenty years – can we think about deliberately slowing down expansion.' I had rarely heard a more clear summary of the planners' present-day outlook, and I told M. Stoleru that his views were largely my own.

Chapter 3

SOME KEY INDUSTRIES

LYON, once 'the capital of silk', is today a capital of chemicals and engineering. Grenoble is famous no longer for its gloves, but for electro-metallurgy and nuclear research. In the Limoges area, even porcelain is beginning to seem less important than uranium and hydro-electricity. On every side, traditional French luxury products have been yielding first place since the war to modern heavy industries. This was felt to be essential, if France was to be able to compete as an industrial nation.

The policy seems to have been justified, and several industries have made striking advances, both technically and economically. As a result, this nation traditionally renowned in the arts has begun to change her colours; and some of the national pride that the French usually feel towards cultural achievement has come, since the war, to be focused instead on science and industry. Far more than in cautious Britain, public and politicians alike have responded enthusiastically, even naïvely, to ambitious or imaginative new plans; and it seems no coincidence that most of the initiative and ideas for the Channel Tunnel project came from the French side, although Britain, being an island, would have stood to gain most from a scheme that in her feebleness she has once again shelved.

The single-vault suspension bridge across the lower Seine at Tancarville, the road tunnel under Mont Blanc, and the futuristic new airport at Roissy, north-east of Paris, are some of the post-war public works of which the French are ingenuously proud. Of course during de Gaulle's reign such grandiose schemes were sometimes conceived more with an eye to prestige than economic advantage. But this is not a charge that can be laid against France's earlier long-term efforts, in the first years after the war, to rebuild her basic industries: railways, fuel and power, iron and steel, cars and aeroplanes, machinery and chemicals.

THE RAILWAYS: ARMAND PRE-DATES BEECHING

France's State railways – in their management, if not in their financing – provide an example of the technocratic system at its best. Thanks to this, France's trains are reputed as amongst the most modern, swift and comfortable in the world, and many nations send experts to study the Société Nationale des Chemins de Fer Français as a model of how to run their own railways. When Louis Armand became president of the SNCF in 1946, and began to modernize, he had several advantages over Dr Beeching, who set about a similar task in Britain seventeen years later. French railways, nationalized in 1938, ended the war with four-fifths of their engines and coaches destroyed, and a high percentage of the rolling-stock, track and stations also out of action. But this proved a blessing in disguise: Armand could start with a clean sheet. First he closed down 6,000 miles of uneconomic branch lines; or rather in many cases he simply never reopened them. Research technicians were given generous budgets to prepare new locomotive designs: as a result, France today not only exports electric and diesel engines in some numbers, but her trains hold the world speed records. SNCF electric engines have reached 207 m.p.h. on trial runs, while passenger trains on regular runs often cruise at their legal maximum of 125 m.p.h.

Armand also invested heavily in electrification. The electrified track has nearly trebled since 1938 and today accounts for 24 per cent of length and carries over 76 per cent of traffic. Most of the main lines from Paris to other big cities are electrified. Everywhere the emphasis is on longer trains and more powerful engines. The average train in France is much longer than in Britain: British Rail, while carrying no more freight than the French, do ten times as many train-miles. This helps to give France the edge in efficiency and lower costs. Punctuality is secured by a system of penalties for drivers who are late without cause, and the SNCF's high record of punctuality is one reason for its low accident rate.

T–TNF–D

Thanks to modernization and streamlining, the SNCF has been able to reduce its staff from 514,000 in 1938 to 276,000 today – compared with Britain's pre-Beeching 1963 figure of 747,000. Of course this saves money. Yet despite this glowing picture of technical progress and efficiency, the SNCF in recent years has been running up an annual deficit which has grown alarmingly. Several reasons are given: the continuing heavy cost of long-term investment and modernization; the pensions paid to the many thousands of laid-off railwaymen who are still alive; growing competition from air and road transport; and above all the fact that the Government tacitly helps to subsidize industry by keeping freight and other charges down. The deficit is met by the State, but falls on the taxpayer, and until it is reduced, the SNCF will not be able to fulfil its boast that the way to solvent finances runs through inspired modernization. Plans have now been carried through for drastic closures of more branch lines and their replacement in many cases by local buses. At the same time, following the Nora report, the administration and financing have now been reorganized and streamlined so as to give the SNCF more autonomy and force it to operate on commercial lines like a private company. As one SNCF official told me, with a certain complacent French logic: 'Our financial situation may be bad, but our economic situation is very good.'

'WHITE COAL' FROM THE MOUNTAINS AND 'LIQUID GOLD' FROM THE DESERT

The rapid growth of industry, and of private prosperity, has put strain, as in many countries, on France's resources of fuel and power. The two main domestic sources of energy, coal and electricity, were both nationalized just after the war, and in both cases technical advance helped for a time to exploit natural assets to the maximum. But as modern industry came to prefer oil to coal, so France had to look more and more to imports for her energy supplies: the percentage of her needs covered by imports rose from 48 to 75 between 1960 and 1974. The exploitation of sizeable natural gas deposits in south-west France was partly able to offset the dependence on imported oil, but these reserves will not last much longer. And when the energy crisis hit the western world in 1973–4, France suffered as much as any country. Rocketing oil prices brought the trade deficit in her fuel bill for 1974 to 48,000m francs. This new and dangerous situation has led to a complete rethinking of France's energy strategy since 1974. Ways are being sought of economizing in fuel. The nuclear programme is at last being speeded up – amid furious ecological controversy – and new forms of energy, solar and geothermal, are being pioneered. But first, let us look at earlier post-war developments.

As soon as the State took over the coal-mines after the war, it subjected them to the same rigorous modernization as the railways. This was done so well that productivity became for a while the highest in Europe; by 1955, output per man was 23 per cent above the pre-war rate, compared with a rise of only 6 per cent in Britain. This meant a useful saving in manpower in a country where labour has been short. As with railways, nationalization seems to have been more effective than in Britain, one reason being the high level of French technical progress due to the output of talented engineers from the three prestigious Ecoles des Mines.

But French coal is mostly poor in quality and hard to extract, and therefore tends to work out as more expensive than imported coal. So, as the coal era in Europe began to wane, France started to limit production in the 1960s. Annual output, which after the war had been pushed up to 60 million tons, had been cut right back to 25 million by 1973. Many of the mines in the Lille area, almost exhausted, were closed down and tens of thousands of miners were redeployed. Then the world energy crisis produced a panicky about-turn in policy, with plans to push production up again to 45 million tons. However this was soon found to be uneconomic, so poor were the remaining mines; the coal board's deficit, always high, reached nearly 3,000m francs in 1974, and this had to be met from State funds. The present compromise solution – still a costly one – is to hold annual production at about 37 million tons until there is enough nuclear energy for the mines to be run right down.

For Electricité de France, the main problem is quite different – it is simply that of trying to keep pace with a demand that doubles every ten years. The EDF was created in 1946, out of myriad little private companies operating 14,000 different concessions. Today it is an efficient empire with a staff of 95,000. The élite of the EDF, including some of the cleverest *polytechniciens*, plan provisions forty years ahead, sneer at English power-cuts, and work out how to extract every drop of power from a country rich in hydro-electric resources, the *houille blanche* ('white coal') as it is sometimes called. The EDF has built or shared in the building of more than thirty dams in France in the past thirty years, mainly in the Alps, Pyrenees and Massif Central, and along the Rhine and Rhône. These rank as some of France's most notable post-war constructions. But the most widely publicized EDF operation has been the construction of the world's first tidal power dam, across the estuary of the river Rance at St-Malo, in Brittany. Inaugurated in 1966, this dam uses a new type of 'bulb' turbine invented by the French, and extracts power both as the tide rises and as it ebbs. Thus it goes one better than the old tidal water-mills which worked only one way. It is a vast bulwark of concrete, 800 yards long. Tides on this estuary rise up to forty feet and are among the strongest in the world; even so, the dam produces only 0·5 per cent of French electricity, and must be regarded as an exciting technical experiment rather than as a major practical asset.

The third principal domestic source of raw energy is natural gas. The deposit struck in 1951 at Lacq, in the Pyrenean foothills near Pau, is the largest yet found on the west European mainland outside Holland and now supplies France with a third of her gas consumption. 'Le gaz de Lacq' has been one of the clichés of modern French industrial pride – and with some justification. Some 230 acres in the valley west of Pau are covered with a network of brightly painted pipes and cylinders, yellow, red, blue and so on; each colour is for a different industrial function. At night the security flares from the thirty-two operational wells blaze out for miles across the valley like a city on fire. This is modern industry at its best: clean, aesthetic, open to view. It is perfect, save for the pervasive odours of methylmercaptan and sulphur.

The big State-backed company that exploits the Lacq conces-

sion, the Société Nationale des Pétroles d'Aquitaine (SNPA), has
built there one of the world's largest sulphur-producing plants.
All around you can see the great pale-yellow mounds. The gas,
once de-sulphurized, is piped direct for consumer use to Paris and
elsewhere, or is sold separately as propane or butane, while some
of it supplies raw material for new petro-chemical and plastics
factories that have sprung up round Lacq. The deposits in the
Lacq area provide the equivalent of some seven million tons of
coal a year, or nearly a third of France's gas consumption; but
the natural reserves will begin to run dry after about 1983, and
scientists do not expect any major new discoveries. By the end of
the century, there may be no more natural gas in France.

This adds an even greater urgency to the need to find ways of
offsetting oil imports, which had been rising steadily to reach
over 92 million tons in 1973. Oil, in France even more than in
most countries, is a complex political issue. Most of France's oil
comes from the Middle East, though until 1971 as much as 40
per cent of it came from the Algerian Sahara, where the French
had discovered it in colonial days. But in 1971 the Algerians
nationalized the remaining French companies and paid them scant
compensation. It seemed a blow to France at the time, but she was
rapidly able to make up the loss by increasing imports from elsewhere. She even found that her pro-Arab policy in the Middle
East stood her in good stead, for during the 1972 crisis over Iraqi
oil she was able to get much better terms than her rivals, the big
American and Anglo-Dutch companies.

This was a small victory for the policy that France had pursued
ever since the 1920s: that of securing for her oil industry some
measure of independence from the international giants. Her aim
has always been that French State-backed companies should
carry out at least half the importing and refining of the oil that
France needs; and it was with this in view that, in January 1966,
the Government merged the two principal State concerns into a
new body, the Entreprise de Recherches et d'Activités Pétrolières
(ERAP), and put in charge of it a leading technocrat, Pierre
Guillaumat. He was briefed to try to do for France's oil industry
what Mattei had done for Italy's; that is, not only to push aside
the French private companies (of which the main one is the

Compagnie Française des Pétroles) but to challenge the big foreign ones. ERAP in 1976 merged with SNPA to form an even bigger giant, and today markets its own brand of petrol under the trade name 'Elf'. It has had some success in making oil-prospecting deals with Middle East countries and thus breaking the American and Anglo-Dutch monopoly there. Thanks to ERAP and CFP, about half of France's oil imports are now controlled by French companies. But this nationalistic policy has antagonized the big foreign oil firms as well as France's EEC partners. It does not really save France money, and has political rather than economic motives.

Oil imports are now levelling off, and are expected to begin falling steadily after 1982, when the intensive new nuclear programme starts to take effect. France is the world's fourth atomic power (she completed her first reactor in 1956 and exploded her first bomb in 1960), but for more than a decade she deliberately put brakes on applying this energy for making electricity on any scale. One reason was that she wanted to avoid the early British mistake of hurrying uneconomic prototypes into use; she preferred to concentrate on research, so as to bring down costs and to complete the perfection of reactors that would be genuinely viable. Then in the 1960s another more decisive factor was that a decline in world oil prices made it harder than ever for nuclear energy to be run at an economic price, and on top of this the French failed to develop successfully their own type of nuclear fuel. Nuclear energy was in 1970 still supplying only 3 per cent of France's electricity.

Another reason for the delay was that in nuclear matters France under de Gaulle tended to follow a strongly national policy. This was not entirely her fault; since about 1957 the United States, for political and military reasons, withheld from the French certain forms of nuclear co-operation which she had granted to the British. But France did her share too of rejecting US help.

Yet the French go-it-alone policy has borne some fruit over the years. France's own scientific post-war record in this field was outstanding, especially considering that she had to start virtually from scratch in 1945, without the war-time experience of the other major powers. The Commissariat à l'Energie Atomique (CEA) has harboured some brilliant scientists (its first high commissioner, in 1945, was Frédéric Joliot-Curie himself) and it pioneered much important research in, for example, the production of plutonium and the use of natural rather than enriched uranium. Thanks to these efforts, France was able to avoid having to buy enriched uranium from the United States. As the world's fourth largest uranium producer, she has enough on her own soil to last for many years: some 60,000 tons have been located so far, mostly in the Massif Central, where the CEA has encouraged the public in the lucrative sport of taking geiger counters with them on Sunday picnics. France's own nuclear technology is highly advanced, especially in the field of fast breeder reactors.

A speed-up of the nuclear programme had begun even before the world energy crisis, but it was rapidly seen to be not enough. With oil imports accounting for 66 per cent of the nation's total energy needs, what was France to do to reduce the strain on the balance of payments? She has reacted more vigorously than many other EEC countries. One official response since 1974 has been a campaign to economize in fuel. Factories, offices and individuals have responded by cutting down wastage or installing fuel-saving devices. And the official aim is to reduce consumption objectives over the next decade by as much as 16 per cent without jeopardizing industrial growth or living standards. But over-all energy needs are bound to go on rising. So the only real solution is to seek alternative sources – but where? The coal and gas reserves are approaching exhaustion, and the best sites for hydraulic power dams have all been harnessed. Drilling for oil off the west coast of Brittany began in 1975: prospects are thought to be good, but the oil, if found, will take some years to exploit in any quantity, and France certainly has no off-shore bonanza on her horizon like Britain. Meanwhile, experiments with new kinds of energy are being intensified. At Melun in the Paris area, and elsewhere, some 10,000 homes are now equipped for heating by natural hot water from underground springs, and it is planned to increase this to 500,000 homes by 1986. For some years a research centre in the Pyrenees has been pioneering the harnessing of the sun's energy, and now a number of houses capable of using solar energy are being built experimentally. But it will be many years before these ventures can make any large practical contribution to France's energy supplies.

There remains the atom. In 1974 the new nuclear programme was launched, and France is now building power stations at the rate of some 5,000 extra mega-watts a year; some of the new stations will have a capacity of 1,300 MW each, as large as any in the world. By the end of 1975 work had started on 12 new stations, and plans were announced for a further 18 for the period 1976–8. It is not yet certain how economically viable this operation will be, but at least the French have now had the practical sense to give up the expensive luxury of reliance on home-produced natural uranium gas-cooled reactors. Soon after de Gaulle's departure in 1969, the Pompidou Government decided the only sane economic choice was to switch to American-type light water reactors, even at the price of some dependence on foreign technology. To power the new stations, several such reactors are now being built by a French company under licence from Westinghouse. At the same time, France is increasing nuclear collaboration with other European countries, even though a common EEC energy policy is still a long way out of sight. France is taking the lead in a European consortium now building an isotope separation plant in the Rhône valley.

The nuclear expansion has come under heavy criticism, both from some economists, who consider that costs have been rising too fast for the stations to be viable, and especially from a strong ecological lobby. The issue has become highly political, and in a number of areas there have been demonstrations against plans to build power stations locally.* The Government in such cases has backed down, but it is determined to go ahead with its over-all programme. If this is adhered to, the nuclear share in total French energy supplies will rise from a mere 1·8 per cent today to about 25 per cent in 1985, when 72 per cent of electricity will come from nuclear sources. It is hoped that dependence on imports will thus drop from 75 per cent of total energy consumption today to between 55 and 60 per cent in 1985.

* See p. 247.

RENAULT, PEUGEOT, CITROËN:
SWEET FUMES OF SUCCESS

French technical flair is no monopoly of the big State industries, as anyone knows who has tested the hydro-pneumatic suspension of a Citroën CX or driven a tough Peugeot 604 for thousands of bumpy miles without a mishap. Ever since the pioneering days of Panhard and Louis Renault in the 1890s, the car industry has held a place of honour in this land of creative engineers; and to-day the emphasis is still on daring new ideas of design and construction. It is this that has helped it to weather the post-1973 crisis better than many of its foreign competitors.

After the war this pilot sector of French industry rebuilt itself brilliantly, and by 1959 had secured a strong position as the world's fourth largest car-producer and France's chief exporter. The industry bases some of its success on the average French-man's mania for cars, remarkable even by the usual standards of this car-mad modern world. The French have the highest level of car ownership per head in the EEC,* and their cars are relatively cheap. They have built a kind of popular mystique around the various national makes – the robustness of Peugeots, the bizarre ingenuity of Citroëns, the lightness and economy of Renaults, these have become legendary. Since the war France has concentrated, first, on small economy cars such as the Renault 4 CV and the curious Citroën 2 CV, and now, increasingly, on larger, elegant saloon cars such as the Peugeot 604 and the big whale-like Citroëns which, for advanced techniques, comfort and design, have few rivals in their class.

The present annual production of well over two-and-a-half million cars, 55 per cent of them exported, comes from four big firms, one nationalized (Renault) and three private: Peugeot, Citroën (90 per cent owned by Peugeot since 1976), and Simca (controlled by Chrysler). Each firm has a distinct individuality, and this gives flavour, if not always efficiency, to the industry as a whole.

Renault throughout the 1950s was the foremost showpiece of

* Some 288 per 1,000 people, compared with U.S.A. 495, Sweden 323, West Germany 280, Britain 251.

French State industry. And though it went through a bad patch in the mid-1960s, today it has recovered much of its earlier dynamism and remains a remarkable example of 'State capitalism', of a public manufacturing firm operating just like a private one, in a competitive field. It was founded in 1899 by Louis Renault, a young self-taught mechanic who in the manner of Ford or Nuffield built it over the next forty years into one of the leading car firms of Europe. In 1944 he was charged with Nazi collaboration; the State confiscated his empire and, this being the era of nationalization, they decided to hold on to it. They installed some inspired technocrats to run it on commercial lines, and straight away made it into a torch-bearer for French industry. Starting almost from nothing, it built up its own production of machine-tools. Its huge factory at Billancourt, in south-west Paris, was the first in Europe to use automation, in 1946. And in 1948 there began to pour off its assembly lines a remarkable new baby car, the Quatre Chevaux (4 CV, i.e. 4 h.p.), which had been planned secretly during the war by Renault technicians.

The 4 CV was a symbol of the social philosophy which has guided the Régie Renault ever since, first under Pierre Lefaucheux, and then under his successor as chairman, Pierre Dreyfus. An idealistic kind of technocrat, Dreyfus regarded the car as a social instrument to which every family has a right. Therefore his firm concentrated on massive turnout of relatively small and cheap cars, the models gradually growing in size only as French incomes and living standards rose. Thus in 1956 the 4 CV began to give place to the slightly larger Dauphine, one of the most brilliant and attractive small cars ever made, which sold well over two million; and the Dauphine then in turn gave place to the rather larger R10.

The other feature of this social philosophy is the idea that a firm owes its workers not only a wage but also as full and happy a life as possible. With discreet State backing, Renault after the war steadily led the field in welfare and labour relations – often to the annoyance of more staid private firms. Not only does the Régie spend an unusual amount of money on social clubs, housing, education and other schemes for its workers, but in 1954 it inaugurated a new kind of labour charter, the Convention Collective. This committed the firm to regular 4 per cent annual wage increases, and in return the unions agreed not to strike except as a last resort, when all negotiations had failed. This charter was later copied in the mines and in some private sectors.

The firm's approach to its workers is one of discreet paternalism. They were the first in France, in 1963, to be given a fourth week's statutory paid holiday. And whenever there is a problem in the factory, or a change of company policy, the chairman sends a personal letter to each worker's home. These measures help to explain why Renault was virtually free from strikes for fifteen years, from 1953 to 1968. What is less easy to explain away is why the 1968 strikes, when they came, were fiercer and lasted longer at Renault than in almost any other French firm, and why again in 1971–2 and in 1975 Renault was the scene of bitter strikes. Perhaps the key to this paradox is that at Renault the ideological aspects of the strikes are ascendant over the material ones. In most French firms, the workers wanted better pay and conditions: at Renault, they already had these, and a number of politically sophisticated and well-paid *cadres* and technicians struck out for what they saw as the next phase, the assumption of control by workers over their firm's destiny. Once again, but this time in a different way, Renault was setting the pace in France!

Renault in the 1950s was also a pioneer in the field of exports. At a time when most French manufacturers were still slumped in protectionism, Renault's leaders foresaw which way the world car market was likely to move in the 1960s and sensed that France could not afford to be left out of this new competition. Though the Régie has never managed to break into the North American market on any scale, elsewhere its exports have soared, especially to other EEC countries: today, in Germany itself, Renault sells more cars than Mercedes does!

Citroën, Renault's closest rival, could hardly be more different. From 1934 until the short-lived tie-up with Fiat in 1968, Citroën was entirely controlled by the Michelin tyre company, which had bought it when its founder, André Citroën, went bankrupt. The Michelin family empire is the most arrogant, conservative and fanatically secretive in French industry, and Citroën took its colouring from them: it was a caricature of the old-fashioned family concern, where unions and workers were treated with a chilly paternalism and modern methods frowned on – Citroën in France would scorn advertising and publicity, take little trouble with exports, and handle many domestic clients with cavalier contempt, while sales were still based on old-fashioned personal contact and interview. American doctrines of planned obsolescence were equally disregarded: Citroën believed in making cars that would last and could be kept in production, like the 2 CV, for 20 years or more. And such was the firm's record of mechanical genius that it was able to get away with these strange methods, and in the 1960s it made the best progress of any French car firm.

Now that Michelin, after an abortive affair with Fiat, has virtually sold out Citroën to Peugeot, the approach is changing. But even today, visitors are rarely welcomed at Citroën's parent factory in Paris, nor at the big new automated plant in Rennes; and the Normandy testing-ground for new models is guarded by ten-foot walls and patrols of dogs. But the dogs have something worth guarding: Citroën's dedicated team of designers work two decades ahead of production, and the firm relies on the reputation it has created for unrivalled advance in design. This has become a mystique in France, but it is rooted in reality. Those cars with their weird shapes are solidly reliable: the internals are designed first, then the body shape is planned round them. The 2 CV may look like an old tin can, but it rarely breaks down, costs less than 12,000 francs, does fifty miles to the gallon, and has been called 'the world's most intelligent car'. Born in 1948, it was still coming off the lines in 1971 at the rate of 225,000 a year (including its newer and slightly less inelegant sister version, the Dyane). The big frog-nosed Citroëns, DS, ID, and the new CX, are noted for their road-holding, comfort, and hydro-pneumatic suspension which makes them flop gently when they stop, like tired elephants. They have been the official ministerial car in many countries, including France itself. De Gaulle had a fleet of fifteen at the Elysée Palace, and he owed his life twice over to their excellent wheels and brakes – once, in a night storm, when a tree fell across his path, and then when he was shot at by the

OAS and his chauffeur had to make a quick get-away on bullet-punctured tyres.

Peugeot is also a family firm, and its recent record has been much better than Citroën's. Its factory at Sochaux, near the Swiss frontier, is owned by a wealthy and clannish Protestant dynasty: six of the twelve members of the Board are Peugeots and a seventh, the managing director, is a son-in-law. There is pride at Peugeot, and some secretiveness, but little of the feudal arrogance of the Michelins. The accent is on prudence and reliability; this is the only large firm in France to pay its suppliers in ready cash. Peugeot cars, like their makers, are sober and discreet, and have a quality that might seem more English than French They are famed, above all, for their robustness. Exports are high, and Peugeot is no longer the smallest of the Big Four, for its sales have far overtaken those of Simca. In 1975 the Government chose its latest luxury model, the 604, to replace the Citroën DS for official purposes – a notable prestige victory!

When Chrysler were looking for a foothold in Europe, they first made overtures to Peugeot, and met with a proud rebuff. Then, in 1963, they bid for the ailing Simca; and the Government allowed the deal, since it saw no other way of saving the firm. So today Chrysler hold 69 per cent of Simca's shares. After a difficult period, Simca is now at last doing rather better, and holds 11 per cent of the domestic market. It has always seemed a somewhat nondescript firm in its style of cars; but some of its newer models, notably the 1308 Alpine, have shown more flair.

In the first years after the war, the French car industry's task was simply to meet the needs of a hungry domestic market that in 1945 had only a million cars on the road. Tariffs were high, foreign competition was slight, demand far exceeded supply, and people wanted cars quickly and cheaply, without frills. Then horizons began to widen. When Renault attacked the American market, in 1957, initial success was on an unexpected scale. The Americans had never seen a car as small or as cute as the Dauphine before; they bought 200,000 in three years, often as playthings for wife or kids. But Detroit hit back by building its own small cars, the 'compacts'. Then Volkswagen arrived in the

United States to challenge Renault, and after 1959 French imports there began to tumble. Shortly afterwards Italy, France's biggest regular client, also withdrew much of her custom by imposing austerity measures to deal with her own economic crisis. The proportion of exports in France's car production fell from a half to a third between 1959 and 1964.

The French began to realize that having four separate rival firms was a luxury; they must group together, with each other or with outside partners. In 1959, soon after the Common Market came into existence, Dreyfus had in fact proposed to Volkswagen and Fiat a kind of non-aggression pact, with delimited spheres of influence and no rivalry over new models. He was turned down. When Dreyfus put the same idea later to Henry Ford II, he was told, 'We'll lick you because we're stronger.' Then, while Dreyfus continued to woo the Germans, the Government began to try to persuade Citroën and Peugeot to link together. But in 1966 came an unexpected *coup de foudre*: Peugeot ditched Citroën and announced a new association with Renault. Rapidly this helped to restore the fortunes of Renault, which during the mid-1960s had appeared to be losing its old verve and flair. Believing that in the new conditions of world competition he could no longer rely on one star model, Dreyfus had swung to the opposite extreme and in 1962 brought out *four* new models – unprecedented in Europe for one firm in the same year. This proliferation put up costs, and in the difficult slump years of 1963–5 Renault, as one French writer put it, 'held the world record for fall in production'. Fortunes change swiftly, however, in the mercurial car industry, and even before the Peugeot deal Renault's sales were mounting again: they rose 28 per cent in 1966. Today Renault alone turns out more than a million private cars a year, some 60 per cent of them for export. Several established models – notably the compact little R5 and the larger, sturdy R16 – have been brilliantly successful. In 1976 Dreyfus retired, to be replaced by Bernard Vernier-Palliez: he is a more cautious man, who is busy diversifying the firm into production of bicycles, boats, sports equipment and so on, in view of the uncertain long-term prospects for the automobile.

But what of proud Citroën, isolated amongst its peers? Despite its technical prowess, the shortcomings of its haughty commercial policy began to tell, and in the late 1960s its sales dropped seriously on the French market. Capital reserves, too, were falling. Citroën began to realize that in the new age of battle between giants it might be forced to modify the splendid paradoxes of its policy, and so it reached for *ententes* with more orthodox firms. So when in 1968 Agnelli of Fiat offered to create a new Citroën–Fiat holding company in France with 45 per cent Fiat participation, the Michelin family said yes. But de Gaulle, personally, said no. He knew that Citroën would soon be virtually swallowed up by the far larger and more dynamic Fiat, Europe's number one car firm. Finally, however, he accepted a compromise whereby Fiat's share in the new holding company would be initially only 15 per cent. But neither Fiat nor Citroën found the ensuing partnership very satisfactory, and in 1973 it was finally broken off without having helped either side very much. Commercially minded Fiat and capricious, inventive Citroën should in theory have proved complementary; in practice, they were too different in temperament and philosophy to find much point of contact. '*Les intérêts composent toujours, les passions jamais,*' commented one motoring journalist, quoting Beaumarchais. It was another failure for the ideal of inter-EEC mergers beloved of the European federalists. So Citroën, on its own again and now losing money faster than ever (the deficit was 1,000m francs for the first year of the energy crisis, 1974), turned again to its earlier would-be saviour: Peugeot. This time the Michelin family sunk their pride in a big way; they sold out to Peugeot some nine-tenths of their interest in Citroën. Helped by a massive State loan, Peugeot by 1976 had become the effective master of the two firms, which jointly are now larger than Renault. They control about 19 per cent each of the French market, compared with Renault's 35 per cent. Renault's technical association with Peugeot continues, but is likely to be phased down, for obvious reasons.

During the crisis years of 1974–5, France's motor industry suffered worse than that of Germany or Japan, but less badly than the British, Italian or American. After the 1973 boom year, production fell by between 5 and 10 per cent over each of the next two years. Even Renault was hit, due partly to a 10-week strike in its Le Mans factory in 1975 which cost it 100,000 vehicles and helped it clock up a 400m franc deficit for that year. But by early 1976 French production was climbing again fast. If the industry seems to have weathered the crisis relatively easily, this is thanks partly to the emphasis it has always placed on smallish, economical cars, the kind well-suited to the new motoring climate. The industry has made its mistakes since the war, but its career on the whole has been brilliant – thanks to technical flair and, finally, a degree of commercial acumen. It has rationalized and modernized more fully than any other branch of French industry, and has learned that the only way to stand up to General Motors is to imitate it, and unite. France in 1966 pushed Britain out of second place among Europe's car producers, and her present annual output of around 2,800,000 private cars is not far behind Germany's. However cost inflation is so serious that firms are finding it ever harder to make a profit. The crisis has brought home the lesson that world saturation is not far round the corner, and production is bound to slow down again.

CARAVELLES AND AIRBUS – BUT CONCORDE?

The post-war renaissance of French aviation was more striking than in any other sector of French industry. It was at such a low ebb just after the war that its leading firm, Sud-Est Aviation of Toulouse,* was reduced to making gas-generators and refrigerators. Eight years later it was making the Caravelle, and today Airbus and Concorde – three aircraft of high technical distinction, whatever the commercial doubts about Concorde.

This was the full measure of the French triumph in the 1950s: to have succeeded in bringing out the Caravelle under such adverse conditions, at a time when the British and American industries with their war-time experience were still far ahead. If the French tend to boast about it rather too much, maybe it's because they know they were once the leading pioneers of early aviation, and so in this field they are even more prestige-conscious than usual. Prestige was the driving force behind the Caravelle's

---

* Its name was changed to Sud-Aviation in 1957, after a merger with another firm, and then in 1970 to Aérospatiale, after further mergers.

take-off, as it is today behind the Concorde. Fortunately, in the case of the Caravelle it made splendid economic sense too.

France's aircraft industry led the world in the first part of the century; by 1945, after working half-heartedly for the Germans and then lying fallow, it was nearly derelict. All the advanced techniques and expertise were across the Channel or the Atlantic. For the next few years French factories looking for employment had to fall back on making British or American models under licence: Sud-Est, for instance, made de Havilland fighters. The first new French national venture, the Armagnac, a heavy four-engined plane turned out by Sud-Est in 1949, was not a great success and was spurned by Air France in favour of Constellations.

But down in Toulouse, capital of the French aviation industry since the 1914–18 war, a team of gifted designers and engineers set about preparing for the real come-back. Their company, Sud-Est, was one of several aircraft firms that had been nationalized in 1936, and in 1946 the Government put at its head an exceptionally vigorous and able young administrator, Georges Héreil. He rapidly rebuilt the firm's workshops and began to plot with the Government how best to restore France's position. With over 90 per cent of the world's construction in American hands, the problem was to find a weak point, an aircraft that no one else had yet made. The answer, it seemed, was a fast, medium-range jet. So in 1952, the Government gave Héreil the go-ahead and the funds for the Caravelle.

Héreil took a gamble that few private firms – and certainly none in France – would have dared. Believing that the Americans would not bring a similar kind of jet into service before the early 1960s, he insisted that the Caravelle be ready by 1959 in order to exploit the world market. This meant taking the unusual risk of investing 400m francs in an initial batch of fifty Caravelles before any airlines, even Air France, had placed orders. For three years the technical team headed by Pierre Satre, and known as *la République de Toulouse*, worked round the clock. The operation was almost wholly French, save for the Rolls-Royce engines. The first trial flight was in 1955, and Air France had the first Caravelles in service by 1959, as planned. They were an immediate success, and other airlines such as Alitalia and SAS began to buy in some numbers. The Caravelle's speed (500 m.p.h.), its silence, its comfort, its resistance to fatigue, put it ahead of other aircraft in its class. On a trial flight to Rome, it was blessed by the Pope.

As many as 280 Caravelles were sold, to 34 different airlines, before the aircraft was finally taken out of production in 1972. But Héreil largely failed in his greatest ambition, that of breaking into the American market. He persuaded United Air Lines to buy 20 Caravelles, but other US airlines fought shy, partly because the Americans were planning something better themselves. When the Boeing 727 appeared in the early 1960s as the Caravelle's expected rival, it had already sold 131 machines eighteen months ahead of its first flight. This shows that the Caravelle's dent in the American-dominated world market, though impressive by European standards, was relatively modest.

So in the 1970s, in a bid to ensure that Europe has a share in the new supersonic jet market, Aérospatiale and the British Aircraft Corporation have been building the Concorde. Prestige once more is at stake; and throughout this troubled Concorde affair the French have seemed noticeably more concerned about it than the British. When the Labour Government, for economic reasons, wanted to cancel the project, the French, for reasons of prestige as much as anything else, wanted to go on. But French technical pride and devotion are also involved, not only prestige: visitors to Toulouse have always been impressed by the enthusiasm and dedicated ambition of the men at work on the prototypes.

Concorde may have been misconceived commercially, but in terms of technology it is another triumph for French aviation. The designers and engineers were let down by the politicians and commercial experts. The endless Franco-British wrangles and delays over Concorde at political level have not, however, proved that joint projects of this kind are impossible; simply, that they need to be tackled differently. Increasingly it is impossible for one European country on its own to make a major aircraft today: Europe needs to combine, even more than in the car industry. But this needs to be done mainly on a technical and financial level, with minimum interference from Governments. This is the lesson of Concorde, now being applied to the four-nation Airbus which Sud-Aviation – today renamed Aérospatiale – has been building at Toulouse in collaboration with German, Dutch and British firms. Governments (excluding the craven British) supply the money and over-all blessing; the firms do the rest. Airbus is a relatively cheap, large-capacity (300-seat), medium-range, sub-sonic machine. The first models went into service, with Air France, in 1974. Sales at first were sluggish, for the plane could not have been born at a less happy moment, with world passenger traffic contracting. But Airbus soon proved its worth so well that in 1975, a difficult year, it was the world's best-selling large passenger aircraft after the Boeings, and new orders for it out-stripped the combined sales of its two closest American rivals, the TriStar and the DC-10. By April 1976 there were 17 Airbus A-300s in service and 39 more on order or option: clients included Lufthansa and Korean, Indian and South African airlines. The aircraft was proving invaluable on middle-range European routes, and in today's climate it makes far better economic sense than Concorde.

Aérospatiale has also been increasing its output of helicopters, military and civil, of which it is Europe's leading producer. It sells about 300 a year, to some 70 countries. The firm makes a handsome profit on these, as it does on its large output of miss-iles. But losses on Concorde are so great that Aérospatiale has been running ever more deeply into the red. Since Héreil's depar-ture in 1962, it has also suffered from faults of management. So in December 1975 the Government brought in one of France's top air force officers, General Jacques Mitterrand – brother of François! – to take charge of the firm, with the aim of trying to rationalize production and cut costs.

Aérospatiale may be France's largest aircraft firm, but it is far from being the only one. Marcel Dassault's private company has a brilliant record in the production of military aircraft, and his Mystères and Mirages have been sold in large numbers all round the world. France's aircraft industry may be only half the size of Britain's in terms of personnel, but its productivity is far superior, and well over a third of its sales come from exports. Civil aircraft production may now be going through a difficult period, as in many countries, but this does not alter the fact that France's post-war aviation revival has been in every sense remarkable. There are several underlying reasons for this success. The Government not only helped and encouraged the aircraft industry to recover; it has promoted the most intensive system of air education outside eastern Europe. The aeronautical Grandes Ecoles have expanded fast and enjoy high prestige. Private aero-clubs flourish, too, and there are 23,000 licensed pilots in France. Since Blériot's day and earlier the French have been an air-minded people, always ready to hero-worship *ces hommes magnifiques dans leurs machines volantes*; and the idealistic pilot Saint-Exupéry, who died while on service in the air in 1944, is still the most popular of all authors with French youth. So the success of Caravelle and Airbus stems from this background of national enthusiasm and scientific prowess.

SHOES AND SHIPS AND SEALING-WAX: EFFICIENCY OR PRESTIGE?

Almost all the big industries described so far are either in State hands, or, in the case of cars and aircraft, are led by State firms that have set the pace. And most of them have been very successful. With the older, more fragmented industries, mainly privately owned (shipping, textiles and chemicals, for instance) the picture is often rather different.

Electronics is an example of a largely private industry that has done quite well; but this is because the State relies on it heavily for civil and military purposes and is accordingly generous with contracts and research grants. A modern, highly competitive industry such as this cannot be allowed to languish as if it were turning out *lingerie* or cargo-boats. One French electronics firm, the Compagnie Générale de Télégraphie Sans Fil (CSF), has made progress with radar and invented the SECAM colour TV system that has been one of the main prestige weapons in de Gaulle's armoury.

Today the Government has reluctantly come to accept that national independence, and even European independence, in the electronics field is just not possible; American techniques are too far ahead. So in the 1960s the French began operating a dual policy. On the one hand, they encouraged American investment in electronics. The Bull take-over was permitted, and IBM was allowed to build up its strength in France. IBM France, with its new factory at Montpellier and its splendid research centre in the hills behind Nice, is one of the most impressive firms in the country; the staff and management are all French, with only limited supervision from their American parent. On the other hand, the second element in French policy was to try to develop a co-ordinated national computer-building programme, with purely French firms. Known as the 'Plan Calcul', this policy was launched in 1967 with a great roll of drums, and the new partially State-backed Compagnie Internationale pour l'Informatique (CII) was soon producing 25 computers a month in its Toulouse factory. But CII rapidly found itself unable to compete viably against the American giants, and so in 1973 the owners of CII formed an alliance with Siemens (West Germany) and Philips (Holland) in a bid to create a European computer industry large enough to be workable. But the bid failed: in 1975 the European consortium collapsed, and the Government was faced with a choice between nationalizing the CII, or inciting its private owners (Thomson and GCE) to sell it either to Siemens or to an American group. Putting efficiency and economy before national pride, they chose the final course. And today the major part of CII's heavy computer production is in the hands of the American-controlled giant, Honeywell-Bull (Honeywell having by now taken over General Electric's interests in Bull). So nearly all France's growing computer industry is now US-dominated. This may all sound immensely complicated, as such business deals often are, but it proves again the sad and simple point that inter-EEC mergers or alliances have appeared less attractive or less feasible than reliance on American investment and know-how.

Charges of prestige-hunting were however levelled against the decision to build the world's longest and most modern passenger liner, the 55,000-ton *France*. This splendid ship was built at St-Nazaire and launched in 1962 – an ornate palace geared to rich American tastes, with fine French *cuisine* added. For several years it did good business on the North Atlantic route, but then came cost inflation and the energy crisis, and by 1974 the *France* was running at a huge loss. That year, in the wake of other dinosaurs such as the *United States* and the *Q EI*, it was taken out of service, after only 12 years. Today it is gently rusting in the Quai de l'Oubli at Le Havre, waiting to be sold to the Brazilians as a floating hotel – or some similar fate – as a former Derby winner is sold off cheap for carting coal. So disturbed was the French public at this waste of a fine ship, and waste of a national status-symbol, that when the singer Michel Sardou wrote a lament for the *France*, his record went to the top of the hit-parade and sold 512,000 in two weeks. 'La France a trahi le *France*' was the burden of his song. But the earlier critics of prestige-hunting had been proved all too right. The 400m francs of public money could have been better spent on something less spectacular, such as the new hospitals that France still badly needs.

The *France*, owned by the State-controlled Compagnie Générale Transatlantique, was built at a time when the French shipbuilding industry was in the doldrums. In the 1960s, even more than in Britain, French shipyards were hit by the new world conditions, and several of them closed: Nantes and St-Nazaire, the two main shipyard centres, were among the most depressed of French towns, where strikes were frequent. Then the Government encouraged a policy of rationalization, and this for a while brought results. In 1971 the Chantiers de l'Atlantique at St-Nazaire signed a contract with Shell for five 500,000-ton oil tankers, the largest in the world. But then came the oil crisis, and a sharp decline in the world demand for new tankers. By 1975, the Chantiers were having to rethink. They still had full order books for three years, and were far better placed than Tyne or Clyde. But Onassis had just cancelled orders for a couple of 500,000-tonners and the writing was clearly on the wall. So what next? The Chantiers are now being forced to plan their second major production turnabout in a decade, having already moved from liners to tankers at the end of the liner age in the mid-sixties. Old-fashioned and cautious private firm though they may be, they have recently come up with an ingenious idea. They are planning by 1980 to switch some 4,000 of their staff of 10,000 to the building of pre-fabricated factory components for the Third

World. Pieces of factory and equipment will be made in the Chantiers, where the expertise and machinery exist, then shipped out in giant vessels, maybe converted tankers, to a Third World where the demand for new factories is growing fast. Market research indicates that the scheme could be viable. This is a good example of the resilience of much of French industry in the face of the recent crisis.

The chemical industry has also been managing to adapt. It has expanded faster than any other French industry since the war, and has some good, well-modernized firms such as Péchiney and Boussois-Souchon-Neuvesel. But it is probably one of the French industries most vulnerable to the new world conditions, since this is a particularly competitive field, demanding expensive research and constant progress. Rhône-Poulenc, the third largest French chemicals firm, was so badly hit by the recent recession that in 1975 it lost 800m francs and had to lay off 4,000 staff. This gives some idea of the latent weakness of the industry. France has to rely heavily on imports of chemical ingredients from Germany and the United States; and though there has been some successful regrouping, notably a merger between Péchiney, Ugine and Kuhlmann, France still lacks really large chemical firms able to compete equally with Montecatini, Bayer, or ICI.

It is evident that many of the most efficient industries in France tend to be owned or closely supervised by the State. Whether this makes a case for yet more State control of the economy is an ideological question as much as a practical one. The greatest hazard of State control, at least under a régime such as de Gaulle's, was the one that constantly asserted itself during his reign: the confusing of national prestige with more pragmatic motives. Of course pride in achievement is a legitimate spur to progress, and in any country there is bound to be a national element in this pride. This is the spirit in which the Caravelle was born, and the great dams along the Rhône, and many other valuable post-war successes, not forgetting the tapestries of Aubusson. But in other cases, the choice of priority was more contestable. The liner *France*, the Concorde, the Rance tidal dam, the attempt to 'do a Mattei' in the oil industry, the promoting of SECAM colour TV against weightier support for the German PAL, some aspects of the nuclear programme, all these were interesting projects, but time has shown that some of them were an unwise extravagance. Pompidou, however, proved much less of a glory-hunter than de Gaulle. From 1969 onwards, very few major new prestige projects were launched, while certain industries were put on to a more competitive basis. National pride now counts for less, and economic viability for more. Giscard, since 1974, has taken this new trend even further. One of his closest advisers, Lionel Stoleru, a master-mind behind the new 'realist' policy, told me, 'We are now trying to cut our cap according to our cloth. In the civil field, only the space programme remains as an expensive luxury that we shouldn't really afford, though that's now a European rather than a purely French problem. Concorde is another such luxury – I'd like to scrap it, but now it's too late.'

Chapter 4

THE YOUNG FARMERS' REVOLT

FRENCH agriculture since the war has been an absorbing human drama, not merely a technical affair of subsidies and fertilizers. In few other sectors of French life are the human conflicts between change and tradition more acute, or more revealing of post-war France as a whole. An old peasant society is dying; and a new, energetic one of modern-minded young farmers has been painfully taking its place.

The delayed industrial revolution in France has provoked sudden transformations that in Britain or Germany were spread gently over several decades. The vast and static community of small farmers, once a source of stability to France, has become an anachronism and a burden. Mechanization of the farms has made economic nonsense of this huge population, and since the war over one half of it (nearly five million people) have moved to the towns, where life is easier and labour short. Of those who remain on the small farms, many of the older ones are sunk as deep as ever in their seclusion and fear of progress; they are the pariahs of the nation, rather than the paragons of an idyllic and simple life. But a strange thing has happened: a new generation of young farmers, with a totally different outlook from their parents, began to arise after the war, not from the rich estates of the northern plains but from the desolate smallholdings of the south and west. They promoted a new creed of modernization and technical progress, and have been forming themselves into producer groups and co-operatives. They seized from their elders most of the key posts in the farmers' unions and pressure groups, and even impressed some of their ideas on the Ministry of Agriculture. Whereas in industry this kind of impetus has come above all from official technocrats, on the land much of it has come from the farmers themselves. They have already done much to break down the old idea of *les paysans** as an isolated social class, and to bring the small farmers closer into the community. Even cautious scholars have described their movement as a 'revolution'. This chapter is largely the story of their efforts, in the first decades after the war, to pull peasant farming, in one generation, from the Middle Ages to the point where it can meet the consumer needs of a modern urban society. Their struggle is not yet won – French farming still faces difficulties, and the Common Market has not yet helped it as much as was hoped. But an irreversible process is in motion.

THE JACISTS, PISANI AND THE ARTICHOKE WARS

France is the richest agricultural nation in Western Europe, and also one of the poorest. Blessed by her climate, by a fertile soil and plenty of space, her output is far greater than any of her neighbours'; yet the standards of her subsistence farming would be unthinkable in Britain, Holland or Denmark. For in France there are two agricultures, as it is often said. On the one hand, the big wheat and cattle farms of the Paris basin and the north-east plains, which for some decades have been as modern and rich as any in Europe; on the other, the small farms of much of the rest of the country, poorest of all in the Massif Central, the extreme south-west and much of Brittany. The pattern is diverse, varying by region and produce, and this makes it hard to generalize even about the poorer areas. In Brittany and the Vendée, for instance, there are still too many people on the land, and few local industries to draw them away; yet in parts of the Massif Central the rural exodus has reached its safe limits, and not enough young people are left to replace the old when they retire.

The laws of equal inheritance, dating from Napoleon and earlier, have been one main cause of the small size of farms. Even until recent years, so great was the peasant's suspicion of town and factory that a son would stay tamely to receive his share of his father's land rather than seek his fortune elsewhere. Today the

* The word *paysan* denotes the whole social class of poorer people who earn their living from the land, whether as farmers or labourers. It is a less archaic and pejorative term than 'peasant'. 'Countryman' might be a fairer translation.

laws are still valid, but the sons move away more readily. Farms have gradually been growing larger, through rationalization. The average size has more than trebled since 1882, while the total number has dropped in the same period from 3·5 to 1·1 million; yet many are still too small to make economic sense under modern conditions. Over 50 per cent of all farms have less than fifty acres, and of these the average is only twenty-five acres.

Before the war all but a small sector of agriculture lay sunk in a kind of lethargy and fatalism. The gulf between the peasant and the new industrial workers in the towns grew steadily wider; *paysantisme* was more than a profession, it was a way of life, a doctrine that nothing could or should disturb 'the eternal order of the fields'. The notorious 1892 reforms of Jules Méline, then Minister of Agriculture, had pushed up high tariff walls round France to protect the farmers from outside storms – but they simply caused stagnation. Later Governments then followed the Méline line.

It was not until that weird interregnum, the Vichy period, that the stalemate really began to be broken. In agriculture, the influence of Vichy is a subject of some controversy. Led by Pétain himself, a man from a peasant family, Vichy promoted a massive 'back to the land' movement, and tried to set up a regionalized 'corporatist' structure, with the peasants forming a kind of state-within-the-State. This, by modern thinking, is pure fascism, and it had some parallels in Italy and Germany at that time; and yet in its French context it may have done some good. The system had not in practice got very far by the time Vichy ended; and the local farmers' syndicates it had set up to deal with local problems were quickly swept away by the Liberation. But even Vichy's harshest critics sometimes agree that these syndicates may have helped to sow the seeds of the practical peasant collaboration and local unity that was lacking in France hitherto and is developing, in a different way, today.

When peace came the immediate task, as in industry, was physical reconstruction. In 1945 food production was down to half its pre-war level, due to the fighting and especially to the mass deportations to Germany. The First Plan made farm machinery its top priority outside industry, and the results were striking. The number of tractors rose from 35,000 or so in 1938–45 to 230,000 by 1954, and farmers were encouraged by law to form State-aided groups for the joint buying and use of machinery. Productivity rose rapidly, and output was soon well above its pre-war level. At the same time, the much-needed rural exodus was gathering pace. But after about 1948 the real danger emerged: rapid industrial growth and its attendant inflation hit the farmer badly, for food prices did not keep pace. By 1950 industrial prices had risen 50 per cent higher than agricultural ones, compared with their pre-war level; by 1958 the disparity in growth was more than three to one. Yet for much of their spending, for fertilizers and machinery as well as clothes and household goods, farmers had to pay industrial prices out of a rural income. In 1958 at least half the peasantry was still barely above the bread-line.

The 1950s were marked by continual rural protests and disturbances, with tractors barring the main roads. The leaders were Right-wing demagogues of the old school. They demanded the remedy of higher price-supports and other forms of direct aid, but were utterly opposed to the real, more drastic solution of changing the structure of the small farms. Here the old peasant leaders found alliance with the rich farmers of the Paris basin who controlled the main union, the Fédération Nationale de Syndicats des Exploitants Agricoles (FNSEA). Together they formed a powerful lobby in Parliament. And so until its death in 1958 the Fourth Republic gave them what they asked for: price supports, based on a sliding scale that pegged food prices to rises in industrial ones. The farmers welcomed this system, but it helped the big, well-organized farms more than the small ones, unable to compete with the chaotic system of marketing. Discontent went on, reaching a peak of violence in 1957. There were tractor blocks, the angry slogans, the mild stoppages, the burning of surplus crops, the wild-mouthed demagogues – inevitably these gave French townsfolk, as well as foreigners, a picture of the French farmer as a comic and ignorant anarchist, always complaining, his head firmly in the sand. Yet his plight was genuine, even if partly his own fault. It was time for a new outlook, and new leadership.

And it came. All this time the new young radicals were quietly marshalling their forces in the background. By about 1957 they began to make their presence felt. It was not a haphazard movement. Like so many of the progressive influences in post-war France, it was rooted in militant Leftish Catholicism: nearly all the young leaders came from the Jeunesse Agricole Chrétienne.

The JAC youth movement had been started by the priesthood in 1929. Its aim was to combat the spread of atheism, at an epoch when the conflict in rural France between clergy and Marxists was at its height. In the 1930s village priests ran the local JAC branches and devoted them to prayer and Bible meetings, with a little social activity on the side. But during the war the JAC took on a different tone, more secular, but no less serious. Among the very young sons of small farmers, mostly still in their teens, there occurred one of those strange psychological changes that seem to have marked the destiny of France at that time. The danger and responsibility of their war-time activities, often in the Resistance, gave them an early maturity and seriousness. Many of them began to ponder deeply on how they could avoid a life of certain hardship and poverty short of leaving the soil which they felt was their home. Some, deported to Germany, saw there the example of small farms that *could* be run on modern lines. But how could it be done in France?

From about 1942 little groups began to form to plan the future. The JAC's secretary-general, René Colson, an inspired young peasant from the Haute-Marne, toured the country organizing meetings and firing other young peasants with his ideals. The initiative in the JAC was now out of the hands of the priests, and the accent was on learning economics, self-help and sharing of labour. A liberal-minded priest from the Aveyron department, in the south of the Massif Central, has told me: 'Young boys who had left school at twelve or so were thinking and deciding for themselves – it was amazing, and quite new in France. The war had produced a surge of independence, both from family and from priests. The role of the priest in the JAC now changed – instead of a didactic leader, he became an equal. Most priests, of course, resented this. But for me, it was an eye-opener to meet these uneducated young Jacists who yet had far more calibre and more *sérieux* than my most gifted *lycée* pupils of the same age. They were determined to cure their sense of inferiority and make themselves articulate. One boy round here taught himself public speaking by treating his cows as an audience; another, a very rough type, kept his beret on at meetings so he could be forced to make a speech as a penalty. That was how he cured his shyness.'

One aim of the JAC in the early post-war years was to give its members something of the general culture they had missed through leaving school so young. A Breton farmer has described how the JAC 'changed his life' by introducing him to art and history, by widening his horizons outside the brutish world of the farm, and giving him some hope that the peasants *could* improve their lot. The JAC organized amateur theatricals, singing contests and sports, for there were few cars and no television in those days, and young peasants had to find their own ways of fighting loneliness and boredom. The JAC's most important work, however, was professional. Local groups set about studying modern accountancy and the latest farming techniques – all much neglected by the older peasant generation. But the Jacists soon found that to apply these new ideas in practice was not so easy. On most farms the way was blocked by fathers who would have nothing of new methods and in many cases even tried to stop their sons leaving home in the evenings to study. In this patriarchal society the conflict of generations grew acute, and many Jacists saw little hope save to wait maybe ten or twenty years for father to retire. But the JAC was well organized nationally, with central committees and a newspaper. The next step, so it seemed by the mid 1950s, must be to carry their campaign into national farming politics and press for reforms of the whole structure of agriculture.

This was especially the view of Michel Debatisse, who took over the leadership of the JAC soon after Colson's early death in 1951. Debatisse, today the most influential farmer in all France, was typical of the JAC of those days. He was born in 1929 in the village of Palladuc, in Auvergne. His parents had a thirty-five-acre farm on a hill, where the soil was almost as thin as the wooded landscape was lovely. The few dairy cows, poultry and vegetables barely gave them a living. Michel grew up without toys or much comfort, though he was lucky that this was one of the 25 per cent of French farms that had running water. He left school at thirteen and joined the JAC. Soon he was running a local drama group, touring the villages by bicycle on summer evenings. He was a squat, thin, badly dressed youth, but his ugly face had – and has – a fierce kind of strength, and he rapidly began to develop wider ambitions. There was little he could do, so he felt, in Palladuc, but he saw that in Paris no one was really trying to help the small farmers constructively. He began to write articles for the JAC paper, and by 1950 was in Paris part of each week, editing it.

By about 1955 Debatisse and his friends were reaching the age when people generally leave the JAC and settle down to raising a family of their own and running a farm. Yet they felt that their campaign had hardly begun. Where could they carry it next? The main union, the FNSEA, was in the hands of much older and richer farmers from the north, and seemed hardly likely to welcome them. But the FNSEA had a moribund youth section, which the Jacists saw as a stepping-stone. When they made some innocent proposals for reviving it, the FNSEA leaders saw no objection, little suspecting what a Trojan horse they were letting in. So in 1957 the Debatisse faction took over the key posts of the Centre National des Jeunes Agriculteurs (CNJA) and began to use it as a militant and vocal pressure-group. As a first step towards breaking down the isolation of the peasant, joint meetings were held with industrial workers' unions; a most unusual step in France. Debatisse toured the country, stirring up the support of young farmers, Marxist and Christian alike: though a practising Catholic, he was no sectarian when it came to farming. Other CNJA leaders were dispatched to glean the latest ideas and techniques from Kansas, Denmark or the Ukraine; today it is rare to meet a member of that team who is not widely travelled.

The CNJA also began to form new links with the Plan and with the young technocrats who came to power with de Gaulle in 1958. Immediately they discovered a similarity of language and interest. Planners and civil servants began to consult the CNJA on what to do about farming; and Debatisse was elected one of the youngest-ever members of the Government's Economic and Social Council. The breakthrough was beginning.

Debatisse and his friends proposed that Government policy be switched from price supports to investment and structural reform. Above all, they questioned the hitherto sacred rights of property ownership, which they saw as a strait-jacket round French farming: they wanted drastic measures to persuade older farmers to retire, to take land away from unproductive hands and give it to new tenant farmers working in groups. And whereas many of the older FNSEA leaders still clung to the pre-war Mélinian doctrine that the rural exodus was a grave social danger, the CNJA saw it as necessary and good, but asked simply that it be 'humanized' to avoid distress.

The new Gaullist régime soon ran into trouble with the older and richer farmers. The Rueff financial reforms of December 1958 had stripped away many of the precious price supports, including the sliding scale. Rural discontent again grew: the Amiens riot of February 1960, where more than one hundred police and farmers were injured, was one of the worst since the war. But the Gaullists did not placate the old guard as the Fourth Republic had done. Michel Debré, the reform-minded Prime Minister, had an ear for the CNJA's ideas: he drew up a *loi d'orientation* partly inspired by them, and in the summer of 1960 narrowly succeeded in pushing it through Parliament, despite active opposition from the FNSEA and its allies. Above all, this law proposed a new Government agency to buy up and redistribute land; a modified form of what the CNJA wanted. For the first time a French Government committed itself to tackling the question of farming structures, and turned its back on the heritage of Méline.

But the orientation law was no more than an outline of principle, and the Government proved very slow in applying the decrees that would put it into force. The CNJA began to suspect sabotage by Ministry officials in league with the FNSEA. The Young Farmers' rising irritation suddenly reached flash-point at the end of May 1961, when a seasonal glut knocked the bottom out of the potato and vegetable markets in western Brittany. At Pont l'Abbé on 27 May farmers set fire to ballot-boxes in local elections and filled the streets with tons of potatoes sprayed with petrol. Then at Morlaix, a market town in north Finistère, 4,000 young farmers invaded the streets with their tractors at dawn on 8 June, seized the sub-prefecture in protest, and held it for several hours. This was the epoch of *putsches* in Algiers, and the newspapers delightedly drew the parallel. But these farmers were not terrorists: they were relatively prosperous growers of artichokes and other early vegetables, in the rich coastal plain between Morlaix and St-Pol-de-Léon. When their two leaders, Alexis Gourvennec and Marcel Léon, were arrested by the police, sympathy riots spread throughout the west. Down as far as the Pyrenees and Languedoc, roadblocks and banners were out in force. It was the largest and most effective peasant demonstration in post-war France, and it marked a decisive turning-point.

For the first time French farmers were demonstrating *for* progress, instead of against it. For the first time the riots were led and organized by the new leaders, not by the old demagogues. *'L'Agriculture de Papa est morte'* read the triumphant banners in the streets of Morlaix. Gourvennec, an ex-Jacist, was only twenty-four; an arrogant, well-spoken young man with something of the looks of Gérard Philipe. He and his fellow-Bretons were protesting at the marketing system, and not for the first time: the previous year, in a rather less violent version of their famous 'artichoke wars', they had sent lorry-loads of artichokes straight to Paris to sell on the streets, after the Breton middlemen had refused them a fair price. The growers were furious because the Government had continually urged them to produce more, and yet had done nothing to reform the archaic marketing system, so that prices always collapsed in a good season. Gourvennec and the farmers of his region were highly organized and far from poor; their actual problems were rather different from those of a region like Debatisse's. But both types of young farmers shared the same dynamism and the same reforming zeal, whether the reforms they needed most were of markets or of land.

The Government responded quickly after the Morlaix affair. Gourvennec had friends in the Ministry, and it is often alleged that some of them had secretly advised him to stage the riot in order to get things moving! In August de Gaulle appointed as Minister of Agriculture the most forceful and modern-minded figure to have filled that post in this century. Edgar Pisani, tall, black-bearded, eloquent and flamboyant, looks something like a cross between Ustinov and Svengali. He is an ex-prefect, and very much in the new 'technocratic' mould. During his four-and-a-half years (1961–6) in the usually unwanted job of Minister of Agriculture he showed a greater understanding of the farmers' real needs than any of his predecessors. He at once drew up a *loi complémentaire* of decrees to activate the 1960 law, and got them approved. This Pisani Law, as it is called, established a new pension fund to encourage old farmers to retire; an agency for buying land (already outlined in the earlier law); stricter rules against absentee landlords; and measures to encourage farmers to form into groups both for marketing and for shared production. This law has remained ever since the basis of Government policy for the modernizing of agriculture; in fact, the more recent 'Mansholt Plan' for the Common Market as a whole is inspired by the same principles. But although the Pisani Law has often been described as the boldest and most realistic step ever taken to reform French planning, in practice its application in the 1960s was slow because of lack of funds and bureaucratic delays, some of them, possibly, deliberate.

The law marked a victory for the Young Farmers, who rapidly began to infiltrate the FNSEA council itself. Today the new leaders share the power evenly in the Federation with the big northern farmers, and the old-style peasant demagogues have everywhere fallen away. But if Debatisse and his friends have won a political battle in Paris, they have not yet won the war in the fields. There is a new mood today in French farming; but, inevitably, the old structures are giving place more slowly.

SLOW DEATH OF THE PEASANT

The past twenty years have seen a tremendous effort of modernization on the farms. The results have been spectacular, but uneven. In many cases, huge rises in productivity have simply led to awkward surpluses, and this has not been helped by the anomalies of the EEC's price-fixing system. In other cases, productivity remains low, or the farmer still cannot get fair prices because of failures to reform the marketing system. There are still many problems to be solved. But down on the farms themselves, there is no doubt of the new spirit among nearly all except the older farmers. Everywhere the old order is steadily being swept aside by new men and ideas. And some of the outward contrasts in this age of transition are striking enough to the casual visitor. In a Brittany farm kitchen a huge TV set stands by the ancient open fireplace, but there is no running water; near Avignon, one son in a farmer's family hoes potatoes while his brother goes to work at the nearby plutonium factory; in the chalky uplands of the Aveyron, an old man vacantly minds the cows while his son brings home fertilizer in a smart new Simca. Techniques and home comforts are slowly improving, from a very low level; and for good or ill the peasant's life is becoming 'urbanized', as it already is more or less completely in Britain. But the deeper changes, and the obstacles to change, are psychological. What is at stake is the peasant's rooted individualism, and his emotional attachment to his own piece of land.

Believing this to be the greatest barrier to progress, the new farm leaders made land ownership reform an important part of their policy. This, in France, is a highly complex problem. Until the end of the last war the feudal tradition of land property was strong. Some small farmers clung proudly to their own ancestral acres, but many others worked on a system of *métayage*, paying their landlords a tithe, usually half their produce. Often the landlord was the all-powerful local *châtelain*, and his *métayers* were little more than serfs. If one of them gave offence, maybe by not going to Mass enough or hinting Left-wing views, he risked eviction. One of the keenest of the new ex-Jacist leaders, Bernard Lambert, who has a small farm in a very feudal area near Nantes, spoke to me with bitterness of the pre-war days: 'My father was a *métayer*, and would always lift his cap to the *châtelain* and call him "*Monsieur notre maître*". Once, when my father won a radio in a raffle, the landlord confiscated it because we were in debt. No wonder there are so many communists among farmers!'

A Socialist law in 1946 replaced the *métayage* system with a tenancy statute (*statut de fermage*) which gave much greater security from eviction and put a normal annual rent in place of the tithe. This is in force today: *métayage* has almost disappeared except in parts of the south-west. But the *statut de fermage* has created new problems. In some areas it is not applied fairly, because the tribunals are on the side of the landlords and the tenant gets victimized. In many other cases it works to the tenant's disadvantage in a quite different way. Because rents are fixed very low (they vary according to produce but average, say, sixty to eighty francs per acre a year), the landlord has little incentive to keep the farms in repair or make improvements. Many farm-houses are half in ruins, which harms efficiency and helps to drive the young into the towns. Lambert told me: 'I've spent a hundred and ten thousand francs on new cowsheds and other improvements here, which I vitally needed but my landlord wouldn't pay for. Yet, if he chucks me out, they belong to him.'

Despite the drawbacks of the statute, most young farmers prefer to be tenants, not owners; land prices have been rising fast, and they would rather sink their limited capital into live-stock and modern machinery. Probably more than half of all French farm land is rented. But many of the older farmers cling tenaciously to the idea of property. And despite the low rents, land is still considered a good investment by many non-farmers too, city speculators and others, who will snap up any good estate that comes on the market. For a variety of reasons an ambitious young farmer usually finds it extremely hard to acquire new land, whether for rent or sale, if he wants to enlarge his farm to an economic size.

So one central innovation of the Pisani Law, directly prompted by the Young Farmers, was to set up Sociétés d'Aménagement Foncier et d'Etablissement Rural (SAFERs): regional agencies with powers to buy up land as it comes on the market, make improvements on it, and then resell it to the most deserving, who are usually young farmers wanting to make good use of modern techniques. The SAFERs also have some rights of pre-emption, at fixed prices, thus acting as a curb on speculation. If a farmer wants to sell a plot of land, say, for 10,000 francs to a speculator, the local SAFER can step in, offer maybe 8,000 francs, and have the matter settled by an independent court.

This was greeted as the heaviest blow ever struck in France at the sacred rights of property. In practice the scheme has worked slowly, for the SAFERs' funds have been limited. They have also been impeded by the usual French legal delays, sometimes of up to five years for each transaction. And their powers of pre-emption are so hedged with limitations (due to concessions to the old guard of the FNSEA) that much of the most needed land eludes their grasp. However, gradually the operation has gathered steam, and over the past fifteen years it has enabled some 50,000 farmers to enlarge their holdings; it has handled the buying and selling of more than thirteen million acres, some ten per cent of the land that has come on to the market in that period. Though the SAFERs' success varies by region, they cannot be counted a failure.

Another land problem has been the parcellization of the soil, and French Governments have been trying to solve this since 1940. Fly over many parts of France and you will see a crazy quilt of thin strips; quite a modest farmer may often have ten or twenty different little fields, not next to each other but scattered over miles. This is partly a result of the equal inheritance laws, as farms were split up between sons and then the parcels changed hands. And it often makes modern mechanized farming extremely difficult.

The policy of *remembrement* – literally, the piecing together of limbs – was initiated by Vichy and has continued ever since. By subsidizing up to 80 per cent of the legal, surveying and field costs, the Government tries to entice farmers to make rational swaps of their fields. The results have been variable: far better among the big, go-ahead farms of the north than in the sluggish south. After a long resistance to *remembrement*, farmers in many areas are now coming to accept it more easily; in fact, in some places, the policy is now held up by shortage of official funds rather than by lack of local co-operation. Since 1945, a total of 25 million acres have been *remembrés*. Even so, in the small-farm districts the process of educating the peasants to make this kind of change can still be a long and arduous one. Nowhere else does the conservatism of the older peasants show itself more keenly, or their emotional attachment to the soil show a worse side. A farmer may eventually accept the idea in theory; but when the work actually starts, he will be struck with sentimental horror, and refuse to give up the field where his father taught him to plough, or the apple tree his grandmother planted – even if he is offered as good in return, and his costs are covered!

In the Aveyron, a poorish, upland department of small live-stock and potato farms, *remembrement* was the main issue in the 1965 local elections. Several village councils that had earlier decided to go ahead with it were thrown out by the older voters. The commune of Privezac provided a *cause célèbre*. In 1963 it had voted 90 per cent for *remembrement*. So surveyors arrived and drew up a plan. Then there were protests. The village split into two clans, but *across* the traditional rural lines of Reds against Whites, teachers against priests. In the pro-*remembrement* camp the young Catholic Jacists were led by the Socialist mayor, an ex-teacher. Against them were the older farmers led by the deputy mayor, a Catholic ex-officer. When Government officials came to inspect the crisis, the police had to protect them. And when bulldozers arrived to tear down hedges and start the re-grouping, the old guard charged them on tractors and tore up the surveyor's markers. Several people were arrested, and the *remembrement* finally went ahead.

In many cases the conflicts are the fault of the officials, who reshuffle the land without tact. The job needs psychologists, as much as surveyors. And not all the young guard are so in favour of the policy. 'Is it worth raising fire and blood in a commune just for this?' said one. 'Better, surely, to get rid of the surplus farmers first, and then regroup. After all, *remembrement* doesn't in itself make farms any bigger.' Yet, in many areas, it has been helping to make farms more efficient and to create a more flexible rural society, less obsessively attached to its *petits coins*. And the farms *are* getting bigger, too, which is more important. In one typical Aveyron commune their number has halved since 1911, as people sell out to their neighbours, or drift away. But the young farmers reckon that only one farm in five is large enough to be viable today. It is partly a question of waiting for the old generation to die; half of all French farmers are over fifty-five. They block not only land redistribution, but also the kind of inter-farm sharing of work and equipment that alone, as the young realize, can enable the small farm to survive. The conflict of generations within families is often bitter. Realizing this, the Pisani Law set up a fund – which has since become EEC official policy – to help old farmers to retire. After a slow start, this fund is now bringing results and has benefited some 400,000 families. But the pensions are modest – rarely more than 4,000 francs a year.

In the Aveyron, a hardy region that furnished the JAC with many of its best leaders, several of the most dynamic ones have persuaded their fathers to retire. Down a muddy track near the department's main town of Rodez, I went to call on a former president of the JAC, Raymond Lacombe: the man who had once kept his beret on at meetings so as to be forced to make speeches! He is a tough little man of forty with coarse peasant features, but a mind sharp as flint; his wife is better spoken than he and comes from the Ardennes, finds the Massif Central a bit lonely; three kids are playing on the floor; the modern farm kitchen is spotless but there are no luxuries. Lacombe said: 'I was my father's tenant till last year; now he's retired and just looks after the animals a bit. We built this house for ourselves, so we don't have to share. We're luckier than most. I've got forty acres, with cows, pigs, corn and barley. I've raised money to buy a tractor and I share other equipment with friends; father wouldn't have done that. Recently I've bought a piggery and our net income's doubled. But costs rise so fast that forty acres isn't viable the way it used to be. If I could I might get out, though I love this place. On twelve farms round here, there are only four young people left.'

It is the same story nearly everywhere in France. In Lacombe's commune the population has dropped since 1911 from 717 to 399; it could safely lose another 200 without economic stress if the farms were fully modernized. In many places the exodus is even more striking: in the centre of Brittany I met a couple *all ten* of whose children had left. Less than 14 per cent of the

French now work on the land, against 35 per cent before the war.

It is usually the girls who leave first. More than the actual discomfort, they hate the isolation, the drudgery and sense of inferiority, and they rarely want to marry a farmer, even a prosperous one. Then the boys go too, in search of wives and a decent living, or because they are deprived of all responsibility on the farm so long as father is in charge. In one recent national survey of fifteen- to twenty-nine-year-olds still on the land, half the boys and three-quarters of the girls intended to leave. In the old days they stayed out of duty or tradition; today, if they stay it is by choice. Some men remain on alone through apathy, habit or a kind of vocation: in many isolated country districts the proportion of bachelor farmers is frighteningly high, and their life must be lonely and narrow beyond belief. The suicide rate in France is higher among farmers than in any other profession: one farmer in nine aged between 36 and 45 commits suicide.

The nearest industrial town is the usual venue for the émigrés; or, in many cases, Paris. There are more Aveyronnais in Paris than in the Aveyron. Until recently parents often tried to stop their children from going, and regarded the towns as wicked and corrupting. But this has changed. Too many children have come home on visits obviously uncorrupted and happier. And TV and other modern changes have broken down much of the old suspicion between farm and town. One Breton farmer with three sons told me: 'It would be nice if one of them felt he'd like to stay, but I certainly shan't stop them going. It's really up to me, isn't it, to make my farm attractive and viable for them to want to take it over.'

If all farms were large and modern enough, the farming population could well drop to 10 per cent or less (in Britain it is 4 per cent; in the US, 8 per cent) without any fall in output, and this is precisely what is now being applied as EEC policy under the Mansholt Plan. It is a question of controlling the exodus. In few areas has it yet reached its reasonable limits; in the Aveyron many farms are without successors, but when they fall vacant they always find ready buyers among other farmers.

The real problem is to ensure that it is not simply the dullards

who stay behind, and that enough young people of calibre remain
as active farmers to carry through the modernizing process efficiently. Hence the EEC's new policy of grants for dynamic young
farmers to encourage them to stay. Debatisse and his friends see
clearly that for this to work it is also essential to make rural life
more attractive and varied, with more comfort, culture, education
and social stimulus.

At this point in time the French rural world, as in many
Western countries, is in a bleak period of mutation between two
cultures – the old folk culture, rapidly passing away, and a new
modern one not yet properly installed. In the old days there was
great poverty, but also a certain warmth and tradition that helped
make it bearable. Many of the older people today speak of those
times with feeling. In Breton moorland farmsteads young people
drew round the fire on winter evenings to hear wise old women
reciting Celtic legends. Auvergne had a whole world of traditional
dances and music. In the Aveyron, and many other parts, there
were *veillées*, where neighbours would gather in one farm to weave
baskets or shred maize, and make it the excuse for a good party.
And then, the harvests! In Auvergne, a farmer told me: 'When I
was a boy, at harvest-time, the seasonal labourers would come up
by hundreds from Clermont-Ferrand and every night in the
village hall there'd be gay parties and dances. Today the work's
done by two men with a combine-harvester, and the labourers
work in the new Clermont factories and go to the movies.'
Today, folk culture rarely means more than putting on cos-
tumes for an annual fête to please the tourists. Even the JAC's
music and drama activities of the post-1944 period have declined:
the young have left the farms, or prefer to go off to the towns on
their motor-scooters in the evenings. And the modern world is
taking the place of the old culture, as the TV aerials sprout above
the cow-byres. Some farms, where electricity is just arriving, have
moved in one step from oil-lamps to the electronic age, as a TV
set may be the first gadget they buy. Certainly, modern comforts
and amenities are spreading: it is quite usual to see a huge new
electric cooker in the kitchen of a shabby and crumbling farm-
house. Over 50 per cent of farmers have cars; often they are those

charmingly ugly two-horse Citroëns that bounce so readily down any rutty track.

But the lag behind living standards in the cities, or on farms in a country like Britain, is still great. Few small farmers yet feel they can go away for an annual holiday (maybe there is no one else to milk the cows) and many older farmhouses are in a terrible state of repair. Though the percentage of farms with running water has doubled since Debatisse's childhood, Lacombe told me: 'We've been on the mains only since 1968. Before that we used a small well, and when it froze in the winter, I had to fetch water with my tractor every day from a spring 400 yards away. It was tough. Many farmers round here can't build modern piggeries simply because they've still got no water. Most of them do have electricity now, but it's hard to get a telephone laid on if you want one.'

The cultural hiatus, too, means that while the peasants have lost the old art of enriching their own lives, they often seem to be waiting for others to bring them new commercial entertainment. One Aveyron farmer's wife told me: 'Before the war, the families here would group together in the evenings for *entr'aide* work-parties. Now there's just a cinema in the nearby town, and far less real social life.' When someone does open a local dance-hall (as a shopkeeper has done in Lacombe's village) it is usually a great success, but such initiatives are rare. Eager people like Lacombe do what they can: he has even drawn up a project for a new social centre in his nearest large village, with library, lecture-rooms, etc. and he has had it scheduled in the regional section of the Plan. But there are not so many Lacombes, and they have other duties, too. What the countryside badly needs, and lacks, are professional *'animateurs culturels'*.

It is in education that the farmer feels his isolation and inferiority most keenly. In theory, every village child has exactly the same State education as the most privileged Parisian. In practice, it is not quite like that. In thinly populated areas some children still have to walk six or eight miles each day, and it is hardly surprising that many of them even fail to finish their primary schooling. A Government system of *ramassage scolaire* has started recently, with buses collecting children for school from lonely farms; it has made progress, but it lacks funds. Moreover, isolated schools often have only one single class spanning the whole age-range, and this holds back the brightest. And the teachers tend to be the dregs of their profession. Not until rural education improves will many of the brighter young couples feel like staying to bring up a family on the farm.

In higher and technical education, however, there have been great strides forward. Hundreds of full- or part-time agricultural colleges and evening institutes have been opened in recent years. The pressure on the Government for these has come, once again, from the young farmers, who will often also form their own technical study groups and hire specialists to come and teach them. Some of the pioneering work is rather touching: a young farmer's wife in the Aveyron told me of her patient efforts to get a group of ill-educated wives in her commune to study modern techniques of farm management and accounting, tasks that are traditionally left to the women on small farms.

In putting an accent on technical expertise, and the sharing of effort and equipment, the younger generation realize that it may be the only way to save the family farm. Mechanization has spread rapidly since the war, with tractor numbers rising today to over 1,300,000. It is true that often the tractors have been badly used, especially by older farmers, who tend to buy them proudly as a status symbol without having large enough fields or the right know-how. A man accustomed all his life to an instinctive *rapport* with oxen or horses will often be unable to run a machine. It breaks down, or incurs heavy running costs, and the farmer grows bitter that his panacea has failed him.

The younger ones have generally gone about things more intelligently. In Normandy a Young Farmers' leader with a 300-acre cattle and wheat farm told me: 'We formed a group of twenty-two farmers, and bought a silage machine, harvesting equipment and several tractors in common. We share all costs. It's quite an accepted way of working now, but nearly all of us are young. You'll rarely get the old doing this.'

This kind of group farming is entirely new in France, and cuts across deeply ingrained habits of individualism. More than 2,000 groups were at first formed privately, and in 1964 they were endorsed by a Government decree granting financial aid to encourage others. Besides helping with costly mechanization, the groups bring other advantages too. Salaried labourers are scarce today, most of them preferring to work in factories; so the groups can provide a pooling of labour for many jobs, and especially the chance of a rota system for milking and minding livestock. This gives the farmer the possibility of taking a week-end off, or even a holiday. The groups also facilitate specialization of produce, increasingly necessary in the new context of the Common Market. Above all, they enable farm units to grow larger and more viable without destroying their family farm basis or the individual's responsibility. Today there are some 5,000 groups.

Some groups have failed and split up, in the Aveyron and elsewhere, either because the older members failed to co-operate; or because the principle of shared decisions was too much for the peasant spirit; or, quite often, because the women kicked against the need for joint accounting. But in one part of the district a group experiment is taking place that could be of some significance for the poorer regions of France. At Espalion, in the lovely valley of the Lot, a middle-aged farmer called Belières has grouped some twenty small farms into a Banque du Travail. This carries the sharing idea a stage farther: each man-hour is set a price, according to the type of work, and if a farmer spends a morning helping a neighbour, or lends equipment, he is credited accordingly in the labour bank. At the end of the season, gains and losses are paid off, like a game of poker. It is a way of getting a group to work together without anyone feeling cheated, and its success at Espalion has led to other banks springing up elsewhere in France. Now Belières has launched a more ambitious scheme: through the local SAFER, the bank itself has bought 320 acres on an empty plateau about thirty miles away, and it plans to grow crops there. Some of the younger farmers have been persuaded to move there, and have had houses built for them in the nearest large village, eight miles from the new estate. This is a first step towards an American-type solution of the isolation problem in a motor age: the farmer lives in town and commutes by car to his fields, like a city worker. Both this and the 'bank' itself may seem simple enough notions to Anglo-Saxons or north

Europeans; but they represent an unprecedented breach in the French autarchic tradition. Some Aveyron farmers are sceptical: 'Will it work? People may not be ready for this kind of thing yet. Farmers are used to living close to their fields and their animals; until recently, they tended to sleep *in* the cowsheds with them.'

Although there are bound to be difficulties of this sort, it is certain that group farming will increase. It also seems likely that, within a decade or two, the new farm leaders and the Government will have largely succeeded in their aims of reforming farming structures. Whole areas will have been pulled up towards the level of the big rich farms of the north. The growth in the size of farms, *remembrement*, departure of surplus population, improvement in rural culture and comfort, technical modernization: all this is going ahead steadily, as one generation succeeds another. This battle is half won, and the new leaders have already turned to the next one: the reform of markets, the checking of over-production, the adapting of output to the entirely new and different needs of industrial buyers.

But the Jacist revolution has not touched, and will not touch, the whole of peasant France. There are wide areas where either the soil is too poor or the people too old and backward for much progress to be made. Such areas are the stark hinterland of Brittany, and the ruggedest parts of the Massif Central, much poorer than the Aveyron pasture-lands I have described. Only a score of miles from Gourvennec's smiling coastal artichoke plains, you can find grim upland hamlets where no one is left, apart from a few old people. The Lozère (east of the Aveyron), most backward and depopulated of all French departments, is in the same predicament. Here people eke out a living from useless polyculture, that inevitable curse of so much poor-soil farming: a patch of vines for the family's own vinegary wine, a cow or two and some mangy chickens, cabbages struggling to grow on a chalky hillside. Meat is a once-a-week luxury; children, if there are any, are kept from school to help with the chores, and sleep in haylofts. The working day is sixteen hours, and a family's income may be less than £700 a year. Yet the farmer is afraid of getting loans for modern improvements, for this type of peasant fears debt above all else. In a poor part of Brittany I met an old farmer who, rather than spend money on mending the broken gates and gaps in his hedges, made his wife and children stand guard in turns all day, to stop the cattle from straying.

This particular attitude is still common, and this world can only be left to die: it is too late for it to evolve. As the more desolate areas depopulate, their future will lie with afforestation and tourism – such regions are often among the loveliest. In parts of the Massif Central large-scale planting of new timber forests has begun, partly under the aegis of the State, and is providing employment for some local peasants. In Provence, the Dordogne, the Cévennes and elsewhere, many hill-top villages are now virtually deserted save for the tourist trade; thousands of farmsteads, as they become vacant, are being bought up by Parisians and other city dwellers for use as homes for holidays or retirement. In some areas, the farmers themselves are beginning to hire out their farms to tourists in the summer. Both sides benefit: the farmers get extra income and can manage to take a holiday themselves, while the tourists from the cities join in local country life and rediscover what for many of them are their lost peasant origins. This trend will certainly develop, and it contributes to the healing of the old breach in France between *paysan* and *citadin*.* Meanwhile, in many lonely regions, the Government is now creating national parks, with sports and holiday centres, and wild-life preserves. In this vast and beautiful land of France, as productivity steadily increases in the fertile zones, there will no longer be any need for peasants to scratch at the soil of ungrateful uplands. These can be left, as in the United States, to the splendours of nature.

CO-OPERATIVES STEAL A MARCH
ON THE CAPITALISTS

The process of modernization, which alone can enable the family farm to survive, is also in turn a kind of threat. For modernization can lead to mass-production, mass-processing and mass-marketing on a scale far beyond the means of the individual farmer: it can lead to the creation of huge farms that are run like a manufacturing industry, controlled by big companies. This is happening in

* See pp. 366–8.

several Western countries. The new patterns of urban living demand a large regular supply of standardized, well-packaged goods.

In the United States giant processing firms, often with their own farms and plantations, have sprung up to meet and, in turn, to stimulate this new demand. But in France the farmer is peculiarly ill prepared for this revolution. His own values of farm-fresh quality, so closely tied up with the genius of French country cooking, are at the opposite end of the scale from the industrial values of packaged efficiency. Until recently he has tended to find an alibi in the French housewife, who has been slow to accept frozen food. But change is inexorable, as cities swell beyond the capacities of local markets, and as the opening of frontiers forces France to adapt to other countries' needs and ways.

Yet today France finds herself, not only with backward farms and markets, but also with a feeble and fragmented processing industry. It is ironical that a nation that has a peach glut nearly every summer still has to import many of her tinned peaches from America for her out-of-season needs. In 1968 France destroyed 80,000 tons of rotting, surplus peaches and then imported the same quantity of tinned peaches! Several big American firms have understandably been trying to take advantage of this situation to establish useful footholds in the Common Market. As with computers or typewriters, they either try to take over French firms or set up their own French factories. And the cries of protest have been even louder than in industry, for what often seems to be at stake is not only national pride but the farmer's personal independence.

Short of buying their own land, which they usually cannot do in France, the best way these firms can operate is to make a contract with the farmer for his produce; and the firm usually demands an exclusive contract. It provides the seeds or foodstuffs, and insists on supervising every stage of production so that its own very precise standards shall be met. This, retort the French farmers, reduces the farmer to a peon, or at best a mere salaried worker, deprived of responsibility: it is a menace to the traditions of French farming, and all the worse when the capital is American!

This issue of 'vertical integration', as it is called, became one of the talking-points of French farming in the mid-1960s. Other countries have been facing the same problem. In Britain farmers accept the necessity for the trend, but make sure that by forming co-operatives they keep their own share of the processing industry and stop the firms winning a monopoly. In France they have finally succeeded in doing exactly the same. But for some years the issue was clouded with rhetoric and passion, because the farmers were so ill prepared for the struggle, and because of latent anti-Americanism. Two spectacular new American intrusions in 1964 (a Libby's tomato factory in the Languedoc, and a Purina poultry slaughterhouse in Brittany) set French pulses racing and put war-cries like '*Alerte au colonialisme américain!*' into the headlines.

Libby's was invited into the Languedoc by Pisani only as a last resort, after he had failed to stir up the archaic French canning industry to modernize itself and so help cope with the Midi fruit glut. Libby's was ready and eager to step right in with a minimum 15,000 tons a year. On top of this the Languedoc irrigation scheme,* boycotted by the vinegrowers, was in need of other outlets and new clients. So Libby's won its permit, and in 1964 opened a factory for tomato juice and canned tomatoes at Vauvert, south of Nîmes. At first the local farmers bristled with suspicion. 'They'll treat us like United Fruit treats Guatemala!' they said; 'peons! That's all we'll be.' But many of the more go-ahead farmers *did* sign contracts with Libby's, including many who had not grown tomatoes before. They got a below-market price (14 instead of the usual 16 centimes a kilo); but they were given the security of assured sales, as well as yields two or three times the local average thanks to Libby's seedlings and techniques which they were obliged to implement scrupulously. Despite many mistakes and errors of tact on both sides, the operation began to run quite smoothly, and has offered an Englishman an amusing picture of the head-on clash of French and American minds and methods!

In Libby's office at Nîmes in 1965 I met the director of field operations, Mr Bundy, a boyish and somewhat humourless Californian agronomist who after two years in the area spoke no

* See pp. 215–6.

more French than *bonjour*. For him, it was just another technical job in a backward country; next year it might well be Latin America. His walls were covered with scientific organization charts of every farm: when to sow, when to water, when to harvest. The local peasantry regarded them wide-eyed with wonder. Then I called on the president of the contractors' association (a defence group formed to negotiate with Libby's), who turned out to be anything but a peon. André de Flaux, a witty and sophisticated middle-class farmer with the charm and looks of Yves Montand, owned a big estate next door to his friend Lamour. 'The trouble with these Americans,' he said to me coolly, chain-smoking *Gitanes*, 'is that they blindly applied Californian growing techniques without first studying the climate, the soil or the people. Every little decision had to be referred back to Chicago. But they've learned, slowly. The other trouble is that they send people here who won't learn French and so have no direct contact with us. It causes a lot of inefficiency: three lorry-loads were lost once, just because instructions were misunderstood.'

'But,' he went on, 'I'm basically pro-Libby's and it's all working better now. At least they're quite affable, now that we've shown them we're not Puerto Ricans. We formed an association which negotiates group contracts. They didn't like it at all at first, but it helps us keep some power. I agree with Debatisse: it's very bad for a farmer to depend solely on one contract. But most of us here grow other things too. I've got 600 acres altogether.'

To the Government's delight, the Libby's venture *has* had precisely the desired effect in stirring up local French competitors. A big farmers' co-operative in the same area, Conserveries Gard, planted 1,250 acres of peach- and pear-trees and in 1967 opened its own factory which is now one of the largest fruit-canning plants in Europe – much larger, in fact, than the local Libby's operation. Conserveries Gard has gone soaring ahead and is very efficient. Many farmers, including de Flaux, are under contract to both – and Libby's is now widely cited, even by Left-wing critics, as an example of justified and useful American investment in France.

This was less true of the large chicken slaughterhouse opened in 1964 in a village near Rennes, Brittany, by Duquesne-Purina, a firm largely controlled by the mighty American Ralston-Purina group. Purina brought nothing new in techniques or efficiency; it simply further depressed a national poultry market that was already, as in other countries, suffering from over-production. Purina is primarily a feedstuff producer, and the farmers it placed under contract were obliged to buy its feed in return for selling it their birds. By offering them above-market prices, it threatened to put the local co-operatives out of business. The Breton farmers went on the warpath, and extra police were called in to protect the slaughterhouse. Bernard Lambert, the local Left-wing leader whom I happened to see at that time, told me: 'This is an under-hand American attempt to seize the French poultry market and put our farmers in servitude.' In the event Purina agreed to limit their output to 5,000 birds a week (one-sixth of capacity) and the affair steadily subsided. But more than Libby's, it proved the *cause célèbre* that impelled French farmers to start actively planning the struggle against 'capital integration'.

This they have now been doing, as in Britain, by developing their own co-operatives – very successfully. The co-operative movement has expanded eightfold in the past seven years, notably on its processing and marketing side. One national chain of co-operatives makes and sells a well-known brand of yoghourt, Yoplait. Another has a sizeable frozen-food factory. So successful is this movement that the 'vertical integration' problem has now virtually disappeared. French farmers have found their own strength; they have been able to steal a march on the capitalists. They have also been protected by the Government, which tends to veto plans for take-overs by foreign firms in this sensitive food-processing field.

Co-operatives began in France some seventy years ago. They are largest and best-organized in the dairy sector, especially in Normandy and Brittany. They have obvious advantages for the farmer: the danger is that in a really large bureaucratic co-operative the small farmer may feel almost as lost as when tied to a big capitalist firm. The Co-opérative de Landerneau in Brittany, one of the largest in Europe, is often accused of being a trust in the hands of the big local farmers, where the small farmer simply hands over his produce on contract as if to Purina.

The young farmers' policy towards integration has tied in with their views on land ownership and group farming, thus adding up to a new economic attitude to the profession as a whole. Michel Debatisse explained it to me in 1965: 'The farmer *must* keep responsibility for his produce – that is the basis of our *métier*. If he becomes a mere wage-earner, tied to a firm, he will be "alienated". We must try to stop farming going the way of industry in the last century and being proletarized. But of course we believe in technical progress, too, and we see the need for modern integrated markets and large-scale processing to serve the new mass-consumer needs. The only answer to this dilemma is for the farmers to group together and take charge of a large part of the processing and marketing business themselves, in peaceful co-existence with the capitalists. But each farm will retain some individuality. The family or two-family farm offers the only sound moral basis; we don't want *kolkhozes*. What we do want is a new attitude to land ownership. The peasant's implacable attachment to his own acres, even when he is no more than tenant, must be replaced by the idea of the land as a common resource or working tool, as fishermen use the sea without owning it. The right to work on the land must be divorced from the right to own it.'

This revolutionary talk about land was aimed not so much against the big firms (who are rarely landowners) as against what was then seen as an almost equally serious menace, that of the *cumulards*, speculators who buy up land and then put in salaried managers and workers to farm it. In 1962 the Young Farmers in Normandy decided to make a public example of one of the most illustrious of all *cumulards*: at dawn one day, 700 of them burst in upon the actor Jean Gabin in his country home, and told him they would 'break the whole place up' unless he agreed to sell or lease the two farms he ran on this basis. Being a kind and liberal man, he apparently agreed. The farmers' argument was that many of them had farms too small to be viable, yet could not find new land. Gabin's farms, they knew, were modern and well run, and his staff well paid. But the farmers did not want to be wage-earners.

Since these crises of the 1960s, the farmers have largely won their battles and *cumulards* are no longer a problem, even less than capitalist integration. Debatisse and his generation, ageing ex-revolutionaries now nearing fifty, today control FNSEA and the other seats of power and have modified a great deal of their radical talk about 'the land as a common tool'. The issues they and other farmers face are significantly different from those of even five years ago.

MARKETS, COMMON AND CONFUSED

French farmers had originally set high hopes on the agricultural Common Market, when it was first mooted a decade or so ago. They saw that France was starting off with the lowest agricultural wholesale prices of the Six and the largest volume of production. Thus it seemed inevitable that the gradual alignment of prices and the dropping of tariffs and other barriers among the Six would benefit French farmers more than the others. Had not France agreed to the Common Market partly because she felt that her gains in agriculture would compensate for Germany's probable gains in industry? So, when the setting up of a common farm policy ran into repeated delays and crises in the mid-1960s, French farmers grew angry – 'We planted Common Market seeds, and look, the wretched crops have come up national,' said one of them, while others made jokes about *choux de Bruxelles* that were failing to sprout.

Finally they have sprouted, though in a somewhat blighted form. Now that the EEC's Common Agricultural Policy (CAP) has become a kind of reality, farmers' feelings about it are very mixed. It has not proved the panacea that many of them had hoped. For one thing, France's partners greatly increased their own production during the 1960s and so they no longer offer her the once hoped-for prospect of ready markets for her surpluses. For another, whereas in Pisani's time the Government wisely switched the emphasis of domestic aid from price supports to structural reforms, the CAP with its accent on fixed prices is having the reverse effect, and only since the coming into operation of the 'mini-Mansholt' plan in 1972 is the CAP beginning to tackle the basic problems of reconversion of small farms. It is true that the CAP's high level of fixed prices in most sectors has

helped most French farmers to earn a better living than before –
and this goes some way to explain the relative calm of the farming
scene (Midi vinegrowers excepted) since 1967. But the system
helps the rich more than the poor; and by leading to large surpluses which Governments then have to dispose of, it falls heavily
on the taxpayers of the Community.

The economic basis of the common farm policy is extremely
complex. Summarized in a few words, it consists of a Community
levy imposed on agricultural imports into member countries and
then redistributed to their farmers in the form of price supports
and export subsidies. This protectionist system aims to boost
farmers' incomes and to encourage the Communtiy to become
more self-supporting in food. It helps mostly those countries that
are food exporters rather than importers; that is, it helps mainly
French farmers, even if not quite as hoped. But it has proved
expensive for the national budgets of all concerned, because the
price supports and other subsidies have been allowed far to
exceed the size of the levy, thus leading to heavy annual deficits.
This is because the EEC, yielding to pressure from various
farmers' lobbies, originally fixed the prices for most products
around the level of the highest then obtaining and not the average.
For instance, if wheat was cheapest in France and dearest in
Germany, it was the German rather than the French price that
was chosen for the CAP. This has simply encouraged farmers to
over-produce in many sectors, knowing that their surpluses will
be bought up anyway and then dumped on world markets. By
1969 the butter surplus – '*der Buttenberg*' ('the butter mountain')
– had topped 400,000 tons, and by 1975 the CAP was costing
well over £2,000m a year or 3 per cent of national resources –
three-quarters of the total sums spent by the Six on education!
Political horsetrading, too, has falsified the price policies. For
instance, the Community now has a large wheat surplus thanks
largely to the massive output of the large north French farms; yet
the wheat farms of Bavaria and some other parts of Germany
remain mostly small and ill-organized, and their owners have
successfully pressured the Bonn Government into insisting on
high wheat prices. And Paris, for reasons of high policy, has
yielded to Bonn's wishes in return for some favours elsewhere.

Inevitably this has discouraged farmers from shifting some of their production – as the French would like – from wheat to meat, where the EEC still has a shortage and has to import. Though the EEC has several times tried to reduce the official prices in sectors where there are surpluses (these include sugar, and some fruit and vegetables in season, as well as cereals and most dairy products), the farmers' lobbies have never allowed it.

As the CAP's subsidies are paid on quality, irrespective of the size or efficiency of the farm, inevitably it has benefited most those farmers that need it least. The large farms of northern France with their high productivity have done handsomely; some farmers now earn £10,000 a year or more. But small farmers in the South and West, struggling on £800 or so a year, have profited hardly at all. The CAP is simply widening the notorious gap between the 'two agricultures'. The same problem exists to a lesser degree among France's partners, and it is clear that the CAP's unified price system is crazily unsuited to countries where farming is so disunified. Only about a tenth of the CAP's funds are devoted to what is called 'guidance', that is, to grants for improving structures and reconverting uneconomic farms. However, there are signs that the EEC is now taking this more seriously; and since even the price support system at least rewards efficiency and modernization, the CAP is cautiously welcomed by the more forward-looking farm leaders, Debatisse and others. CNJA leaders told me, 'The CAP has altered the entire focus of our farming – if we have a grievance today we go lobbying in Brussels, not Paris, and farming seems to be the one area where national frontiers really are being destroyed.'

Those sectors where French farmers have benefited most from the CAP include cereals, sugar, wine, and certain dairy products – the EEC's share in over-all French cheese exports, for instance, rose from 10 to 68 per cent in 1958–69, suggesting maybe that Germans and others were now eating seven times as many Camemberts as before! In the case of fruit and vegetables, the situation is more variable, for France is not as well equipped to deal with marketing as her better-organized Dutch and Italian partners. The same applies to eggs and poultry, and to pig-breeding and beef: though production is huge, distribution methods are often so out-of-date that France cannot compete adequately with her partners. In fact, the past few years have made it more evident than ever that one of the greatest problems still facing French agriculture is marketing.

The chaos of French marketing is legendary. Though matters are much better than they used to be, produce may still change hands several times on its way from farmer to housewife; or it may sometimes travel hundreds of miles from its country farm to the Paris markets, only to be shipped back for sale not far from where it came from. Margins between producer and retail prices are still the highest in Europe. Even milk generally doubles its price between farmer and consumer; while for fruit and vegetables, in summer the margins may rise to 300 or 400 per cent.

An important aspect of the problem is that the small farmer has only recently begun to acquire any effective knowledge of marketing himself. He has therefore been ill equipped to stand up to the skilfully rapacious middleman. No Government has had the courage to fully reorganize the middlemen; their lobby is too powerful. But a few gentler reforms are under way, and are proving effective. Modern marketing centres have been built in a number of towns; and, more important, farmers have been encouraged to form into sales groups and co-operatives to gain more control of the market.

The complexities of the marketing issue vary greatly from one type of produce to another, and are closely linked to the problem of surpluses. The central features of this situation are firstly, underproduction of meat, especially beef; and secondly, seasonal gluts of fruit and some vegetables. The Government and the EEC are trying to cure the former by encouraging farmers to switch from cereals to livestock, and the latter by developing the canning industry, reforming the markets and regulating them in periods of glut. These policies have been making progress, but only slowly. In theory, if production were well organized, France could not only satisfy her own needs but grow rich on exports. At present, her over-all export surplus in foodstuffs is only about 10 per cent. In crops and animal products it is 35 per cent, but there is a big deficit in tinned and processed foods of all sorts.

The need to regulate production is seen most sharply in the

conflict between wheat and meat. Since long before the days of the CAP, wheat prices have been fully controlled and guaranteed by a Government Board, set up in 1936 by the Popular Front with the aim of helping the small farmer. In practice, it has always helped the large ones rather more, for improved techniques have sent the yields shooting up since the war on the rich estates of northern France. The small farmer's prices are protected too; but he usually has neither the soil nor the techniques to profit so much. Meanwhile, the new affluent society wants to eat less bread and more meat. France, land of the *biftek* and Europe's heaviest meat eater after Belgium, shares the European shortage. Yet Government and EEC efforts to turn wheat farms over to meat have usually fallen foul of two obstacles in addition to the enticingly high prices of wheat: these are the corruption of the meat markets, and the farmer's distaste for the servitude and financial hazards of cattle-rearing. A go-ahead young farmer in Normandy, with a relatively large cattle *and* wheat farm, told me how the farmers feel: 'Whatever the Government may want, *I'm* stepping up my emphasis here on wheat – it pays far better. The meat market keeps on collapsing, and prices are guaranteed only at a low level. Wheat needs less investment, and is given better loans; if you rear a calf, you have to wait three years to get your money back, and there's often the risk of disease. But the corn harvests are nearly always good. Above all, cattle demand constant attention with never a week-end off, and hired cowmen are hard to find. Farmers nowadays won't accept this any more; they want leisure like people in towns. Group farming, with rotas, will help, but it won't solve everything.'

Other farmers I talked to felt the same. The Government in the late 1960s began some not very successful attempts at market reform. It shifted the grotesque central Paris meat market to an expensive and grandiose new home in the suburbs, at La Villette; but this prestige operation proved a costly flop, for the meat-traders virtually boycotted La Villette's *abattoirs* and preferred to slaughter their meat locally. The Government has also incited the setting up of a national chain of new slaughterhouses which have helped a little to standardize buying and to offer the farmer reasonable prices. Slowly, too, the producers have been learning to group together to control their own sales. They have been helped by the rapid growth in France of large retail supermarkets, which will buy their produce direct, thus circumventing the middlemen. But what my Norman friend called 'the *mafia* of corrupt little dealers and butchers' is only slowly yielding ground, and many small breeders, often isolated and ignorant of the market, still tend to get cheated.

The farmers' marketing groups, backed by the Government and known as Sociétés d'Intérêt Collectif Agricole, have had good results in stopping prices from tumbling in a crisis, but they have seldom put them up in better times. In the Aveyron, Lacombe told me: 'We started a meat SICA here in 1962. It certainly saves us a lot of time and trouble. We don't have to go to the market individually, a SICA lorry collects our livestock and sells it for us. And the dealers don't cheat us so much any more, because the SICA is beginning to know the markets as well as they do. But the trouble is, only 20 per cent of the breeders round here will join the SICA – there's individualism for you! – and this destroys much of its effect. If, when prices start to fall, we retaliate by withholding our produce, the non-SICA people simply jump in and get better prices. The SICA *is* growing, but it's a slow process to educate the older farmers to use it.'

Hitherto, the retail price of *le biftek* has always been political dynamite, and has inhibited the Government from raising it to help the farmer. But the French housewife will clearly have to get used to paying more. The whole problem is partly caused by her, for it is her notorious choosiness about cuts that leads to wastage. The Government has sometimes made efforts to widen and educate her taste, by publicity campaigns showing that the less popular cuts are also perfectly edible, but these have not been very successful.

In the fruit and vegetable sectors, too, new SICAs have played a part in buffering farmers from the effects of seasonal gluts in some areas. Soon after the 1961 artichoke war, Gourvennec formed a SICA in north Finistère and has succeeded in imposing minimum prices on local middlemen. If prices threaten to drop lower, then the SICA withholds produce. This has been tried and proved successful, several times, with artichokes and cauliflowers.

Never again, after 1961, have artichokes, sold in the Paris shops for 1·20 francs a kilo, earned the Breton grower a mere six centimes. Here at least, by grouping together, the farmers have won a control over their produce that they never had before, and have grown as strong as their buyers. But the men of north Finistère are exceptionally dynamic and disciplined, and Gourvennec is an unusual leader. Some even call him a fascist; he has a commando team of local thugs, some of them paratroop veterans who fought in Algeria, and several times they have wrecked lorryloads of artichoke plants about to be sold by non-SICA members to other parts of France.

It is not certain how far his example could, or should, be followed elsewhere. Down in the south of France, in the fertile, fruit-growing plains around Nîmes and Avignon, there is no Gourvennec and the problems of glut have not yet been solved so easily. Output has quadrupled in the past ten years, notably of apples, peaches and cherries; in a good season the wholesale price of a kilo of peaches may tumble to thirty centimes, while the retail figure stays at well over a franc. The farmers, furious, resorted to riots and destruction in 1963, and in 1965 to the more sophisticated practice of offering passing motorists pamphlets and free peaches. But the farmers themselves are partly to blame for the trouble. The Vaucluse peach SICA does not work properly because 80 per cent of growers are too individualistic to join it.

High transport costs are one main reason why profit margins are so high and producer prices so low, especially for areas as far from Paris as Finistère and Provence. This is often a reason, too, why the small farmer of the centre or south-west finds it so hard to compete with the big farms of the Paris basin. Some of this may be inevitable in a country as large as France; but not all of it. The French centripetal tradition, added to the blindness and muddle of the market, means that far too great a percentage of national produce goes to or via Paris, simply because the local dealer does not know where else, outside his own little area, to send it. And local markets' lack of mutual contact can still lead to extraordinary price disparities, with eggs or livestock of similar quality fetching 50 per cent higher prices in one town than in another fifty miles away.

It was largely with the aim of curing these problems that the Government after 1958 started building a number of new *marché-gares*, big modern markets beside railways on the outskirts of Lyon, Toulouse, Nîmes and a dozen or so other provincial centres. They are linked by telex with each other and with Paris, and thus are able to help direct produce to where it is most needed and to reduce excessive price fluctuations. They simply provide a new venue for the farmer to come and sell to his dealer, who will then put the stuff straight on a train. Certainly, they have enabled quicker and more open transactions and shipments than in the old congested markets in town centres. But beyond this, they have proved something of a disappointment. The dealers and the middlemen themselves are still the same, using the same methods. No one has yet succeeded in reforming the old-fashioned French system of direct wholesale buying, which is often unfair on the producer. One or two experiments at introducing the fairer Dutch auction system – *vente au cadran*, or dial selling – have collapsed for pure reasons of temperament and habit.

The largest of all *marché-gares* was opened in March 1969, at Rungis near Orly airport, just south of Paris, and the notorious Paris central market, Les Halles, was transferred there almost in its entirety. For a century Les Halles had physically handled much of the food for the Paris region – it was a huge blood-sucking spiders' nest of middlemen where vested privilege, greed and muddle went hand in hand. It was also colourful and quaint, and many a nostalgic tear was shed at its transfer. Today, tourists can no longer jostle with *les forts des Halles* in their blood-stained aprons, as they drink their onion soup at the Pied de Cochon after a theatre or night-club. This central area, near the Rue de Rivoli, is now being redeveloped: a blow has been struck for modern planning, and for the decongestion of central Paris. This has helped to improve the marketing circuits, for the middlemen are not finding it so easy to reconstruct their mafia in their sleek new premises. But if marketing in France has improved considerably in the past five years, it is due much less to the *marché-gares*, which already seem outdated, than to the huge development of the co-operatives doing their deals directly by telex with the supermarket chains and wholesalers. They and other influences

have helped to reduce the middlemen's numbers and make them
group together and behave more honestly. The farmer is learning
gradually to influence the market and adapt himself to its needs,
just as the industrialist does. Inexorably, the farmer is turning
himself from peasant into businessman.

This kind of trend towards more modern methods has been
noticeable among France's vinegrowers. Many of them have
grouped into co-operatives, and under the Government's lead
have been putting a new emphasis on quality rather than high
output for its own sake. For some years this policy appeared to
be making progress, but in reality this crucial sector of French
agriculture remains the most volatile and archaic of all. Of
France's vast tribe of 1,300,000 vinegrowers, only a fraction are
efficient full-time producers of good wines; the majority, especially in the Languedoc,* are petty growers of inferior plonk on
ill-organized parcels of land. The CAP, far from helping them,
has brought the added menace of Italian competition.

To understand this problem, one must first realize that there
are two separate wine industries in France. First, the minority
industry of *appellation contrôlée* vintage wines, like Burgundies,
Beaujolais and Bordeaux. They have rarely caused much problem, and their sales both in France and abroad have been rising
happily. True, the Bordeaux fraud scandals of 1974 caused a
temporary setback to clarets, but this was soon overcome. The
second group are the growers of cheap wines that rarely get
exported but make up over two-thirds of France's total output.
These growers, most of them in the Languedoc, are especially
vulnerable to price-collapses in a bumper year, and their lobby
is politically powerful and sometimes physically violent. The
Government has generally pandered to it, and under the Fourth
Republic it spent millions of francs each year on buying up and
destroying surpluses. Wine was subsidized irrespective of quality.
The Laniel Government in 1953 then introduced a less negative
and wasteful policy: in a bid to curb chronic over-production, it
offered subsidies to farmers for uprooting poor vines and replacing them with other crops. By 1957 some 275,000 acres of vines,
5 per cent of all vineyards, had been uprooted, mostly in the

* See pp. 214–6.

poorer districts of the centre and west. However Algerian independence later introduced a new situation. Before 1962 nearly a quarter of the wine drunk in France was Algerian, but when these imports dropped away, France's own over-production became less of a problem. The uprooting policy was largely suspended after the early 1960s, and, instead, the Government began to encourage the replacing of poor vines with 'noble' ones, more likely to find a market. For although French domestic consumption has been falling slightly* – from 58 to 54 million hectolitres a year in the period 1963–73 – with prosperity the French increasingly want to drink better wines, as do their foreign clients.

This vulnerable sector of agriculture is more closely supervised by the Government than any other, with a complex system of price controls. Wines and vines alike are scrupulously graded and inspected, and under recent measures the very poorest wines have been banned from the market altogether and diverted for making vinegar or pure alcohol. Many farmers have responded to the call for quality, so that without lowering of standards many acres of vines are upgraded each year from *vin ordinaire* to *appellation contrôlée*, or else to the intermediate category, *vins délimités de qualité supérieure* – and very drinkable these are too. Even in the Languedoc, where the peasants are famous for their stubborn conservatism, VDQS vines have been gradually replacing the lesser breeds. But the growers will not go further than this; though the Government has built in the Languedoc one of the largest new irrigation networks in Europe, the growers have refused to take advantage of it and replace their vineyards with more profitable crops.

There is still serious over-production of cheap wine in a year of bumper harvest. At first it was hoped, after the creation of the CAP, that a solution for this problem could be for France to find new export outlets within the EEC. And indeed, between 1958 and 1969 French exports to the rest of the Six doubled for *appellation contrôlée* and quintupled for VDQS and *vins courants*. This was due partly to the raising of quotas and partly, maybe, to the psychological impetus of the Common Market. The Germans, Dutch and Belgians have been drinking more and more cheapish

* See pp. 456–60.

imported red wine (and so indeed were the British, until the sinking £ and increases in excise taxes pushed the lowliest plonk into the luxury bracket).

But French farmers soon found, to their alarm, that their Italian rivals benefited much more than they did from northern Europe's growing taste for table wines. Worse than this: Italian wines, more cheaply produced, less carefully graded, and often more robust than French ones, began to flood the French domestic market too. Under EEC rules, France could not legally prevent these imports, nor stop the fortifying of her own wines with the stronger Italian ones. Some south Italian wines are 14° or 15°, against an average 10° in the Midi. Inevitably, the big firms, such as Nicolas, that sell cheap wines *en masse* to the French consumer, have been taking advantage of this, blending Italian with local produce in order to create an anonymous but fuller-bodied wine. By 1972, Italian imports were up to 8 million hectolitres a year.

This coincided with a series of bumper French harvests in the early 1970s, and also with the general economic crisis that reduced consumer demand. The growers were left with enormous unsold stocks, and though the Government, as was its practice, bought these up for distillation, the growers considered the price guarantees too low to allow them a living. So, in the summer of 1975, came the inevitable explosion. As so often before in this century, the Languedoc wine lobby resorted to violence in order to pressurize the Government. This time, their aim was to get restrictions imposed on Italian imports. They occupied Perpignan cathedral as a gesture of peasant revolt. They disrupted the tourist trade by blacking out signposts, while at the same time wooing the infuriated tourists by offering them wine at about a franc a bottle. They blockaded the port of Sète, where many of the Italian imports arrive in transit. The Giscard Government, scared of social unrest in a period of mounting economic crisis, yielded to their demands by flouting EEC rules; in September it put import duties of 12 to 16 per cent on Italian wines. Rome was furious, and so was Brussels; the Commission's President, M. Ortoli, himself a Frenchman, warned that the 'wine war' was threatening the EEC's credibility. The EEC even began the painful process of arraigning France before its Court of Justice, but it failed to come up with any remedies for the real cause of the crisis – European over-production. In Europe's landscape, the wine lake was left to expand beside the beef and butter mountains.

Nor did the duties reduce Italian imports enough to satisfy the growers. Early in 1976 there was more and worse violence – riots and demonstrations throughout the Midi, in which a farmer and a policeman were killed near Carcassonne; attacks on lorries and depots of importers of Italian wines, in which hundreds of thousands of hectolitres were destroyed. Some of the big merchants retaliated by boycotting Languedoc wines. In many areas, angry farmers and riot-police were in a state of near-war. Finally, in April, a scared Government made more concessions to the growers: it promised new loans and tax concessions to those facing real hardship; it agreed to control the quality of imported wines more strictly, within the framework of EEC rules; it decided to set up a special 'Office du Vin' to help rationalize the industry; and it coaxed an extra subsidy out of the EEC to help pay for distilling a surplus of 12 million hectolitres.

Once again the Midi found that violence pays. But, once again, the real problem of chronic over-production has simply been expensively patched over, not solved. One curious feature of this crisis has been that French and Italian rivals have found that they face a common problem; they both over-produce. Italy, too, has her multitude of poor and angry peasants whom she has to placate. In 1976 the EEC did finally take one modest step towards an over-all solution: Italy and France agreed on a long-term programme of the uprooting or quality improvement of some 375,000 hectares of vines, aided by CAP funds. However in France the real trouble today is that poorer growers have discovered, to their cost, that replacing bad vines with superior ones does not necessarily bring them in more income. Under French rules, vines producing *appellation* or VDQS wines are limited to an output of 20 hectolitres an acre, whereas for *vins courants* there is no limitation and output can easily rise to 80 hl an acre. Yet the price differential can be as low as 20 per cent for the producer, who thus retains an incentive to go on producing a lot of cheap and unsaleable plonk – so long as the State agrees to underwrite his surpluses by buying them for distillation. It is a vicious circle. Much of the Midi wine is so thin and poor that French and foreign consumers, now more selective, are increasingly spurning it. Thus, in a typical bumper harvest year such as 1975, France's total production was 75 million hectolitres, of which some 55 million was consumed by the French and 6 million exported – leaving 14 million to be distilled, largely at the taxpayer's cost. It seems there can be no final solution until the Government has the courage to break the vicious circle – that is, to increase differentials (presumably at the consumer's expense), or else to find ways of putting restrictions on output per hectare. But this would lead to a terrible backlash from the aggressive, Poujadist-minded Languedoc growers, who still see it as their inalienable, ancestral right to produce as much as they wish. Politically, such a solution may not be possible until the old generation has died away.

A NEW ERA FOR FARMING

Agriculture – vinegrowers apart – is no longer the stormy political issue that it used to be in France, in the days when it made and unmade governments under the Third and Fourth Republics. Steadily it has slipped towards the sidelines of national life, overtaken in gravity by other problems such as education and labour relations. The farmers stayed strangely silent during the student and worker troubles of 1968; and indeed, since their last bout of widespread unrest, in 1967, they have rarely demonstrated on any scale.

To some extent, this calm is evidence of the progress that has been made, almost imperceptibly, towards solving the basic problems. With the agricultural population now down to 13 per cent of the whole, the rural exodus has achieved its purpose in many areas. Modernization of farms is going ahead fast. And though many small farmers still remain in acute hardship, their numbers are dwindling into an ever smaller and therefore less influential minority; to put it callously, they have become a social rather than a political problem.

Another reason for the calm is that ever since Pisani's departure in January 1966 the Government has pursued a policy of appeasement. Edgar Faure, Pisani's redoubtable successor, began to woo the farmers demagogically with higher subsidies – here he showed himself far less radical than as Minister of Education two years later – and this policy has since been merged into that of the CAP and followed by the Ministers after him, under both Pompidou and Giscard. In a sense, the policy has paid off. Whereas farmers' average income in real terms rose hardly at all in 1964–8, it climbed fast in 1968–73, by as much as 6 per cent in some years. Then came the economic crisis, which at first hit farmers much harder than salaried workers; their costs, notably of fuel and machinery, rose dramatically, yet they were not able to counter inflation by making heavy wage demands, as workers could and did. In 1974, farmers' real incomes fell by 10 per cent. There were some demonstrations, especially in the poorer dairy and livestock-breeding regions such as Brittany, but on the whole the farming world reacted less angrily to the crisis than one might have expected. Perhaps, after five fat years, they felt they could tolerate a drop in revenue. Perhaps also Debatisse's close friendship with Jacques Chirac, by then Prime Minister, counted for something. Anyway, in 1975 the Government again came to the aid of the farmers, especially the poorer ones. It pumped in emergency subsidies and tax concessions totalling an extra 2,700 million francs for that year, including an ingenious '*aide à la vache*' – a direct grant of 160 francs per cow for a maximum of 15 cows per farm. This was to compensate for the serious fall in meat and dairy prices the year before. As a result of these measures, farmers' real incomes fell by less than one per cent in that peak-of-the-crisis year, 1975. Meat prices picked up, while it was the wheat farmers who suffered from falling world markets and a poor harvest. The chronic fragility of the whole situation was underlined again the following year, more sharply than ever, when the severe drought lost the farmers a total of 6,000 million francs and caused another estimated 10 per cent drop in real income.

The national farm leaders today are pursuing a policy of tacit though critical co-operation with the Government. The Young Farmers' movement of two decades ago has completed its seizure of power; Debatisse is now president of the FNSEA, and his moderate-progressive views are accepted doctrine. He and his friends have won their battle to save the family farm as the basis of agriculture. Their ideas on the collective use of land are also making progress – witness the growth of group farming – but they have trimmed these ideas into something more practicable. Power has made them into cautious pragmatists. They still regard themselves as the champions of the small farmer, but they believe that the best way to help him is through alliance with the Government and the big farmers, not through conflict with them. Debatisse has even done a deal with the rich farmers who share the power with him in the FNSEA; he leaves them a free hand to pursue their lucrative export drives, while they in turn support his campaign for structural reforms to help the small man. And since Debatisse has most of his troops well in hand, the small farmers have not, as one might have expected, marshalled their tractors on the roads against the injustices of the CAP.

This is not to say that they all support Debatisse's pragmatic compromises. There is a crypto-Communist movement, mainly of older farmers, that fights against the CAP and the Government; but it lacks the leadership to be effective. There are Right-wing groups that still hark back to the ideas of Dorgères or Poujade; but they too have little influence. And there is Bernard Lambert and his friends, Left-wingers who belong mostly to the PSU and have broken with Debatisse; they hold that vertical integration remains a menace and that the small farmer is still being 'proletarized' (their favourite word) through his dependence on capitalist wholesalers. They have links with Leftist movements in factories and among students.

They are the first to point out that farmers' incomes have not been rising faster than industrial ones, so that the gap between the two remains at about 30 per cent. And clearly, the problems of French farming will not be solved until this gap is narrowed. There are two answers: a reform of the price system, and structural reform. The CAP must be revised; the cost of the Government's support for agriculture is now running at 6,900 million francs a year, of which 5,600 million goes to the CAP, and most of this is spent on price supports. These are no real solution to the farmer's problems, any more than a pain-killer removes the causes of toothache. Productivity per acre has more than doubled since 1949; but if this simply leads to a glut, it hardly seems worth the money invested. Of course it can be argued that, as agriculture completes its modernization, so supports will become less necessary; it is the transitional phase that is expensive, as in the reconversion of any industry. There is some truth in this – and there would be more, if the price supports were going to those who need them. At any rate, the EEC is now beginning to tackle structural reform more seriously. Dr Mansholt's original blueprint, issued in 1968, scheduled big reductions not only in the farm population but also in the amount of land under cultivation; many upland farm areas, he said, could never be made economic and should be turned over to tourism or afforestation. This plan ran into political trouble, but now at last a modified form of it, the 'mini-Mansholt', is being applied. While pensions are being increased to help older farmers to retire, new grants are also being offered to help young ones to establish themselves, especially if they can show that they have a long-term plan. Since on 75 per cent of farms belonging to elderly farmers there is now no successor, it is recognized that the problem, in many areas, has become that of encouraging a dynamic young generation not to leave but to stay. At the same time, the Government is offering grants to farmers in mountain areas to become 'gardeners of nature', that is, to form themselves into groups as herdsmen and as protectors of the heritage of forest, stream and pasture. This seems to have something in common with the Debatisse ideal of 'the land as a common tool'.

Thus, gradually, a new philosophy of the use of the soil is taking root. It still faces sentimental opposition from an older generation, for it runs contrary to the deeply held notion that every acre must be cultivated, and owned as private property. But it seems clear that within a generation the pattern of farming will be very different from what it is today. Huge areas of southern or central France will have become parks or reserves, or pastures worked on a group basis; farming will be confined to intensive production in the more fertile regions, where the farmers will work in co-operatives. The Young Farmers had the foresight to scent out this revolution a generation ago, and today they are winning. So the old idyll of the small farmer with his few cows and patch of vines draws to its end; it was rarely such a happy idyll anyway. The French farmer of tomorrow will be more prosperous – if less picturesque.

Chapter 5

THE BATTLE FOR THE RETAIL TRADE

THE defects of the agricultural markets, and of small industry, too, have found themselves repeated throughout much of the distributive and retail trade. With its high profit-margins and low turnover, its lack of enterprise or real competition, no other sector of French life has seemed so backward – at least till recently. Today, French commerce is swinging from one extreme to the other, and the sudden challenge of the new hypermarkets is altering mentalities. France's 800,000 little shops and middlemen are being forced to re-adapt. On balance, they are still too numerous and too small for the nation's needs; Napoleon's jibe about Britain as a nation of shopkeepers has always seemed to apply more aptly to his own country.

France's small-shopkeeper class emerged from the war with a muddy black-market reputation. 'Les BOF' (*beurre, œufs et fromages*), the generic name for dairy shops, became a phrase of contempt to denote a whole selfish crypto-collaborationist class of petty tradesmen, vividly described by Jean Dutourd in his novel, *Au Bon Beurre*. After the war the reputation changed, but scarcely improved; in 1955 this was the class that provided the Right-wing rabble-rouser, Pierre Poujade, with the hard core of his support, in opposition to the growth of big industry and of workers' salaries. Although already protected by a tax system that hit mainly the larger stores, the small ones did what they could to resist progress or the growth of modern rivals. The BOF mentality persisted; the basic aim was to keep prices and profit-margins high even if it meant selling less, and few shops stopped to consider that a reverse policy might yield better results. In the main towns there were a number of larger stores, mostly old-established ones like Printemps. But their margins, too, were excessive; and the nation that had invented the department store in the nineteenth century failed to develop it as much as her neighbours.

The past decade or so, however, has seen a remarkable transformation. The first French supermarket was not born till 1957; today there are 3,850 of them and the larger ones, the *hypermarchés*, are the largest stores in Europe. For better or worse, American methods have been creeping in, together with a spirit of salesmanship and competition that for France is entirely novel. Price wars, also a new phenomenon in France, have cut some profit-margins in groceries and consumer durables. And in face of the supermarkets, the old, small shops are trying to group together, or else are slowly dying out. In some cases, their angry self-defence has taken violent forms.

A JESUIT GROCER'S CRUSADE

Government reforms, foreign influences, the growth of new suburbs and ways of living, have all played their part in pushing these changes forward. But the original catalyst was an inspired young grocer called Edouard Leclerc, in a small town in Brittany. Had it not been for his persistent crusading ever since 1949, the old order would never have cracked so easily. He was the first with the courage to use discount methods, and so challenge the conspiracy of industry, shops and middlemen to keep prices high.

Leclerc has been one of the truly amazing figures of modern France, and has variously been likened to St Vincent de Paul, Danilo Dolci and Rasputin. Whimsical, boisterous, conceited and religious, he entered commerce not for personal gain but with a driving sense of social mission. Today he still owns only three stores himself, all in Finistère; but all over France at least 300 others, each independently owned, use his name and apply his methods and prices under his strict control. The secret is to buy direct from the maker or producer and sell to the public at near-wholesale prices, cutting your own profits to the bone. In Britain or the United States this might seem either quite familiar, or else some kind of sales trick. In France, applied straightforwardly, the innovation went some way towards forcing other shops to bring down their prices too. And though his personal impetus is now largely spent and he is no longer in the forefront of the scene, it is impossible to deny the key role that he played in the 1950s, in preparing the way for the supermarkets and the new spirit in commerce.

In a land where shops are usually handed down from father to son, Leclerc could hardly have come from a more unlikely background. His father was a senior army officer, scholar and gentleman farmer; and young Edouard, like several of his brothers, was destined for the priesthood. But after ten years in Jesuit seminaries he quit, because he could no longer face celibacy – and because his true vocation was already clear to him: to serve his fellow-men by breaking a wicked system. In 1949, at the age of twenty-three, he opened his first barrack-like little store in his home town of Landerneau, near Brest, and began by buying biscuits from a nearby factory and selling them at 25 per cent below usual prices. Soon he was dealing in the whole range of groceries. At first the local tradesmen simply laughed at this crazy young amateur. But the public flocked in, and Leclerc's turnover shot up. By 1952 the Finistère tradesmen were alarmed, and made their first combined effort to destroy him. And they used the weapon which has been used against him and others, many times, ever since: they persuaded manufacturers and wholesalers to threaten to stop supplying him.

For the past fifty years there had been a *de facto* system of price-fixing in France. Industry set the minimum prices of its goods and boycotted any shop that went below them. The shops themselves liked this system – in fact it was they who had instigated it, for it prevented tiresome competition. It was theoretically illegal, but never prosecuted; and it benefited everyone except the consumer. No one for many years, until Leclerc, had dared challenge it.

Soon his supplies began to suffer from the boycott. So he wrote to the Government to complain, and to explain his aims. High officials in the Ministry of Finance had probably never heard of this strange idealist in a far corner of France; but his plight happened to chime with some of their own preoccupations for stopping inflation. In August 1953 the Laniel Government in one of its rare moments of effectiveness signed a decree that strongly

asserted the illegality of imposed prices and refusal of sale. The
measure, re-affirmed by the Gaullists in 1958, and again in 1960,
remains the key to all post-war progress in distribution. Without
it, Leclerc would have perished and the new supermarkets might
have had the greatest difficulty in starting. So Leclerc was saved,
and began to carry the campaign outside Landerneau. In 1955
the first of the chain of Centres E. Leclerc began to spread across
Brittany. Then, in 1958, two engineers from Grenoble invited
him to open a centre in that city – the most dynamic and booming
in France, but on that account also the most costly to live in. It
seemed ideal terrain for his first real national offensive, and he
agreed. Almost at once an enterprising Grenoble business tycoon
hit back by opening six local cut-price stores using somewhat
similar wholesale methods. All over Grenoble, retail prices began
to fall. The Leclerc centre itself, not surprisingly, did not do very
well in the face of this competition. But Leclerc did not mind; he
had achieved his aim. Grenoble soon became known as one of the
cheapest towns in France.

So in 1959 he found someone to start his first centre in Paris,
in the working-class suburb of Issy-les-Moulineaux. The national
grocery trade was by this time really scared. The chairman of the
grocers' union came to his inaugural Press conference at Issy and
heckled for an hour. 'You are a Government puppet, Leclerc!'
'No!' shrieked the journalists delightedly, 'the housewives are
with you, Leclerc!' A few days later, a leader of the Petites et
Moyennes Entreprises federation described Leclerc as 'a bowl of
vitriol hurled in the face of French commerce to disfigure and
dishonour it, to the profit of the big capitalists and international
trusts'. Poujade held a rally in Paris and called Leclerc 'that
defrocked priest, lackey of the Jewish-plutocrat trusts!'

By 1960 there were sixty Leclerc centres; and a few other new
discount shops, such as the Grenoble ones, were daring to copy
him. Now the menace was strong enough for the Grands Magasins and the chain-stores to grow alarmed, as well as the small
shops. Monoprix with its 200 local branches, Prisunic with 180,
and others, are the equivalent in France of Woolworth's or Marks
and Spencer; and they owed much of their prosperity to the fact
that, while charging prices only slightly below those of the

boutiques, they did their own wholesale buying and so could make a double profit. This might involve a mark-up of 20 per cent on the manufacturer's price plus 30 per cent on the wholesaler's – compared with Leclerc's over-all margins of 8 to 12 per cent.

These stores declared war on Leclerc. First they tried the American strategy of the 'loss leader', highly publicized shock reductions on a few obvious articles, such as detergents, while maintaining the main range of prices. This, in Leclerc's mind, is not real price-cutting at all, but clever salesmanship. But it had some effect on an ill-prepared French public. So Leclerc hit back, by extending the range of his own centres from groceries to textiles, where mark-ups in France are often appallingly high, even up to 100 per cent. When a chain of new Leclerc textile centres sprang up across France, selling at 30 or 40 per cent below normal prices, they had an obvious success. Then the big stores decided to take their legal courage in their hands and put pressure on Leclerc's suppliers (who often were their own associates or subsidiaries) to boycott him. They managed to break the 1953 law discreetly, not by open boycott so much as by deliberate inefficiency: pretending goods were out of stock, sending the wrong goods or delaying deliveries. In other cases owners of Leclerc centres were offered bribes to desert him, and some accepted. The boycotts multiplied, and the whole Leclerc experiment looked like collapsing. So Leclerc appealed to the Prime Minister, Michel Debré. And again he was listened to. The Government was worried about rising prices. So it issued, in March 1960, a loud and sharp new warning against breaking the 1953 decree; and it had the Gaullist authority to make itself obeyed.

After this, the trade's machinations against Leclerc changed into something nearer normal competition. In a town where a Leclerc shop flourished, other stores felt obliged to lower their prices to near his level. Thus he won his basic campaign. He never intended to go further than this and seize control of the bulk of the trade himself. Even at the height of his influence, his centres have never accounted for more than about 3½ per cent of the retail trade in their sectors. His aim was simply to provoke – and to pioneer methods that other, more commercial chains could copy. This they later did. In fact, it is unthinkable that his own network could ever have been more than a catalyst. His own highly personal methods are more a kind of inspired free-booting than organized modern trade. In many of his ventures, his impudent charm, his verve and his persuasiveness seem to have played as important a part as his low prices.

He holds several dogmas. One is that it is immoral for a shop to spend money on gay and expensive décor and equipment, and then pay for it by raising prices. The supermarket that he opened in Brest, like his original little store in Landerneau, was of an austerity that East Berlin in the late 1940s might have found it hard to beat: a big, tawdry warehouse full of packing-cases and mountains of tins and sacks of potatoes. It is true that many new French supermarkets go to the opposite wasteful extreme, and then wonder why they make a loss. But it is doubtful how far the French housewife today wants quite such grimness in return for cut prices.

A more constructive dogma is that 'commerce' must give way to the notion of 'distribution'; the tradesman exists simply to put goods on the market at the minimum extra cost to the public, concentrating on large, rapid turnover and allotting himself a fee for his services. It is a Socialistic attitude rare among small French shopkeepers. A Leclerc grocery centre will operate on a margin of 8 to 12 per cent, of which only 2 or 3 per cent will be net profit; in a traditional shop, the net profit alone may be 10 to 20 per cent. Leclerc's whisky is often 6 francs cheaper than the same brand in a normal shop.

A thousand small shops, mostly grocers, have closed since 1954 in Leclerc's stronghold of north Finistère; and it is not hard to see why. Whereas a small shop will perhaps buy one hundred kilos of fruit and vegetables a day from a middleman, Leclerc will bring five tons on a lorry direct from the Nantes central market and undercut the local shop by 30 to 70 per cent. This shows how much the middlemen are often still profiteering at the expense of both consumer and farmer. On one occasion, Leclerc brought in 300 tons of Bulgarian strawberry jam by boat to Brest, and sold it at far below usual jam prices. When a local chain-store manager, some time later, asked his Paris head office how they had come to

miss such an attractive import deal, he was told, 'We tested that
jam, and found it quite unfit for consumption.' 'But Leclerc's
been selling it for a year and no one's got ill.'

It is a joke that Leclerc likes to tell. Half his crusade has been
deadly earnest; half is schoolboy spirits, Robin Hood against the
bad barons. And he enjoys mockingly exploiting the legend he has
helped to create of himself. Half the week, he is campaigning
across France or the world, and the other half he spends modestly
with his wife in a small house in Landerneau, his only luxury a
Mercedes which he changes each year. His tiny office in a corner of
the Brest shop is piled with old bottles and packing-cases, and
there I called on him in 1965. He has clear blue eyes, a cheeky
smile, a soft, excited voice, and a very personal manner as if he
were straight away letting you into some secret. 'No, I don't feel
I'm a prophet. I run shops as a way of formulating my ideas.
Maybe what I'm doing *is* close to religion though, because it's
social justice, economically viable charity. Distribution touches all
aspects of man. As for Christ, I admire him as an amoral being,
the first to chase the tradesmen from the Temple. I go to Mass,
but don't know if I'm a Christian.' Then, voice ecstatic but eyes
laughing: 'My philosophy is to be happy. In the struggle for
happiness one finds the sense of eternity. Life goes past, ideas
drive their course, God is a . . .' The phone rings. 'Yes? . . . Well,
cut *all* our prices, *all*, d'you hear?' Receiver down. 'Sorry, where
was I? Oh, yes, God is a river of life that flows through all. It is
enough to drink of this river, to live.' 'Monsieur Leclerc, what
of the criticism that you are a tool of the Government?' 'When
the Government need me, they ask. The Government uses lots of
people, not only me. No, I am not its mistress; *une gaule me
suffit.*'

Brilliant publicist, sharp businessman, genial fanatic, Leclerc
has had an influence out of proportion to the size of his sales.
Sometimes the mere threat of a new centre in a town was enough
to send prices down. Once, stopping overnight in Tours, just for a
joke he called on a house-agent and said he was looking for ten
local premises for shops. The price-cutting panic was widespread.

Today, the glossy new supermarkets have taken over from
Leclerc on a far vaster scale. Certainly, their bulk-buying is more

suited to the new needs of France than the old ways of the little groceries. But how far has there been a real change of heart? Are the supermarkets really applying some of Leclerc's methods, or are they concealing the faults of the old system behind a modern façade?

THE LITTLE SHOPS VERSUS THE HYPERMARKETS

When the Bon Marché opened in the Rue de Sèvres in 1852, it was the first real modern department store in the world. Soon it was followed by Printemps, Galeries Lafayette, Samaritaine and the other Paris giants that are still there today. Gradually they began to form branches in the provinces, and chains for cheap consumer goods – the Prisunic chain belongs to Printemps, and Monoprix to the Galeries Lafayette. But the big stores and their chains were soon overtaken in scope and efficiency by their Anglo-Saxon counterparts. Their growth was stunted by their high-price policy, by their *ententes* against competition, and by the general stagnation of the French economy until the 1950s.

Then in the late 1950s the growth of new suburbs and spending power gave a cue for the appearance of a few self-service super-markets. Though they were influenced by Leclerc, their main ideas and techniques were borrowed not from him but from the United States. In 1955 the Paris branch of the National Cash Register Company began to invite groups of leading French shop executives to his headquarters at Dayton, Ohio, to attend the famous sales courses given by Bernard Trujillo. The aim was to inspire the modernizing of French shops and so push up the sales of cash registers. It succeeded brilliantly, and Trujillo has possibly had even more influence on French commerce than Leclerc. Over 4,000 Frenchmen have been to Dayton, and France has provided Trujillo with 30 per cent of his foreign pupils – far more than Britain.

He teaches the doctrine of rapid turnover, of large shops with a wide range of goods, and of the loss-leader or, as he puts it, 'islands of loss in an ocean of profit'. It is all within a general motive of profit, and therefore not quite the same as Leclerc's more radical philosophy. Trujillo's French pupils, especially the younger ones, listened in amazement to this gospel; and back home some of them began to try to apply it.

The change started to make its impact around 1959. This was about the time that Léon Gingembre of the PME (nine-tenths of whose members are tradesmen) was breaking with Poujadism to face up to the Common Market, so it all fell into place. An extreme example of the change is a man such as Hubert Delorozoy, owner of a new chain of stores in outer Paris and one of the most vocal figures in the world of French commerce. Until about 1958 he was a strongly Poujadist believer in the old small shop. Then he went to Dayton three times. Today he will proudly show a visitor his big new supermarket at Corbeil with its gaudy lighting, its crowds, its rows of clicking registers and its competitive prices. The aggressive sales atmosphere is reinforced by megaphones blaring details of the latest bargains. It all seems centuries removed from the old *épicier du coin*; yet, regrettably or not, its noisy materialism seems as typically 'French' as the quiet, unambitious order that is passing away.

After a slow start, the supermarket movement has made something of a breakthrough in France in the past nine years. A new breed of shop executive recognizes the advantages of Trujillo's methods. And those who feared that the conservative French housewife could never be wooed away from her local grocery, with its human contacts, have been proved wrong. The number of supermarkets, nil in 1957, rose to over 1,000 by 1969 and over 3,850 by 1976. Their share of the total retail trade in food rose from a mere 4 per cent in 1969 to 25 per cent by 1976 – though this is still modest by United States standards, where 30,000 supermarkets have 72 per cent of the food trade. Supermarkets may be more numerous in Britain than in France, but in France they are much larger. The French, in this as in other fields, are acquiring the American taste for gigantism. Not content with the word *supermarché*, the French have coined '*hypermarché*' to denote the larger giants – Carrefour's new one outside Marseille, with 22,000 square metres of selling space, is the largest store in Europe, and several others in France are not much smaller. There is nothing quite like these stores in Britain. You can find them out on the periphery of any sizeable French town, where the land is relatively cheap and there's plenty of room for car parking. Behind a row of some forty to fifty checkout desks, the lights blaze down on a garish emporium that has none of Leclerc's austerity and will as happily sell you a TV set, a double bed or an off-the-peg suit as a packet of frozen snails or a tin of caviar. The delicatessen counter alone may be, say, 50 metres long. And the stores are generally open till 10 p.m. On Saturdays, the whole family comes to pile its week's supplies on to a giant trolley that only the husband can have the strength to wheel out to the car. It is all a far cry, not only from the *épicier du coin*, but even from modest Sainsbury's.

The most dynamic, intelligent and successful of the new supermarket chains is Carrefour. It was founded in 1960 by a small shopkeeper from Annecy, Marcel Fournier, who borrowed some ideas from Leclerc and some from Trujillo, and proceeded to apply them on a large scale with tremendous flair. In 1963 he opened the first *hypermarché*, near Orly, south of Paris (the French definition of *hypermarché* is simply a supermarket with more than 2,500 square metres selling space). This amortized its installation costs within three years and attracted a diverse clientèle. Some were Leftish intellectuals from the new colleges and science centres south of Paris, who disapproved of ordinary 'commerce'. Others were local tradesmen who found it cheaper than buying from their own wholesalers, partly because they could avoid tax declarations. One café-owner would carry away 80 bottles of Pernod a week, and never ask for receipts.

Today France has 350 *hypermarchés*. Carrefour and its associates run 38 of these giant stores in France, and several abroad including three in Britain – near Cardiff, Southampton and Wolverhampton. The struggle to establish these stores in Britain was not easy, for opposition from local commercial interests and from municipal bureaucracy was even stronger than it had been in France in the early days, when Carrefour not surprisingly suffered some of the same persecution as Leclerc. In several French towns in the 1960s Fournier found his building permits blocked by local councils, under pressure from the small shops. He won through, at least for long enough to be able to expand massively, and several newer supermarket chains have since followed the trail he blazed. But not all of them know how to apply the new ideas as intelligently as he or Delorozoy. Some stores belong to the 'integrated' combines such as Prisunic, who have simply added a self-service format to their existing chain-store methods and have not really adopted the basic techniques of fast turnover and low costs. Many are too small, with too narrow a range of goods; or they stay fixed to the idea of high profits; or they spend too much on costly prestige overheads of décor and large staff. Other supermarkets have been crippled by shop-lifting, which is rampant in France, and can only be combated at the cost of expensive outlay on detectives and concealed mirrors.

Some stores, far from being too small, are *too* large. In certain towns, the craze for the new gigantism has been carried too far and supply has run ahead of demand. Too many firms have been anxious to get in on the act, and they have over-estimated the market. Toulouse has six new hypermarkets, probably more than it needs. Many inevitably fail to make a profit, and in some towns there have been closures.

For all these reasons it is clear that progress in French commerce is extremely uneven, and cannot be assessed purely in terms of the huge increase in the average size of shops. Though there is a new spirit of competition, there is also much wastage and inefficiency. Thus, retail margins as a whole have not dropped appreciably.

Most of the large firms have at least been reacting positively to the modern challenge. Among smaller shops and middlemen, there tends to be a sharper contrast between a minority who are also adapting, and a majority who are not. Some middlemen have gone out of business; others have reacted by grouping together in face of Leclerc and the combines. In the grocery trade their numbers have dropped strikingly since 1945, from 3,000 to 600. A few have even started their own supermarkets.

As for the myriad little shops of France, a minority of intelligent owners realize that, if they want to maintain their place, they will probably have to adapt to fulfil specialized needs. Since

Delorozoy opened his Corbeil supermarket the nearby grocers have floundered, but a little quality leather shop has done a roaring trade, sharing some of Delorozoy's clients but not competing with his goods. It is the same story with Carrefour; nearly all the little general stores near the hypermarkets have closed, and been replaced by coiffeurs, dry cleaners or house-agents.

Gingembre is trying to push as many of his flock as possible in this kind of direction: 'There will always be some things,' he told me, 'that the small shop can do better than a large one – personal repairs and deliveries, or specialized luxury goods where economies are not important. American experience proves this. It is simply a question of adapting French commerce to it without too much hardship. My job is to goad the shops to change, but to protect them while they are doing so.'

He will have a hard task. The majority of France's small shops are slipping gently into decline, but not into death. Even more than the farmer, the small tradesman tends to cling tenaciously to his dying business, neither modernizing it nor moving to something else. The steady growth of population and spending power is artificially prolonging his life, but without curing his rooted obsolescence. There are still some 700,000 shops in France; one per 72 people, against one per 86 in Britain and one per 100 in the United States. While small groceries are killed off by the supermarkets, at the same time the general rise in consumer spending produces a crop of new luxury specialized shops, and multi-boutique 'commercial centres' in the new suburbs.

Only in certain urban areas are the old shops dying out in any number. Elsewhere, especially in depopulating villages or older suburbs, it is easy to find an extreme example of the *malaise*: the dingy general store that ekes a bare living by selling everything from tin-tacks to poor-quality fruit, and often acts as a café for its few faithful clients. It is true that the superficial outward picture may in other cases be rather different. Even in out-of-the-way places, many little shops parade new glass fronts, neon signs and fresh paint, thanks to a system of loans that enables them to make some concessions to changing public taste. But this and the laden, well-dressed windows may simply be masking old-fashioned attitudes to sales and profits, and a primitive lack of accountancy that serves mainly as an alibi for the shopkeeper in his staple occupation of tax-evasion.

A Government sociological survey carried out among 300 average small-shopkeepers showed that nearly all of them were quite satisfied with their own methods, and blamed their difficulties on the State and on the big shops who 'got all the advantages'. Although pessimistic about their long-term future, nine out of ten were hostile to forming mergers or other link-ups in order to survive; each hoped to 'last a little longer than the others' by developing personal contacts with clients and counting on their loyalty. 'We are sellers, not mere distributors,' some of them said proudly. 'The French housewife likes us to advise her – happily she's not yet Americanized.' In most cases it was the women who showed the most negative attitudes, typical of the older French *petite bourgeoisie*: suspicion of State and community, reliance on family links and habitual loyalties, miserliness, hatred of change.

As on the farms, there is often a difference of outlook between generations, save that in commerce the percentage of brighter sons who stay is even lower. They leave for industry or management, while the dull ones remain to inherit a family concern that needs no qualifications. And the average age of shopkeepers is fifty-five. Leclerc hates them, and has publicly suggested they should be forcibly retired and turned over to road-building. More probably, they will be left to die out, and the Government will make increased efforts to train the new generation to a different outlook.

The Government has used one other weapon to modernize commerce, and that is fiscal reform. In 1965, after six years of delays, it found the courage to push through Parliament a much contested Bill that revised the French profits-tax system in such a way as to penalize the firms with large margins. This was the famous value-added tax (*taxe sur la valeur ajoutée* – TVA) that had already been adopted in Germany and is now standard practice throughout the EEC, including Britain (VAT).

Hitherto, manufacturing firms and wholesalers had paid a value-added tax of some 20 per cent of their gross profit margin on each article, while shops simply paid a 2·75 per cent local tax on their sales turnover, irrespective of profits. A shop with an average 50 per cent mark up would therefore pay only one-quarter more tax than one with 20 per cent on the same range of goods, and this encouraged high profit-margins. Shops could, if they wished, use the TVA system instead, but only the Leclerc centres, Carrefour and one or two others had low enough margins to make it worth it; and as a result Leclerc was branded, quite unjustly, by the rest of the trade for being 'privileged' by the wholesalers' tax system.

The new law, in force since 1968, does away with the turnover tax and extends the TVA to the retail trade on a scale varying from 25 per cent for cars and TV sets to 7 per cent for most ordinary foodstuffs. Propelled by Leclerc, the Government first put the idea forward in 1959, but the trade fought it every inch of the way, and with some success: the final Bill contained some concessions to the small shopkeepers, who would have been hit hardest. Those with a turnover of less than some 20,000 francs a year (about 400,000 shops and servicing firms) are *altogether exempt* from the TVA, while a similar number of others in the medium range are assessed for a modified tax on a lump-sum basis. The reason put forward for this is that small shops have such archaic methods of accountancy that this new tax on each article sold would be far too complicated for them, whereas the old tax was on over-all turnover. There is some truth in this; but it is even more true that the Government finally funked a reform that would have spelt rapid death to many shops and caused widespread unrest. So the very small shops, privileged under the old system that gave such an alibi to tax-evasion, are still protected. Yet the TVA as a whole has been undoubtedly beneficial in its influence on French commerce. All medium-sized and larger firms are affected, and by providing them with new incentives to reduce their profit-margins, the TVA has encouraged them to streamline services and management and to put more stress on investment. Even in its half-hearted French version, the TVA is clearly a positive and useful innovation.

Despite these concessions, France's small shopkeepers are far from satisfied. Recently a militant minority have turned to violence, in a desperate crusade against the supermarkets. Not long after May 1968, a 'neo-Poujadist' movement of some ferocity sprang up in the area north of Grenoble, and from there spread across France. It was led by a young café-owner, Gérard Nicoud, who saw that the students and workers had won something, at least, through their violent tactics in May, and so decided to copy them. He and his followers raided local tax offices to burn documents, they blockaded main roads, assaulted Ministers, sent out pirate broadcasts. When a Carrefour hypermarket near Lyon went up in flames in 1970, sabotage was whispered, though never proved. Nicoud has several times gone to prison, or into hiding. He considered himself a martyr for a noble cause – 'We've plenty of dynamite tucked away,' he said. His immediate militant following, though nation-wide, is limited; but most shop-keepers sympathize with his grievances, even if disapproving of his methods.

He has been compared to Poujade, but is really very different. Poujade was an old-style demagogue who moved into politics; Nicoud is more of a modern-style extremist, despising political action, a kind of Right-wing *gauchiste*. Yet Poujade, though less violent than Nicoud, was in fact more reactionary. He wanted French commerce to stay as it was. Nicoud, fascist though his approach may be, is more progress-minded. He accepts the need for small shops to become modern and efficient, and despises those who are not. He simply wants the family businesses to be helped to survive, and charges the Government with trying to kill them by siding with the supermarkets. He is a typical product of the post-1968 period, as Poujade and Leclerc in their very different ways were of the 1950s.

Pompidou's Government became rather frightened of Nicoud and his sympathizers. It was anxious at all costs to avoid riots and disorders in a pre-electoral period. Thus in the spring of 1972 it decreed a series of measures to help small traders, on the lines demanded by Nicoud. Some of these decrees were humane and reasonable (increase in pensions for elderly tradesmen, grants for young ones wanting to convert). Others were blatant vote-catching. One measure was a new tax on the supermarkets, to help finance a fund for small traders wanting to retire.

The Government also appeased the small traders by forbidding the big stores to practice 'loss-leaders' and, notably, by making it much harder for them to get building permits. In 1973 the Minister of Commerce, Jean Royer, a well-known right-wing reactionary, pushed through Parliament a blatantly demagogic law that made further expansion by the hypermarkets almost impossible. Under this law, a firm wanting to set up a new store of more than 400 square metres in a small town, or more than 1,000 square metres in a larger town (over 40,000 inhabitants), must not only seek an official building permit but also get the prior approval of new local committees specially set up for the purpose. Since, under the law, the committees are composed largely of local tradesmen, most of the applications by the super-market firms have been turned down. In 1973–6 Carrefour was able to start building only two new stores in France, and both of these were on sites vacated or sold to it by other firms, i.e. already marked out as supermarkets. Denis Defforey, the new director-general of Carrefour, told me: 'The Royer law makes it extremely hard for us to expand. We can do so only by building extensions to our present stores, or by trying to take over permits already granted to other firms that have since gone broke. It's all very retrograde, and the consumer suffers most, since our prices are lower.'

The Royer law has been retained under Giscard, and today the Government is still anxiously trying to hold a balance. On the one hand, not to restrict too much the development of modern commerce, essential in the fight against inflation. On the other, not to provoke a sensitive and angry minority, representing perhaps a million voters. It is clear today that, as the problems of France's small farmers and small industries begin to find a solu-tion, small shops are now the biggest danger area. The conflict between the *hypermarché* and the *épicier du coin* is far more dramatic than in England or most Common Market countries. It clearly illustrates the dilemma of France in transition.

There are still some specialized corners of the French commer-cial world where vested privilege and restrictive practice are far more iniquitous than in the general retail trade, yet nothing has been done to cure them. The worst case is pharmaceutics. Any visitor to France will have noticed that in this land of high prices the chemists' shops have the highest ones of all. This is because the chemists cling on to an old privilege that forbids the sale of their goods in other kinds of shop; and they exploit this through a price-fixing cartel with minimum mark-ups of 32 per cent. Cases have been quoted of the same drug costing four times as much in a chemist's shop as when sold wholesale for medical purposes. The Rueff-Armand Report in 1960 proposed that the monopoly be removed, and a number of ordinary chemical goods and medicines be authorized for sale anywhere, as in many countries. But the Government has not yet dared act; the chemists are powerfully organized, and are in close league with the industry, which also profits from the price-fixing. Watchsellers and butchers pose similar problems. All three trades have this in common, that they demand some special expertise: watch-shops do repairs, a butcher has to know how to cut meat, and a chemist needs a diploma to prepare medicines. They can therefore easily dig their heels in whenever anyone tries to reform them. 'They represent the worst aspects of the medieval guild spirit,' an official in the Ministry of Finance told me, 'and I'm afraid they'll be the last strongholds of the bad old France to be swept away.'

WANTED, A FRENCH 'WHICH?'

It is partly the consumer's own fault that French consumer prices are not lower. After the war the housewife grew so used to the steady rise in prices that she ceased to question them, and in a land so snobbish about quality, anything cheap came to be regarded with suspicion. Soon after the war the Government carried out an experiment that consisted in cutting cheeses in identical halves in a number of shops, and giving them different price-tags; most people chose the dearer halves. With price-fixing so widespread, the notion of a valid 'bargain' never really developed. In the past few years, however, the influence of Leclerc and the new competition has helped to make the housewife more price-wise, at least for ordinary goods. But there are still few firms that have succeeded in putting across the idea of quality *plus* cheap mass-production in the manner, say, of Marks and Spencer; and amid the welter of new goods and their myriad different brand-names in the shops, the buyer is handicapped by the relative lack of disinterested advice from consumer bodies.

The various private consumer associations have always been too small, too poor and too split by petty rivalries to have much effect. This is not very surprising. The French are notoriously bad at this kind of spontaneous civic initiative and expect the State to take the lead. The consumer bodies find they cannot get subscribers. In one specialized field, however, that of photography and household electrical goods, an inspired kind of consumer venture has produced remarkable results. In 1954 a bold young man called André Essel founded a body with the snobbish-sounding name of Fédération Nationale des Achats des Cadres (executives' shopping federation). This is primarily a chain of discount stores, in a field where mark-ups are exceptionally high – often 50 per cent for TV sets or cameras. By buying wholesale Essel was able to undercut other shops by 20 per cent or more, and has played a big part in forcing prices down elsewhere. The Grands Magasins and the older TV and electrical shops detest this debonair and thrusting ex-journalist; but they have not been able to destroy him, and his turnover has risen several hundred-fold in twenty years. The FNAC is also a kind of club, with a matey atmosphere in each of its three big modern stores in central Paris; most of its clientèle are *cadres*, 75 per cent of the record sales are classical music, and you can sit down for a snack or a drink while selecting your new Leica camera or Marconi pick-up. The FNAC has 140,000 subscribers to its monthly consumer magazine, *Contact*, which exists partly to publicize FNAC goods, but manages to be objective too; it does much testing in the photo and electrical field, and recently advised members against buying the FNAC's top-selling photo flashgun, when it detected a fault. The FNAC has also extended into the provinces, with new stores in Lyon and Grenoble. Its new bookshop in Montparnasse, the largest in Paris, has been phenomenally successful, selling three million books in two years – at discount prices – and causing twelve little bookshops in the area to close down. The FNAC also has a cultural club, that sells theatre and concert tickets at greatly reduced prices, as well as staging its own productions.

The FNAC, though valuable, is not a true consumer body. As usual in France, the initiative for founding a strong and wide-ranging one has had to come from the Government, which has recently set up a National Consumer Institute. This provides the private consumer bodies with some funds and facilities for the regular scientific testing that alone can give teeth to consumer protection. It has also started to publish a monthly consumer magazine, with a circulation of 80,000. This is modest compared with *Which?*'s 500,000, but at least is an improvement on the 15,000 subscribers of the previous leader in the field, published by one of the private bodies. Consumer protection is thus slowly making progress in France.

One task of an effective French consumer organization will be to help to ensure that the new mass-market does not bring with it too great a loss of quality and variety. This is a problem in many countries today, but especially in France, and many Frenchmen are aware of the danger. I have already suggested that, in certain industries, the old French traditions of individual quality and craftsmanship are not adapting easily to the new mass-consumer needs. In commerce there is the same dilemma. It may be senti-mental to shed a tear about the passing of the old corner grocery; and the new supermarket, if properly run, may well be cheaper and more efficient – but will it make life pleasanter? One of the arguments flung against Leclerc and Carrefour is that they bring in an un-French uniformism.

In the long term this may prove a more fundamental problem than the more practical and immediate one of modernization. And it gives less cause for optimism. It is already clear that before too long the ideas of Leclerc and Trujillo will prevail over the *ancien régime* and commerce throughout France will become efficient and progressive. The present movement is irreversible; it is simply a matter of time. The transformation is a necessary one – but what kind of world will it bring in its place? To the surprise of many experts, the old idea that the French housewife could never be wooed away from her familiar local shops and buying habits has now been disproved. In fact she is proving more adaptable than the shopkeepers, and will readily follow American methods when they are properly applied. Inevitably, some human quality will be lost, at least in the larger and more impersonal supermarkets. That is the price of efficiency. But an experience like that of the FNAC suggests that it might still be possible to combine a personal style, and attention to quality, with modern methods. In commerce, as in other fields, the issue for this nation is how to modernize without losing the essential French qualities.

Chapter 6

NEW LIFE IN THE PROVINCES

UNTIL about two decades ago the French provinces were second to none in Europe for lethargy and bourgeois narrowness of spirit. Bourges, Reims, Dijon and a score of other towns, with their soaring cathedrals, their graceful old streets and their calm reflection of history: how delightful they were to visit, and how tedious to live in. Ipswich or Nottingham might be far uglier, but were never quite so dead.

In no other country was the contrast more striking between the dazzling capital and the rest, '*le désert français*', as it was sometimes called. Nowhere was 'provincial' quite such a term of contempt as in Paris – even the Larousse dictionary defined it as 'gauche, undistinguished'. French literature is rich in monuments to Parisian writers' hypnotized love-hatred of their home towns, from Flaubert's Rouen to Mauriac's Bordeaux; for it is a French paradox that the deadness of the provinces has gone hand in hand with strong local attachments, and many a Parisian would proclaim 'Moi, je suis Auvergnat', or Angevin, or Limousin, but would never dream of going back to make a career there. In this most centralized nation on earth, Paris over the centuries sucked the blood out of her provinces. Their intellectual life, their talent and initiative, their powers of decision on the smallest matters of local government, were all drawn to Paris. Even heavy industry settled in Paris, or in a few favoured regions in north-eastern France.

Since the war this situation has been slowly changing. The rural exodus, and the growth of new industry, prosperity and mobility, have brought a new liveliness and self-awareness to many provincial towns and their regions. This time Paris has been unable to hog all the new wealth and progress, as she did in the nineteenth century. In fact, the ill-planned recent overgrowth of

Paris has made it such a nerve-racking city to live in that many sophisticated Parisians are reversing their age-old scorn and beginning to move out to the provinces. New factories and theatres, new university institutes and town-planning schemes, are making provincial life more tolerable. Regional development has become today's obsession, a pillar of Government policy: 'la grande affaire de la nation', Pompidou called it.

But France still has a long way to go towards real decentralization. Though in two respects – in industrial development, and in social and cultural vitality – there has been progress, government remains as centralized as ever. That is why larger towns, such as Bordeaux or Lyon, are still far from being true regional capitals in the manner of Turin, Stuttgart or Edinburgh. Though the State since the war has handed out vast new sums of money to the provinces, it still keeps control of how most of it is spent and has not given up effective sovereignty. The regional assemblies created in 1972 have not proved very effective, for they have been allowed little real power of decision. And since then the Giscard Government, like its predecessors, has baulked at further devolution. Until this is granted, France's regional revival must remain limited – and the centralized power of the State will continue to be a cause of discontent.

TODAY'S OBSESSION: REGIONAL DEVELOPMENT

Some of the roots of French centralization go back deep into history, to the Capetian monarchs and even to Roman times. For more practical modern purposes, they date from Napoleon. Before his day, under the *ancien régime*, France's thirty historic Provinces were governed by *intendants* – rulers centrally appointed by the king, but with large local powers of decision. It was a system of decentralized administration that worked perfectly, without being federal. Then, in 1793, a violent conflict between the two main factions of the Revolution led to a victory of the Jacobin extremists from Paris over the milder provincial Girondins, and a few years later Napoleon with Jacobin aid decided to impose the authority of Paris more sternly. He carved up the provinces and replaced them with ninety-one arbitrary 'departments', named after often obscure rivers. Brittany, for instance, now had no legal existence; Rennes, its chief town, became the capital of Ille-et-Vilaine. In charge of each department Napoleon placed a Prefect, a strong ruler answerable to Paris for everything. This is the Jacobin heritage under which France still labours today. The system has many advantages, and not solely political ones; but it has hindered the regions from developing their own personality.

Throughout the nineteenth century the political dominance of Paris encouraged other forms of centralization too. When the railways were built, for political and strategic reasons their network was traced like a spider's web round Paris with few good cross-country lines, so that even as late as 1938 it was quicker to go from Toulouse to Lyon via Paris (683 miles) than direct (340 miles). When heavy industry grew up, some of it settled near the coal and iron-ore mines, in Lorraine, Flanders and the upper Loire, but much of it went to Paris, to be near the sources of finance and the vital lobbies of Ministries. Yet at this time the growth of new techniques and transport was, in other countries, encouraging decentralization.

Gradually all the big banks became centred in Paris, while the snobberies of the literary salons joined with the hold of the Sorbonne over the State university network to deprive the provinces of much of their intellectual resources. And the ordinary population came too, hungry for work. The great Parisian building programmes of Baron Haussmann in the 1860s saw little counterpart in the provinces, and this helped draw to the capital hundreds of thousands of destitute peasants, for the rural exodus was now beginning. The statistics are astonishing. From 1851 to 1931 the population of Greater Paris went up by 4·4 million, that of Flanders and the Lyon–St-Etienne region by 1·8 million, while that of the rest of France went down by 1·2 million. Paris's share of the French population rose in this period from 5 to 15 per cent, and by the 1931 census many lesser provincial towns were smaller than they had been in 1800. In Britain, London saw a similar growth, but it was at least shared by many other towns too. No wonder that France, even today, has fewer large towns than Germany, Britain or Italy.

This may hardly seem a defect today, in an age now preoccupied with pollution, over-population, and the quality of life. But France after the war had no choice but to urbanize, if she was to compete in a capitalist world. From an economic point of view, her problem had been not so much the actual size of the towns as the imbalance between Paris and the rest, and the consequent waste of resources. By 1939 a high percentage of the private wealth of France was concentrated in Paris, or in country châteaux belonging to Parisians; and workers' salaries in Paris were 40 per cent higher than in the provinces. All this time France had been investing eagerly in countries like Morocco or Senegal, where the legacy of her inter-war colonial development still catches the eye. But she neglected her own provinces, notably the south and west. The notion began to grow up of 'two Frances', with the country divided diagonally from Caen to Marseille. To the east of this line, Paris and 85 per cent of the industry, the big modern farms and Parisians' rich playgrounds on the Riviera; to the west, a territory more thinly populated than Spain (except in Brittany), with backward farms and towns without industry. Only since the war has this imbalance caught the public attention. Slowly, it is being rectified.

Since the 1930s several forces, some spontaneous and some in the form of Government action, have been helping to revive the provinces. First, the pre-war decentralization of a few car and air-craft factories, for strategic reasons, may have had a little influence. The natural pull of Paris was already beginning to wane, so the demographers tell us, due mainly to the over-all industrial stagnation and population decline. Then came those ubiquitous blessings in disguise, Vichy and the Occupation. A number of dynamic leaders and firms withdrew from Paris and the occupied zone in the north to the 'free' Vichy territory. Cut off from Paris for two years, the southern provinces under Vichy were forced to act and think for themselves. And right up to the Liberation, the strait-jacket of the war put a curb on the usual procedures of central bureaucracy and gave local initiatives, whether Resistance or collaborationist, a chance to flourish. Lack of transport crippled the circulation of national newspapers outside Paris, and gave the provincial daily Press a chance to build up a strength it has since managed to maintain.

After the war the sudden up-swing in the birth-rate took place everywhere, not just in Paris, and gave a new psychological impetus to stagnating provincial towns. There was also the renewed rural exodus, this time faster than ever. Paris was still the immigrants' chief target, and its population swelled rapidly; but so did that of other towns. Between 1939 and 1954, for the first time since 1890 Paris's population increased less than that of the rest of France. Since the war Greater Paris has grown from six to ten million; but many other towns have trebled in size and Grenoble has quadrupled. In a world over-populated with the billions of Asia, this may seem a dubious achievement; but France is still under-populated for her size and resources, and the smallness of her towns has been a reason for their dullness as well as a curb on her own economic strength. Paris is the only town to have passed its optimum size: its congestion, its high costs, its growing commuting problems, all contribute to its current neurosis and have begun to drive some people away. Engineers, professors and executives begin to see that life in some other towns, in the warm south, or near the sea or mountains, may be more human and pleasant, even if less intellectually exciting. Among younger middle-class people, a new and astonishing anti-Paris snobbism has even started to replace the old anti-provincial snobbism. And of the many thousands of such Parisians who have left the capital for new jobs in the provinces, very few later regret it.

The 1975 census results showed, very strikingly, that for the first time in centuries more people are moving from Paris to the provinces than in the other, more traditional direction. Net immigration into the Paris region fell from 700,000 in 1954–62 to 377,000 in the next census period, 1962–8, and then to a mere 87,000 in 1968–75. A closer breakdown reveals that this 87,000 figure would in fact be *minus* if foreign immigrants to Paris were excluded. In fact, some 20,000 Parisians are moving to the provinces each year, very often back to their own native province, and this is greater than the reverse movement. It is a profound historical change, and concerns workers as well as middle-class people.

The growth of car-ownership, of faster trains and domestic air services, have all helped to make a life away from Paris seem less like exile to a cultured family used to its stimulus. With a working week in Nancy or Toulouse, and then a week-end in the capital, a cake can be had and eaten. This new mobility has had its effect on staid provincials, too, and so has the growth of television and tourism. Towns have slowly been coaxed out of their isolated slumber, and made more aware of each other and of the outside world. All this is common experience, in any modern country, but in France with its long neglect it has been especially striking.

These changes have been largely spontaneous. In the general context of post-war France some degree of provincial revival has been inevitable, whether encouraged by Governments or not. But the State has closely supported it – with varying success – and is trying to channel and control it.

'*Aménagement du territoire*' as the French call it (regional development in the widest sense) was almost unheard of before the war. After 1945 it soon became a major preoccupation of Monnet and his planners. In 1947 Jean-François Gravier, a young geographer attached to the Plan, published his famous book, *Paris et le désert français*, which brilliantly analysed the economic aspects of the problem. He showed how the neglect of the west wasted the country's resources, and how the congestion of Paris and other key areas led to inefficiency and high costs. France, he said, could not become a modern nation unless she remedied these faults. The rural exodus was right and inevitable, but new jobs must be found for these people within their own home areas, not the other side of France.

The warnings of Gravier and his colleagues deeply impressed the civil servants and politicians, and many of their proposals became accepted as the basis of official policy. Soon after the war the Government began to encourage the formation of local 'expansion committees', and in 1950 it instituted the first scheme of subsidies and tax concessions for firms prepared to shift their factories from Paris or open new ones in the backward areas.

These steps met with a few successes – for instance, a big new Citroën factory at Rennes – but in general they were too weak and haphazardly directed. So, in 1955, rules were imposed to prevent the creation or enlargement of factories in the Paris area. Soon

The twenty-two new Regions and their capitals

afterwards, a start was made with regionalizing the Plan; and the ninety departments were grouped into twenty-two new economic regions, roughly corresponding to the old provinces. The department kept its existing functions; but the region had a new super-Prefect in charge of economic co-ordination, for the department was now clearly too small a unit for this.

At the same time the subsidies for new provincial factories were increased, especially for the west and south-west. These incentives were not at first very successful, and most firms preferred to move their factories out to somewhere nearer the capital, such as Rouen or Orléans. But gradually a momentum has developed, and in 1968–74 the industrial growth of the West, seen in terms of numbers of new jobs, was four times the French average. The incentives have played a part in this. The Government has also come to accept that in the more difficult and unpopular areas it must take the lead itself. Therefore it has initiated such schemes as new atomic and spatial centres in west Brittany, and irrigation and tourist projects in the Languedoc.

The Government soon realized that the only valid way to counter the appeal of Paris was not by setting prohibitions against it, but by stimulating rival centres of attraction. Therefore in 1965 it designated eight of the largest towns as *métropoles d'équilibre*,* and declared the aim of building up their populations to between 500,000 and a million (the Lyon and Lille conurbations are already beyond a million). This policy in itself may have been little more than a gesture, but at least it officially emphasized the need to endow other towns with some of the same amenities and metropolitan qualities as Paris. It was soon working so well that a new danger appeared: some of the *métropoles* were attracting too much of the activity of their region and were thus creating their own 'desert' around them. So from 1973 the eight *métropoles* were left to find their own equilibrium, and a new plan was launched for encouraging middle-sized towns.

New multi-purpose arts centres (Maisons de la Culture) have been built in some big towns, though not always with the happiest results. Several of the Grandes Ecoles have been transferred from Paris; provincial universities have been encouraged to grow faster than the Sorbonne, and have now at last been granted a certain autonomy under the Edgar Faure reforms. Finally, in addition to these cultural measures, a reform of State administration has regrouped the official services in each department under the authority of the Prefect rather than of their respective Ministries in Paris. These measures have certainly stimulated regional growth and probably have promoted efficiency too. But except in the university world there has been very little decentralization of authority as far as public services and finances are concerned.

* Marseille, Lyon, Toulouse, Bordeaux, Nantes, Strasbourg, Lille and Nancy/Metz.

Nevertheless, within the self-imposed limits of their *étatiste* ethos, the Gaullists' enthusiasm for the regions has been patent enough. *Aménagement du territoire* has been elevated into a science and a doctrine, the subject of endless speeches, books and conferences, and in 1963 a new Government department was created to take charge of it – the Délégation à l'Aménagement du Territoire et à l'Action Régionale (DATAR), which has been highly successful under its three talented directors, first Olivier Guichard, then Jérôme Monod, now François Essig.

For all the failures and delays in the application of policies, there is something well founded about the enthusiasm. France today presents her planners with some of the exciting challenge of a virgin land. It is one of the few parts of Western Europe where there is still the space, and the resources, for really ambitious possibilities. And as one talks with Lamour about the future of the Languedoc, or with eager DATAR technocrats about the new industries of the Béarn or the Rhône-Rhine canal, one gets just a glimpse of the vision that inspired the early developers of the New World. Whereas in Britain it is a question of patiently rebuilding the town-centres of old eyesores like Birmingham and Newcastle, in France only Flanders and the pre-war Paris suburbs present this kind of congested mess. Elsewhere, Corbusier-style ideas can have their fling: linear cities on virgin plains, factories in the depths of unknown valleys, tunnels under high mountains. True, there is the usual French chasm between theory and achievement; but at least a start has been made. Since the war this freedom of space has favoured the harmonious siting of new factories, such as the gleaming blue-and-white power station beside the Oise near Beaumont, which must strike any tourist on the road from Calais to Paris. And France is lucky to be making her real industrial revolution in this age of mobility and clean fuel. One has only to contrast the sparkle and cleanness of Grenoble and its modern industries with smoky nineteenth-century St-Etienne in its coal-grimed hollow, virtually the only large French town as dour and ugly as its score of English industrial counterparts.

Many French executives and politicians, even at the most local level, are mesmerized by geographical obsessions that sound extraordinary to English ears. Towns are pieces on an enormous chessboard, and the mere drawing of lines across a map yields some strange reality of its own. Towns are seen constantly in relation to each other, like battalions of little magnets. Transposed into English terms, a local French dignitary or official might talk like this: '*Swindon, bien que dans l'orbite londonienne, peut profiter d'une certaine vocation bristolienne, et tout en s'inspirant du rayonnement intellectuel oxfordien, elle se situe bien pour remplir un grand destin au carrefour des grands axes de demain – de l'agglomération birminghamoise jusqu'à Southampton aux portes des Amériques, et de l'hinterland*' – current *franglais* – '*galloise jusqu'à Harwich, plaque-tournante de l'avenir scandinavien*'. Everything is seen in terms of 'les grands axes de demain'. Does the mayor of Swindon talk like that?

The new enthusiasm is beginning, in some places, to percolate from the State technocrats to the local organizations – chambers of commerce, municipal councils, *conseils généraux*.* Their preoccupations are changing, from the details of their own little budgets and the jealous guarding of their own interests, to a wider co-operation with the State, and with each other, in schemes of expansion. It is a slow process, and there is plenty of obstruction; but gradually the relations between State and citizen, on a local level, are evolving beyond the old questions of political doctrine and privilege towards economic and social matters. Often the arguments are as bitter as before, but they are rather more practical. Recently I happened to overhear an animated conversation in Caen between a group of *conseillers généraux* of the Calvados department. A decade or two earlier their debate might have been about, say, the Church schools issue, or conscription in Algeria, or the wickedness of Mendès-France in attacking the local *bouilleurs de cru* (home distillers of apple alcohol). This time they were discussing whether a new international airport should be built at Caen or at Deauville, and whether the new motorway to Paris could be ready in two years or three. These were matters for the State to decide, finally, but the local dignitaries were determined to have their say.

A new kind of regional spirit is beginning to appear, notably among the younger generation now pushing their way to the top

* The elected councils of the *départements*.

in many local councils. It is a very different spirit from the old sentimental attachments of 'Moi, je suis Auvergnat'; in fact, it is quite the opposite, for it is based on a new mobility. The dynamism and the keenest local pride often come from young citizens who have moved in from elsewhere, who are prepared to put down roots but will still want to keep in touch with the rest of France. This is different from the outlook of the old Breton whose pride is never to have ventured on to foreign soil east of Rennes.

This new spirit has been awakened partly by the decline of French nationalism and the rise of Europe. The French – despite the misleading impression formerly given by de Gaulle – are less nationalist than they used to be. Most of them still believe, however vaguely, in a united Europe, despite the recent setbacks to that ideal. They know that it could one day mean more importance for the regions of Europe, as nations fade. In the brave, early years of the European ideal, all the prophets – Gravier, Lamour, Armand – were stressing that Europe was the great chance of the French regions, just as without regional revival France would be lost to Europe. Armand wrote: 'The regions can renew their personality through European union *without having to do it through the monster that is Paris.* If Lyon were a little more Milanese, Toulouse a little more Spanish, Lille a little more Flemish, we would all be the better for it.' Alas, it is not going to happen overnight. The EEC's moves towards a common regional policy have not yet been exactly a success. But if the EEC were to recover from its present doldrums and again start making progress towards economic union, it is likely that this would lead the regions of Europe to assert themselves – economically, if not politically – and to form new links across frontiers. Already there have been signs of it as, for instance, Lorraine with its new Moselle Canal to Coblenz feels the pull towards the Ruhr and the rise of a new economic Lotharingia.

In the past few years the pattern of regional development in France has come into a steady focus. All the larger towns that ring Paris (Caen, Evreux, Rouen, Amiens, Reims, Orléans and others) are doing well. Some are sites for new overspill universities; all are favourite spots for new industry. But to the north and east the already highly industrialized regions of Flanders and Lorraine are now in some difficulty because of the nature of their industries: coal-mines and textiles around Lille, impoverished iron-mines around Metz. In the west, the campaign to introduce badly needed new industries has borne fruit in certain areas, notably around Bordeaux and Nantes, on the coast, and at Rennes and Pau, inland. But much of the south-central part of France is still in trouble. In fact, latest figures show that the old pattern, which I mentioned earlier, of a France split in two halves – rich, industrialized east, and poor, rural west – is becoming out of date, and a new, more complex pattern is emerging. The zone of demographic decline, of ageing population and industrial depression, is no longer the west, but a broad strip of territory cutting across France from north-east to south-west – it starts in the Ardennes and the Meuse, skirts northern Burgundy, then broadens out to include most of the Massif Central (Auvergne and Limousin) and ends up in the Pyrenees. These areas, inland and mostly hilly, are now where the main problems lie, much more than the west coast itself where only Brittany is still in serious difficulty. So in 1975 the Government, with a loud roll of drums, launched a new development programme for the Massif Central, which happens also to be the home region of both Giscard and Chirac – coincidence? It will prove an uphill task to attract new industries to the remoter parts of this sprawling massif, where the population is slowly drifting away. 'Perhaps it's too late to save the Limousin,' one DATAR man told me, like a doctor at a death-bed.

For some years the foremost expansion zone of France has been the south-east – the whole area from Lyon down to Marseille and eastwards to the Alps. Some of this growth has been due to Government stimulus, notably in prompting huge new tourist resorts along the Languedoc coast, a new industrial complex at Fos, west of Marseille, and a 'scientific park' just inland from Cannes. But for the most part, firms and their staff have flocked readily to an area that has many advantages – its climate, its tourist delights, its natural resources and its good position between the Mediterranean and the heart of Europe. The growth of the south-east has in some senses been almost *too* fast for the nation's healthy equilibrium. The brightest star of all in this area is

France's 'little Chicago in the Alps', *venue* of the 1968 Winter Olympics and winner of every French gold medal for post-war regional development: the astonishing city of Grenoble.

THE ARROGANT ADVANCE OF GRENOBLE

A young nuclear scientist took me up in the funicular to the old fortress on the cliffs beside the city. We watched, as the sun set over the jagged Vercors massif, and the ranks of new skyscrapers below us glittered from pink to grey. There it sprawled in its flat valley within a ski's leap of the high Alps, France's little answer to the New World, *ville-pilote*, showpiece of a nation's future.

'My wife and I are hard-core Parisians,' said my friend, 'and we were rather dubious when we moved here eight years ago. But few of the thousands of Parisians who've settled here recently want to go back. It's not like moving to the provinces, it's living in the France of tomorrow.'

In the 1820s Stendhal wrote of his native town: 'What could I add, if I were God?' He was referring to the landscape; Grenoble itself was little more than a sleepy village. Some things have not changed since Stendhal's day: the Alpine freshness in the air, the close backdrop of snow-peak or steep forest behind every street, the hardy traditions of the mountain people of the Dauphiné. But man has added plenty else, without waiting for God. The valley of the Isère beneath its toothy rocks pullulates with some of the most advanced industries in Europe, electro-chemicals, electro-metallurgy, heavy machinery and nuclear laboratories. The population, 80,000 in 1945, reached 360,000 (including suburbs) in 1969. Eight people in ten are immigrants to the town; one in seven is a student or scientist. The crowds in the streets are youthful and cosmopolitan, and there is a new social informality still rare in the provinces. 'You can wear ski-clothes in a smart restaurant,' I was told, 'and no one minds or notices, as they would in Lyon.' There is even an air of self-assertive brashness that some people find more American than French.

It is this unusual marriage of touristic setting and intellectual and economic dynamism that sets Grenoble so far apart either from a more conventional French town like Dijon, or from the average British industrial centre, even from a so-called boom town like Coventry. Since the war Grenoble has become something of a legend in France, and the open-mindedness and enterprise of its new élites have made it a pace-setter in many diverse fields. What Grenoble does today, France does tomorrow. In 1960 the first French family planning clinic opened here, in defiance of the anti-contraception laws; Edouard Leclerc here started his first centre outside his Brittany home base; the university (now split into three) is the least provincial in the provinces, with the highest percentages both of non-Dauphinois and non-French students; as a nuclear headquarters Grenoble is second only to Paris; and in 1965 it became the first large French town to stage a 'municipal revolution' by electing a young mayor from the new technocratic class, rather than from the traditional élites of bourgeois *notables*. And these recent achievements were preceded by others, mostly more fortuitous, dating back into history: the first funicular in France, the first Syndicat d'Initiative, the first scheme of family allowances, the pioneering of hydro-electricity, the most courageous Resistance fighting (in the Vercors, 1944), and even the origins of the French Revolution.

What has made Grenoble so special? It has not been due to any particular Government pressure, nor, until 1965, to municipal dynamism. The twofold answer lies in its surrounding mountains. Grenoble's industrial strength originates from the nearby invention of hydro-electricity in the last century; and today it is the skiing, above all, that attracts the young élites from Paris and elsewhere, for no other big town is so near the mountains. The rest is a snowball effect; the more factories and intellectuals come, the more others tend to follow.

Grenoble was no more than a quiet burg noted for its glove industries when, in the 1860s, some French engineers experimented with a new idea of drawing electric power from the high waterfalls of the Belledonne and Chartreuse mountains. Thus the age of 'white coal' (*houille blanche*) was born. Factories large and small came to settle near the new sources of power – some of them were little paper mills which you can still see today clinging to the sides of steep clefts in the Chartreuse, for the electricity at first was not on the grid. And Grenoble has never looked back. The population doubled between 1872 and 1926, at a time when most of France was stagnating. By the 1950s the largest firms were Merlin-Gerin (electro-metallurgy) and Neyrpic (turbines and hydraulic research), both among Europe's leaders in their fields. The university was also developing fast, especially in science, spurred by the presence of Professor Néel and other outstanding physicists. It was this that persuaded the Government, in 1956, to choose Grenoble as the site for France's principal nuclear research centre, which today has a staff of 2,000, a third of them specialists.

Since then industry has taken a new direction. The older metallurgical firms, based on the *houille blanche*, seem to have passed their prime; Neyrpic and another big one, Bouchayer et Viallet, have been taken over by outside companies. But some equally large and more advanced industries have arrived to work closely with Grenoble's reservoir of research scientists; Pechiney, one of France's leading chemical firms, has opened electro-chemical research laboratories with a staff of 2,000.

This town offers much the most successful example in France of close and fruitful co-operation between universities and local industry. In the United States, or even in Britain, this is not so uncommon; but French professors with their ivory-tower traditions have tended to scorn practical work, and hence the lag today in French applied research. Grenoble even eighty years ago managed to create a different outlook, when pioneering electrical industries first began to settle in this remote university town. In 1892 the world's first university course on industrial electricity was held here, and the links have steadily strengthened ever since. Today the firms give little in the form of direct grants, but they constantly commission the science faculties for special jobs of research, while, in return, the university specialists make full use of the firms' laboratories and practical experience. This situation helps to entice brilliant scientists from Paris, as well as the kind of advanced industries that especially rely on research. As one example, Professor Néel's invention of a new form of powder magnet has led to the creation here of two factories specializing in this.

The late Dean of the Science Faculty, Professor Louis Weil, as ebullient and engagingly conceited a man as most leaders of this city, took me on to the roof of the Nuclear Studies Centre and showed me his and Néel's kingdom – a 300-acre site beside the Merlin-Gerin works where 30m francs' worth of new reactors and cyclotrons were taking shape. 'It's the human contacts,' he told me, 'that are so much easier here than in most towns. We seem to be creating a new sort of open society, unusual for France. I'm sure the skiing has a lot to do with it. It's easy to settle thorny problems of liaison with some top industrialist or civil servant when you're up in a funicular with him. Everyone here goes skiing.'

These links are one reason why Grenoble is the best example in France of what economists call the 'multiplier effect': investment breeding further investment. Whereas in some places – such as Lacq or Rennes – new industry has implanted itself as an alien growth, here it perfectly animates its region and is animated by it. This, plus the tourism and the three cosmopolitan universities, are creating a new kind of social ambience that offers pointers to the way the rest of France may be about to move. In most other towns, despite the new liveliness, the old bourgeois hierarchies are still largely in place. Here the original nucleus of conservative Grenoblois are being pushed aside by the flood of immigrants, and a certain new classlessness is emerging, unusual in a land where class divisions are still much more rigid than in Britain. People in Grenoble are judged for themselves, rather than for being 'Monsieur le Président' of this or that. But though the old barriers are down, a new organized pattern of society is only just beginning to emerge and many of the newcomers feel a bit rootless.

The town combines its pioneering spirit with the street animation of the Midi, and the people in their bizarrely assorted clothes seem to have come from everywhere – from the coal-mines of Lorraine, the farms of Auvergne, the Mezzogiorno, Texas, the Champs-Elysées. It is a town of youth, and of *cadres*; at least 35,000 people earn their living directly off science or studies. In the chic little downtown *pizzerie*, strolling guitarists (usually students) sing modern American folk-songs – and you might be in Chelsea. In the cafés and cocktail bars, fashionably dressed young people discuss skiing, business, student politics or their love-lives with equal aplomb – and you might be in Cannes or Manhattan. Grenoble is the least provincial spot in the French provinces; it may lack the 'soul' of an older cathedral city, but is finding its own, new kind of soul.

The State's direct contribution to the boom has been largely confined to the nuclear centre and to the universities' handsome research grants. But the Gaullists, in order to show the flag, also provided the most splendid modern Préfecture in France, all glass and marble and fitted carpets.

Today the Prefect watches warily over the most remarkable municipal situation in France. Throughout the boom years of 1945–65 the *mairie* remained, surprisingly, in the hands of the old guard of Grenoble-born *notables*, in turn Socialist or Gaullist by label but reactionary by temperament. And the new immigrants were not yet sufficiently organized or civically aware to dislodge them. During those years almost nothing was done for town-planning. The city spread its tentacles along the valleys, and rents and land-prices shot up unchecked. I remember admiring a new ring of peripheral skyscrapers in southern Grenoble in 1959, and coming back six years later to find that other rings had grown outside them, like the layers of a tree, and the city centre had virtually transplanted itself in that time from the old town to the southern 1959 periphery. It reminded me of the posters in Texas, 'Don't park your car in this lot: there'll be a new building in an hour.' This was all very exciting for boom-worshippers, but inconvenient for people living in a city that had vastly outstripped its public services.

Then in 1964 a certain Hubert Dubedout of the Nuclear Centre found that his water supply kept failing in his fourth-floor flat. Thousands of others were in similar plights, for the mother city of hydro-electricity was served by a water system unchanged since 1883. Dubedout launched a public campaign to get the mayor to do something, and he succeeded. Encouraged by this, he and a few young friends from the city's scientific *élite* formed a non-party group to contest the local elections of March 1965. Allying with the Socialists, and helped by Communist abstention in the second ballot, they succeeded to everyone's surprise in dislodging the Gaullist-conservative ruling coalition from the *mairie*. The intellectual immigrants of Grenoble had found their force at last; nearly all of them voted for Dubedout.

Today he is mayor of Grenoble. He is an ex-naval officer and an electronics engineer from Pau, in his early fifties, slim, good looking and disdainful in manner; a man generations apart in spirit from the usual mayor of a large French town. When I first met him, at a pompous lunch in the Préfecture for the elderly *notables* from nearby villages, he winked at me in front of the Prefect as if to say, 'I feel as much an outsider here as you.' He is the prototype of the new French technocratic pragmatist, a kind that normally steers well clear of the intrigues of municipal politics. His victory had a few echoes in other towns in the 1965 elections, and was greeted by the political observers in Paris as a national portent. Grenoble had set the pace once again.

Dubedout and his energetic team revitalized the *mairie*, and then worked hard to get Grenoble ready for the Winter Olympics. Besides preparing a huge new ice rink, this involved a complete overhaul for the town as a whole. New airports and motorways had to be built, a new railway station and post-office, skating-rinks and an Olympic village to house 4,000. Three-quarters of the total cost of 1,000 million francs was borne by the State; the town had to find most of the rest, and some of the burden fell on rate-payers. But the lasting benefits will be enormous: Grenoble acquired in two years the modern infrastructure that would other-wise have been spread over twenty.

Thanks to the happy coincidence of Dubedout and the Olympic Games, Grenoble now has the town-planning policy it so badly needed. Yet all did not go so smoothly. First, several of the small communes on the edge of the town used their powers of veto to hold up the general projects. In one case, a Socialist mayor refused to let a road to the Olympic village pass over his territory because he feared it would bring new housing, and he did not want his village to change. Then, the defeated mayor, Albert Michallon, waged a vendetta of comic-opera extravagance against Dubedout. Michallon, a doctor from an old Grenoble family, is a witty, flamboyant playboy who had been elected mayor in 1959 on a

UNR ticket but was always something of an embarrassment to the Gaullists. Careless of civic management but a fanatic for prestige, it was he who secured the Games for Grenoble, and when he lost his seat as mayor he remained chairman of the Olympics organizing committee and refused to stand down. He and Dubedout proceeded to block each other's plans, and Dubedout said the *mairie* would boycott the committee until Michallon resigned. François Missoffe, the Minister of Youth and Sport, then somehow succeeded in reconciling the two rivals, and Michallon even said publicly, in his own fruity style, 'Dubedout and I are henceforth *cul et chemise. Lui, c'est le cul.*' When the Dubedouts have replaced the Michallons throughout France, perhaps municipal affairs will be more efficient – but less colourful.

Dubedout started out with no ambitions in national politics beyond the horizons of Grenoble. Yet, locally, he soon found it impossible to remain detached from party politics. He supported Mendès-France, when the latter chose a Grenoble constituency for his brief and ill-fated political come-back in 1967–8; and today he rules in alliance with the Socialists and with erratic and grudging support from the Communists. He has joined the Socialist party and become one of its most brilliant figures, though he still plays little active part in national politics. But he is sometimes talked of as a possible Prime Minister, should Mitterrand one day become President of France. Locally, Dubedout is constantly harassed by local Gaullists and extreme-Right elements, and especially by the *gauchistes* on the new campuses – it seems no surprise that Grenoble, avant-garde as ever, is the most politically aware and effervescent town outside Paris, with the largest share of active *gauchistes*.

Dubedout managed to steer a course between all these hazards, to become re-elected in 1971, and to embark on some remarkable experiments. His superb new 37m-franc *mairie*, all fountains and modern art, glass and marble, is no mere showpiece but the headquarters of a campaign to create a new style of municipal government.* He has been trying to associate the citizens actively with every daily phase of government – a new idea in France – and not merely to 'administer' them, in the usual French manner. He has

* See pp. 276–7.

succeeded, too, in persuading the suburban communes to join with Grenoble in a voluntary association for planning and management – also rare in France. Just as he is much less a politician than a technocrat, so he is less technocrat than humanist, aiming to galvanize the whole community into working to improve its own quality of life. Can he succeed, without falling victim to party jealousies? Can his ideas spread elsewhere? He has run into much trouble locally, and some of his schemes have suffered setbacks, but I remain cautiously optimistic.

He recognizes that the town's phenomenal expansion must now be matched by social and civic developments, too. In fact, it is uncertain that the town can grow indefinitely. Some economists now talk of 'saturation', and soon there will be little building space left in the confined plain. Grenoble's expansion was always something of a freak, in the light of its geographical position, 350 miles from Paris and off the main through routes. Lyon, sixty miles away, may lack Grenoble's zest but is far better suited as a capital. But will Grenoble keep its unusual pioneering spirit if its growth is slowed? So far, it seems to have offered the best example in France of success breeding success, of mystique and achievement linked in a chain reaction. It is something of a Californian phenomenon, with new human energy responding to environment. Grenoble also, most significantly, affords some glimpse of what the French can do once their natural talents are released from the conventions and structures of the past which mostly still weigh on them so heavily. Above all, it is an example of spontaneous growth and private initiative, with the State for once playing a secondary role.

In other parts of France this is less often the case. But since about 1960 some other towns have been growing livelier, too, and the contrast between Grenoble and the rest is less striking than it used to be. The spirit is catching on, whether it be due to the dynamism of a few local people, to special Government efforts, or to unplanned social or economic factors. I shall now describe a few typical areas where change, or the forces resisting change, are especially interesting.

CAEN, RENNES, AND THE TRAVAILS OF BRITTANY

Five hundred miles from the Dauphiné Alps, on the rolling plains of western Normandy, Caen, like Grenoble, is a thriving university and industrial city. It has been growing faster than most French towns of its size, but not simply of its own accord; the special efforts of a dynamic team of civil servants in the 1960s made it one of the few striking successes of the Government's decentralization campaign.

Caen is the regional capital of Basse-Normandie, comprising the three departments of Calvados, Manche and Orne. This is an average French region with some industry and much agriculture, marked by an even higher level of rural over-population than in Brittany. There has been a steady rural exodus since the war, most of it towards Paris rather than local towns. So the Government decided to try to develop Caen as a local counter-attraction to Paris.

When the Gaullists came to power and the regions were created, a fanatical young *sous-préfet* called Robert de Caumont was appointed to co-ordinate the economic development of Basse-Normandie, and he made it his vocation to build Caen into a great metropolis. The conservative city council of stolid Normans were even more lifeless than in pre-Dubedout Grenoble, nor did Caen have the spontaneous magnetism of Grenoble; so the State had to make the running. De Caumont, then still in his twenties, was an extreme example of the new school of young French technocrat-civil servant, energetic, apolitical, obsessed with expansion and forward planning, concerned to find human solutions but often too over-educated to possess the human touch. He spent four years in Normandy coaxing or bullying mayors and businessmen into action, and visiting Paris to entice factories down to Caen or to wheedle extra money out of Ministries.

Rarely can one civil servant have done so much for an area. He brought new firms, he had new suburbs built, he helped animate this poorer western half of Normandy with a new regional awareness – hence the councillors I heard arguing about airports. In 1964 he and the Prefect launched a 'return to your homeland' campaign by writing to young *émigrés* and local boys away on military service, telling them that the region had changed and there were now new factories offering work. Later the industrial drive began to bear fruit more rapidly, and Caen and its region for a time led France in the growth of fresh employment. There are new Renault and Citroën factories, and others making television sets, electrical machinery and steel; and the exodus of youth has been slowed right down. Caen's population of 180,000 (with suburbs) is now more than twice its pre-war figure.

From Caen a main road runs south-west through the hilly *bocage* country, and finally arrives at Rennes, the capital of Brittany. This hitherto sleepy city is today no less active than Caen, but in a very different style. Far more than at Grenoble or Caen, or almost anywhere, its revival has been sponsored from within its old self, and draws its spiritual strength from the culture and pride of this most nation-like of French provinces. Though the Government is anxious to help economically backward Brittany, at Rennes the re-awakening has been led and animated by its exceptionally vigorous *centriste* mayor, Henri Fréville. He has been able to prove, like Dubedout, that even in centralized France a mayor of a large town, given the right courage and energy, can get some things done without having to be a stooge of the Government.

Rennes, which survived the war almost intact, is a dignified, unsmart, animated town of old grey buildings, with a less complacent and a more metropolitan atmosphere than Caen. Where the Normans are phlegmatic and almost Teutonic, the Bretons are humorous and individual – the Welsh of France. For centuries their capital was a great centre of army, law and learning; but it had no industry at all, and by about 1950 seemed depressed and poor. Yet *émigrés* kept arriving from the desolate, over-populated hinterland, and this being mother Brittany, they were less keen than in many parts of France to make straight for Paris. It was essential to find new work for them in Rennes.

This was the situation facing Fréville, a middle-aged, bespectacled history professor from the university, when he won the *mairie* in 1953 on an MRP ticket. His first and biggest *coup* was to persuade Citroën that Rennes was just the place for the big new factory they wanted and could not build in or near Paris. From that day the Rennais began to recover confidence in their future, and Citroën today has 8,000 workers there. A few other industries have since arrived, too, and efforts have been made to develop Rennes as an electronics centre in collaboration with the big science faculties. It is not easy, for most firms are reluctant to move 220 miles westwards from Paris, despite the 25 per cent installation subsidies. But since the war the population of Rennes has risen from 100,000 to 220,000 without (until the 1974 crisis) unemployment. Fréville, a radical idealist, has made efforts to provide cheap but good-quality housing and to endow the new estates with the kind of social and cultural equipment that usually is so conspicuously lacking in the modern French dormitory suburbs.*

Thanks to Fréville, and to many other less discernible factors, there has been a marked change in social atmosphere in Rennes since the early 1950s. The director of the theatre company told me: 'There's a totally different spirit, a revolution. The older Rennais haven't changed much, but they've been submerged by the new ones – the student generation, the technicians from Paris, the peasants arriving with the open outlook of *émigrés*. It used to be a dead town where, as they'd say, "Nothing ever catches on except fire" [there was a big fire here in 1720]. Today there's a new kind of curiosity and sense of adventure: you can see it in the growth of the ciné-clubs, the popularity of composers like Schoenberg, or our own success with plays by people like Brecht and Osborne.' A university lecturer told me: 'Rennes has been transformed completely. It used to be dead after seven at night; now some cafés are still full well after midnight.'

Rennes is also the centre of a modest Breton cultural revival, though this is due more to the enthusiasm of a few local intellectuals and folklorists than to wide popular feeling. As the *coiffes* and handicrafts die out in the villages, so the Breton culture and language clubs grow in the towns. This may be a bit phoney and not especially significant. Nevertheless, Rennes has the vocation to be an authentic regional centre and is already the capital of a

* See p. 352.

'region' comprising the four Brittany departments. It is providing a magnet for the province's rural exodus, while its new factories and housing-estates offer the sociologist an absorbing study in peasantry transformed overnight into city-dwellers. Behind the pleasant blue-and-purple façades of the blocks of flats in the new suburbs, Fréville has deliberately tried to jumble the classes together – Breton peasants and Parisian technicians.

Rennes' revival is well ahead of that of the rest of Brittany. It stands on the province's eastern frontier, half turned towards Paris. To its west are 150 miles of a rugged and still poorly developed peninsula, one of France's more depressed areas. Long distances to Paris with inadequate transport services, backward farms and too-numerous peasantry, declining traditional industries and too few modern ones, a slump in the naval roles of Brest and Lorient – all these factors have been working against Brittany. Over the past ten years or so, the Government has made special efforts to help Brittany: it has poured in funds, attracted new industries, modernized the infrastructure. Great progress has been made. But the province still remains vulnerable, largely because of its isolated position. When recession spread in France in 1974–5, the Bretons found themselves among the worst hit. They reacted in their usual militant and volatile manner, and there were angry demonstrations against factory closures. Other Bretons, the tiny minority of nationalists who believe in violence, resorted to their bomb attacks again. But these two kinds of unrest – economic and political – are largely unconnected. The terrorists do not command wide sympathy and, while most Bretons certainly want more regional autonomy, they are not separatists and their first concern is for a better economic deal.

The problem here is that Brittany has still been failing to attract enough industry for its large 2½-million population; and the prime reason still seems to be its isolation at the extremity of a France whose focus has been moving eastwards towards the EEC centres of gravity. What is the solution? Most Breton leaders feel that one long-term answer is for Brittany to try to loosen its economic over-dependence on Paris, not through separatism but commerce, by turning its focus out seawards again and towards its British and Irish neighbours; that is, to resume the old trading and maritime role that it held before the bear-hug of Napoleonic centralism. This might not need to depend on political devolution. The sea-facing concept has been actively endorsed by the Government planners in Paris, who have recently launched for the whole Atlantic coast the strategy of '*Eurocéan*'. 'The under-developed west of France,' one planner explained to me, 'must no longer be thought of as on the periphery of the EEC, but as its forward zone, Europe's gateway to the West, its watery frontier with the Americas.' For all the fanciful rhetoric, the idea could make sense.

Some of the more dynamic Bretons are already putting it into practice. Alexis Gourvennec, victor of the artichoke wars* and today the best-known figure on Brittany's economic scene, formed a North Finistère pressure group in the mid-1960s that lobbied intensively in Paris, and in 1968 was instrumental in persuading the Government to allocate massive funds for Brittany, including some 6 million francs towards building a deep-water port at Roscoff. In fighting for this port he was gambling on Britain's entry into the EEC and the new trade outlets that would follow. The existing means of transporting Breton vegetables to Britain were unsatisfactory and slow. A direct ferry to Plymouth was the answer – but who was to run it? Gourvennec's SICA approached various ferry companies, who all turned the project down as unlikely to be viable. The SICA had no alternative but to launch their own company (today called Brittany Ferries), to the scorn of the other firms who expected them to fail – '*Vous n'êtes pas des armateurs mais des amateurs*', they were told. But by hiring the right skills the farmers succeeded. In 1973 they launched the now successful daily ferry service to Plymouth, which has done a lot to develop trade between '*la petite et la Grande Bretagne*' – vegetables, heavy freight and tourism. It is believed to be one of the rare examples in the world of local farmers starting up their own shipping line in order to take control of their own destiny.

Gourvennec later opened St-Malo–Plymouth and St-Malo–

* See p. 129.

Portsmouth lines, and is planning one from Roscoff to southern Ireland, but this expansion has not been without controversy. Gourvennec, as I stated in an earlier chapter, deals ruthlessly with those rash enough to oppose him. When in 1975 the German TT Line decided to start a Southampton–St-Malo service to compete with Brittany Ferries, the not exactly Left-wing Gourvennec formed a cynical alliance with the Communist-led seamen's union at St-Malo who were objecting to the flag-of-convenience *Mary Poppins* with its foreign crews. He sent bus-loads of 250 commandos from St-Pol to St-Malo, paying them 150 francs a day each – and the poor *Mary Poppins*, blackballed also at Southampton, slunk back to Hamburg. Gourvennec then ran into heavy criticism, in France and abroad. Many people felt that his action was a disgraceful violation of the EEC spirit of free enterprise, and the Bonn Government lodged protests. But Giscard's Government did not lift a finger against Godfather Gourvennec; they knew just how powerful and useful he is in Brittany, and that it is better to have him as a friend than a foe.

Gourvennec often uses strong-arm methods of this kind. When I asked him to explain them, he said: 'I admit we sometimes behave illegally, but it's for valid reasons. Pious declarations get you nowhere; violent demonstrations often do. But mind you, we never injure people.' He is a stocky, rough-featured peasant who now lives the jet-hopping life of a tycoon, but he keeps his Breton accent and prides himself on his earthiness and rejection of high-life graces. At a banquet in a top Paris restaurant to celebrate Brittany Ferries, he brushed aside the Mumms and Château-Laffittes and said to the waiter, '*Donne-moi un bon coup de rouge, mon vieux.*' He is also an idealist with the gift of the gab. Like most Bretons, he feels Brittany will increasingly benefit from British and Irish entry into the EEC. 'Our ferries are part of a policy of putting Brittany on the centre of the map,' he told me. 'The main north-south axis of Europe is too far east. We want to see a grand new highway, through Spain and up the west coast of France, cutting across Brittany to Roscoff, to link with the motorway from Plymouth to Birmingham and Glasgow – the great axis of tomorrow! In modern times, the Celtic lands have ignored each other too long. Modern Brittany knows far too little of modern

Wales and Ireland. We must return to the close historic links of our ancestors – through culture, tourism, trade.'

A second Breton vision today is that the area might become oil-rich, like Scotland. France's first major search for its own offshore oil began in 1975 in the Atlantic 60 miles west of Brest. Conditions proved difficult at first, but prospects of finding oil or natural gas in quantities are thought to be good. And the Bretons, amid their economic malaise, have been clutching at this hope of a brighter future. In Brest, where in 1975 unemployment was running at more than 10 per cent, I was told: 'If oil is found, our troubles will be ended. There'll be a huge spin-off of jobs, and Brest will become a boom-town, like Aberdeen.' Many local people are still bitter against Paris for its cancellation in 1972 of plans for an oil refinery at Brest. The oil firms thought it too remote. But if oil is found offshore, this decision could be reversed. The only danger, as one local journalist warned me, is that 'Breton imaginations easily outstrip the facts. For some people, the black gold is already flowing in the streets. We Bretons are a nation of dreamers – and just as our ancestor Merlin sought the Holy Grail in these forests, so today oil wells have become our mystical Grail. If oil proves as elusive as the Grail did, the ugly backlash of disappointment could have political repercussions.'

At best, the oil could not be commercialized before 1981. Meanwhile Brittany's traditional small industries have been proving vulnerable. Unemployment in 1975 was well above the national average, a sharp slump in the building trade being a main cause. Scores of small firms closed as the crisis worsened. Though the Government in recent years has managed to woo some electronics and light mechanical firms to western Brittany, most heavy industry considers it too remote. Not nearly enough new jobs are being created to keep pace with a continuing exodus of some 12,000 a year, mostly young people, from the poor farmlands of the interior. Traditionally, these people have made for Paris, but the appeal of the capital is now waning. Surprisingly, the 1976 census figures show that for the first time in many decades more Bretons are returning to the province than leaving it. Most are retired people, but younger ones, wooed back by official incitements of job prospects, are liable to end up resentful.

Recent factory strikes and sit-ins have shown something of the bitterness of local feelings; for instance, the workers in the electrical plant of Joint Français at St-Brieuc, who went on strike for eight weeks in 1972, were angry at being paid 30 per cent below Paris levels.

To this must be added a slump in two other key industries, pig-breeding and fisheries. The deep-sea fishing of Lorient and Concarneau has recently been badly hit by foreign competition, rising costs, falling prices and Atlantic over-fishing. At Lorient in 1975 I saw a number of trawlers laid up: 'Two years ago,' I was told, 'before this fishing crisis, we invested 300 million francs in buying 34 new trawlers. Now we are left looking silly, with a lot of debts, and boats we no longer need.' And on top of this, there hangs over Lorient the Damoclean sword of the 200-mile limit, due to be ratified in 1977. In the office of one fishing-fleet owner, there were maps of British waters on the wall. My host then opened a cupboard: pinned inside was a map of what the new limit would mean to Lorient – 'I hide this away,' he said, 'for when the fishermen see it they go berserk with panic.' The new ruling will put up costs, because fishing rights will have to be paid for. The main issue is British and Irish waters, crucial to Lorient, for there is far more fish there than in French waters. 'We desperately hope,' I was told, 'that Britain will agree to the Nine sharing their 200-mile zones on a Community basis. But is it likely? The trouble is, the EEC has no fishing policy. We've created *Europe verte*, of a sort, but not *Europe bleue*.'

A tenacious, assertive, but not always realistic people, Bretons have tended for years to blame their troubles on Paris's 'neglect' and failure to help them. Many still do so. But the charge is not nearly as justified as it used to be. Since the late 1960s, the Government has poured more money into Brittany than any other region. The ports and the telephone and road networks have at last been impressively modernized; Grandes Ecoles have been transferred from Paris, new electronics and space-communications centres set up, and nuclear centres established; handsome grants are offered for new industry. Some private firms have responded, though not enough. Finally, Giscard's 1975 reflation programme was especially generous in the new funding it offered for Brittany, and the green light was at last given for Brest to enlarge its tanker-repairing facilities by building a giant new dry-dock to take 500,000-tonners and so rival Portugal's.

Though Bretons may not always admit it, their province has come a long way in the past decade or so, and it is apparent in the new building on every side. Except in the desolate interior, this does not *look* a depressed area. By the time of the energy crisis it seemed to be finally on the way to solving its economic problems. But 1974–5 were such poor years that there seemed a danger of the progress being cancelled out. This worried the Government because of Brittany's political sensitivity, which is less a matter of terrorist extremism than of more general resentments. It is true that the Front de Libération de la Bretagne and other nationalist movements have several times staged bomb attacks in recent years, leading to the arrests of scores of their members including priests, but the influence of the FLB should not be exaggerated. Though it arouses a general kind of sympathy in local breasts, most Bretons disavow this kind of extremism, and separatism is much less widely popular than in Scotland. But – except in dealing with terrorism – Paris usually goes out of its way to placate Breton sentiment; its handling of the *Mary Poppins* affair was a case in point.

Regional awareness has been growing in Brittany, as in some other parts of France. It is partly cultural: for instance, Alain Stivell, the folk-singer who sings in Breton, is today a cult hero with numerous imitators. Bretons are also demanding more say in their own affairs, but, as we shall see later in this chapter, their new regional assembly has proved little more than a rubber-stamp body. The neo-Jacobins in Paris are not keen on the provinces managing their own destiny. But Bretons' demands for more real autonomy are bound to grow, especially if, as in Scotland, oil is found and the Bretons consider it theirs. Probably they will weather the current economic crisis, if the rest of Europe does. And they have the men, like Gourvennec, to lead them into a new future, with new links across the sea. However, sooner or later the Government will have to do more than dole out money and placate them if it is to help them find fulfilment.

LANGUEDOC, TOULOUSE, THE AVEYRON

At the other end of France, the Languedoc presents the opposite picture: a sluggish area where the State has had to take the initiative. This coastal plain between the Rhône and Catalonia has much the same climate as Provence; and with its good soil, thick population and strategic position astride the main routes into Spain and the south-west, it seemed ideal for development. But its race of lazy vine-growers needed a strong push from outside. So the Government chose the Languedoc for two of the more important development schemes in modern France: the canal, the biggest irrigation network in Europe; and the largest State-sponsored tourist project in history. It all seemed like a technocrat's dream: *carte blanche* to make bold new strokes across the map. But the Government was anxious not to repeat the mistakes in some countries of alienating the local population. To carry out both projects it set up Sociétés d'Economie Mixte, directed by the State but associating local municipalities and some local business interests. They have had some success in terms of public relations – except when it came to uprooting the vines.

The vine has been described as 'the Languedoc's sole wealth – and its greatest tragedy'. This province, named after its ancient dialect, the 'tongue of *oc*', was the most powerful in France in the days before Napoleon, and stretched to the west beyond Toulouse. In the early nineteenth century factories were flourishing along this coast, and one of the first railway lines in France was that from Montpellier to the port of Sète. But the vine killed this brief era of industrial expansion. When French wine consumption rose rapidly in the nineteenth century the Languedociens found they could produce plenty and cheaply on their sunny slopes, and it was much less trouble than building railways. Today the thick vineyards roll for scores of miles on every side, and life is easy when the grape grows fat on the red earth and needs little attention. The vines and the climate have united to produce a slow, conservative, unenterprising temperament. Only when their prices or markets are threatened will the growers get excited and take action. In 1907, in 1953, and again, much more recently, in 1975–6,* they staged some of the worst farming riots of the

* See pp. 156–60.

century. Today they are as defensive as ever about their interests. 'Pasteur says, wine is the healthiest of drinks,' shout their big roadside posters; or, 'Water is polluted: drink wine' – and the poster shows a little boy polluting the water in the manner of little boys. After all, the growers have to do something to counter the Government's anti-alcoholism campaign.

The monoculture of cheap wine was dangerous for the region's economy. Yet it could not really be diversified unless there was water for growing other crops. In 1940 Philippe Lamour, novelist, man of action and farming leader, escaped from the Occupation in the north and bought an estate at Bellegarde, south of Nîmes, at the eastern edge of the Languedoc, near the fertile, fruit-growing zone of the lower Rhône. There he settled, and after the war gave himself the mission of rescuing the Languedoc. 'We must save the "French desert" before it is too late,' he wrote – and he persuaded the Fourth Republic to build the canal which had lain dormant as a project since 1851. Lamour is an unusual and striking personality, a kind of freelance technocrat and man of ideas. He is versatile, charming and human; it amuses him to disconcert romantic-minded girl secretaries by announcing his surname most seductively to them down a telephone. '*Vous cherchez l'amour, mademoiselle? Me voilà.*'

He formed a company that dug a wide master canal from the Rhône to Montpellier and built dams in the Cévennes behind Béziers. Soon a network of little canals began to transect some of the vineyards. Lamour and two or three other local pioneers uprooted their own few vines and proceeded to demonstrate that the same acreage of apple- or pear-orchards could earn six times as much as vines, if properly irrigated. The vinegrowers were invited to follow suit. And how did they react? They formed 'committees of defence against the canal', they rioted in the streets of the big towns with banners saying 'Death to Lamour!', they behaved, in short, like farmers a hundred years ago who were afraid those new-fangled trains would run over their cows. Agitation finally subsided, once the farmers realized they would not be *forced* to uproot their vines; but today hardly a single vinegrower has yet destroyed a single acre. The canal simply ran into debt through lack of clients, and Lamour had to sanction what at first he had regarded as intolerable: use of the canal to irrigate vines. But only 18 per cent of the 57,000 acres actively using the canal's water are under vine. The water is used mainly in the non-vinegrowing plain south of Nîmes, where yields of fruit, asparagus and tomatoes have risen sharply.

But it is in the foothills behind Béziers, far to the west, that the vineyards are the poorest, with soil often unsuited for VDQS, and here the farms could benefit most from transformation, using the water from the Cévennes dams. Yet it is here that the small farmers are the most stubborn. France's leading viticultural expert, Professor Milhau of Montpellier University, explained to me: 'A lot of those vineyards up behind Béziers are on quite the wrong soil and ought to go. But vinegrowing has been in those lazy farmers' blood for centuries – it's a religion. The other big problem is that many of the vines are hired out on a share-cropping basis by absentee landlords, middle-class people who live in the cities. And they can't be bothered to make changes – you see, the vine round here is considered *un métier noble*, it's not ungentlemanly like pig-breeding.'

Despite this considerable failure with the vines, the canal in itself has been a technical and administrative success. Several foreign countries have copied the ideas that underlie it. Provided that the problems of marketing and fruit surpluses can be solved, the areas not under vine will probably succeed in becoming, as is planned, a 'French California'. The growth of ventures such as Libby's shows that a new dynamism, linked with the canal, is beginning to have the desired influence on the region, at least around Nîmes. But it will take a generation or more before the 'tyranny of the vine' fades to the right proportions in the areas to the west, where it is strongest. And not until then is the canal likely to become economically viable.

The tourist project, like the canal, was Lamour's original idea, though its official endorsement, in 1962, must be credited to the Fifth Republic, not the Fourth. Between the mouth of the Rhône and the Pyrenees lay one hundred miles of splendid sandy beaches, hitherto largely unexploited because of the mosquitoes, the marshy lagoons just inland and the flat, relatively unbeautiful scenery. But Europe's tourist hordes were growing each year, the Riviera and the Costa Brava were saturated: where were the extra crowds to go? and how was France to remove the threat to her tourist balance of trade, caused partly by the lack of space and high prices in Provence?

As the Government pondered these problems, it seemed that the ideal solution might be to build a chain of new popular resorts along this coast, and so help re-animate the Languedoc too. First the Government made war on the mosquitoes, successfully, with a chemical process that killed their larvae. Then it prepared a master-plan for six resorts, and in 1963 began buying up land at key points. This was done secretly, through third parties, to avoid sudden speculation. Surprisingly the secret was actually kept, and nearly 7,000 acres were acquired on the cheap before the project was revealed at all, whereupon prices shot up all along the coast, sometimes a hundredfold. But round its own little enclaves the Government marked out wider zones, where under a new law it gave itself the right to regulate prices and, if it wished, pre-empt land at its own figure. Thus, in the places that matter, speculation that might have ruined the project at an early stage was kept right down; and even the severest critics of the régime admit that this part of the operation has been a great success. 'No Left-wing Government in France could have done it,' a Marxist professor at Montpellier told me: 'It needed the connivance of the big financiers.'

A special inter-ministerial committee in Paris master-minds the project, while a series of locally constituted Sociétés d'Economie Mixte are in charge of providing the infrastructure and public services for each resort. When the land is ready for building, most of it is sold or leased to private firms who are now constructing the hotels, villas and casinos, and will run them on a profit basis as anywhere else. But they have to adhere closely to the architectural master-plan, which is the charge of Georges Candilis, the brilliant Greek who was le Corbusier's assistant for ten years. This is capitalism, but controlled. 'We want to avoid the anarchy of Florida or the Costa del Sol,' I was told.

Another important aim was to keep rents and hotel prices down and to encourage rather more 'social' and 'popular' tourism than on the Riviera. This was a main reason for the anti-speculation measures, linked with the official campaign to dissuade quite so many Frenchmen, and others, from preferring the beaches of cheaper lands like Spain. So the Touring Club de France, the Club Méditerranée and other such bodies were encouraged to buy land in the Languedoc for holiday camps and modest villas; and some low-cost flats will be subsidized by using them out of season as lodgings for Montpellier students. All this makes good sense, in an age of mass tourism. Unfortunately, the Government has found that this policy conflicts with other realities. Under the Fifth Plan alone it invested 350m francs in the project, and has come under heavy pressure from its financial partners, the State and private banks, to amortize its costs quickly. It finds it can get far higher and quicker returns by encouraging luxury flats and hotels than it can from 'social' tourism, and more of these are being built than was planned originally. The private flats are selling well to rich Parisians, Germans and others; but there is not yet much sign of the promised cheaper holiday housing, apart from a number of camping sites. 'This is a commercial victory for the Government, but a moral defeat,' said one local sceptic. In their final form, the resorts will have more in common than was intended with the rich new development around Cannes, even if, with their Corbusier-style sun-terraces and garden cities, they will show little visual resemblance to a traditional seaside town.

Thousands of acres of cypresses were first planted to act as windbreaks, new roads were built, and dredgers set to work on preparing pleasure-ports. In the summer of 1969 the first tourists began to arrive at the first of the resorts, la Grande Motte, south-east of Montpellier, and Port Barcarès, near Perpignan. Candilis and his colleagues have built Cannes from scratch in the middle of nowhere, in the style of Brasilia – and the effect is weird. When I first visited la Grande Motte in March 1969 I found the strangest urban landscape, with the first tendrils of tourist activity beginning to sprout up through the concrete jungle of the huge building site. A few boutiques and cafés had already dared open their doors. Two salesgirls in a beauty shop were waiting for clients who did not come, staring with expressions of utter sadness at the workmen outside the window. It was like a shot from Antonioni. But two summers later, la Grande Motte was finished. The pleasure-port with its 1,800 boats is now as busy as any on the Côte d'Azur. Coloured sun-blinds cover the honeycomb façades of the notorious pyramid-shaped blocks of holiday flats. The visitors seem happy – though I'm not sure that such an artificial and futuristic setting would be to everyone's taste for a holiday. However la Grande Motte is always full in high summer now – and it can take 40,000 tourists at a time.

When the nine new resorts are all completed, they will contain 300,000 tourist beds, half as many as on the whole Riviera. Work is going ahead only a little behind schedule, and the number of visitors to the coast rose from 500,000 in 1965 to 1,640,000 ten years later. Foreign investors have been showing an increasing interest – not only the Dutch and Germans but also the Japanese and British. A Japanese supermarket consortium has taken over the pleasure-ship *Lydia*, berthed high and dry on the beach at Port Barcarès and now used as a casino and fun-palace. Near Perpignan the British are developing a £6·5 million nudist resort, with 500 bungalows, marina, discotheque and so on. It is to be called Aphrodite. 'Nudism is a growth industry,' said the architect. Most of the clients are expected to be French and German, rather than British; but one wag pointed out that this is not very logical, as it is the French and Germans who can still afford to buy clothes.

There is one other development that in some ways has done more than anything, so far, to reanimate the Languedoc – and that is the arrival of several hundred thousand repatriate *pieds noirs** from Algeria. Some 25,000 settled in Montpellier alone in 1962–3, swelling its population by one-fifth. The absorption by France of over 800,000 *pieds noirs*, most of them in the Midi, has been one of the great unsung achievements of the 1960s, and bears witness to the elasticity of the economy as well as to the Government's astuteness and the tolerance of the French. There has been remarkably little friction of any sort, and though there was some

* When the first French settlers arrived in Algeria, the barefoot Muslims called them after their black shoes – and the nickname has stuck.

initial hardship in the refugee camps of Marseille, Government resettlement grants have helped virtually all the *pieds noirs* to find new homes, jobs or businesses. Some who at first settled in the north found they did not like the climate or the local temperament, and many of them have drifted back south where they find closer affinities. The ones in Montpellier are mostly Oranais, either of Midi origins themselves, or else of Spanish descent like many Montpelliérains. This and the climate make them feel at home, even though they no longer have flocks of Muslim servants. Though in Oran or Algiers they produced the thugs and diehards of the OAS, back in France those same characteristics of toughness and perseverance show the bright side of their medal; they have bought up dying farms or businesses and are making them buzz. In the Languedoc, their hard-working vitality acts as a catalyst on the local rhythm of life, especially in commerce. In some parts of the Midi, especially around the Garonne, they have helped to stimulate agriculture by importing a new outlook as well as the modern techniques they used on the much larger estates of North Africa. As someone said, 'They see the Midi as the kind of challenge to them that Africa was in the last century.'

In one village near Montpellier, the sole local café had been quietly stagnating for years; then some *pieds noirs* bought it up, modernized and enlarged it, and now it is full every night with young ex-Oranais playing with the juke-box and pin-tables. In Montpellier I had an intriguing experience. It is today a town of quite exceptionally pretty girls with brown skins and bold figures, dressed in gaily coloured slacks. Sitting near an animated nest of them, in one of the student cafés in the town's main square, a memory came into my mind that I could not at first identify. Where had I seen girls precisely like these before? Then I remembered. These girls were like the hysterical crowds of *Algérie française* youth in Oran in the May 1958 revolution. And Oran, in the old days, had the loveliest European girls in the world. Later I was told that the café I had been sitting in was the *pied noir* student headquarters.

A hundred miles or so to the west, the sprawling region known as Midi-Pyrénées is one of the most backward and neglected –

save for its turbulent capital, Toulouse. This city of rose-red brick provides the most fascinating example in all France of the paradoxes inherent in the conflict between State regional policies and local attitudes. On the one hand, you can look at this conflict as Government dynamism struggling against local inertia; or else, as local tradition and character trying to assert itself against stifling Parisian centralism. The Toulousains are a people with an exceptional pride in their ancient and lovely city, and with a long anti-Paris tradition; they are also by nature rather lazy, and have long been suspicious of modern industry. Yet the Government in the past decade or so has chosen Toulouse as the number-one testing ground of its campaign to promote new activities in the most outlying provinces. Helped by a local rural exodus to Toulouse which has provided a huge new labour pool, the Government has massively implanted new industries and scientific centres and encouraged the immigration from Paris of new modern-minded élites. Thus today there are two Toulouses, two societies, new and old, the one imposed on the other – and they uneasily co-exist.

Since the *mairie* has remained largely in the hands of the 'old Toulousains', local initiative has played a lesser part in the city's phenomenal post-war development than has the State or spontaneous population factors. Not only has the city drained much of the surplus farming folk from the poor smallholdings of its hinterland, it has also taken in 30,000 *pieds noirs*, to add to the 25,000 Spanish exiles who settled after the Civil War. Sixty years ago Toulouse was a sleepy market town. Since 1939 its size has more than doubled, to reach 450,000 (with suburbs), a growth rate second only to Grenoble's. Recently it seems to have crossed that mysterious threshold where an ordinary town begins to take on the atmosphere and habits of a metropolis: the suburbs grow larger than the city itself, townsfolk become commuters, Paris-style quick-lunch bars and night-clubs spring up, and you can no longer reach the open country in a pleasant walk from the centre.

But Toulouse's development has had to face economic difficulties, due to geography as much as to local lack of enterprise. It is out on the rim of the EEC, and not even on the sea (like Bordeaux), nor on a major river route. It is in a cul-de-sac; its nearest neighbour, Spain, lies across high mountains. Toulouse often regards its vocation as to be 'the gateway to Spain' and to open up new markets there for France. But this is not easy, so long as Spain's political insularity remains, and until a new tunnel is built under the Pyrenees, a project often discussed but slow to take shape. In the meantime, why should new industry want to settle in a town so badly placed? To counter this problem the Government decided to make a special effort, using as its starting-point the existing aircraft and armament factories that had been set up here around the time of the First World War in order to be as far from the Germans as possible. In the 1920s the city's aerial vocation had taken another stride when Mermoz, Saint-Exupéry and others pioneered flights to Africa, and southerly Toulouse was chosen as their base. Then, after the Second War, the Government developed it as the capital of the French aircraft-building industry,* first with the Caravelle, now with Concorde and Airbus.

The Government was aware also of a need to diversify, to avoid any reliance on the kind of older heavy industries (such as armaments) whose transport costs would suffer from Toulouse's position. Aeronautics seemed to link naturally with electronics, so Paris decided recently to make Toulouse the key centre in its drive to expand this industry. It implanted the French firm, CII, and enticed subsidiaries of two American ones including Motorola.† A complementary step has been the decision to make the city France's leading centre for scientific research and higher studies in electronics, aeronautics and space. The two principal aeronautic Grandes Ecoles have been moved here from Paris, and scores of other scientific colleges and institutes have been set up. The science faculty (now a separate university) has been expanded, and Toulouse today has more students (40,000) than any other town outside Paris. The aim is to sidestep geographic isolation by making this '*la capitale de la matière grise*', where advanced industries and research centres can help each other. The interaction is not yet as successful as in Grenoble, but a start has been made. And the new grey matter comes to Toulouse quite willingly

* See pp. 112–16.
† See p. 85.

– the relative nearness of mountains and sea, the warmth, the architecture, a better-than-average cultural life, all these are reasons why Parisians have been readier to migrate to new jobs here than to most parts of France.

Two Toulouses. You can see the contrast, architecturally: like some enormous Neapolitan vanilla-and-strawberry ice, the old city, all mellow rose-red brick, is ringed by a white circle of new flats, factories, colleges and laboratories. The Government has grafted this brisk and gleaming super-structure on to the old one. Two populations, two mentalities and ways of life, co-exist uneasily and are only just beginning to mix. One, the new élites, the energetic scientists, pilots, professors and managers, and with them the *pieds noirs* and other immigrants with their pioneering instincts. The other, the 'real' Toulouse – its bourgeoisie secluded within their graceful pink palaces in the city centre, easy-going and southern, historically disdainful of industry, patriotically involved in the living past of a city that once ruled the whole Languedoc. *L'anti-Paris* Toulouse has been called, and tribal memories linger of the brutal colonization of the city by Paris after the suppression of the Cathars in 1220. So today's economic and intellectual 'colonization', however well-meant, is also treated warily.

This rivalry with Paris has been a hindrance in local affairs, as elsewhere in France. You have only to get stuck behind a fuming lorry in one of the city's endless traffic jams, or trudge through the mud of an unkempt pavement, to realize that all has not been well with local government. Toulouse for many decades has been a Socialist and Radical stronghold, and until the 1971 local elections the *mairie* was in the hands of a fiercely anti-Gaullist, left-of-centre coalition, while most councillors were from the 'old Toulouse' population hostile to Paris. Hence mayor and prefect tended to obstruct each other's schemes, and public services lagged far behind the city's growth. 'Paris is holding back funds because we have *mal voté*,' the town clerk complained to me, and, like Fréville, he made a snide remark about Bordeaux's advantages under Chaban-Delmas. But the fault was on both sides.

The chief casualty of this feuding has been the former mayor's grandiose project of Le Mirail, a suburb designed by Candilis on

Corbusian lines and due to house 100,000 people. Under the cross-fire of ministerial vetoes and local bungling and corruption, Le Mirail fell far behind schedule; badly sited, with inadequate services, it failed even to find enough tenants. Its grim symmetry of elephantine white-and-brown apartment blocks became indeed a white elephant.

Toulouse finally fell to the Right in the 1971 local elections, and the new Mayor, Pierre Baudis, is a Giscardian, in alliance with the Gaullists. This is now leading to easier co-operation with Paris. There are signs that the State is now putting more cash into essential bilateral municipal schemes, and not just into boosting industry and research on its own terms. But is it right that a town should be penalized for its political views? Moreover, French centralism applies not only to government but also to business; almost all the banks in Toulouse are run from Paris, and most of the big local firms have their headquarters in Paris or overseas. This helps to explain why locally owned industry has proved so lethargic. Toulouse's prestigious aviation and electronics firms may be technologically very advanced, but recently they have proved vulnerable to the economic crisis, and the difficulties at Aérospatiale and with CII have caused these factories to contract and have increased local unemployment. This may be a transient phase. But meanwhile, in other respects, Toulouse cannot really be called a modern industrial town, yet. Thousands of tiny firms in textiles, leather and food-processing – most with fewer than 10 employees each – are dying out as fast as the big ones grow, so the employment situation is not improving very fast.

There are signs however that 'old Toulouse' is now waking from its ancient slumber to embrace the industrial age and to tackle its growth problems more energetically. Symbolically, the former president of the Chamber of Commerce, a seigneur worthy of the local folklore museum, was in 1971 ousted by a younger Toulousain industrialist with whizz-kid ideas that include building an international trade centre. A few newer local firms, notably in textiles and chemicals, are showing unwonted enterprise: one is doing a roaring export trade to Germany in Carnaby Street-type leather clothes. And, another portent, the new mayor's alderman for public relations is none other than a young Arizona-trained executive at Motorola, also a local man. The previous mayor was a Socialist of the most conservative brand, the opposite of Dubedout. There is no special virtue in Toulouse moving Right, save that in this case, because of the personalities involved, it happens to mean a more forward-looking brand of local government and smoother links with Paris. At last the old Toulouse is beginning to come to terms with the new Toulouse and to apply the motto, 'If you can't beat 'em, join 'em.'

This today is a fascinating example of a medium-sized provincial town beginning consciously to realize its vocation as a big international city, rather as Manchester did a century ago. Toulouse is taking a new look both at its future and its past. There is a conscious revival of regional culture, as in Brittany – typical of it is the newly created 'Ballets Occitans', a brilliant young folklore troupe who are reviving the rich local heritage of song and dance. But – in culture, politics or industry – the issue facing Toulouse, as other towns, is whether this new regionalism is to be a defence against Paris, or is to work with it and with Europe. Toulousains are pro-Europe, and they are throwing off some of their old insularity. But their pride is still offended by their lack of real autonomy. So long as Paris continues to hold the strings, Toulouse's vocation as a real provincial capital – in the German or even Italian manner – must remain limited.

Another and very different problem is that Toulouse's growth may create a 'desert' round it, almost as bad as the old *désert français* caused by Paris. Instead of radiating and animating its rural hinterland, Toulouse simply drains its population; several departments round here, notably the Gers, the Lot and the Ariège, are among the poorest and emptiest in France. The rural exodus may be necessary in itself, but it is dangerous if it simply creates a void for miles around; and in some parts of these departments there is not enough labour or resources left for repairing roads and buildings or fallen telephone wires. In some areas tourism might help to provide a solution; but it will need heavy investment in new services, and in creating and staffing the national parks now being created. Another solution, now being applied, is to develop the medium-sized and smaller towns, especially the capitals of departments, and build some of them up as counter-poles of influence to Toulouse, just as Toulouse is to Paris. In many such towns the local artisans and cottage-industries have died away, and not much has yet taken their place. It is usually hard to persuade new industries to settle in a small out-of-the-way place, if it is far from Paris. Sometimes, on main roads in the Massif Central, one sees hopeful hoardings on the edge of little towns: 'Industrialists! Choose Noirétable for your new factory! We shall be proud to welcome you!' One wonders how many inquiries they receive.

The Aveyron, north-east of Toulouse, in the south of the Massif Central, is an example of a department literally fighting for its life. It is on a knife-edge between considerable new prosperity and further decline, with strong forces pulling in both directions. Its population, now 279,000 over 3,426 square miles, has dropped by a third since 1886, and on many of the chalky upland *causses* the villages are dying. But the Aveyronnais are an unusually tough and enterprising people, more prepared for an uphill struggle than the soft plainsmen of the Languedoc. Their young farmers, as I have shown, are already fighting with some success to improve and modernize agriculture, the Aveyron's main industry. But they cannot operate in a void. They need flourishing local centres, for markets, shopping, schools, social and cultural life, especially if the next generation is to find a life on the land congenial. The nearest big town, Toulouse, is one hundred miles away over difficult winding roads.

The Aveyron's one real industrial town, Decazeville, collapsed into irremediable depression a few years ago when its coal-mines wore thin and ceased to be competitive. When the State began to close them down, 800 miners protested by staying at the bottom of a pit for several weeks over Christmas 1961. The miners were offered resettlement in State mines in other parts of France, but they stubbornly wanted to stay in their own area, and demanded that new industries be provided. Yet no industry wanted to come to a dying coal town on a remote branch railway line.

It was a new blow for the Aveyron. Fortunately its capital, Rodez, has fared much better, and today is an unexpectedly thriving and go-ahead town of some 45,000 people. All around, for scores of miles, there is nothing but chalky plateaux, and brown hills with straggling farms. But Rodez itself, in the valley of the river Aveyron, is an oasis of modernity with its Parisian shops, newly decorated hotels and many new blocks of flats. It benefits from its position on one of the main tourist routes through the Massif Central, and also from being the marketing capital of a large agricultural area, although not a rich one. Another secret of its success is that though people emigrate from the Aveyron they do not forget it. Its boundaries are much the same as those of the old province of Rouergue, and so it is less artificial than most departments and keeps its own regional pride. Many of its *émigrés* make their fortune in Paris but keep up the old links: men like Marcellin Cazes who founded and ran the famous literary café, Chez Lipp, at St-Germain-des-Prés, and then came back to die at his old home in Rodez in 1965. Similarly when a big Paris chemical factory had to be evacuated for strategic reasons in 1939, its managing director chose Rodez of all remote places, because that was where he came from. Today, with 800 workers, the factory is one of the causes of Rodez' prosperity. Another cause, oddly enough, is the town's vocation as a centre of boarding-schools: 'It's really our chief local industry,' I was told. 'There are 10,000 schoolchildren here.' Because the air is so fresh, and venial distractions so few, many parents would rather send their children away here than, for example, to Cannes with its fleshpots. And so the streets of this unlikely backwoods Seaford are regularly full of crocodiles of uniformed pupils, led by nuns or priests or young State *surveillants*.

Finally, Rodez has succeeded in reviving its local artisanal industries. Woodwork, furniture, packaging, decorative iron-work – a score of little firms of this sort have sprung up or expanded since the war, whereas in the smaller towns of the Cévennes, to the south-east, the old silk and hosiery industries are dying. Rodez is just large enough, and sufficiently enterprising, to benefit from the new urban trends in France, and so acts as a catchment centre in a region of heavy rural exodus. The problem is to help less enterprising or fortunate towns to do the same.

With this in view, the Government since 1972 has embarked on what it calls its '*politique des Villes Moyennes*'. The aim is to help towns of between 20,000 and 100,000 inhabitants to attract new industry and to improve their town-planning and other amenities, so that they can become vital local centres and thus counter-balance the pull of the big towns such as Toulouse and Lyon – just as, in the 1950s and 1960s, the policy was to build up those big towns to counter-balance Paris. Special grants and other incentives are now given for new industry in these medium-sized towns. The towns are also being encouraged to sign contracts with the State, whereby they receive subsidies to help them with urban improvements. The first town to sign such a contract, in 1974, was in fact Rodez, which in return for some State aid is now com-mitted to a programme of renovating its historic centre, creating pedestrian precincts, improving parking facilities and so on. More than twenty other towns have signed these contracts – towns as diverse as Annecy and Dieppe, or Vannes and Béthune (in the Lille mining belt) – and some sixty others are preparing to do so. These contracts are basically for improving the environ-ment, rather than for helping the economy directly, but the argu-ment is that unless 'quality of life' in these towns is made more attractive, new firms will not be enticed to settle in them. The policy is meeting with some success, on a modest scale, and is in line with the Government's new objectives of combating an excessive drift to the big cities that would leave much of France depopulated. The policy also marks a certain retreat from the kind of centralized technocratic control used, for instance, in the Languedoc schemes. A town, once its programme has been approved, is left to get on with the job itself.

Of the other *métropoles d'équilibre* besides Toulouse, the one now changing the fastest is Bordeaux. Until about 1958 it had the reputation of being the least active of France's larger towns, and after the war it fell from fourth to sixth place, overtaken in size by Toulouse and Nice. Its narrow-spirited mercantile ruling class, straight out of the pages of Mauriac, still clung to the illusion of Bordeaux as a great seaport. They rebuilt the damaged harbour after the war, only to find that half its cranes stayed idle. The end of France's colonial links, the decline of the shipping trade for coal and wood, the relative loss of ground by Bordeaux wines to those of Burgundy and elsewhere, all spelt stagnation to the city and its port, which, apart from the wine, and the wood of the Landes forests, had no industry on which to depend.

But the ambitious young mayor, Jacques Chaban-Delmas, was a Gaullist of exceptional influence, and after 1958 his hour came. Using his new prestige as President of the National Assembly, and then as Prime Minister, he persuaded the snobbish and cautious burghers to accept a change of course. More important, he could now secure the right funds and decisions from Ministries. Over a hundred new factories – most of them small ones, admittedly – arrived in Bordeaux from 1960 to 1965. Today, large areas of the city are being rebuilt or extended, new bridges and ring motorways have been completed, and the new university campus is one of the largest and most attractive in France. Most important, a big new deep-water port for tankers and container ships was opened in 1976 at Le Verdon, 60 miles north of the city on the tip of the Médoc peninsula. The local claim is that it will eventually be the largest roll-on-roll-off container port on Europe's Atlantic coast, and a rival to Rotterdam. Its south-westerly position is seen as its crucial asset. The port's director told me, 'We are relatively so near the Americas and Africa that we can cut three or four days off the return Atlantic voyage to, say, Le Havre or Rotterdam, and this could save a big ship a million francs.' And he added with usual French modesty, 'We shall transform the geographical economy of Western Europe!'

Marseille is a much greater port, with a scarcely less distinguished mayor, Gaston Defferre. But he is not exactly a Gaullist. Despite his difficulties with the State administration, his record of housing and other public works has been striking: a Métro; a tunnel under the Old Port to help cure traffic jams that are amongst the worst in Europe; and now, the rebuilding of a large part of the city's centre. This brash, torrid, proletarian town is the second in France (population, over one million), and it remains the first seaport of the Mediterranean despite a certain decline in its traditional sea-trade. Now, thirty miles to the west, a large new port and industrial centre has been built at Fos, near the Rhône delta. With its tanker berths, refineries and steelworks, it has been marked out to become 'the Europort of the South', quite as much as Le Verdon. Unfortunately, its industrial development has been badly affected since 1974 by the crisis in the steel industry; and Marseille, instead of collaborating with the Fos venture, has regarded it with a certain rivalry. Fos is not yet the success it was planned to be; it typifies both the good and the bad side of the new French love of grand-scale industrial planning. But it would be premature to write it off as a failure. It will benefit eventually from the new Rhône-Rhine canal, due to be completed by 1985.

Lyon, like Marseille, benefits from a good strategic position, and is booming. Its new international airport, opened in 1975, is much the largest and most modern in France outside the Paris area. Part of the centre of Lyon, an area known as *La Part Dieu*, has been rebuilt and now contains – controversially – one of the largest new business and commercial complexes in Western Europe. Of the other *métropoles*, Strasbourg has been stimulated by its European role and by the new trade along the Rhine. It has attracted its share of new industry, but feels the pressure of German competition. At Lille, the difficulties of textiles and coal are balanced by the rise of the steel industries at nearby Dunkerque; the town is doing all right, but not brilliantly. Over in the west, the graceful city of Nantes has many of the signs of new prosperity, with animated streets and some fine modern shops and other buildings. Rather like Bordeaux, it is a town with a strong conservative tradition, now acquiring a new vitality.

The eighth and last of the *métropoles* is a hybrid: Nancy-Metz, twin capitals of Lorraine and inseparable rivals. Nancy is the aristocratic university town, Metz the energetic centre of heavy industry. They complement each other well, and their province was, until not long ago, one of the most prosperous and successful in France. But today Lorraine has run into trouble. It is one of the few regions of France where the problem is out-of-date industry, rather than lack of industry. The great iron-ore mines, basis of Lorraine's wealth, are beginning to wear thin; even on the home market they can no longer easily compete with higher-grade imported ore. Recession has also hit the Moselle coal-mines and the outmoded Vosges textile firms, both typically vulnerable sectors. Even the steelworks are now contracting, too. Wendel-Sidelor, one of the largest French steel combines, decided in 1971 to close nineteen plants in Lorraine, in order to switch investment to its vast new steelworks at Fos, where conditions for productivity are far more favourable. This threatened the jobs of 12,000 Lorrains, and caused an outcry. The Lorrains are unusually hard-working, skilled and resourceful – just the kind of labour that industry likes. This makes them all the more indignant about their present troubles, but it will probably help them to win through. Moreover, they recently acquired a protagonist of international repute: Jean-Jacques Servan-Schreiber, the controversial Radical leader, who won a famous by-election at Nancy in 1970 on a local issue, and has since vocally championed Lorraine against what he calls the 'colonization' of Paris.

FACTORIES, MOTORWAYS, TELEPHONES: A VARIABLE RECORD

THIS survey of a few typical towns and regions may have shown how uneven the success of the policy of industrial decentralization has been. The greatest achievement is that the growth of industry in the Paris region has been slowed right down and finally halted altogether. The statistics are revealing. From 1954 to 1962, the number of industrial jobs in the Paris region rose from 1,371,000 to 1,453,000, while the figure for the provinces rose in about the same proportion, from 4,041,000 to 4,222,000. This was no great feat for decentralization. However, from 1962 to 1973, the Paris figure dropped from 1,453,000 to 1,376,000, while that for the provinces rose from 4,222,000 to 4,892,000 – that is, by 15 per cent. This is some victory for the persistent efforts of the Government's regional development board, DATAR.

Yet we must add three qualifications to this success story. First, since 1973 the economic crisis has inevitably slowed growth in the provinces, though hopefully this will prove temporary. Second, firms have been more inclined to set up new plant in the provinces than transfer existing plant from Paris. Third, the regions which have most benefited from the new industry are not necessarily those which need it most.

The first point is too obvious to need further comment. As for the second, in the 1950s a number of smaller firms did transfer their plant from Paris, but by about 1960 nearly all those firms wishing to make this kind of move had done so, and the trend slowed right down. More recently the Government has imposed heavier restrictions on extensions of plant in the Paris area, and this has impelled a few more firms to uproot themselves completely – for instance, some electronics factories now installed in the Bordeaux, Nantes and Brittany areas. But in general it is true that the gradual shift in industrial balance between Paris and the provinces has been due to the dynamic growth of the latter rather than to transplantations. Renault and Simca, for instance, have expanded by opening several new factories in the provinces, although they both keep their central plant in the Paris area.

The third point is the most serious. Statistics confirm that a Paris firm will readily put a new factory within 150 miles of the capital, but will usually be less keen to go farther out. On the whole it is the towns of what is called '*la grande couronne parisienne*' – Amiens, Reims, Orléans, Rouen, etc. – that have attracted most new industry, together with some a little farther out, such as Caen and Le Mans. Their revival is at least one step forward, for in 1950 the 'desert' began at the edge of Paris, certainly to the west and south. But it does not solve the general imbalance and waste of resources. A number of towns much farther away, especially in the south-east of France, have also found it quite easy to attract new industries – Grenoble is the best example but not the only one. However there are large areas of the West and South-West where the smaller towns especially are seriously lacking in employment. Since 1955 the Government has been seeking to correct this imbalance with a complex system of incentives. Subsidies for new factories' installations costs are nil in the case of towns within the greater Paris orbit, but could go up to 25 per cent in many of the more remote or under-privileged areas, and cover up to 60 per cent of costs in the case of transfers of plant *from* Paris. There are also tax exemptions in many parts of France, and other forms of aid. In 1956–73, over 4,500 operations benefited in some form from these incentives, although they have had variable success – better in some specific towns (such as Nantes, Bordeaux and Clermont-Ferrand) than in Brittany or the southern Massif Central. In 1976, DATAR stepped up the grants, in order to combat the effects of the economic crisis, but it is doubtful how far cash incentives in themselves can be the solution. For many firms they present an attractive bonus, but are rarely decisive when it comes to choosing a location. Other factors usually weigh more heavily, such as the need to keep fairly near to the financial and commercial world of Paris, the fear of not finding enough skilled labour in the remoter areas, or the high transport costs over long distances. So, although the 'French desert' has become much smaller, it does still exist in some areas.

Some firms have hesitated to take the plunge for fear that they could not persuade their executives and senior technicians to settle in the provinces. Often it is the wives who are cautious about moving from Paris to find themselves in a new town without friends and without a good *lycée* or university for the children (significantly, it is university towns, such as Caen and Grenoble, that have expanded the fastest). Or if *cadres* are ready to decentralize, the skilled workers prove more stubborn. For, although there is a new mobility in France among the educated classes and the emigrating peasantry, the third section of the nation (the urban workers) still tend to be sedentary in their outlook, as in many countries. Like the miners of Decazeville, they will rarely move to find work elsewhere, and especially not from Paris. This remains a problem for the DATAR planners. But at least the attitudes of *cadres* and their wives, and of many technicians, have been evolving radically in the past decade or so. Today, more young middle-class Parisians are moving to new jobs in the provinces than following the classic route of Julien Sorel – seeking fame and fortune in the capital. It is almost *more* chic now to say that you live and work in Avignon or Annecy than in the *treizième* – a strange reversal. And nearly all these emigrants are happy with the results, especially when they move to the sunny South, or near to the sea or mountains. The rhythm of life is much calmer than in Paris, the children can have more fun, there are even good theatres and concerts in many towns, and gradually you can recreate a new social circle. 'I've had two nervous breakdowns in Paris, and now I'm happier here,' said an executive of a new electronics factory, on the balcony of his chalet overlooking Lake Geneva at Thonon.

But though such people will readily emigrate to the cheerful South, they will think twice about settling, say, in Limoges, or Charleville in the leaden-skied Ardennes. So, for this and other reasons, the over-all pattern of regional development remains strikingly uneven. Where there *is* a really dynamic local initiative, even in a small town like Falaise, or else a special Government effort, it usually bears fruit. But if the general policy has not worked better, it may be partly the Government's own fault. The Left has often accused it of not being tough enough with firms, or of yielding to pressure from the Patronat – which is less concerned with environment or unemployment than with competitiveness and thus tends to prefer the *status quo*. Citroën spent years successfully resisting official efforts to persuade it to shift its huge main factory from the Quai de Javel near the Eiffel Tower; on the other hand, it is reported that in order to get the CSF to set up its electronics plant in Brest, the Government resorted to threats of suspending its valued State contracts. It is hard to say which case is the more typical. The Government does sometimes allow its own rules to be broken, and it has not done all that it might to decentralize its own industries. It is true that several State aircraft and electronics plants have been moved out of Paris recently, but it is partly the State's fault that so much of the car industry is still in the Paris area; Renault's main factory remains at Billancourt.

There might even be an element of truth in Left-wing allegations that the campaign for developing the South and West has become a bit two-faced since the mid-1960s. The development of the Common Market and of German competition has made it more imperative than ever to build up French industry where it is already strong – in the eastern half of the country. Heavy industrial firms in the Rhône Valley and Alsace have been allowed to expand at full tilt. This may have been right and necessary in the short term; but there have not always been the resources to carry out both policies at once. As one Socialist put it to me, 'The two main planks of the régime's industrial policy, concentration of firms and deconcentration of their plant, often contradict each other.'

It is often argued, too, that industrial decentralization would be more successful if the State were to move more of its own central decision-making services to the provinces. It is because the big nationalized banks and other powers of financial decision are all in Paris that so many firms tend to keep their head offices there even when their factories are elsewhere. Centralization of the banks is a late phenomenon that was continuing even in the 1930s, and though today the process is halted, it is only beginning to move into reverse. One of the three largest State banks, Crédit Lyonnais, bears the name of a city that before 1914 was a great banking centre but today, as one Lyon financier told me indignantly, 'It is little better than a village in terms of banking autonomy.' He added: 'It is this, as much as anything, that hinders Lyon from becoming a real capital like Frankfurt or Turin. At least civil servants are now aware of the problem, and you can discuss it without being thought some sort of Girondin terrorist.'

In 1975 another of the biggest State banks, the Banque Nationale de Paris, took a momentous step. It transferred its regional management offices from Paris to the regions themselves. Hitherto, if a client, say, in Marseille, wanted a loan, the decision would be referred to the bank's south-eastern regional office located *in Paris*, at its headquarters! But now, new centres for dealing with such questions have been built in the towns themselves, in green parks in the outskirts – first in Lille and Lyon, with others to follow. This kind of physically decentralized decision-taking has long been the norm in many countries, and France is now timidly and belatedly following suit.

There is now a move to transplant lock-stock-and-barrel to the provinces certain national services, which do not thereby cease to be centralized units, but which at least stop cluttering up Paris. Thus the BNP recently transferred its main technical and publishing department to a site outside Orléans, and in 1975 a third big State bank, Société Générale, moved its securities department, involving 1,200 people, to Nantes. These moves have been successful, as have the recent transfers of certain Grandes Ecoles from Paris to Toulouse, Rennes and elsewhere. The Government is even beginning to transplant one or two of its own ministerial services: the Quai d'Orsay has moved to Nantes its department that deals with French citizens resident abroad; while the State meteorological office is being shifted to Toulouse.

These moves are useful, in terms of helping to decongest Paris and create new jobs in the provinces. But they are still on a very limited scale; most Ministries refuse to take part. Moreover, such moves rarely imply any major decentralization of decision-making to the regions. It is true that the regional Prefects now have their own budgets for certain local projects and activities, and no longer have to refer every decision to Paris.* But, in a country where the State tightly supervises financial life, all the main services of the Ministry of Finance remain in Paris, and for matters such as funds or permits for industry, all must still go via Paris. This encourages private finance to stay in Paris too, and industrial firms to keep their head offices there. A firm may put new factories in the provinces, but keep all its centres of decision in Paris, with the result that domestic air flights will be filled with executives virtually commuting two or three times a week. A few older firms, with family roots in a town, have been trying gamely to keep their head office by their works – Michelin at Clermont-Ferrand is one – but it entails incessant tiresome journeys. Another big firm, Pont-à-Mousson of Lorraine, was always proud of keeping its offices at Nancy near its plant, but one day when I called there I was told: 'Sorry, there's no one you can talk to here. The top staff have all just moved to Paris.' They had capitulated. Sometimes this happens because, if you want influential directors on your board, you must choose Parisians. Not only the banks and Ministries are there, but also the foreign clients for sales. What foreign importer bothers to tout round Lyon or Bordeaux, when he will go as a matter of course to Turin or Stuttgart?

This was the picture at least until very recently. Today the Government is finally making an effort to break the vicious circle. It has tightened restrictions on new offices in Paris, which still has 40 per cent of all French office jobs, for 20 per cent of the population. It has created a new body called the Association Bureaux Provinces – similar to the Location of Offices Bureau in Britain –

* See pp. 271–2.

which is trying to woo firms of all kinds to establish their offices away from Paris. The Government is also using its full armoury of publicity to promote Lyon, Nice and Strasbourg in particular as centres for office headquarters, not only national but international. It is now putting almost as much stress on decentralization of services as of industry, but it is still too early to assess the results of this policy. By the summer of 1976, no firm of any note had agreed to move its headquarters to the provinces, although a number – following the lead of the BNP – had begun to increase the size and the powers of decision of their various regional offices. It seems that no real progress is likely until the Ministry of Finance, and one or two other Ministries, set a firm lead by decentralizing their own decision-making structures, thus obliging the rest of the financial world to follow suit. If the vicious circle were broken in this way, the provincial cities with their new liveliness and prosperity could become centres of decision as well. But the decision is basically a political one, and is not likely to find an easy solution in the present climate.

Finally, France must complete the modernization of her structure of transport and communications, if regional development is to be a full success. Here great progress has been made, but the pattern remains uneven: rail and internal air services are excellent; but the motorway programme suffered years of delay and only in the past few years has been tackled seriously; and France is still struggling to make up the notorious backlogs in her telephone system.

In de Gaulle's day, national priorities were selected too much in terms of prestige. The Mont Blanc tunnel, opened in 1965 at a cost of 100m francs, is a marvellous piece of engineering and a useful new link with north Italy, but for some years the investment remained partly wasted because the roads leading to it in that part of France were so poor. They have now been improved. The Pont de Tancarville, the Moselle canal, the Rhône and Rhine dams, the long suspension bridge across the mouth of the Loire, opened in 1975, these are fine achievements, but more is needed. The Pyrenean tunnel scheme is hanging fire. The Channel Tunnel has been postponed indefinitely – alas, not through any fault of

France. Finally in 1975 the Government gave the go-ahead for a project that has been in the air since the eighteenth century, even earlier than the Channel Tunnel: the building of a wide canal linking the Rhône and Saône to the Rhine. This 145-mile canal will take eight years to build, at a cost of 5,600m francs, and will run from Chalon on the Saône to the Rhine near Mulhouse. It will provide Europe with its first complete Mediterranean-to-North Sea waterway, and it will help Lyon to trade with Germany and give Marseille a better chance to compete with Rotterdam for the commerce of the Ruhr. Those feeling sore about it, however, are the Lorrains, already in economic trouble; an earlier rival project for a canal from the Saône to the Moselle, via Nancy, has been finally cancelled.

Railway links between Paris and the main cities are among the fastest and best in the world; but inter-town services, though vastly improved since the war, are still inadequate. Internal air services have now developed rapidly after a slow start. Throughout the 1950s they were held back by narrow-sighted objections from the SNCF, whose interests are not lightly cast aside by the Government because of the money so heavily invested in it after the war. But soon internal air traffic could be neglected no more. The lack was even holding up the factory policy: at least one firm selected Savoy for its plant largely so as to be near the international air link from Geneva to Paris. Since about 1960 Air Inter, the State-run domestic affiliate of Air France and the SNCF, has expanded rapidly – its passenger traffic doubled in 1964–6. Toulouse, for instance, is now linked to Paris by eight flights a day each way. Yet it was only in 1965 that Toulouse, Lyon and Bordeaux became linked with each other at all. Recently these inter-city flights have developed fast. Limoges provides a striking example. It started direct flights to Lyon two years *sooner* than to Paris. Today it also has daily flights to the little town of Aurillac, 100 miles to the south-east. And Limoges' annual passenger traffic grew from 2,800 to 65,000 in 1971–5.

The road network has been a sore subject of debate in this car-mad country. Critics have been ready to point out that although France has some of the highest petrol taxes and other motoring charges in Europe, her record of motorway building was for many years even slower than that of Britain. In 1967, France still had only 490 miles of motorway, less even than Britain (620), and far behind Italy (1,300) and Germany (2,200), although since then things have improved. However, this comparison has always been misleading. France enjoys the legacy of about the best network in Europe of secondary roads and traditional main roads: they are straight, well surfaced (except in cobbled Flanders), well engineered in hilly areas, and a delight compared with most roads in Britain. In most places they are still quite adequate for their traffic. The problem, however, is that in a few key places, mainly on the edge of big towns, or on certain trunk routes in summer, the traditional network has become inadequate. It is thus quite usual to be able to drive for scores of miles at top speed between towns, and then get stuck for hours in some bottleneck.

In 1969, after long delays, the motorway programme was speeded up. By mid-1976 France had 2,260 miles of motorway; it had overtaken Britain and Italy and was now in second place in Europe behind Germany (3,600 miles). The main reason for this spurt is simple: the Government has finally called in private enterprise. For many years it would neither spend much money on motorways itself nor allow private firms to build them. An exception was allowed for the autoroute from Nice to Fréjus, built at great speed with private capital, because it was 'touristic'. But elsewhere roads had always been considered a public service, so they advanced slowly at the whim of State budgets. Then the Government began to realize that bottlenecks might hold up industrial traffic, thus hampering the economy, or even keep foreign tourists away. Finally in 1969 the energetic Minister of Equipment, Albin Chalandon, persuaded the Cabinet to let him entrust some financing to private hands. The decision was opposed by *étatistes* like Michel Debré, who felt it would lead to a 'dismantling of the State', but Chalandon easily found takers for his new projects, and by the early 1970s private firms were at work on several new motorways.

A 750-mile motorway down the length of France, from Lille via Paris and Lyon to Marseille, was laboriously completed (save for the Lyon bypass section) by the State in 1970, and it has cured many of the summer traffic jams at places like Montélimar in the

Rhône valley. Since then, State and private firms have completed motorways from Paris to Caen, to La Ferté-Bernard (near Le Mans) and to Tours; from Lyon to Grenoble; from Marseille via Nice to Italy; and from Orange (on the Lyon–Marseille motorway) across the Languedoc to Narbonne. This last route carries the full weight of summer tourism into north-east Spain, and before it was built the notorious Béziers bottleneck was a congested mass of infuriated tourists. But the final stretches of motorways on the main tourist routes into Spain, both around Perpignan and around Bayonne in the west, have yet to be finished. One problem in populated districts like these is that the sacred French rights of land ownership make sliproads and expropriation a slow and costly business, lasting up to four years. This is why, though France may have better roads linking towns than Britain, it still has fewer modern bypasses.

It has been decided that the economic crisis since 1974 will not affect projects already nearing completion, such as the much-needed Paris–Metz–Strasbourg motorway, but restrictions on funds will cause delay on others scheduled, such as the equally needed Bordeaux–Toulouse–Narbonne link. The crisis has barely reduced traffic, but it has put up building costs hugely, and the motorist has to pay for his new motorways. As in Italy, there have always been tolls on these, except on a few short stretches near main cities; today they run at up to 1·5 francs per kilometre. The ensuing partial boycott keeps some of the old roads clogged up and thus lessens the value of the investment; it is reckoned that motorway traffic might rise by 30 per cent if there were no tolls. But the Ministry of Finance has never allowed the Ministry of Equipment adequate funds for motorways, so many years ago tolls were decided on as the only answer, and private firms have since been allowed to follow suit. The already highly taxed French motorist still has some right to feel aggrieved.

With the Post Office telephone system, matters are still much worse. In no other public service is France more backward. In Britain, telephones tend to break down or yield wrong numbers; in France, they work rather better mechanically, but there are just not enough of them. Over a million names are on waiting-lists for telephones, and it is estimated that another million or so would apply if they did not consider it hopeless. Despite some recent progress, in 1974 the number of lines per 100 people (11·5) was still among the lowest of any industrialized country, below Spain (12·1) and far below Britain (22·5), Germany (19·6) and Sweden (48·3 – the highest figure in the world). Trunk lines in France are still so inadequate that over 30 per cent of long-distance calls fail to get through at first demand, and this shortage cancels out some of the progress that has been made recently in automatizing the system. During the day, you may spend ages dialling fruitlessly a number in some other part of France. The dismal queues waiting to make trunk calls in many a post office are a disgrace for a nation that calls itself modern; and many new factories and offices, especially in the provinces, have to survive for months with only one or two lines. This situation wastes thousands of business man-hours a day, and in a number of cases it has dissuaded firms from decentralizing their plant from Paris. And as if all this were not bad enough, the French telephone service is not only the most inefficient but also one of the most expensive in the Western world. A new subscriber has to pay 500 francs for the privilege of being connected – even if he is simply inheriting a telephone that already exists in the flat into which he is moving, and thus no technical work is required. This sum, like all subscribers' dues, is regarded as a Government tax. And the built-in attitude of the Post Office staff is that subscribers are '*administrés*', not clients. When you get your telephone bill, if there appears to be a mistake on it, you must first pay it in full before you have any right to query it.

The failures of the telephone system have never been due to lack of expertise or technology, but simply to lack of investment and proper organization. After the war, France built the world's longest coaxial cable and pioneered the world's first experiment with long-distance automatic dialling equipment. But, as so often in France, there was then a failure to apply research to practice. Today, she is in the forefront of nations developing the videophone, conference calls networks, the touch-tone (press-button) instrument, and other modernistic devices. Yet three homes in four are still without an ordinary telephone to set beside their washing-machines and other expensive gadgets. One cause of the backlog is that post-war Governments showed a curious tendency to regard the telephone as a private bourgeois luxury rather than an essential tool of modern business. The early plans totally ignored the subject. Another trouble has been that the Postes et Télécommunications is a Ministry run on an outdated civil service basis and has been given little chance to operate the service on proper commercial lines. Added to this are its own internal problems: the vested interests of its bureaucratic staff, the antiquated quality of much of its routine equipment, and – an unavoidable handicap – the cost of keeping up local exchanges and wires in a country as scattered as France.

In the past decade, the Government has had some change of heart, and has been struggling, with modest success, to make up the backlog; since 1967 it has been promising 'top priority' for the telephone. One improvement is that the P. et T. can now float loans, instead of having to finance development from its own State income. Its budget for the telephone increased between 1971 and 1976 from 18,300m to 47,900m francs. And this has borne results: the number of subscribers rose by 70 per cent from 1970 to 1975, so that France now has almost one-quarter as many telephones per capita as Sweden, against one-sixth as many a decade ago – bravo! In 1975, for the first time in ten years, the number of new telephones installed (1·2 million) was actually superior to the number of new demands. So the waiting list has been slightly cut, and the average time a new applicant must wait for an instrument to be installed and connected dropped in 1975 from sixteen to a mere eleven months – fantastic! Modern offices are now actually being built ready equipped with lines. Moreover, the number of inter-city automatic trunk lines was trebled in 1970–75. Some 95 per cent of the network is now automatic (in Brittany and some other areas it is 100 per cent), and internationally so – a peasant on a Breton farmstead, provided he is lucky enough to have secured a telephone, can now lift his receiver and dial Tokyo or São Paolo, whereas five or ten years ago not only would he have had to ask the local village operator and then wait several hours, but the local exchange would have been shut down totally outside office hours. Finally, the P. et T. are catching up with the normal practice in most countries by actually building public telephone booths – at many bus stops, in the streets, outside post offices – whereas previously you had to go inside a post office (when it was open) or use a noisy café, or late at night try the police station. A curious footnote to this saga is that the price of a local call from a public box (40 centimes) is the one item that has not risen in price in France during the steady inflation of the past decade. I have never checked the reason for this, but I assume it is an attempt to placate that angry horde of would-be subscribers who have to wait so long for their own telephone.

They are still having to wait. Demand, especially private, has risen much faster than was forecast, and this is why the backlog has not been reduced faster. While 87 per cent of French homes now have a refrigerator, only 25 per cent have a telephone – and the days are past when the average working-class family thought such an instrument quite outside its grasp. They now expect it. So the P. et T.'s current target for 1982 is to increase the percentage of homes thus equipped to seventy, and cut the average wait to two weeks. Can it be done? In recent years it has become clear that effective modernization needs not only money but a basic administrative shake-up, and this has been blocked by the unions at the P. et T. and their fear of change and reduction in manpower through automation. Recently, plans were put forward for hiving the telephone service off from the ordinary postal service (which has entirely different problems) and putting it on a proper commercial basis, like Electricité de France, but the unions said no, and the plan has been shelved. Here is a classic example of how the State will often prejudice its own modernization policies, through fear of taking measures that would lead to internal unrest. But France is not alone in this.

ENVIRONMENT: THE NEW VOGUE FOR 'A MORE HUMAN KIND OF GROWTH'

Modernization, increased production, these have been the obsessions of French planning since the war. But now the French, like other industrial nations, are suddenly becoming more aware that this kind of expansion is not an end in itself; that it simply creates other problems. Even if the telephone service became totally efficient, if France were laced with a network of new motorways, if all the backward regions got the new factories they need, if power were truly decentralized, even so there would still be a lot left to solve. The coin of urban and industrial growth has another side to it – and today, phrases like 'protecting the environment', 'pollution', 'quality of life', have become quite as much in vogue in France as in Britain or the United States. France, too, now has her doom-men writing doom-books, preaching what in a sense are the opposite of Gravier's warnings – that the 'French desert', having been made to bloom, might return to being a desert, this time not through neglect but through over-exploitation.

This problem of the environment has seemed less acute in France than in some countries because, after all, France has so much space. Unlike Britain, she does not have to fight to protect every acre of greenery. And the French have been right to set the highest priority, hitherto, on modernizing their archaic economy and on industrializing in order to compete with their peers. But now they are becoming aware that this process needs much more careful control. France's vaunted wide-open spaces are not inexhaustible. Already, many a beauty-spot has been sacrificed to a new factory or refinery. Pollution has been allowed to spread because the cost of checking it might interfere with cherished productivity targets. And, for all the high ideals of the planners, the capitalist régime has connived at speculators buying up lovely stretches of mountain or coast for property development, especially on the Côte d'Azur.

Public opinion has recently become far more sensitive to these issues. Opinion polls indicate that most Frenchmen now regard them as high priorities. In 1969, a public campaign dissuaded the Government from allowing a promoter to build a fashionable ski-resort in the Vanoise National Park in the Savoy Alps. Two years later, another campaign induced the Government to step in to prevent the siting of a new oil refinery in the Beaujolais wine country. Similar battles have been waged over projects in the Paris area.* The Government hitherto had seemed too lax about the environment. Its concern had been usually to find the most economic and profitable solution, and so it was far too indulgent

* See next chapter (Paris).

towards the promoters and financiers whose help it thought it needed. But in the early 1970s there were signs of a change. In 1971 Pompidou created a Ministry for the Environment, with the Gaullist, Robert Poujade (no relation to Pierre), as Minister. He made some spirited declarations, and began to spend his limited budget on buying up forest land and small bits of coast, on mobile teams to check noise, and on warning devices for measuring air pollution in factory zones. It was a brave start, but it only nibbled at a huge problem. Although air pollution in the Paris area has been reduced by fuel regulations, river pollution of the Seine below Paris remains severe. On the Mediterranean coast, the problem is the most serious. The new industrial complex at Fos has been pouring tons of sulphur dioxide daily over the Fos/ Marseille area which contains 2,500,000 people. However, one can understand the Government's dilemma: if it imposes stricter anti-pollution rules, will it not frighten away the new industries it has been so anxious to entice there? At present there is a tax on pollution, but many firms have found it cheaper to pay this than to install costly anti-pollution devices. As Charles Hargrove of *The Times* wrote, 'This practically amounts to a licence to pollute.' Of course the problem is not limited to the Marseille area. The whole Mediterranean has been clogging up with filth, the Italians being the worst offenders. Jacques Cousteau, the under-water explorer, warned that 'the Mediterranean is being asphyxiated', and in 1976 Prince Rainier of Monaco launched an international campaign to halt the catastrophe. Helped by the many coastal research laboratories already at work on the problem, he began to clear up his own little stretch of coast, and with some success. 'The beaches will at last be clean again this summer,' said a member of Cousteau's diving team, 'and even the fish are coming back to Monaco.' But it will take much time and money before the whole coast can be saved.

In the past four or five years there has been a steady and striking change in public opinion. The French have come to realize that, like other countries, they may have to temper their hectic expansion drive in order to spend more money on clearing up the mess it causes. There has also been a growing revolt against modern urbanization for its own sake. Already in 1972–3

Pompidou came under wide criticism for his indulgent attitude to new Paris skyscrapers,* and the feeling grew generally that the official vogue for an American-style 'gigantism' was going too far. Throughout France, people began to feel that more of the nation's new prosperity should be spent on better '*qualité de la vie*' (Chaban-Delmas' slogan, not a very original one).

I drove recently through a small town in central France whose entry signboard announced its attractions, in the French manner: '*Visitez Châteauneuf; sa piscine chauffée municipale, ses zones industrielles, son église XIIIe siècle.*' What a significant, almost symbolic, new order of priorities it represents: the French, as a nation, are today putting even more emphasis on modern amenities and environment than on the industrialization that has obsessed them since the war, or on their cherished historical heritage.

The coming to power in 1974 of a new French President with a new outlook happened to coincide with this shift in public feeling. Far more than Pompidou, Giscard is a sincere and passionate environmentalist. He has said recently: 'For the nation that we are today, city-dwellers uprooted from our rural origins, to be modern must mean to live amid greenery and to be able to stroll on foot. Our town-planning must fulfil the citizen's desire to return to the warm human contacts of the old rural or small-town way of life.' So, no more gigantism. Giscard is at once a modernist and a nostalgist; he believes in post-industrial Corbusian concepts of factories-amid-meadows, and also in conservation and restoration. His '*ville à la campagne*' ideas have sometimes been ridiculed as 'an aristocrat's daydream'. But there is no doubt that when in 1975 he launched his famous slogan, 'A more human kind of growth', it did find a genuine public response.

So two separate objectives are being pursued. The very necessary modernization of public services (communications, energy, etc.), still far from complete, is going ahead. And parallel with it there is now a new emphasis on environment, not only on conserving what exists, but on new projects – urban, touristic and so on – with 'quality of life' in mind. Giscard has said that he thinks the two objectives are complementary and should be harmonized.

* See pp. 304–6.

However, they are not always so easily compatible. Consider, for instance, the furore over nuclear power stations. Since 1974 the State has embarked on a massive policy of building new stations,* in order to combat the long-term energy crisis. But this has led to violent protests and demonstrations in several parts of France, notably from the population around the proposed sites, in Brittany, Provence, the upper Seine valley, and elsewhere. Some of this reaction is purely political, from the far Left, and some is from ecological fanatics. However, some of it reflects a genuine public disquiet over health hazards, alimented by a report in 1976 from a team of scientists themselves working for the Government, who called for a three-year halt to the nuclear programme in order to study safety. They alleged that the new reactors were badly designed, cooling circuits were potentially dangerous, and no proper thought had been given to disposal of waste. The Government promptly denied that health hazards are as great as this, and is still going ahead – although more cautiously. In some places informal referendums have been held, and where a majority of the local population is truly worried, plans for the site are dropped. Thus in 1976 the Electricité de France officially shelved a programme for equipping all Brittany with nuclear power, owing to local hostility. Nevertheless, some observers felt that the Bretons were once again being a little wild and illogical in screaming at the Government to help their economy and then rejecting its plans to do so.

In other fields, the policy of harmonizing the two objectives has not run into such trouble. One of Giscard's first actions on coming to power was to veto certain major new development plans for Paris itself, which, he felt, might harm the city's landscape and environment.† This met with general approval. He has also introduced a controversial land reform that is supposed to make it easier for cities to protect their historic centres against speculators.** And above all, Giscard has turned his attention to protecting what is left of France's beautiful coastline. This had become desperately urgent. In 1971, a Government report on the Côte d'Azur property boom had warned that this coast, from Marseille to Italy, was 'being gradually obstructed by a wall of concrete' and would be 'completely saturated long before 1985'. Between Antibes and Cagnes a block of holiday flats *one kilometre* long and 16 storeys high had been built beside the beach, screening the sea from view. It was too late to pull this down, but Giscard at once took action by vetoing or rescinding permits for certain other plans for mammoth 'marinas' or leisure/property complexes on this coast. A sharp brake was also put on the activities of the notorious Guy Merlin, who by 1975 had become France's leading property developer through building 'walls of concrete' along parts of the Normandy and Vendée coasts and elsewhere. Appealing to the average petit-bourgeois' growing desire for his own holiday flat by the sea, and offering generous mortgages, Merlin threw up ugly six-storey strips along some of the finest unspoilt Vendée beaches, and destroyed some nearby woodlands in the process. Commercially, it was all a huge success. At first local councillors and other *notables* welcomed Merlin, glad at the prospect of more tourists in this not-very-prosperous area, but some of them later regretted it. Merlin was accused of creating 'human rabbit-hutches' and of 'sarcellizing'* the coast. Finally, a new and tougher Prefect was appointed, and Merlin was forced to modify all his future projects.

All over France stable doors were now being shut, even if some horses had escaped. In 1975 the Government activated a more general policy for the coast. It created a Conservatoire de l'Espace Littoral, conceived originally by Olivier Guichard when Minister of Equipment and modelled on Britain's National Trust. With a tiny initial annual budget of 12m francs, it began work hopefully, with the aim of buying some of the lovelier stretches of threatened coastline, tidying them up, and then reselling them to local communes, holiday clubs or other bodies, on condition that they developed them aesthetically. In the South of France, the gorgeous Ramatuelle peninsula south of St-Tropez, and the *calanques* near Cassis were among the first areas to be earmarked. It was also decided not to repeat the 'gigantism' of La Grande Motte's pyramids, on the Languedoc coast, in any future State-sponsored tourist development. Opinions today remain divided about the Languedoc scheme, which I described earlier in this

* See pp. 335–7.

chapter. At least it has been coherently planned and properly equipped, and is thus a great improvement on, say, much of the post-war Spanish or Côte d'Azur building. But those towering, tight-packed pyramids are not to everyone's taste.

In the late 1960s the Government began planning to do for the Aquitaine coast – the 150 miles of splendid beach from the Gironde down to Biarritz – what it had done for the Languedoc, but this time very much more modestly. There were to be no skyscrapers, no big futuristic resorts. The prime aim was to conserve the landscape and natural resources. Much money was spent first on tidying beach areas, improving sanitation, and so on. Nine new tourist zones were marked out, but these were to be integrated into existing resorts, such as Hossegor and Lacanau, rather than built Brasilia-like on their own as at La Grande Motte. New holiday property was restricted to three storeys and a low density, and was to be placed either just inland – around the lovely lakes and in the huge forests of the Landes – or perpendicular to the coast, not parallel to it. All very splendid for the environment – but so much so that the required private investors were largely frightened off, fearing that such strict conditions would kill profitability. One would-be promoter told me, 'The Germans, our best flat-buying clients, want to be right on the beach, or they won't come.' After much delay and bargaining, and a few concessions by the State, some investors were finally found, and in 1975 building started. The project has been criticized for the delays, but not quite fairly; after all, as the technocrats in charge of it have pointed out, there is no hurry, and it is surely wiser to spend time first on getting the environmental aspects right, than to throw up speculative eyesores that are later regretted.

This approach is typical of a new Government ethos that infuses not only Giscard and his advisers but the DATAR and many other planners. Even in Brittany with its struggling economy, almost as much State attention is now being paid to protecting the coast from touristic over-building as to enticing new industry. When I toured the entire Atlantic coast in 1975 and then reported my findings to my friend Jérôme Monod, then head of DATAR, in Paris, his first question was: 'Do you think we are doing all right? – are we succeeding?' I was about to assure him that, yes, all the new factories I had seen, at Brest, La Rochelle, Bordeaux and so on, certainly seemed to mark a step forward, when he added, 'I mean, shall we manage to save it, that coast?' That is a new attitude. Even five years ago, he would have asked first about the factories.

The same ethos is behind the new Villes Moyennes policy, described a few pages back. The contracts with these towns are essentially for urban renovation and restoration. One of them, La Roche-sur-Yon, capital of the Vendée, has won a 40 per cent State contribution to its 16 million franc programme to provide pedestrian precincts, parks, better public transport, and so on. When I visited the town in 1975, I saw that Napoleon's famous main square with his horseback statue had been allowed to degenerate into an untidy car-park and cheap-jack market. Left-wing strikers had scrawled on the base of the statue, and banners announced some publicity rally – '*Opération faisans – Pernod – Europe I*'. 'Yes', said the ebullient town clerk, 'it's part of our programme to clear all this up and give Bonaparte back his dignity.' Not far away, at La Rochelle, I found the Socialist mayor embarked on even more ambitious schemes of his own, without seeking State aid. This charming old fortified seaport has some of the finest Renaissance buildings in France, and if properly cleaned up could almost rank beside Bruges or Dubrovnik. So the mayor has cancelled some earlier projects for large-scale rebuilding, and the narrow streets of the ancient town are now being turned into paved precincts. The mayor even has a scheme for banning cars from the whole town and providing free communal bicycles as public transport. He has bought quantities of stolen bicycles from the police – at one franc for thirty! – and will scatter them round the town for people to pick up, use, and deposit by the kerb where they wish. A similar scheme in Milan has worked well, despite thefts. The mayor of La Rochelle hopes that his bicycles will prove too decrepit to be thought worth stealing.

This environmentalist trend is taking many forms in France today and – unusual for France – is as often due to local or private initiative as to State schemes. Throughout the country there are new open-air or heated public swimming-pools, well-equipped leisure and sports centres, advisory clinics, elegant new homes for old people, renovated castles, new museums, street telephone booths that have not been vandalized, and campaigns against noise and litter. In short, the French, like the Germans and others, are now belatedly turning to the kind of welfare and leisure amenities that we in Britain take such pride in having pioneered so many years ago. And with their eagerness, thoroughness, sense of style and more lavish budgets, they are fast overtaking us in many areas. At this rate, every Clochemerle in France will soon have its *piscine chauffée municipale*.

ANDRÉ MALRAUX'S 'MAISONS DE LA CULTURE'

A better 'quality of life' means also better facilities for the arts. The post-war cultural revival in the French provinces has roughly paralleled that in Britain – save that, as you might expect, it has been due rather less to private or local initiative and rather more to State policy. The progress, and the disappointments, have been considerable. Until 1945 or so the gulf between Paris and its 'desert' was nowhere so evident as in the arts and intellectual activity. Paris was a spider that sucked the talent from the rest of France. A few painters or writers worked sunnily in Provence, it is true: but these apart, no intellectual or writer worth his salt dared stray from the magic circle of the capital. The 62 regional repertory companies of the *belle époque* had dwindled by 1930 to a tiny handful, killed by local apathy as much as by the cinema.

The revival began soon after the war when a few talented actor-producers decided to forgo the Parisian rat-race and set up 'reps' in other cities,* helped by State subsidies. This policy has continued, and it has found ready audiences even in unlikely industrial towns. The growth of leisure and affluence, university expansion, the arrival from Paris of young teachers and *cadres*, all this has helped to end the local stagnation and create a new demand for the arts. Led by Aix and Avignon, scores of summer festivals have sprung up. Music, too, has developed. In some cases town councils helped provide subsidies for all this, but in many others

* See pp. 261–3

they acted as a damper. So the State has intervened. The bridging of the cultural gap between Paris and provinces is part of the official doctrine of *l'aménagement du territoire* – after all, it has practical uses, too, if it helps entice reluctant industrialists and *cadres* to migrate from the capital!

Many of the theatres used by the new 'reps' were small or improvised. Many sizeable towns had none at all, and other live arts were often badly catered for. This inspired de Gaulle's Minister of Culture, André Malraux, to embark in the early 1960s on the grandiose policy of building a network of luxurious multi-purpose arts centres, the Maisons de la Culture. These, he declared, would enable France 'to become again the world's foremost cultural nation'. (What a remarkable admission that she had ceased to be so!)

Malraux was an enigma. Novelist and Left-wing revolutionary in the 1920s and 1930s, aloof and mystical historian of art in the 1940s and 1950s, he then spent his eleven years (1958–69) at the Ministry of Culture as an emotional public apologist of Gaullist nationalism; and many people who had admired his early career came to regard him as unbalanced, a bit of a crank, even a crypto-fascist. But this mandarin was more complex than that. His close personal loyalty to de Gaulle dated from the war years, when he was a leader of the *maquis*. During his years in charge of culture he was probably closer to de Gaulle than any other Minister; and while he shared something of his master's didactic and authoritarian approach, his actual ideas, like de Gaulle's, were often liberal and unorthodox. Within the régime his influence was usually liberal in defending films and books from censorship; but he won discredit for acting vindictively towards certain individuals who crossed him, such as Jean-Louis Barrault. Whatever he did was done with great fervour, usually for some ideal; many of the strands of his earlier thinking remained evident in his actions as Minister, notably his scheme for the Maisons de la Culture. After a promising start these centres ran into severe difficulties in the later sixties, and since Malraux's retirement in 1969 the whole policy has been modified. But it has been such an interesting experiment that the story is worth telling in some detail.

Some ten Maisons are in action today – far fewer than were originally planned to be ready by now. The basic formula – still largely valid – is as follows. In each case, State and town council go fifty-fifty on building costs and annual subsidies; an association, made up of delegates from both sides plus members of the public, supervises general policy; but an artistic director appointed in practice by the Ministry is in full charge of programming. It is this attempt at State/town partnership that has caused much of the trouble, for in many cases philistine municipalities and highbrow Malraux did not see eye-to-eye on what the Maisons should be for. It was Malraux's lofty aim that they should present only works of quality and spread Paris standards throughout the provinces – 'In ten years' time,' he claimed, opening a Maison at Amiens in 1966, 'this hideous word "provincial" will have ceased to exist in France.' His second aim was to destroy the notion of culture as a bourgeois preserve, and to draw a new social class into theatres and art galleries. This was Malraux, man of the Left, and here his ideas were not so very different from those prevalent in Britain. But Malraux, mandarin of art, went much further. For him, art was a means whereby the soul attains to God (see *La Métamorphose des dieux* and *Les Voix du silence*), and so with a Gaullist missionary zeal he sought to colonize the French desert with this divine truth.

It was therefore a matter of doctrine that the Maisons should be highbrow and not find a place, as many people would like, for mere entertainment or for local amateur activities. But here was one of the basic contradictions of the whole policy. The highbrow doctrine was hard to reconcile with that of bringing culture to the masses. It presupposed that workers needs must love the highest when they see it, and would flock in. Which of course they did not. In practice, Malraux's ideals have not been working out quite as he planned. The directors of his Maisons have had to take a more pragmatic approach, as they struggle with low budgets, local prejudices and sheer lack of available top-line talent. It was to Malraux's credit that, regardless of politics, he chose as directors the best men available – and these were, not surprisingly, nearly all Leftist anti-Gaullist theatre men, of the stamp of Brook or Wesker. The undoubted *artistic* successes of the Maisons in their early years were due more than anything to the quality of these men. Malraux gave them their head, and backed them in their local battles.

One important function of the Maisons, quoting Malraux again, has been to provide for the 'interpenetration of the arts'. Under one roof there should be three or four different halls, with facilities for plays, concerts, film shows, library, cabaret, lectures, art exhibitions. Thus a film lover, once drawn inside, might begin to take an interest in sculpture, or an opera fan in poetry. But this sensible idea was prone to difficulties. The Malraux policy posed the question: where does 'art' end and 'entertainment' begin? In Britain, too, 'interpenetration' is in vogue for our modest local arts centres; but most people in Britain would cast the net wider, and allow that the staging of pop concerts, amateur drama or even handicrafts, might be a way of initially enticing a mass audience into the centres and destroying the popular fear of 'culture'. The French, or at least an educated minority, are probably less wary than the British of the *avant-garde* or 'difficult': the problem exists nevertheless, and has given rise to some destructive conflicts, notably at Caen.

This was one of the first of the Maisons de la Culture. In a sense it pre-dated them, for it was designed in the 1950s as an ordinary municipal theatre to replace the one destroyed in the war. When it was ready, in 1963, Malraux entrusted the running of it to Jo Tréhard, a lively Leftish young man who had been producing the town's 'rep' in a converted Nissen hut. He found himself with a palatial foyer and a fine modern stage and auditorium, but little space for 'interpenetration' activities. Nevertheless he pushed ahead with the Malraux policy, which he supported; he aimed his programmes at the 'new wave' of Caennais, the thousands of university students and the technicians and *cadres* from Paris, and he won a big success. *Avant-garde* plays, concerts and debates, unusual in a staid town like Caen, picked up eager new audiences. With its small reading-room, art gallery and attractive lounge-bar, the Maison was always an animated social centre. French universities generally lack clubs and extramural amenities, so the Maison gave the students a focus they badly needed. It did at least as much for Caen as the Playhouse for Nottingham, where some of John Neville's problems were strikingly similar to Tréhard's. Its resident drama company tried its hand at Sophocles and a Britten opera, while other plays were imported from Paris: Madeleine Renaud in Beckett's *Oh! les Beaux Jours* played to full houses. Besides film shows and recitals, there were lectures by guests from Paris such as Alain Resnais and Roland Barthes. Tréhard tried to break with the highly conventional and reverential French attitude to culture and to build up more informality and audience-involvement. It was not easy in a town like Caen: some of his keenest opponents were the old university literature professors who, as he put it, 'think drama ended with Victor Hugo and have barely heard of Brecht'.

Not only the professors but the older philistine townsfolk too were furious with Tréhard's policy. Their idea of theatre was light opera, and boulevard comedies on tour from Paris: that was what they'd had before the war. The town council supported them, partly for electoral reasons (they were far more numerous than the minority of highbrows), and began to plot Tréhard's removal. The council juridically owned the building itself, and shared with Malraux a power of veto over the director. The first crisis came in 1964-5, and Tréhard was saved only when a pressure group of *amis de la Maison* formed itself and rallied enough signatures to convince the councillors that his policy had best be left alone. This was followed by an uneasy truce. 'I'm still having to go carefully,' Tréhard told me in 1966; 'I even put on *The Merry Widow* once, to appease the council, though I'm ashamed of it.' Then in 1968, when political intolerance flared up in Caen as in the rest of France, the council forced another showdown with Tréhard and secured his removal. The State replied by cutting off its funds. So the building ceased to be a Maison de la Culture and became an uninspired municipal theatre. When I revisited Caen in 1969 the building was locked and empty at 7 p.m., a time when normally it had been full of students. Posters on the door announced a Humphrey Bogart film and an insipid boulevard comedy for the following week. And Jo Tréhard I found gamely trying to salvage the wreckage of his policy (with modest State help) in an ugly little converted church hall in the suburbs, barely better than his original Nissen hut. It seemed a local tragedy worthy of Brecht.

Since 1971 matters have improved a little in Caen. Local elections that year threw up a new mayor who was more sympathetic to Tréhard and allowed him to hire the big theatre for certain productions. Tréhard died in 1973, though the policy continues unchanged for his successor. But it remains not a Maison but a civic theatre – and the council at least can claim that that is what it was built to be. At St-Etienne, a similar quarrel affected Jean Dasté, the distinguished pioneering theatre producer whose 'rep' had done excellent work in that hideous town ever since the war. A palatial Maison was built for him as a reward. But just before it was due to open, in 1968, there was a change of mayor; the new one, unlike the old, thought Dasté a dangerous highbrow and refused to let him take over direction of the centre. Dasté has now retired, but his successors face the same problem. As at Caen, their company is simply allowed to use the centre occasionally, but only the smaller of its two theatres – the larger one is used for *fêtes*.

Both these disputes were over 'brow' (and while a minority in France may be abstrusely highbrow, the average Frenchman may be little keener on culture than his English counterpart – even if, due to his education, he pays greater lip-service to it). Other crises have been more directly political. At Bourges, for instance. Here, where there is no university, the Maison de la Culture had even more influence than at Caen. For several years in the 1960s it revitalized the life of what had been a sleepy old market town, as dead as its cathedral was lovely. Bus companies even revised their time-tables to take villagers home at night from the Maison; and some touring variety-shows decided to give Bourges a miss in future through lack of support. The director, Gabriel Monnet, was a young man of the same stamp as Tréhard, but with standards a little less restrictive. Cutting his suit according to his cloth in a city with little intellectual tradition, he gave shelter to local painters, amateur actors and folklore enthusiasts in the corners of his ample premises, a large converted building with several halls. But this was not allowed to prejudice his professional programme, as highbrow and ambitious as at Caen. Monnet, a gifted producer, staged the French premières of new experimental plays, ran them for fifteen performances (remarkable, in a country town) and won enthusiastic notices even from the Paris critics. In the single month of October 1964 there were plays by Chekhov, Pirandello, Rilke and Shakespeare, as well as ballets, concerts, films and lectures. Of course the quality varied: not all was up to the Paris standards Malraux wanted, but much of it was. Despite his local popularity, Monnet too ran into trouble in that fatal summer of 1968. He left his Maison open during the May strikes, and incautiously did not prevent a few young people from gathering there and holding sessions on the Sorbonne model. This so infuriated the conservative mayor of Bourges that he accused Monnet of every Left-wing crime and forced his removal. Monnet went off to run a theatre company in Nice. Today the Maison is still open, but without its own theatre company, and without Monnet's *éclat*.

Britain, too, knows this kind of provincial cultural feuding, but it is generally over finance rather than ideology. The Maisons de la Culture have fallen easy prey to the French talent for political extremism and lack of compromise – and especially in the aftermath of May 1968. The Maisons are frequently denounced by the bourgeoisie as hotbeds of Leftism, yet boycotted by the *gauchistes* as being too 'institutional' and part of the Establishment. The directors are caught between this crossfire. Tréhard told me: 'The Catholic bourgeoisie think I'm an atheist or Communist because I like modern drama, while some Left intellectuals despise me as a Gaullist (which I'm not) because I've been working for Malraux. I'm no *étatiste*, but I admire Malraux – politically, he's left me entirely free in my choice of material.'

Given the tense and uneasy basis of most State/municipal relations in France, this kind of partnership may not be the right formula for such cultural ventures. But what is the answer? Of course it might be pleasant to see French towns with more autonomy and civic initiative, running their own centres themselves – as one or two have done, notably in Toulouse. But local finances in France do not easily stretch to this, and frankly it is frowned on by the Ministry, who want to keep centralized control. In this particular sphere, State interference does seem justified, on balance: there is no doubt that the Ministry has more idea of what a Maison de la Culture should be than most provincial mayors, and as one official said to me, 'If we left these councils to their own devices, half of them would run their Maison as a glorified Rotary Club-cum-funfair, with an eye on their own re-election.'

Malraux himself in November 1968 publicly admitted that the formula of the Maisons had not been entirely successful and needed rethinking. Since his departure the following summer, the cultural austerity policy has been discreetly relaxed, and Maisons now invite cabaret artists and pop singers of the more respectable kind (Raymond Devos, Moustaki, etc). But not do-it-yourself amateur shows: these are still taboo. New Maisons continue to be built, slowly. Those at Reims, Rennes, Nevers and Chalon-sur-Saône are working quite smoothly. At present the most active is, needless to say, the Maison at Grenoble, opened during the 1968 Winter Olympics. It cost 30m francs, and of its 4m-franc annual budget some 2·6m comes from subsidies and the rest from membership and box-office. It is a palatial modern edifice of glass and concrete, far grander than the Royal Festival Hall in London; there are three separate theatres, one of them ambitiously designed with a revolving auditorium. The staff number 87, and there are 30,000 subscribing members. Dubedout, needless to say, fully backs the director's artistic policy. But who knows what might happen, even in Grenoble, if Dubedout ceased to be mayor?

The same precarious dependence on municipal whim is evident at Amiens, which I visited in 1971. This Maison just about ticks over, and is typical of the successes and hazards of the whole policy. Costing 12·5m francs to build (in 1966), it is a large, light, open-plan building, elegant and welcoming. Until 1972 it was the home of an excellent State-backed modern ballet company, and besides their productions it has offered a mixed bag of serious films and plays (from Racine to Weiss), as well as concerts, etc. There are book and record libraries, and a painting room for children. I found a relaxed, club-like atmosphere, rare in French official institutions and due much to the personality of its then director, Philippe Tiry. In the large refectory/bar, ballerinas in tights after rehearsals gossiped and joked with students using the place as a café, or with visiting Paris critics, or local worthies. In short, the Maison is a haven for that minority (10,000 *abonnés*, mostly young people) who use it. Before 1966 the town had no cultural focus.

But Tiry was walking a tightrope. The limited audience means that plays can run on average only two or three nights: thus even the most successful runs at a deficit and needs its share of the annual subsidy (town and State each give 800,000 francs). One solution might be to raise the price of seats, which are deliberately kept low (rarely above 8 to 10 francs) for sound social reasons. To raise them might deter those less-well-off categories (students and workers) whom the Maison primarily aims to attract, and thus further limit audiences. It is a familiar vicious circle. As a result, the limited subsidy severely restricts the extent of programming, and the Maison is used far below capacity: each of its two fine modern theatres has a live show on average one night in six. And matters are not helped by the fact that a large part of the prosperous Amiens bourgeoisie prefers, somewhat naturally, to go to Paris for its culture, only just over an hour away by fast train or motorway.

Even the Maison at Grenoble is seriously under-used too, in proportion to its size and initial costs. The prime reason, again, is lack of budget rather than lack of audiences. Overheads are huge. Can provincial towns really afford these luxuries? Were the Maisons not built on too unrealistically grandiose a scale? Most people now think so. At Amiens, Tiry was under the same kind of pressure as Tréhard, to allow the Maison to be used more widely, for the kind of activities that *could* make a profit – amateur drama, touring operettas, Rotary banquets. This, his critics said, would not only help his budget but make him more popular. But he held to the Malraux policy. At the time of my visit, *The Merry Widow* on tour was relegated to a local cinema while the Maison's larger theatre stood empty. It is a highly debatable policy. Do you give people what they want, or what you think good for them? Tiry has now resigned, and the ballet company (which keeps its State subsidy only on condition that it stays in the provinces, though it is of international quality) has moved off to Angers, a town with a stronger musical tradition where a Maison is about to open. And the *mairie* of Amiens has fallen to the Communists, who are determined to try to combine culture with popular appeal.

Will they have any more success than a non-Communist municipality in helping the new director to woo workers into the Maison? This has always been considered one of the failures of Malraux's policy, in his bid to unite the highbrow with the popular: though Monnet at Bourges managed to raise the percentage of working class in his audience to 6·5, at Grenoble it is only 3·5, and at Amiens with all its factories only 2 per cent. Many workers seem to have been frightened off by the cathedral-like nature of these *temples de la culture* – dare the uninitiated enter? Probably the problem can be solved only by long-term changes in French education, which is still class-ridden and gives workers a feeling of exclusion from culture.*

The 'cathedral' policy was abandoned by Jacques Duhamel, who became Minister of Culture in 1971. He was a very different figure from Malraux, a sensible, if not very inspiring realist. The new Maisons he sponsored are smaller, simpler, and cheaper than the old ones; the State still pays half the building and running costs. This policy has been continued by Duhamel's successors, Maurice Druon, and then Michel Guy. In some towns, the new policy is to disperse several small buildings around residential districts, rather than have one main centre. In this way it is hoped to get closer to local audiences, and to be less intimidating. It sounds a sensible idea. In Annecy, a '*maison de la culture sans murs*' is working brilliantly on these lines. And there are other towns, of course, especially larger ones, that do not need or seek a State-backed Maison de la Culture: their existing buildings are adequate. This is true of Lyon, with its commercial theatres and opera house, and of Avignon.

Since 1974, Michel Guy has helped the Maisons by strengthening the system of programme exchanges network and giving them a proper budget for subsidizing tours. Under the Sixth Plan of 1970–75, funds were also increased for building further arts centres of the new, more modest kind. The recent economic crisis has caused a cut-back, and the existing Maisons are struggling to cope with soaring costs and frozen budgets. However, the scheme for a national network of arts centres in scores of towns has not been abandoned, despite the delays and setbacks and changes in

* See pp. 465–7.

policy. The Maisons do mark a positive and original step forward, and they have answered a need. They will probably survive, even if not as originally planned – and the author of *l'Espoir*, who died did not depart in 1976, with his hopes entirely unfulfilled.

The post-war drama renaissance helped pave the way for the Maisons de la Culture. This is one more token of the spontaneous rebirth of France in that period, following the inter-war years when provincial theatre was virtually dead. At first the struggle was tough, but soon the State and a few councils began to provide grants. Today, at least thirty fixed companies are flourishing, in addition to the Maisons; and some of them, notably Roger Planchon's Théâtre de la Cité in the Lyon working-class suburb of Villeurbanne, have won international fame. Jean Dasté at St-Etienne, Maurice Sarrazin at Toulouse, Hubert Gignoux first at Rennes and then at Strasbourg: these and others, equivalents of John Neville at Nottingham, forwent a career on the Paris boulevards to stay and animate the provinces. And a town like St-Etienne can hardly have seemed promising ground at first. This kind of private initiative has been growing, and is no longer so rare in the arts outside Paris. It has been strongly encouraged by Michel Guy, who has offered a number of companies the security of long-term contracts, and increased subsidies despite the economic squeeze since 1974.

The Comédie de l'Ouest at Rennes, now led by Guy Parigot, has had an amazing success. It has patiently created an audience for serious theatre, in a region with no modern dramatic tradition. Today it tours thirty north-western towns each year with near-capacity houses for Sophocles, Brecht, Strindberg, Beckett. In the tiniest Breton upland villages its posters are everywhere; eight towns have even built themselves new theatres to house its tours. It has also performed in Britain, Poland, Holland, etc. On its home ground Shakespeare is by far the most popular author (in the provinces with their insular Racinian standards, Shakespeare often represents a modern break with tradition). Another British play, *Look Back in Anger*, caused something of a storm in Brittany, and set older Catholics distributing tracts against it. The clash between cultures, in fact, is almost as strong as at Caen.

Fréville, the mayor of Rennes, has helped the company a lot, and in 1968 he and Malraux rewarded it with a large new Maison de la Culture which Parigot directs. Until then, the company did not have its own theatre; for its performances in Rennes it had to borrow the old municipal theatre which is really the preserve of the antiquated local opera company. Parigot's former partner, Georges Goubert, told me: 'They haven't changed their décor since 1870. Our audiences are twice the size of theirs, and far younger. But it's a tradition in a town like this to go on croaking out *Faust* and *Carmen* year after year with third-rate singers; and Fréville can't really get rid of them, though he'd like to.'

Planchon's problems have been much worse. He was able to develop his astonishing experimental theatre partly because he was helped by the Left-wing municipality of Villeurbanne. With social views on the arts that outshine Wesker's, over the past twenty-five years he has gone all out to build up a working-class audience. Aided by a few local industrialists and works committees, he has staged lunch-hour excerpts in canteens and on factory floors, while in the evenings a fleet of buses bring workers to the theatre on its hilltop above the yellow tenement-skyscrapers of unlovely Villeurbanne. The operation is a success and the theatre has 150,000 season-ticket subscribers.

The rich theatre-goers of adjacent Lyon, snobbiest city in France, at first took no notice of this young Bolshevik crank. When he became famous and began to do seasons in Paris, the Lyonnais, surprised, would go and watch him there; but few of them would venture in their evening dress to sit among the workers on their own doorstep. And when, in 1965, the Government wanted to reward Planchon for his work by providing him with a Maison de la Culture, the Lyon city council refused to share the costs with Villeurbanne, so the project collapsed. Planchon's existing theatre was modernized a few years later, but without Lyon paying for it. Then, in 1972, the Government honoured this brilliant pioneer by allowing his company to take over the mantle of the famous Théâtre National Populaire,* which the late Jean Vilar founded in Paris. Planchon's Théâtre de la Cité keeps Villeurbanne as its base, but is allowed to call itself 'TNP'

* See pp. 620–23.

and has become, in a sense, officially recognized as the foremost drama company of France. This is the apogee of the provincial cultural revival.

Other arts besides theatre have been flourishing too, and not only in towns with Maisons de la Culture. In Lyon, for instance, despite its bourgeois conservatism, the growth of sheer activity in the past fifteen years has been striking. The number of art exhibitions was twenty-four in March 1966, against seven in March 1956; of concerts, thirty-three against thirteen; of theatre performances, one hundred and five against nineteen. This suggests that well-to-do people are now much readier to find their culture on the spot, rather than save it for visits to Paris. Not, however, that all the new provincial culture is of high quality. Inevitably, the work of some repertory companies is mediocre. Of all the arts, music fares worst. The thirty provincial *Conservatoires* are mostly moribund, and few of the eight traditional opera-houses have much vitality left, apart from Marseille. In the Lyon figures quoted above, it is significant that opera performances alone went down from twenty to thirteen. The brilliant summer festivals, at Aix, Besançon, Royan and elsewhere, are exceptions in the provincial musical field; but they are brief, and are nourished largely by visitors and performers from Paris and abroad.

It hardly needs repeating that the development of the universities has played a part in the awakening of the provinces. The four large towns that have grown fastest, Grenoble, Besançon, Caen and Toulouse, all have universities. The student population in such towns is often five to ten times higher than before the war, and is growing on average about twice as fast as that of Paris. The students animate the streets and cafés, and provide audiences for the new art and drama centres. Though the pull of Paris remains strong for the more brilliant students and professors, an increasing minority of them are beginning to realize that working conditions are often easier in the provinces. Moreover, the universities' new semi-autonomy* is further adding to their liveliness.

There have also been some attempts at decentralization in

* See pp. 502–5.

another State-controlled sector, radio and television. It was not until 1963 that the old ORTF* began to develop regional TV news and magazine programmes, partly in order to combat the influence of the provincial Press, most of it anti-Gaullist. These programmes may have done something to stimulate regional interest, but their political tone was carefully controlled from the ORTF in Paris. The charming and otherwise liberal Gaullist who ran its Brittany station told me in 1965: 'With only fifteen minutes of local news a day, do we have time to air local criticisms of Government policy? We, the Government, are doing all we can to promote regional progress. The time isn't ripe to let people here in Brittany criticize us openly, just when we're really doing something for them. They're too immature.' I had rarely heard a more candid résumé of Gaullist paternalism.

In 1973, the ORTF set up a Third TV Network which drew many of its programmes from regional studios, and this regional system was further extended when the ORTF as such was disbanded in 1975 and the three TV channels were each made autonomous while remaining under State tutelage. Today this third network, FR3, has studios all over France. Each regional station does a daily twenty-minute local news bulletin and a fifteen-minute documentary for its region. Some of this magazine material is also networked, and in addition the regions sometimes produce their own full-length documentaries which are shown nationally. The regions thus see each other's work, which is a good thing, and the studios help to give much-needed free-lance work and publicity to local actors, musicians and others. Some of the documentaries are of high quality, made by excellent directors, but they are nearly always on non-controversial subjects, such as history, the arts, or local customs. And the news bulletins remain rather formal and official, giving more screen time to the doings of local politicians and prefects than to strikes or other discontents. '*Télé-préfecture*' these bulletins have sometimes been dubbed. For in fact the regional stations' autonomy is highly circumscribed; they are controlled from Paris by the head of FR3, Claude Contamine, a tough Gaullist who showed his political mettle in the old ORTF days. The stations do not have the same

* See pp. 630–49.

organic links with their regions as Britain's ITV companies or even the BBC in Scotland. They can reflect regional doings in a picturesque, anodyne way, but their contribution to real local debate and vitality remains perforce very limited.

The regional Press itself at first sight presents an encouraging contrast. Here, for once, the influence of Paris on the provinces is minimal. The Occupation, and the war-time restrictions on transport, destroyed the pre-war circulations of the Parisian Press in the provinces, and allowed the local papers to build up a relative strength that they have since maintained and even increased. Since 1939 sales of provincial dailies have risen from 5·2 to 7 million, while sales of Parisian ones have dropped from 6 to 4 million. Astonishing as it may seem, the French morning paper with the highest circulation is not a Paris one but *Ouest-France* (750,000 copies), published in Rennes, with forty-four editions covering twelve departments. This is followed, in the provinces, by *Le Progrès de Lyon* (500,000), *Le Dauphiné Libéré* of Grenoble (420,000) and *La Voix du Nord* in Lille (415,000). There are eighty-one provincial dailies, and the larger ones are solid empires with fine new offices and presses, making many of the Paris dailies look like struggling poor relations. In Caen, which is little farther from Paris than from Rennes, *Ouest-France* has three times the sales of all the Paris papers together!

All this, however, is not quite the evidence it might seem of a thrusting new regional spirit. Most of these papers are editorially trite and parochial. In many cases they have built up their strength by killing off smaller rivals and have established a virtual monopoly in their area. They feel that, in order to keep this, they must appeal to everybody and not risk alienating any section of readers by flaunting bold opinions. Though in a general sense they are mostly anti-Gaullist, with a few courageous exceptions (*Le Provençal* in Marseille, *La Dépêche du Midi* in Toulouse) they rarely take a strong editorial line on anything that matters; they deal objectively but duly with national news and, worst of all, most of them dismiss international and foreign affairs on a page or two of poorly edited agency messages. For most local people this has been their sole source of news and political comment, apart from the State radio and TV and perhaps the Europe No. 1

radio bulletins; the intelligentsia take *Le Monde*, one of the few Paris papers to have much sale in the provinces, or weeklies like *Nouvel Observateur*. Far more than before the war, the big local papers put their whole accent on pages and pages of local news; and opinion surveys show that this is what the readers turn to first – they no longer care much about politics. The coverage is thorough, and reasonably objective, and no doubt it has helped a little to promote the new regional awareness; but alongside the very occasional article on a real public issue, there are endless columns of accounts of civic banquets or what the French call *histoires de chiens écrasés*, trivia of the silliest sort. When the commercially aggressive *Dauphiné Libéré* staged a battle-royal with the staid *Progrès de Lyon* in 1965 for circulation in overlap districts, the Grenoble paper won by exploiting trivia, and by every kind of gimmick such as big prizes for quizzes and full pages in polychromatic colour. Soon after this the two papers reached a truce and agreed to collaborate. Even the wide circulation areas of the larger papers give a misleading idea of their coverage, for the multiple editions are so localized that there may be no news at all of the regional capital in an edition sold in another town thirty miles away. Most of these papers appeal to the lowest common denominator, and they pander to parochialism rather than encouraging true regionalism. The new regional movements in France are taking place in spite of them, rather than through them. They have the power to be leaders, but they abuse it.

Chiens écrasés, culture snobberies, reactionary mayors, villages that reject town-planning schemes or *remembrement*: the *esprit de clocher* is still far from dead in France, despite the decline of the old ideological factions and the progress of the new generation led by the Dubedouts and de Caumonts, the Lamours and Planchons. There are still plenty of intellectuals who find life isolated and stifling in the provinces – especially those who have not yet lived in Paris. But change is coming fast, and the real test will be to see how many of the ambitious leaders of the new generation renounce the traditional path of Julien Sorel. Roger Planchon is one instance. People are beginning to realize that Paris is often the parochial place; at home and abroad, for good or ill, its legend is waning. It is the hard core of Paris writers and intellectuals, with their heads firmly in the sand, who are often to blame for the gulf of suspicion between capital and provinces, and theirs will be one of the last bastions to fall. They still prefer to live or gather round the parish-pump of St-Germain or Montparnasse and will rarely leave the capital save for a villa or a beach in Provence. They know nothing of the provinces and, unlike writers in England, they will not live in them. Mauriac, who for all his love–hate kept his provincial roots, once wrote: 'An artist out of touch with the provinces is also out of touch with humanity.' Precisely. Post-war French novels are not noted for their humanity.

A few younger artists and writers are beginning to resist the lure of Paris when they win recognition, and to remain in the provinces. J.-M.-G. le Clézio, one of the better young novelists, lives in Nice – not that Nice is exactly typical. Several young little-known writers in a symposium held by *Arts* magazine stressed how much more 'real' and 'deep' they found life in the provinces; and if any renaissance emerges to take French creative writing and art out of its present sterile phase, it might well come from the provinces, as it did, in a sense, in Britain a number of years ago. For the present, the new cultural activity in towns like Caen inevitably takes its tone from Paris. The provinces have not yet found a creative style of their own, apart from the somewhat self-conscious folklorism of Breton, Provençal or other groups.

Are French provincial towns livelier than English ones? Oxford and Cambridge apart (which have little equivalent in France), on a cultural level there is possibly more activity in a French town, certainly more highbrow activity. But spontaneous initiatives, though numerous, rarely seem to take root; successful activity is nearly always carefully institutionalized, as in the Maisons. It is likely to be a long time before Bordeaux produces its Beatles. On a wider level, social and civic as well as cultural, there is not the same range of community activity and interest as in Anglo-Saxon towns. The reason lies partly in the French character, and partly in the prefectoral system which does not always make it easy for a town to be master of its own destiny.

PREFECTS AND MAYORS: CAUTIOUS REFORMS

There are many people in France today who look longingly at the German *Länder*, the Swiss cantons or the English boroughs and county councils, and wish they had something similar. There is a whole school of thought, led by people like Jean-Jacques Servan-Schreiber, which holds that France will never properly be able to modernize its structures and its habits unless it develops a more genuine regional democracy. On the other hand, there are plenty of civil servants in other countries who admire the strength and lucidity of the prefectoral system, and envy the projects that a powerful central administration has been able to carry out in its regions.

In terms of practical results, no less than of ideology, it is extremely hard to draw up a fair balance-sheet of the French system, which is much criticized by the French themselves and is now under reform. Though a town with a vigorous mayor, like Rennes or Grenoble, could certainly benefit from more autonomy on the English model, yet in an area like Caen or the Languedoc the main driving force and ideas seem to have come from the State; or rather, they have come from a few dynamic individuals, prefects or others, who serve the State without necessarily sharing the Government's views. Though the prefect is still the political servant of the Minister of the Interior, under modern conditions his daily functions have inevitably become more economic than political. Often his working relations even with anti-Government mayors and communes are perfectly good, whenever they share the same aims of progress and expansion.

Prefects and mayors in fact are frequently victims of the same common enemy: a centralized State machine that despite some earlier reforms is still too slow and bureaucratic for modern needs. This is one of today's two main problems of local government. The other is much more fundamental: a century and a half of State tutelage over local affairs has sapped the spirit of civic initiative. No wonder the State has to make most of the running, not only in a big town like Caen but in ten thousand smaller communes; no wonder the reaction of so many of them is wary or apathetic. And this is a vicious circle. So long as the State nanny holds its children so tight, they will not break their legs – but they will not learn to walk either, and they will not feel any incentive to try. Why bother with civic or regional initiatives, when the State decides all? This is often the attitude. Pressure for reform grew steadily in the 1960s, and finally in 1971–2 the Pompidou Government pushed laws through Parliament that gave the communes a shade more financial autonomy and set up, timidly, new regional assemblies. But these assemblies have very limited powers and are not directly elected, so that effective control remains in the hands of the State. The Government claimed that the reforms should be regarded merely as a first step, to be developed later; but when, in 1975, Giscard made plans to act on this and to extend the powers and franchise of the regional bodies, he came under such pressure from his Gaullist allies, those neo-Jacobins, that he was forced to shelve the project. So today the French still have a long way to go before regional democracy becomes a reality.

The system is still based, today, on an uneasy balance of power between State and commune, with each possessing a virtual veto on the other's projects and often using it. There are over 36,000 communes, most of them small villages, while others are towns like Lyon or Marseille. Unlike the departments, they are real traditional entities, often with strong local pride. Each has a mayor and council, local men locally elected in the normal way; but the mayor, once elected, becomes a servant of the State, responsible to the prefect. Many of the council's decisions, and also (at least until the 1971 reforms) the spending of its budget, have always required formal approval by the prefect, who also has the right to suspend mayor or councillors from office, or take over some of their duties. The council derives its modest budget from local taxes and State subsidies, and spends it on local services and public works. This system depends on good relations between mayor and prefect; and there is no doubt that a wealthy commune with a good mayor can initiate a great deal, if he has the prefect's backing. But a great many local services, for which in Britain the council is autonomous, in France require the collaboration and aid of the relevant Ministry in Paris or of its local officials acting in liaison with the prefect. For instance, the council has to help pay for building new schools, but the State runs them. Much the same is true of hospitals. Council housing, main roads and bridges, and larger civic projects such as a Maison de la Culture are usually built or maintained jointly by commune and State, and though the commune can in some cases go ahead on its own, it will rarely feel it has the money for the luxury of forgoing State aid. So the commune is dependent on the endless delays and muddles of the Ministries, or on arbitrary last-minute budget cuts by the Ministry of Finance. Or if it has *mal voté*, it may even face Government vengeance or blackmail. Many communes, especially the smaller ones, feel either powerless or resentful; and sometimes they in turn will block State projects for their area. In theory, the State may have the right to override such obstructions. In practice, for obvious political reasons, it is generally more cautious, whether it is dealing with *remembrement* in the Aveyron or Lyon's Maison de la Culture; and it will prefer the carrot to the stick. So the *status quo* of mutual vetoes remains, wasting endless time and effort. Under the new reform, a commune can now spend its budget as it likes, without having to secure the prefect's rubber stamp. But as that budget remains very limited, so does the commune's effective autonomy.

On the level of the department, a locally elected *conseil général* acts as a kind of enfeebled county council, with its own little budget for some services such as secondary roads, public assistance, drainage. It meets only twice a year, its budget has to be approved by the Ministry of the Interior, and in practice it usually does what the prefect tells it. It is elected on a 'rotten borough' basis, heavily weighted in favour of villages rather than towns, and its members are usually elderly. It has the constitutional power to wield more influence than it does, but lacks the energy. So people tend to forget about it. The department is run by the prefect and his staff, in themselves an admirable institution. Prefects are high civil servants of at least the calibre of senior ambassadors. They are usually men of culture, personal presence and impartiality, with little personal concern for the intrigues and squabbles between Government politicians and communes, though inevitably they get caught up in them. A prefect has a luxurious flat in his *préfecture*, he wears a blue and gold uniform on official occasions, and if he dies in office he is buried with full military and civil honours. He is appointed by the Ministry of the Interior, and like a diplomat he is moved from post to post every few years, partly so that he should not get too involved with his 'subjects'. As conceived by Napoleon, his first task is to maintain law and order and to keep his Minister informed of local opinion and possible trouble. This system has served the State well in stormy periods, from Napoleon's own to the great strikes of 1948 and the crises over Algeria in 1958–62. Today the prefect still controls most of the police and, whether a Gaullist or Giscardian, he is expected to act as a 'spy' for the Government on local political developments. But the bulk of his work is elsewhere. Besides supervising the communes and the *conseil général*, he has to co-ordinate the ever more complex activities of the various Government services within his borders. He is assisted by a staff of sub-prefects and specialists, of whom the brighter younger ones have usually come from the Ecole Nationale d'Administration.*

Prefects and their senior staff are clearly the source of much dynamism and progress in France. But it became increasingly clear, as the post-war years went by, that in terms of administration alone some changes were badly needed. The department had become too small a unit for modern economic planning; and as the problems of local development became more complex, there were increasing failures of co-ordination between the prefect and the specialized services of each Ministry in the department. In 1964 a double reform, regional and prefectoral, sought to apply remedies.

First, the departmental services of the Ministries were regrouped and placed under the authority of the prefect. This has helped quite a lot to harmonize local administration. Previously, the *préfecture*'s own technical and specialized staff frequently duplicated the work of local officials of, say, the Ministry of Health or Public Works; and the prefect as he went about his department might come across a new hospital or bridge, for instance, that Paris was building without having informed him. Now, the prefect is a channel for everything, and though many technical matters

* See pp. 49–53.

still have to be referred to Paris, at least he has the authority to settle the simpler ones. Gravier quotes the case, in 1957, of a Ministerial decree being needed to authorize the social aid bureau of a small town near Dunkerque to accept a legacy from a local widow; and often, before 1964, local mayors would complain to me: 'I can't put up a monument or change a street-name without consulting Paris.' Now that these matters can be settled locally there are not only fewer delays; they are now decided by officials with some knowledge of local factors, instead of by grey men in Paris who might never have heard of the commune in question.

This reform has helped shake local bureaucracy out of some of its inertia and routine. It has given an opportunity for certain procedures to be modernized – to move in one jump, as it were, from quill-pens to computers. But it causes problems. In many cases the *préfectures* do not have the staff to carry out the new work properly, and many petty officials are either unable or unwilling to adapt themselves to the changes in routine. In many cases, it simply means that the same people are dealing with the same things, though in the name of the prefect, not of Paris.

The most serious criticism of the reform, however, is that it was fanfared by the Government as a great feat of decentralization, when it was nothing of the sort; it was merely deconcentration. By reinforcing the prefect's powers so strongly the State probably increased its own influence over the communes, which previously might play off one inefficient Ministry against another. Some Left-wing critics even saw the reform as a sinister move by the Gaullists to extend their hold over certain spheres of the civil service. Local schoolteachers, for instance, a notoriously Left-wing breed, were previously appointed by the university rectors (often men of similar Leftish sympathies) in conjunction with the Ministry of Education. Now the nominations pass via the prefect. There is no doubt that, in general, the prefects use their powers wisely and impartially, and the new system is more efficient than the old. But it is not democratic.

Some of the same arguments were true of the 1964 regional reform. This grouped the ninety departments into twenty-two regions solely for the purpose of economic planning; in other respects, they kept their old functions. The departments are all much the same size, though their population may vary from over a million (Bouches-du-Rhône) to the Lozère with 81,900. Their size was conceived in Napoleon's day so that an official in his capital could travel by stage coach to any part of his domain and back 'between sunrise and sundown'; but the motorcar has killed all that. The departments have remained artificial, without acquiring the emotional significance of the old provinces, so that when a man from Avignon says '*Je suis du Vaucluse*' he is stating a legal fact, but when he says '*Je suis provençal*' he is making an emotive statement.

It was however the economic rather than the human artificiality of the department that prompted the reform. In many areas big new projects such as the Languedoc canal cut across departmental boundaries and caused problems of liaison; and the economic future of a region such as Brittany, or the Auvergne, clearly could no longer be considered only at the level of their impoverished departments. So the prefect of whichever department contained the chief city was named *préfet de région*, with a sub-prefect beneath him specifically charged with co-ordinating economic growth. In each region, a new consultative body was set up to advise the prefect, a Commission du Développement Economique Régional (CODER). A quarter of its members were designated by the Prime Minister, the rest were delegates from the *conseils généraux* and from local bodies such as trade unions and chambers of commerce. At the same time the Plan was given a special chapter for each region, which the prefect and his staff were supposed to prepare in consultation with the CODER. Some aspects of the annual State budget were also regionalized, so that instead of the spending of every franc being decided in Paris, the prefects were given lump sums to dispose of in certain spheres such as housing or roads. Major projects, such as inter-region motorways, remained in central hands.

This reform, like the prefectoral one, marked a definite step forward. Most of the new regions do correspond roughly to the old provinces – Brittany, Burgundy, Auvergne, Provence, Lorraine and so on. Therefore they mean something to people, and their creation has done a good deal to stimulate the growth of the new regional spirit. They show that at least the Government is interested in the regions, even if it wants to keep total control. Any mayor or other local individual prepared to co-operate with the regional prefect may find himself caught up in an excited atmosphere of dynamic activity.

Politically the situation is very paradoxical. In practice you may find people of various views working together in the field: Gaullists and Socialists, Catholics and Marxists, unite in their work if they are more interested in progress than ideology. There is plenty of discussion, and the prefects and their staff are often ready in private to take notice of criticism and advice of a practical kind. But the Gaullists remained extremely reluctant to formalize democratic opposition and decision; they feared this would give a cue to the old 'corrupt' party system and give old doctrinal quarrels a chance to re-assert themselves against the new technocracy. The CODERs were a *façade*: they met only twice a year, they had no proper funds or secretariats, they were not properly elected, and there was little evidence that the State ever took much notice of their advice. The town clerk of Toulouse complained to me: 'The CODERs have to accept a *fait accompli* from the prefect. The trouble is, in France, the opinion of the opposition isn't respected. Our old regional expansion committee here went off at half cock, because the local people felt that all the decisions were taken by mysterious hidden technocrats and it wasn't worth their trying.'

It was argued in Paris that if democracy *were* encouraged, if more autonomy were given to the regions or communes, in the short term it might lead to anything but practical progress, at least in many places. Among the older guard of mayors and other dignitaries, the *esprit de clocher* and sectarian, non-expansionist attitudes are still entrenched. Many Gaullists have felt that it might be wiser, before trying to revive local democracy, to wait for the new generation to establish its take-over. There might be some sense in this. The mayor of a small town is often an elderly lawyer or doctor with a sense of political tact, but without economic ideas or the desire for change. Many communes will refuse to fit into any general project unless they feel certain to benefit: some on main roads have been known to veto plans for a new motorway or bypass through fear of losing trade. One notorious case has concerned the Electricité de France, which despite its splendid new power dams and reactors was obliged for years to retain an antiquated system of tariffs and charges that varied from commune to commune and thus made computerizing of accounts impossible. This was simply because each commune felt it had some special advantage to maintain, and refused to help the EDF to harmonize its tariffs. Rationalization has thus taken many years and is only now achieving results.

Some anti-Government mayors and councils tend to be against progress just because it is identified in their minds with the State. Maybe, if they were given more power, this attitude would change. But if communes were more autonomous it might, in some places, raise the problem of Communism. Several large towns are in Communist hands, notably Le Havre and Nîmes. In practice their municipal control of affairs works quite smoothly, because they know they have to co-operate with the State – and because, to be fair, they often do have a progressive civic policy. But if they had more power and money of their own, they might form virtual Communist enclaves which, in the case of a port like Le Havre, could hold to ransom the national economy.

Another problem is that the municipal election system, a Gaullist creation, tends to produce homogeneous single-list councils with no opposition. A party wins all seats, or none. This hardly stimulates democracy and free discussion. Although an élite in France is now actively interested in regionalism and town-planning, this has hardly spread yet to the man-in-the-street, perhaps in part because of the failures of TV and the local Press; and the general public level of civic awareness and responsibility is low by British or American standards. In Nancy a local journalist told me: 'The municipal council here is old and mediocre. There are lots of lively young people, engineers, teachers and so on, who are interested in the problems but won't try to take part in public life – they feel it's too difficult to dislodge the old ones.' In other areas the picture is brighter, and the assumption of power by a new generation really seems to be happening. This is true in some country districts where the JAC revolution in farming has had its repercussions in many local elections. In the elections in the Maine-et-Loire in 1959, the average age of councillors fell at one swoop from sixty to thirty-five. Almost everywhere in France the traditional position of the *notables* is slowly declining; though they may still hold on to the formal positions of power, their influence and prestige is falling. The transfer to a new generation with a quite different outlook is ineluctable.

The star case is, of course, Grenoble. Here Dubedout is trying to break the old French habit whereby a citizen delegates all responsibility to those he has elected and then washes his hands of it. This is so not only in relations between citizen and State. Mayor and council, too, once chosen, are left to get on with the job: the citizen may grumble and protest, even loudly, but he does not expect to participate. He considers himself, and is considered, '*un administré*'. At Grenoble, Dubedout believes that '*la démocratie de participation*' at a local level is an essential first step, to build up later to regional democracy. Basing himself on the non-party '*groupe d'action municipale*' which he founded privately in 1964 to campaign for the water-supply, he has encouraged the creation of civic associations in different wards of the city, he holds public debates on local matters and organizes civic exhibitions. He has made some progress, save that he finds it hard to keep the associations free from party feuding. The Communists in particular accuse him of seeking to depoliticize civic life, which they want to keep as an arena of the class struggle.

Grenoble's example has been spreading fast, but not always with the happiest results. Several hundred other *groupes d'action municipale* (GAMs) have been formed spontaneously throughout France in the past few years. Many of them started out as genuine non-party bodies, to canvass for the improvement of local services or to help animate the life of the suburbs. But increasingly they have become politicized. A national federation of GAMs has been formed, which has allied itself with Mitterrand, and most GAMs have simply become local opposition pressure-groups in towns with pro-Government councils. In towns ruled by the Left, they barely exist. Dubedout's own GAM has lost its old identity and become merged with the municipality. Some non-party civic associations flourish outside the GAM network, but they are not numerous. This is one more sad example of the political polarization that re-awoke in France after May 1968 and has again been growing since 1974.

One of Dubedout's achievements in the 1960s was to persuade the suburban communes to link with Grenoble itself in a voluntary association for joint town-planning and certain joint services. This has had some success, but it has been hampered by the inevitable feuds between councils of very varied political colouring.

This whole question of the regrouping of communes has come to the fore in the past ten years. There are two types of problem: (a) the spread of conurbations far outside their old municipal boundaries (as in Grenoble) to engulf old village communes which are now suburbs yet cling fiercely to their independence; (b) the depopulation of small rural communes, which ought no longer to exist as administrative entities. The map of France's communes has barely altered since the nineteenth century. There are still some 36,400 of them, more than in Germany, Italy and Benelux together. Over 3,000 have less than 100 people; one has three people, and most of its statutory municipal council of nine live elsewhere! Yet to persuade them to merge, as a modern economy requires, is not easy. Not only do mayors and councillors want to avoid losing office, but the ordinary citizen too is sentimental about his commune. The village *mairie*, the mayor with his sash conducting a wedding or opening a local fête, this is something very real in France.

Therefore the Government, for electoral reasons, has proceeded warily over mergers. In 1967 it began to tackle the urban problem by imposing *communautés urbaines* on four large conurbations where it felt conditions might be favourable: Bordeaux, Lille, Lyon, Strasbourg. In each case, central and suburban communes each keep their own identity and mayor, but are grouped into a joint council, with a joint budget for equipment and many public services. This has been working fairly smoothly, despite the inevitable rivalries and frictions between Left- and Right-wing suburbs, and it has since been copied voluntarily by five smaller conurbations, including Brest, Le Mans and Dunkerque. The chief problem is that the duplication of some services and staff at commune and *communauté* level is proving an expensive way of running things, and a project is now being studied that would regroup the major conurbations into super-communes with directly elected councils, while the existing communes would retain their identity within these. This would be roughly similar to the new two-tier system of the metropolitan counties in England; but it might throw up the same disadvantages.

In most places the Government has preferred the carrot to the stick. It encourages communes, urban or rural, to group themselves into 'syndicates' or 'districts' for joint planning, or for the pooling of budgets for services such as roads, water, housing – and thousands have now done this. Then in 1971 it passed a law allowing substantial loans and tax advantages to communes that agree to total mergers. The prefect in each department was ordered to consult with the mayors and draw up a schedule of proposed mergers by July 1972. But the response was feeble. Most small communes fear that to be swallowed up by a large one would mean the loss of 'human scale' (as many of them put it) and also higher taxation. This is the reaction even when a village of, say, 200 people is invited to merge with a larger one of 1,000. And when a village near Lille was faced in 1972 with a project of integration with either Lille or Roubaix, the mayor exclaimed angrily, 'We are in the position of Poland in 1939, trapped between Germany and Russia!' All over France, you could almost hear the bells of all the little Clochemerles tolling their sympathy for his *esprit de clocher*.

In the past fifteen years, over 10,000 communes have grouped into 'syndicates' or 'districts' but only 1,300 have merged totally, and most of these have been small villages. Certainly the commune is one of the few genuine civic entities in France and should not be tampered with lightly. There is probably no harm in allowing villages to keep a certain sentimental identity – including the folklore of the mayor with his sash – so long as they can be rationalized into larger units for administrative and economic purposes. Thus the mayors of smaller communes would become largely honorary, with little more to do than make bride and groom sign their names. This is probably the path to follow, but rationalization still has a long way to go. In some towns the failure to achieve even a district has been a handicap: at Caen, the Right-wing town and Left-wing suburbs have refused to collaborate, so that rich Caen has not paid a sou towards the growth of the new satellite towns which are adding greatly to its own trade and prosperity. Thus the planning of an area in rapid expansion has been rendered difficult. It may seem a paradox that this powerful and elephantine State cannot, or will not, deal with the flea that tickles its ear. But when there are 36,400 fleas you have to be careful, and the communes' jealous exercise of their legal rights has been one price they exact from the State for its intrusions on their privacy in other respects.

These intrusions have been lessened by the law of 1970 which makes it no longer necessary for the commune to present its annual budget to the prefect for approval. Even so, it still needs his backing for the financing of most services, since its own powers of raising revenue have remained limited. This has been especially irksome for larger towns. Marseille and Lyon have had to depend on the State for nearly every stage of the building of their much-needed underground railways. A new law in 1966 slightly increased local revenue by creating a new municipal tax on salaries in place of the old turnover tax. More important, towns are now allowed to raise public loans for financing public works: Marseille was the first to make use of this, in 1972, with a 120m franc loan from private banks. But this has far from solved the problem. With rising costs, most towns have been running increasingly into debt and have had to push up the rates much faster than the level of inflation. Rates and other local taxes rose on average 22·5 per cent in 1975, while inflation was 10 per cent. Some larger towns are beginning to face, on a lesser scale, exactly the same problem as New York: rocketing costs in city centres are forcing businesses and inhabitants out into the suburbs, so that the central commune finds its local revenue dropping, and city centres are emptying or, as one French paper put it, 'becoming Harlemized'. In 1975, the mayors of thirty-nine leading towns of all political shades – from the Communists to the Right – joined together to present the Government with a document setting out their grievances and their sense of desperation, and demanding more financial help. In some cases, the situation is partly their own fault: they have embarked on over-ambitious projects which the rate-payers are reluctant to pay for. But the real issue is that French towns are still under-financed. As the mayors pointed out, they have to pay for 50 per cent of the equipment of their towns while their income is only 15 per cent of that of the State. And although the State has recently allowed them new forms of local tax-raising, it has also imposed VAT on their expenditure, thus taking away with one hand more than what it has given with the other. Whereas in Germany a city handles 60 per cent of all local financing, in France the figure is still only 18 per cent. It is only very slowly that a reluctant State is allowing local councils to evolve towards the kind of economic semi-autonomy that they enjoy in many other countries.

An even more important question is whether the State will ever allow any real measure of self-government at the wider level of the region. What are the prospects for the kind of limited regional autonomy that the Italians have daringly set in motion since 1970, and that Britain is now preparing, at least for Scotland and Wales? In France, the *conseils généraux* are feeble, and the CODERs of the 1960s were a farce. Many political thinkers are aware of the drawbacks caused by this gulf in the democratic structure, between the commune on the one hand and the national parliament on the other. The one unit is in many cases too small, the other too big. The gulf has become even more manifest since the war, owing to the decline of the old locally based political forces – partisan and aggressive – and the rise of the new technocracy imposed from outside, which at the level of the region or department has tended to mean yet more State control. Many technocrats working for the Government have stressed the need for some regional level of democratic decision. Lamour told me: 'Our projects are useless unless they are followed by valid local initiatives. Once we have given the impetus, we want to be able to leave them in local hands.'

The Government has been cautious, for obvious reasons. Ten centuries of centralism have held this diverse nation together, and the State does not want one flick of the legislative pen to send it flying apart. De Gaulle prepared a timid regional reform in 1969, which was defeated for reasons that had little to do with its own merits or defects. Then after a decent interval Pompidou took the issue off the shelf again. First, some 400 new urban cantons were created; since the *conseils généraux* are elected by cantons, mainly rural, this reform removed something of their 'rotten borough' basis and has brought a little new life to them.

More important was the law of 1972 that replaced the CODERs with two new bodies in each region. One of these is purely consultative, an economic and social council of local delegates. The other goes a little farther. It is made up of the deputies and senators who represent the region in Paris, plus certain *conseillers généraux* and town councillors chosen from among themselves. This regional assembly has a small budget of its own, derived from local taxes and the tax on driving licences, up to a ceiling of 20 francs annually *per capita*. From this it can finance some local projects on its own initiative. The regional prefect must also consult it regularly on all planning matters.

These reforms have been judged too timid by those who want real regional democracy in France. They point out that the assemblies' powers of decision are limited to the use of their own budgets, which are so small that the prefects in practice keep the authority. And the prefects will always look to Paris, where their future careers are decided. Within each region it is the prefect who has the staff and the facilities for drawing up detailed projects, and he tends to present these as a *fait accompli* to the assemblies, who have neither the resources nor the know-how for this kind of planning work. So most of them are in practice mere rubber-stamp bodies. Nor do they have the moral authority of a direct popular mandate. They are mere colleges of existing local dignitaries, and so they tend to be conservative, and the already heavy work-load of deputies and senators has simply been increased. It is true that in one or two regions a somewhat different pattern has emerged, and a Left-wing assembly under a strong leader has succeeded in imposing its will on the prefect; thus, in 1975, the Provence assembly, chaired by Gaston Defferre, rejected the prefect's annual proposals and voted in its own. This can be done, but it is a rare case, and largely a matter of personalities.

At least the reform has marked some step forward, and the Government in 1972 was at pains to stress that it was intended to be '*évolutive*', a first step towards possibly more radical measures later. At least the region has for the first time been legalized as an institution, like the commune; before, it was a mere administrative planning convenience. 'It is unrealistic to expect France to move overnight from extreme centralism to a federal system,' said one official advocate of the reform; 'we must go step by step.' In fact Giscard at the time of his election in 1974 made it clear he was in favour of moving on to the next crucial phase – direct regional elections. But then the following year came the separatist flare-ups in Brittany, Languedoc, Alsace, and especially in Corsica where autonomists killed two policemen in a series of angry riots. The Jacobin-minded Gaullists took fright, fearing a break-up of the State if there were any political devolution. Chirac declared that only 'dreamers and irresponsibles' could demand direct elections. And Giscard, under pressure from his Gaullist allies, backtracked, declaring on television in December 1975 that France was not a nation of the size of the United States or Russia, and could not expect a federal structure. The regionalists, disappointed, asked cynically: 'but what about West Germany, or Yugoslavia, the same size as France or smaller?'

The Government has two main fears. First, that devolution would encourage secessionist tendencies in certain regions such as Brittany and Corsica. Second, that directly elected Left-dominated assemblies in certain regions would increase the influence of the Opposition. The Government has been worried by the experiment in Italy since 1970, where Emilia and Tuscany elected Communist-led assemblies and, it is generally agreed, thereby helped the rise of the PCI. 'Once a town or an area falls into Communist hands in France, it's hard to win it back,' a member of Pompidou's staff told me in 1972; 'we've seen that in places such as Le Havre and Nîmes.' Moreover, since 1975 the Government has been surreptitiously attempting to reduce the influence of the regions by increasing the prerogatives of the *préfets de département* at the expense of those of the *préfets de région*. Thus, for instance, the important new national employment fund has been put in the charge of the former, not the latter, at local level. It may be a subtle move to re-confirm the department as the main administrative unit. Yet, as the regionalists never cease to point out, the department is a purely artificial unit while the regions, or most of them, correspond to some historical or cultural reality.

Giscard has declared that he is not opposed to further regional reform in the longer term, but democracy must first be strengthened at the local level, in the communes, where it is closest to people's daily lives. So, at the end of 1975 he put Olivier Guichard, Gaullist baron and creator of DATAR, in charge of a commission of mayors and other *notables*, with the task of advising on ways of strengthening and modernizing the commune. The commission was expected to propose an increase in local finances, and possibly a breaking up and regrouping of the larger cities into smaller communes within urban districts – somewhat on the lines of the new British system – so that in these places the citizens can feel closer to local government. This could have advantages. But there is also the fear that these changes would be used as a pretext for shelving true regional reform *sine die*. It is asked, could the French ever afford or tolerate such a complex multi-tier system of democracy? – first Brussels and Strasbourg with its new direct elections, then Paris, then the region, then the department, then the urban district and finally the smaller commune inside that. Probably not. But the regionalists feel that if any of these tiers is to be sacrificed, it should be the archaic and artificial department.

By 'regionalists' I do not mean local autonomists, but those national figures, such as Philippe Lamour and the late Louis Armand, Michel Crozier, Jean-Jacques Servan-Schreiber and many others, who believe that some devolution at regional level is essential, if French society is to be properly modernized. Michel Crozier has stated clearly his belief that direct regional elections would throw up a new and dynamic generation of younger local politicians – a whole fleet of Jimmy Carters – to break the somewhat sterile grip of the older potentates, whether of Right or Left, Chaban-Delmas or Defferre, who have ruled their local fiefs for too long. Crozier also says it is silly to fear the separatists, who represent only a marginal extremist fraction, even in Brittany and Corsica. He cites the West German example: the division of the nation into *Länder* after 1945, far from weakening Germany as some people hoped it might do, has been a source of strength and one cause of the 'German miracle'.

Crozier quotes recent opinion surveys by sociologists, which show that the French as a whole feel far more loyalty to region than department, and that 71 per cent are in favour of direct regional elections and only 8 per cent hostile.

Crozier has powerful backing. Jean Lecanuet, the Centrist leader, has come out in favour of regional elections and so even has François Mitterrand. Jérôme Monod, while still head of DATAR, wrote in 1974 that 'an irresistible current will lead one day to universal suffrage' for the regions. Giscard himself is believed to be still basically in favour, though forced by political necessity to bide his time. He is known also to share the view of many people that the present number of regions, twenty-two, is far too great, especially when set in a European context. Regions such as Auvergne or Champagne/Ardennes, with little more than $1\frac{1}{4}$ million people, represent less than 0·7 per cent of the total population of the EEC and cannot measure up against the German *Länder*, or the main Italian regions or, say, Wales. It would be absurd to expect them to look after their own economic development. Moreover, while most of the regions correspond roughly to the old provinces of France and thus to some cultural reality, some – such as Centre, or Pays de la Loire – definitely do not, and are simply groupings of departments that had no better place to go. The argument is that France should be regrouped into about eight or ten big 'European-size' regions, equal say to Hesse or Piedmont. Thus the two Norman regions would be united, as would Alsace and Lorraine, and so on. These new units would take their place in a '*Europe des régions*' where, as the power of Brussels and of the Strasbourg Parliament increases, so that of the nation state wanes and that of the regions grows. This at least is the dream. In France, 'European federalists' and 'regionalists' have usually been the same people, and it has been their faith that, as Europe unites, so France's centralized structures would crack under the weight of economic reality and influences from France's more decentralized neighbours. But this may take a very long time.

Chapter 7

PARIS, THE BELOVED MONSTER

WHILE dull provincial towns turn into lively ones, Paris, lively already, has become something of a madhouse. Frenetic and congested, it has been ill prepared either physically or psychologically for the new pressures of growth and prosperity. Parisians, a restless and self-willed breed at the best of times, find their nerves stretched taut by the traffic jams, the noise, the often inadequate housing, the lack of space and services. People are late for appointments, snappy down the telephone or choking back an irritation that the plumber will not come or the shops are overcharging. Life is much simpler in the provinces.

No wonder that Parisians' feelings have grown so fiercely ambivalent towards a city that has always inspired deep loyalties and whose personal spell, even today, is not lightly broken. 'Paris, what a monster!' is a phrase I have continually heard people use, almost lovingly. And so the two Parises co-exist: the unpleasant modern town of practical daily life, and the strong, secret personality of a city whose insidious beauty and vitality still manage to survive the odds against them and even to renew themselves. For these reasons, many foreigners like myself find Paris a fascinating and exciting city to visit for a month or two but we no longer want to live there, as so many francophiles and expatriates did in the decades before the war.

Even Parisians are coming to realize that their city has lost some of its old uniqueness and lustre, though opinions may vary as to why this is so. One explanation is political: Paris, far more than the provinces, bore the brunt of the upheavals and humiliations of the war and post-war years, from Nazi parades on the Champs-Elysées to the last sickening months of the Algerian crisis in 1962, with terrorist bomb-attacks and armed police raids all over the city. And Parisians, despite their new wealth and stability, have not quite emerged from the shame of these events, which were then followed by the student riots of 1968, much worse in Paris than in the provinces. The fact that the Latin Quarter, even today, tends to fill up with grim-faced riot police, whenever any student unrest is expected, hardly adds to the city's gaiety.

But some of the trouble at least is purely practical. Paris has paid the price of nearly a century of neglect of town-planning. The Ville Lumière that the tourist sees is bright with new paint and whitened façades, but it hides realities: the congested commercial districts, the lack of parks, the crumbling tenements and, outside the old city gates, the sprawling wilderness of pre-war suburbs, ill-equipped with hospitals, schools, public transport or even water. As the population has swollen, these problems have grown too, and they have soured the life of the whole city.

Just at the moment when greater Paris seemed to be on the verge of seizing up like an engine without oil, the problem at last began to be tackled seriously. First of all, the housing shortage has been partly cured, and today the outer suburbs are ringed with a white phalanx of new blocks of flats like some vast Stonehenge: the older ones are unbeautiful and ill planned, but at least they provide essential roofs. In the early 1960s, the Gaullist master-planners set to work on the whole shape of the city, eagerly colouring the maps in their offices with grandiose designs for garden cities and urban freeways. The French do not do things by halves; after years of total disregard, the future of Paris has now become a public obsession, the subject of scores of books, reports and conferences. Up through the waste land of the old slums and suburbs, the first shoots are appearing of a new, daring, possibly beautiful city. Many of the new projects are, as in London, highly controversial. And, with the population and its needs growing fast, the whole operation is also a race against time.

GIANT-SCALE PLANNING FOR THE YEAR 2000

When Baron Haussmann, prefect of the Seine department in 1853–70, drove his broad boulevards through the congested bowels of the old city, he turned Paris into the best-planned and most elegant modern capital in Europe. Today the boulevards are

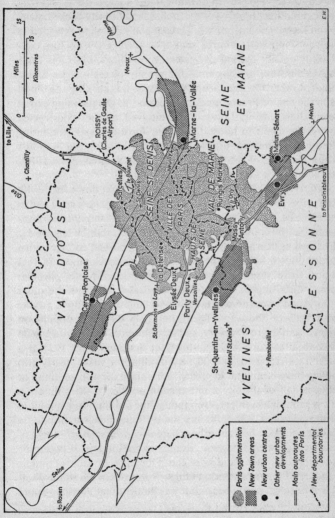

The eight departments of the new 'Paris Region', showing the two parallel axes of the new urban centres.

still her most distinctive feature, and in recent years they have helped to keep the growth of traffic under some control. But they. never cured the problems of the archaic and densely packed quarters in between them, nor was Haussmann's planning extended to the new industrial suburbs that after 1870 grew up higgledy-piggledy outside the old city gates. Aubervilliers, Les Lilas, Issy-les-Moulineaux, lovely names for ghastly places – these and a hundred other townlets arose while Paris was sucking the blood from the rest of France, and they became, as the planning expert Peter Hall puts it, 'a vast, ill-conceived, hastily constructed emergency camp to house the labour force of Paris, presenting almost the limit of urban degeneration'.* Auguste Renoir's pastoral canvas of the Seine at Argenteuil, painted in the 1870s, was soon blotted out beyond recognition.

After 1918 this industrial growth slowed right down. But, with land prices so low, a different type of excrescence now appeared in the suburbs, the individual *pavillon*. The Parisian *petit bourgeois* found that he could afford to realize a dream that he has always cherished as dearly as the Englishman: a suburban cottage with a garden. But instead of the English ribbon-development of that period, there was anarchy. Some 80,000 little red-roofed *pavillons* spread their ungainly rash of assorted shapes across the outer suburbs, and were among the few new buildings put up in greater Paris between the wars. Then after 1945 the city's population again began to grow rapidly, and new blocks of flats were flung up piece-meal to cope with it, slowly at first, and after 1954 at a faster rate rising to 100,000 new dwellings a year. Nearly two million have been built in greater Paris since the war, to house or rehouse half of the city's nine million people. In sheer numbers this is some achievement, even though the old slums are not all of them yet cleared. But only since the 1960s has much attempt been made to plan the new suburbs coherently. At first, stray blocks of flats were planted anywhere, usually in vacant gaps between the old suburbs where land was cheap because of lack of public transport. London's solution of new towns out in the country was at first rejected, partly because it was thought that Parisians could

* *The World Cities* (World University Library, Weidenfeld & Nicolson, 1966).

never be persuaded to become thirty-mile commuters, and partly because of the difficulty in France of attracting new light industries quickly to the areas.

Inside Paris itself, the main problem is still congestion of every sort. By 'Paris itself' I mean the municipality of twenty *arrondissements* within the old city gates, known as the Ville de Paris. Since 1911 its population has steadily declined from 2·9 to 2·2 million. But the people are still packed as densely as on Manhattan: 84 to the acre, against 43 in the equivalent area of London. Green parks cover 6·9 per cent of the Ville de Paris, against 15·4 per cent of London and 17·3 per cent of New York – and the only Paris parks of any size are at either extremity, Boulogne and Vincennes. The open spaces by the Seine in the city centre are deceptive; and the patch of dusty scrub that bears the royal name of Tuileries is not of much practical use as a park.

In the eastern and northern districts, thousands of antiquated little factories and depots lie cheek-by-jowl with residential tenements, polluting the air, and blocking the traffic with their lorries. Apart from the boulevards, most streets are narrow, and there are more cars in the city than parking spaces for them, so that it becomes a major exploit to find room to unload a van. The noise of the high-pitched French car engines reverberates in the chasm-like streets, and, though drivers are not supposed to use their horns, they do. Compared with much of Paris, even a poorish London district like Battersea or Lambeth seems a haven of space and calm. Offices have spread into old-fashioned residential districts quite unsuited for them, while Paris *intra muros* still holds many of the records among major Western cities for poor housing (most of the new building has taken place in the suburbs). At the 1968 census over a quarter of the dwellings inside the Ville de Paris were classified as decaying or insanitary, while 48·4 per cent were 'overcrowded'. Some 70 per cent were built before 1914, and 45 per cent had no lavatory. Large family flats are especially scarce: the average size of a Paris flat in 1968 was 2·3 rooms, against 3·1 in London and 3·3 in New York.

The well-known character of Parisians seems to me to aggravate this situation, in a kind of vicious circle. It is their egotism and lack of civic spirit that have helped to get their city into this mess;

equally, their intolerance and hyper-tension seem peculiarly ill suited to putting up with the results. A Londoner is tempted to observe, smugly, that a more phlegmatic or community-minded people would have found more effective ways of living with their difficulties, if not of solving them. Many Parisians themselves agree with this diagnosis.

One of the troubles is that local government in the Paris area is notoriously weak and divided. The municipal council of the Ville de Paris has for the past century had even less autonomy than an ordinary French commune, however small; it has been allowed no mayor and has been governed directly by the prefect of the Paris department. This is because the State has been haunted by memories of 1789, 1848 and 1871, and would allow little power to the dangerous Paris populace. May 1968 did not help to reassure it. So the city council has had neither the scope nor the resources to tackle the problems on the scale needed. For the same political reasons the State has never encouraged it to fuse with the hundreds of suburban communes into an effective co-ordinating body in the manner of the Greater London Council. All over-all planning for the Paris Region is controlled by the State. And these communes, many of them Communist, have proved equally reluctant to co-operate or merge their identities.

But now at last Paris is to get its own mayor. The Government has decided that, with slum clearance and the steady *embourgeoisement* of the population of the Ville de Paris, the citizens are no longer such a menace. For many years now they have elected a healthy Right-of-centre majority to the city council, and can therefore be trusted. So, under a law passed in 1975, Paris will elect a mayor at the municipal elections of March 1977, and he will have the same considerable powers as in any other town, save in matters of police; the city will still have a special Prefect of Police, for obvious reasons of Government security in the capital. Above all, it is the new mayor and no longer the departmental prefect who will now be in charge of the city's 30,000 municipal employees. And the city council should now have the moral authority to take much more initiative in town-planning affairs.

This will hopefully improve the administration of the Ville de Paris, but it will not solve the problem of lack of co-ordination between the communes of the conurbation. It may even make them more resentful of the city itself. For a hundred years now these communes have been quite inadequate for their tasks. The late-nineteenth-century urban growth engulfed existing village communities that at once became paralysed by what faced them – how could the mayor of a peaceful townlet, like Asnières or Montreuil, cope with the needs of the new flood? And the State did little to help. Hence the ugliness and physical chaos of these suburbs has been matched by their lack of public equipment; only recently has real progress been made in providing them properly with hospitals, sports centres, theatres, university colleges or even adequate *lycées*. All the culture for which Paris is famous has rested within a small circle between Montmartre and Montparnasse; the rest was *la banlieue*, a melancholy hinterland of shacks and seedy cafés where children play in the weeds of vacant lots.

Most of the main offices, too, are in central Paris. Yet to travel there for daily work or an evening's enjoyment can be hard, because of the shortages of public transport. The Métro network does not extend very far outside the Ville de Paris – apart from one new express line – because of jealous rivalries with the SNCF at the time of its building, in the 1900s; the SNCF's own local services radiate effectively from the central stations, but with few inter-suburban ring lines, while suburban bus services are equally rudimentary. In the 1950s, when the housing shortage was at its worst, some workers would have to get up at 5 a.m. to make a two-hour journey into central Paris and out again to their factory, arriving back home at 8 p.m. This is now less of a problem, since it has become easier to find a flat near one's work; but the average time a day spent commuting in the Paris area is still sixty minutes (110 minutes for those living in the suburbs), and could be much reduced if transport was less centripetal. The rush-hour traffic jams at the main exit-routes are worse than in London.

Such are the main problems still facing the planners today. The Fourth Republic made little effort to solve them: its few early post-war schemes all fell foul of bureaucratic and political disputes and muddles. And this failure is one reason why the

Common Market preferred the more manageable city of Brussels for its headquarters, and Paris, as someone put it, 'muffed her chance to become the capital of Europe'.

In the mid-1950s, however, a project finally began to take shape for actively limiting and controlling the growth of Paris. This ran into criticism. Many people argued that to check the economic growth of Paris like this, and especially the building of offices, would hinder it from competing with other Western capitals; big new international concerns looking for a base would turn instead to London, maybe, or Rome, or Frankfurt, and this would not be in France's interests.

These views were shared by Paul Delouvrier, the brilliant civil servant and former delegate-general in Algeria who in 1961 was appointed head of a new Government office charged with planning and supervising the city's future. This was later merged with the new Région de Paris, similar to the twenty-one other economic regions, and Delouvrier became its Prefect. He found that the census of 1962 showed that the region was growing even faster than had been thought: its population had gone up 1·1 million since 1954. This further convinced Delouvrier that sharp limitation of growth was going to be not only economically undesirable but also very difficult, and in 1963 he won de Gaulle's support for a change of policy to one of planned expansion. Two years later he decreed the grandiose Schéma Directeur, or directive outline, that still forms the basis of all today's activity.

The Paris region comprises 5,000 square miles in a radius of thirty to sixty miles from the city centre. The Schéma deals with the whole of this area, thus allowing planning on a sweeping new scale. Delouvrier anticipated that the Paris region, 8·5 million in 1962, would grow spontaneously through birth-rate and immigration to 12 million by 1985, and 14 or possibly 16 million by the year 2000. Delouvrier's estimate also assumed that other big French towns would double or treble their size in the period 1962–2000: it was not that the provinces were again to be bled white by Paris, rather that France's delayed urbanization and rise in population were both happening so fast. The issue, as Delouvrier saw it, was not how to prevent the growth of Paris but how to prevent it from happening chaotically. The Schéma took over and extended the earlier unquestioned plans for central renovation, and complemented them with titanic new suburban projects.

The basis of its thinking was that Paris would be asphyxiated unless it was made polycentric. Although the main centres of power and wealth are to remain inside Paris, the Schéma has planned five new cities on the perimeter, each with a population rising eventually to about 400,000, and each with its own complete social, cultural and commercial equipment, unlike the present suburbs. The 'new towns' solution, hitherto rejected, is now espoused eagerly, but not quite on the British model. Instead of radiating round Paris, these cities are aligned on two parallel axes astride the Seine and Marne, pushing towards the sea. On the south side, Melun-Sénart and Evry (near Corbeil) and St-Quentin-en-Yvelines (west of Versailles); on the north, Marne-la-Vallée and Cergy-Pontoise. These towns are to have their own light industries, for a million extra jobs will have to be found in the region by the year 2000, mostly in the tertiary sector. Building of the new towns began soon after 1970, and by 1976 was well advanced despite inevitable delays. Some towns had acquired more than 30,000 new inhabitants and impressive new public buildings.

Not all the new population is going to these cities. The smaller existing towns of the Paris region, such as Senlis, Meaux and Etampes, most of them so lifeless and dreary in the 1950s, have already been revitalized in the past few years as commuter and light industrial centres. Other new towns of medium size will be built in the gaps of the existing conurbation, as is happening already. And here is the crucial point: the planners hope that if these towns can be built in the right way, with the right amenities, then gradually they will be able to absorb and wipe out the older suburban chaos in between them. But it will take a very long time. To start by razing to the ground the existing mess and then rebuild from scratch would be too costly, and would arouse too much hostility. At least the planting of new towns in the middle of the mess will help to provide the needed services and will ease the suburbs' dependence on central Paris; and this is already happening in some places. Nanterre, for instance, west of Neuilly, boasts a new theatre and a notorious new university among its modern housing estates. There are also plans for zoning the decongestion of central Paris. The business milieu has been extended westwards from the Champs-Elysées to La Défense, beyond Neuilly; and some university centres and colleges are moving out to the south or north-east. Thus the famous Ecole Polytechnique, in the heart of the Latin Quarter, now has a new home at Palaiseau, west of Orly.

The Schéma also planned new networks of intersecting motor-ways, and 60-m.p.h. express Métro services far into the suburbs. Some of these projects are now completed. A new ring motorway outside the city gates, the Boulevard Périphérique, is far more effective than the makeshift old North and South Circular Roads in London at allowing traffic to bypass swiftly the centre of the city. Access motorways have been built since the war towards Lille, Rouen, Tours and Lyon, and others are planned. A new ring motorway in the outer suburbs, linking such places as Versailles, Orly and St-Denis, is now being built and will be completed by about 1983. It is badly needed, as suburban traffic grows, but its proposed western section has run into opposition through fear of its spoiling the forests between central Paris and Versailles. Plans for one or two new radial access roads, linking the outer suburbs to central Paris, have in fact been abandoned since Giscard came to power; the reasons were not so much the economic crisis as a new policy of dissuading too much traffic from entering the central area. Plans for France's first rapid elevated 'aerotrain' – a French invention – to be put in service on a new line from La Défense to Pontoise, and to run at 110 m.p.h., were also postponed indefinitely, in 1975. In this case, it *was* a crisis economy measure.

However, the energy crisis came just too late to prevent the completion of the most important of the Schéma's transport projects: the ambitious new international Charles de Gaulle airport that opened at Roissy, north-east of Paris, in 1974. It is now sharing the traffic with the older Orly airport, south of Paris. With its modernistic architecture and highly efficient systems of access to aircraft, it is on the whole a success. But the two main airports are so far apart that there can be tedious delays for those obliged to go from one to the other to change planes.

The Schéma Directeur at least shows boldness and imagination, and has been welcomed by most of those who accept its premise about the inevitability of the growth of Paris. Even the Marxist writer Michel Ragon, a leading architectural critic, has said: 'It is thanks to courageous and clear-sighted civil servants like Delouvrier that Paris will perhaps be saved.' But plenty of other people, on the Right as well as the Left, have criticized the Schéma as being far too grandiose, technocratic and inhuman, as 'a pipe-dream of polytechnicians' or 'a Gaullist attempt to revive the "royal myth" of imperial Paris'. Much of this opposition is purely political, but some is more objective. One fear has been that plans on this giant scale might simply encourage more immigration than ever. And what about the size and siting of the new cities? – why, it is asked, first reject the British models for their artificiality, and then make this *volte-face* with projects several times the size of Stevenage? Might it not be wiser to enlarge existing towns, like Orléans, Reims and Rouen, which are much farther from Paris but could be less than thirty minutes away by 'aerotrain'?

There may be some force in these arguments – and especially in the view often put forward that the Schéma has neglected a proper green-belt policy like London's, and has allowed the conurbation to spread over too vast an area. Much therefore will depend on how the new cities are built. The aim is to provide them with civic centres, theatres and so on, at the same time as the building of the flats. To some extent this is happening, but public funds are short; and despite the new co-ordinating powers of the regional Préfecture, it cannot always bludgeon the various Ministries into ensuring that the ideals of the Schéma become a reality.

This is the central dilemma: the ideas and the spirit of the planners are decades in advance of the cumbersome French legal and administrative machine, and of the habits and attitudes of most ordinary civil servants and local councillors. The Schéma has come up against serious difficulties: lack of funds, bureaucratic and legal delays, human and political opposition. For instance, work on the big project at La Défense was held up for years by the failure of the Government's bridges and highways department to start widening the Pont de Neuilly; on several matters the SNCF is still caught up in rivalries with the Paris public transport authority; and the slow, tortuous process of granting building permits, though designed to favour planned development, often simply has the effect of inhibiting private initiative.

In order to remove one anomaly, the three departments of the region (Seine, Seine-et-Marne, Seine-et-Oise) were redivided in 1967 into eight smaller but more logically shaped ones. Hitherto the small Seine department with Paris at its centre had formed an island in the middle of the Seine-et-Oise, and this concentric pattern hampered administration in a period of rapid growth. But the new divisions had a patent political motive too: they involved constituency changes with the ill-disguised aim of helping to break up the notorious 'Red belt' of the Paris suburbs. This simply aggravated the suspicions and hostility of many of the Left-wing communes towards the Government's over-all plans for the region. Yet the Préfecture badly needs the co-operation of the region's 2,000 communes, whose powers of obstruction are the same as elsewhere in France.

A number of mayors, on the Right as well as the Left, complained that the authorities failed to consult them adequately when drawing up the Schéma. And they may have had some justification. It was the State officials, even more than in the provinces, who did all the real thinking and decision-making. As one planner put it to me, in typical Gaullist tones: 'How on earth can you expect the mayor of some wretched suburb to grasp the kind of problems *we* are facing? Their arguments would simply have held things up.' This tended to be Delouvrier's own attitude; and his technocratic arrogance made him so unpopular with a number of small-time Gaullist mayors in the region that in 1969 the Government found it politically expedient to replace him.

While the larger urban communes resent State officialdom for political reasons, some of the smaller ones outside the conurbation have opposed the Schéma because it threatened their rural peace. In the village of Le Mesnil St-Denis, eight miles south-west of Versailles and barely a mile from the bounds of tomorrow's megalopolis at St-Quentin, I called in 1966 on the Right-wing mayor, Raymond Berrurier, a local solicitor and a most fruity character. He received me with old-world courtesy and talked charmingly and plausibly: 'Here, we're trying to keep the human scale and save the landscape from these skyscrapers. I've formed a national association for preserving the Ile-de-France, and we're at war with Delouvrier. What we need in France are more civic trusts and commissions of inquiry. That's what I admire about Britain. In this country, people's opinions aren't consulted. Even so, my association's managed to make some progress. For instance, when Citroën were planning a new factory at Bièvre, a village near here, we fought them, and managed to get the authorities to reduce its planned size – it would have spoilt the village. Here at Le Mesnil, there are three little factories; but each of them signed a contract with me, before it arrived, promising not to get too big. So, when one firm later wanted to expand, I obliged it to move elsewhere. You see, I don't want my village to change.'

I bade him farewell, reeling before his mixture of civic good sense and reactionary nonsense. One cogent argument against his point of view is that there is little in the unlovely Ile-de-France worth 'preserving', apart from the *châteaux* in their great parks, which the Schéma will not touch. Le Mesnil itself has little charm or character. Though Berrurier himself died in 1967, his outlook and his pressure-group are still very much alive. But most of the larger communes at least do accept the basic need for change, even when resenting the District politically.

But however progress-minded a commune may be, the task of creating a sizeable new town on its territory is generally quite beyond its resources.* How can Evry, original population 5,100, build itself a city the size of Rouen? The French are now adopting the solution of new-town development corporations, with local powers of control somewhat on the British model. Without some such bodies, there are dangers of the new suburbs growing up in piecemeal chaos, as already seems to be happening in some places where private speculators have set to work on their own schemes. The Government has the power to stop this speculation: it can

---

* As there are no 'rural districts' in France, the whole national territory is divided into communes, and an isolated village will generally be the headquarters of a commune covering several square miles.

block the sale of land in the development zones. But it has been very lax. Anxious to shore up public funds with help from private finance, it has sanctioned thousands of private building schemes that break the strict zoning rules of the Schéma. The authors of the Schéma were often furious at such sabotage of their plans. But the trouble in many cases came from higher up, from the well-known links between President Pompidou and the big banks. Finally, after a good deal of outcry, the Minister of Construction, Albin Chalandon, promised in 1972 to allow no more derogations in the Paris area. His successors have managed, more or less, to apply this policy.

The shortage of public funds, both for cheap housing and for essential services, has severely slowed down the application of the Schéma. This has been true especially of road-building. The much-needed Boulevard Périphérique moved forward at only two-and-a-half miles a year; its cost, 72m francs a mile, was ten times higher than that for a similar road in the open country, largely because of the price of land expropriation in Paris. And the magnificent new market at Rungis, with its costly installations, has been doing almost as much harm as good because of the traffic jams it provokes in the area; some people driving to nearby Orly miss their planes because the road is blocked by columns of food lorries. This is because the authorities, when they planned the market, failed to ensure that new access motorways were provided at the same time – a typical example of lack of inter-ministerial liaison in France.

In the past ten years, public funds have increased. Some of the new money, at least, is being spent on renovating the old suburbs, and on providing outer Paris with the community services that are essential if life there is to be tolerable. There are signs of progress: for instance, whereas no new hospitals at all were built in Greater Paris in 1934–60, ten were completed in the 1960s. New theatres, colleges, swimming-pools and libraries are at last beginning to enliven *la triste banlieue*. For many years the task appeared Sisyphean, and the population of the Paris Region continued to swell by some 125,000 a year: the traffic jams mounted up, and the schools, clinics, telephone exchanges, even the cemeteries, were full to bursting. Happily, in the mid-1970s a new factor has occurred to help the planners. The annual population growth has slowed to 100,000 and is likely to drop further. Decline in the national birth-rate is one reason, another is the new trend of Parisians to go and live in the provinces. Delouvrier's forecast of a minimum 14 million population for the region by A.D. 2000 has now been reduced to 12 million. So the race against time, to save the Ville Lumière from the twilight of asphyxia, is likely to be won after all. The improvements in the past few years, the new schools and hospitals and theatres, the new hypermarkets and urban ring roads, are very remarkable – even if often higgledy-piggledy and far from beautiful.

ROMANTIC 'VIEUX PARIS' AND THE SKYSCRAPERS

The Schéma Directeur has little to say about central Paris itself (the Ville de Paris), for here planning is the resort of the municipal council – in theory. In practice, this hitherto weak and conservative body has left the Government to take the initiative for most major decisions. But though city councillors may have been indignant at their dependence on the prefect, they have not lacked powers of veto – and it was the consequent stalemate between council and State, persisting throughout the Third and Fourth Republics, that led to the almost total absence of effective town planning inside Paris from Haussmann's day to de Gaulle's. Governments were too weak or short-lived to challenge the city fathers with controversial projects. Thus an essential measure such as the removal of the huge food markets (Les Halles) in order to decongest the city centre, first mooted in the 1920s, was repeatedly contested and shelved by the council right up till the 1960s. Time and again it rejected imaginative proposals, by Le Corbusier and others, for the city's future.

De Gaulle's return in 1958 brought at last a more forceful and coherent Government approach. And as the council now had a Gaullist majority, it was generally ready to fall in with the new plans. So the next few years saw some serious attempts to check the mounting chaos of Paris without spoiling its beauty. Les Halles *were* finally removed, to a new home in the suburbs. The blackened façades of public and private buildings were scoured

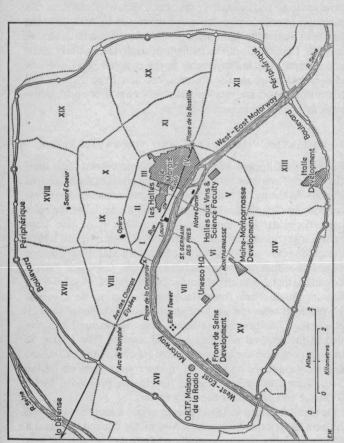

Central Paris, showing the principal new roads and development areas (the Roman figures mark arrondissement numbers).

clean. A start was made on renovating historic areas such as the Marais. The aim was to keep a working balance between aesthetic and practical needs, in a city where so much is worth preserving but so much needs to be rebuilt. Paris cannot become a museum-piece, like Venice; she needs new roads and buildings, like any modern metropolis, but these must be made to blend with the old. This has been the guiding policy of the planners, and for some years it seemed to be working quite well. Despite a few aesthetic blunders, the good aspects outweighed the bad, and compared with London there was not much ugly piecemeal rebuilding of central office areas. It was only in the early 1970s that things began to go wrong, as Pompidou's Government showed itself less concerned with aesthetics than de Gaulle's and more lenient towards the high-rise developers. Parisians became alarmed at the threat of 'Manhattan-on-Seine'. No one was more alarmed than Giscard himself, who on coming to power in 1974 clamped down heavily on the laissez-faire policy of 'gigantism'.

The earliest and most grandiose of the post-war skyscraper projects – at La Défense, two miles west of the Arc de Triomphe – is well away from the city centre and therefore has not run into so much criticism. It was conceived under the Fourth Republic; but, lying outside the city limits, it could not be blocked by the city fathers. The State managed to associate three local communes with a public organization that is now completing what has been called one of the most ambitious and exciting urban renewal schemes in the world. A towering cluster of twenty-six office and apartment blocks are acting as overspill for the saturated Champs-Elysées area and may come to rival it as the city's main business centre. This sharply accentuates the historic tendency of Paris, like London, to shift its centre of gravity steadily westwards.

The area chosen was a 1,700-acre site astride the tip of the straight axis that runs from the Louvre up the Champs-Elysées to Neuilly. The existing mess of tenements and seedy little factories was first gradually cleared, and a grandiose station, complete with 'drugstore' and boutiques, was built for the new express Métro line that comes in from St-Germain-en-Laye. A multi-level ring motorway complex was constructed round the edge of La Défense to take some of the heaviest traffic in France, for this is the main route to the north-west suburbs (an earlier plan, for the whole complex to go underground, was abandoned). In the middle are the skyscrapers, a strange assortment of shapes and colours, treacle-brown and steely-grey, gleaming in the sunset. They stand austerely on a traffic-free platform and will finally contain offices for 40,000 workers, as well as 6,000 flats, with parking below ground for 20,000 cars.

At first, in the early 1960s, a few big firms such as Esso leapt at the chance to move out from the cramped Champs-Elysées area, and they swiftly took over the first completed towers. But then came a long period of delay, as other candidates were put off by spiralling costs and the consequent lack of finance slowed operations to a halt. The Government was finally able to salvage the whole project only by sanctioning, in 1968, a much higher density than originally planned: several towers now rise to forty storeys or more and, seen from the Louvre or the Concorde, they dramatically pierce the skyline behind the Arc de Triomphe. Some modern architects saw this as providing a splendid crown to one of the world's greatest urban vistas – 'The Champs-Elysées,' Michel Ragon has written, 'will become in comparison old-fashioned and provincial, a mere corridor for cars.' Others feared that the towers would ruin the harmony of this famous avenue. And in 1974 Giscard himself cancelled a much-contested plan for so-called 'mirror towers' that were to stand at the centre of La Défense and provide a glinting kinetic backdrop to the Arc de Triomphe.

Even so, La Défense has had fewer critics than some of the other new projects – notably at Maine-Montparnasse and on the Seine riverfront near the Eiffel Tower, for these are sited much closer to central Paris. The old Maine and Montparnasse railway termini have been shifted southwards, and on their site three titanic monoliths have been planted: two rectangular blocks each 250 metres long and 60 high, and between them a 209-metre sky-scraper in similar style, much the tallest building in central Paris (excluding the Eiffel Tower). The ensemble contains flats, car parks and offices (Air France has moved its headquarters there) and eventually there will be a garden too, but this, needless to say, is slower to materialize. The whole project ran into fierce public criticism, not only because of the skyscraper's squat shape (like a huge replica of the much-loved Shell building in London) but because of its siting: it dwarfs the nearby Invalides and Ecole Militaire. But the promoters claimed that a lower or slimmer tower would not be viable in view of land prices and other costs in Paris. The Gaullist Government fell in with their wishes. And downstream from the Eiffel Tower a series of 85-metre blocks have emerged along the Left Bank, in what used to be a tawdry and slummy district. At least they are pleasantly spaced, set on various levels amid small private gardens, and in terms of urban renewal they are an improvement on what this area used to be like. But they too are helping to turn Paris into any anonymous high-rise city.

It is the same story in some other parts of the city. The necessary and overdue renewal of run-down areas – large parts of the fourteenth and fifteenth *arrondissements* – suddenly developed into high-rise smallpox. This was not so until about 1970: many of the new buildings completed in central Paris under de Gaulle or earlier were individually elegant and blended with their surroundings. This was true of the Y-shaped UNESCO headquarters opened in 1958 near the Ecole Militaire. There have also been some more dubious achievements, it is true, such as the barrack-like new university science block that brashly affronts the romantic old quais of the Ile St-Louis, and the new international artists' centre just across the river in the Marais. The latter marks a not very inspired attempt to keep to a traditional style, whereas French architects are usually more successful when being really modern with plenty of glass and steel.

None of these buildings were very tall. But soon it was the turn of the skyscrapers, as Paris belatedly got caught in the kind of boom in office building that London first knew in the 1950s. Other projects followed those described above: notably, a planned cluster of fifty-eight towers near the Place d'Italie, each over 80 metres high, to contain flats for 60,000 people and 450,000 square metres of shops and offices. Paris now has over sixty new buildings worthy of the title of 'skyscraper', and the city's familiar skyline has been changing fast – amid much controversy and misgiving. There are two kinds of debate: the practical and social, and the aesthetic. On the practical side, no one denies that slum clearance and renewal are urgent priorities in many outer *arrondissements*; but when the Pompidou Government and its allies, the promoters, claimed that high-rise redevelopment of these zones alone made sense financially, not everyone agreed. The Government also argued, controversially, that if Paris was to maintain her role as a European business capital, then more office space was needed and this too must be high-rise. But there were counter-arguments. One, that the high-rise buildings would add to the already severe congestion of inner Paris: under the Italie scheme, for instance, the population of the area concerned would swell from 27,000 to 60,000, and although the new housing would be of far better quality than the old, this would not solve problems of traffic jams, pollution and urban stress. Another argument is more political: with land costs so high, the new housing is mostly expensive and middle class, while the former slum dwellers have been evicted to new homes in the outer suburbs. Thus inner Paris has become increasingly a bourgeois 'ghetto' – to the fury of the Left.

The aesthetic debate has been even more bitter. Of course there are many Parisians, mostly older ones, who object to sky-scrapers or modern buildings in any form and want their city to stay unchanged. Their point of view does not have much influence. A more widely held view is that a big city, even Paris, *is* enhanced by a few really tall buildings, even if they are not very beautiful in themselves. The Eiffel Tower caused fury in its day, but today few lovers of *vieux Paris* want it pulled down; and even the wedding-cake pomposity of Sacré Coeur has come to seem acceptable because of its gleaming hill-top position. But a sky-scraper, especially a broad one, does pose more delicate aesthetic problems than a church or a slim spike of steel. Indeed, many modern architects see Paris's vocation as essentially a feminine city of slender towers and spires, and not of square blocks. The Gaullist planners seemed to accept this initially. At least they tried to group the skyscrapers in clusters – as at La Défense and Italie – or in some harmonious relation to each other, rather than let them sprout piecemeal as in much of London outside the Barbican. And – apart from one or two striking lapses such as Montparnasse – they kept them away from the beautiful heart of the city astride the river. But the lapses then grew more frequent, and along the edge of this inner perimeter the new towers have been altering the whole city's physiognomy. The boulevards may stay unchanged, but look what overshadows them.

In de Gaulle's day, when the influential Malraux was Minister of Culture, officialdom was generally alert to such dangers, and this compensated for the weakness of public opinion. Though Malraux is said to have approved personally of the Montparnasse scheme – an odd piece of taste – on many other occasions he was vigilant and effective. His conservation committees scrutinized all new designs – and in Paris you cannot so much as cut down a tree without official permission. When the Ministry of Agriculture wanted to build itself a nine-storey office block in the Faubourg St-Germain, it was obliged to reduce the plan to five storeys, the same height as the rest of that graceful old quarter. There have always been formal rules about the height of new buildings – 31 metres in central Paris, 37 metres in the outer *arrondissements* – and in Malraux's days these were usually abided by. But, under Pompidou, official permission to break them was given more and more readily, as the Government bent to the desires of the developers.

If public opinion were more effective in France, or if the city council had more power, it might have been possible to check such abuses. But the council, for reasons I gave earlier, has generally done what the Government wanted: and while this lack of opposition was sometimes the ally of enlightened town planning (as in the case of the transfer of Les Halles) it could also be its enemy. As for public opinion, given that most broadcasting is in State hands, that the Press is generally weak, and that the French are not the most civic-minded of peoples, it is little surprise that this has not had more impact. It is hard to imagine in Paris the same kind of intense and effective public campaign that has been waged in Britain over Stansted Airport or the Piccadilly scheme. In Paris, the public and the Press make protests and express alarm, but they have tended to feel helpless as to the outcome –

and this has been true not only of the skyscraper issue but of others such as the Left Bank motorway. However, after about 1971 the concern over the 'Manhattanization' of Paris was spreading even in official circles: by 1972 Pompidou himself became worried at the criticism, and in June of that year the Prefect of Paris produced a new plan for limiting the spread of high-rise buildings. Then Giscard came to power, with 'environmentalist' views that happened to coincide with the shift in public feeling.* Some of his first actions were to cancel the Left Bank motorway project and to demand a revision of the Les Halles project (for both, see below). He also hit out at skyscrapers. Besides cancelling the 'mirror towers' at La Défense, he vetoed the plan for a 180-metre tower in the Italie scheme, on the grounds that it would spoil the aesthetic scale of the area and also add to congestion. Permission for high-rise buildings is now granted much more rarely. 'No one today would get away with the Tour Montparnasse,' said an official in 1976.

Even if high-density building is now banned, the age-old congestion of central Paris is still very far from cured. There are many areas that could be torn down and rebuilt on more spacious lines without spoiling the city's character. But this calls for a most careful policy on such matters as new offices, slum clearance, road improvements, and restoration of old buildings. The policy on new office building has been haphazard. In theory they are not allowed in the inner *arrondissements*, where much commercial activity is already far too cramped, especially in the teeming areas round the Bourse. If a landlord pulls down a block of flats, he can put offices in the new one only if it also includes the same residential space as before. But in practice offices have been creeping, often clandestinely, into old residential blocks quite unsuited for them, in bourgeois districts such as the sixteenth and seventeenth. The Government finally accepted that to limit Paris office space artificially might harm France's economic growth as a whole. However, by about 1974, the boom in new office building had begun to collapse through sheer excess. British developers in particular had moved into the Paris market on a big scale about

* See p. 246.

the time of Britain's entry into the EEC, and were responsible for massive new building in various parts of Paris. Then came the economic crisis, with its cut-back in demand, and by 1975 some one million square metres of office space was standing empty in Paris, much of it in such choice sites as the new La Défense blocks. So the problem for the time being has solved itself. The Government's policy today is to attract international firms to settle their headquarters in Paris, but to encourage other companies to transfer their offices to the provinces, and thus it is again restricting new central Paris office building.

Slum clearance is another matter that has been approached somewhat spasmodically. A number of 'insanitary zones' have been designated, mostly in the poor and over-populated quarters of east and south Paris, and notably in the thirteenth and nineteenth districts a number of streets have been torn down and replaced with better-spaced municipal housing; but not more than about 40 per cent of the worst of the Paris slums have been cleared since the war, and new ones fall into decay each year. Any tourist can find these slums if he looks, stinking alleys with crumbling façades and dank courts, where large families live huddled without water and sometimes without electricity – the 'other Paris' from the chic of the Avenue Montaigne or the Opéra with its Chagall ceiling. Just as war-time destruction helped France's post-war railways to become more modern than British ones, so Paris planners sometimes envy London's East End for the Blitz! But this can hardly excuse the delays in Paris, which are largely due to lack of public funds, sometimes aggravated, it is true, by the slum-dwellers themselves. Many of the older ones resist being uprooted: the Parisian is often strangely attached to his filthy but warmly human *quartier*, and he resents the fact that his new home will probably be in some lonely suburb while his own street, because of land prices and profiteering, will be replaced by bourgeois housing.

Another principal cause of congestion was, for many years, the concentration in Paris of the nation's central food and wine markets. The latter, the Halle aux Vins, was finally removed in the early 1960s. Under the Fourth Republic the authorities had repeatedly failed in their efforts to winkle the wine-traders out of their ancient stronghold near the Jardin des Plantes; their political lobby was too strong and their legal resistance too cunning. Then de Gaulle came to power, and simply banished them by decree. It so happened that the Sorbonne Science Faculty badly needed more premises, and the wine market seemed the only suitable site, so an ugly new science block was erected, literally on top of the wine vaults. The traders have since then been gradually transferring themselves to the suburb of Bercy, where a new market is being built. It is one of the most notorious Gaullist victories for rational planning, if not for aesthetics.

The central food market, Les Halles, took longer to shift. Zola called it 'the bowels of Paris' and every morning it blocked whole square miles on the Right Bank with its lorries. Whereas London's little Covent Garden is mainly a market for samples, and the bulk of the goods it buys and sells stays in the docks or stations, Les Halles physically handled a large part of the nation's food. Some 6,000 tons of fruit and vegetables, in addition to meat, were brought into the heart of Paris each day, some of it at peak business periods. But the rich middlemen of Les Halles were always strongly opposed to change: they made fat profits out of the organized chaos, and they had built a powerful lobby to defend their interests, with plenty of allies on the city council. Thus it took many years of pressure and persuasion by Government and planners before the city fathers finally agreed, in 1963, to the transfer of Les Halles. The meat market has been regrouped – expensively and inefficiently – at La Villette, in the north-east suburbs, and in March 1969 the fruit and vegetable sections finally moved to a huge new *marché-gare* built for them at Rungis, near Orly. Here marketing is certainly better organized and more honest. No wonder the middlemen are angry.

The future of the 86-acre site vacated by Les Halles was finally decided in 1976, after a seven-year wrangle. First, after 1969, several rival projects were submitted. Only on one point were all agreed: part of the zone would be made into a small park, for there is no greenery at all in this grimy and teeming corner of the city. But there the agreement ended. A Right-wing lobby wanted luxury flats and smart shops round the park, while 'modernists' wanted the renovation to be part of a much wider scheme for remodelling this drab district of Paris, right up to the Gare du Nord. In 1971 the city council with Government backing opted for a cheaper compromise solution: an international commercial centre round the garden, with office buildings, a huge hotel, and other facilities. Deep underneath would go a large new Métro station for the new express line across Paris. So a huge hole was carved out, and work on the Métro began. But Giscard, on coming to power, ruled that the earlier Government plan was too soulless and commercial, its big new buildings out of keeping with the scale of the area. There was a further long delay, while new plans were prepared, and meanwhile the gaping 'Hole of the Halles' became a standing Paris joke. Only in July 1976 did Giscard approve the sketches for a new and much more classic design, with no business or office centre, but a formal garden a little like the Tuileries. In the middle will be an ornamental pond with a glass bottom, giving light by day to an underground forum with library, arcades and shops. These in turn will light up the pond by night. It sounds attractive, but the Press commented that the disappearance of the business centre will cause a second 'hole' – this time, in the city budget, which stands to lose 120 million francs through the loss of the proposed office space.

Unfortunately, the renovation of Les Halles has involved the removal of the famous nineteenth-century Baltard pavilions that housed the markets, graceful wrought-iron structures that many people thought should be preserved. There was something of an outcry in 1971, and a counter-project took shape for incorporating six of the twelve pavilions into the renovated site. But the Government said no. One pavilion has been reconstructed on a new site in the suburbs, and some of the others too may in the end find new homes; the rest will be destroyed. Certainly none remain at Les Halles. Thus modernization has won another anguished victory over conservation. A few hundred yards to the east, a mammoth new cultural centre has been completed on the patch of waste ground called the Plateau Beaubourg, and was opened in January 1977. Conceived by President Pompidou and now bearing his name, it is a multi-storey transparent structure of glass and steel, blazing out into the night, housing a museum of modern art, galleries, restaurants and reading rooms, a public library for a million volumes, and a modern music institute directed by Pierre Boulez.* In its way it is attractive, and at least highly original, and will certainly fill a need in the life of this humdrum, commercial part of Paris. The much-debated question is whether its blatant modernism is in keeping with the area.

The removal of Les Halles and the lorries has eased, but certainly has not cured, the over-all congestion of traffic in Paris, although, in certain places and at certain times, it can still be worse than in London. As on main roads in the provinces, the motorist's progress tends to be either very fast or not at all. You may sweep majestically down the Champs-Elysées, and then get stuck for half an hour in the bottlenecks between Concorde and the Opéra. Except at peak hours, traffic moves at a spanking pace along the new Seine embankment roads and the main boulevards; but just you try negotiating one of the main exits from Paris at 7.30 on a wet evening, caught for hours in a slow-drifting sea of horn-blowing Gallic frustration.

This is the legacy of Haussmann and after: a few broad roads masking a honeycomb of narrow ones, ill served with exit routes and ill adapted for the building of modern traffic islands. Until the early 1960s the city authorities did somehow manage to keep abreast of the problem, and in 1960 traffic was still moving as fast as ten years earlier, despite a doubling of volume. This was achieved by the building of underpasses along the Seine and elsewhere, by widening some streets and by creating the most extensive one-way system in Europe: even major roads like the Boulevards St-Germain and de Sebastopol are now *sens unique*. However, by 1960 or so *ad hoc* improvements of this sort had reached their physical limits, short of much more drastic rebuilding. Yet traffic was continuing to grow by 10 per cent a year. A more expensive – and controversial – road programme was then put under way in the mid-1960s. Tunnels were carved under the Louvre and the Place de la Concorde for a fast new west-to-east motorway across the city near the Seine. This was completed in record time – a remarkable operation – so that now at most periods of the day is it possible to cross central Paris, say from Boulogne to the Gare de Lyon, at some speed. But the road goes

* See pp. 627–8.

only one way. When, in 1971, plans were announced for an east-to-west motorway along the Left Bank, running directly opposite Notre Dame, there was a public outcry at the threat this posed to the loveliest part of Paris, especially to the famous *quais*. The city council, in a rare moment of effectiveness, persuaded the Pompidou Government to modify the project, so that the road would be roofed over from view. But the *quais* were still doomed. Then in 1974 Giscard, in the most striking of all his conservationist measures, banned the project outright, and crossing the bottleneck in front of the Palais Bourbon still remains a problem for the motorist. At least in the past few years exitways from central Paris have been greatly improved, especially in the west, in the Boulogne and Porte de Maillot areas, where an elaborate network of tunnels and flyovers links the central area to the Boulevard Périphérique and the Autoroute de l'Ouest. Lovers of old Paris do not all approve of the Los Angelization of that unloveliest of parks, the Bois de Boulogne. Commuters generally do.

Fast new roads do not in themselves solve what has been one of Paris's biggest problems, that of parking. This was at its worst in the early 1970s. Since then it has been improved in some areas – by installing underground garages and parking meters – but is still a nightmare in others. More cars are now owned in Paris than there are kerbside or garage spaces for them, and some Parisians thus have no option but to keep their cars outside the city limits. Thousands of cars each day are left illegally in no-parking areas, and the police are lenient – too lenient – about dealing with them. In the 1950s a 'blue zone' was instigated covering all the central districts and limiting all parking during working hours to ninety minutes: the motorist adjusted a cardboard disc inside his windscreen, showing the time he was due to leave. This system required some honesty and brought in no public revenue apart from the fines; it was chosen rather than parking meters as the lesser of two evils, since it was feared that Parisian cunning would rapidly find ways of robbing or cheating meters, and that Parisian pride would never abrogate the citizen's 'right' to free public parking. It was also thought that meters in lovely Parisian avenues would be unaesthetic. Four times in the 1960s the city fathers rejected police proposals for paying meters, and by 1969 Paris was the only major world city without them. Finally, in 1971, the police got their way, and the first meters cautiously made their appearance on some central streets – only to be met with a wave of sabotage. Paper-clips, chewing-gum and false coins were shoved into them; some were sawn off in the night. This campaign was partly the work of angry motorists, but some of it was hooliganism – a schoolgirl of nine caught clogging up meters with paper-clips cheerfully admitted, 'All my friends do the same.' But gradually the sabotage subsided, and the meters are now here to stay. Gradually they have spread throughout central Paris, virtually replacing the disc system. There are now over 26,000 of them, and Parisians have come to accept them. At the same time fines for using non-parking areas have been increased much faster than inflation, and are now between 50 and 120 francs. All this has helped to make short-term parking in working hours much easier in certain business areas, especially around the Champs-Elysées. But it has done little to solve the still acute problem of evening or overnight parking in entertainment or residential districts, where the narrow streets between high nineteenth-century blocks were simply not made for a dense car population. To go to a dinner-party in Passy, or a café or cinema at St-Germain-des-Prés, involves an acute parking problem that is not yet shared anywhere in London, after 6 p.m., except around Leicester Square and Soho. After circling around for anything up to an hour, one arrives late, furious and apologetic, vividly reminded of the basic statistics: 84 people to the acre in central Paris, 43 in London.

Ten years ago this Paris figure was 114 to the acre. As many people move out to new homes in the suburbs, and as slums are cleared and replaced by more spacious middle-class housing or by new offices and shops, so the population of the Ville de Paris has been falling dramatically – from 2·8 million in 1954 to less than 2·2 million today – a process which is speeding up, not slowing down. Less than one Parisian in four now lives within the city gates. This drop is a great help in many respects: it relieves unhealthy congestion, and makes the provision of schools, clinics and other facilities much easier. But it hardly solves the car problem, for the new middle-class Parisians are virtually all of

them car-owners – unlike the old slum-dwellers – and business
and entertainment activities have been multiplying in the premises left vacant. Far fewer Parisians live in the Latin Quarter than
in the old days; far more go there, by day or night, to shop, eat,
or seek culture.

One official solution has been to build car parks underground.
Numerous large ones have opened in central Paris in the past
twelve years, often financed and run by private firms who let
many of the spaces on long leases. Other spaces are for general
use at three francs or so an hour. But often, like the parking
meters, they are not fully utilized, for the Parisian, spoilt by the
long years of the disc system, still has some objection to paying
for parking. Yet he regards the daily use of his car as an inalienable human right; individualist to the last, he will often spurn
public transport even where it is adequate, and insist on taking
his car into town in the imprudent hope that he, unlike the next
man, will succeed in beating the jams and finding a parking space.

This prejudice is slowly being overcome, now that public
transport is at last being made more efficient and comfortable.
Ten or even five years ago, London's public transport was undoubtedly better than Paris's, but now we are seeing a strange
reversal of roles – as London buses and tube trains get dirtier,
slower and more infrequent, Paris's transport has had a face-lift.
It seems to me a typical symptom, almost a symbol, of the
changed fortunes of the two countries. Paris buses always used to
move splendidly fast whenever the traffic was clear, but there
were far too few of them; now their numbers have been greatly
increased, and new and more comfortable vehicles introduced.
There are even a few London-type double-deckers, called *impér-
iales*, but these have never really caught on, if only because the
public retains a notion that they are likely to fall over. Down
many boulevards and avenues there are now traffic-free bus lanes,
so that the buses move even faster than before. Smart new bus
shelters have been built everywhere, with detailed bus-route maps
and even telephone kiosks – and you are now expected to queue
in an orderly Anglo-Saxon manner, instead of pulling one of those
numbered queue-tickets from a machine and then waiting like
some convict for the conductor to call your number. What is

more, the *carnets* of tickets are now usable on bus or Métro alike, and all buses have automatic punchers, so that (unlike London) there are no more conductors. A new *Carte Orange* runabout season ticket, costing some 40 to 80 francs a month depending on zone, can be used on any bus, Métro or local S N C F train routes in the Paris area; introduced in 1975, it had secured a million buyers within the first six months. Thanks to all these new factors, the number of passengers using Paris buses, which had been falling alarmingly for several years, rose 20 per cent in the last months of 1975 and was still rising in 1976. Quite a revolution.

Buses have long been acceptable to the bourgeoisie. But the old Métro, with its nostalgic stench, prison-like automatic barriers, long Kafka corridors and sad ticket-punchers like *tricoteuses* at the guillotine, for years remained defiantly a working-class institution. 'So sorry I'm late,' says Marie-Chantal, archetypal French deb, in a well-known Parisian joke of the fifties, 'but my brother Claude had taken the Jag, brother Pierre had taken the Mercedes, so I took the Métro – do you know it?' London's debs have been cheerfully boarding trains at Sloane Square since the days of W. S. Gilbert. But London tube-trains, with their plushy seating, were for long a cut above even the first-class carriages of the Métro.

In the past few years the Régie Autonome des Transports Parisiens has done much to brighten up central stations, such as the Opéra, with chic modern décor. It even tried to remove the familiar, acrid smell by introducing perfumed trains, but this experiment was short-lived. If the smell has grown less with the years, it is simply because Parisians now wash. A number of platforms have now been lengthened to allow longer trains. Another improvement has been to build the new deep-level de luxe express Métro network embracing both city and suburbs. The first line, from La Défense across the city centre to Boissy-St-Léger, suffered from serious technical hold-ups: the expensive new tunnelling machinery literally broke its teeth on the hard chalk of the Paris sub-soil, and much of the work had to be done by hand, at a slower rate than for the original Métro in the 1900s! The first sections of this line, from La Défense to the Opéra, were finally opened with a triumphant flourish in 1971 – several years behind schedule. By 1976 the whole line was complete, save for a short central section near Les Halles. The gigantic stations are of an opulence exceeding anything in Moscow. This first express Métro line is 27 miles long and has cost 4,000m francs: there are many who argue that this is a false priority, angled towards prestige, and that more money should have been spent instead on improving and extending the ordinary Métro lines. The public transport system may be improving, but Marie-Chantal and her business friends still prefer to use their cars. Or they take taxis, if they are lucky enough to find any.

Taxis in Paris are in theory more plentiful, but in practice more scarce, than in New York or London. There is one for 360 people, against one for 677 in New York, and one for 1,350 in London. Yet at least a thousand stay locked up in their Paris garages each day for lack of drivers. One reason is that Paris taxi-drivers operate one of the most effective closed shops in France. When a driver dies or retires, his taxi-licence changes hands on a private black market for some 30,000 francs. The Rueff-Armand report in 1960 proposed the massive issue of new licences by the police. The 15,000 drivers replied with threats of a strike. In the end, in 1961, the police did persuade them to accept a small increase of 1,000 licences; but the rest of the reform, including a suppression of the black market, has never been applied And as the city grows, the shortage of taxis becomes yearly more acute. Incredible as it may seem, there are fewer taxis in Paris today than in 1931 (13,500 against 21,000) despite a huge increase in population and business. Moreover, the drivers exploit their control of the situation by sticking to conventional meal-times, so that taxis are scarcest when they are most needed, between noon and 2 p.m., or between 6 and 8 p.m. 'In New York or London,' Art Buchwald has written, 'taxis drive their clients towards their destination; in Paris, you accompany the *chauffeur* towards his garage or his restaurant.' The drivers try to justify their closed shop, and their attitudes, by pleading that the traffic jams are slowing down their turnover and reducing their earnings. More taxis, they say, would mean worse jams. But this is illogical; if there were more taxis, there might be fewer private cars on the streets.

If Parisians still have to live in a congested city, at least it is a whiter and smarter one than some years ago. The official policy today is to clean and restore old buildings, as much as to prevent ugly new ones in the city centre; and of all changes in France since the 1950s, the whitening of Parisian façades is often the one that first strikes the casual visitor.

Twenty years ago, this capital of European gaiety and chic gave an overriding impression of greyness and lack of paint. It was sometimes picturesque, as in parts of Montmartre and the Latin Quarter, but more often just depressing, as in the dour commercial quarters around the Rue Lafayette or the Gare St-Lazare. Then in the mid-1950s a large number of shops and cafés began of their own accord to modernize their fronts, with glass, chromium or marble and fresh paint. Owners found that their new boom in trade made them able to afford these changes, and their clients were beginning to expect it. By 1958 the glittering transformation was remarkable, even in many poorer streets. But it was very superficial: on upper floors, house façades were still black and peeling, while passages and courtyards behind the chic shops were often a morass of decay, grime and bad sanitation. Landlords, of course, lacked the direct trade incentives of their business lessees.

Then came Gaullism. In 1958 Pierre Sudreau, the new Minister of Construction, issued a solemn public warning that the decay was not merely unaesthetic, it was also eating at the fabric of the city. But he found it hard to act, because ground rents of most older buildings were still fixed so low that landlords had a valid excuse for not making improvements.* So in 1959 a law was passed allowing phased rent increases, so long as part of the money was spent on cleaning façades *and* courtyards and other basic repairs. At the same time, a forgotten law of 1852 was cunningly revived, that had made the *ravalement* (literally, 'scraping') of façades compulsory every ten years. Then Malraux, whose Ministry was responsible for the upkeep of State buildings, set an example by cleaning, first, the Marine Ministry building in the Place de la Concorde, followed by the Foreign Ministry on the Quai d'Orsay and others. And a few private landlords were

* See p. 327.

induced to follow suit, along eye-catching streets such as the Champs-Elysées.

At first, most people laughed at Malraux and Sudreau: 'What! Get Parisians to clean their houses? It's the kind of law you just can't apply, in France.' But surprisingly it has worked. Today over two-thirds of the city's façades have been *ravalé*, many of them in poorer districts, and the work goes steadily ahead. Each year a number of streets in selected areas are designated by the Seine *préfecture*, and notices served on landlords. Fines for failing to comply within a given time are 1,000 francs; but full *ravalement* may cost up to 100,000 francs, so at first it is cheaper to pay the fines. That is why, in many streets, you can often see an odd black sheep that has failed to copy the new whiteness of its neighbours. But this happens surprisingly rarely. Public opinion has accepted *ravalement* more readily than anyone expected, in a city not famed for its individual house-pride, and it is one sign of the big psychological changes in France since the war. Very often landlords are under strong pressure from their tenants to comply; and if they feel unwilling or unable to afford it, sometimes they sell the building to an association of tenants who then get the work done.

While the town council devoted 40m francs in 1960–64 to assisting private *ravalement*, the State spent 10m francs in the same period on cleaning public buildings. Private stone buildings, most of them nineteenth-century, are generally scoured by a form of wet sand-blasting, while the more delicate stones of older or more precious buildings, such as the Louvre or Invalides, are treated with a special process of pressurized water jets, which takes time and is costly of labour. Today nearly all the famous buildings are restored to their original pale sandstone hues. Most Parisians approve the results, though some do not. 'The Opéra's like a wedding-cake,' they complain. But earlier fears that the cleaning might cause damage seem to have been unjustified, even in the case of the delicate fabric of Notre Dame. Now that the first newness has weathered a little, the effects of the *ravalement* look particularly fine. It may prove to be one of Malraux's few enduring achievements as Minister of Culture, and it has now been extended to the provinces.

Malraux also set about restoring the neglected historic quarters of Paris, and notably the Marais, rather more forcefully than any Minister of Culture before him. Before his arrival, the public authorities and a few rich individuals had both done something, with limited means, to purchase and restore a few of the thousands of lovely old *hôtels particuliers* in Paris. But many others were falling gently into ruin. Then in 1962 Malraux initiated a law that obliges landlords to play their part in the work and cost of restoration, under pain of expropriation, and thus enables the authorities to tackle whole areas rather than just individual buildings. Armed with this law, the city council made a modest start by selecting a nine-acre pilot zone in the centre of the Marais for intensive restoration.

The Marais, between the Hôtel de Ville and the Bastille, was in the seventeenth century the most fashionable and aristocratic quarter of Paris. Since then it has slipped steadily into decline, and today much of it is a slum area, insanitary and overcrowded. Hundreds of its elegant sixteenth- and seventeenth-century houses are still standing; but many of them have been carved up internally into tenements or even depots and workshops, or covered over with ugly superstructures. A few, such as the Hôtel de Sens and the Hôtel d'Aumont, had been rescued by the city council in earlier years. Now the plan is to work outwards from the pilot zone and gradually restore the whole Marais: slum-clearance without demolition. The traditional artisan activities of the area, jewellery, leather-work and toy-making, are being encouraged to remain or return. Some of the modern additions, including garages and a chemical depot, will be cleared away, and a quarter once famed for its greenery will be given back its gardens.

State, city and landlords each spent some 17m francs on restoring the pilot zone in 1967–72. It involved removing about a third of the zone's population of 1,200, mostly poor people, to new homes in the suburbs. Some working-class people were allowed to remain; but landlords, in return for their share of the costs of the scheme, may now charge what rents they like once the houses are restored, and though the authorities claim that they want the area to be socially mixed, it is easy to see it becoming largely a *quartier de luxe*, as it was in the days when Louis XIII held court there in the Place des Vosges.

Many people on the Left strongly resent this solution, although they are otherwise in favour of restoring old Paris. But with public money so short, it may be the most realistic answer. Several areas besides the Marais urgently need attention, and it will all take a very long time; it therefore seems unavoidable to appeal to private capital and snobberies. In the Marais the authorities are merely exploiting the already marked vogue on the part of rich Parisians to return to live in the city's historic centre. The adjacent Ile St-Louis is the focal point of this movement. Its *quais* have been fashionable for many years; now the equally lovely old stone buildings in the island's interior, hitherto working-class slums, are being restored privately at great cost and turned into bijou flatlets, smart antique shops and modish candlelit restaurants in ancient, vaulted cellars. Precisely the same trend is engulfing the old hill-villages of Provence and, as if to underline the point, the food in the new 'bistros' is fashionably '*provençal*'! In the Marais, slum-clearance is less easy; but people like Zizi Jeanmaire and the Prince de Broglie had already moved there, to privately restored buildings; a two-room flat in the Place des Vosges may now fetch 330,000 francs; chic boutiques are opening up all round; and there is now a fashionable Marais arts festival every summer. Just to the north of the Marais, the city council decided in 1976 to renovate the old St-Martin canal, now a derelict waterway bordered by slums and parking lots. The canal is to be cleaned and restored, and lined attractively with gardens and promenades.

These are not the only parts of the city which are changing, socially, under modern economic conditions. Although certain areas, such as Passy and much of the seventh, have for many years been strongholds of the *haute bourgeoisie*, most of Paris has hitherto tended to be rather more socially intermixed than London, partly because of the way the Haussmann-era blocks were built, with flats of varying size and quality under the same roof. This was later intensified by the housing shortage: middle-class people took flats where they could find them, and if the controlled rent was low, they felt disinclined to move. So one might often find quite smart people living at a poor address, behind the Gare de l'Est, for instance, or in the nineteenth. This simply increased their reluctance to entertain at home.

Today all this is gradually changing, as the housing shortage eases and areas are rebuilt. While some rich and fashionable people move into the ancient city centre, others, possibly as rich but less fastidious or cultivated, move out to glossy new luxury housing estates towards Versailles, with names like Résidence Elysée and Parc Vendôme. Steadily the Parisian prejudice against living in *la banlieue* is being eroded, and a nation of commuters is arising. Inside Paris, rents and leasehold prices have been rising so fast, especially for new flats, that many working people too are moving out to the suburbs; and previously humble districts, notably in the thirteenth and fifteenth, are rapidly growing more bourgeois, just as Camden Town or Islington are. But in Paris this is due mainly to new middle-class blocks of flats, as at Italie, and rarely to the conversion of older houses as in London. Communists and Socialists see the trend as a deliberate move by the authorities to reduce the city's Left-wing vote, and are demanding that more cheap State housing be built inside Paris.

The central districts of culture, café life and entertainment are also slowly altering their character or their fashions. The Champs-Elysées grows steadily more brash and commercialized: it is now the stronghold of the rapidly expanding new trades of advertising and public relations, and of the fashion-model world, the movie business and a good deal of organized gay-Paree tourism. As the Edwardian elegance of Fouquet's dims into the past, so the giant new car showrooms rise up beside it, and so do the quick-service beefburger bars with their oddly Americanized names, and the baroque new 'souks' and 'pubs'. The stately private homes around the Etoile have mostly been transformed: one of them now houses a new Champs-Elysées gimmick, 'le Sir Winston Churchill Pub', a plushy and amusingly phoney imitation of London.

Perhaps not too many tears need be shed for the Champs-Elysées. More disquieting is the rapid 'Champs-Elyséefication' of St-Germain-des-Prés, a quarter that up till now had always provided such a contrast to the materialistic glitter of the Right Bank. This enchanted kingdom of literary cafés and old market streets, satiric cabarets, bookshops, art shops and plain working Parisians, has always been something of an intellectual madhouse

– but on its own authentic terms. Now it is being colonized and exploited, and is under massive invasion from a new commercial-ized, trend-conscious arti-smartiness, the Parisian equivalent of some of the more dubious aspects of late swinging London. Op-art boutiques in weird styles have swarmed down the boulevard; *yé-yé* discothèques blare from the bowels of quaint old houses; in the Rue St-Benoît the modish new *faux-bistros* crowd thicker than in Chelsea; and if parking anywhere in Paris is difficult, here at night it is hysterically impossible, as the big smart Citroëns slither on to the pavements of alleys built only for hand-carts. To crown it all, in 1965 a new multi-storey 'Drugstore' of laughable brash-ness planted itself at the very heart of St-Germain, right next to the distinguished old Café Lipp and opposite the Deux Magots. Its gaudy lights blaze out at night like Blackpool pier, and its multiple shops, snack-bars and cinema, all open till after mid-night, attract crowds of goggling visitors, Parisians and others, who have little kinship or sympathy with the *milieu* of Aragon and Sartre they are supplanting. Over the decades, Parisian artists and intellectuals have remained remarkably loyal to the cafés on this square; but now they are giving up the unequal struggle.

The fifth *arrondissement*, around and behind the Sorbonne and the Panthéon, I find the most attractive part of Paris nowadays. Modern change is adding to its vitality, but without yet spoiling it. Some buildings, down by the river facing the islands, have been expensively restored. Just inland, the Rue de la Huchette and other quaint and narrow old streets teem excitingly with students, bohemians and foreigners of every colour. Up on the hill, in a strange bohemian hinterland, picturesque squalor, cheerful mod-ernity and academic traditionalism go hand in hand. *Risqué* caba-rets and off-beat *bistros* stand close to the walls of ancient and venerable colleges; in the crumbling Rue Mouffetard and the Place de la Contrescarpe, Champs-Elysées-style cafés merge with old shops or stalls that evoke the Medina of Fez. And in the peeling old stone-floored houses of the *quartier*, impoverished artists and writers co-exist with working-class families, and with a few young émigrés from smart Passy homes who find it fun to deck out the romantic little attics as stylish modern flatlets. Here the Paris of Mimi and Rudolf whispers its last enchantments.

Montmartre, on the other hand, today seems hardly worth a mention. Artists no longer live there, and though the Butte with its steep steps and streets retains some of its visual charm, the whole area is in the grip of a grasping and vulgar tourist racket. The Parisian folk-songs in the cafés, the comic local characters, the careful folksy décor, are all calculated, down to the last franc, to entice the tourist; and Montmartre has lost nearly all of its old authentic life.

With their glittering neon lights, and glass and marble, the streets of central Paris have changed astonishingly in their outward aspect since the mid-1950s; and, as befits a Latin city of terrace cafés, the style is superficially more dazzling than in London. It is by no means confined to Paris: in the smallest village today, you can find shops with new plate-glass fronts, a blaze of light half the night. Around 1955 the hitherto conservative French commercial world suddenly went overboard for modernism and modern design: much of it is unoriginal and imported and some of it is vulgar but, on the whole, it shows a better sense of harmony and stylistic gaiety than its counterparts in Britain, America or Germany.

In theory the authorities try to supervise the new developments. In the Place de l'Opéra, for instance, the colour scheme for electric publicity signs has to be blue-and-white. On the Champs-Elysées, too, no red signs are allowed, in an effort to avoid the worst horrors of Piccadilly Circus or Times Square. Yet a new gaudiness seems to be creeping in. In Paris you need a building permit to modernize a shop or café, and the designs are scrutinized; but permits are given far too easily, and there have been some serious lapses of taste. How did the St-Germain Drugstore get by? According to one account, the promoters originally submitted designs as horrific as possible – a familiar trick – and then accepted modifications.

Paris today is a stimulating place for the visitor lounging in a boulevard café and watching the world go by. But it is a tiresome place to work in. Certainly, the mood is less ominous and sour than in the Algerian crisis years when the streets were full of sten-guns; but peace and stability have brought an upsurge of materialism and have not done much to ease the Parisians' hardness. *Odi et amo.* I love and hate the Parisians for their ruthless intelligence, their bitter-sweet sophistication, their zest and their cruelty, and I grow tearful at the cabaret-song clichés about the chestnut-trees and the dear little *bistros,* because I know their tarnished magic is still real. But I do not want to live there. Some of Paris, mainly the Latin Quarter, I find as invigorating as any city in the world; the rest is strained and unaccommodating. In Paris people often seem to lack the time or the self-discipline to be generous or fully human: many of the more sensitive ones are today acutely aware of this and of what Paris does to them, and so they try to insulate themselves within their home lives and small circle of friends, or they leave.

But these are difficult years of transition for Paris, after the decades of upheaval and neglect. Maybe, if and when the practical problems are solved and the renovation is done, then a calmer, easier, less self-destructive city will arise, blending the best of old and new. It would be unwise to underestimate how far the *malaise* of Paris today has purely practical causes. But there is something else, which cannot be solved merely by ending the traffic jams or clearing the slums. Paris no longer appears as the world's unrivalled generator of art, ideas and *douceur de vivre*. To find out why, we must first look at some of the underlying social, intellectual and cultural changes in post-war France.

Chapter 8

THE HOUSING INJUSTICES:
A LEGACY OF NEGLECT

ANYONE returning to France today after twenty or so years' absence might be surprised at the rows of new blocks of flats in every town and suburb – a common enough sight in most parts of the world today, but an achievement in its sorry French context. Since the 1950s the French have finally been shocked out of their neglect of housing by the pressures of rapid urbanization; and the nation that built almost nothing from 1914 to 1954 has somehow managed since then to house or re-house some twenty million people. New dormitory towns have risen up, where the traditional French way of life is painfully adapting itself to the very different needs and patterns of modern suburbia. But the housing problem, though much less serious than a decade ago, is still far from solved. Rather, it has changed its nature. There is no longer really a shortage; in fact many flats are standing empty, and people on average are far better housed than even ten years ago. But the complex system of subsidies and controlled rents has led to injustices nearly as great as the ones it was supposed to cure. Many affluent people are living in low-rent flats, while other, poorer families can hardly afford their new 'social' housing. And there is still far too much decrepit, insanitary housing for a nation that calls itself modern. In 1976 the Government finally committed itself to drastic reform of this whole situation.

THE TYRANNY OF BUREAUCRATS
AND SPECULATORS

It often used to be said that the French submitted to bad housing because they preferred to spend their money on other things. I do not think this is nearly so true today: the French are becoming quite house-proud, when they get the chance. But the millions still searching for better homes within their means are finding out the hard way that nations, like people, have to suffer for their past. The backlog of neglect will still take many years to cure; and even today the building programme is inefficiently organized. Until a few years ago France's housing shortage was often described as her 'foremost national disgrace'. This is no longer quite true: crash building programmes are bearing fruit, and since 1968 housing has been replaced by education as the nation's number one disaster area. Even so, there are plenty of black spots remaining, especially in the slums of old cities.

Whereas Britain and Germany began massive rehousing right after the war, the French (perhaps wisely) gave priority to industrial recovery. In 1952 France was still producing only about 75,000 new homes a year. The annual rate then began to shoot up fast, and in the 1960s it was running at about 400,000, to reach 550,000 for 1975. But Germany had been building half-a-million new homes a year ever since 1953; and Britain, with less war damage than France and a slower population increase, had by 1967 completed five-and-a-half million against France's four million. The activities of 'Shelter' and the scandal over *Cathy Come Home* show that in Britain, too, the housing shortage endures; but France's was, till recently, more widespread. For one thing, the French have had to fight against the appalling archaism of much of their existing housing. Certainly there has been dramatic progress: between 1954 and 1973 the percentage of homes without running water fell from 42 to 3·4, and of those without flushing lavatories from 73 to 30, while in the same period the proportion of homes with bath or shower rose from 10 to 65 per cent. But the 1968 census classified 31·6 per cent of homes 'over-crowded' (that is, with more than four people in three living rooms) and a 1973 enquiry found that 65 per cent of all French houses date from before 1914, many of them in shocking repair. And though the quality and amenities of the newest flats are steadily improving (few today are built without bathrooms) on average they are still less well finished and well equipped, and with smaller rooms, than their counterparts in northern Europe.

The social problems and hardships caused by the housing crisis have been obvious enough. According to a survey in 1965, one in four of the 800,000 annual abortions in France was directly connected with it. Often it might disrupt a marriage, or dissuade a worker with a family from moving to a better job in another district. The Press has been full of horror stories: I remember in 1957 the case of a young Paris hospital orderly and his wife and baby, who could not find lodgings and finally were granted a room inside the hospital. But the baby cried at night and disturbed the patients. Terrified lest they be thrown out, the witless parents resorted to putting sticking plaster across its mouth – and it suffocated to death.

For workers there are now at last plenty of State-built flats; but their rents and fixed charges have been rising so fast that many of the poorest people for whom they were intended can no longer afford them. There are now masses of smart flats around, but rents and prices of new ones have soared fantastically, especially inside Paris. A working-class family will probably have a car and TV, but may still live in a tenement, or else in a new flat that is cramped by many modern standards; a middle-class family may dine out extravagantly and take holidays in Greece, yet be reluctant to invite their friends to their home. In the past such things were attributed to the French disregard for home comforts, and preference for food, clothes and pleasure. But today many Frenchmen would gladly spend more on improving their living conditions, if only they could do so at a fair price. The problem today lies not with French domestic habits, but with former Government policies and the crazy structure of the property markets. This is one of those typical sectors of French public life where State investment has had a low priority because it does not offer quick returns of productivity.

Much of the trouble stems back to August 1914. On the outbreak of the First World War one of the Government's first actions was to freeze all rents, in order to protect soldiers' families from profiteering landlords. It was a fair war-time measure. But in the difficult post-war period it was maintained as a permanency, and no inter-war Government had the foresight or the electoral courage to lift it. Thus developers had little incentive to promote new buildings; new rents, too, were blocked. No more than

1,800,000 homes were built in France between the wars, a quarter of them simply reconstruction of war damage, while Britain and Germany each built over four million. The low rents gave landlords a valid excuse for making no improvements or repairs, so that many houses fell into premature decay. This helps to explain why, even today, so many buildings in France look woebegone.

After the Second World War, the upsurge in the birth-rate and the rural exodus soon brought the crisis to a head. Many privileged people were living practically free, at 1914 rents shrivelled away by inflation; many others were homeless. So in 1948 a coalition Government passed a bold law. This permitted gradual long-term rent increases for existing flats, so long as part of the money was spent on repairs; and it freed rents henceforth on new private building. The law, vigorously applied, was partly successful in its twofold aim: to encourage both repairs and new building.

But the controlled increases in pre-1948 rents have been far outstripped by the rapid rises in the newer ones, caught up in the spiral of inflation, and there is still a wide price-gap between flats of similar quality in the two groups. Moreover, the 1948 law did not repeal one crucial clause in the 1914 law that grants a tenant virtual freedom from eviction, even on expiry of lease. Families, often quite wealthy ones, will thus cling stubbornly to relatively cheap flats they may have occupied for generations; and this limits the market, especially for the people who need it most, the young couples with growing families. The market, instead of being flexible to suit demand, is still artificially divided into three sectors: old controlled rents, new cheapish State housing (also controlled), and new uncontrolled housing which is often unreasonably expensive.

The categories of State housing – the equivalent of 'council housing' in Britain – are many and complex, the commonest being the *Habitations à loyer modéré*, built by public agencies (led by the State, but partly municipal) with money from long-term Treasury loans at 1 per cent interest. Some 197,000 HLMs were built in 1974, two-thirds for rent and the rest for ownership; and 130,000 other low-cost flats received other forms of public aid, partly derived from a regular housing tax on firms to the tune of 1 per cent of their wage bills. These figures rise steadily each year (in 1959 only 90,000 HLMs were built) but they must be set against the demolition or collapse beyond repair of nearly 200,000 old houses a year. Given the rise in the population, it is only in the past few years that the supply of new 'social' housing has caught up with demand. The quality of the newer HLMs is generally fair and their rents, though rising fast, are still much lower than those of the open market: a three-room flat in the Paris suburbs will cost around 500 to 600 francs a month, including central heating and maintenance. Waiting-lists for the better-sited flats are often full, and are subject to some graft and political intrigue; your own political views may or may not help you find a flat, depending on who controls the local HLM office. Moreover, though the HLMs are supposedly reserved for lower-paid workers, they are frequently infiltrated by junior *cadres* and civil servants, who would rather sink their pride than pay the prices of the open market. This does not ease working-class resentment.

Rather than increase the burden on the Treasury, the Gaullist Government stepped up its efforts to woo more private capital into building investment. But the response has benefited the luxury market far more than the 'social' sector. Inevitably, financiers and developers are still reluctant to invest in low-rent flats; they prefer free rents and quick returns. So the 1960s saw an extravagant boom in new luxury housing, especially in Paris and on the Riviera, with ready buyers among the newly rich. And the losers have been the middle-income groups as well as the poor; for not only are middle-range flats over-priced, but mortgages are harder to find than in many countries.

Before the war urban flats were mostly rented. Today there is a growing trend towards owner-occupation of new flats, especially by middle-class people with some capital. It satisfies their property-owning instincts, it provides developers with quick dividends, and it suits the Government for political as well as economic reasons. But not everyone can raise the money. The State has its own generous mortgage system for a small number of owner-occupied HLMs, but funds for these are limited.

The Government has recently made some efforts to create a mortgage market, inspired partly by foreign models. In 1966 it authorized the deposit banks and insurance companies to institute twenty-year loans at 8 or 9 per cent interest. This met with a reasonable response, and has meant that an average four-room flat in the suburbs or provinces costing, say, 200,000 to 300,000 francs is at last within the range of a young middle-class family without capital. Previously, the only hope was to borrow from the banks who, with luck, might lend up to 60 per cent but at 10 to 15 per cent interest repayable within ten years. The Government also launched a modest new savings-bank scheme for housing, with some initial success. But it has not yet tried on any scale the solution to the housing crisis practised in Britain and elsewhere, that of massively enlisting private savings. This may be an opportunity wasted; for the French, who have never in the past been great savers, are at last, with their new prosperity, taking private saving much more seriously.

Yet progress here is likely to remain slight, until the flagrant speculation of land and property is finally checked. This has been the biggest obstacle of all to cheaper and better housing, and, more than anything, it has sent the free rents soaring. It also limits the number and quality of H L Ms, simply because so large a part of their precious funds has to be spent on the initial buying of land.

It may seem a paradox that a country with so much virgin open space should suffer from the kind of speculation usually associated with land shortage. But the French have generally rejected the policy of commuter towns deep in the countryside, and even the planned new Paris satellites mark only a modified new departure. The French urban tradition is one of close city living, and this has pushed up land prices all round the perimeters of towns, as well as inside them. Prices in urban areas rose twentyfold in 1945–57, far more rapidly than over-all inflation. This is a paradise for any-one wanting to make easy money. In an area scheduled for massive development, such as La Défense or the western suburbs of Toulouse, prices have risen anything from twenty-five- to a hundredfold in a few years. Today a square metre of land may cost 15,000 francs on the Champs-Elysées or in parts of Nice and Cannes, 8,000 francs in a smart suburb like Neuilly, and 2,000 francs or more in many other parts of Greater Paris or the

Riviera. No wonder that the HLM agencies have abandoned most of the Ville de Paris to bourgeois housing.

Scarcely less grave than land speculation is profiteering over property, which often is allied to corruption or embezzlement. There are proven cases of officials being suborned by developers to push through the building permits for some dubious luxury-housing project; or of the real financing and conditions of a scheme being dissimulated by its promoters in order to allay suspicions. To be fair, one must add that only a minority of developers are dishonest and unscrupulous. But corrupt practices are so widespread that the State tends to turn a blind eye; to make a purge might implicate too many of its own officials, or might deter the business world from investment in building. Sometimes, however, a scandal bursts into the open of its own accord: in 1961, a fashionable and gifted architect, Fernand Pouillon, was imprisoned for embezzling funds for a smart new block of flats in Paris; and in 1964 a highly respected Marseille development company, the Urbaine Immobilière, was found guilty of massive tax evasion and of cheating its own contractors and clients.

In theory the Government has long had plenty of legal means to take stronger action than it has dared. One of the first Gaullist measures, in 1959, was to pass a law giving birth to the *zones à urbaniser par priorité* and the *zones d'aménagement différé*: sectors of private or public land marked out either for immediate public development (ZUPs) or reserved for future use (ZADs). In these zones the authorities have the right to forbid sales of land, to pre-empt and, if they consider the price demanded too high, to have it fixed by a tribunal. The idea is an excellent one, as with the SAFERs in agriculture; and in France, where so little land is municipally owned and where the rights of private property tend to be held sacred, it is probably the only way to make coherent town-planning into a reality. But funds have generally been too small for much effective pre-empting.

The ZUPs and ZADs are still in force today (save that the former now have a rather different statute and are called ZACs – *zones d'aménagement concerté*). They were the creation of Pierre Sudreau, who made great efforts during his four years as Minister of Construction (1958–62) to lay the foundations of a better housing policy. This remarkable man ranks beside Pisani as one of the best of the 'technocrat' Ministers of the Gaullist era. But his reforms were not effectively followed up by his successors. Not that this was entirely their fault. In the late sixties and early seventies several distinguished Ministers of Equipment and Housing (as the post came to be called) tried one after the other to push through the anti-speculation measures which they knew were essential. One after the other they fell foul of the timidity of the Government, especially under Pompidou, in face of the pressures of big business. Pisani first, in 1967, proposed some new taxes; the Government shelved all of them but one, a tax on high-density building, which actually became law although, owing to devious machinations against it, it was never applied. Albin Chalandon, who succeeded Pisani in 1968, arrived with 'liberal' economic views, in favour of a free market, but gradually he too came to realize the necessity for tighter control of speculation. In 1971 he tried to revive Pisani's plan for a tax penalizing those owning vacant unused land in urban areas, and added to it a project for speeding up the cumbersome French expropriation procedures. Gaullist deputies at once threw up their hands in horror – how many of their electors were landowners, large or small, who stood to suffer from such changes? In a pre-electoral period the reforms were unthinkable, and so were shelved again. It was not merely that Pompidou had compromised yet again with his big-business allies: there are fourteen million land or house owners in France, many with no more than the odd acre but all eager to be able to benefit from speculation if ever the chance arose.

After Giscard came to power, at last something effective was done. It was seen that land speculation was not only causing social injustice by raising housing costs, it was also threatening the fabric of many historic city centres. Prices there were now so high that promoters felt obliged to build to a high density, while residents were fleeing to cheaper and more spacious homes in the suburbs, leaving behind them empty streets or slum ghettoes full of poor immigrants – an American-style phenomenon, alien to the French city-centre residential tradition. The Ville de Paris is not the only city that has been depopulating: between 1968 and

1975 Lyon lost 70,000 people and Bordeaux 44,000, both to the profit of their suburban communes. Giscard's action was to encourage his Minister of Equipment, Robert Galley, to prepare a new law which was hurried through Parliament by the end of 1975. This imposes a legal density limit of 1 in all city centres (in Paris, 1·5); that is, on a given site, if you put up single-storey buildings you can cover the whole site, but if you build to an average of two-storeys you can cover only half the site, and so on. The law also gives town councils the right to pre-empt central sites at market prices, and the right to impose special taxes on any promoters breaking the density rules. The aim is that councils should use this extra revenue to finance new green spaces, other civic amenities, and low-cost housing near the city centres.

The project came under fire from all sides – from the Left who thought it was too weak and could easily be evaded by speculators, and especially from sections of the Right who complained of 'creeping municipalization' and infringement of the sacred rights of property. But Giscard, unlike Pompidou, stuck to his guns despite pressure from his allies: the law went through and is now being applied. At least it is a step in the right direction, though it does have inadequacies. One fear is that it may give mayors too much of a temptation to connive at high density because of the extra revenue it will bring them. This can only be tested with time. A much more serious criticism of the law is that it applies only to central areas of cities, and thus will do nothing to limit the speculation which is causing so much harm on the edges of cities and in smaller towns and villages, that is, where most of the new low-cost housing is sited. New moves in 1975 to bring in a general land tax were quietly shelved; in the present economic climate even Giscard would not dare that one.

Government regulations are responsible for the artificial division of French rents into three categories, which frequently leads to injustice. In the same street in an average town, a middle-class pre-1948 block may have three-room flats controlled at around 200 francs a month, while similar flats in a post-1948 HLM block next door might be 400 to 500 francs, and scarcely superior ones in a new block down the road might have 'free' rents of 800 to

1,200 francs. And these privileged pre-1948 rents give rise to all kinds of rackets. Sometimes, for instance, a family in a large flat will sub-let one room furnished for as much as their whole rent. Or a big Paris flat may remain virtually unused, rented by a rich widow on the Riviera who comes to Paris only once a year and yet has legal security of tenure. Or an outgoing tenant may succeed in extracting key-money (supposedly illegal) from his successor, of maybe up to 200,000 francs. Or a Paris flat may be sub-let furnished to foreign diplomats or other visitors, at a colossal rent. This practice, too, is illegal; but it flourishes, and few foreigners in Paris have not suffered from it. How well I remember Madame C. in Passy, coming round each month for her 800 francs *in cash* for my simple three-room flat (that was 1958; the price might be treble now), always seeming a little nervous that I might call her bluff and report her, which I never dared to do.

The Frenchman today is coming to care more about his home, and increasingly he wants to own rather than rent it. This tendency has been encouraged by the Right-of-centre Fifth Republic Governments, and the percentage of French homes owner-occupied rather than rented rose from 41·6 in 1962 to 45·5 in 1973. The French are also spending a larger part of their income on housing. Since the war the figure has risen from 3·4 to 13 per cent, and is now comparable with British, German and American levels, as it never used to be. But, because of the contortions of the market, many people spend only 3 or 4 per cent while others, no less well-housed in proportion to their incomes, spend 15 or 20 per cent. Millions therefore could spend more without hardship, but millions of others are spending more than is fair. It is a problem not of poverty but of fairer organization by the Government, whose failure to do better has been a symptom of the weakness of social justice and morality in France. Despite the efforts of men like Sudreau and Pisani, the de Gaulle and Pompidou Governments did not tackle the problem at its root. This was partly because a régime preoccupied with prestige and industrial progress set a comparatively low priority on housing, and also because so many of the Government's big-business allies were profiting from the situation.

As over land speculation, so in the wider field of housing and rent policy, Giscard has at least proved himself far more effective and progressive than Pompidou. In 1975, he commissioned two of France's most brilliant public servants, Raymond Barre and Simon Nora, each to make detailed proposals to him, the first on ways of improving the State system of financing low-cost housing, the second on ways to preserve older housing from falling into ruin. The Barre Commission concluded that the 15,000 million francs of State annual subsidy to HLMs and similar housing was being used both uneconomically and unjustly because the right people were not benefiting from it. HLM rents had risen so sharply that the poorest people, for whom they were intended, could no longer afford them and thus stayed in their old unhygienic slums. On the other hand, the quality of the newer HLMs was quite good but, because there was no proper means test for applicants, many well-salaried people were moving into them, and thus benefiting from subsidies intended for the poor. The period of shortage was now over; there was now plenty of newish housing, so that those with a little money could pick and choose. As a result many of the older HLMs of the fifties era, poorly built, badly sited, but over-priced, were now standing empty. Some 50,000 flats were empty in the Paris region alone. The wheel was coming full circle. As a remedy for this waste of resources and lack of justice, Professor Barre (a leading economist, who a few months later was to be appointed Prime Minister) proposed quite simply that the system of financing should be inverted: subsidies should go not to the agencies building the HLMs and similar housing but to the recipients, that is to the tenants or would-be owners. Thus rents and prices would be raised to an economic level, but individuals would be helped to pay for them according to their means. The capitalist ethos and the lowest income-groups would benefit together, at one stroke. Brilliant.

Simon Nora followed a parallel line of thinking, in suggesting that there was now too much construction of new housing on new estates, and funds should be switched to renewal of older housing, especially in town centres. He pointed out that 16 million people – mostly the very old, or young couples – were still living in homes classified as 'uncomfortable' (that is, without indoor sanitation, and often over-crowded). He blamed the 1948 rent control law, which was still dissuading landlords from making the necessary improvements. He went on to demonstrate that, while in some cases these older dwellings were beyond repair, in most cases it would be cheaper to modernize them than to build new ones. He argued eloquently that to restore older housing would be to improve France's architectural heritage and give new life to city centres; the French no longer wished to live in soulless suburban estates, they wanted attractive surroundings and would be happy to live in the centre of cities if the housing quality and amenities were right. This was a theme totally in tune with Giscard's own conservationist views, and with the new public mood. Nora, like Barre, proposed subsidies for families on a means basis, rather than for the builders. Nora and Barre were both of them opposed by the promoters and the building trade, for obvious reasons, but they may be getting their way. In July 1976, Robert Galley announced a new Government project that is inspired by both the reports. There will still be some direct aid to the low-cost housing agencies, but there will also be a huge new scheme of subsidies and State mortgages for those wanting to rent or buy this housing, all on a sliding scale according to income. The Bill is likely to have a hard passage through Parliament. But it represents one of Giscard's more striking social reforms – as well as usefully stealing a march on the Left, just before the elections.

A PAINFUL ADJUSTMENT TO LIFE IN THE NEW SUBURBIA

Approaching Paris from the north, from Chantilly, you see a sign to the left, 'Sarcelles, Grand Ensemble', and the eye follows it down to the forest of grey-and-white rectangles stretching across the plain below. To many Frenchmen that signpost reads 'Brave New World': this was one of the first and still the most notorious of the new Paris suburbs, and has given its name to a new 'disease': sarcellitis, or new-town blues. Its criss-cross streets bear names like Allée Marcel Proust and Avenue Paul Valéry, but there is little poetry in the flat utility façades of their build-ings; the town has 80,000 people, yet for over fifteen years there was no *lycée*, and the civic centre arrived fifteen years after the flat-dwellers it was built for. In the noisy, perfunctory cafés, young *pieds noirs* and slum evacuees play with pin-tables or argue about racing bets; in the Parc J. Kennedy, beside the new flats, children scrabble at sand in the playgrounds; a notice in a shop window pleads with lonely housewives to join some religious fellowship. For students of Harlow or Stevenage, it is all very familiar – and yet different. In many ways, Sarcelles is a paradise of fresh air and modern plumbing after the old slums – and yet, what opportuni-ties were missed! To the French it seems more than a town, it is a portent, an emotive concept like St-Tropez or Verdun: a victory in the grim battle for more housing, but at what cost to the human spirit?

The French woke up late to the social problems of modern mass suburbia, but now they are fascinated and disturbed by them. At last they realize that to build enough new flats is not the only answer to the housing problem: there must also be rational, human town-planning. But the French social temperament, still family orientated and unneighbourly, adapts ill to these new con-ditions. Without some community living the new suburbs remain lonely and soulless; yet steps to promote it are often resisted in the sacred name of French privacy and individualism.

In the first decade after the war, while the British were fast at work on their New Towns, in France virtually the only concerted new building was the reconstruction of the ravaged centres of towns like Caen and Le Havre. Elsewhere housing was simply thrown up piecemeal, block by block, wherever there was a suit-able gap or land was cheap. But by the mid-1950s, as the building programme at last gathered pace, a more coherent approach was clearly needed. So Pierre Sudreau launched the policy of the 'Grands Ensembles', self-sufficient suburbs each with its own shopping centres, *lycée* and so on. In some ways they are not so different from the British models, save that they are usually closer to existing cities and consist of flats rather than houses.

Sarcelles, the largest of the Grands Ensembles and the arche-type, was started in 1956 and is virtually completed, housing

80,000. Others, not so large and rarely as ugly, have grown up in other parts of the Paris region and elsewhere. They were born of necessity, and at least they have fulfilled their basic aim of re-housing; in Sarcelles, for instance, one inhabitant in three has come direct from the Paris slums, while most of the others never had a home of their own before, but were sharing with relatives or living in cheap hotels. But the rehousing has created new problems in turn, and the Grands Ensembles have come in for heavy criti-cism. Why cannot even low-cost housing be more attractive? Why are the suburbs not provided with better social and cultural equip-ment, more transport and local industries? Why are their citizens not leading happier and fuller lives? These questions have been posed and analysed without cease in a stream of books, theses, conferences and sensational newspaper articles. The French, so conservative about their living patterns, seem to be finding the new-town experience far more traumatic than the British. Life there is scrutinized as if it were the planet Mars, or some new biological discovery.

The first main criticism, of Sarcelles in particular, was of crude architectural planning. Unlike the wide-spreading new towns of England, the French ones are usually built with higher density, in the usual south European urban manner. This may not in itself be a drawback; in fact, it may promote a feeling of urban warmth and animation, whereas the long, tidy lanes of English suburbia can often seem lifeless and depressing. But at Sarcelles the density has taken on a fearsome geometry. Its central quarter, dating from the 1950s, is an austere gridiron of straight avenues and grey box-like blocks, mostly five storeys high, some rising to sixteen. There is a fair amount of space, with trees and gardens, in contrast to the ultra-high density of most of central Paris; but this does not really atone for the rectilinear concept which horrifies so many visitors. Ian Nairn castigated 'the intellectual arrogance and paucity of invention of this loveless, pre-cast concrete desert'.* Sarcelles, in fact, sprang from a clumsy attempt by French archi-tects to apply some of le Corbusier's ideas without properly understanding them.

Modern town-planning, neglected and misunderstood in France

Observer, 3 January 1965.

for so long, has fortunately made great strides in the past ten years
or so, since the early days of Sarcelles. At last the French are
beginning to realize what le Corbusier had been preaching at their
deaf ears since the 1920s. Was ever a prophet so not without
honour save in his country of adoption? When the great Swiss
died in 1965, one of his French devotees told me, 'Good: *now*
perhaps the French will take him seriously!' But even before his
death there were signs of a thaw. This evolution of thinking is
noticeable even inside Sarcelles. Its newer quarters, built in the
mid-1960s, are markedly less monolithic than the old ones, and
the new blocks are grouped in some harmonious relation to each
other. The design and quality of individual buildings and flats
shows a similar improvement: whereas the older ones have severe
barrack-like façades of stone and concrete, the new ones are much
gayer, with balconies, larger windows and façades made of
coloured synthetic materials. Though costs must always be kept
very low, improved techniques and productivity have finally made
it possible to add a few frills for the same relative price. Likewise
the newer workers' flats now have larger rooms, the luxury of a
small bath in place of a shower-tub, and soundproofing that is still
imperfect but less of a farce than it was in the days when *les bruits
des voisins* were major causes of unneighbourliness and 'sarcellitis'. Having broken the back of the housing shortage, the
Ministry is now turning its attention to improving quality.

Slowly but surely, therefore, French cheap-housing standards
are creeping up towards north European levels. After the horrors
of the early period, some of the newer estates and suburbs are
beginning to show quite a pleasing sense of landscaping, design
and detail. Among low-cost developments, I am thinking for
instance of Aillaud's ingenious pastel-coloured, serpent-shaped
ensembles at Pantin (eastern Paris) and Forbach (in Lorraine).
As for the smarter bourgeois estates, some of those just west of
Paris are as elegant as any of their type in Europe.

And yet the French have a habit, often baffling or irritating to
foreigners, of leaving even some of their best-designed new
projects with an untidy, unfinished air. A smart new building may
remain for months surrounded by rubble or weedy waste-land;
sleek flats will co-exist cheerfully with shacks or rubbish-heaps

which no one seems to be bothered to remove. Sometimes this is due essentially to delays over expropriation of adjacent land. At Sarcelles, for instance, where the streets are kept neat and tidy by the firm that is building the town, a few scattered privately owned sheds and villas nevertheless manage to survive incongruously amid the new geometry, defying the lawyers' efforts to remove them. But in many other instances, the cause of this untidiness seems to be a kind of aesthetic blindness of the French to surroundings that do not interest them: thus a smart restaurant often does not bother to decorate its *toilettes*. Once the main job has been done, people worry less about clearing up the bits; it is a typical facet of that slapdash French perfectionism that puts more stress on form than on detail. Notice how the French love elegant new cars, yet often leave dents and scratches unrepaired. I think this national trait, at all levels, is partly a hangover from the defeatism and lethargy of pre-war decades, and is certainly on the wane today. The success of the *ravalement des façades* campaign is one sign of this, and the new concern for personal hygiene may be another. But the trait still exists, and like the other forms of ugliness, it may add marginally to suburban *malaise*.

The aesthetic failings of the earlier Grands Ensembles have been slight, however, compared with their administrative troubles. The French system of local government, and the economic structure of the housing industry, are both of them peculiarly ill-suited to this kind of venture, so that two inter-related difficulties have arisen. First, when the houses are built there is little money left over for the social equipment that alone can turn a dormitory into a living town. Second, civic progress is often frustrated by conflicts between the new town and the old semi-rural commune on to whose territory it has been 'parachuted'. The two largest new towns so far completed in the Paris region, Sarcelles and Massy-Antony, both afford striking examples.

At Sarcelles the main operation of building, renting and upkeep has been carried out with impressive efficiency by a body known as the SCIC (Société Centrale Immobilière de la Caisse des Dépôts). The Caisse des Dépôts is a huge State finance house; and the SCIC, its subsidiary, is France's leading building promoter. Its own work is scrupulous, and free from any breath of scandal. But its official brief is simply to provide houses quickly and cheaply, and the Government neglected to insist that it also be given the funds for the next stage. Of course basic shelter must be the first priority, but the inhabitants, deprived of their fair share of schools, sports grounds or public transport, have been quick to point out cynically that it is the flats, whether rented or sold, that bring back the investment.

Responsibility for providing public equipment has been divided rather vaguely between the SCIC, the relevant Ministries and the local municipality; and here the trouble began. In June 1964, in the middle of Sarcelles, I noticed a splendid hole in the ground, some 200 yards square and fifteen feet deep: 'That,' I was told proudly by the SCIC, 'will be our civic centre, with a big Maison de la Culture, library, skating-rink, scores of shops including a giant Prisunic, 400,000 square metres of offices and underground parking for 2,500 cars. Any day now, work will begin.' I came back *two-and-a-half years* later: the hole was quite unchanged, a bit muddier in the January rain. What had happened? First, there were municipal elections. The Grand Ensemble is adjacent to the old townlet of Sarcelles, population about 4,000, which until 1965 held most of the seats on the communal council. But the afflux of new working-class votes produced an inevitable swing to the Left, and in March 1965 Sarcelles elected a council with a Communist-Socialist majority, most of its members from the new town. (This has been a common pattern in many such places: one alleged political motive behind the Gaullists' rehousing policy, that of breaking up the monolithic 'Red Belt' of the older suburbs, seems to have been a complete failure!) The new Communist mayor, Monsieur Canacos, a technical worker, was damned if *he* was going to help the State with its Maison de la Culture. For a long time he refused to commit his 50 per cent of the needed funds. Finally, in 1966, some kind of agreement was reached; but neither commune, nor SCIC, nor private business showed much haste to sink capital in so ambitious a project as the civic centre, and it was not until the winter of 1968–9 that building work began in the muddy hole. Three years later, the centre was not yet completed.

At Massy-Antony, in the southern suburbs, the problems have been worse. The State authorities deliberately planted this Grand

Ensemble astride two communes in different departments (Antony in the Seine, Massy in the Seine-et-Oise) in order to provoke maximum administrative difficulties and so draw the fullest lessons for the future. They certainly got what they wanted. The town has been built by a *société d'économie mixte* comprising State and private interests plus the two existing communes, which already were quite populous; but the communes' role has been largely obstructive. First, the Socialist mayor of old Antony rejected plans for a new separate commune for the ensemble, since it would have deprived him of some territory and power. Then the mayor of old Massy began systematic opposition to the new town. Most of the ensemble is in Massy, not Antony; but the burghers of the sleepy old market-town of Massy, most of them small tradesmen, farmers and *rentiers*, have been ill-equipped to cope with the growth of a big modern suburb. They fought it, and building might never have started at all, had not the State, in 1958, made rare use of its ultimate right of veto over communal obstruction and sent bulldozers out over the cornfields while the farmers were in the act of harvest. This incident did not make for happier relations. The former mayor of Massy, an old-style reactionary Socialist, saw little reason to spend his precious budget on the new town. For some years he succeeded in blocking the *dossiers* of joint projects that needed his formal support, notably for a sports centre. And so the young slum evacuees in the new town were condemned to play football on improvised pitches amid car parks and vacant lots. The irony was that the mayor derived much of his electoral support from those who suffered from his policies, for most of the new Massiens are Left-wing. Today there is a new and younger Socialist mayor, far more reasonable, and matters have improved.

Such conflicts did not augur well for the projected new cities of the Schéma Directeur. The French system aimed hopefully to breathe life into a Grand Ensemble by grafting it on to the living tissue of a traditional town. But is it reasonable to expect these old communes to take civic and economic responsibility for big new suburbs? Is it not like putting a car factory down in a cornfield, and then compensating the farmer by making him managing-director? And even though the political problems are often ephemeral, the financial ones remain. However co-operative a mayor (and few have been as tiresome as at Massy), his own resources just do not stretch to the vast task of providing a new town with what it needs. A commune's finances derive mainly from taxes on local shops and factories; yet these are the very things that the new towns initially lack. And the State has shown little willingness to be flexible and provide special funds: it sticks to its own formal rules, that the commune must pay its routine share, 30 per cent for new hospitals and schools, 35 per cent for sports facilities, 50 per cent for Maisons de la Culture and so on. The delays and shortages are therefore often the fault of the State (Massy is an exception) and can be due to inter-Ministerial rivalries, if the Ministry of Health, say, or Education, refuses to come to the relief of one of the Ministry of Construction's new schemes. Hence the results. At Massy, transport links with Paris and nearby factory zones are poor: one Métro line to the Luxembourg, and a few crowded buses. Most people, it is true, have cars, but not all can park near their work. Throughout the Paris region there was for many years a lack of effective liaison between the town-planners and the transport authorities.

The consequent fatigue and waste of leisure-time hardly needs stressing. A worker in a new suburb spends, on average, ninety minutes on travel each day; he is away from home eleven or twelve hours, and may be too tired in the evening to do more than watch TV, which helps to explain these towns' lack of social animation. A remarkable article by Boris Kidel in *l'Express* in May 1963 compared the lives of three typical skilled car-workers and their families, from Renault, Opel (near Frankfurt) and Ford (Dagenham). The article showed that the Frenchman's lot was tougher than that of his counterparts simply because he lived on the wrong side of Paris from Renault. The German bicycled for twenty minutes through open country to his work; the Englishman had a thirty-minute motor-bike ride from his Hornchurch bungalow; the Frenchman struggled for ninety minutes each way in train and Métro, from his flat in north-east Paris to the Billancourt works, leaving home at 5.30 a.m. and getting back at 7 p.m. Yet, having acquired his precious HLM in the days when you accepted what you could get, he now had no right to a transfer.

Maybe this is an extreme case, even a piece of special pleading by the (then) Left-wing *l'Express*. But it has some general truth.

French planners have finally learned from these early mistakes. The Grand Ensemble concept was officially abandoned in 1972, and since the early seventies work has begun on nine 'Villes Nouvelles' – five in the Paris region,* others outside Marseille, Lyon, Rouen and Lille – which are altogether superior. They are inspired to an extent by the previously rejected British model, and one of them, Cergy-Pontoise, has even hired British consultants. But they are planned to be much larger than either the Stevenages or the Sarcelles – most have a target size of 200,000 to 500,000 – and it is claimed that this will make it easier to provide them with full amenities. Each town is being built by a specially created local body which co-ordinates planning, land buying and so on, and this obviates much of the feuding between communes or lack of liaison between Ministries that bedevilled the Grands Ensembles. These new towns really *are* getting their factories, offices, shops and civic amenities at the same time as the flats, instead of years later. And in many cases the modern architecture is varied and striking, and the density much lower than in places like Sarcelles. Cergy already has a majestic new civic centre that includes the local prefecture. Evry, south of Paris, with its bright multi-coloured flats, is the star case. Its new town has only 30,000 inhabitants to date, but already the largest multi-purpose centre in France has been completed there. It is known as the Agora, and has three theatres, a skating rink and every other kind of sport, dance halls, a library, a youth centre, and hypermarkets. Local employment for women and office workers is still in short supply, but there are several new factories nearby, one of them using 80 per cent local labour. For those who commute to Paris the SNCF has even built a special new railway line, its first since 1937, with fifty trains a day each way. A recent opinion survey found that some 88 to 90 per cent of the new inhabitants of Evry were happy with their homes and with the local shops, while 72 to 77 per cent were satisfied with the local schools and entertainments, and with the amount of greenery.

This indicates that the French can and will adapt happily, in

* See p. 293.

time, to a new style of suburban living. But elsewhere it has not been so easy. In the older Grands Ensembles, the failures of planning simply aggravated the psychological difficulties of the French in changing to this new style. On the older estates like Sarcelles, if the lack of local jobs is one cause of housewives' boredom, another, much greater, is their relative lack of Anglo-Saxon neighbourliness or of any tradition of women's clubs and associations, and their wariness about making friends or pooling resources with strangers. Much has been said and written about this.

Sometimes the picture painted is too black. The inhabitants' reactions vary immensely: certainly, many of them feel a sense of incompleteness, and yet without any doubt the majority *are* happier than in their old slums. A sociological survey at Sarcelles in 1968 found that 80 per cent of the inhabitants were 'happy to be living there' once they had settled in. A little flat with all mod. cons. where the family can bolt the door and build its nest, a playground outside for *les gosses*, blue sky with no smog – these are their first priorities, and these at least they find. Few consciously object to the grim geometry of Sarcelles; some even yearn to go and live there. 'That's a true City of the Future for you!' enthuses the teenage working-class heroine of a sensitive novel* about life in the HLMs, on her first visit to the place; 'kilometres and kilometres and kilometres of houses houses houses houses – and sky, and sun, houses full of sun . . . and green spaces, enormous, clean, superb, like carpets, with a notice on each one, "Respect the Lawns and Trees and See They Are Respected", notices which seem to have some effect here as the population are no doubt progressive like the architecture.' Ian Nairn should meet *her*.

After some initial problems, such as learning how to use baths and refuse-chutes and modern lifts, many families settle down devotedly to their new domesticity and soon develop what has been called '*le réflexe petit-bourgeois*'. This means, first, an avid materialism, a buying spree of furniture and electrical gadgets, usually on hire purchase and sometimes beyond their real means: the new towns are rife with skilful sales-touts, who can often

* *Les Petits Enfants du siècle*, by Christiane Rochefort (Grasset, 1961).

persuade wives into rash commitments while husbands are at work. Poor families also tend to be feckless at first with gas and electricity, unused to the new luxury of meters on deferred payment. Some households thus find themselves paying up to 60 per cent of their income on fixed charges, including rent; and the rents, though reasonable for what is offered, are usually much higher than their old ones in the slums and not always so easy to meet on a worker's salary. Many budgets are helped out by State housing allowances, averaging 120 francs a month; even so, the sharp change in spending habits and living standards, with no immediate corresponding rise in salary, often spells recurring financial crisis during the first months in a new home. This has been reckoned as a common cause of nervous breakdowns in the Grands Ensembles, and according to some reports in the Left-wing Press, it even drives a number of respectable wives and mothers to part-time prostitution in a desperate effort to make ends meet.†

Possibly this whole issue has been exaggerated. Though the financial difficulties are often real enough, it is partly a question of learning how to adapt to new middle-class ways of being budget-wise, and this the workers usually manage in time. But the other aspect of the petit-bourgeois reflex goes deeper, and derives from one of the strongest traits in the French character, the attachment to family rather than community. In their old slums, for all the discomfort, people were close to friends and shops they had known for years, and often were surrounded by relatives too. Put them down in a new setting, and they draw in their horns. Their first reaction is to close the door, enjoy the new privacy and comfort, and cling to what still remains that is familiar: the immediate family cell. Friendly calls by neighbours are resented, or are assumed to have some ulterior motive. However much people like their flats, they show a deep emotional wariness towards regarding the *milieu* of the Grand Ensemble as 'home'.

Sometimes this reaction takes a violent or hostile form. Some

† See *Nouvel Observateur*, 23 March and 4 May 1966; also Jean-Luc Godard's film, *Deux ou trois choses que je sais d'elle* (1967).

people strongly resent their enforced removal from the slums; others, whose old homes are still standing, retreat back to them after a few experimental months in a Grand Ensemble. Women find the adaptation hardest, and sometimes, as the lonely days drag on, they will take to making special journeys back to do their daily shopping among the old friendly faces. In a few cases, the *ennui* of the new towns can lead even to illness or suicide, or, among teenagers, to a kind of listless petty vandalism. But, though the newspapers enjoy building up sensational scares, most sociologists and social workers deny that the level of delinquency or nervous illness is in fact much higher in a Grand Ensemble than elsewhere; it is simply that the causes are different.

Most inhabitants react more placidly, and their *malaise* is more subtle and less conscious. They vaguely resent the lack of social warmth and ambience, but they answer this by retreating into their own ambience rather than by working together to create a public one. At Massy, a complacent middle-aged clerk in an HLM told me: 'Some newcomers here were unhappy and sus-picious at first, but now they're getting to like it. Here we sun-bathe on our balconies at week-ends, we watch TV, or we drive into the countryside, which is only ten minutes away. Yes, we'd like more sport, but we don't need more clubs or social life, the French are too individual and *renfermés* for that. Personally, I don't see these new towns creating a new collective spirit in France.'

The inhabitants do resent a shortage of utilitarian facilities that they could use as individuals: schools, clinics, transport, jobs, sports fields. But when it comes to general social or cultural amenities, or even entertainment other than sport, they often fail to patronize what they are given. And this is true even of that noble French institution, the café or *brasserie*. The rarity of pave-ment cafés is one of the most striking lacunae of the new towns, at least to the casual eye. It is due partly to a new anti-alcoholism law, that limits cafés in new suburbs to one per 3,000 people, but also to the reluctance of most cafetiers to try their luck in this strange new *milieu*. Massy, with 30,000 people, still had only three cafés in 1969, one-third of its legal ration, whereas a tradi-tional town of its size might have a hundred. The cafés that do emerge are mostly overlit, functional places with stone floors, bare walls and a vaguely listless atmosphere – juke-box or TV blaring, a few youths playing with pin-tables. Usually there is not enough traditional café warmth to tempt the locals away from their own TV sets. In one sense this is a sign of progress: the cosier their new flats, the less need the French feel to visit cafés.*

There are plenty of shops in the new towns. Sarcelles has five separate *centres commerciaux*, each one grouped round a traffic-free precinct, cheerful and pleasantly designed, strikingly similar to their English counterparts. But, though the housewives gladly use them for their daily needs, for the 'serious' buying of clothes, furniture or other such items, they still prefer to go off to shops in a real town, be it Paris or St-Denis. It is all part of their reluctance to put down roots.

And yet, within each new town there is always a small minority of people who think and react quite differently from all this, and who create little cells of extreme animation. These are the pioneers, usually the more educated ones, who instead of drawing in their horns are inspired by the challenge of turning the concrete desert into a spiritual flower-garden. Sometimes they are militant Catholics; or eager Communists; or social workers with a sense of mission; or cultural enthusiasts. However opposed their ideologies, they usually find that they have a lot in common.† It is them against the rest. Thanks to them, Sarcelles has its evening courses of drama, German and basket-work, its high-powered visiting lecturers from Paris, its ciné-clubs, its youth centre, and its large public library run by a young bearded campaigner who treats the civilizing of the city as a military operation, and can tell you at once from the coloured pins on his wall-map how many people in each block have discovered Dostoyevsky. The only trouble is that these manifold socio-cultural activities are often badly attended, and are kept alive by the same little band of loyalists, who circulate from one to the next.

As far as culture goes this is perhaps not so surprising, and not so different from the pattern, say, in Stevenage. After all, Sarcelles

* See p. 414.
† See pp. 580–82.

is hardly a university town like Rennes, with a ready-made audience. But in another respect the French experience does differ significantly from the British: the pioneers have not had much success in providing obvious civic self-help activities. Baby-sitting, crèches, help for old people or invalids, youth movements, courses in domestic science or civics – good works of this sort are carried out on limited budgets by various official or semi-official bodies, but usually in a rather formal, juridical manner, and without overmuch public response. Even in a middle-class setting, a young housewife in a prosperous new suburb west of Paris told me that she was treated with some suspicion by the neighbours when, purely as a public service and without asking for payment, she tried to start up a crèche. 'She must be a Communist – she's trying to get at us,' was the initial reaction of many bourgeois mothers who really would have liked nothing better than to be able to leave their small children in safe hands for an hour or two. Because the woman was not someone they knew, and because she was doing something 'unofficial', and was not a paid social worker, she was suspect. Finally, the crèche did get going, and was a great success, but it took great patience. A nation with little tradition of voluntary public service, where most welfare work tends to be institutionalized, is naturally finding it hard to adapt to the informal community living that life in the new towns demands. Slowly, new habits are forming. But in the meantime, where officialdom fails to provide what the citizens need, they show little initiative for taking remedies into their own hands.

You must travel four hundred miles and more from Sarcelles, to the Pyrenees and Provence, to find two of the more successful cases of pre-1970s new-town pioneering. Mourenx, west of Pau, is a rare example in France of a Grand Ensemble all by itself in the open country, unattached to an older community. It was built to house the workers of the new industries of nearby Lacq; and the big State company that exploits the gas-fields has co-operated closely with the SCIC in trying to ensure that Mourenx is as much a showpiece of modern French town-planning as Lacq is of French industry. Aesthetically this policy has paid off. Set in the gentle green foothills of the Pyrenees, Mourenx, with its white towers, lawns and piazzas, and Béarn-style flower-boxes, looks quite beautiful, especially on a summer night; and though there is much the same rectangular pattern as at Sarcelles, the effect is far less monolithic. Socially the town has been through the usual crises. The workers arrived here from all corners of France, notably from the mines of the North, and many at first were lonely and *dépaysés*: '*Maman isolée! ne restez plus seule au foyer, venez chez nous*,' was the significant appeal by a religious club that I saw in a shop-window on my first visit, in 1960. But gradually the families settled down and found contentment, seduced by the warm southern climate, the scenery, the sea and mountains close at hand: all schoolchildren are taken for skiing classes once a week in winter. It is a town made up almost entirely of young married couples with children, and nearly every family has a car, for the workers of Lacq are quite well paid. Civically, too, it is ahead of most Grands Ensembles. In the early years the SCIC and the Lacq company (SNPA) made the mistake of running the town as their own private operation in which the inhabitants had no say; there were even uniformed SCIC wardens to keep people off the lawns. But in 1963 the population rebelled, led by their mayor, a schoolmaster from Normandy. Tired of being treated as 'minors', they demanded control over their own local affairs, as in any other commune. The SCIC backed down, gracefully, and today the Mourenxois, thanks to their show of public spirit, seem to have achieved a kind of civic maturity that is still rare in the new towns. Not that life is all roses. Although the rank-and-file workers are content to stay, the prosperous executives and scientists of Lacq have mostly shown a reluctance to settle in the chic villas built for them at Mourenx, and are tending to drift away to Pau and elsewhere. But at least Mourenx is proving that it *is* possible for a Grand Ensemble to overcome its teething troubles.

The same is being proved, more effectively, at Bagnols-sur-Cèze in the Rhône valley, twenty miles north-west of Avignon. Here, in a lyrical Provençal setting of vineyards and blue-grey hills, a new dormitory for the workers and scientists of the big Marcoule atomic centre has been cunningly grafted on to the ancient and beautiful little market town of Bagnols, through the talents of the architect Georges Candilis. The three medieval towers of the old city are carefully balanced by three white towers of flats in the new town; the modern buildings with their gaily coloured sun-blinds and shutters blend as easily with the landscape as the weathered stone of the old Gothic churches; and in a space between the two towns, a new shopping-centre forms a meeting-point for the two populations. The harmonious result won Candilis, in 1959, the first official French Prix de l'Urbanisme.

Bagnols has architecture, scenery and climate on its side and more besides. The town is composed of two rival élites. On the one hand the 5,000 'vieux Bagnolais', who like all Provençaux have history in their blood, and have been used since pre-Roman days to welcoming and assimilating successive waves of newcomers to their epic homeland. They are proud of their old town with its fine museum, its ramparts, its Roman tower. The other élite are the 12,000 'nouveaux Bagnolais', known as 'Marcoulens', technicians and skilled workers from all over France, mostly well paid, and generally happy to settle in this sunlit valley. Their lives are subsidized by their employers at Marcoule, the Commissariat à l'Energie Atomique. At the large and handsome swimming-pool and lido in the new town centre, the sons and daughters of physicists and farmers flirt and splash under the white light that seduced Cézanne, and life seems far nearer to St-Tropez than to Sarcelles. And yet, even this idyll is not perfect. The ideal of the planners for a fusion of 'old Bags' and 'new Bags' (as my scribbled field-notes describe them) has not yet been realized. Although many of the 'old Bags' have been rehoused in the new flats among the newcomers, the two groups still practise, not so surprisingly, a certain *apartheid*. It seems to be largely the fault of the Marcoulens: aloof and clannish behind the prestige of their Grande Ecole diplomas, their top-secret nuclear work and their keeping-up-with-the-Duponts society, they tend to look down on the old Bags as '*paysans*'. And the old Bags in turn resent what they regard as patronizing pretentiousness. Real friendships between the two are not common: the case of a Norman at Marcoule, who married a local artist and learned Provençal, is a rare exception. Yet the mutual coolness is usually masked by civility and rarely develops into conflict. And the new generations are breaking down their parents' barriers. One technician told me, 'At home, my son plays only with other little Marcoulens: but at the *lycée* and the lido he makes friends with Provençal children too, and doesn't seem to differentiate.'

In most other respects, adaptation to the new suburban living has been swifter and easier in Bagnols than in less privileged Grands Ensembles. But nearly everwhere in France, and not only in Bagnols and Mourenx, a certain thaw has now begun to be felt in the new towns. In Sarcelles, in Massy, in a score of other such places, families are slowly and tentatively breaking with age-old habits and forming new loyalties, almost despite themselves. *Natura abhorret vacuum.* The influx into the new working-class suburbs of a certain number of *cadres*, and of energetic and gregarious *pieds noirs*,* is beginning to produce a new social ferment and class fluidity that is still rare in Paris and other older towns. And though the family *foyer* is still generally held sacred against intrusion, on neutral territory the barriers of unneighbourliness are beginning to come down; neighbours who, for the first year or two, do no more than exchange a wary 'Bonjour, Madame' on the staircase, may finally meet at some local fête, find that they share the same problems, and become quite friendly. At Mourenx a young social worker, Mlle Auger, told me of her efforts to promote basket-work and pottery classes for housewives, and voluntary baby-sitting: 'Women here feel a lack of something, they're not sure what. Their new homes are so easy to run, it leaves them with leisure – for what? I believe they come to my classes in order, above all, to meet new people and form new links that they don't seem to manage to do on their own doorsteps.'

Mlle Auger also referred, as others have done, to the 'new French élites' that the Grands Ensembles are throwing up: the pioneers, the do-gooders, the apostles of community-living, people like herself. The new suburbia seems, in fact, to bring out the best and the worst in the French: this new, uncharacteristic social spirit: and an atavistic petit-bourgeois egotism and withdrawal. And these two are now in battle for the soul of France. Or rather, that is one way of putting it; there is also another point of view. Some people claim that the Grands Ensembles are leading towards

*See pp. 219–20.

a dangerous collectivism, alien to the glorious tradition of French privacy and individualism. The novelist Marc Bernard in his book on Sarcelles* writes:

Some of our animators inveigh against this passive, closed-door spirit and condemn it; I'm not sure that they're right. I fear that by trying to improve things they may make them worse. There's such a powerful current drawing us towards collectivism these days that anything that slows it down and blocks it should be desirable, even to be encouraged. It wouldn't be a bad thing to hold courses on individualism in all the Sarcelles of the world.

But this seems to me to ignore the facts of a town like Sarcelles, where usually it is the active ones who are the individualists. The answer must be to strike a balance. New towns are inevitable, and if the French are to live in them happily they must develop some kind of community living. It is a question not of stifling their individualism but of providing it with new kinds of social outlet – without running to the un-French extremes of the *kibbutz* or *kolkhoz* or, worse, of the undiscriminating conformist good-neighbourliness of American 'organization-man' suburbia.

For the Grands Ensembles to flourish in this way, it seems to me that initially the State and the communes will have to play a large part. They will have to provide the equipment and a staff of 'animators' to make the towns congenial, for in officialized France these will not easily appear of their own accord. The larger and richer communes are in a position to take some initiatives themselves. It is significant that two of the most interesting examples of 'animation' in the new suburbs of a big town are at Rennes and Grenoble. At Rennes, the new housing estates happen to be *inside* the communal boundaries of this prosperous city, whose enlightened mayor, Henri Fréville,† has set up a 'cultural office' that co-ordinates various State and municipal services: it has animators in each suburb who have created local civic units to run their own arts clubs, crèches and so on. And at Grenoble, Hubert Dubedout** has built a new suburb that would, he claimed,

---

* *Sarcellopolis*, Flammarion, 1964.
† See pp. 206–8.
** See pp. 201–4.

'go to the farthest limits of social integration': not only have old people's homes, student hostels, and flats for varying income groups all been placed together in the same blocks, but the same buildings are serving as schools during the day and socio-cultural centres in the evenings and at weekends. The project has had its teething troubles, but it shows social imagination of a kind still rare in France. Such initiatives demand a strong lead, probably from an official personality – and when a new suburb is being built in a smaller commune, this lead must usually come from the State. Ideally, it should be only a first step towards a more spontaneous kind of community life. The real question it poses is whether the State in France will ever wither away, whether a crèche will ever be an informal circle of housewives, instead of a unit in some Fédération Nationale, governed from Paris by complex legal statutes dating back to the law of 1901.

UTOPIAS OF THE NEW RICH: 'IS PARIS 2 BURNING?'

If you've money in the bank, then the dilemma of collectivism versus individualism loses much of its force. For poorer people wanting a new home, there is little choice but an HLM amid rows of similar HLMs, but for a few there is all the glory and diversity of the open market: a chic town flat in Neuilly at over half a million francs, a modern *'maison de campagne, style anglais'* in the woods of the Ile-de-France, or a bijou apartment with sun-terrace and built-in barbecue on one of the modish little estates west of Paris, with names like 'le Parc Montaigne' or 'la Rési-dence Vendôme'. Some of this type of housing lies inside Paris; but Parisian prices and rents have soared so high, for new pro-perty, that most of those with middle or upper-middle incomes are obliged to move out of town. The Parisian businessman is being forced to learn the Anglo-Saxon habit of commuting.

The Ile-de-France is thus rapidly changing its social character. Until very recently civilization was regarded as ending at the gates of Paris; outside, there was only the despised *banlieue*, and beyond that, little but the empty plains and forests of the Paris basin,

broken only by the royal *châteaux* in their great parks. The Ile-de-
France had never known much equivalent of the stockbroker belt
in Buckinghamshire, the tea-shops of Tunbridge Wells, or Betjeman's mid-Surrey with its colonels and tennis-girls. Towns like
Etampes and Senlis, thirty miles from Paris, were closed and lifeless. A few film-stars and writers, it is true, owned smart villas in
discreet villages like Montfort-l'Amaury; and it was just socially
acceptable to live, say, in St-Cloud or St-Germain-en-Laye. But
for most of the bourgeoisie, Paris alone counted.

Today, while the rich commute at week-ends to their *châteaux*,
say, in Normandy, or by Caravelle to the *Côte*, thousands of
not-quite-so-rich Parisians have developed a new craze for week-
end country cottages.* And throughout the middle classes, by
force of necessity the old snobbism against *la banlieue* is dropping
away, and a new counter-snobbism is being carefully fostered, for
a certain style of smart Americanized suburban living. Out to the
west of Paris, around and beyond Versailles, the spare land is
rapidly filling up with these chic little housing-estates and their
tennis-courts, *piscines* and boutiques. A small flat or *pavillon* here
may cost 250,000 francs or more, with poor credit facilities, but at
least that is little more than half what it would be inside Paris.
And in this suburbia the young, short-haired executives are bask-
ing in a new, un-French ideal. Some drive their Peugeots or
Citroën IDs across the Bois to their offices; others sit reading
Le Figaro on early trains to the Gare St-Lazare as if on the 8.44
from Sevenoaks. And France will need her John Betjeman to
hymn the tennis-court life of this new world.

The most apparent difference between all new housing in
France and in Britain is still, of course, that the French build flats
and the British build houses. But even this is now changing. The
French do not live in flats by choice; flats were thrust upon them.
'In the heart of every Frenchman there slumbers a *pavillon*,' writes
Marc Bernard, and opinion surveys reveal that 82 per cent of
Frenchmen yearn for nothing better than a little house with a
garden, just like an Englishman. The anarchic rash of *pavillons*
built outside Paris in the inter-war years shows how far the

* See p. 411.

French will go towards realizing this dream when they get the chance. But, to meet the post-war housing crisis, officialdom leaned towards flats rather than rows of houses because they were cheaper and quicker to build. There was also the French tradition of in-city living, countering and frustrating the secret dream of the *pavillon*. Today, however, conditions are changing. The housing crisis has eased a little, affluence is growing, the middle class has caught Anglo-Americanization like the measles – and the decline of pro-Paris snobbery means that people are readier to move right out to where land prices are still low enough for the mass production of little commuter villas with gardens. Even the Government is now sponsoring a few English-style HLM estates of this type. As for private building, you will find full-page advertisements in papers like *Le Monde* offering '*la joie de vivre authentique et profonde*' of modern five-room villas '*à la manière anglaise*' with lawns and crazy paving. At Le Mesnil St Denis, south-west of Versailles, the American firm of Levitt and Sons has built an estate of 520 villas of this type, ranging from about 150,000 to 200,000 francs; no more expensive than their equivalents twenty-five miles from London. In the first three weeks the 'show' villas had 35,000 visitors, and the whole estate was subscribed twice over. Buyers were *cadres moyens*, engineers, doctors, older people wanting to get out of Paris or newly weds with some capital.

The most interesting factor is that on this type of estate, and at this social level, a most unprecedented neighbourliness soon develops. Often there are no hedges between the gardens and no one minds; yet these same people, in their old Paris flats, often never got to know their neighbours. Of course flat-dwelling is far less conducive to neighbourliness than house-dwelling (this partly explains the difficulties in the Grands Ensembles) and when there is no too-close neighbour to make a noise through the ceiling, or mess up the communal stairways, he no longer need be shunned.

The experience of these garden-estates in France is still far too recent for any firm conclusions to be drawn; but it seems that their new American-style communal spirit may bring with it some American-style dangers. In their old flats the French at least tended to be tolerant towards and uncompetitive with neighbours, so long as each left the other in peace; you could be rich or poor, black or yellow, living in sin or addicted to drugs, and no one cared so long as you were discreet. On the new estates, people show signs of being more choosy about their neighbours, less tolerant of social non-conformists, more envious of the next man's smarter car or niftier spin-drier. This has not yet reached American proportions; but it might be moving that way.

Preoccupation with material status, *le standing* as the French call it in their charming *franglais*, is growing inevitably in the newly affluent middle class, and housing is one of its first considerations. Someone put it to me: 'An executive can ask you to his office, where his surroundings reflect his standing; or he can entertain in a smart restaurant; but his flat may give him away.' House-agents and promoters are now playing skilfully upon these snobberies and these desires, and in the past few years a publicity campaign unique in France has gone into persuading people that a new earthly paradise of ease and elegance awaits them beyond the western gates of Paris. '*Le murmure des Eaux Vives au sortir de Métro!*' promises one advertisement for an estate with its own park and fountains at the end of the Métro to Palaiseau. Another full-page spread, rich in house-agents' *franglais*, plays on the theme of Californian-style luxury at Le Parc Montaigne, near St-Cyr: '*Les tennis-quick . . . avec des amis; piscine . . . pour goûter la détente d'un " crawl" ; centre commercial, lieu plaisant du shopping; barbecue chez soi . . . été comme hiver; dressing-room en acajou; cheminée . . . une joie intime . . . dans une atmosphère de vacances.*' Or again, '*Il prend son drink au Drugstore . . . ils vont au club de bridge.*' I am not making this up. This is France in the 1970s. Luridly the glossy colour-ads offer a world of mahogany and fitted carpets, of parasols and wide sun-terraces amid beeches and poplars; and the public follow. The show-flats in their nouveau-riche way are often almost as enticing as the advertisements have suggested, and visiting them has become a popular Sunday afternoon sport, a sort of window-shopping enjoyed also by workers who couldn't possibly afford to buy. But others can and do buy: starved by decades of poor housing, and seduced by the agents' slogans of '*le luxe à la portée de tout le monde*', many young couples readily take the risk of signing away their capital and committing themselves to larger monthly payments than they can easily afford.

A remarkable estate that helped set the new trend is Elysée Deux, at La-Celle-St-Cloud, built in the mid-1960s by a sharp and ambitious young promoter, Robert de Balkany. Here the five-storey blocks of elegant flats (many with two bathrooms) are set amid pine-trees on a hill-side, and surround a shopping-centre whose chief features are a luxury first-run cinema, a sauna bath, a night-club whose metallic décor has been designed to harmonize with modern Courrèges fashions, and a 'drugstore' roughly similar to the new ones in central Paris. It is called Le Drugwest and it serves Franco-American dishes to the sound of Western music, amid a jazzily sophisticated décor of glass, dark wood and huge yellow and orange Chinese lanterns. It is immensely popular, lively, plushy, modernistic, and I can think of nowhere else I would sooner take a foreign visitor to show him what the new France is like. Though Elysée Deux as a whole and the Drugwest in particular owe a lot to America, they do retain a curiously French flavour, sharp, brashly chic rather than vulgar, that I cannot help finding attractive and stimulating. De Balkany's policy has been to entice moneyed people out to suburbs like this by trying to *recreate* the chic, the appeal, the amenities of central Paris. Hence the Courrèges nightclub, the first-run cinema, the Drugwest; and hence the name: Elysée Deux, a new little Champs-Elysées. Even the local coiffeur has transferred from the Champs-Elysées. This policy has not worked ideally; some of the promised amenities, such as youth centre and swimming-pool, have arrived late or have not been properly looked after. But on the whole these '*banlieusards de grand luxe*' are happy with their new home.

The success of Elysée Deux did, however, go to de Balkany's head. In 1966 he began work on a much vaster project: a luxury city for 20,000 people on a 250-acre site just north of Versailles, complete with theatres, churches, smart hotels, exotic gardens, night-clubs, a new Drugwest open all night, and 'the largest shopping-centre in Europe'. And this Xanadu he baptized, inevitably, PARIS DEUX. 'The idea is not new,' proclaimed a four-page advertisement in *Le Monde*, with touching modesty: 'Louis XIV once transported Paris to the countryside. He, like us, felt the imperious need to do so. And so, 300 years later, on almost the same spot, we shall build a quintessence of Paris and recreate an art of living unique in the world.' True to his policy, de Balkany first built the new Drugwest at Paris Deux as a 'magnet', before any dwellings were finished. Then a giant publicity campaign, costing 3,500,000 francs or more, drew in the crowds and the clients: 200,000 came in four weeks to see the Drugwest and the show-flats. But the Left, the Press, even the Government grew restive. Would de Balkany be able to honour his contracts and his promises? Suppose he failed to sell enough flats in advance and his project collapsed, half finished? Was it all a confidence trick? And anyway, why spend the nation's resources on these snobbish absurdities when millions of workers were still homeless or in slums? *Le Nouvel Observateur* sharply attacked Paris Deux, alleging that its publicity was phoney and its information to clients misleading: '*Paris 2 Brûle-t-il?*' the paper inquired hopefully in front-page banner headline. (This was the time of the première of Clément's film on the Liberation.) Delouvrier was also hostile, and wanted to see the whole project go up in flames: it was just the kind of development that might sabotage the careful long-term planning of his Schéma Directeur. But de Balkany had influence in high places, and the Right-wing Pompidou intervened in the role of von Choltitz, if hardly for the same reasons. All the Government did was to induce de Balkany to modify the scale of Paris Deux – and to change its name to 'Parly Deux', after the Paris municipal council had threatened legal action over the 'sacrilegious' abuse of the city's name!

Parly Deux is now nearly completed. Like Elysée Deux on a larger scale, it is quite attractive in its flamboyant way. The bronzed young bodies of the new-rich lounge in summer by the eight outdoor swimming-pools, *à la Californienne*. The flats (a four-roomer costs from 300,000 to 500,0000 francs) are reasonably elegant, no block having more than six floors – and though the show-flats are grotesquely furnished, a buyer need not copy their style. The Parlysiens I talked to seemed quite happy. One fact is certain: the Paris of tomorrow will soon have its Parly

Deux by the dozen. This new-affluent bourgeoisie has now found what it thinks it wants: all-night drugstores, built-in barbecues, mahogany dressing-rooms and the rest. And whatever the sins of speculators, the trend in France towards this 'new art of living', this 'authentic and profound *joie de vivre*', seems irreversible.

Chapter 9

NOVELTY AND TRADITION
IN DAILY LIFE

THE new franc (one hundred old francs) was introduced in 1959: fifteen years later a large percentage of people, educated people, still felt unwilling to calculate in anything but old francs, and not through want of arithmetic. It is one example of the way that personal habits and rooted methods of thinking are still slow to change in this ancient country, even under the impact of economic revolution. In preceding chapters we have seen how the French are adapting unevenly, often bemusedly, to change forced on them by technical advance and sheer modern necessity: new gadgets like tractors or built-in barbecues they may seize on eagerly, but basic changes involving social attitudes often seem harder to accept. In their private and daily lives, and in their new leisure and spending habits, the same is equally true, and in this chapter I shall trace how certain modern styles of life are being seized on with frenzied appetite, while certain others, in practice more necessary, are being shunned. The formalism and stratification of French traditional society does not easily adapt itself, and today the French are often the prisoners of their own rigidities.

A SLOW DISMANTLING OF
THE BARRICADES OF CLASS

These rigidities can be seen especially in French social divisions. Despite the tradition of civic *égalité*, this is still a less egalitarian society than the United States or Scandinavia, or even the Britain of today. Britain has often been regarded as the land of caste, second only to India, but in practice, though the British are far more class-conscious than the French, I think they are today less class-divided. In Britain, with its new social fluidity, the classes are fascinatedly aware of each other on a personal everyday level. In France class distinctions are taken very much more for granted and are rarely discussed with the same passionate human interest – it would be hard to imagine a French *Look Back in Anger*. Though most children go to the same primary schools, and though there is certainly more fluidity than before the war, yet there is still little sense of a classless meritocracy where a worker's son can rub shoulders with a banker's or a general's. The bourgeoisie retains much of its aloofness, its ignorance of the lives of workers or peasants, and the different strata mix surprisingly little.

You have only to wander round France to notice how the working classes, despite their new prosperity, are less assertively emancipated than in Britain. There are some parts of central Paris, notably around the Faubourg St-Honoré, that still have the air of elegant upper-class preserves in a way that is true of no part of the West End of London. Or contrast the democratic hubbub of Heathrow airport with the chic, expensive atmosphere of Orly. Workers in France, even when they can afford it, are reticent about thrusting their way forward to share in the bourgeoisie's own public world of smart shops, theatres and airports, and their own tastes are not publicly catered for on the same scale as in Britain. It is one reason why there is less vulgarity in France than in Britain today, but also less justice.

The causes of these abiding class rigidities lie deep in French history and character. The desire to avoid open conflicts between groups has led to a protective formalization of French life which over the centuries has pushed each class into its fixed place. Animosities are often bitter, but they are oddly depersonalized. Conflicts take the form of economic pressures, political demands and attitude-striking: the taking of pot-shots from behind sheltered barricades, rather than the British hand-to-hand jousting. A French worker may resent and fear the alien bourgeois world, but when he meets a bourgeois he is likely to treat him naturally as a simple fellow-citizen, without the chip-on-the-shoulder awkwardness common in Britain. For, paradoxically, there is a real and strong method of *égalité* and mutual respect between all individuals, when regarded as citizens rather than as members of a class. And this *égalité* produces a kind of legal fiction that the gross inequalities of income, opportunity and way of life do not exist.

Class patterns are certainly changing in France today, but less through a merging of different classes than a blurring of the outward distinctions between them. Under modern conditions their interests and habits are drawing closer. A skilled worker may own the same kind of car as a bourgeois, and off-duty he may dress the same way; like Lancashire mill-girls, the new working generation is giving up its old class 'uniform' and is dressing like the middle class, so that it becomes harder to tell them apart. But the real barriers remain, despite progress towards integration in the new suburbs.

One reason often put forward for Britain's post-war social revolution is the enforced mucking together of war-time; the French did not have this kind of experience, being split up and paralysed by the Occupation, even though in other ways this was a catalyst. But the social rigidity is due more than anything to the way the bourgeoisie has managed to retain virtual control of the secondary and higher education systems. Strange as it may seem, education in France* is in many ways even more closely divided on class lines than in Britain with its public schools. The State *lycées*, though in theory free and open to all, are in practice still partly a preserve of the middle class, and they alone provide a passport to higher education and the best jobs. The percentage of workers' children who go to university is slowly rising but is still less than three per cent, far lower than in Britain. And inside the middle class, the cachet of a Grande Ecole diploma produces a further distinction, separating the higher professional élites in industry from the lower bourgeoisie. These gradings stay for life: once a *cadre* always a *cadre*, and there is less opportunity than in Britain for an able man to win promotion from the shop-floor or from junior clerical ranks. According to one survey, of the 2,530 most famous or powerful people in France today, from Giscard to Bardot, only 3 per cent have come from working-class homes, while 68 per cent of France's ruling élite is recruited from the top 5 per cent of the population.

* See pp. 465–7.

Much of this is due not only to bourgeois opposition but to the reluctance of humbler people to push their way forward via the *lycées* into an alien world. There is still a feeling of 'us' and 'them': the feeling that used to be much stronger in Britain than it is today. A worker's son will sometimes enter the white-collar middle class by training to be a primary teacher or a *fonctionnaire*; but he will rarely aspire to be an engineer or doctor. Within his own lifetime a man does not change class; and though his son may do so through the right education, his social mobility remains restricted. His accent may not give him away so quickly as in Britain; but his family background will cling to him more closely.

Inside these barriers the character and the influence of each individual class have been changing considerably, and nowhere so much as in the aristocracy. In the days before 1914 the French nobility set the tone in France and in all Europe for taste, gallantry and prowess. Unlike their often-so-Philistine counterparts in Britain, they were the guardians of national culture, and gifted young bourgeois like Marcel Proust were drawn to their *salons* as the natural forum for their talents. But in the past decades the nobility has been pushed into the sidelines of national life, though not extinguished. Few young writers or artists seek their patronage today; French culture has changed its form and passed into other hands, those of a bohemian wing of the bourgeoisie. More recently, the aristocracy has suffered a new blow through the loss of another of its fiefs, the army. Since the end of the Algerian war the army has been stripped of much of its prestige and power and reduced to an instrument of modern technological warfare; no longer does it seem able to offer, as it once did, a glorious and dignified career to the sons of the provincial nobility.

Yet many of the great families, the de la Rochefoucaulds, the de Cossé-Brissacs and the rest, are managing to keep their identity and their pride, by coming to terms with the modern economy. If they had done this sooner they might have kept more influence today, but in the nineteenth century their lordly code of values led them to scorn business and vulgar competition, and so they let the new empires of banking, industry and technocracy fall into the hands of the bourgeoisie. Today, late though not quite *too* late, they are taking up salaried posts in industry, in banks, in the senior civil service, as the only answer to financial ruin. Economically they are thus merging into the upper bourgeoisie, just as, socially, in the last century and earlier, many bourgeois families succeeded in merging into the nobility and prefixed the lordly 'de' to their names.

With their landed fortunes eroded by inflation, taxes and social changes, aristocrats often have to devote part of their new industrial incomes to the upkeep of their cherished family *châteaux*, if they want these to remain habitable. Other *châteaux* are falling into ruin, or have been sold; a few, the historic ones, are helped along by State grants. A family may spend week-ends and part of the summer in its *château*, and most of the year in its flat in Paris, usually in one of the dignified older quarters such as the Faubourg St-Germain. Here the great families for the most part live unflamboyantly and discreetly, clinging together in their own exclusive social world, inviting each other to formal cocktail parties or to an occasional ball or banquet with echoes of past glories. And the rest of France tolerates and ignores them. For although the French public adores foreign royalty or the idea of an English *milord*, it cares not a jot for its own nobility, whose doings find little place in French gossip-columns. It is one typical facet of the stratified privacy of French society. Snobbishness certainly exists, but not in the national limelight; it is provided by those bourgeois social-climbers who do still hanker for *la noblesse* and who make a pastime of collecting invitations to the right homes. '*Mais je suis reçue par les de Rohan-Chabot!*' said one insecure middle-class girl I know, in tones of pride. But if the rest of France lets them be, if they are not constantly Hickeyfied like the Duchess of Argyll, perhaps this privacy has helped the aristocrats' own true qualities of *finesse* to endure. Many of them seem to be cultured and gentle people, less grasping than the bourgeoisie. Many are liberal, though they rarely feel the desire or need to renounce their titles publicly like a Wedgwood Benn. The aristocrat's pride in his family name remains deep. Though the big clan-like family is on the wane in France, the nobility is one of its last strongholds, and the emotional security of their pedigree is still powerful.

Family influences are declining in the upper-middle class: the *grande bourgeoisie* and, just below it, the *bonne bourgeoisie*. The professional and money-making class retains much of its strength as the central ruling élite of France: de Gaulle was a typical product of the *grande bourgeoisie*, as Michel Debré, a lawyer and son of a professor, is of the *bonne bourgeoisie*. But the bourgeoisie's nature is changing as France changes. Traditionally its power was based on property, passed down through family hands and so necessitating close family loyalties and careful marriages. Today the bourgeois family firm is yielding place to the managerial corporation, and bourgeois property like that of the nobility has been hit by economic change. So instead, the upper bourgeoisie now relies increasingly on income from élite salaried positions; and as it still controls the higher rungs of the educational ladder, a near-monopoly of these jobs is well within its grasp. The new technocratic power groups, whether in public or private services, are mostly from this class; and the general rise in prosperity has poured new money into the pockets of successful surgeons, lawyers, architects and others of the professional bourgeoisie. These economic changes tend to weaken family links by making individual members of the class more self-sufficient.

The 'arranged' marriage has now almost disappeared, and so have large dowries. And with this has come greater personal freedom. The stifling world described by Mauriac and others, where family honour was placed way ahead of individual happiness, is relaxing its bonds. A grown-up son or daughter can today more easily escape from the family orbit without being treated as a rebel and outcast. But, by English standards, this is still relative; and even in Paris, the smart bourgeoisie of Passy or Neuilly remains rather more formal and conventional, rather less open to bohemian or other outside influences, than its London counterparts. Not only is there stronger social pressure to *sauver les apparences*; but, except in the small and artificial socialite world of *le tout-Paris*, one is much less likely than in London to find people of different interests and intellectual *milieux*, Left-wing thinkers and go-ahead bankers, young technocrats and way-out artists, mixing together naturally at the same parties and gatherings.

The upper bourgeoisie still makes strong efforts, largely successful, to preserve its social *milieux* against *parvenus* from lower down the middle classes. However, a new middle-middle class is arising in its own right, and its numbers and influence have been growing fast without necessarily bursting through the barriers above. Economic expansion, especially of the new tertiary services, has thrown up from the ranks of the lower bourgeoisie a new property-less but affluent group: sales and advertising executives, skilled technicians, *cadres moyens* in industry and public service, and those shopkeepers, craftsmen and small industrialists who have managed to adapt to the times. This is an aggressive status-seeking world of new social mobility, still in the process of forming its own standards and tastes. These are the people who aspire to share Elysée Deux and Parly Deux with the older *bonne bourgeoisie* (the *grande bourgeoisie* and the intellectuals keep well away).

Elsewhere in the middle classes the rise of prosperity has been spread most unevenly. Many older people especially, their savings or investments eroded by inflation, and no longer able to count so much on help from their families, are living in genteel poverty. And a large part of the traditional *petite bourgeoisie* has slumped into decline, notably the millions of self-employed artisans and small traders now outclassed by the new consumer economy. Even the *petits fonctionnaires* in public service (postal workers, clerks, primary teachers) have seen their wages rise much less fast than in the private sector. Their ranks are now being infiltrated by the sons and especially by the daughters of the peasantry and of some workers – young people who prefer soft jobs as clerks or typists to the drudgery of farm or factory. The change gives them the status of *classe moyenne* rather than *paysan* or *ouvrier*, but in the case of a worker it may not benefit him financially.

Most of the four million peasants who have left the land since the war have joined the ranks of industrial workers, though some have penetrated the middle classes, becoming tradesmen or, as above, office employees. And the gap that these and other rural émigrés have left behind them has caused class structures in the villages to alter far more radically than in the cities. In the old days, as Henri Mendras has pointed out,* the village was ruled by an élite of local *notables* – the *châtelain*, the curé, the school-teacher, the lawyer – who acted as intermediaries between the peasants and the rest of the nation. But since early in this century these *notables* have begun to drift away or lose influence: *châtelains* today often have jobs in Paris, while the calibre of local teachers has declined and so has the role of the curé. And the peasants, fewer in number but more educated and forceful than before, have begun to take affairs into their own hands and produce their own élites. Laurence Wylie† has described how the village of Chan-zeaux, near Angers, was ruled on semi-feudal lines till 1939 by the *châtelain* (who was also mayor) and the priest. But when the old *châtelain* died, the land was split up between heirs, many of them absentees, and the estate began to fall into ruin. The priest retired, and the village was left without leaders. Finally, the villagers elected one of their own number, a former cartwright, as mayor, and began to form committees to run the commune themselves, which they are now doing with great success. In recent elections the new *châtelain* received fewer votes than any of the twelve other council members: top of the list was his own *fermier*! And the *châtelain*'s children, who in the old days would address the local carpenter and his wife as *le père X* and *la mère X*, now respectfully call them *Monsieur* and *Madame*. The *châtelain*, a pleasant and liberal man, runs an insurance firm in Paris and uses part of his profits to keep up the *château*, as I was told on my own visit to Chanzeaux recently. But other neighbouring *châteaux* have been closed or sold: one has been bought by a new-rich Parisian family, and another by a garage-owner in Nantes who has put in a manager and runs it as a farm. Not far away, in another corner of this highly traditionalist region of western France, the Young Farmers' leader, Bernard Lambert, told me how his own relations with the local gentry had altered since the days when his father, a *métayer*, was victimized by his landlord. 'Some of them are quite human nowadays,' said this fiery young Left-winger: 'You

* *Sociologie de la campagne française*, pp. 72–87 (PUF, 1965).
† *France: Change and Tradition*, pp. 181–9 (Gollancz, 1963).

should meet my neighbour, the Comte de Cossé-Brissac!' To prove his point, he lifted the phone: '*Écoute, mon vieux, je t'envoie un journaliste anglais – d'accord?*' Astonished by the *tutoiement*, I took my leave of the Lamberts in their ugly, squalid little farm-slum, and drove under cover of truce through the social barricades to the baronial hall where the young gentleman-farmer count and his charming wife gave me *un scotch* on a Louis XV sofa: '*Oui, c'est un brave type, Bernard – un peu excité, un peu farfelu, mais il est bien.*'

Perhaps these are extreme examples. In some other parts of France there is still a good deal of conservatism and suspicion between rich farmers and small ones. But the trend is in the direction of Chanzeaux, and Mendras predicts the day when 'new peasant élites' will have entirely taken over from the old *notables*, when the small village will have lost its social importance save as a farmers' co-operative centre, and the new hubs of rural life will be the country towns, thriving with culture and agricultural technocracy. Increasingly, as transport and education develop, farmers are using the local towns rather than the villages as centres for marketing, shopping and entertainment; and as the farmers become more urbanized, so the townfolk penetrate into the country, buying up old houses and villas for week-end or summer visits. In Provence, and to the south and west of Paris, as many as half the houses in some villages are used for this purpose.

Thus one of the sharpest of French class distinctions, that between *paysan* and *citadin*, is beginning to fade as the two grow closer in styles of life and knowledge of each other. But the other sharp distinction, that of *ouvrier* and *bourgeois*, may prove harder to erase, since it derives not from mutual ignorance but from the direct economic and social subordination of one class to another, whose urban conditions of life may not be so very dissimilar.

The workers, as I have suggested, are becoming more bourgeois without necessarily assimilating into the lower bourgeoisie. Nowadays they watch the same TV programmes, sometimes go on the same kind of skiing or camping holidays, even dress the same way. And they are beginning to develop the same property-owning instincts and material aspirations, at least when they move into new flats. A university professor near Toulon told me: 'My *femme de ménage* is a practising Catholic and a good Communist and her husband is a dustman. When she comes tomorrow we'll have a good chat about the TV play we'll both be watching tonight. Her young daughter is a *coiffeuse* and one of the most elegant girls I know – her wedding photo was all over the local papers.'

Together with this goes an inevitable decline, as in Britain, in the old working-class emotional solidarity born of hard times. Someone said to me: 'People aren't so willing any more to spend their Sundays selling *Humanité-Dimanche*. They'd rather take the family off into the country in their new 2 cv.' Though they still vote Communist by tradition, and though a political rally in Paris or some other towns may still draw out the crowds, the class is beginning to lose some of its old sense of pride and self-identity. It is also becoming less homogeneous as its better-paid upper échelons, such as the envied '*métallos de chez Renault*' and other skilled workers, develop new proletarian élites who, without becoming middle class, often find that their interests are closer to those of their own factory *cadres* than of low-paid workers in the old artisanal firms. The new, milder image of the Communist Party is a reflection of this new working-class passivity, and abandonment of the ideal of revolution.

Labour relations in France, though outwardly calm outside short, sharp periods of crisis, exist in a climate of suspicion and cold-war stalemate. It is this which can so easily give rise to a sudden flare-up, such as that of 1968. Nowhere are the class barriers so evident as in industry. As compared with the fluctuating, troublesome, but very human situation in Britain, in many French firms there is a lack of direct discussion between employers and workers. The sociologist Michel Crozier, who has closely analysed this problem,* regards it as initially the fault of directors and *cadres* in most cases: in all aspects of labour relations, and not only in times of dispute, they prefer to keep their distance through fear of losing authority. The failure of the *comités d'entreprise* is one symptom of this. The workers resent the barriers, but are too proud or class-inhibited to make their own efforts to break them, and instead they plough their grievances

* *Le Phénomène bureaucratique* (Editions du Seuil, 1963).

into voting Communist. Bargaining therefore is usually done collectively, on a national level with the Government as arbiter. It is another example of the French tendency to formalize and depersonalize inter-group relations, in order to avoid awkward conflict. But conflict is sometimes not so much avoided as postponed, for this situation builds up tensions which can be resolved only by occasional violent theatrical outbursts. This was the significance of the 1968 strikes.

If I have drawn a somewhat severe picture of French class divisions today, it is because change has been so much less apparent than in Britain. But change has begun, and the French themselves are aware of it – especially since 1968 – and of a break in the ice-pack after the long 'alienation' of workers and peasantry from any control of the nation's destinies. On the Grands Ensembles, newly prosperous workers and middle-class families are beginning to make personal contacts that they never knew in their older homes. The new young generation, less bound than their parents by family conventions and appearances, are also strikingly less concerned about class distinctions; and, as at Bagnols, a teenager who at home has friends only from his parents' *milieux* will mix easily at school with children of all sorts. This is likely to develop as more workers' children enter the *lycées*. But often in past French history change has proved deceptive: society has shown a talent for regrouping under pressure of new conditions and then simply hardening its ranks once more. It is too early yet to say whether the new suburban contacts, the new youthful friendships, will produce a new climate or be absorbed into the existing system.

FAMILIES AND WOMEN:
FEMININITY NOT FEMINISM

France has often appeared *par excellence* a land where the family reigns supreme, focus of the individual's loyalty and affection, of his economic interest – and even of his legal duty, for the rights and obligations of family ties were clearly defined in the still operative Code Napoléon of 1804. Many a Frenchman has spent his youth in a world where he was expected to regard cousins,

uncles and grandmothers as more important to him than friends
of his own age, and where the family's needs and demands were
put before those of the local community or even of the State: 'I
cannot pay my taxes: you see, I've a duty to support Aunt Louise,'
has been a stock French attitude.

Today, when set beside the waning of family life in Britain or
America, France at first sight appears much of its old self. Once I
called up a girl I knew in Paris who lived with her parents. 'Do
come round this evening,' she said, 'I'm giving a little party.' Of
the thirty people present I was the only non-relative, and it was
not any special family occasion. Admittedly this was *la noblesse*,
where family still rules most strongly, and therefore it was an
extreme case. Lower down the social scale, there are plenty of
signs of change at work, and especially in the bourgeoisie. The
focus of loyalty is steadily narrowing from what sociologists call
the 'extended family' to the 'nuclear family': from the big multi-
generation clan to the immediate home cell of parents and children.
The trend varies from class to class. In the property-less lower
bourgeoisie the nuclear family has for many decades held more
importance than the clan, and therefore the change is less marked.
But in rural areas the big patriarchal peasant families are steadily
losing their influence as young people drift away to the towns. And
in the all-important upper bourgeoisie, as property gives way to
income, as family managements disappear and sons disperse to
new salaried careers in other parts of France, so does the close
network of the big family gathering, subject of a thousand bitter
novels, become less necessary for the individual's future and
security, and also less easy to maintain. Many young couples are
today likely to prefer pleasure motoring, or foreign holidays, or
the privacy of a week-end cottage, to the old traditional family
reunions on Sundays and in August. It is hard to be precise on
this subject, for French sociology, though abundant with data
about working relations and economic habits, shows a typical
French reticence about invading family privacy. Therefore I cannot state for sure that the average French bourgeois, say, meets his
uncles and cousins 5·7 times a year against 13·8 times in 1938,
though this might be so. But even this putative 5·7 would still be
near the European record. 'I had to cancel my holiday in Greece

this summer,' a sophisticated girl teacher of twenty-five told me, 'because, you see, my grandmother got ill and my mother was worried.' I doubt if her English equivalent would often display such a sense of duty.

On another occasion a friend of mine who is a successful young civil servant invited me to spend Sunday in his parents' prosperous country home near Paris. There I met four generations of them, from his grandmother of ninety-two to his own children and their hordes of little cousins, twenty or more people, and myself one of the only two outsiders. It was delightful, relaxed and very French. In other words, though clan loyalties towards more distant relatives may be fading, an adult's ties with his own parents and even with *their* parents often remain surprisingly close; and though between teenagers and parents there is less deference and formality than there used to be, children usually still live at home until married. Obsessive relationships between adults and their parents, especially between sons and mothers, are still a constant theme of French novels, and show how much this subject still preoccupies the French: witness Marguerite Duras's *Des Journées entières dans les arbres*, about an old woman's destructive love of her worthless son, or Jacques Borel's 1965 Goncourt winner, *L'Adoration*, about a man's inability to break the umbilical cord of emotion, or Robert Pinget's *Le Fiston*, which treats of an old man's tragic mooning about the son who has left home without trace. If many younger French people today are trying to lead more emotionally independent lives, it is often not without a sense of guilt, or an awareness of the pain it causes to their parents who cling for security to a different family tradition. This may be so in any country: it is especially sharp in France.

The immediate post-war rise in the birth-rate, *le bébé-boom*, perhaps did more than anything to strengthen the prestige and social importance of the younger nuclear family. This rise played such a key psychological role in the post-war French recovery that today, after more than thirty years, baby-making and baby-rearing are still regarded as a kind of prestige industry, as in Russia. The young mother filling her H L M with cots and nappies is now saluted as of more value to the nation than the old family patriarch holding up the pillars of society. Stimulated by the large child-allowances, the average size of families has swelled since the war, notably in the working class: on a small income, once a first child has arrived and the wife has given up her own earning-power, it is often more economic to go on and have two or three more, so large are the allowances. And in the middle classes too, now that property counts for so much less, the laws of equal inheritance are no longer such a disincentive to having several children. However, in the past ten years or so the birth-rate has been falling, as it has in other Western countries, especially in the middle classes. This has become a cause for concern, for France is still under-populated in proportion to her size. In 1976 Giscard brought in new measures to strengthen the family and to encourage couples to have three or four children rather than merely two. Baby-rearing remains a prestige industry, at least in official eyes.

These factors, plus the typically Latin adoration of small children, have led to a veritable *culte de l'enfant*, as it is called. '*Mais comme elle est mignonne, la petite!*' you hear them drooling in parks and streets. The French are usually generous and truly kind to their small children, and though a Frenchman may still react with narrow selfishness towards neighbours and officials, he will often make big personal sacrifices for his own children. More than in many countries, the golden ideal is to get married young, settle down and breed: the pregnant woman enjoys a privileged social status, special stores for her like Prénatal ('*tout pour la future maman!*') proliferate in every town, and the new suburbs pullulate with the kind of images of fecundity that Agnès Varda satirized in her film *Le Bonheur*. Some others, like her, suspect uneasily that this sacred cult has gone too far; and when another director, J.-C. Averty, defied it in a surrealist TV series in which babies were peeled, sliced, minced in machines and sold in butchers' shops, the public giggled in embarrassed outrage, some of them inwardly relieved to see a taboo exposed and the Baby-King ridiculed. It was rather like *Private Eye* satirizing the Queen.

The rise of the nuclear family has brought an increased element of sincerity and comradeship to married life. Couples are marrying younger than before the war, and are freer to make their own choices; arranged marriages have disappeared except in a few older provincial families. This does not mean that every match is a love-match; French girls can be shrewdly practical as well as romantic, and often have an eye for the character, position and prospects of their fiancés. Nor does it mean that bourgeois parents do not still fight much harder than in Britain, and often with more success, to prevent their daughters making 'unsuitable' marriages across the barriers of class or religion. When she meets her Jimmy Porter the bourgeois French girl may well have a secret affair with him, but is still most likely to heed parental advice not to marry him. But this is becoming less so, and Jesse Pitts reports:

> An upper-class girl graduating from Sciences Po wants to marry a young Jewish man who works in movie-producing. Her parents offer her the alternatives: stop seeing the young man or leave their home. She leaves their home and goes to work for 750 francs a month in an advertising agency. Before the war nobody would have employed her; ten or twelve years ago the job did not exist. In 1962 she can live her own life long enough for the parents to capitulate.*

The increased sincerity of marriages has its counterpart in an easier attitude to divorce, which is still highly disapproved of in theory but has become so prevalent that in practice it is often socially acceptable. The divorce figures, after a steady rise in the post-war years, have now levelled off at about one for every ten marriages, some 25 per cent above the British rate but below that of some countries. In this secular State divorce poses few of the legal problems that it still does in Italy. Although it is expensive, it is now almost as common in the working class as in the bourgeoisie – and twice as common in Paris as in the provinces. According to the opinion surveys, religious conviction or fear of scandal or family dishonour are no longer the main factors inhibiting divorce, when marriage is on the rocks; fear of harming the children, or of financial stress, or of loneliness, rank higher. Depending on your views, you can see this as a decline in morals, or in social hypocrisy.

A bill passed in 1964 removed many of the last remaining legal inequalities between husband and wife, as regards property-

* *France: Change and Tradition*, p. 296.

ownership and grounds for divorce; and this was claimed as one
of the final steps in a series of post-war measures for the social
emancipation of women. Further legislation in 1975, under
Giscard, made divorce virtually as easy as it is in Anglo-Saxon
countries, and removed all final inequalities between the sexes in
divorce matters. But the most significant fact about Frenchwomen today is that, apart from a small and untypical band of
feminist pioneers, they are not very interested in this kind of
equality. They care for femininity, not feminism; and all the
foreigner's silly clichés about the Frenchwoman, chic, seductive,
flirtatious and sexy, derive from this one abundant truth.

Women in France have rarely been segregated or treated as
inferior, in the manner of Spain or Italy. The Frenchwoman
regards herself, and is regarded, as the equal of man – *equal, but
quite different*. Given an opportunity to play the *same* role as a
man, legal, professional or social, she will often shy away in fear of
losing her femininity, and the men will cheer her for it! France is
still the land, cliché or not, of *la petite différence*: it is not the land
of suffragettes, nor of the women's clubs beloved of Anglo-Saxon
amazons. The 'Women's Lib' movement exists in France, but it
has much less appeal than in Anglo-Saxon countries. Woman's
role in the family, and in society, is a powerful one; but she lives
and sees herself in relation to that family and to individual men,
not to other women or the community as a whole. This is splendid, save that, today, this profound psychological orientation finds
itself under pressure from all sorts of new factors, economic and
social: women are being pushed and tempted towards a different
kind of emancipation, and they feel deeply torn between this and
their traditional feminine role. All the sociologists speak of this as
an 'age of transition' for the Frenchwoman. Let us look at her
dilemma more closely.

Frenchwomen were given the vote in 1945, by the reformist
Liberation Government under de Gaulle (not himself noted for
his feminism). But they have not done much with their new rights:
80 per cent are said to vote the way their husbands suggest, and if
the rest have any political influence of their own, it is towards
conservatism. De Gaulle, because he stood for peace and stability,
always had a higher vote among women than men, and since this

may have helped to keep him in power, he had no need to regret his post-war gesture. Women today are not legally barred from any office of State. But they seldom appear on political platforms; and after an initial burst of post-war feminist enthusiasm, their numbers in the National Assembly have dropped steadily, from 30 in 1945 to 9 in 1973, compared with the 26 British women MPs. In the 1973 elections only two per cent of the candidates were women, many of them Communists; and in all the shifting ministries of the period 1945–74, only three women reached even junior office. This state of affairs has been due more to women's own disinclination to enter public life than to male bias. They have preferred to wield influence behind the scenes – with Madame de Pompadour as their prototype, not Jeanne d'Arc – and I am sure that Madame de Gaulle had more influence on France's internal affairs than all French women politicians together during the 1945–74 era. When Giscard, dedicated reformist in all social matters, came to power, he tried an entirely new tack. He brought women from outside politics into his Government. Simone Weil, a brilliant and liberal-minded lawyer, became Minister of Health, and was so persuasive and successful that all the opinion polls were soon showing her as the most popular Minister and she was even being tipped as a future Prime Minister. 'The best man we've got in our team is a woman,' Chirac is said to have remarked. Françoise Giroud, brought in from being editor of *l'Express* to a new post of Secretary of State for the Feminine Condition, has not made quite the same impact, and her job has sometimes been regarded as a piece of Giscardian window-dressing. In 1976 Alice Saunier-Séïte was brought in from the academic world to the hot seat of Secretary of State for Universities. By 1976 there were five women in the Government, and this was claimed to be a world record. But it must be noted that the three most prominent of them were not career politicians; they were co-opted from other professions, like technocrats. Giscard has proved that women can be highly effective in government. He has not yet begun to prove that Frenchwomen are interested in political careers.

In ordinary working life, however, women have not shown the same reluctance, and in most careers there is now virtual equality.

A girl of good family is no longer expected to lead an idle life at home before marriage; she goes out and gets a job. And in the universities the proportion of girl students has risen from 25 per cent in 1930 to 47 per cent today. In 1972 a girl of nineteen came first in the passing-out exam of the Ecole Polytechnique, that hitherto male preserve. In the liberal professions women's numbers have also been rising, and now account for about 15 per cent of the whole – 20 per cent of university professors, 18 per cent of lawyers, 9 per cent of doctors. There is a woman prefect, and has recently been a woman ambassador. Only in industry and big business is there still something of a masculine bias against women in directors' chairs: but here too they are infiltrating, for example the brilliant Mme Gomez, now chairperson of Waterman (France).

Conversely, in the poorer classes, where for decades wives have habitually gone out to work, the rise of prosperity has now enabled many of them to give up their jobs and devote themselves to the home. In this *milieu*, to have a wife who does not work is often a status symbol. Because of this trend the total number of women at full-time work, $7\frac{1}{2}$ million, is actually no more than it was in 1900, despite the growth of population. But women still account for a higher proportion of the total labour force in France (34·3 per cent) than in Britain (31 per cent), though less than in Germany (37 per cent). And France is nearer than most countries to achieving the ideal of equal pay for equal work.

The main point to draw from these figures is that, in the educated classes, far more women are at work than before the war. And yet relatively few of them emerge as actively career-minded. A woman will work before she is married, and maybe again when her children are grown up or if her marriage collapses; but there is still a certain prejudice in bourgeois France against the young housewife, however gifted, who leaves her small children with a nanny or *au pair* girl and continues a full-time job. In Britain we know the problem of the young graduate wife by the kitchen sink, full of guilt at wasting her expensive education; in France, the guilt tends to be the other way round. And even before marriage, as one feminist at the head of a big agency put it to me: 'These young girls come with their degrees looking for jobs, but there's nothing they really want to do, they're just waiting for the right man.' It is all a sign, in the eyes of some indignant feminists, that Frenchwomen are not yet fully emancipated.

A small but militant feminist movement has gained ground in the 1970s, stimulated by the events of May 1968 which awoke the spirit of revolt in so many fields. One of its leading champions is Delphine Seyrig, the actress. As compared with the American and British movements, it is not concerned with general chip-on-the-shoulder protests against 'male chauvinist piggery' (the term does not exist in French) but devotes itself solely to concrete ends, that is, to securing better rights for women in precise fields. It has fought for battered wives, and has organized women's strikes in factories. The whole movement is diverse and spontaneous. It does not seek, like some Anglo-Saxon bra-burners, to turn women into men. On the contrary, '*Le droit à différence*' is one of its slogans, a specific rejection of certain male values, such as careerism and competitiveness, and a stress on feminine qualities.

This is very typically French. Most Frenchwomen are still hesitant to share a man's privileges. This was noticeable during the campaign for the 1964 Matrimonial Bill, which finally abrogated the old laws whereby a wife had to obtain her husband's permission to open a bank account, run a shop or get a passport, while much joint property was legally the husband's and the divorce courts were obliged to regard a wife's infidelity as more serious than a man's. The feminist pioneers fought successfully to push the bill through, but it was not particularly popular with women as a whole. As one leading feminist said to me: 'Many women felt that the bill implied a mistrust of the husband. They felt they did not need equality, but would rather use their charms on a man to win their way.'

To live for one man, to use charm or guile to woo or persuade him, to devote feminine skills to pleasing him, feeding him, rearing his children – this may be a woman's instinct anywhere, but especially in France, and the French male provides her with an enthusiastic alibi. It exasperated Simone de Beauvoir, and in *Le Deuxième Sexe* (1949), a book that has less meaning in an Anglo-Saxon context, she gave her compatriots some tart precepts on how to escape from their self-imposed 'inferiority'. That famous book had some influence in intellectual circles, and in the first post-Liberation years there was even a small upsurge of feminism, linked to the existentialist movement. But since then, de Beauvoir and her co-militants have seen their influence wane.

Men and women alike have a fear and contempt for the independent, no-nonsense, masculine type of woman so common in England, and those Frenchwomen who do emerge as leaders of their sex are usually subtly and exquisitely feminine people such as Hélène Gordon-Lazareff, editor of *Elle*. Another such person, Christiane Collange, the mildly feminist but highly seductive assistant editor of *l'Express*, told me: 'Whenever I go to make a speech about the rights of women, I'm always especially careful to look *soignée* and appealing. Feminism here gives people the willies.'

So there is not much feeling of solidarity among Frenchwomen, and consequently very little of the club-activity of women's institutes and guilds in Britain or the legions of American sororities. Until recently the strength of family links made up for this lack of clubbiness and in fact was a cause of it. But with the dispersal of families and the move to new suburban homes, the French housewife is beginning to feel her isolation. 'Put the young bourgeoise down in a new flat,' said one critic of this mentality, 'and what'll she do? Still spend half the morning telephoning Maman to discuss what to cook her husband for dinner.' Or else she may overwork herself trying to do a job and run a home all at once, yet fail to ease her burden by linking with neighbours in self-help. I have described this problem on the Grands Ensembles, and how new attitudes are gradually emerging born of necessity. In other aspects of life, too, changing conditions are compelling women into a different realization of themselves. The new opportunities for higher education and careers, new forms of leisure, greater social tolerance about sex and birth-control* – these are opening wider horizons and providing escapes from what de Beauvoir called 'the slavery of the female condition'. And, consciously or unconsciously, women are faced with the problem of reconciling this new kind of emancipation with their prized femininity and emotional urge to depend on a man's world. This is their central dilemma. It is a confused question, much

* See pp. 390–97.

debated in France today, especially in the form of '*le foyer contre le travail*'. I quote from one of the best known of the many recent books on the subject, *Le Métier de femme*,* by the sociologist Ménie Grégoire:

> The feminists of the early 1900s who fought to snatch away from men some of their privileges would be very disappointed to see how much the equality that they demanded embarrasses women today. It is time to give a clear picture of the formidable confusion in which most women of the present generation find themselves: they try to reconcile everything while sacrificing nothing. We are in the century of the feminine *mauvaise conscience*. Every mother who keeps on with her professional job knows this perpetual feeling of duty ill performed. She lives by stealing time away, from her children, her employer, herself.

This desire to depend on a man's world, on happiness brought by a man, may bring its ecstatic rewards, but also it makes French-women especially vulnerable and subject to strain. For there is no doubt that Frenchmen, those notorious egotists, exploit their advantage both emotionally and in practical ways; they even refuse to help with the chores because it is considered unvirile. Both before and after marriage a woman usually has to fight harder than in most countries to keep her man's interest in her; and though this is certainly one reason why in their forties and even fifties Frenchwomen often remain so chic and sexually alert, it may also explain those tense, sharp expressions, the hard lines around the mouth. They lack the puddingy relaxedness of English matrons.

My own subjective reaction is just this: often I find French-women ill at ease and brusquely defensive compared with men. Why is it that French secretaries, when telephoned by a stranger, are usually so much more curt and unhelpful than their bosses? '*Il n'est pas là – moi, je n'en sais rien, rappelez,*' they snap. without offering to take a message. Yet when you do finally contact the boss, he is often charming and ready to help. Why, at a dinner-party, does the conversation even of a clever and educated woman appear conventional and slightly stilted? Why are women, rather than men, the chief guardians of French formalism, less prepared

* Plon, 1965.

than men to modernize a business or adapt to new office routine, or to get on christian-name or *tu* terms with friends instead of the endless *Madames*? Why does the natural feminine reserve of a Frenchwoman so often have an uneasy edge to it, as if she wanted to assert herself but was not quite sure how, lacking either the passive shyness and sweetness of a Mediterranean or Oriental woman, or yet the assured and emancipated ease of a northerner?

For the answers, *cherchez l'homme*. If anyone is still unemancipated, it is the French male, in his attitude to women. He may behave with gallant charm to a woman he loves, or desires, or wants to flirt with; he is still backward at treating a woman as an equal, as a social human being, when there is no sexual undertone. Possibly that is why at the dinner-table a clever Frenchwoman does not always feel at ease in men's conversation; and I am certain that it is often because French bosses are tiresome and inconsiderate that secretaries vent their irritation on outsiders. The qualities of the Frenchwoman – warmth, subtlety, finesse, loyalty – often lie buried, and they expect *you* to make all the effort to woo them out of their defensiveness. After all, they have much to endure: they bear the brunt not only of Frenchmen but also of many of the practical strains of living in a city like Paris today. And it is only fair to add that there are plenty of unprickly exceptions, especially among the younger generation, who are beginning to develop a new ease and confidence. Among the middle-aged middle classes the rudeness and strained defensiveness are worst.

It is in her sexual attitudes that the unresolved semi-emancipation of the Frenchwoman appears most clearly today. Generally she is *sérieuse* and romantic, though not necessarily virginal before marriage; and with part of herself she welcomes the growing climate of freedom and frankness between the sexes. But another part of herself is still under the shadow of all kinds of complexes and conventions, the legacy of a traditional Catholic society. She is often unsure whether she really wants sexual freedom, or what to do with it. And this is true of Catholics and agnostics alike.

Of course the idea of the Frenchwoman as *légère*, or of France as the land of unfettered *amour*, has always been one of the silliest of foreigners' clichés. It sprang largely from the tourists' inability to distinguish between the strict codes of French domestic life (which usually he never saw) and the manifest tradition of public tolerance which readily sanctioned conspicuous minority activities such as Montmartre night-life or the free-living world of the Left Bank bohemia. If you are on your own and outside society, then the guardians of morality ignore you – and so for many decades Paris has been a favourite refuge for foreigners wanting privacy and freedom. Even today, many of those couples living so romantically in sin on the Left Bank are expatriates. But if you belong to one of the rigid compartments of French society, then you must obey its hypocritical rules.

The tourist is often misled, too, by all the charming billing and cooing that goes on in cafés, parks and buses. But this, too, is an aspect of *public* tolerance: so long as there is no one around who knows you, then no one minds or stares, as they do in some countries. You virtually do not exist, and so you can do what you like. And anyway, demonstrative flirtation is all part of the French romantic game, with men expecting women to be coquettish and women expecting men to be *galant*. But how often, among the unmarrieds, does it end up in bed? Much less, nowadays, than in London, where far more young people live on their own away from parents.

Certainly there is more sexual freedom among the young than there used to be. On the one hand, French parents now more easily allow their daughters to go out with boys; young people have more leisure and more money for getting away on their own together; and the younger clergy are now much more liberal about sex. In some student and working-class circles relations have become very free, and some teenage girls are developing the complex, familiar in Britain, that they *ought* to lose their virginity. But though she may no longer be so chaste, the French girl of any age or class remains strikingly *sérieuse* in not giving herself unless she thinks she is in love: she rarely goes in for the kind of promiscuity common in Scandinavia and rapidly spreading in Britain. And all the evidence suggests that French unmarried girls as a whole, especially in the provinces, are still among the most virginal in Europe, outside Italy and Spain. There is a true story that when, in Lyon, a dead baby was found recently in a hostel for working girls, and all 144 inmates agreed to a police request that they be medically examined to see who could be absolved from suspicion, all but seven were found to be virgins. And a Kinsey-type survey carried out in 1960 by the leading French public opinion institute IFOP found that 70 per cent of married women under thirty *claimed* to have been still virgins on their wedding night. But things are changing. In 1972, a similar survey by the leading sexologist, Dr Pierre Simon, found that only 45 per cent of women claimed to be still virgins at their marriage. So either Frenchwomen are becoming less chaste; or else they are becoming more prepared to tell the truth.

In many respects the social codes are becoming more tolerant. Not only has divorce become more acceptable, but the *fille mère* with an illegitimate child is no longer such a social outcast: her title has been officially changed to *mère célibataire*, she can legally call herself *Madame* if she wishes, and there are plenty of State and private organizations to help her with her problems or look after her child. Even pre-marital sex, according to the survey, is no longer regarded by most women as a dishonour or a crime but simply as 'rather a pity' or 'rather stupid'. Yet when family respectability is directly at stake, the codes still hold firm. It is still the ideal of almost every family in France, Catholic or not, to lead its daughter a virgin to the altar (or *mairie*); and one Frenchman told me he was deeply shocked when he visited friends in West Germany and 'The parents gave me the impression they wouldn't really have minded if I'd slept with their twenty-year-old daughter.' According to IFOP in 1960, more than half of French mothers then still thought a girl should not be allowed out with a boy till she was nineteen, and many still acted on it. And only 27 per cent of girls under thirty said they approved of pre-marital sex even between fiancés, while few admitted having practised it.

Again according to IFOP, two men in three want to marry a virgin, or at least get engaged to one. Jean-Pierre Mocky in his shrewd and witty film *Les Vierges* (1966) suggested that modern French girls are inhibited by male taboos about virginity, above all else. He gave a satirical account of five young Parisiennes all longing to leap into bed but frustrated by various social hypocrisies and especially by their boyfriends' terror of deflowering them: 'I do not accept shop-soiled goods,' says a snobby playboy to his fiancée. As in any Latin or Catholic country, virginity in male eyes is still something of a sacred property, and the most dedicated womanizer will often draw back when confronted with *une jeune fille*: virgins are for marrying, not seducing. Mocky's portrait was deliberately overdrawn, but I think there is some general truth in his point that many French girls are at heart readier for sexual emancipation than society, and especially male society, will let them be.

There are still many strong conventions and *idées reçues* about sex which are only gradually being eroded by changing practice. The most damaging result of this climate is that there are still prejudices against proper sex education. Under pressure from parental opinion rather than from the Church, sex education was formally banned in schools until quite recently (though some teachers give clandestine lessons under the heading of philosophy or biology), and many mothers are still too inhibited to explain anything directly to their daughters. The nationwide debate about birth-control, which has been raging since the 1960s, has made a breach in this wall of silence. In some schools, unofficial extra-curricular sex-education classes were started around 1970, and they had some success. Finally, in 1976, sex education was required to begin at the age of eleven or twelve, and instruction on the use of the pill and contraception became compulsory in all secondary schools, including those run by the Church. There was very little opposition to this, even from Catholic quarters, and latest opinion polls show that the French are now massively in favour of sex education. Public opinion has changed enormously in the past few years. However, many older Frenchwomen, who have not benefited from this, still carry throughout their lives a burden of superstition and guilt about sex. I admire French girls for their romantic *sérieux* and, when it is a true choice, for their chastity: but often it is not a true choice, it is muddled up with fear, inhibition and convention.

While the pre-marital 'affair' may be rarer than in many countries, after marriage the pattern changes and I suspect that adulterous intrigue is as common in France as anywhere. Many French people resent this national image, fostered in countless novels and films from Flaubert to Godard: when in 1964 Godard made a film about a modern Bovary with the title *La Femme mariée*, the Gaullist censors sprang to defend French marital honour and forced him to change '*La*' to '*Une*'. There are many people who argue, rather more to the point, that adultery has grown less common, now that fewer marriages are arranged and divorce is easier. On the other hand, the growth of travel and prosperity has probably tended to encourage infidelities, at least in the bourgeoisie where adultery is more widespread than in the working class. There are no statistics: I can only suggest that, in a land where so many women are still torn between Catholic ideals of chastity and the impulses of hedonistic romanticism, the extra-marital affair is more likely to prove the norm than the pre-marital one.

I am also impressed by how very discreet, indeed secretive, the French are about their love-affairs – even when both partners are unmarried and it is not a question of trying to preserve appearances or to avoid hurting someone else. Except in a small Parisian bohemian *milieu*, lovers rarely live together openly, and, however free you both may be, it is considered vulgar to 'flaunt' your liaison by moving as a couple in your own social circle. London has now become more permissive about this than Paris, where even the very young go about together in couples much less than in some countries. Nor will a Frenchwoman easily confide her private life even to her nearest and dearest: a French friend of mine told me she once shared a flat with her most intimate girl friend, who all the time was having a serious affair with a married man in the same town; the girl never dropped a hint of it, and my friend only found out afterwards, accidentally. And when on another occasion I told an emancipated upper-class Parisienne how disconcerting I found it, when with a group of young French people, even quite bohemian ones, that one could never tell who was involved with who, she said: 'Don't worry, nor can we. In France, we like to keep people guessing. I was shocked when I went to London as a young girl and everyone asked me who my boy-friend was. I said, "In France we don't have boy-friends."

When I am with my lover and our friends, no one knows we are lovers. We each go out with other people sometimes too, and trust each other to be faithful. My private life is my own. I'd hate other people to know what I was up to, they'd simply gossip and make it seem cheap. And then it would get back to my family, who'd be mortally upset, so why should I cause them needless distress?'

You can call this a sign of civilized delicacy in a society – just as you can call the relative lack of discussion of sex and sexual morality a token of French maturity when set beside the endless naïve self-analysing of British and Americans who, as someone once said, 'have sex on the brain and that's not the right place for it'. In France *il y a des choses qui se font mais dont on ne parle pas.* De Gaulle was a good Catholic and some of his Ministers had mistresses; *bien sûr, c'est normal,* but a public man's private life is his own affair so long as he's discreet – except maybe in an extreme case involving criminal conduct, such as the 'Scandale des Ballets Roses' in 1957, when the elderly Socialist President of the National Assembly, M. le Troquer, was involved with some friends in orgies with girls under sixteen. But as for John Profumo's little fling with a high-class tart, the national crisis *that* affair caused in Britain was greeted in France with hilarious amazement: it is hardly conceivable that a French Minister's public career would be judged by peccadilloes of that sort, or that the French public would be surprised or outraged to learn of them, or that he should be expected to answer questions in Parliament about them. Even the divorce cases of well-known people usually take place in private in France, and though they may cause gossip among their friends, they are rarely reported in the newspapers.

This may be a sign of civilized delicacy, but I cannot help feeling that on the ordinary social level there is also a good deal of hypocrisy involved. Just as the lack of discussion of sex might be as much a sign of taboo and refusal to face facts as it is a sign of maturity, so the concealing of a love-affair is often part of a social pretence that restricts the freedom of people's lives. 'Ah yes,' sighed my upper-class Parisienne, 'of course it would be nice in a way if we could be together more openly as a couple, maybe live together. Of course having an affair under these conditions *is* a strain in many ways, with all the subterfuge it involves, often it's hard to spend the night together when we'd like to. But you can't have everything. Things just aren't like that in France.'

This climate of intrigue does at least help to keep the French romantic temperature running high, with the titillation of *fruits défendus*. It relates closely to the French male attitude to women, which is still at heart very Latin: women are prized feminine possessions, to be courted and desired but also to be protected from other men. Therefore, as an essential alibi of a masculine society, *amours* must be discreet. For all the apparent freedom and equality for women in France, there is still a slight hangover of this Latin mentality. Women who break the rules, by being too assertive or self-dependent, by trying to live on their own terms or develop their own morality, are not approved of and, much worse, are not found attractive. And most women accept the *status quo* because what they treasure above all is French male appreciation of their femininity. This they are given, abundantly.

It might even be claimed that the French have found the ideal balance between Italo-Spanish female subservience and Americo-Nordic destruction of the prized *petite différence*. Many women, at least, think so. An English girl who has lived and worked for some years in France told me: 'In England when you're working in an office with men, they either treat you as just silly, or if you're good at your job they forget you're a woman. In France, they manage to treat your work seriously *and* flatter you as an attractive woman, and I prefer that.' A French girl married to an Englishman and living in London said: 'For all the difficulties of being a woman in France, at least one is supremely a *woman*, and I find that more deeply satisfying than English comradeliness.' And several other Frenchwomen who have lived in Britain or America have told me, in effect: 'In your country, couples are bound by affection and respect, but they seem to remain a bit separate; in France, there's a sort of *complicité*, a forming of a unit against the world, and perhaps that's why so many marriages don't work, because romantic aims are pitched too high.'

The Frenchman's demonstrative delight in female company is therefore the Frenchwoman's greatest compensation for her various difficulties – and she relishes it, even when she knows it is no more than skin-deep. It gives to relations between the sexes a

certain romantic tenderness and intimacy, a subtle pleasure in
being together, that is not always equalled in more emancipated
but less philogynous countries. The Frenchman may often be a
sexual egotist, but his egotism is not brutish or in-turned. Partly
to flatter his own vanity and sexual power, he is more sensitively
concerned than most males to see that the woman, too, is fulfilled;
and *donner le plaisir* is for him as important a part of love-making
as his own satisfaction. Hence his reputation as a lover, which
according to Jean-François Revel* is far better justified than the
Italian's.

So the Frenchwoman is offered an atmosphere where she is
easily tempted to indulge her deep-seated romanticism, in a land
where words like *plaisir* and *séduire* have overtones of emotional
delicacy that are lost in literal translation. In a recent interview in
Elle, a middle-class divorcée of twenty-four says:

On a envie de savoir si on séduit . . . de se confirmer un petit peu
vis-à-vis des hommes. Beaucoup de femmes font l'amour uniquement
pour sentir qu'elles plaisent. Ce qui est important dans l'amour, c'est
de séduire, et puis d'être limpide brusquement à quelqu'un; de le
rencontrer vraiment; c'est la chose la plus belle qui existe . . .

and *séduire* means something not easy to translate: to win power
over someone through the giving of pleasure.

There are drawbacks, however, to this tender idyll between the
sexes. Not only are women made vulnerable and sometimes
strained by the emotional dependence on male egotism; but men
are not easily prepared to treat them as friends or ordinary social
equals. Many Frenchwomen regret this lack of easy-going
camaraderie: in France, a close friendship between a man and a
woman does not so often develop without ceasing to be platonic
or at least giving rise to gossip. A girl who knows both Paris and
London said to me: 'In London, if a man takes me out to dinner,
I know I can ask him up to coffee in my flat afterwards, out of
politeness – and it needn't mean any more. A Frenchman will
always take it as *une invitation*.' In England, in ordinary conversation you can use carefully ambiguous terms like 'boy-friend'
and 'girl-friend' which have no real French equivalent: *amant* and

* *Pour l'Italie* (Julliard).

petite amie have much more precise connotations and cannot be used so casually. 'Mon amant et moi . . .' would cause raising of eyebrows; 'My boy-friend and I . . .' does not. And a woman who in England might be described as 'having an affair with' or 'involved with so-and-so' in France would be 'la maîtresse d'un tel', with its subtle indication of male ascendancy. These verbal nuances indicate the national differences of attitude.

The Frenchwoman today is often unsure which male attitude she prefers. In a way she is pleased to be reminded so continually of her femininity – she regards a suave pass as rightful *hommage*, and the English approach she may find boorish and unflattering. But she is also beginning to look enviously at the more easy-going and emancipated Anglo-Saxon world; and that is the direction which younger French girls, students and teenagers, are now following. Among younger couples, for instance, a wife now does expect her husband to help her with the chores, and she no longer so easily accepts a man who will not take her own views and ambitions as seriously as his own. A very young divorcée told *Elle*: 'I lived for two years with a boy. He saw it as a one-way exchange. I agreed to share his life, take an interest in his work. Not he. My concerns were unimportant to him the moment they were mine. So I left him.'

Thus a new kind of attitude is now emerging among the post-Bardot, post-Sagan generation – a new assertiveness, but still very man-orientated. The present age is indeed one of mutation for the Frenchwoman: the old pattern of 'femininity, not feminism' is certain to be modified, though how fast or far remains to be seen. Some emancipation on Anglo-Saxon lines is inevitable. But male exploiters of the present *status quo* are not the only people who feel that the French ideal of womanhood contains much that it would be sad to lose. Françoise Giroud, herself something of a feminist, told me that she thought the French version of *le couple*, intimate and equal but different, might prove a stronger bulwark than other styles of marriage for protecting the warm human cell of parents and children against the forces that in some modern countries are threatening to destroy it. So the issue for the Frenchwoman today is how to become happily emancipated (in her relations with men both social and sexual, in her community

relations with other women, in her career and intellectual interests)
without sacrificing *la petite, et précieuse, différence*! She wants
freedom, but her own kind of freedom. She doesn't want to be an
amazon in the Crusades. At heart, she would rather stay at home
and be wooed by a troubadour. And France would be the poorer
without its troubadour spirit:

> Bertrans, En Bertrans, left a fine canzone:
> 'There is a throat; ah, there are two white hands;
> There is a trellis full of early roses,
> And all my heart is bound about with love.'*

BATTLES FOR BIRTH-CONTROL AND ABORTION

There is one domain where Frenchwomen have especially lacked
emancipation hitherto, but where suddenly a revolution has been
taking place, in a climate of controversy bordering on national
crisis. Until about fifteen years ago, birth-control was almost as
taboo from public discussion as in Spain. Ever since 1920, this
secular State had imposed anti-contraception laws which liberals
often described as scandalous, criminal, or 'medieval, when compared with the family-planning policies of Tunisia, France's
former protectorate'. And it seemed that nowhere did the
Frenchwoman suffer so much from society as in the privacy of her
own married life.

During the 1960s, the campaign of a group of pioneers forced
a breach in the curtain of social prejudice, and brought the whole
issue into the open. Today, birth-control is publicly debated
without cease, even on State television; and the Gaullist Government was finally pushed into repealing the 1920 laws, so that all
modern forms of contraception are now legal. Public opinion
too has been changing fast, but the battle is not yet entirely
won.

The aim of the law passed in 1920 was not religious but demographic: to help repair the human losses of the First World War.
It prohibited all publicity for birth-control, including advisory
clinics, and it banned the sale of contraceptives except for certain

* Ezra Pound, *Near Périgord* (Faber and Faber, 1928).

medical purposes. Since then it was frequently side-stepped and had long been overtaken by most educated public opinion; but only since 1967 did it come under reform, and over the years it caused untold hardship and frustration, especially to poorer people who could not afford the luxury of trips abroad to foreign gynaecologists. Most French couples have always resorted to the time-honoured methods of *coitus interruptus,* uterine washing or periodic abstinence. Or they have resorted to abortion; and, since this was illegal until 1974, they often did it themselves. Deaths from clumsy self-abortion were estimated to run into thousands a year. Abortions were legal only when the mother's life was in danger – and most doctors interpreted this cruel law with a stupid literalness. In one case a woman of thirty-nine who had had four miscarriages, four still-births and seven live births, four of them producing abnormal children, had great difficulty in persuading the doctors to sanction an abortion (which by then would have been legal) when she was pregnant for the fifteenth time and acutely ill.

A few thousand rich and informed women were able to avoid these problems. They would go off regularly for their diaphragms or abortions to private doctors in London, Geneva or Morocco: 'Elle va en Suisse' became a stock whispered joke at smart Paris parties. But most couples had neither the means for this nor, more relevant, the degree of knowledge or initiative to take other, less costly steps themselves, such as finding one of the few French doctors who would help with birth-control. And millions of working wives, faced with the horrors of raising a large family under French housing conditions, came to regard sex and their husband's desires with panic, and greet the menopause with relief. So the lack till now of birth-control has been one main reason why the sex-life of the French, despite their romanticism, despite their warmth and skill as lovers, has not always been the paradise of fulfilment that foreigners often imagine. But few novelists ever dared say so.

This was the picture until recently. Now it is changing rapidly. In 1956 a courageous young woman doctor, Madame Marie-Andrée Weill-Hallé, was the first to declare war on the 1920 law by founding with a few colleagues the Mouvement Français pour le Planning Familial. Its first advisory clinic was opened, in *avant-garde* Grenoble, in 1961, and by 1966 there were nearly two hundred all over France. The Government turned a blind eye: though the clinics could well be regarded as illegal under the 1920 law, Ministers were anxious to avoid a showdown with informed public opinion that might make them look ridiculous. So a kind of tacit truce was observed between MFPF and Government: but the former, in order to keep its side of the bargain, had to resort to the most bizarre procedures in order not to flout the law too openly. When a woman visited one of its clinics, she was put in touch with one of the 1,500 or so French doctors who agreed to work with the Movement, and he would probably fit her for a diaphragm. But the sale or import of these was supposedly illegal. So, by an arrangement with the IPPF, the woman sent a ten-franc postal order and her prescription to a British clinic in south London, which then posted her the cap in a plain envelope. Sent singly, by letter post, they usually escaped customs checks; an initial attempt to import them in bulk packets often led to seizures. Dr Pierre Simon, one of Dr Weill-Hallé's most militant colleagues, told me: 'Whenever I went to London, I would bring back dozens in a suitcase for my patients. Once, the customs officer at Orly inspected my case, and they dropped out all over the floor. All the women near me giggled sympathetically, and then the officer laughed too, and told me to clear out quickly or he'd get into trouble.' It seemed to be a sign of the changing times that in the 1960s London should be providing Paris with aids to sexual pleasure.

This was by no means the only example of the Government's hypocritical handling of the 1920 law. On the pretext that they limit syphilis, male condoms have always been freely on sale in chemists' shops (some 40 million were bought a year, or just over two for each adult male); and even the pill began to be available in the mid-1960s, on prescription – officially, for curing a variety of obscure diseases. A number of officials at the Ministry of Health privately encouraged the MFPF, and so did some Ministers, though they could not say so in public: when the Movement invited the Minister of Health to the opening of its first Paris clinic, in 1961, the reply came back: 'He cannot of course appear openly on such an occasion, but he sends you his best wishes.' Hypocrisy is at least preferable to repression, and one might be tempted to argue that the law had been so cleverly turned by usage that it scarcely needed reforming. But this was not really so. Not only did the law add greatly to the hesitance of doctors and manufacturers, but the Movement could never dare publicize its clinics openly. It had to rely on 'bush telegraph', mainly among the bourgeoisie; and class barriers and female reticence to talk about sex are such that most working women never knew of their local clinic. The Movement has been a remarkable and rare example in France of effective unofficial civic action on a national scale; but, lacking official funds, it had to rely mainly on voluntary staff working in poky and obscure premises.

Since de Gaulle, his wife and many of his Ministers were loyal Catholics, official Vatican policy counted for much in the Government reluctance to end hypocrisy and reform the law openly. Just as the easing of Vatican attitudes in 1964–5 helped to bring reform much closer, so the stiffening of Pope Paul's position in 1966 had a parallel influence in Paris. The French hierarchy, like Cardinals anywhere, are today divided and confused about the subject; but among rank-and-file French Catholics there has been in recent years a massive change of heart, which neither the *humanae vitae* encyclical of 1968 nor the Pope's anti-sex outburst of January 1976 have reversed. Priests no longer come to family planning meetings to heckle and protest, as they used to in the early days; many of the younger ones even advise their penitents how to seek advice on birth-control. Several Catholic bodies are now taking an active part in this kind of education, and many of the MFPF's own leaders have been practising Catholics.

But the old-guard Catholics, opposed to reform, have been active and numerous too, and one of their leaders was that *éminence grise*, Madame de Gaulle. For various reasons, partly electoral, the Government in the mid-1960s was wary of offending this group. When in 1966 the Socialists and their allies put repeal of the 1920 laws into their programme, the Government saw that the issue was gaining popularity, and that it could no longer afford to stay silent. So it set up a commission of inquiry into the use of the pill, whose findings it then conveniently ignored. It managed to go on sitting on the fence in this way till after the 1967 elections, clutching at straws of medical doubt about the pill or the coil as alibis for inaction. But by then the national conspiracy of silence had been shattered. There was now a crescendo of discussion about birth-control – in the Press, in polemical articles by feminists such as Ménie Grégoire in papers such as *Elle*, in films such as Autant-Lara's *Journal d'une femme en blanc* (the story of a bold young doctor who fights for birth-control in her hospital), and even on State TV, where admittedly the evidence was sometimes carefully slanted in favour of the *status quo*. Public opinion was evolving; and by now demographers, and economists too, though insistent on the need to keep up the birth-rate, doubted that under modern conditions the 1920 laws were still relevant for this purpose.

Finally the Government capitulated. It allowed a progressive-minded Gaullist deputy, Lucien Neuwirth, to put forward his own reform bill which with discreet official support went through Parliament at the end of 1967. The new Act legalizes the sale of contraceptives (under certain conditions) and also the giving of advice about birth-control. But Parliament was not its last hurdle. Certain Ministers hostile to the reform then tried to sabotage it by withholding their signatures from the decrees needed to put it into force. One was Joseph Fontanet, Minister of Labour under Pompidou, an old-style Catholic. Thus the decree authorizing sale of the inter-uterine coil was held up for five years and not finally signed until 1967; the same was true of the decree legalizing birth-control propaganda and setting up a national centre for advice and information. Other aspects of the new law came into force more rapidly. Diaphragms are now imported commercially in bulk (mostly from Britain) and are on sale freely to all over eighteen (those below this age must have parental and medical agreement). The pill requires a doctor's prescription but not parental approval even in the case of girls of fifteen or sixteen. A patient was supposed to present the chemist with a record card and vouchers, signed by her doctor, each time she bought pills: but this measure was criticized for treating married women humiliatingly as if they were drug addicts, and it has never been enforced. In one respect the French law is more liberal than custom in Britain: it draws no formal distinction between married and unmarried women. This is left to each doctor's discretion. The authors of the law accept that, nowadays, contraceptives are needed as much by the unmarried as the married; they are now all available free on the national health service, for people of any age.

The effectiveness of the Neuwirth Act will in the long term depend on the amount of support it gets from the medical profession. Today French doctors' views are changing, though until recently few of them would have anything to do with birth-control. Often her own doctor is the only person a woman knows to whom she can turn for expert advice; and often in the past she turned to him in vain. In 1962 and again in 1966 the Council of the Order of Doctors, the supreme medical body, declared formally that contraceptive advice, and changes in the 1920 law, were none of a doctor's business. Most older GPs, whether Catholic or not, were bound by a professional instinct that they had best keep out of the controversy, and few of them bothered to learn anything about modern birth-control. Before the passing of the new law, only 4 per cent of doctors collaborated with the MFPF, while perhaps a thousand others gave contraceptive advice privately. Even today, many GPs when consulted by a worried and ignorant patient still tend to give her a lecture on the joys of motherhood and refuse to offer advice. But since the new law, things are changing rapidly: doctors tend to be cautious and legalistic, and it was the old law that held them back. An estimated three doctors in four now accept the need for birth-control.

Yet the Frenchwoman herself, wed or unwed, has proved slow to take advantage of the newly offered liberation from anxiety, pain and restraint. According to a survey in 1975, the percentage of Frenchwomen between 15 and 50 who regularly take the pill has risen since 1968 from 5 to 22, while another 7 per cent use coil or diaphragm. However a further 13 per cent still prefer such methods as *coitus interruptus*, while more than half of Frenchwomen with an active sex-life use no contraception at all. Although even back in 1962 some 57 per cent of women – according to one survey – said they favoured the sale of contraceptives, and of the rest only one in four was opposed for moral reasons, when it comes to applying those views to their own personal lives they are more hesitant – even today, when the opinion polls report that over 90 per cent of the French regard birth-control as desirable. Old-style, anti-sex Catholicism may be receding fast in France, but it has left behind a widespread legacy of semi-conscious guilt, superstition and prudery, even among women who would profess themselves atheists. Dr Weill-Hallé told me: 'If we have lagged so far behind Britain in family planning, the reasons have been much less legal or religious than psychological and social. The first task of our staff at the clinics has usually been to try to *déculpabiliser* a new client, to rid her of her complexes about coming to us.'

Owing to lack of sex education until very recently, many girls enter marriage with the haziest ideas. In the 1960s, a woman who ventured to try out an MFPF clinic and was satisfied (as they nearly always were) might still be unlikely to recommend it to her friends; it was almost as if she had discovered some secret opium-den, a source of guilty delight. These prejudices are fast disappearing in the middle class, where – as in Britain – mothers increasingly bring their sixteen-year-olds to the family doctor and say, 'Please put this girl on the pill before she gets into trouble.' But the working classes are still far more reticent, and often there has been a political element in this: because the MFPF clinics were not a State service but a bourgeois-led enterprise, many women, or at least their husbands, tended to ask themselves, 'What financial trust is drawing the profits from this new trade? Is the Patronat behind it all? Watch out, it may be another capitalist trick.' Matters were made worse by the traditional Communist suspicion of birth-control. Stalinists thought it a bourgeois trick to weaken the numbers of the working class, and for years it was municipal opposition that prevented the MFPF from setting up any clinic in the Paris 'Red Belt'. Today however, in line with its new liberal image, the Communist Party has moved in favour of birth-control. Attitudes are thus changing in the working class, but it may be another few years before birth-control is generally practised. The reticence seems to me to illustrate, once again, the lack of club-like solidarity among Frenchwomen – were it not for this, one might have expected the bush telegraph to spread more rapidly. It illustrates, too, the Frenchwoman's personal conservatism and fear of change, even when offered change for the better. Were it not for this, the sheer weight of some kind of grass-roots movement of opinion might have broken down legal and medical resistances more quickly.

This affair seems typical of the manner in which many social and economic changes are taking place in France today. First, an intolerable situation is allowed to build up without anyone taking action. Then a handful of pioneers set to work, and progress slowly follows, haphazard, empirical, unauthorized, usually resisted by the strong social forces always at work to protect the harmony of the *status quo* against conflict. Then, finally, legal or structural reform is sanctioned, not so much to facilitate as to regularize changes that have already taken place.

Much the same has now happened more recently in the case of abortion. Their legal battle for birth-control won, the pioneers turned their attention to abortion reform in the early 1970s. Here France's legislation was on much the same repressive level as that of Germany and Italy: abortion was sanctioned only when the mother's life was in danger. The number of abortions in France dropped after the spread of contraceptives, but in 1974 was still running at perhaps half a million a year, many of them clumsily performed and of course in secret. Only a minority of women, about 30,000 a year, had the funds or know-how to go to that new Mecca of abortion, Great Britain. As with birth-control, the Government was for years afraid of reform for electoral reasons. Pompidou was said to be in favour, and his Health Minister even prepared a draft project in 1972, but the Government did not dare put it before Parliament. Not only was opposition from old-style Catholics much stronger than in the case of birth-control, but the Order of Doctors too was far more wary. A 1972 survey showed that some 40 to 50 per cent of doctors were opposed to abortion even in the case of rape or incest or when the girl was under 15, and 39 per cent would not approve it even in the case of a foetus found to be seriously malformed. Ordinary public opinion was much more advanced: 91 per cent favoured abortion in cases of malformed foetus, or when the mother's mental or physical health was in danger.

The 'Bobigny affair' in October 1972 helped to mobilize public opinion behind the growing campaign for reform. A girl of sixteen in the Paris suburb of Bobigny was arrested and prosecuted for getting an abortion as a result of rape. She was defended, successfully, by the well-known radical lawyer, Mme Gisèle Halimi, who tiraded against the cruelties of the existing laws. As soon as Giscard came to power, he saw that reform should be delayed no longer, and instructed his Health Minister, Simone Weil, to prepare a bill with all speed, which of course she did. Opinion polls were now showing 73 per cent of the French in favour of abortion. But there was also an active anti-abortion lobby, calling itself '*Laissez-les-Vivre*', while in Parliament many Gaullist and Giscardian deputies were strongly opposed to reform, either on religious grounds or else – like Michel Debré – because of the harm they feared it might do to France's already waning birth-rate. However, Giscard was determined to push the bill through, even if it meant splitting his coalition – which it did. In November 1974, on a free vote, two-thirds of the Gaullists and their allies opposed the reform, and it was passed thanks only to the support of the Socialists and Communists!

The law gives Frenchwomen of any age, married or single, the right to claim an abortion with the minimum of formalities within the first ten weeks of pregnancy. After this, termination can take place only if there is thought to be a grave risk to the health of mother or child, verified by two specialists. Abortions are not free, but guidelines have set fees in public hospitals or clinics at between 400 and 700 francs – well within the means of most women and far less than the old illicit back-street rates. The law is now in application, but with very variable results, since a great many doctors, nurses and directors of hospitals are refusing to co-operate. In many cases they plead grounds of conscience, which they have the right to do. In others, they claim that they lack the staff, beds or facilities to carry out what many of them regard as an unnecessary operation since it is not curing sickness. Some hospitals will accept only single girls under twenty or mothers over forty with several children already; but this is against the spirit of the law, which allows the woman alone to decide whether or not she wants the child. Many doctors find excuses for delaying the abortion, so that the ten-week limit is passed and then legally it becomes much more difficult. By March 1976, when the law had been in force over a year, only one public hospital in two was accepting women for abortions. This initial reticence was only to be expected, given the mentality of the French medical profession. However, the law *is* making progress and will finally be accepted nearly everywhere. Already the number of deaths through clumsy self-abortion has fallen dramatically, and so has the number of departures to clinics in London or other nearby foreign cities. A woman who finds that her local public hospital will not help her can now go perfectly legally, provided she has the means, to a private French clinic. So, a great battle for social justice has been won, France has caught up with civilized practice in countries such as Britain, and the law has caught up with, even overtaken, reality.

TOWARDS AN AMERICANIZED AFFLUENCE

Material change is rarely so traumatic as psychological change; and if in their family and private habits and social attitudes the French are still uneasily torn between old and new, they show fewer complexes about adapting to the more practical aspects of modern affluence. After some initial consumer resistance, they are now throwing themselves into *la civilisation des gadgets* with a hearty materialist appetite.

The statistics suggest that individual prosperity has risen faster in France since the war than in almost any other part of Europe (except perhaps West Germany), though admittedly from a lower starting-point than in some countries such as Britain. But are the French today really as prosperous as the Germans, and much more so than the British? It is a question often asked, and not easy to answer – especially in face of the seeming discrepancies in the French standard of living. A casual visitor, seeing the smart cars parked outside the tenements, the drab-coated workers emerging from glittering boutiques, and other perplexing contrasts, may conclude either that criteria of wealth are different from those in Britain or that distribution of it is more uneven. And to a degree he will be right, on both counts.

In a period of rapid inflation and of fluctuating currencies, such as that of the past few years, it is foolish to try to reach any firm conclusions about changes in living standards within one country, let alone to draw comparisons between countries. However, here are some approximate statistics on France from official sources – OECD and EEC. The real purchasing power of the average French worker's salary is estimated to have risen by 170 per cent between 1950 and 1975; and in the middle and upper income groups it has risen faster still. According to other figures, over-all private consumption rose by 174 per cent in 1950–74. Thus average incomes, in real money terms, have nearly trebled since the late 1940s, the date by which they had regained their pre-war levels. So which country today has the highest standard of living? The statistics are surprising. In 1974, according to OECD, France had an annual gross domestic product per head of $5,060, well behind that of Switzerland ($6,970), Sweden ($6,880), the United States ($6,600) and West Germany ($6,200), but far ahead of Britain ($3,370) and Italy ($2,710). These figures are to an extent artificial, since they reflect the weakness of certain currencies as much as standards of living; if a nation devalues by 15 per cent against the dollar, this does not mean its living standards fall by that amount overnight. However, they offer some guide. We must then deduct the differing proportions of national production ploughed back into investment (higher in Germany than France, and lower still in Britain), and must then take into account differences in the cost of living, which by 1976 was about 10 per cent higher in Germany than France and 20 per cent higher in France than Britain. From these various calculations it may be fair to say that, of these three peoples, the British were until about 1960 the richest and are now the poorest, while the Germans have moved from third to first place. But even this calculation does not fully answer the question about living standards, which depend not only on purchasing power but on factors inherited from the past, notably housing: a man who owns a cottage may rise to the same level of income as his neighbour in a mansion, but without thereby having the same standard of living. This is why French families often seem to be less comfortably off than their English counterparts, despite higher spending power: they are less well endowed with a legacy of good housing and other such amenities. And they still spend their money in different ways. Although the styles of living and spending habits of the two countries are moving steadily closer, it is still true that the French spend more on pleasure, whether it be food, leisure or holidays, and less on comfort and possessions. But the gap is narrowing, and now that they have improved their housing the French have overtaken the British in standard of living within the past ten years. Their expansion is steadier, swifter and more firmly based. Some experts have predicted that by 1985 they will be the richest people in Western Europe after the Swedes.

But will they, by 1985, have also succeeded in distributing their wealth more fairly? The fruits of new prosperity have been spread more unevenly than in post-war Britain: during the Gaullist period in particular, the rich were getting richer proportionately faster than the poor. Expansion under a liberal economy, and the shortage of technicians and skilled workers, have tended to favour those with higher salaries or running their own businesses.

The French upper bourgeoisie today are certainly better off, on average, than their English counterparts: one reason is that they rarely inflict on themselves the same burden of private school bills for their children, and so they can often afford two long, expensive holidays each year, and plenty of smart meals and clothes – especially if they live in a flat with one of the old controlled rents. The group faring next best in the race for prosperity are probably the skilled workers in growing industries; under conditions of full employment, they have seen wages rise fast without their having to fight for it. Yet for some years the gap between workers and *cadres* was tending to widen. From 1956 to 1964 *cadres'* average spending power rose 39·4 per cent, that of foremen and technicians 16·6 and of workers 25·4; by the end of 1968 a *cadre supérieur* was earning on average twice as much as a *cadre moyen*, nearly four times as much as a skilled worker and six times as much as an unskilled worker. However, during the past few years of rapid inflation, wage differentials have been narrowing again, as in many countries. Workers, by threatening strikes, have managed to maintain their spending power, while the middle classes have been feeling the squeeze. And ever since May 1968 Government policies have favoured the lower-paid. In the period 1970–75, the spending power of workers rose 33 per cent and of directors 7 per cent, and in this same period the average wage differential between *cadres supérieurs* and workers paid by the hour fell from 6·3 to 5·4. Yet these differentials remain greater in France than in Britain or most other north European countries or indeed the United States. And a principal reason is that a French *patron* or senior *cadre* is much less heavily taxed. The well-to-do Frenchman not only pays less direct tax, he also has a long tradition of successful tax evasion, especially if he is self-employed. And he clings tenaciously to these privileges. Hence the outcry when Giscard in 1976 finally introduced a modest capital gains tax,* even though most other industrial nations have had a tax of this kind for many years.

Some progress at least has been made in the last few years in helping the lowest-paid workers. The official minimum legal wage, which aims to protect them against exploitation or sheer starvation, for years after the war did no better than keep pace with rising costs, and in May 1968 barely exceeded two francs an hour. After the strikes it was dramatically raised by 35 per cent, and after further increases it stood at 7·55 francs by the end of 1975. These rises have much outstripped the pace of inflation – and so, for the first time, a humble manual worker can begin to look for more than mere subsistence living. Thus, for those in paid employment, real hardship is finally receding. But there are plenty of other poorer categories, self-employed or non-employed, who still fail to find any share in the new affluence, whether or not through their own fault. Many small farmers, shopkeepers and artisans are far worse off than factory workers. Old age pensions are low, so that old people living away from their families are often in real poverty. And there are plenty of older middle-class people, living on fixed incomes whittled away by inflation, who form a new sub-proletariat. If one Frenchman in ten is really well off, two in ten are still close to poverty.

* See p. 672.

But what of the others, the mass of better-paid workers and junior or middle employees – *le Français moyen*? With the help of family allowances, and in many cases of a second income from wife or grown-up child, the average net revenue of a household in this bracket is today around 3,000 francs a month; and, provided they can find a decent home, most of them could be considered reasonably prosperous. The working classes are eating far more meat than before the war and, another sign of prosperity, are even beginning to adopt the middle-class habit of saving part of their earnings. Cars, television, summer holidays by the sea and other middle-class privileges are changing their lives. The percentage of homes with refrigerators has risen since 1954 from 7 to 90 (in Britain, it is 82); with washing-machines, from 8 to 72 (in Britain, 69); with television, from 1 to 84 (Britain, 94); with cars, from 21 to 64 (Britain, 56). After years of resisting a mass-consumer economy in the name of individualism, the French are now embracing it more eagerly than the economists expected. You have only to notice, as you drive through France, how the old faded house-wall advertisements for things like Byrrh apéritifs have been giving way to strident new hoardings for the latest household gadgets.

Food and drink today account for no more than 26 per cent of the average family's budget, compared with 50 per cent before the war. Spending here is still rising in absolute terms, at nearly 2 per cent a year, but not nearly so fast as in other sectors. For instance, private spending on transport, travel and telephones has risen 190 per cent in real value since 1950, and its share of the family budget has increased in this period from 5·4 to 10·9 per cent. Over the same years the sector described by the statisticians as 'health and hygiene' has risen by over 200 per cent, from 5·9 to 13·4 per cent of the budget – in other words, the French are getting cleaner. Consumption on clothing, home equipment and leisure activities has seen similar increases and within the sector of leisure, café- and restaurant-going are in relative (but not absolute) decline compared with the rapid advance of television, cars and sport. These dry statistics confirm that affluence is pushing French spending habits closer to the British or American models. There is still, relatively, a greater emphasis in France on enjoyment, but the gap is closing, and the former reluctance of the French to spend their money on useful possessions is now sharply waning. And the patterns of pleasure-spending are changing, too; the old traditions of occasional lavish ceremonial expenditure, on a big annual banquet or family outing, for instance, are giving way to more routine and private activities, such as week-end motoring trips or visits *à deux* to *bistrots*. And some may feel that this is making France a duller and a less French place.

Another symptom of this change: the French now spend as much money on their homes and making them comfortable (21·8 per cent of their budget) as the British do. In each country, about 40 per cent of this sum goes on rent or mortgages, and the rest on fuel, furnishing and decoration. *Le bricolage* (do-it-yourself odd-jobbery), which used to interest the French so little, has now become a major pastime, linked especially with the new middle-class vogue for buying up derelict country villas for week-ends. And even in respectable suburbs, a bourgeois husband is no longer so likely to consider it undignified for the neighbours to see him painting his own front door on a Sunday. In equipping the home, a family will pay less attention than before to the formal salon and more to smart new gadgets for the kitchen – somewhat paradoxically seeing that the housewife puts less emphasis these days on serious cooking. But in working-class homes a big refrigerator is usually a better status-symbol than smart chairs, and many of them keep their *frigo* or washing-machine in the *salon* for show.

Armed with these luxuries the housewife spends far less time than before on household chores, but they still take her nearly twice as long, according to one estimate, as in the United States. The main reasons for this, obviously, are that the French housewife still has fewer gadgets than the American and still takes her cooking far more seriously; also, as I have noted earlier, the Frenchwoman gets less help from her husband, and is shy of collective self-help with other wives. It is noticeable that launderettes have caught on far less widely in France than in many countries: literally as well as metaphorically, the Frenchwoman has a distaste for washing her dirty linen in public, nor does she feel the same urge as an Anglo-Saxon for a neighbourly chat.

In one or two other respects the French seem not quite sure how to deal with their new domestic affluence. Take furniture and décor for example. Many sophisticated couples with a smart modern flat show a bias against filling it with modern furniture, and go out of their way to install antiques, often with incongruous results. Modern designs, readily accepted in the office or restaurant, are still regarded by many people as cold and inhuman in the home – witness Jacques Tati's horrified satire on this style of living in the film *Mon Oncle*. I think that this bias is now declining, and many well-to-do people now have new flats most elegantly furnished in a modern manner, often with Scandinavian influences. But the French are still drawn more strongly than the British to their own classic tradition, to those spindly straight-backed Louis XV chairs and formal settees that decorate so many bourgeois salons. The French have little equivalent of the comfy vulgarity of English pre-war style; their taste is either for the classical or the ultra-new. Neither in furniture nor in domestic décor have they yet found a satisfactory modern style of their own. Influences have frequently been foreign, either Scandinavian or Italian. But today they are now beginning to try harder, and with more success. One of the most fashionable of today's decorators, a suavely enigmatic and bearded figure called Slavik, has forged ahead on his own with some rococo innovations that can be seen, in Paris, at the St-Germain Drugstore, the Elysée Deux Drugwest, the Bistrot de Paris in Rue de Lille and the Sir Winston Churchill pub near the Etoile. Parisian décor is at its best when using glittering surfaces of glass and metal, and then in its flamboyant way it often achieves an elegance and lightness that far outclasses London.

In the important French domain of clothes and fashion, affluence has brought with it an increase in the general level of public taste – paradoxically, just at a time when Paris has been losing its pre-eminence as world trend-setter. But the true *milieu* of Parisian *haute couture* has always been restricted to a few thousand rich society women. And although it is true that this little *milieu* has lost some of its importance, and that there are fewer supremely elegant women to be seen in Paris these days, at the same time good taste has become more democratic and has spread much wider. Many of the simpler of the new fashions are nowadays quickly copied and mass-produced by the big stores like Le Printemps, at prices within the reach of secretaries and even of some factory-girls; and, ever since the war, papers such as *Elle* and *Marie-Claire* have been drumming notions of elegance into the heads of ordinary Frenchwomen who, as a general breed, never used to have any special claim to be so very well dressed. More recently, men as well as women have been strongly influenced by the new fashions from Italy, Scandinavia, and especially from London, and in 1966 the mini-skirt and the trouser-suit began to invade the French teenage market. French fashion experts are quick to point out that this English invasion is strictly limited to the very young and to day-time clothes: in clothes for more adult women, and for evening or formal wear, the French claim to be holding their own. But wherever the influences may come from, there is no doubt that the ordinary not-so-rich French girl dresses more carefully and elegantly than even ten years ago, let alone before the war.

Elle, Marie-Claire and one or two similar women's magazines can take much of the credit for this, and for the improvements they have prompted in décor, housekeeping skills, and especially in hygiene. Just before the war, when Frenchwomen were among the dirtiest and smelliest in Europe, *Marie-Claire* took the lead in a public campaign to get them to wash more. After the war this developed further, other papers joined in, the public responded, and the post-war rise in the sales of soap, toothpaste and cleansing creams has been phenomenal. If the provision of bathrooms in the new flats has been one factor in the new cleanliness, the women's magazines can claim a share in the triumph too. Marcelle Auclair, founder and principal columnist of *Marie-Claire*, told me: 'French girls used to disguise their dirt with powder and make-up on top of it. Now they wash properly, and clean their teeth. Haven't you noticed how the Métro stinks much less than it used to?'

Flip through these magazines' pages, or even through those of a more intellectual glossy such as *l'Express*, and the same pattern of phrases will strike you again and again from the advertisements: '*Après les sweaters d'hiver, voici les fully-fashioned des beaux jours* ... *New! Smart c'est Dacron! Votre Shopping Club* ... *Le véritable wash and wear* ... *Le drink des gens raffinés* ... *Les chips*

Foder . . . Night Cream pour la nuit . . . le meilleur after-shave . . . Pour les bébés, Baby Relax.' These, and many others, I culled at random from single issues of *Elle, Marie-Claire* and *l'Express.* Whatever has been happening to the language that Proust and Pascal spoke? In the past few years there has been, understandably, a great intellectual outcry against this invasion of French by Anglo-Saxon words: *franglais* it is called, and a professor at the Sorbonne, Etiemble, wrote a book denouncing it. But I think the invasion has sometimes been misunderstood. It is not that ordinary French people have been voluntarily abandoning their language; rather, they have been the victims of a commercial conspiracy. Modern techniques of advertising and public relations have been recent arrivals in France, but have now swept through the land with hurricane force. The professional *milieu* decided that the French could be conditioned to accept a commodity as new and smart if it were given an Anglo-Saxon name. The clothing and cosmetics worlds virtually adopted English as their *lingua franca*, and house-agents have been doing the same. Some of this inevitably spilled over on to journalists and others who have picked up the new habits of speech, but only superficially; although the advertisements may talk about *un drink* and *le shopping*, a Frenchman is still more likely to invite you to *prendre un verre* and his wife will *faire les courses*. If they do use the English words, it will be usually as a kind of joke. In fact, by the mid-1970s, the craze for *franglais* words in advertisements, which had been growing throughout the 1960s, seemed to be already on the wane. It was a mode, which might pass, like any other.

Even so, the Giscard Government grew alarmed, notably at the more permanent invasion of English terms into the everyday vocabulary of French business and technology. Words like *le management, le marketing, le pipeline,* became common currency simply because no one seemed to have invented adequate French equivalents. At the end of 1975 Parliament adopted a Bill presented by a Gaullist deputy, Pierre Bas, that from January 1977 made illegal the use of any foreign words – wherever a French equivalent can be found to exist – in advertisements, official documents, and even on radio and television. *Franglais* may be struck a death-blow. The law was greeted with some derision in the Press, most papers pointing out that it was absurd to try to impose legal curbs on something as spontaneous and fluid as language. The British laughed at it as a typical bit of French legalism, and in *The Times* Bernard Levin even wrote a leader in French lamenting, as a francophile, what he called 'this cultural crime of a crackpot nation that will impoverish its own tongue through this protectionism'. He and many others expressed the view that a language will die unless it is in permanent evolution, fertilized by new blood from outside – and it is now the turn of the French to import English words, just as the English language was so much enriched by French terms in past centuries. Admittedly, the *franglais* had probably gone too far and shown itself ridiculous, so that possibly some kind of curb was needed. But it seemed doubtful whether a law of this kind was the right answer. The feeling in 1976 was that no tribunal would really dare to apply the new law literally. It would, you might say, be laughed out of court.

The alleged Americanization of France is a matter I shall return to in the final chapter. In the context of modern domestic living and affluence, I would merely make the point that Americanization is not necessarily the same as modernization. Because the Americans happened to do it all first, any other country that tries to modernize may appear to be aping America. But though the French may naïvely describe their new *brasseries* as 'drugstores' and their new *salons* as 'living-rooms', the flavour often remains recognizably French.

LEISURE: FROM THE TWO-HOUR LUNCH TO 'LE WEEKEND ANGLAIS'

The French are a hard-working people, in their own not-always-so-constructive way; and though they have traditionally set high store by *le plaisir* – self-indulgence in brief intervals between toil or duty – only now, with their new affluence, are they facing up to the different modern concept of *le loisir*. 'Leisure used to be synonymous with idleness, at least for the working classes,' writes the sociologist, Joffre Dumazedier, 'but today it has acquired the status of a *valeur*, like work.'* And it has won official recognition as such. Since the war, in France as in Britain, Governments and local bodies have shown a new concern with the need to help people use their free time positively.

In their new leisure habits, as in so much else, the French are steadily becoming more like other people. The Englishman who deserts his darts in the pub or his cricket matches, and the Frenchman who tires of his *bistrot* or *boules*, both of them turn today to watching much the same kind of TV programmes, or listening to the same records, or driving their little cars to the same kind of crowded beaches and camping sites. 'Modern leisure will be uniform and mutually imitative,' Dumazedier told me. In New York they are copying Parisian terrace-cafés; London is filling up with coffee-shops, *bistros* and *discothèques*; Paris is building 'pubs' and 'drugstores'. Yet there are still some respects in which the French attitude to leisure differs noticeably from the British, especially in the way they like their free time divided up: that is, in the French preference for longer annual holidays rather than for shorter working hours.

The French take the longest holidays in Europe. Just before the war workers won the legal right to two weeks' paid annual leave, a third week was added in 1956 and a fourth, under union pressure, in 1965. Now the legal minimum is twenty-four working days a year, or virtually five weeks. Holidays have become a major national obsession. Nearly one third of the population take more than five weeks away from home each year, and in the middle classes it is perfectly usual to spend all August by the sea or abroad, and then go skiing for a fortnight in winter. Added to this, the number of official public holidays (14 July, 1 May, 11 November and the rest) has been growing, and now accounts for ten days a year. And whenever one of these falls on a Thursday or Tuesday, many a *cadre* will *faire le pont* by taking the Friday or Monday off as well, to give himself four free days in a row. And yet, this does not mean that the Frenchman fails to work hard. It is simply that he works differently. Executives will frequently stay in their offices from 9 a.m. till 7 or 8 at night, while in an average factory the working day is from 7.30 a.m. to 5.30 or

* *Vers une civilisation des loisirs?* (Seuil, 1962).

6 p.m. The legal working week is often extended by voluntary overtime (save during the years of short-timing that followed the energy crisis), and until May 1968 the minimum in industry was forty-five hours, about the longest in Europe. Under the agreement reached after the strikes, it had now been progressively lowered to forty hours in most industries. But given the transport problems in many suburbs, the working man's effective week-day leisure time is in some cases little more than it was before the war – and this helps to explain, as I have suggested, the dearth of evening activity in places like Sarcelles.

I think there may be several reasons for this emphasis on annual rather than daily leisure: the strains of city living, especially in Paris, and the rarity of private gardens, both give the French more incentive than the British to go on holiday; and despite the decline of family ties there are still very many people who regard leisure as best spent visiting parents or relatives in the country. There is also, in the moneyed classes at least, a new spirit of restlessness and wanderlust. Nor do the French have much tradition of indoor hobbies, in the English sense: the only French word for 'hobby' is the quaint *violon d'Ingres* which implies not so much an amateurish pastime as a secondary professional pursuit at which one excels.

There is, however, one important respect in which the French are moving closer to the British pattern; they are giving up work on Saturdays, and as they have no word of their own for the Saturday-plus-Sunday leisure unit, they are forced to borrow ours. *Le weekend* is growing in social significance. Most factories are now closing on Saturdays, and the unions recently switched their main demand from longer holidays to the universal five-day week – a claim which they won, by and large, as a result of the 1968 strikes. In Paris ministerial offices an experiment began in 1966 to give up Saturday morning work in favour of longer daily hours, and it has been welcomed and generalized. The middle classes go away for the week-end far more than they used, and some workers are beginning to follow suit. Many more families in all classes would have done so much sooner, were it not that the French have hitherto inflicted on themselves the illogicality of State schools closing on Thursdays, not Saturdays. There were pedagogic reasons for this, and a large number of parents too were in favour of it – especially in working-class homes, parents were often quite glad to have their children out of the way on Saturdays. Recent reforms, while keeping the mid-week holiday, have now abolished Saturday afternoon school in an effort to lighten the burden of school work. So the week-end craze goes from strength to strength.

You have only to stand beside one of the main roads out of Paris, at 7 or 8 p.m. on a summer Friday, to see the extent of the new week-end vogue. Even as long ago as May 1958, at the height of the crisis that brought back de Gaulle, the sight of that army of cars, piled high with suitcases, cots and children, misled a British correspondent into writing a scare story about the threat of civil war: 'Mass flight from Paris begins' ran his front-page headline. Today, as in 1958, it is not the threat of paratroops from Algiers, but the growing strains of daily life inside Paris, that incites a steadily increasing number of people to make for the week-end quiet of the country, and as likely as not they will go neither to a hotel nor to relatives but to their own little country cottage. The *résidence secondaire* has become something of a cult among middle-class Parisians in the past few years. Today they own over 350,000 of them within an orbit of 100 miles of Paris; and in the Yonne department, around Sens and Auxerre, 20 per cent of all housing falls into this class. Many are old farmsteads, left empty by the rural exodus and now made over to the new bourgeois sport of *bricolage*. Others are new week-end villas for the well-to-do. Some 30,000 of these are built a year in France.

If there is not more evening leisure in France, it is partly because so many people still prefer to keep to the old tradition of the two-hour family lunch. This has always been the principal meal of the day in France; and although in Paris the habit is dying under the *force majeure* of suburban commuting, in the provinces everything still tends to close down from 12 to 2, and husbands come home from office or factory and children from school. The Frenchman still regards lunch as something of a necessary human right; and even when pressed for time on a long car journey, rather than snatch a sandwich he will probably insist on stopping for a full-scale meal, and think you odd if you suggest driving straight through. In Paris, professional or upper-class people who live centrally invite friends home to lunch during the week almost as much as to dinner. And foreigners, such as diplomats and journalists, easily pick up the lunch habit too: living in Passy, half an hour door-to-door by Métro from my office at the Opéra, I used to go home to lunch as a matter of course.

It is a practice that can be pleasant in one's own life, but is irksome when everyone else is doing it too. Though in Paris today it is now becoming a little easier to get a hair-cut, or collect laundry, or go shopping during the lunch-hour, it is still hard in the provinces and especially in the Midi. In Toulouse, even the big new *hypermarchés* close from noon till two. In Paris, it is only in the past few years that a few of the larger banks and stores have begun to stay open over lunch. The Parisians with their new American business influences are now coming to realize what a drag this two-hour break can be on a modern economy. At the same time change is being forced on them, willy-nilly, by the drift out to the suburbs. The past few years have thus seen quite a revolution in Greater Paris, where the percentage of employees who go home for lunch has dropped from 60 to 15 since 1958: most factories and many larger offices have opened canteens, while snack-bars and cafeterias have been springing up fast in central Paris to cater for those with limited means. Many firms have finally changed over to a uniform one-hour break, usually welcomed by a majority of staff, which enables them to close an hour earlier in the evenings or, more probably, to cut out Saturday work. The conflict has often been acute: many firms delayed the change-over for years simply because it was strongly opposed by those employees who did live fairly close, and the staggering of hours to suit both sides was not possible. So those of the staff who lived in the suburbs found a cheap lunch where they could, and then had to spend an hour or more killing time. Or else, in defiance of sense, they still made a long trek home.

It is usually the younger people who accept the change most easily. A journalist told me: 'Our office is too small to have a canteen, but the girls bring sandwiches, and most of us seem quite pleased with the new system.' But older people often grumble at having to change their habits: 'It's upset my whole family life,' said a saleswoman in her forties; 'I used to get home in time to cook a big hot lunch for my husband and children, who go to school near-by, and we'd have a cold meal at night. Now, I have to stay at work and eat in the canteen, my family get the maid to cook them lunch, and I have to prepare a hot meal for myself in the evening. In some other cases, it is the senior executives who have opposed the change most strongly: they hold dearly to their three-hour business lunches (either as a necessity or a useful alibi!) and they want their secretaries' lives to be accommodated to theirs.

The pressure for earlier office closing has not been nearly as great as one might have expected, even from young people, and the French often seem not to know what to do with extended evening leisure when they get it. They are almost as conservative about the time of dinner as about lunch: it is usually set for 8 or at earliest 7.30, and they will rarely shift it earlier in order to spend a full evening doing something else. Evening events, whether club meetings, cinemas or theatres, therefore do not start until 9 or possibly 8.30, and as so many people have to get up early for their work, most serious leisure activity is left for the week-end.

Personal expenditure on leisure activities has more than quadrupled in real terms since 1950, and its share of the average budget has grown from 9·7 to 14 per cent. Workers and even farmers are today aspiring towards leisure spending as never before. One symptom is the immense development of horse betting, known nationally as *le tiercé* (three-horse bet): though still less of an obsession than in England, its turnover has nevertheless reached seventeen francs a week per head. The mysterious letters 'PMU' outside a café mean that it houses one of the 3,000 branches of the Pari Mutuel Urbain, the semi-public body that controls all betting in France and draws in an annual profit of more than 1,000m francs.

Another trend towards the British pattern is that leisure money is now spent increasingly on possessions and equipment, rather than on more transitory, if intense, enjoyments. The French are buying thirteen times as many music records as in 1950, eight times as much photographic and film material, three times as many toys and musical instruments: yet the share of café-going in the average leisure budget has dropped from 40 to 26 per cent. Thousands of little old *bistrots*,* formerly haunts of alcoholism, have gone out of business. Others struggle on, with falling custom, and their owners swell the ranks of the discontented small-tradesman classes (Gérard Nicoud, their militant new leader, is, significantly, not a shopkeeper, but a café-owner). Even the larger, modernized terrace-cafés and *brasseries*, though they still do a brisk trade in most places, have lost some of their old importance as centres of social life and gossip; people tend to spend more of their time at home, at least in the new suburbs. Many cafés, faced with a relative decline in their trade in wines and spirits, are now trying to diversify their appeal. Many have introduced juke-boxes and pin-tables (known as *le baby-foot*), and so manage to fill themselves with strident youth, even at the risk of driving away staider clients. Others, in parts of southern and south-eastern France, are becoming mainly venues for games of *boules* or *pétanque*, both a type of bowls. The French have not yet caught up with bingo, which is probably too much of a community game for their temperament – and, dare one suggest, too fatuously unintelligent? But many cafés in poorer areas have installed TV as in Italy, and the clients sit hushed all evening in the semi-dark – what a change from the old days of public chatter! They drink less, argue less and have become, you might feel, more docile and less picturesque.

So are we to infer that the French are growing less sociable, or simply that they are transferring their sociability from the café to the home? And if so, does this mean a decline in the alleged French trait of domestic inhospitality? I am quite certain that younger professional or upper-class people, freeing themselves from some of the formal standards and obligations of their parents, are today becoming more casual and informal in entertaining friends as well as relatives, and are therefore readier

* In England this word, without its final 't', is taken to mean a small French-type restaurant; in France, it is more correctly used to mean a little café selling wines and often, but not always, some simple food.

to do it more often. Often they will extend you a casual invitation to supper at a few hours' notice although they may add, apologetically, '*ça sera à la fortune du pot*', half ashamed at betraying the old ceremonial standards. How much they entertain may depend on where and how they live. Generally people are more hospitable in the provinces than in Paris, where daily and professional life is so hectic that many families prefer to hug their privacy to themselves. The deeper you go into country areas the warmer the welcome, and once or twice I have found young farmers almost embarrassingly hospitable, as in Greece: '*Mais restez chez nous jusqu'à demain, vous pouvez coucher dans le grenier.*' Even in big towns the hospitality can be overwhelming: during five weeks recently spent doing research in Toulouse, a town where I had no friends when I arrived, I was asked home to lunch or dinner by *seventeen* French families, some of them several times. In Paris, on the other hand, a friend is likely to greet you with, '*Il faut que tu viennes dîner à la maison, on te fera signe*', and then do nothing.

Yet even Parisians can often be hospitable when they get away from the frenetic Parisian rat-race. I knew an English married couple in official jobs in Paris who became friendly with two French civil servants. There were cordial business lunches, and sometimes the couple asked the French to parties and were then assured, '*Vous devez dîner chez nous*', etc., and of course nothing happened. Until, one day, the English couple and both the Frenchmen and their wives found that by chance they were all going to spend August in villas in the same part of Auvergne. Holiday addresses were exchanged, and the usual promise of hospitality, which the English took with a pinch of salt. But lo! – in Auvergne, the phone rang, dates were fixed, their French hosts piled lavish meal upon lavish meal with the utmost grace and warmth. The English had broken through the barrier; they were *des vrais amis* at last. But, back in Paris, the iron curtain descended again. Of course, this is a big-city disease not confined to Paris; the French in London have just the same grievances.

Among the bourgeoisie and the nobility the old tradition of formality is still quite powerful. And though, today, there is more impromptu entertaining *à trois* or *à quatre* than there used to be, a certain gulf seems to exist between this and the formal dinner or *réception* with everyone in their best clothes and everything just so. The Hampstead or Kensington norm of regular little dinner-parties for six or eight, elegant but informal, is still infrequent. I think that the Second World War, just as it produced a greater loosening of class barriers in Britain than in France, also prompted the English to relax their formal standards, whereas in France, conversely, formality was a means of maintaining national pride under the Occupation, of showing a stiff upper lip to the invader. This might be one reason why the convention still lingers so strongly that, if you are to give a party in your own home, then it must be done perfectly or not at all. Another reason is that far more bourgeois families still have servants than in England, and this makes formality easier: 'I cannot have anyone to dinner this month,' a leisured housewife once told me, 'you see, my maid has hurt her leg.'

'*A la fortune du pot*' may mark a breach in this tradition, but anything more involves, at least at a certain social level, champagne buckets and waiters in white coats, and workmen called in to redecorate the *salon*. And so, unless you are hailed in the street and bid to supper that night, you probably won't be asked for a year. In Parisian 'society', dinner-party habits are still Edwardian by most London standards, with printed invitation cards, probably evening dress, white-gloved hired waiters, rigid conventions about serving the correct food and wines; and, very possibly, much of the expensive silver, glass and china will have been borrowed for the occasion from relatives! When it comes to giving a drinks party, if it is not one of the noisy *surprise-parties* of the very young when left on their own, then it will pobably be the opposite extreme – a prim little *cocktail* or *vin d'honneur*, always with the same neat *canapés* and conventional talk, a style that still epitomizes most social gatherings among the well-to-do over-forties and has set the tone for diplomatic receptions all round the globe. Younger people, it is true, are trying to desert this tradition. Sometimes they now give *saucisson-et-vin-rouge* buffet suppers where you eat off your lap. But the French often appear ill-at-ease when trying to be informal like this, and except in very modern flats this casual style rarely seems suited to their furniture or décor. Consequently, they do not give parties very much.

FROM ESCOFFIER TO 'LE WIMPY ET CHIPS': UNE ÉPOQUE TRAGIQUE

In almost every subject I have touched on so far, from farms and factories to family planning, I have suggested that the changes now emerging are imperative and fundamentally for the better, and that if some of the old subtle quality of French life is being lost in the process of modernization, this is a price that France must pay, for the time being. But there is one sanctum of French civilization, dear to all our hearts, where change is much harder to welcome and where today's modernization may not be worth the price it entails.

The shiny new snack-bar, the quick-grill and the deep freeze, having conquered half the free world, are now infiltrating the last and most cherished of citadels, *la vraie cuisine française*, which is not in need of reform save that it demands too much time and trouble for a modern nation in a hurry. Foreign influences, which have done so much to raise standards of eating in post-war Britain, are in a different way having quite the reverse effect in France; and so the quality of restaurants, once uniformly high, has been growing erratic and unpredictable.

This decline, it must be stated, is very relative: you still eat better in France than anywhere else. The *malaise* has not yet spread widely beyond Paris and a few leading tourist centres. In the ordinary provinces, *la vraie cuisine* manages to stand fairly firm. And even though French standards may be slipping, this nation continues to eat with a great deal more seriousness and discrimination than any other in Europe. Older people in particular still talk and think about food to an amazing extent, comparing in detail this week's *poulet à l'estragon*, say, with last week's in a way that the English, even today, might find boring or in bad taste. Eavesdrop on a conversation in street or bus, and there is still a large chance it might be two men enthusing over the flavour of the *quenelles de brochet* in their favourite *bistrot*, or working wives comparing the subtleties of ten different cheeses. And although the younger middle class with its 'drugstores' may be growing more indifferent to gastronomy, both the peasantry and the workers are affording to eat better than before the war and are helping to keep up the traditions. So the situation is not yet desperate. But there are clouds blowing up, larger than Charles Forte's hand.

I have often thought that, in the difficult years before, during and just after the war, the Frenchman clung to good eating partly as a compensation and a constant in a shifting world: his *cuisine* went on tasting the same, it did not turn sour or betray him as so many ideals of liberty and patriotism had done; and its near-aesthetic pleasures did not, like the enjoyment of art or books or women, make spiritual or emotional demands on him in return. But today he may feel less need for this kind of solace; or if not, there are so many other material compensations available too. Television, cars, foreign holidays, smarter flats and other possessions have all developed huge new rival claims on the Frenchman's attention and budget – and especially on his wife's time. In the middle classes, fewer wives have servants than before the war, more have jobs, and life has grown more hectic. So today the bourgeoisie will as soon toss a couple of steaks under her new electric grill as spend hours over a *plat mijoté* as her mother or her mother's *bonne* would have done. Many younger middle-class people even take a conscious pride in reacting against their parents' self-indulgent gourmandise, and some young wives feel the need to assert themselves by refusing to be a slave in the kitchen.

So I doubt if today the average young middle-class family really eats very much more excitingly at home in France than in Britain (where standards have risen so much). They still, however, eat a little differently: table wine is still far cheaper, fresh French bread is uniquely and compulsively chewable, the French are still much more likely than the British to know how to dress a salad or cook vegetables, and there is a wider variety of fresh foods available in shops open everywhere until eight or after. But the family *pot* of which you are invited to *prendre la fortune* will probably be no more than a conventional roast veal or chicken dish, followed by cheese or fruit; and the housewife rarely troubles herself with complicated sweets or puddings. When she entertains more deliberately, just as in Britain, a young hostess may now tend to desert traditional recipes for 'amusing' foreign experiments. She may prepare a *paella* or *moussaka* discovered on summer holidays, or adopt the modish new American barbecue habit, or even acquire one of the widely advertised Japanese *hibacki* kits. English breakfast foods like kippers and cereals have been creeping in, and one shop near the Opéra called 'Produits Exotiques' turned out to be full of goods from Kelloggs and Crosse & Blackwell.

These trends horrify the gourmets – and so does the fact that, after a long resistance, housewives and shopkeepers finally show signs of thawing towards frozen foods. For many years after the entry of frozen foods into Europe, in France the gastronomic tradition prevailed: shoppers shunned goods which they felt lacked flavour and freshness, so grocers did not stock them and the habit barely caught on. Even today, the French eat only a quarter as much frozen produce as the British or Germans. But the figures are now creeping up: several of the more advanced farmers' co-operatives are now doing their own frozen processing, and deep-freezes in the modern supermarkets are growing larger. And whereas in Britain the big-selling frozen foods are ordinary things like peas, beans or fish fingers, the French prefer much more complex deep-frozen pre-cooked dishes such as *cassoulet* or *bouillabaisse*. In most shops you can buy frozen snails or frogs' legs. So the French have at least transplanted their own gastronomy to the deep-freeze rather than aping Anglo-Saxon tastes.

The decline in gastronomic fervour among the younger bourgeoisie has inevitably affected not only home cooking but also restaurants, which have suffered from this and from other new economic and social pressures too. Before the war food was exceptionally cheap and many people ate out a lot as a matter of course; but by 1950 the number of meals served daily in Paris restaurants had dropped from a million in 1939 to 250,000, due partly to rocketing prices but largely to the war-time development of office and factory canteens. Many restaurants closed. Since

1950 this tally of daily meals has crept up again to 400,000, but the number of really good restaurants has not increased. Instead, the shortening of the lunch-break, together with other modern trends and foreign influences, has thrown up a rash of new snack-bars and self-service cafeterias alien to the French tradition.

The snack-bars are a good deal less successful than the cafeterias. The latter sometimes adopt absurd *franglais* names like *Le Self des Selfs* (just off the Champs-Elysées), but at least the food they offer bears some relation to French classic dishes (you can get an *andouillette* for about 8 francs, and maybe a *choucroute* or a *petit salé aux lentilles* for a little more) and though mass-produced it is quite edible. The cafeterias are crowded, cheerful places, popular with office-workers at lunch-time, and compare very favourably with their English equivalent such as Jolyon. They now account for one in four of the restaurant meals served in Paris.

But the new counter-service snack-bars and light-lunch places seem to me hybrids – an attempt to adapt the New York coffee-house or the Forte's or Wimpy formula, while keeping something of the style of a French terrace-café. An energetic caterer, Jacques Borel, even started a small chain of Wimpy Bars in association with J. Lyons: you can get *un wimpy* for about 3 francs or *avec chips* for 4, *un super-wimpy king-size* (5 francs) or *un breakfast anglais* flavoured with ketchup from an authentic round red squeezy Lyons flask and washed down, if you wish, with something as out-of-place as Beaujolais. This kind of bar has never really caught on with young French people. And the French public still find it very hard to get the kind of cheap but edible snack that for 40p or 50p you find everywhere in Britain, in pubs or snack-bars.

It seems inevitable and not necessarily regrettable that the French should want to move over to the snack or light-meal habit for at least one of their main meals of the day. France has always been a nation of over-eaters, where the middle-aged *crise de foie* has been an occupational disease, and where too much stress has probably been set on the tradition that a meal must, *de rigueur*, contain three or four full courses. In theory it ought to be perfectly possible for the light snack and true gastronomy to co-exist, each for different occasions, for J. Lyons to lie down with *carré d'agneau aux herbes* and with the *cuisine* of Lyon.

Today, both in restaurants and at home, people are tending towards smaller and less complicated meals, with fewer rich sauces and *plats mijotés* and more emphasis on good-quality meat cooked simply, or on expensive but unelaborate dishes, such as oysters, whose consumption has risen enormously. With the nervous speeding-up of life, far more care is now being given to dieting, and those who can afford to lunch each day in classic restaurants will often take only one or two courses – a remarkable break in tradition. But the catering industry is not adapting easily to these changes.

For some years there has been a *malaise* among many of France's 50,000 or so restaurants. A minority are still doing very well – the new cafeterias and *brasseries* catering for cheap lunches, the smart expense-account places such as (in Paris) Ledoyen and Lasserre, the 2,000 or so really good classic restaurants still patronized by gourmets and the new 'amusing' haunts in Paris or in tourist centres, frequented by French gay young things and by some foreign visitors. And so, if you stroll through St-Germain-des-Prés or St-Tropez, or around any business district at lunchtime, you may get an impression of crowded prosperity. However, the ordinary *bistrot du quartier* of the average suburb or town, hitherto the backbone of the French tradition of good eating, is far less likely today to be full of customers, and has been letting its standards slip. So the industry is being polarized towards (*a*) strictly functional modern eateries, Anglo-Saxon style, (*b*) specialized restaurants of various types, for gourmets, tourists or tycoons.

One of the worst of the new problems facing the *restaurateur* has been the immense rise in labour and other costs. Before the war nearly all restaurants were family concerns or else they exploited under-paid labour, and in either case their own costs were slight. But today staff are protected by new social insurance schemes and working regulations, and this is a main reason why restaurant prices have risen faster than the general cost of living.

Clientèle has consequently fallen away, and many owners have reacted short-sightedly to this by pushing their high prices even higher and inflating themselves out of the market. There is also a growing shortage of good young chefs, even though they can usually command good pay. Many a son of an old *patron-chef* decides that he would rather work in an office or factory, where the hours are easier, than follow in his father's rigorous footsteps; and so the old family *bistrot* dies or falls into less worthy hands. And in the smartest restaurants an increasing proportion of the most brilliant French chefs have been wooed away to better-paid jobs in New York or even London. Waiters, it is true, are in less short supply than in Britain, for the young Frenchman is still much less likely than the Englishman to feel he is demeaning himself in this job. But here again factory and office jobs are a lure, and the French are now beginning to import foreign catering labour.

Another hazard is the increasing normalization of foodstuffs, inevitable *quid pro quo* of the modernization of French agriculture. Here once again the French are beginning to copy American methods, with mixed feelings. The broiler has begun to oust the farm-reared chicken; fertilizers and machine-sowing are helping to make potatoes, vegetables and fruit larger and more handsome, but not always more succulent; bread, so it is thought, has lost some of its old flavour, and Charente butter, instead of being dumped on the table in a rich golden lump, now tends to come in tiny, wrapped packets. Though the supply of fresh and non-synthetic food is still far wider than in Britain, it is easy to see which way things are moving.

There is an even more dangerous American import too: the tourist. Many French gourmets claim that the biggest single cause of decline in restaurant standards, at least in Paris, is simply this: some chefs are corrupted by not having to work hard to please the new hordes of wealthy foreign visitors, notably Americans, who do not understand French cooking and sometimes are scared of it. Once I saw a newly arrived couple in the Franco-American Pam-Pam restaurant near the Opéra, gamely exploring a dozen *escargots* each and washing them down with strawberry milk-shakes. On another occasion, in the 1960s, some

French people I know were lunching at one of France's best restaurants, the Pyramide in Vienne, when an American party came in, ordered their meal from the great Monsieur Point, and then asked for Cokes to drink with it. 'Get out!' said Point, and he threw them out. My friends cheered him for it. Maybe the British and even the Germans are often as barbaric. But the Americans are the worst. And they enable some shameless restaurateurs to make a fat living out of French *cuisine* that is as phoney as a mock-Tudor pub.

All these new influences have combined to make restaurant standards far more erratic than they used to be. Some *patrons* are resisting them with heroic success, others are not. And so today, whether in a smart or a simple place, you often have no idea in advance whether or not you will get a classic dish correctly cooked and served, and whether or not you will get value for money. This never used to be so before the war. And I think this is why the fat red *Michelin* is no longer such a reliable guide; it has been betrayed by its own standards. Its elaborate system of grades and symbols worked ideally in days when standards were firm and unfluctuating, but today it is beginning to face the same kind of hazards as *The Good Food Guide* in Britain, and has not yet really succeeded in adapting to them. Its tastes are formal and expensive, like those of some elderly, rich uncle; and its small corps of inspectors, with such a vast field to cover, are often slow to spot the decline in an established place or the arrival of a better new one. In many towns I find that *Michelin* simply does not include the best restaurants, at least in the lower-middle price range.

If the young French bourgeois cares less about gastronomy than do his parents, this may not mean that he cares less for dining out. His tastes are shifting: today he may want his restaurant to be 'also something of an amusing spectacle', as one gourmet said with scorn. Until recently nearly all the good restaurants popular with Parisians for dinner were sober, brightly lit, ordinary-looking places, either conventionally elegant (like Fouquet's) or plain and shabby (like many of the greatest *bistrots*). But now, in the wake of London, a new atmospheric modishness is creeping in. To meet a new public demand, a number of restaurants have modernized their décor in a rustic or arty-crafty style, probably installing canned music or even a guitarist. And frequently they recoup these expenses by skimping the quality of their food, hoping their new clientèle won't notice. The vogue now is the small 'intimate' restaurants with the accent on *ambiance*, open very late and probably helped along by dim lights or candles: yet in the old days the French thought it barbaric not to be able to see clearly what they were eating.

Just as in London, a number of new restaurants have opened in beautiful old historic buildings, artfully converted, and frequently run not by professional restaurateurs but – heresy in France – by moneyed amateurs. They like to specialize in such *à la mode* dishes as *viandes aux herbes de Provence grillées au feu de bois*, which you might regard as today's French cult equivalent of *steak Diane flambé* in an English country pub. This trend is most obvious around the Latin Quarter, on the Ile St-Louis, and in parts of Provence itself. All around St-Germain-des-Prés, in new haunts with names like Le Bistingo, Le Steak House or La Brocherie, the candlelight flickers on well-bred young faces and 'Provençal' décor, the peasant cuisine is what the *Gault–Millau* guide calls '*style camping élégant*' – and who could ever guess he was not in Chelsea?

One obvious aspect of this vogue is that hitherto despised foreign *cuisines* are now coming into their own in Paris. The French (who rarely get as far as Peking) have always been acutely and chauvinistically conscious of other nations' inferior cooking, and gourmets would seldom accept even the best Italian, Russian or Tonkinese dishes as anything more than quaint or amusing. But today amusement and quaintness are just what many people want. Of course, there have always been some foreign restaurants in Paris, notably those nostalgic little Russian ones that arrived after 1917; but until recently they formed a kind of ghetto, patronized by their own national exiles or by a few tourists and curious intellectuals. Now foreign food is becoming *à la mode*. First in the late 1950s came the wave of *pizzerie*, all Chianti-flasks and Amalfi posters and waiters in Neapolitan costume (many of them Corsicans) singing *Torna a Sorrento* as they flicked their *pizze* into the oven. Now Spanish, Greek, Danish, Arab and even Japanese restaurants are spreading in Paris, while the *pieds noirs* have imported *couscous* and *méchoui* to scores of menus throughout France, and a few Tonkinese and Italian ventures are appearing even in provincial towns where till now foreign food was unknown.

Many of these new places are perfectly authentic and of reasonable standard, run by their own national chefs. Others, notably the slick new quasi-Anglo-Saxon ones, have a good deal less to do with gastronomy but are quite funny. The glossy St-Germain-des-Prés Drugstore, for instance, offers a mixed Franco-American menu that includes barbecued spare-ribs, 'club sandwiches', hamburger steaks and *Chien Chaud dit Hot Dog* – and this for its French public, not just for tourists. Nearly every large provincial town or new suburb now has its 'drugstore'. It is easy to laugh at them, but in fact they do perform a useful service and the food often tastes better than the silly menus would suggest. The drug-stores are open late, every day of the week, and offer a range of shopping facilities in their little *boutiques*. It is highly convenient to be able to stroll in at midnight, even on a Sunday, and buy a novel or razor-blades or chocolates. Where in an English town can you find such service at such an hour?

As for the British, for decades our island cuisine was a stock topic of mirth in Paris. But now the Parisian passion for mimicking all things English has scaled new heights: to observe this, go to Slavik's extraordinary new London Tavern at St-Germain-des-Prés, run by a young couple from Auvergne with help from Watney's and Fortnum and Mason. Here, amid an implausible baroque pastiche of a Victorian pub, a well-dressed crowd (French, mind you) can be seen gobbling up *le London Lunch* (*rosbif et Yorkshire pudding*, 15 francs), *le Buckingham salad*, *le rice crispies* and *le Toffy cup* (*sic* – toffee ice-cream) and maybe washing it down with one of nine recherché blends of tea at 4.50 or 5.50 francs a pot, just as in an English pub. Scores of other so-called 'pubs' are now springing up all over Paris and even in the provinces, discreetly backed by certain British whisky firms and breweries. I even found a new 'pub' for the French colony at Douala in the Cameroun. Most of these 'pubs' offer indifferent *franglais* food at Champs-Elysées prices, and represent the last word in current French attempts to re-create not the real England but their own make-believe England.

Some Parisians take such places with a snobbish seriousness, others enjoy them as a bizarre joke. In either case the appeal is very different from that of the less outrageous new restaurants from the Orient or Mediterranean. French tourists on their foreign holidays have been discovering that Spanish, Greek, Italian or Austro-Hungarian food is not always as coarse or unsubtle as they had been told; and so, back home, they carry these new tastes into their own Parisian dining-out. And although these new foreign restaurants inevitably fill a far less crucial need than in Britain, I do feel they have added some variety and liveliness to Paris.

The true gourmets are still numerous, and they are now staging a kind of counter-offensive against the general decline in taste and standards. Many well-to-do people, and especially older ones, have developed a passion for hunting down and cultivating little unsmart, out-of-the-way *bistrots* where the cooking and the wines are still superb. Before the war this was more a matter of spontaneous routine and there was no need to be so selective: now it is becoming a cult, a retort to the ungastronomic cults of the gay young smarties.

Much the most original and highly publicized development in serious French gastronomy during the past decade or so – and probably the most important since Escoffier – has been the rise of what its inventors call 'La Nouvelle Grande Cuisine Française'. This is a highly inventive new style of cooking that rejects the rich, high-calory ingredients such as cream, butter, egg-yolk, sugar and brandy that have decked out so many of the great classic dishes. It returns to a greater simplicity, using the finest raw materials and cooking them in their own juices. The self-appointed leader of this school is Paul Bocuse, now aged 50, whose luxury establishment at Collonges-au-Mont-d'Or, outside Lyon, wins top star-ratings in all the guide-books and is widely regarded today as the best restaurant in the world. Bocuse is as well known in France as any leading actor or singer; he is known by his friends as '*l'Empereur*', and has his own Press officer. His colleagues and disciples, following the same style of cooking, now run a number of the most highly praised restaurants in France: they include the brothers Troisgros at Roanne, Roger Vergé at Mougins (near Cannes) and Jean-Pierre Haeberlin at Illhaeusern (Alsace), all with the rare three-stars in Michelin. These and a score or so other restaurants in France offer unusual new dishes, cooked rapidly and lightly in an almost Oriental style, and daringly blending flavours: for instance, a purée of mixed spinach and pear preserves the fresh taste of both. Nearly all these places are very expensive – say, in the 150-francs-a-head range, including wines – because this kind of cuisine requires a great deal of time and skill, and the finest ingredients. Some food-lovers – and I fear I am one of them – find the results a bit too chi-chi and over-refined, and prefer the more robust tastes of maybe less healthy dishes such as a good *cassoulet* or *civet de lièvre*. But the Nouvelle Grande Cuisine has become immensely popular with many gourmets, either because of its qualities, or for snob reasons, or because of its low calorie content in an age of increasing concern about diet. One of Bocuse's best-known fellow-chiefs, Michel Guérard, has taken the style even further by inventing what he calls *la cuisine minceur*, and is now running a kind of luxury health-farm for gourmet-minded slimmers in a smart country hotel near Pau, where you can combine exquisite eating with an intake of less than 500 calories per four-course meal. When I telephoned him, the receptionist said, 'The Master is holding a seminar, please ring later.' Guérard, Bocuse and their friends do in fact consider themselves as high-priests or prose-lytizing *maîtres-à-penser* of a new form of what the French have always regarded as one of the greatest of the arts. Recently they ran a five-day gastronomic cruise aboard a liner off the south coast of France, complete with course of lectures. One of the pundits on board was a doctor, president of the Société des Médecins Gastronomes. The theme of his talk was that rich and heavy eating need not add to one's weight if it is combined with plenty of sexual intercourse. As he left the ship, with his pretty young Japanese wife on his arm, he said, 'I've lost four kilos on this cruise.'

There are still enough serious and well-heeled eaters in France to ensure that the really good restaurants – whether traditional or Nouvelle Grande Cuisine – continue to stay full and prosper. And I must stress that the new phoney Parisian trendiness that I described earlier has not yet infected the provinces very much, where cooking is usually more authentic and cheaper than in Paris. And although value-for-money may have declined in the smarter restaurants along tourist routes, there are hundreds of small out-of-the-way hotels and *bistrots* throughout France where you can still eat superbly for 20 francs or so. Another positive factor is that the working classes still seem to care about their food: though a young Parisian bourgeois may today have little better taste than a similar Londoner, at a lower social level the gulf between standards in the two countries is still immeasurable. Witness the French *relais routiers* for lorry-drivers, and the British transport 'caffs'. Working families now have the money to buy much more meat and fresh vegetables than before the war, and meat consumption is the highest in Europe after Belgium. As the working-class wife, unlike the bourgeois wife, is less likely than before the war to have a job, she may spend more time on elaborate dishes. Henri Gault, co-author with Christian Millau of a leading guide-book, told me: 'Wives in this class still cook *pot-au-feu* or *bœuf en daube*, and their husbands expect it. At the small factory near where I live, workers bring dishes like *petit salé aux lentilles* or *bœuf bourguignonne* in canisters for their picnic lunches, cooked by their wives, and they heat them up in the factory. But at Sarcelles, where the working class *s'embourgeoise*, all that is disappearing.'

Although many French may now have become negligent about gastronomy, they still have it in their bones. In Britain it is still something of a self-conscious minority interest, often verging on the pretentious or vulgar. Scratch an Englishman guzzling his *tournedos Rossini* in a plushy Midlands roadhouse, and you will find a ketchup-and-chips man, even a Wincarnis man; scratch a Frenchman in his 'drugstore' or candlelit vault, and you will often find a gourmet playing truant. Recently in Grenoble I went to an ordinary routine luncheon in the Préfecture for some local councillors: we had *lotte à l'armoricaine* followed by *pintadeau farci aux morilles*, with superb cheeses and *profiterolles* – all of it memorable and magnificent. Does an English local council ever entertain like that?

But how long can it last? What will have happened in France in ten or twenty years' time? Frozen foods, packaging, snack-bars and industrialized catering will sweep their way forward through sheer necessity and economic momentum. Jacques Borel, the clever young tycoon in the vanguard of this movement, told me: 'In France, as elsewhere, the future is with the big chains. Individual restaurants just won't be viable any more – all but a few. Restaurants today should be run by accountants, not by *patrons* who see themselves as artists. Not many people ask for elaborate sauces any more, so sauces can go to hell, they're too much trouble. And if Paris today is copying New York ten years late, be sure that in France the provinces *always* copy Paris, twenty years later still. I'm not saying that gastronomy will die, but it'll end up confined to just 200 or so expensive restaurants, as in Britain.'

Borel, who now owns more than 100 cheap restaurants in addition to his Wimpys, has the convincing air of a man who knows what he is doing. But there is one possible alternative to the picture he gives of little islands of real cooking in an ocean of hamburgers. It might be possible to make industrial labour-saving techniques into the ally of classic recipes, not their enemy. Methods of dehydration and deep-freezing have been rapidly improving, and a *coq-au-vin* mass pre-cooked in this way under the guidance of an expert can be almost as good as the real thing, whatever the purists may fear. This at least is the view of Gault and Millau, leading French gastronomic experts. Christian Millau told me that a dish expertly pre-cooked, then properly frozen and de-frozen, was barely distinguishable from the same dish freshly cooked, and was generally much better than a similar dish served up in an average-quality restaurant. He saw this as the inevitable prospect for the future, and as a gourmet he was not distressed by it. A number of French firms are already pioneering in this field, allying science to traditional quality. One day it may seem as unusual to order a freshly cooked dish of this kind as it is today to buy hand-made clothes or furniture.

Even so, something may be lost, and the individual restaurateur will become a rare craftsman like the designers of handprinted fabrics or leather-bound books. Nearly all gastronomes agree with Borel that the present polarization is bound to proceed and that the number of 'serious' restaurants will fall. They will continue to find clients – but how long, in practice, will they keep up their standards? For centuries the greatness of French *cuisine* has depended on its grass-roots tradition: it has belonged to workers and peasants as much as to the rich, it has not been imposed from outside by an élite as in Britain. Its genius has grown from the marrow of the nation, like music in Germany, sport in Australia, art in medieval Italy. Cut away these grass-roots, replace them with snack-bars, push gastronomy into a ghetto for specialists, and it might well wither. So the French will sacrifice their high level of daily cuisine on the altar of modernism, and a new generation will grow up, not noticing what has been lost. Borel is sending sauces to hell – and Pierre Grobel, a leading gastronome, laments, '*La base essentielle de la cuisine, c'est la sauce. Mais la sauce se meurt. Nous vivons une époque tragique!*' Paul Bocuse may not agree.

THE HOLIDAY OBSESSION: HAPPINESS IS A TAHITIAN STRAW-VILLAGE IN SICILY

If *cuisine* is ceasing to be national indulgence number one it is easy to see what is taking its place. *L'Express* wrote recently: 'Is not the myth of holidays a specifically French phenomenon? We are the first to have made it a national institution, a collective dream. Psychologically, the French think about holidays all through the year.' Of course others do so too: the post-war growth of tourism is not confined to the French, and the number of people who take holidays away from home is still lower in France than in Britain. But *l'Express* may be right in a way; there are few countries where the annual urge to get away from it all has grown quite so powerful, or where failure to do so is quite such a cause of discontent. In London many of us work peacefully through all the dog-days of summer; in Paris by the end of June people are talking of nothing but *les vacances*, and their irritation with the city has grown visibly near breaking-point.

Before the war the well-to-do took long holidays, but few others did so. Now French wage-earners have secured for themselves the longest annual paid leave in Europe, and the numbers taking holidays away from home each year (51 per cent of the population) are twice as great as in 1939. Many workers now leave home for the sea or mountains, and many others would do the same if they felt they could afford it. Even farmers, who account for nearly half of the 50 per cent of stay-at-homes, are beginning to dream of the holidays they've never yet had in their lives: *Nous aussi, nous voulons voir la mer* are the placards you sometimes see in summer along the routes to the crowded beaches. Only 9 per cent of farmers, and 12 per cent of farm-labourers, take holidays.

The strongest element in the new holiday cult seems to be an urge towards a 'return to nature'. Previously the French city-dweller often felt ill-at-ease in the deep country with its despised, alien peasantry; he preferred urban resorts like Biarritz with casinos and promenades, or else the orderliness of some family *château* or villa. But today the vogue is all for going native, and millions are happy to lose themselves amid the lonelier mountains or beaches of this huge and still unspoilt land. Hotels and *pensions* with their mounting prices have lost ground heavily to the new craze for cheap camping holidays: the numbers who practise *le camping* have risen since 1950 from one to well over five million a year, and though in August it may look as if all of them have flocked at once to the Côte d'Azur, in fact, there are plenty elsewhere too. Skiing, sailing, swimming, cycling and other holiday recreations have also increased hugely in popularity. And whereas the less sophisticated Englishman usually likes to re-create his own home environment on holiday, in his well-equipped caravan, his Butlin's camp or his jolly boarding-house, the modern Frenchman tends to prefer as complete a change as possible, to wear as little as weather and decency will allow, and to scrabble amid pine-needles in a tent. Caravans are still rare, and have low social prestige.

Maybe this return to nature marks a subconscious national desire to compensate for the desertion of agricultural traditions.

Certainly it is a reaction against urbanization, to which the French are not adapting easily. Sociologists are therefore unsure whether the frenetic urge to escape to a new life is a token of healthy adventurousness or of maladjustment. One of them, Michel Crozier, blames the holiday mania on the rigidities and tensions of French society and office life where he says, 'no one is truly at ease or in his right place, and so the French *need* holidays more than, say, the Americans'. Many Frenchmen are thus looking not only for change and relaxation on holiday, but for a social liberation they do not find in their own lives. Many of them, it is true, still take the long, quiet, traditional family holiday amid lots of relatives, in *grand-mère*'s villa in the Dordogne or *tante Louise*'s *château* in Burgundy; but this habit is declining, and instead there is a new emphasis on holidays at once more collective and more individual – on the *colonie de vacances*, the holiday village or big skiing party, where everyone is democratically equal, yet liberated from the emotional ties *chez tante Louise*.

Most surprisingly, the French have begun to tour outside their own frontiers as much as the sun-starved British, and this never used to be so. The reasons may be partly economic (Spain and some other nearby countries are still a little cheaper than France) but they are also psychological. The rise of Europeanism and the decline of French nationalism mean that the French, although still chauvinistic, are much less insular than they used to be, or than the British still are: at least they have grown much more aware of other peoples and curious about how they live, even though they still feel highly competitive and touchily superior. The growth of air and car travel have obviously played their part too. The foreign travel allowance has generally been more generous than in Britain, though of course it tends to follow the ups-and-downs of balance-of-payments crises. French tourist spending abroad rose sixfold between 1950 and 1959, and by 1973 one French holiday in five was spent abroad, a higher proportion than in Britain, where the tradition of foreign travel is much greater and the climatic incentive for it much stronger. And so the nation that in the old days ranked beside Italy as one of the leading tourist countries of Europe found itself by 1965 on the verge of deficit. Although revenue from foreign visitors to France is still rising, French tourists now spend as much money abroad as the industry earns from foreigners in France.

Three million people now go annually to Spain for a night or more – excluding those who cross the frontier on day-trips – and a minority venture much farther, to Israel, Morocco, Russia or Greece (now flooded with French philhellenes). These are usually the more educated French, and on holiday abroad they often give the impression of being more culture-conscious than other Europeans. In the south of Spain the beaches are crowded with reddening Teutons and Britons, and the churches and museums, relatively, with Frenchmen in shorts absorbed in academic guide-books. This impression may be misleading: there are plenty of Frenchmen who also want to redden on beaches, but for obvious reasons they are still relatively more likely than a northerner to stay in their own country. Even so, Frenchmen by virtue of their rigorous education still seem to pay higher attention than most peoples to cultural sightseeing: some through snobbery or a sense of duty, many with real feeling and scholarship. Even house-agents in France, advertising villas in Spain, consider it a useful selling-point to add when they can, 'Fascinating medieval abbey near by'.

All that I have said about the new French holiday ideals could be summed up quintessentially in one magic phrase: Club Méditerranée. This is the Great French Dream made reality, sorely deserving its French Scott Fitzgerald. It is probably the most remarkable organized holiday venture the world has yet seen, and its gigantic success reveals a great deal about the spirit of the French today.

It all began in 1950 when Gérard Blitz, a tall blond athlete from Antwerp, founded a small informal holiday-camp on Majorca with a set of US Army surplus tents, and was surprised when as many as 2,600 people answered his advertisement to join him there. The idea snowballed and became a permanent holiday club, currently providing 425,000 people a year with holidays. Today it operates a total of more than seventy 'villages' all around the globe (you must never call them 'holiday camps'!):

a dozen or so are those famous little straw-hut summer villages around the sea that lends the Club its name, but the majority now are more solidly built bungalow villages, many are open all the year, and sixteen are in winter ski-resorts. Blitz is no longer actively in charge – he has handed over to Gilbert Trigano – but his inspiration is still felt. Like Edouard Leclerc, he has been something of a visionary at work in a cut-throat competitive field, and today the Club applies skilful organization and packaging to his own philosophy of human happiness.

Today's luxury [he has written] is not comfort but open space. Adventure is dead and solitude is dying, in today's crowded resorts. But if you can no longer go on holiday alone without finding yourself in a crowd, it ought to be possible to go off in a crowd in order to find yourself alone. The individual has a horror of promiscuity, but he does need community. And so he needs a very flexible holiday community where at any moment he can join in, or escape – a strange cocktail of *la vie de château* and *la vie de sauvage*.

And the Club's villages have been carefully developed to satisfy some of the deepest French desires: individualism amid camaraderie; sophistication amid primitive return-to-nature; a blend of sport, sensuality, culture and exotic foreign settings; a harmless once-a-year escape from the barriers and tensions of French society into a new kind of never-never-land fraternity. Today this is still the formula even though, victim of its own success, the Club has inevitably been veering from spontaneous towards pre-packed primitivism – and also towards greater comfort.

Borrowing the enchanted model of the Polynesian village as the most 'natural' human social unit, Blitz built up his colonies on the tracks of another no less romantic tradition, the Odyssey. The prototype is at Corfu (Corcyra) near Ithaca, others are on Djerba (authentic island of the lotus-eaters), at Foca not far from Troy itself, at Palinuro, and at Cefalù beyond the Sicilian straits of Scylla and Charybdis, at Al Hoceima in Morocco towards the Pillars of Hercules, as well as in Israel, Spain and Yugoslavia, and many other countries. There is even one in the Tahitian motherland itself (patronized mainly by Americans), while new ones have been opened as far afield as the Ivory Coast, Bulgaria, Mauritius, and even Cuba.

In many of the Mediterranean villages you sleep down by the beach in little round Tahitian thatched huts, two or three to a hut; and many of the more dedicated Club members go around all day in next-to-nothing but a *paréo* (gaudy Tahitian sarong), uniform of the new utopia. In some villages you can also wear flower-garlands. Phoney and embarrassing? Possibly, to some people. But the appeal to the imagination, especially to a real craving for a kind of comradely naturalism, is genuine enough. Virtually no money changes hands within the village, save in the form of pop-art beads, worn like a necklace, for buying bar drinks or cigarettes. Meals, served in elegant open-air patios, are plentiful and excellent; and wine is unlimited and included in the basic fees. Everyone, staff and members, calls everyone else *tu* and by first-names (astonishing, for France); and the staff, known as Gentils Organisateurs (GOs), help discreetly to imbue the Gentils Membres (GMs) with *le mystique du Club* in which many of them apostolically believe. Yet (unlike in some holiday camps) no attempt whatever is made by the staff to force individuals to join in activities. You can skulk in your hut all day, or wander alone into the hinterland, and no one will mind or notice. And there is plenty to do for those who wish it: nightly open-air dancing and sing-songs, sports from water-skiing and snorkelling to judo and volley-ball, all included in the basic fees. There are also daily open-air concerts of classical records, as well as lectures and debates in some villages and, in response to members' demands, an increasing supply of live culture in the form of touring dramatic groups (such as the then Belgian National Theatre) and chamber orchestras performing under the stars in bathing-trunks or jeans. The Club's appeal is essentially middle-class, and it is as different from Butlin's as Rupert Brooke from Tommy Trinder.

Et in Arcadia ego. Bleary-eyed I cross Arcadia's frontiers one Saturday morning at seven, at the Gare de Lyon. Our first rendez-vous is a café opposite the station. Parisienne secretaries with rucksacks, heavy fortyish Belgians with moustaches, a few stray

English clutching dictionaries, we emerge like insects from the chrysalis of our city selves, warily greet each other and begin to unfurl our new wings. The Italian train rattles south: we are bound for Cefalù in Sicily, sixth largest of the summer villages (1,130 beds). In my compartment: a young woman who works at IBM-France, a petite Brussels ballerina, and an engaging curly-haired Parisian student who's already 'done' Cefalù the year before and is an expert on *ambiance*. By Turin, we are on *tu* terms; by Naples, we know each other's jobs. In the high season the Club runs special *trains-dansants* across Italy, where GMs can vociferously break the social ice in the bar and rock the train almost off its rails; but, this being September, there is no bar and no dancing. Even so, the time passes as gaily as a thirty-five-hour, second-class train journey reasonably can. (It is probably more sensible to go by one of the chartered air flights, but I wanted to be initiated in the Club's mystique the hard way.) At Palinuro, south of Naples, a party from another village climb aboard: they are on a five-day Club excursion to the Lipari isles, where they will clamber down inside volcano craters and live like the Swiss Family Robinson. They are singing, and happy. The train is ferried across the straits, then swings along the built-up north Sicilian coast, past the new oil refineries and the heartrending slums. Finally we tunnel under Cefalù's unmistakable Gibraltar-like rock, the train halts, a bevy of lovely *hôtesses* rush to help us with our suitcases, a man in a comic hat is blowing a trumpet (all new arrivals are greeted, traditionally, by fanfares), and the village's *animateurs* are standing around on the platform in weird fancy dress. It's all happening! In the village I am allotted a hut called Sagouin (it means 'filthy wretch') which I share with a solemn Milanese technician. It is underneath an ancient floodlit tower inhabited by a GO sailing-instructor from Dublin. Other GMs have huts with names like Vinaigre and Hula-Hula. The next morning we new-boys and new-girls are given a pep-talk in a pine grove by Charly, the young *chef de village*, clad in the lowest-slung *paréo* I've ever seen, kept up by will-power. He tells us that the aim of the Club is that we should all be very nice to each other (which the French need to be told, as they aren't normally nice to people they don't know, although here they seem to manage it).

Charly, twenty-five, tells me that he trained as an accountant, then joined the Club after visiting Corfu as a G M one year and falling in love with it and a G O there, now his wife. And so, under his aegis, our Sicilian days and nights slip by.

Here is a typical day. I wake late, after a night partly spent fighting a mosquito (the village *boutique* sells aromatic *insecticcido* spray, but it's probably more effective to sleep wrapped up in a sheet, or ask a G O to get your hut fumigated). A quick visit to the communal ladies'-and-gentlemen's *lavoirs*, where it's slightly unnerving to shave while a very luscious blonde in a bikini beside me is cleaning her teeth with an electric brush. Breakfast (nearly everyone in swimsuits) is an odd meal: you help yourself from a long buffet laden with melon, yoghourt, smoked fish, strong local cheese, semi-hard-boiled eggs and orange juice. Then a bathe, and sunbathe: this is Cefalù's weakest point, for though the village is beautifully situated and landscaped on a slope full of flowers and lemon-trees, in another sense the site is badly chosen, for there is only a small, mediocre sandy beach and most beach-lazing has to be done on rocks or a concrete jetty. But we make do. The more enterprising ones are having sailing-lessons, or Yoga instruction from a blonde called Yogush who attracts large classes. Lunch in the lovely patio with its blue and red parasols is a lavish meal: twice a week there is a vast help-yourself *hors d'œuvre* buffet, Provençal style, stretching about thirty yards. Today for our first course there are excellent *quenelles de brochet*, not an easy dish to cook well for 1,100 people. All tables are for eight, and conversation is general, without introductions. Today I find myself sitting with four young Parisian doctors and their girl-friends, typical hard-core G Ms, swapping anecdotes about previous Club holidays like veterans telling campaign stories ('*Moi, j'ai fait Djerba en soixante-deux – c'était sensass!*') but, significantly, not saying a word about France or their other lives back home. They do not exactly greet me as a long-lost friend, but at least they turn to include me in the conversation, which they probably would not have done in any other setting. After lunch I laze in the sun on the wide dance-terrace beside the circular straw-roofed bar, swapping jokes and money-beads with the Sicilian barmen, and offering *espresso* to a handsome girl psychologist from Abbeville while the hi-fi pipes out Jacques Brel and Pete Seeger – 'I'm not too young to try for the sun'. Waves of happiness lap over me. This is Arcadia's solstice. At six there is more music, this time a recorded Bach concert in an area known as 'le Forum', an alfresco theatre on a cliff where we gaze at the silent sea as the sun sets and a Brandenburg Concerto finds a more perfect setting than any concert hall. After dinner the mood is rather different. Hundreds of us crowd round the bar and terrace as the nightly sing-song and *animation* begin. The GO *animateurs* embark on various carefully rehearsed pranks, and at last Billy Butlin seems to be present as well as Rupert Brooke. One GO, a picturesque bronze-bearded Israeli called Czopp, mimes film-titles which we have to guess. He and another GO (male) waltz sexily in each other's arms. '*Le Conquistador (les cons-qui-s'adorent)*' shouts out one cinélogue. Full marks. English GMs express irritation that they can't follow the French dirty jokes. But other jokes don't need language. Volunteers from the audience are called for, and this brings out some of the unpaid GM *animateurs* who have appointed themselves the life-and-soul-of-the-party and without whom no village is complete. Like little Néron, a tubby forty-year-old so called because he habitually wears his *paréo* toga-style and a laurel-crown. Czopp gives him a pink tutu and makes him do a nutcracker waltz as a *petit rat de l'Opéra* which has us all rolling about. Néron is hugely popular at Cefalù, and we wonder what he is in real life: a respectable bank manager maybe from some sleepy town in the Charente, or a commercial traveller from the Paris Red Belt whose inner personality comes alive for three weeks each summer by the old *mare nostrum*. Or there is René, a gigantic, vociferous wizard-prang type with a big ginger moustache, always clapping his hands and singing 'Ooh-la-la', who tonight is made to lie on the floor as a squalling baby while a lady GM changes his nappies and powders his fly (an old Club classic, this). 'The ideal Club holiday,' remarks someone, 'is a return to childhood.' After this we go through the nightly ritual of belting out the Chanson Village (every village has its own song), its tune borrowed from a Sicilian folk-song and its words strictly non-Sicilian: '*Il y a de soleil et la mer à Cefalù-oo-ooo-oo-oooo! Mais aussi le ponton et les cailloux.*' Then there is dancing, non-stop. The boring French band has gone and tonight we have a new one, a Sicilian long-haired pop group, Mick Jaggers every one, whom someone claims to have seen practising down town in Cefalù cathedral – odd place, Sicily. This new group is excellent. *Ça chauffe, carrément*, and no one chauffes more than pretty fourteen-year-old Jane from Inverness, beset by eager Latins: 'Och, when I tell them about all this back home, they'll just nae believe me.' Her parents look on, tolerantly. After midnight the dance-terrace packs up (there are huts close by, and some people seem to want to sleep), but dedicated night-lifers make their way down the slope to a makeshift alfresco cabaret on the beach, where with our beads we buy *moules marinière* or barbecued spare-ribs, and under the Tyrrhenian moon to the strains of the Beatles' *Sergeant Pepper* we release one or two of our remaining inhibitions. We are cupped in a narrow cove below high rocks; Czopp is handing round *moules*; young couples sit round in tiers on the steps, talking softly, or dance slowly to the music; the mood is dreamy and intimate, Lucy is up there in the sky with diamonds, tender is the night. Alain, my student train-mate (whose romantic career at Cefalù I've been watching with interest), is having his curly hair stroked by Mary from Hammersmith. Pretty Marie-Laure from Boulogne-sur-mer tells me, 'Every man I've danced with tonight has asked me to go back to his hut with him.' Which brings me to the question you've all been waiting for me to answer. Well, Alan Whicker in a BBC film, shot at Corfu, claimed that the Club was entirely given over to the four S's, of which three are Sun, Sea and Sand; but Gérard Blitz back in Paris had told me, 'I assure you that there is no more and no less *libertinage* than on any other kind of seaside holiday,' and I rather fancy he is right. After all, the logistics of the situation are not easy. Married couples have a hut to themselves; but if you come on your own you share with a stranger of your own sex and hut-swapping isn't easy unless your hut-mate happens to hit it off with the hut-mate of your own girl, which by the law of averages can't happen often. In an ordinary hotel with single bedrooms, things are much simpler. It is true that at Corfu, Cefalù and other villages, a towel folded just so over a hut door is an accepted Do

Not Disturb sign, but for how long will your hut-mate be generous enough to stay away? Personally I find the Club's sensuality operates a law of diminishing returns, and the proximity of so many near-naked female bodies all day makes me feel like a sweet-shop owner who doesn't want to eat sweets. So, when the *Sergeant Pepper* record ends, I go back alone to my Milanese and my mosquito. And the next day with fifteen other G Ms I leave for a mule-back trek through the Sicilian mountains – one of the many unusual excursions that are possibly the Club's strongest feature. (From Cefalù you can also do a five-day tour of the main sights of Sicily; at Djerba, you can go on a Saharan safari; and at Corfu you can take a Robinson Crusoe trip to a near-by desert island, where you are cast away for several days with nothing but knives and fishing-tackle.) Sicilian guides take us in Fiats up to the hill-town of Castelbuono where we are treated to a 'typical Sicilian banquet' and chant bawdy French student drinking-songs over much Marsala; then we dance by candlelight in a pine wood and doss down in rough dormitories in a country shack. At dawn the mules arrive and for hours we zig-zag high into the lonely hills, while the muleteers with their Tito Gobbi voices parade their folk-song repertoire and offer us terrible local cheese, tasting like sickly chewing-gum. After more dancing, and a *méchoui* and a siesta, we descend again and are given more Marsala in an ex-monastery-turned-night-club. The trip has been exhilarating and sympathetic, and by now I am firm friends with the girl psychologist from Abbeville, the Parisian electronics expert, the Linotype operator on *Le Parisien Libéré*, and freckled Judy Hillman, Town-Planning Correspondent of the *Guardian*, whom I have sold to one of the muleteers for two million lire after much haggling. Back in Cefalù it is almost time to return to Paris, and my last image of the Club is of Czopp like a pied piper leading us all in a galloping chain-dance as, impelled by the pop-group, we re-echo

> '*Nos soucis et nos peines loin derrière nous,*
> *Nous reviendrons Un Jour à Ce-fa-looo-oo-ooo-oo-oooo!*'

Of what value is this never-never-land for the future of France and of French society? This might sound a ponderous question to ask about a harmless summer frolic, but it is not an irrelevant one. The clientèle is almost entirely middle class: one third *cadres* and the rest petit-bourgeois down to clerks, typists and artisans, but with very few real proletarians. This in its French context is not surprising, even though the prices would be within the means of skilled workers nowadays (roughly 2,200 francs for two weeks including air travel, or for three weeks off-season). As a social catalyst the Club therefore has its limits; but within its broad middle-to-upper range it does seem to have managed some shaking-up of the usual class barriers and inhibitions, however superficially. Its officials enjoy telling the story of two men who struck up a friendship of rare warmth over Samos wine and deep-sea diving in one of the Greek villages: only on the way home did they swap names and addresses, to discover that one was a director and the other a night-watchman in the same factory.

But we are not told what happened to this friendship when they got back home; and one managing-director G M has been quoted as saying: 'At one village I got friendly with one of my clerks: it was all right down there, where everything's so free and easy, but it did make it harder to keep up *les convenances* back in the office.' At Cefalù I found it noticeable that the French G Ms, much more than the foreign ones, preferred to remain anonymous and not discuss their jobs or backgrounds with each other. They wanted to forget about France. Nor has there been any pressure from members for Butlin-style winter get-togethers in Paris: one or two Club attempts at these failed because they simply showed up the social differences that were masked in the villages, and Blitz himself told me with disarming frankness: 'The success of the Club is due to its divorce from daily life: if French barriers dropped, the Club would become less attractive. We found that trying to hold meetings in Paris simply lost us the credit we had won in the villages; French barriers are too rigid.' So this is a kind of compensation-world, almost a Jean Genet territory where men and girls act out the fantasy roles they cannot manage in their own lives – classless democrats, cultured pagans, noble savages, high-spirited friends-to-all-the-world.

I think that the French do, at a certain level, feel a genuine urge to escape from the rigidly stratified society in which they have imprisoned themselves, and therefore the Club is a kind of therapy. It also provides a forum where strangers can be naturally nice to each other without the usual French mistrust. This, in a French context, is important: the atmosphere of the villages is genuinely and unforcedly friendly and co-operative, free from the usual French tendency to split into rival factions. Whether this mini-lesson in civism makes it any easier for GMs to go and spread the same spirit in their tougher lives back home is another matter. But I think that, to a small degree, it might.

The traditional bias against *les vacances collectives* is still quite strong in France, so that many people join the Club with initial misgivings. But most of them seem delighted with what they find. Of course there are plenty of things to criticize, which are largely a matter of individual taste. At Cefalù, our main complaint was of a certain claustrophobia due to the siting of the village on a built-up strip of coast beside a main road and railway with no open sandy shore: Blitz's boast that with the Club you can 'go off in a crowd in order to find yourself alone' fell a little flat. But most of the villages are in much more isolated spots, with beaches where you can wander away for miles. Some people might also dislike the *animation*, the fanfares and the singing, the schoolboy jokes and the few fanatics who wear their *paréos* even on the ski slopes. Actually this is only a small part of Club life and obtrudes only in the evenings; and I think a holiday community of over 1,000 would feel a certain emptiness if there were none of it at all. Therefore I was grateful to the public-spirited volunteers like René and Néron as well as to the GO *animateurs*. I felt at Cefalù there was not, in fact, enough professional *animation* to give the village a strong cohesive atmosphere.

The successes of the Club, in addition to the food, the sport and the cultural excursions, are a certain basic good taste and lack of vulgarity in the way the whole thing is conceived and run. The hundreds of straw-huts or bungalows, for instance, are dotted irregularly among trees in a way that pleases the eye; many foreign holiday-camps are far more monolithic in appearance. I agree with what one Club executive told me: 'Only the French could have succeeded with a holiday formula like ours. In Italy, the position of women would have made it impossible, while the Germans or British would have turned it into jolly boy-scoutism for adults. Our French individualism saves us. Lots of foreigners are members, but the Club's style is entirely French. And our aims are quite different from Butlin's. He tries to flatter workers by treating them as bourgeois; we take people right out of any social context. Butlin gives them cinemas, bingo and such-like; we remove urban life totally, and we certainly don't allow transistors, or washing hanging outside huts.' Considering what hell holiday-makers *en masse* generally are, especially British or Germans, the Club's members *en masse* are surprisingly unirritating and pleasantly behaved. I, too, think that French reserve and lack of clubbability saves them: put people together in a setting like this, and anything above a certain level of clubbability rapidly becomes insufferable.

But the Club's basic structures have now been developing and changing fast, and there is some danger of its unique ethos becoming overlaid. Numbers rise each year (membership trebled between 1963 and 1971) and success has tempted it to widen its activities. It has now become a public company with a 53 million franc capital and shares quoted on the Bourse, most of these belonging to Rothschild and other big banks. Its massive new seven-storey headquarters stands, symbolically, right opposite the Bourse. And Gilbert Trigano, the businessman, has now taken over the running of the Club's affairs from Blitz the man of instinct. Trigano is diversifying. He has opened 'villages' for specialized activities, such as the new one devoted to horse-riding in the Massif Central. He even went briefly into the sea-cruise and cultural-coach-tour markets, but without success. More important, he is now setting his cap at a wealthier clientèle, many of them middle-aged, who will accept the Club's informality but not the discomfort of straw-huts and mosquitoes. So the accent is now on comfort. Though one or two classic straw-hut villages continue to be built for younger or hardier members, most of the Club's new ventures are luxurious village-hotels in bungalow-style solid constructions open all the year. Several are far afield, in West Africa, the Caribbean and the Pacific. I visited the one at Agadir, South Morocco, in January 1968: food, facilities and organization were all better than at Cefalù but the ambience was just not the same – the GMs, many of them middle-aged Belgians, were shy of getting on *tu* terms or doing their own *animation*.

Trigano has even opened a huge four-star luxury hotel in Paris itself, at Neuilly, offering Hilton comfort (and better-than-Hilton food) at near-Hilton prices, and attempting to combine this with something of the Club's ambience. Many of the visitors are American. Trigano, in fact, is now aiming hard and with success at an American mass market and has formed a financial and sales link-up with American Express. The four Caribbean villages are mainly for Americans, and the language there is English. The same applies to the old Tahiti village, and the new ones in Hawaii and Mexico. In 1975, as many as 15·3 per cent of all Gentils Membres were American (54·3 per cent were French, 9·4 Belgian, 7·1 Italian, 4·8 German, and less than 1 per cent British). The Club has opened an office on Fifth Avenue, and in New York and some other cities there are even emotional off-season rallies of 'Nice Members' – 'like scenes from *Nashville*', said one GO. The Americans, unlike the French, go in for that kind of thing. Blitz once talked to me of his vision of five million American Nice Members: 'We have *proof* that our particular holiday formula will appeal to the Americans as much as the French, given a few alterations of comfort and language. America's an under-developed country in its methods of tourism, the style of the hotels is so old-fashioned. So we shall export our techniques to them, just as France has imported American techniques in other fields. The Club will be an authentic French penetration into the American sphere, just as IBM or Motorola penetrate into France.' And in a sense, why not? The new installations retain many of the essential Club features – *animateurs*, free sport, beads and *paréos*, if not the straw-huts – and so long as the original Mediterranean villages do not become Americanized, perhaps one should not object. But even within its own French context, the Club's spirit has been changing under the impact of wider success. Inevitably it has grown more conventional and less of a mad pioneering adventure. Today the plumbing is better and the *paréos* fewer: some new GMs even dare to be seen in cocktail dresses. The back-to-nature veterans of the early Majorca days are being joined by a more sedate clientèle who want their primitivism to be carefully streamlined – and the gap between the Club and other types of holiday is narrowing. It would be sad if the true originality of the Club were to be too far diluted: for Blitz created something rare and inspired, no mean feat in the overcrowded jungle of today's tourism, and his claim is not far-fetched that the Club is 'the pilot-organization of Europe's leisure, laboratory for the holidays of the future'.

There are echoes of the atmosphere and ethos of the Club in some of the ordinary public camping-sites in France, especially along the Côte d'Azur: on the Côte des Maures and the Ile de Porquerolles, in the rocky coves near Cassis, and notably around La Capte, south of Hyères, where everyone is bronzed and youthful and the gaudy blue-and-orange tents fill the pine-forests for miles. This is modern, post-Bardot mass tourism with a vengeance, utterly different from the mood of the classic resorts farther east. The whole trend on the Riviera today, for rich and not-so-rich alike, is away from the Edwardian sedateness of Cannes or Monte Carlo and towards the St-Tropez* or La Capte pattern – film-stars with sand between their toes, pine-needles in your *soupe de poissons*, nudists among the rocks, a juke-box idly blaring Mireille Mathieu in the sun, and all the paraphernalia of *le camping élégant* which the French are able to manage with a lithe Latin flair.

In a more contrived and showmanlike genre, there are other new-style tourist ventures on this coast that reach bizarre heights of flamboyance and ingenuity – notably at La Brague, north of Antibes, and on the Ile de Bendor near Bandol. La Siesta at La Brague is a huge beach-club-cum-night-club that holds 3,000 people and was created in 1962 by a local cement tycoon. It has every gimmick you could ask for, down to a special restaurant for dogs, and a set of old gipsy caravans tarted up to make a smart *boutique* and hair-stylist. The real beach was shingle here, so tons of sand were specially imported by Air France from Acapulco, Tahiti and Sussex: and a real Chinese junk was brought from Hong Kong to lie offshore and serve as a Chinese restaurant.

* See pp. 523–5.

After dark, when the lido is deserted, the night-club takes over, and the network of little open-air bars and dance-floors with their illuminated waterfalls are lit by a myriad flaming torches; you can dance on big metal water-lilies in a pool full of flowers. 'Our image,' the *petite* blonde manageress told me proudly, 'is the marriage of fire and water.' La Siesta is hugely popular with minor film-stars and lesser smarties who pay thirty francs' daily entrance fee; and for all its artificiality I do find it rather lovely in a *Great Gatsby* kind of way, even though these 'men and girls who come and go among the whisperings . . . and the stars' are drinking *le scotch*, not champagne. On this very Riviera where Fitzgerald found the night so tender and pursued his strange ideal, is it possible that forty years later the French, or some of them, are now in thrall to the same *mystique* of spiritual fulfilment through glamour and wealth? Are those flaming torches for some people the same as Gatsby's green light? There are signs of it today in romantic, glamour-dazzled, new-rich France – and not only at La Siesta.

The French are increasingly drawn to the seaside (45 per cent of all holiday-makers went there in 1973, against 23 per cent 15 years earlier) and to the mountains (15 per cent in 1973, 10 per cent in 1958). This means that fewer holidays are spent in the spa towns like Vichy, or with relatives in their country homes. And sea and mountains provide the main setting for the post-war growth of sport in France. The number of private sailing-boats and motor-yachts rose from 20,000 in 1960 to 304,000 in 1973: today the Côte d'Azur is so jammed with yachts in summer that some ports such as Beaulieu have instituted ninety-minute parking-discs for them as for cars. Of all sports sailing and skiing are the most popular: more than 4,500,000 go to the ski-slopes each year, mainly to the French Alps but also the Pyrenees and Vosges or abroad. The building of new ski-lifts and hotels in smart centres like Mégève and Courchevel has meant big business for financiers and developers. Some well-to-do Parisians are now picking up the New York habit of long trips for skiing weekends; they drive all through Friday evening the 380 miles from Paris to Mégève and return early on Monday.

Probably the French are today more *sportif* than the English; or at least they are relatively more devoted than the English to participation-sports rather than spectator-sports. True, the annual Tour de France cycle race is essentially a mammoth spectator-sport, and so are the great car races and league football. But France's 66,000 sporting clubs and associations claim among their three million members nearly a million and a half *licenciés* or certified active participants and these include 440,000 footballers, 62,000 judoists and 37,000 racing cyclists. Fishing and hunting are both more popular than ever. *La chasse* is generally conducted with a rifle, not horse and hounds: in the old days it was the preserve of peasants and gentry, as in Renoir's *La Règle du jeu*, but today it has spread more widely, and in fact so many urban amateurs have taken to the woods on Sundays with their guns that the accident-rate has soared and new licensing laws have had to be enforced.

In international competition the French show up better at individual than at team sports, as you might expect. They did poorly in all the recent World Football Cups and their post-war summer Olympics record has been consistently disappointing, due partly to failures of team training and morale. Their rare gold medals have generally been for aristocratic and individual sports such as horse-jumping. At Munich, in 1972, they were placed seventeenth, with two golds, and at Montreal, in 1976, eighteenth with only one. Front-rank French athletes are rare: but when they do emerge, like the runner Michel Jazy and the swimmer Christine Caron a few years ago, they are lauded as national idols. When, in 1976, Eric Tabarly again won the single-handed transatlantic sailing race, his return to Paris produced a hero's ovation from a huge crowd on the Champs-Elysées, like a Roman triumph: there is now a mystique in France surrounding the taciturn Tabarly, and it is he who has inspired so many thousands of young Frenchmen to become sailing fanatics. In the case of skiing, all the widespread grass-roots fervour did for a few years throw up its due crop of brilliant talent, as with football in Brazil or cricket in the West Indies, and in the late 1960s Olympic medallists such as Jean-Claude Killy and the Goitschell sisters were as popular as any film-stars – 'In a way, they're our

Beatles,' one fan told me. In the 1970s, though skiing is more widely popular than ever, there have not been any new great stars. But these things often go in mysterious cycles – witness the decline of English football and Australian swimming during the same period.

For many years public participation in sports was limited by lack of equipment. More recently, the State and town councils have at least made a big effort to provide public swimming pools, and nearly every little town now boasts its *piscine municipale chauffée*. But there is still a shortage of sports grounds, especially in the Grands Ensembles, and only very recently has sport in schools begun to be taken seriously. The past years have seen some interesting new ventures ('snow classes' for poorer children, and State-subsidized skiing holidays for young workers), but funds are limited, and there are frequent complaints on the Left that all the best ski-runs are falling into the hands of property tycoons who charge high prices and are at pains to keep out *hoi polloi*.

Some of these arguments apply to holiday-making as a whole. One person in five in the eighteen-to-thirty-four age-bracket has still not yet been away on holiday in his life, and often it is because he feels he cannot afford it. The Government, it is true, has been making growing efforts to create cheap holiday-villages and hostels in deserted rural areas, and to develop *colonies de vacances* under trained monitors for poorer children, whose parents cannot afford holidays *en famille*. More than a million children visit these *colonies* annually: you find them all along French beaches in summer, a touching and slightly pathetic sight. But far more public money is needed for what is called 'social tourism'.

If only the French public could be induced to spread its holidays over a longer period of the year, fuller and more effective use could be made of such cheap tourist amenities as do exist. Many of the hostels and camps within the range of modest families are over-subscribed in August and at Christmas, and empty most of the rest of the time. Yet many a Frenchman will stay at home rather than change his habits. Holiday-making in August is typically one of those rooted French traditions that is proving hard to alter, however unrealistic and irksome it grows as the tourist numbers swell each year. Some 80 per cent of French summer holidays are taken between 15 July and 31 August against 70 per cent in Britain and 61 per cent in Germany.

Anyone who has lived in Paris knows how the city goes to sleep that month. It is the time that tradesmen in particular choose for their annual bolt to the country. You can stroll pleasantly in empty streets and even park your car, but your favourite *bistrot* will probably have closed, and in some districts you may find it hard to get a hair-cut, or shoes repaired, or even to buy food. In the prosperous classes, mothers and children generally depart for six or eight weeks at a stretch leaving breadwinners behind for part of the time in silent flats, possibly up to no good. The nation's business slows to a crawl, and those who are still at work often pretend to their friends they are not there. Until recently, in the upper bourgeoisie it used to be such a sign of failure to stay in Paris in August that spinsters in genteel poverty would sometimes spend the month like hermits behind closed shutters rather than show that they could not afford to leave.

Meanwhile the summer traffic-jams and casualties mount up on the tourist routes, and hoteliers faced with spiralling costs find they can no longer balance their budget with so short a season. This is probably the gravest of the problems facing the French hotel industry, which has been in crisis for several years. It has been affected also by staff shortages and by the camping vogue. Even foreign tourists in France spend more nights in camps than in hotels. To meet this vicious circle the Government has given loans for modernization, and thousands of hotels have carried this out: but they have also used it as an excuse to double or treble their prices, and the Government has failed to stop them. But French hotel prices (at least for shared rooms) are still well below the absurd English ones.

A State-led campaign for the wider staggering of holidays has made a small amount of progress in the past few years. The percentage of people starting their holidays before 27 June or after 28 August has risen from 12·7 to 14·6 since 1969. But these results have been only mediocre. Although a few big firms have been induced to close their plants in July rather than August, most others, notably Renault, have refused to do so, for apparently valid commercial reasons, and hardly any will follow the foreign pattern of keeping plants open and staggering their own staff holidays. The Ministry of Education in 1965–8 tried the experiment of staggering school summer holidays, making them start ten days earlier in the north than the south. But the scheme ran up against varied opposition, and was abandoned. Now the Government's emphasis, both for school and for industry, is on a different kind of seasonal staggering: between summer and winter. Since 1970 the school year has been redivided, with two long semesters on the German or American pattern, and a fortnight's holiday in February. Industrial workers too, under a new law, are being encouraged to take at least part of their holiday in February. It is hoped that the growing popularity of skiing will make this scheme attractive – and that at least part of the August crush will be channelled away, not to June or September as originally hoped, but to the winter.

Independently of any State initiative, in central Paris itself an increasing number of theatres, shops and restaurants have come to realize what lucrative tourist trade they lose by closing all August: today, no less than twenty-six of the city's forty-odd theatres are still open that month. But in the suburbs, where there are no tourists, the blinds are still down. The main obstacle to staggering now is purely that of habit. The French are individualist about nothing so much as the right to share the same herdlike conventions and habits.

Hitherto the French have always seemed a sedentary people, each attached to his *petit coin*, seldom venturing to live and work in a new town, returning year after year for holidays in the same quiet places, and rarely touring outside France. Now they are smitten with a new restlessness. The holiday craze is one symptom of this; another is the much greater readiness to migrate to other parts of France. Many professional people are becoming, like Americans, unable to stay in the same place for two days together. Ring up a businessman, even quite a lowly one, and he is sure to be just back from Bordeaux, or just off to Geneva, or on the point of driving his family 200 miles for a short week-end. Much of this is sheer nervous energy, the near-hysterical discovery of the joys of a mobile society. 'Where are you going this Easter week-end?' I asked a Parisian journalist recently. 'I'll drive to Spain, I think,' he said, while ten years ago it might have been Fontainebleau – 'and my dentist is driving to Prague for Easter, and my lawyer's taking his mini-bus to Nice.'

This can be seen, too, in the French passion for their cars. Few people in Europe are so car-mad. Not only do they have the highest level of car-ownership in Europe after Sweden, but they react emotionally to cars as to women: '*Une voiture, Monsieur, est comme une femme,*' my *garagiste* once told me when I complained that my Renault's performance was varying mysteriously from day to day. The French like to drive fast when they get the chance, using their brakes a lot and taking chances. The price they pay is a high accident rate: by 1973 it was some 16,000 deaths a year, over twice the British fatality rate per car-mile and about the same as Germany's. Drink is a frequent cause and big posters of the national road safety campaign remind motorists along main roads, '*L'alcool tue – surtout à 100 à l'heure*' – but the penalties against drunkenness while driving are less severe than in many countries. In 1969 the regulations were tightened in an attempt to reduce accidents, and safety-belts were made compulsory on all new cars. After the 1973 energy crisis, France like many countries introduced new speed limits, initially with the aim of saving petrol. But these were found also to be reducing the accident rate, so they were maintained even when the oil scarcity threat eased. Today the limits are 130 k.p.h. on motorways, 110 on dual carriageways, 90 on ordinary country roads. Fines are stiff, and are usually exacted by the police in cash on the spot. In serious cases, the driver's licence is removed on the spot and he has to complete his journey by some other means. The public has reacted quite well to these measures, and the French are now driving with noticeably more prudence than before 1973. The toll of fatal accidents was down to 13,170 for 1975.

Snobberies about certain makes of car go deep and have their own elaborate and shifting scales of values. Foreign cars are smart: their share of the market has been rising steadily to over

21 per cent. Some British cars have snob-value, Bentleys, Triumphs and even Minis; Jaguars are now a shade vulgar. Mercedes also score high, and have ousted Cadillacs and Chevrolets as the prestige family saloon car. Among French cars, Citroën and Peugeot have most cachet. Though Panhard and Renault were among the great pioneers, the French today care little for veteran cars, a hobby they leave to the quaint English. They prefer modern cars: and though they often do not bother to keep them properly polished or to repair scratches, they are fascinated by speed, power and elegance of line. The buying of sports cars is a craze among the rich. Alfa-Romeo is the most popular make followed by Triumph, Ford Mustang, Porsche, Ferrari and Maserati. It seems no coincidence that the hero of that archetypal modern romantic French film, *Un Homme et une femme*, was a Mustang racing-driver. It all fits in with the world of *Elle* and La Siesta's flaming torches.

WELFARE, HEALTH, ALCOHOLISM AND THE SOCIAL MISFITS

And so this society goes racing ahead in its Citroëns and Alfa-Romeos, towards new horizons of Mediterranean holidays, week-end cottages, emancipated birth-control, amusing new restaurants, and fashions from *Elle*. But what of those who are not in the race? Even in the United States, there are plenty who fail to compete in the drive for prosperity – the aged, the ill, the misfits, the hopelessly poor. In France, as in most Western countries, the State has now formally taken upon itself responsibility for its weaker citizens: it performs this duty with uneven results. In some sectors, Social Security has made huge strides forward since the war; in others it lags, and so do several aspects of social justice.

In the early part of this century France was slower than some of her neighbours to develop social legislation. But there was progress in the 1930s, culminating in 1939 in the family allowances that have played such a part in French post-war resurgence. On paper France's Social Security today looks extremely impressive: its budget accounts for 19·8 per cent of national income, a lower figure than in Germany (22·7) but higher than Britain's 17·4 per cent. Yet in practice the French welfare State probably works a little less efficiently than the British: it was conceived on too ambitious a scale, and since then has been frequently obstructed by vested interests such as doctors and rival private insurance schemes. But the Gaullists must take the credit for having greatly improved Social Security. In the first decade of the Fifth Republic its budget rose much faster than national production, and due to a mixture of State over-generosity and bureaucratic mismanagement it was even allowed to build up a serious deficit. By 1976 this had reached the colossal figure of 8,000 million francs a year and was causing serious worry to the Government. Plans were announced for making economies in the service and demanding higher contributions from the public. In France, employers pay more than two-thirds of the cost of social security, while employees pay only twenty per cent.

These economies have not however altered the general framework of the Social Security system, of which the family allowances are still the strongest feature. So great is the Government's desire to keep the birth-rate high that if you have only one child you get no help; allowances start with the second child, and run at about thirty to forty francs a week for each. In addition, a wife and mother gets a generous allowance if she forgoes a job and devotes herself to the home. Over three million families comprising eight million children benefit from these bonanzas, and 1·3 million families also receive State housing allowances, financed by a direct levy on employers. One typical home I visited in a new HLM was drawing 180 francs a week in allowances, equal to nearly half the husband's net wages: 90 francs for the three children, another 50 because the wife did not work, and 40 francs rent subsidy.

Since the nations of the Nine are committed to harmonizing gradually their various Social Security schemes, where possible at the level of the highest, France's partners have been struggling to improve their family allowances while France tries to make up for her lag in unemployment benefits and pensions. There has been so little unemployment in France since the war that the low level of benefits has not been a great issue, save to those unhappy few who *did* find themselves out of a job. Now a National Employment Fund, first set up in 1963 and greatly extended since the economic crisis began in 1974, helps to retain, resettle and compensate redundant workers in declining industries. A worker made redundant for economic reasons can claim up to 90 per cent of his salary in compensation for the ensuing year. The Fund's *raison d'être*, like that of the family subsidies, is forward-looking and practical as much as humane; if, however, you are very old and so have little value for the nation's economic future, you do much less well out of Social Security.

Old-age pensions have been among the worst of any advanced European country. The Gaullists greatly increased them after 1961, but from such a low initial level that today many people over sixty-five are still living on the official minimum of 610 francs a month. Traditionally old people are provided for by their children in France, and often live with them; but for obvious reasons this tradition is dying, except in some rural areas. Big families are breaking up, and younger people are too busily engaged in their own struggle for better homes, jobs and children's education. According to one recent survey, only one person in ten now around sixty expects help from his relatives in his final years; and of those over sixty, 30 per cent are living quite alone and only 24 per cent with their children. In Britain, although the sense of family is less strong, as many as 40 per cent of old people are living with relatives; and the State does more, too, to help the rest.

Some 2 per cent of French old people are living in State or charitable homes for the aged, where conditions are often grim. Many others eke out an existence on their own, often obliged to keep on part-time jobs well beyond sixty-five in order to supplement their pensions. Those who live on their pensions alone can rarely afford meat, or new clothes, or proper heating, or any kind of entertainment. In terms of Social Security, the crux of the problem is that a proper pension insurance scheme started only in 1945, and today's aged have therefore paid few contributions. It is the formerly self-employed who have had least protection of all, and only after a public inquiry in 1961 had revealed the full depths of their misery were their pensions raised to the present minimum.

Occasionally an article in a Left-wing paper describes in lurid terms what it is like to be old and poor in France. But on the whole this is not a problem that troubles the public's conscience greatly, apart from that of a few religious and charitable bodies who do what they can with limited means. I do not deny that the Government has some conscience, and has been making efforts; but although France's five-and-a-half million over-sixty-fives all have the vote, they do not form an organized lobby like vine-growers or small shopkeepers, and so their problems are not a high electoral priority.

The national health service began, as in Britain, just after the war. Its basic difference from the British system is that the patient pays the doctor direct for each consultation, and has to apply afterwards to his local Social Security *caisse* for a refund, like paying your garage for repairs and then claiming from insurance. And throughout the 1950s this gave rise to growing abuses, as doctors began to charge three or four times the admittedly very low sum of 3·2 francs that the *caisses* were then authorized to refund. In 1960 the Government agreed to revise this figure, by now quite out of touch with economic reality; and it tried to get the doctors on their side to agree to a new fixed scale of charges. The powerful medical union said no. So the Government, to its great credit, sidestepped the union and began to fix agreements with individual doctors. Enough doctors collaborated for the Government to be able to win its trial of strength with the union, who backed down. Today some 90 per cent of all French GPs belong to the service (the rest have private patients), and they are allowed to charge the quite handsome fees (in Paris) of 32 francs for a surgery consultation and 42 for a bedside one – it is a little less in the provinces. Seventy-five per cent of this, and of pre-scription charges, is reimbursed by the *caisses* after a week or two – and after a great deal of bureaucratic form-filling.

The health service in France is therefore not entirely free, but this extra 25 per cent does possibly dissuade people from con-sulting their doctors unnecessarily. Even so, though they are well paid, most doctors today are frantically harassed and overworked, and they complain that their prestige has dropped now that they are little more than civil servants, with most interesting medicine in the hands of a few specialists. All this will be familiar enough to an English GP's ears. Many French doctors work a sixty- or seventy-hour week.

Another problem is that the building of new hospitals has not kept pace with urban growth, especially in the Paris area: many hospitals are old-fashioned and overcrowded, and standards of nursing and of hygiene are not always as high as they might be. French nurses, who are also in short supply, are not famous for their bedside charm.

As in other countries, improved living conditions and medical care have brought a reduction in infant mortality, tuberculosis, poliomyelitis and similar diseases and there has also been a certain decline in that most notorious of all French social scourges, alcoholism. A vigorous official campaign against alcoholism ever since 1954 appears to have borne some results, but it is extremely hard to tell just how much. On the one hand there are several encouraging signs: the huge increase in the consumption of soft drinks, the apparent disaffection of the younger generation for their parents' style of heavy drinking, and the decline in inveterate alcoholic café-going. On the other hand deaths from cirrhosis of the liver or sheer alcoholic excess still run steady at about 22,000 a year, though as these are nearly all old people, it can of course be argued that this figure relates more to past habits than to present ones. The more encouraging fact is that French alcoholic consumption per head has been declining steadily: it dropped about 13 per cent from 1951 to 1969, and the Italians have now overtaken the French as the world's heaviest consumers of alcohol. No other nation is seriously in the running – the American with his Bourbon and dry Martinis downs only 8·2 litres of alcohol a year, and the English beer-drinker a mere 7·1. And prosperity in France has bought an improvement in the quality of what is drunk: consumption of champagne, whisky and vintage wines has soared, while that of the old liver-rotting strong coarse wines and *eaux-de-vie* has dropped.

It was Pierre Mendès-France who as Prime Minister in 1954

first gave official status to the anti-alcohol campaign, and won himself a good deal of derision for his milk-drinking image. But the High Committee he founded for 'study and information on alcoholism', attached to the Prime Minister's office, is still very active and seems to have done something to wean the new generation away from the traditional French ideas that wines and spirits are actively good for the health and that not to drink is unmanly. The Committee prompted the distribution to school-children of five million blotters, and much other literature, which did not advocate teetotalism but warned against excess. The blotters almost led to civil war in wine-growing areas like the Hérault, where even today the anti-anti-alcohol lobby puts up posters on the main road, 'Wine is the healthiest of drinks, said Pasteur'. But the campaign may have made some impact: according to one recent survey, only 38 per cent of young people still think wine is essential to health.

Meanwhile, several anti-alcohol measures have been pushed through Parliament recently. One, strongly fought by the wine lobby, forbids the sale of strong drink in public to children under twelve: it is frequently winked at, notably in the case of wine served with meals, but it does limit the kind of thing that horrified me when I first lived in France, the sight of babes of two and three being encouraged by their fathers in cafés to drink whole glasses of undiluted wine. Another Act restricts the frequency of cafés in new suburbs and in the vicinity of factories and schools.

The problem is still huge, mainly in older slum districts and in backward rural areas such as Brittany. You see few merry drunkards on the streets in France, because wine and *eau-de-vie* do not have that kind of effect, they strike deeper; and the French are heavy drinkers not through neurosis or unhappiness like many Anglo-Saxons but from sheer ancestral habit. It is reckoned that a million French adult males, or one in fifteen, drink more than two litres of red wine a day, and another three million drink more than the litre a day that the doctors generously concede as a safe maximum for a manual worker. Some 1,700,000 adults are medically classified as alcoholics; two thirds of the nation's 450,000 mentally handicapped children are born of alcoholics; and 75 per cent of Parisian delinquency and 50 per cent of road accidents are said to be due to alcoholism or excessive drinking. The annual cost of alcoholism to the State, in terms of medical and social care and loss of production, has been put at 25,000m francs, three times what the state earns from taxes on alcohol. And yet, in a land where four million people derive their living from the wine and spirits trade, every step towards reform, whether by raising taxes or cutting production, is frantically opposed. Often the wine lobby will invoke the most lofty national sentiments to defend its interests. 'It is wine that enabled the French private soldier to win the Great War,' said a deputy in Parliament, while in the same debate a duke from the Armagnac region claimed: 'Wine is the glory of our civilization – vine leaves adorn the capitals of our cathedrals.' Such speakers always invoke the idyll of the innocent small farmer.

One dubious idyll is now definitely ending – that of the *bouilleurs de cru*, or home-distillers. These are the two million farmers who have traditionally had the right to produce for their own consumption up to ten litres of tax-free *eau-de-vie* each year from fruit-trees on their property or from the *marc* (pulp) of their wine-harvest. Many have always distilled secretly a great deal more than ten litres, and a total of some 400,000 hecto-litres (ten million gallons) is believed to have found its way illicitly on to the market each year, bringing tidy profits both to farmers and to racketeering middlemen. Mendès-France was one of those who tried, in vain, to bring the *bouilleurs* to justice: he found the lobby against him too powerful, and in some of the wilder apple-growing regions of Normandy and Brittany it seemed that everyone, even policemen, priests and politicians, was involved in the racket. But in 1960 the Gaullists managed to steamroller through Parliament a law that empowered them to act by decree: and they decreed that henceforth the home-distilling privilege would no longer be passed on by inheritance or sale of property, but must end with the death of its possessor and so gradually die out. *Bouilleurs* are now dying off at the rate of some 50,000 a year. This will not automatically end the illicit distilling, but will make it easier to detect.

However, 70 per cent of alcoholism in France is due not to *eau-de-vie* but to red wine. And it is worst, strangely enough, not in the wine-growing regions of the South but in Brittany and Normandy, and in some wild upland areas such as Savoy. In Brittany the alcoholic death-rate is eight times the national average, and many men drink a gallon of red wine a day. One of the problems is that, in poorer districts, much social and even economic life revolves round this habit: business transactions are regularly conducted over a litre of *rouge* in a café, and in one fishing port a merchant navy doctor had to set up his dispensary in a café. There are Breton villages where the coinage for repaying small services is often a bottle of wine.

Alcoholism is therefore a quite different kind of problem in France from Britain or America. It is essentially connected with social backwardness in rural and slum areas, and is nourished by the extreme cheapness of strong red wine and of crude brandy. Among sophisticated people, excessive drinking of whisky or cognac through stress or neurosis or social habit is probably much less common than in many countries. The best hope therefore is that urbanization, education and improved housing will gradually limit the evil of their own accord. Already, in the middle classes, the convention that no meal is complete without wine is beginning to fade, and often in restaurants you see people sitting down with their *quart de Perrier* or just plain *eau nature*. From 1959 to 1969 consumption of mineral waters rose 99 per cent and of fruit juices 760 per cent! Fruit juice is twice as expensive per glass as cheap wine, which limits its sales in the poorer classes, but in the middle class this gives it a prestige appeal. Vermouth sales are lower than fifteen years ago; but *anisette*, after a decline in the 1950s, has been making a come-back. The biggest advances have been made by the smart drinks – champagne, and especially Scotch whisky, which is now drunk almost as widely as in England.

The sum of these trends suggests that the French, although they may not be drinking much less than before, are at least turning away from fire-water to more sophisticated and less destructive drinks, without having yet taken to that nastiest of all fire-waters, gin. No one, or hardly anyone, demands that the French should become teetotal – this has never been the aim of the anti-alcoholism campaigns. No one denies that the great wines of Burgundy, Bordeaux and Champagne are among France's foremost gifts to civilization. But there is a difference between half-a-bottle of Vosne-Romanée, enjoyed over a good meal, and the Breton hospital wards overflowing with cirrhosis cases and mental defectives.

Along with combating alcoholism, the Government has been making efforts to clear up shanty-towns and vagabondage, but is finding the task Sisyphean. The growth of shanty-towns (*bidon-villes*) is quite a new phenomenon of the past two decades, and is due almost entirely to the arrival of foreign workers.* Often they cannot find proper homes, and so they have been settling in encampments of shacks and disused vehicles outside the main cities. Fifty thousand of them now live in these *bidonvilles*, four-fifths in the Paris area, most of them Portuguese or Algerians. One camp, in the suburb of Champigny, houses 10,000 Portuguese, many of them women and children. They live without drains or electricity, on waste land deep in mud. The Government has been making efforts to resettle them, and claims to have rehoused about 1,500 a year since 1965 in special communal hostels. The families are often glad of the chance to move, but the single workers consider it an affront to their pride, and many prefer to stay where they are.

The tramps or *clochards* present a different kind of problem – save that they, too, proudly resist attempts to integrate them into society. There are some 3,000 in Paris alone, it is reckoned, who are *clochards* by choice, liking the life, hating regular work, and hating above all to sleep in a bed; only a minority have become tramps temporarily through unhappiness, breakdown or unemployment. Usually they despise society and want it to leave them alone; they rarely steal, and are too proud to beg. Really they are quite innocuous, apart from their lack of hygiene and their unsightliness, as they lie huddled on the pavements or slouch along the *quais* tippling their bottles of *rouge*. Many are alcoholics. One Paris *clochard* was a Foreign Legion officer, another a Tsarist colonel, a third an intellectual who even as a *clochard* would give *alfresco* lectures on philosophy in the Latin Quarter for the price of a bottle of wine. Many have been poets or artists. One recently

* See pp. 705–6.

came into a legacy of 100,000 francs but preferred to remain a *clochard*. The police periodically round them up and take them off to an official hostel where they are deloused and forcibly given a shower – a supreme affront to their dignity. This happens to the average tramp about twice a year; but if he can prove means of subsistence, as he usually can (from pensions or odd jobs), the police have no right to hold him. Recently some Right-wing deputies made moves to suppress the *clochards*. But the bill that would have made vagabondage in itself a crime was narrowly defeated. The life of blissful monotony can go on.

But for the rest of France there is no blissful monotony. Unlike the *clochards*, the French are being compelled to march with the times and, as this chapter has tried to show, it involves the upheaval of some of the oldest French traditions and possibly the loss of some of those things most precious about France. The dilemmas are acute: how to adapt to the new while preserving the best of the old – and nowhere is this so apparent as in the changing role of French youth and in the struggle now engaged between reformers and conservers over the proud and classical French concept of education. This is the subject of my next chapter.

Chapter 10

YOUTH DEMANDS AN ANSWER

It was in the corridors of the new Préfecture building near the Bastille, one day in 1965, that I had my own Gibbonian moment of awareness of the rise of a huge new generation in France. Usually one expects French public offices to be filled with shuffling, elderly bureaucrats and messengers, spun about with the cobwebs of the Third Republic. Suddenly in this new annexe, as the clock struck noon for lunch, I was besieged by hundreds of clerks and typists, few of them over thirty. Visibly I saw confirmation of the statistics: there are more than twice as many people under twenty-five in France today as in 1939, although the population has risen only 27 per cent. In many offices the old *huissiers* with their stained suits and sad faces are being replaced by sleek young *hôtesses* with public-relations smiles.

Every Frenchman today professes his faith in *la jeunesse. Une France jeune – soyez jeune – il faut l'esprit jeune –* the phrases tumble daily from the mouths of politicians and the pages of glossy magazines, as though youth were synonymous with virtue. In a country previously dominated by the prerogatives of age and hierarchy, this marks a striking change of heart. '*We* may have failed – but *les jeunes*, they are serious, they are made of good stuff, they will do better than us': this is a comment you sometimes hear from older people still ashamed of the defeats of recent decades. Until 1968 this new generation was reticent and elusive, and few older people, even parents and teachers, claimed to know what it was really like. Their faith in it was based more on hopeful thinking than on reason. Then came the May revolution, and suddenly an entirely different image of French youth was uncovered. Many adults were horrified: 'Youth is *pourri* after all,' they said – while others were encouraged: 'At last, youth has emerged from its docility and shown it's got guts!' But after the dust of May had settled, it became clear that the militants – the so-called *enragés* – were only a minority, and the rest were still something of an enigma; less reserved than before, and readier to shout their grievances, but still mysterious, a world apart.

For many years youth has been given more public attention than ever before in France. And in its name a great national debate on education is now raging. Ever since the war, the highly traditional structure of French schools and universities has been under repeated reform on a scale unparalleled since Napoleon. And since 1968 this movement has intensified.

REFORM IN THE CLASSROOM: LESS HUMANITIES, MORE HUMANITY?

'In *Andromaque*, did Racine respect the rule of the three unities?' A sixteen-year-old at the back of the room, in tieless shirt and informal jersey, stands up and gives the perfect formal answer, with four carefully numbered logical points, exegesis and peroration, just the way he's been taught. The rest of the class, also in a motley of informal dress, listens quietly; the boy sits down, and the teacher resumes his own brilliant didactic performance, tripping his way through the subtleties of literary analysis as only a Sorbonne *agrégé* can. Outside the sun falls on an austere and silent courtyard. It could be any *lycée* (at least, until 1968) – and you can be sure that if one *lycée* class is studying *Andromaque* at a given hour of the week, then a thousand are doing so at the same moment, throughout the French cultural empire from Tahiti to South Kensington.

Much of the best and the worst in the French national spirit can be imputed to this concept of education as inspired academic pedagogy limited to the classroom walls. Teaching has always been deductive, rhetorical, formal, preoccupied with style and expression; the teacher (at least until the 1968 crisis) has seldom had real personal contact with his pupils, and his concern has been to train their intellects. The *lycées* have traditionally provided a bourgeois minority with the loftiest academic disciplining in the world; they have moulded a cultured élite where technocrats can turn to any problem with the same clarity they were taught to apply to Racine, and where literature and the arts have flowered naturally in a society indoctrinated with belief in their supremacy. Scientists and classicists alike in the *lycées* have been given such a strong dose of the same '*culture générale*' till the age of nineteen that in later life they can always find a common language, and so the divorce of the two cultures is less serious a problem than in Britain. Even poorer children, though largely absent from the *lycées*, are put through sufficiently rigorous mental hoops in their junior schools for a foreigner to be frequently impressed by the French working man's articulateness and grasp of ideas.

Long before 1968, this system had come increasingly under criticism for being undemocratic, over-classical, and generally unsuited to the broader needs of a technological age: even the excellent principle of *culture générale* came under fire for its old-fashioned syllabus and didactic methods. Reforms were taking place, but inadequately; many pupils felt that their schooling was out of touch with real life, and this feeling lay behind the May explosion which was quite as violent in the *lycées* as in the universities. Since then, the *lycée* world has remained in some confusion. Whereas primary education is now running fairly smoothly, and whereas the May crisis provoked the Government into an immediate shake-up of the universities, it was slower to deal with the *lycées*, which are only now being overhauled, with reforms due to come into force in 1977.

Between 1945 and 1968 a group of liberal-minded experts in the Ministry of Education managed to push a few innovations between the Scylla of State parsimony and vacillation, and the Charybdis of teachers' conservatism. Some of these measures were frankly utilitarian (to provide the economy with more technicians) but others were humane: to broaden access to the *lycées* and technical colleges, to modernize teaching methods, and to lighten the severities of the fearsome examination system.

Eighty per cent of French schools are run by the State,* on the same highly centralized civil-service basis as *préfectures* or post offices; this makes reform much easier to decide in principle than in Britain but often harder to apply in practice, for it has to be imposed from above rather than proceeding naturally by ground-

* The remainder are still mostly in the hands of the Church (see p. 575).

swell movement from area to area. And the teaching profession, who mostly vote Left but in practice have found it hard to accept change, have never taken kindly to measures imposed by a Rightist government without consulting them properly. It has therefore proved much easier to make purely administrative changes, concerning new types of school or examination, than to alter the spirit and attitudes of French teaching.

Much of the State's effort before 1968 was concentrated on the largely material problems of trying to keep pace with the post-1944 baby-boom, with the growing public thirst for more education and with the nation's need for more specialists. In quantitative terms, the State's record in this period was not too bad. Its budget for education grew nearly sixfold in 1952–68, in real terms; over four million children are today in secondary schools, against 300,000 in 1939; and some 35 per cent of French children are still under education at eighteen, three times the British figure. The raising of the minimum leaving age from fourteen to sixteen was gradually implemented during the 1960s, coming fully into force around 1970. Some children do still leave at fifteen, but only if they join an apprentice training scheme that includes some schoolwork. Despite this progress, there are still big gaps to be filled in junior technical education. Plenty of not-so-bright children are still being thrown into jobs without vocational preparation, through lack of the means of training them.

A deeper-rooted problem is that education still exhibits a striking class-distinction basis. And the barrier is not so much one of money as of custom. Though the *lycées* offer mainly free tuition and in theory are open to all, in practice the most distinguished of them such as the Louis-le-Grand or the Jeanson-de-Sailly in Paris are nearly as much a preserve of a certain class as the £1200-a-year English public schools. There has been less democratization than in post-war Britain; and as only a *lycée* or a private school prepares for the *baccalauréat* or university entrance exam, higher education more or less remains a middle-class monopoly: in 1959, only 3·8 per cent of university students were from working-class homes, and, though by 1973 this figure had risen to 12·5 per cent, it was still far behind that of Britain (30 per cent). In some *lycées* it is the teachers who maintain a snobbish bias against admitting workers' children, but more often it is the workers who exclude themselves, whether for social or financial reasons: a worker may feel, with reason, that his son will lack the right kind of cultured home background to be at ease in the rarefied *lycée* atmosphere, and even though tuition is free, there are always extras such as books, meals and transport.

There have always been brilliant exceptions, it is true, including the present Minister of Education himself, René Haby, son of a penniless widow, who through sheer guts and brilliance worked his way up via a teacher-training college to win that prized higher diploma, the *agrégation*. And today, certainly, as the better-paid skilled workers develop new aspirations, so the number of working-class children in *lycées* is far greater than twenty years ago. But social barriers of this kind are always hard to crack in France without an official helping hand. And so, in an effort to hasten the equalizing process, the Government in 1963 adopted the most controversial of all pre-1968 school reforms: in future, it decreed, there would be only one type of State school for all children, rich and poor, between eleven and fifteen.

Hitherto, though children from all social backgrounds attended the same State or Church primary schools, at the age of eleven the *lycées* took their own privileged stream while the rest went to junior secondary schools where they either left at fourteen or fifteen or, if they were lucky, went on to some kind of technical college. Under the 1963 reform, the junior classes in *lycées* and the old junior secondary schools were gradually to lose their old identities and become merged into a network of new comprehensives for eleven-to-fifteens, the Collèges d'Enseignement Secondaire. Selection from these for entry to the *lycées* at fifteen is not by exam but by teachers' recommendation and school record: thus a bright working-class child has four years' more time and probably more serious encouragement than before to make the jump to a *lycée*.

There are now some 3,000 Collèges d'Enseignement Secondaire, or CES, of which over half are new schools, specially built, equipped and staffed over the past ten years. Of the rest, some 540 are transformed junior sections of *lycées*, still housed in the *lycée* buildings. Others are former junior secondary schools, similarly adapted. About three-quarters of the children in the relevant age-group are now in CES rather than the old type of school. So the process is not yet complete, but it is making progress; and at least in the case of the purpose-built CES it seems to be working quite well. I visited one in a suburb of Montpellier that impressed me a lot: the headmaster, a vigorous young ex-*lycée* teacher, was excited by his experiment and said that about half his children, from varying backgrounds, were going on to *lycées:* 'We're out to destroy the social snob status of the *lycée*, and that's a good thing.'

Like the comprehensive schools in Britain, and for similar reasons, the CES have run into strong opposition – mostly from the *lycées* and from bourgeois parents. Many of the latter were scared that *lycée* entrance would now become harder and less automatic for their less bright children, who would be streamed into despised technical careers. And many *lycée* teachers were worried that the bright children now to come to them only at fifteen might not have been taught properly in the CES and that standards would drop. So the *lycées*, with the backing of middle-class parents, made a bid to keep some control over their junior classes. And to an extent they succeeded. Under a compromise solution reached in the 1960s, though these junior classes had to follow the curriculum and teaching methods common to all CES, they could retain some links with their parent *lycée*. In the case of some of the more brilliant *lycées* in larger towns, this has helped to ensure higher standards and more continuity for the brighter children. But it maintains social discrimination. In practice, opportunities are still not equal. It is still easier to get into a *lycée* if you enter a CES attached to it, and you come from the right background. Indeed, it is hardly surprising that the powerful French upper bourgeoisie and its teacher allies have found ways of preserving some of their class strongholds. But they will have to face a new assault from the Haby reforms of 1977.

Another feature of French education has been the emphasis set on written examinations, on class marks awarded weekly for academic progress, and on sheer brain-slogging even at a very young age. A child has been under pressure from his teacher and maybe from his parents to outshine his rivals, and when he falls a few places down the class's ladder, he is in disgrace. It is a system that often inhibits the less bright child, and though it may encourage the clever ones to achieve their very best, it can also induce intellectual snobbery. It has even been held responsible for some of the rivalries and discords in French adult society.

In the years after the war an experiment in less severe and old-fashioned teaching methods was carried out by a remarkable lady called Madame l'Inspectrice-Générale Hatinguais, who might be described as the Jean Monnet of modern French education. The basis of her scheme was to do away with written exams as far as possible for young children. And so great was her influence that in 1957 the Government pushed one jump ahead of Britain and abolished the French equivalent of the Eleven Plus, the *lycée* entrance examination at eleven. This exam had been much criticized for its academicism and for the level of abstract intelligence it expected: one question in the general paper of 1956 invited eleven-year-olds to comment on the philosophical significance of a passage from Gide in which he described how, as a boy, he once let a favourite marble roll into a crack in the wall, so he grew one finger-nail to a huge length to be able to winkle it out again, only to have lost interest in the marble by the time the nail was long enough, so he bit it off again.

The exam-free system has since been extended to the CES where children for all their four years go through a *cycle d'observation et d'orientation:* a careful dossier is kept of their record, and they are streamed towards either *lycées* or technical schools, with plenty of flexibility to allow for late developers. Those whose studies end with leaving the CES take a voluntary leaving exam; others pass on to their next school without exam if their record is good enough. It is a system that depends on having smallish classes and capable teachers, and appears to have been working reasonably well and producing a more relaxed atmosphere.

Madame Hatinguais also elaborated a number of direct and audio-visual teaching methods, using film, tape-recorders and so on. Many of these have won official blessing, but attempts to introduce them widely have not proved easy, so alien are they to the French academic tradition. The progressive headmaster of a primary school near Paris told me: 'I've tried to introduce new methods here, but my staff, young and old alike, aren't interested. They'd rather go on in the old ways. I've got a handsome new tape-recorder, but I'm the only person who uses it for teaching.' It is the usual French problem of a small number of pioneers fighting against general apathy or conservatism. A major difficulty is that, though primary teachers are in reasonable supply, their calibre and their prestige has been falling. This profession used to be the summit of ambition for a bright working-class child, and the best way of entry into the white-collar middle class via the Ecole Normale; today he is more likely to try for a better-paid technical job in industry and often regards teaching as a last resort. The same headmaster told me: 'Primary teaching only attracts the dregs nowadays – and what do you expect, with the salaries they get? One of my staff resigned because he was earning much less than his wife, an anaesthetist, and felt humiliated.' This idealist was exaggerating the picture a little: primary-school salaries have increased in real terms by over 50 per cent in the past ten years, and now run from 2,119 to 3,981 francs a month according to age. But that is little more than half what an *agrégé lycée*-teacher gets. And the decline in teaching quality was one reason why the pre-1968 school reforms were not more effective.

Although the academic burden of the under-fifteens was lightened in the 1960s, in the senior classes of *lycées* it remained oppressive and was one of the factors behind the 1968 revolt. Here every minute of life is still lived in the shadow of that most sacred and imperious of French institutions, the *baccalauréat*. Taken at eighteen or nineteen, *le bac* is a far more rigorous and brain-searching exam than its rough English equivalent, A-level GCE, and even more essential a passport to success. With the *bac*, a student has traditionally had the right to enrol in any faculty of any French university; without it, all the gates of higher education are barred. As more and more middle-class people come to prize a degree, so more of them try for the *bac*, and the faculties swell uncontrollably. It has been described as the national obsession of the middle classes, dividing the French into two camps, *bacheliers* and non-*bacheliers*; and though the exams are controlled as fairly and strictly as possible, there have been notorious cases since the war of parents paying high prices to bribe examiners or secure advance copies of papers. The French word for cramming is *bachotage*; and hundreds of private fee-paying *boîtes à bachot* have sprung up to cram those who find the large *lycée* classes too impersonal. And of course, the more people of mediocre intelligence try for the *bac*, the higher the failure rate, aggravated by larger classes and declining teaching standards in some *lycées*. Those who fail have not only acquired a stigma and possibly a complex for life; they have spent three or four years on an unvocational academic syllabus that leaves them untrained for anything else and with few other educational outlets. They are lucky to get much more than a mediocre job, as clerk or salesman. And this sheer wastage of national resources has prompted growing demands for reform of the *bac* from many people, except those *lycée*-teachers whose heads are in the sand.

In an earlier age, the rhetorical classicism of preparations for the *bac* was possibly ideal for training a ruling élite of lawyers, technocrats and men of letters. Even today, given the right kind of teacher, its syllabus has many noble virtues as a mental grounding for the more gifted child. And the greatest of these, in principle, has always been its insistence on a high level of *culture générale* rather than early specialization. This was so whether you took a classical or a scientific option. Prior to the 1965 reforms the main option on the arts side, known as *le bac philo*, contained a severe dosage of some nine hours' philosophy a week but also no less than five hours of science; and the principal maths and science options ('*math-élém*' and '*sciences-ex*' in *lycée* jargon) each had nine or more hours a week of philosophy and other arts subjects, as well as a rigorous thirteen to seventeen hours of physics, biology, or higher mathematics. While a typical essay subject in the *bac philo* exam might be, 'Do we find anything in perception that assures us about the reality of its object?', even a *sciences-ex* candidate in his philosophy paper might be expected to tackle, 'Can liberty be conceived when there is no reasonable choice?' No wonder the French scientist or engineer is often a man of such high personal culture, more so than his Anglo-Saxon counterpart.

But the syllabus, and notably the rhetorical and deductive methods of teaching, have tended to develop a turn of mind that is conformist, theoretical and often uncreative, schooled to think and verbalize with great clarity along predetermined lines. And although a brilliant pupil may be able to master the system and contribute his own originality, others get submerged. Doubts have been growing as to whether this pre-*bac* pressure-feeding is the best way to train the imagination, and whether a classical diet of logic and moral philosophy (Descartes, Plato, Kant) is the right initiation for the entire élite of a modern nation. 'I am horrified,' writes one *lycée*-teacher, 'at the hatred that today's young people feel for Racine and Corneille. And oh! those November mornings we spend crossing the Alps with Hannibal.'

For the past fifteen years the air has been heavy with reform. In the early 1960s measures and counter-measures flowed from a vacillating Ministry in a bewildering stream, alienating even those teachers who were sympathetic to change. The syllabus was altered three times, ostensibly with the aim of lightening it. Finally in 1965 the Minister, Christian Fouchet, began to apply wider reforms. Their aim was to make the *bac* more vocational and less encyclopedic. The syllabus and the options were re-arranged and modernized. Economics, sociology and statistics were at last recognized as subjects worthy of a *lycéen's* study, and they went into a new 'modern' option together with maths, history and geography. In the *bac philo*, there is now less philosophy, and more literature for its own sake and modern languages. French literature no longer stops at 1900: it reaches to Sartre and beyond.

This up-dating of the syllabus on the arts side was generally welcomed by students themselves and by the more liberal teachers. But on the science side in particular the changes carried a more controversial corollary: earlier specialization. The science and maths options were shorn of some of their philosophy teaching. And, since 1965, no longer does any option grant entry to any faculty: if you take the *bac philo* you are now unable to enrol in a science faculty except with special permission. Thus at seventeen or eighteen a student has to decide almost irrevocably what path he wants to follow for life. The aim of the reform was not solely to lessen the range of encyclopedic study and bring the *bac* closer to modern life: it was also frankly utilitarian, to force scientists to get down to their own subjects earlier, and to oblige students to be less dilettante about their choice of university work. It was a step away from the tradition of *culture générale* – for this it was much criticized, both before and after 1968. So much so, that a back-pedalling move in 1972–3 reformed the *bac* yet again, and specialization was retarded by a year.

Another change in the *bac*, less controversial, institutes a new lower-grade pass certificate for those who average 40 per cent in their papers but fail to reach the 50 per cent that will be needed for university entrance and for the title of *bachelier*. This is a right step and should reduce the wastage, so long as employers can be persuaded to regard the new pass as some qualification. At present, even the full *bac* rarely opens many office-doors in itself, unless followed by a degree or technical diploma. And industry has severely lacked middle-grade technicians with this kind of diploma.

The shortage of technicians may seem paradoxical when set beside the high prestige of the technologist in France and of the Grandes Ecoles that train him after the *bac*. But this prestige belongs only to an élite and ends abruptly below a certain level. An upper-bourgeois family will be proud for their son to take the *bac math-élém* or *sciences-ex* if it leads the way to a Grande Ecole and a noble career as engineer or technocrat; but they will turn up their noses at his going instead to one of the new *lycées techniques* and taking the *bac technique*, a far more practical workshop exam leading to a middle-grade technical career. Yet the failure rate for the prestige *bacs* is high, and few of the throw-outs are trained for much else. At a big *lycée* in Paris I visited a class immersed in the final strained weeks of cramming for the *math-élém*, and their teacher told me: 'Most of these poor kids will fail. They'll end up in clerical jobs or small commerce. Few of them have the minds for this high-quality theoretical work: they'd have done better in a technical stream, if only their silly parents had let them.' Then the school's *censeur* or disciplinary assistant, a woman from a modest family, told me: 'My son went happily to a *lycée technique* and from there to an electronics college, and now in his blue-collar job he's doing better than most of these kids ever will.' So the bourgeoisie is caught in its own snooty trap. But the human wastage and disappointment is great, and the official aim now is to stream more of the beta-plus minds at an early age away from the élite obstacle race and into technical education.

Most of these reforms were still in the process of being applied when the 1968 crisis erupted. Even before 1968 most teachers had reluctantly come to accept the need for change, although many of them still dug their heels in when it came to applying the details in practice. Had there been more trust between State and teachers, the reforms might have been more effective more quickly. But the Ministry, in typical Gaullist manner, tended to decree new measures high-handedly without consultation, in order to avoid argument and obstruction. It was a short-sighted policy that sometimes defeated its own ends. And the pupils were the victims. Their wrath finally exploded in 1968 – against the teaching methods, and also against the whole atmosphere surrounding their education.

Anyone who visited an average French school before 1968 may have been struck by the rarity of informal human contact between teacher and child, and by the relative absence of a sense of warm, human community where the full personality could be developed. The French themselves have become more aware of it, and of how over the years it has aggravated some of the negative traits of their national character. But it's been something even less amenable to legislation than the deductive *ex cathedra* teaching methods so closely bound up with it. Efforts at change have always run into various obstacles: the ingrained unconcern of many teachers for anything but their pupil's intellects; the monolithic State system, ill suited to a matter as delicate and personal as bringing up a child; and the swelling size of many schools, which increases their bureaucracy. It has required a major uprising – that of 1968 – for the French to be shaken into rethinking the whole system.

In any State school the smallest departure from routine, such as an extra half-holiday, could not, before 1968, be fixed without written orders from Paris; and the precise duties of each member of staff were governed by a statute from the Ministry that could not easily be departed from to suit individual needs except by the usual French methods of subterfuge. In the large *lycées* the civil-service atmosphere reached its height, where teachers stood on rigid ceremony and were called by their formal titles – '*Oui, Monsieur le Proviseur*', '*Non, Madame le Censeur*' – by pupils and colleagues alike. Inevitably most teachers have tended to lack initiative and to behave and think like the civil servants they are. Sometimes an energetic or liberal headmaster would succeed in infusing his school with a certain personality of its own without actually defying the Ministry. But this became harder as the *lycées* swelled in size, to 2,000 pupils or more: 'just pedagogic factories', as someone put it, with even less community spirit and humanizing influence than they had before the war.

In 1965 I visited a superb-looking new girls' *lycée* at Nîmes, a real showpiece, with modern sculpture and gay murals, sunny, attractive rooms and fine equipment. No child, I felt, could fail to benefit from such a setting. But the atmosphere! The Directrice, a plump, elderly tartar of the old school, a Queen Victoria in looks and outlook, resisted efforts by some of her younger staff to introduce clubs or hobbies or social activities, or give the girls any responsibility for disciplining themselves. They were there simply to be taught and kept in order. The largest hall in the school held 350, but numbers had swelled to 1,500 so that any ceremony, such as prize-giving or a school concert, that might help to give some community feeling was virtually impossible. The girls arrived in the morning, received their dose of academicism, and went back home. And the teachers did likewise.

Lycée-teachers work hard, to be sure, and may have to spend several hours each evening in term-time correcting pupils' essays, so rigorous is the academic routine. This leaves few of them with much time, or incentive, for sponsoring out-of-class activities. For the average *professeur* it is a kind of office job: he arrives, delivers his series of lectures, maybe with donnish brilliance, and goes home. Discipline, or the children's out-of-school lives, are not his business. Discipline in a *lycée* has always been in the hands of a non-teaching and usually not highly educated member of staff, the *censeur*, a sort of sergeant-major, assisted by a team of *surveillants*, usually unqualified youngsters of twenty or so earning a little pocket-money while they complete their own studies. They have seen that the boarders keep out of mischief, but it has not been their job to inculcate group spirit or help with character-building.

Usually therefore a *lycéen* will have no one at school to whom he feels he could turn for personal advice or comfort; and if his home life is not easy, this may be a real lack. In primary schools the pattern is much the same as in *lycées*: teaching is scarcely less magistral, and classroom discipline is strict but negative. A class has to line up in order at the end of each lesson before it can leave the room or be dismissed. Only the exceptional teacher will try to break through the wall of formality dividing him from his class, while the bad ones resort to petty tyranny. Truffaut's semi-autobiographical film *Les Quatre-Cent Coups* gave an extreme but not impossible account of what life can be like for a sensitive child (with an unhappy home) at a bad primary school. The obverse of this solemn picture is that at most schools French children are really made to work, and they spend less time than in many countries ragging their masters or being given an amusing time. But these are rarely the happiest days of their lives. For what it is worth, a scientific opinion survey* conducted in 1960 among fourteen-year-olds in several Western countries found that the percentage of those who 'did not like school much' was 26 in France, 14 in Britain, 9 in the U.S.A., and of those who 'liked it a lot', 23 in France, 34 in Britain, 33 in the U.S.A. Whether the purpose of school is to make children happy or make them learn is a matter for the educationalists: it seems to me, as a layman, that both should be possible, given the right sort of teacher.

In France the failures have been largely the fault of the teachers and the system. French children are not especially different from any others, and many of them privately hanker for some more personal encouragement and human contact at school. One eager young *professeur de lycée* told me: 'I find that when I do make the running and express warmth they are very responsive. It's usually the teacher's reserve that drives children to become afraid and suspicious of them.' The American sociologist

* Published by the Institut Français d'Opinion Publique, 1961.

Jesse Pitts has analysed this problem: 'The French teacher makes relatively few allowances for the interests and fantasies of youth. Typically, he ignores his students' needs as children. He often talks to pupils of eleven to twelve years old on a level which supposes an intellectual maturity that they are far from having reached.'* Pitts goes on to explain that the children react by outwardly accepting the teacher's authority but secretly developing among themselves their own 'delinquent community' which rejects and fights against the adult world. The school system represses the child's character, or forces it into private rebellious paths rather than encouraging it to grow as part of a community. And it hardly needs Mr Pitts to tell us how this marks the French for life. Much of the egotism and friction, the lack of civic feeling, and the private loyalties among sectional interests, spring from attitudes inherited at school. One main cause of this state of affairs is that traditionally it is the family, not the school, that is supposed to train character. Parents look on school as a facility, which is not supposed to compete with them as a centre of loyalty; and when a school does try to encourage group activities, or when a teacher goes out of his way to help a child, they often resent it as an intrusion on their own sphere.

In the past few years, a nagging feeling has grown among educationalists that some kind of change is needed – not towards the outmoded English cold-showers-and-fagging system (in its way, almost as austere as the French), but at least towards more out-of-class activities, towards making school life gayer and more varied. For a start, practical steps were taken before 1968 to encourage more sport in schools – more, it is true, for reasons of health and fitness than for Arnoldian ones. All *lycées* are now supposed to have five hours' compulsory sport and physical training a week, and the *bac* itself contains an obligatory gymnastics test. But many schools are still handicapped by lack of suitable playing fields or gymnasia, and the sports staff generally have low prestige compared with the academics, so that unless the instructor is really good the children use the classes as an opportunity to fool about. In primary schools, there was virtually no sport until very recently. At one school I was told: 'An instructor

* *France: Change and Tradition,* pp. 254–5.

comes to give classes once a week, but the kids treat it as a joke and prance around the courtyard with him.' I thought of that hilarious scene in *Les Quatre-Cent Coups* where the boys slip off to play truant in the streets of Montmartre behind the back of the daftly prancing gym teacher. Since 1969, however, the number of hours devoted to classroom teaching in primary schools has been reduced, and the weekly ration of 'physical exercise' increased from two hours to six. The results vary from school to school. In some, the new regulations are being carried out constructively; but many are handicapped, like the *lycées*, by lack of facilities and suitable teachers. In the *lycées* there is only one instructor on average for every 240 pupils. Because of this shortage, the official aim of five hours of sport and physical training a week has never been achieved; the average in fact is less than two-and-a-half hours.

A more imaginative development, though still limited in scope, is the *classes de neige*. Every winter some 70,000 children aged about eleven, mostly from big cities, are transported for a month with their teachers to hostels or cheap hotels in the Alps where they carry on with their normal school work mixed in with afternoons on the ski-slopes. The initiative and the finance has come mostly from town councils rather than the Government: some towns, notably Communist-controlled Le Havre, have even built special centres in the far-distant Alps, to use in winter for snow classes and in summer as workers' holiday camps. The operation is a success and the children, many of whom would not otherwise have holidays, benefit hugely. Such changes show the signs of a crack in the old formula of all work and no play. Sport has increased so rapidly in popularity since the war that even teachers and parents are beginning to accept it as not such a waste of school time after all.

Tentative attempts have also been made to introduce more clubs and cultural activities into some schools. But this has faced opposition from older teachers who regard such things as frivolous and a threat to academic standards. In one of the most distinguished of Paris *lycées*, the Henri IV, the staff prevented the students from forming an orchestra because it might make noise during school hours, and a drama club in the same school foundered after two months because none of the staff was pre-pared to help run it. French schoolchildren lived in such awe of their teachers – at least until 1968 – that they generally lacked the initiative to start such things themselves, unless helped officially. And a teacher who showed too much interest in clubs was often *mal vu* by his headmaster. Fortunately, some of the younger ones went ahead undeterred: at the girls' *lycée* in Nîmes, a charming young woman classics teacher told me: 'The Directrice dis-approves of clubs – but I did finally persuade her to let me form a kind of literary society. I asked the girls to prepare an exhibition on Camus. They were absolutely thrilled; they wrote to firms in Paris for books, films and cuttings, and one of them, a *pied noir*, went to immense trouble to collect material about Camus' Algerian background. It proved to me that French children do enjoy this kind of extra-class activity, so long as their teacher gives them a lead.'

The disparity between such activities in France and elsewhere is astonishing. According to the survey I quoted earlier, in France 11 per cent of fourteen-year-olds have a drama group in their school against 76 per cent in Britain and 78 in the United States. For a school orchestra, the percentages are France 8, Britain 46, U.S.A. 83; for a newspaper partly edited by the children, France 4, Britain 34, U.S.A. 64. 'But,' the French may retort, 'just look at the difference between French and American academic standards in schools.' Surely it should be possible to strike a balance?

Teacher opposition has been one part of the problem: lack of funds was another, for the State, needless to say, has always put out-of-class activities near the bottom of its priorities. *Lycées*, even good ones, usually lack even a proper library; the head-master gets no special funds for the purpose, so new books can be acquired only through parents' donations or the children's own modest subscriptions. And many teachers are quite glad there should not be too many foreign or modern classics around to distract pupils from their real work. Better Kant and Molière, who are on the syllabus, than Pasternak or Faulkner. I am also amazed, in this land of culture, at the lack of time devoted to music and visual arts in the curriculum. Every *lycée* has its music room: as often as not it is locked and silent, in contrast to the sounds of piano and part-song that echo round schools in Britain or Germany. No wonder that French musical life is in crisis and Malraux was forced to admit that the French are not a musical nation. Art, in the land of the Impressionists, the adopted land of Picasso, scarcely fares better. The number of hours devoted to it in *lycées* has been falling, and few pupils over sixteen study any art at all. In one large Paris *lycée* where the art-room in mid-morning was totally deserted, I was told: 'There used to be three art teachers here, now there are two and one may soon be sacked.' As art and music feature hardly at all in the *bac*, they can safely be neglected. The Fouchet reforms ordained a new specialized arts option, a superb idea in theory; but it is restricted in practice to a few of the more cultured *lycées*. In junior schools, where there is no *bac*-fever, a little more attention is paid to these subjects, but less than in many countries. Teachers, when criticized, usually lay the blame on parents' lack of interest. Parents merely want their children to pass exams, and will not press for more art and music until these play more part in exams. And the victim of this vicious circle is French creative culture, recently in decline.*

My final criticism of the French school system, as it was on the eve of the 1968 crisis, concerns the lack of practical training in democracy or leadership – either on American lines where a school becomes a parliament-in-embryo, or as in Britain where seniors become responsible for the discipline of juniors. There are classroom lessons in civics and government but, as one teacher said to me: 'Though we teach them about how Parliament and the communes work, we give them little chance to try it all out in practice. We tell them about Prefects; you make them into prefects. Maybe in England your school prefects have too much power; here, children aren't given enough.' Actual discipline has always been left, in class, to the teacher, and outside it to the *surveillant*, and has been restricted to preventing mischief.

This problem too began to worry the pioneers in the Ministry, and even before 1968 a few tentative attempts at reform were made, such as the setting up of joint consultative committees of staff and 'delegate' pupils – much on the paternalist lines of the *comités d'entreprise* in industry! These proved mainly ineffectual.

* See pp. 588 and 627–30.

The masters were very much in charge, and in stuffier schools the delegates were told sharply, 'Your place here is to listen, not to talk.' But not only the teachers have been to blame. One of the basic obstacles to the development of training in leadership and responsibility has been, and still is, the attitude of parents who see it as usurpation of their own duties. Many a parent would find it intolerable for his little Pierre to be bossed around at school by the son of a neighbour, perhaps considered socially inferior. All French children are equal in law: therefore all must have equal status in the same school – however unequal the opportunities of getting there!

Such, broadly, was the situation in French schools before May 1968. Since then all has been in such confusion that it is difficult to generalize. What is clear, however, is that nothing will ever be quite the same again.

Long before May *lycéens* had been growing restive. There were even a few sporadic demonstrations and short strikes in some places. When in May the Paris university students launched their revolt, *lycéens* all over the country were quick to follow them. Small politically minded groups formed a national *comité d'action des lycéens* which proved as militant as the students. Thousands of other *lycéens*, less political, joined in either because of their scholastic grievances or just for the hell of it. Amazing scenes took place, hardly believable in this staid *milieu* where schoolchildren had usually been seen and not heard. Many *lycées* were 'occupied' by their pupils, like the factories by workers, and red and black flags hoisted over them. Teachers no longer dared sit at their rostra, but either fled the classroom or, the more liberal of them, sat for hours each day on the benches beside their striking pupils, discussing school, politics, sex, careers, life. 'I never knew my girls before except as minds; now I know them as people,' one young woman teacher told me. *Lycéens* suddenly discovered in themselves a social and political awareness that before had been barely latent; and although many reacted stupidly, some showed a remarkable maturity. Parents, invited to take part in the impromptu *lycée* debates, were in some cases astonished to hear thoughtful and persuasive public orations from their own sons and daughters – how the babes had grown up! Other parents, worried above all that the *bac* might not take place and a precious career be jeopardized, sometimes hit back brutally: 'When some parents entered the *lycée*,' teachers told me in one school, 'we had physically to prevent them from setting on their children and beating them up.' Finally however the *bac* did take place, in a sort of way, and the holidays began. Some *lycéens* went off quietly to the seaside with their parents and calmed down; but others, filled with a new fire, embarked on strange projects – I met several, one only fifteen, who planned to spend the summer touring round France spreading the gospel to peasants and workers, like the Bolsheviks after 1917. My favourite anecdote comes from a girls' *lycée* in Paris at the moment of its 'liberation' by a crowd of male invaders from a near-by boys' *lycée*: the main foyer was filled with excited schoolboys calling the girls out on strike, and in their midst was the Directrice, a tiny, round, elderly figure, totally bewildered, clutching at the jacket of a *lycéen* leader, a wild hippy figure towering above her, and imploring him: 'Mais non, Monsieur, je ne refuse *pas* le dialogue! Je ne le refuse *pas*!'

The revolt did indeed open a new 'dialogue' between certain teachers and their pupils, after the decades of indifference; and when the astute Edgar Faure became Minister in July he set about trying to build on this. He was concerned that the ills of the *lycées* could not be cured by reforms *à la* Fouchet of exams and cycles of study; there must now be a more profound overhaul of teaching methods, of teacher-pupil relations, centralized bureaucracy and so on – the fundamental problems, structural and psychological, which were hardest to solve by legislation. So Faure's *loi d'orientation* of 1968–9 provided for relatively few changes in programmes or curricula. His aim was to exploit the idealistic upsurge of May, and to create from it a more human spirit in the *lycées*. Alas, this has not proved any too easy.

His main emphasis was on institutionalizing the teacher-pupil 'dialogue'. And his foremost reform was the setting up of democratic governing boards (*conseils d'administration*) in each *lycée* and CEG. Each board is made up one sixth of parents, one sixth of senior boys or girls (elected by the pupils themselves), and the

remaining two thirds of staff, Ministry officials and local dignitaries, mostly elected but some appointed. The board has no
powers over curricula and exams, which remain in Ministry
hands; but it can virtually dictate to the headmaster a wide range
of decisions concerning the internal running of the *lycée*, the use of
its budget, teaching methods and discipline, and the vexed issue of
weekly class marks. The boards were set up at the end of 1968 and
their success has varied hugely from school to school. Where
there is a strong headmaster, the board is sometimes little more
than a cipher in his hands. In some other cases co-operation is
smooth. In others there is chaos, and some headmasters have been
driven to resigning, with the complaint that their authority has
been destroyed. One liberal-minded *proviseur* of a large Paris
lycée told me: 'My board has become politicized, and in true
French style has split up into little intransigent pressure-groups;
they argue for hours and never get anywhere. I was certainly in
favour of changing the old system, but nothing valid's yet been
put in its place.' The reform is a worthy attempt to decentralize
certain powers away from the Ministry which previously controlled every detail of routine in a school, down to the buying of
blotters. It is also an attempt to give the pupils a sense of sharing
in the running of the school – but this has not yet worked too
well. The extreme-Left pupils (who include some of the brightest)
boycott the boards. In some other cases pupil delegates are
virtually co-opted by an authoritarian headmaster and have
little influence. It could indeed be argued that these cumbersome
'school parliaments' where pupils are in a small minority are not
the right answer to the problems of teaching responsibility and
leadership, but are simply one further demonstration of the
French *penchant* for legalism and institutions. But at least they
are a step away from too much centralism.

   The climate of classroom life, and day-to-day contacts between
teachers and pupils, remained variable and tense after the
anxious *rentrée* of September 1968. The foremost legacy of May
is that pupils have abandoned their former sullen defensiveness
and are now more open and outspoken. They interrupt *cours
magistraux* to ask questions, they make demands on their
teachers and contest their authority. In some cases this has led

to more honest and informal relations; in others, to sterile conflict. A minority of *lycéens*, perhaps 5 per cent, have remained aggressively political since May, calling themselves Maoists, Guevarists and so on, and not hiding their aim of destroying the whole system. They put up posters (which they are allowed to do) and scrawl violent slogans everywhere, so that even the calmest *lycée* may give the superficial appearance of anarchy. In some cases there have been strikes and riots, leading to temporary closures of *lycées*: at the distinguished Louis-le-Grand *lycée* in the Quartier Latin ten schoolboys were injured in May 1969 when a grenade exploded in a scuffle between Left- and Right-wing factions. Although such incidents are rare, and largely confined to a few politically sensitive *lycées* in central Paris, they reflect a general mood of disquiet throughout France.

Teachers have reacted to the new situation in various ways. The conservatives have either sought to reimpose their authority in class, sometimes with success; or else they have given up the unequal struggle and their classes proceed in chaos. 'I can't teach them anything any more – they just shout and won't listen,' one teacher told me; 'ungrateful little bastards, after the years of my life I've given them!' Other teachers, mainly the younger ones, are trying to come to terms with their pupils' new mood and to create from it something positive. They are now putting less accent on the *cours magistral* and more on question-and-answer teaching and work in groups. Sometimes their human contact with pupils is much easier than before, and both sides are glad that the barriers were cracked in the violence of May. Generally it is in the senior classes, especially those cramming for the *bac* or for Grande Ecole entrance, that work proceeds most seriously; lower down the school there is more disorder and less work.

Some *lycées* have swung from one authoritarian extreme to the other of permissiveness. A not illiberal woman teacher in a girls' *lycée* in Paris told me in 1972: 'The girls talk and smoke in class, even in the *bac* classes – it's impossible to control them. If you put your foot down, there's simply a riot or a walk-out. The headmistress makes little effort to impose her authority – she's been given orders by the Ministry to avoid trouble at all costs. I don't want to sound too old-fashioned, but there's been a huge increase in what you might call "vulgarity" – girls playing the guitar in the corridors and so on. The positive aspect is that the old prison-like austerity has gone and the girls are happier than they used to be.'

Outside class, too, there has been a marked relaxing of discipline with sometimes good and sometimes bad results. In a further effort to give the pupils more responsibility Edgar Faure cut down the work of the *surveillants*, and ordained that each *lycée* should have a kind of socio-cultural centre run by the pupils themselves and used for their clubs and other activities. But the *lycéens* have not shown great eagerness to take control of these officially imposed centres, which generally lack the funds and premises for being effective. 'We go to our centre just to smoke and play pop records,' said one *lycéenne* (senior pupils can now smoke in school – except in class, officially!). Other *lycées* simply lack the space facilities for these centres. At the hugely over-crowded Lycée Fermat in Toulouse (3,250 boys), it has been hard to find any room to give the boys for their *foyer educatif*, and the headmaster has shown little interest in providing one. A master told me, 'With great difficulty we've managed to start up a school theatre group and a school newspaper since 1968 – two plusses of the May revolt – but there are no official funds for them. And in a school as over-swollen as ours, is it surprising that there's no sense of community at all? It's just a factory. Two of our masters met by chance on holiday in Istanbul recently and were surprised to find they worked in the same school. They didn't even know each other by sight.'

The decline in the role of the *surveillant* means that the elected head of each class has rather more duties than before: previously he did little but collect exercise books for teacher, now he is expected to keep some order when a teacher is not present. But there is still no attempt to establish any kind of prefect system, and French schoolboys are still remarkably reluctant to impose discipline on their fellows in the name of the school authority. '*Nous ne sommes pas des flics*' (we're not cops) said one; 'it's not our role to dole out punishments.' Pupils have received no preparation for this kind of responsibility, which is alien to the long French school tradition. One or two experiments in a new kind of school community system were made even before 1968, but tended to run into difficulties. At Briançon in the Alps an ambitious scheme was attempted in a *lycée* with a high percentage of boarders from disturbed home backgrounds: the headmaster* tried to create a more humane and easy-going atmosphere by doing away with formal punishment, putting the boys on their honour to behave, and appointing each senior boy as a kind of 'moral tutor' to three juniors, to see that they dressed and behaved properly and were happy – an inspired kind of fagging system in reverse! The scheme was welcomed by the boys at first and worked quite well for two or three years. Finally it broke down because too many seniors abused it and showed little aptitude for it – and also because of parental opposition to this encroachment on their own role.

In 1973, under a new Minister of Education, Joseph Fontanet, an interesting new attempt was made to add extra-curricular variety to school life. Instead of all schools following the same routines, each was now to be allowed to spend ten per cent of working hours in any way it pleased, preferably on non-academic activities. But the experiment has met with only very patchy success. In some cases, enterprising staff have managed to do something worth-while with the new free time. For example, at a *lycée* in Grenoble, 400 pupils and staff spent a week of the ten-week term living with farmers in mountain villages. But in a great many schools, the teachers themselves have opposed the new scheme, through fear that it would lead to lowering of academic standards, or out of inertia, because they dislike having to think up new ideas, or else from opposition on principle to any innovation coming from the Ministry. And as the new scheme is not fully compulsory but remains at the discretion of staff, in some schools it has been virtually abandoned, or else is carried on intermittently in those classes where the teacher is in favour. Some teachers do take their pupils to visit local factories, museums, or other places of interest, or they organize discussions or other projects in the classroom. But as no extra funds have been

* André Rouède: see his book on the subject, *Le lycée impossible* (Le Seuil, 1967).

allotted for the new scheme, scope is limited. And few are the French teachers who are ready to put their heart into the kind of activity that in countries such as Britain is usually considered a normal part of the job. 'It's the usual French problem,' one headmaster told me, 'teachers complain about State control, but then have no idea how to use freedom when they are given it. They lack any initiative, except in making protests.'

By the mid-1970s, the post-May agitation in the *lycées* had largely died down. Teachers found that the new generation of schoolchildren was much more docile and ready to work quite hard, without abusing the relative new freedom that had mostly replaced the old authoritarianism. But the *lycéens* did seem to be lacking in enthusiasm. A teacher in Toulouse told me in 1974: 'They give us the impression that they are not interested in school, they come here just to pass exams, and real life for them is what they get outside, from travel, television, relationships, political activity. The old system had its faults, but there was a certain spirit, which now has gone.' And a pupil at a smart Paris *lycée* told *Le Monde*: 'This place for me is like a supermarket; I come for what I can get out of it, but I feel no attachment.'

During the early 1970s it came to be recognized that secondary education was in need of an overhaul at least as drastic as that which Faure had applied to the universities. Lesser *ad hoc* reforms, like the new schools councils or the 'ten per cent', were not enough. The *lycées* needed to be brought much closer to modern life. Some radical proposals were formulated, notably by a State-appointed commission led by Louis Joxe; but Pompidou, ex-*lycée* teacher, showed himself a conservative in education matters, and by the time of his death in 1974 no serious attempt at change had been made. When Giscard came to power, he at once made it clear that he regarded a new deal for education as a major part of his blueprint for an 'advanced liberal society'. He made a surprise choice of Education Minister, René Haby, a university rector of great force and ability but with no direct experience of politics, and told him to prepare a new master plan. This was hurried through Parliament in 1975 and, despite the varied oppositions it inevitably aroused, was due to come into application in September 1977.

Haby decided that it was necessary to start at the bottom, and to change not only the secondary system but also primary and even nursery schooling. His reforms aim to provide greater equality of opportunity at all stages. First, there is now to be much closer liaison between teaching methods and courses in the voluntary nursery schools and in the primary ones. Then, from the age of six when they enter primary school, right up to sixteen when they either end their education or go on to a *lycée*, all French children will follow exactly the same kind of courses, and these will be far less academic than before. All children, of whatever background, will learn some manual skills, and there will be a greater accent than before on sport, the sciences, and the plastic arts. 'All children will now receive a very concrete, non-theoretical kind of education – quite a revolution for France,' said one educationalist. Some schools had already started to apply these methods before 1977: I met the thirteen-year-old son of a senior civil servant who was doing compulsory carpentry and cookery at his CES. After sixteen, pupils will either leave school and in many cases go to some apprenticeship scheme, or they will go to one of two types of *lycée*, academic or technical. Here too there will be a common curriculum up until the last two years before the *bac*, and it is only in the year of the *bac* itself that real specialization will begin. The *bac* is to be made more flexible, so that instead of the present rigorous streaming into '*philo*', '*math-élém*', etc., it will be possible as in Britain to sit for an interdisciplinary mixture of subjects – for instance, science, economics and languages, which could be useful for many business careers. The only subjects that will remain compulsory right up to the *bac* are physical training and – that most cherished of French disciplines – philosophy. The traditionalists regard this as a certain victory.

The reforms have run into some systematic opposition from the Left, and from those teachers and parents who fear that any change is bound to be for the worse. One liberal professor commented on this: 'People are always complaining about the "degradation" of the system, yet they admit that on the whole there has been progress over the past fifteen years. Even the Communists admit this.' Many people are simply bewildered by the spate of contradictory reforms and tinkerings over the past twenty years and are sceptical as to whether the latest will really produce any final solution. It does at least seem likely to provide more equal opportunity, and to bring school education closer to the needs of modern life. But this could be at a certain cost to academic standards. And, although the new technical *lycées* (a merger of the old *lycées techniques* and junior technical schools) will probably provide for better blue-collar training, it is far from certain that enough provision has yet been made for vocational training for those leaving school at sixteen. Above all, the new reforms in the *lycées* will require the right kind of teachers, with new attitudes. And this remains the great weakness. What needs changing most in the *lycée* system is probably less the syllabus than the methods – the magistral discourse, the lack of inductive inquiry, the reliance on set texts. This French tradition has produced results over the decades that in many ways are most impressive: a verbal finesse, a sophistication of thought and language, which has meant that young people can discourse easily about abstract ideas and make natural use of words like *spiritualité*, *sensibilité*, *poésie*, that embarrass an Englishman. But it can also lead, especially among intellectuals* and bureaucrats, to a frightening orthodoxy.

The old *lycée* system has gone, with all its grandeurs and horrors. Only now, nearly a decade after May 1968, is a coherent attempt being made to put a new system in its place. And this cannot succeed without a new kind of teacher, ready to apply new methods. Inside class and out of it, the key to the whole schools problem lies with the teachers themselves. Most are far more aware of the need for change than before 1968. But their handicap is partly their own lack of the right kind of training. They were taught purely to instil academic virtues into their pupils, and few have much knowledge of modern methods, of psychology, or of what might broadly be called education for civics and leisure. Realizing this, Edgar Faure pledged an overhaul of teacher-training which is now being applied. The normal system, which is based on an academic degree course within universities, is to end; in its place there will be new, more vocational colleges attached

* See p. 552.

to the universities, putting their stress on modern pedagogic training. This will bring the French system closer to that of Britain. The reform has been hotly opposed over several years by the die-hards, but the first colleges are expected to open in 1977. Meantime, there are still some years of confusion ahead, with the pupils themselves as the chief victims. Most recent reforms in education appear to be in the right direction. But – apart from a vague new egalitarianism – no coherent ideal has yet emerged to replace the old élitist one that is doomed. As they reluctantly dismantle parts of their perfectionist academic assault course, have the French really thought out, even now, what kind of humane education, in the broadest sense, they want to put in its place?

UNIVERSITIES: FAURE'S REBUILDING AFTER THE EARTHQUAKE

The great student uprising of May 1968 was led by a number of revolutionary extremists – Cohn-Bendit and others – who were set on destroying capitalist society. They stole most of the limelight, but they were not fully representative. The mass of students who joined their revolt did not want to destroy society *in toto*, so much as to remodel the archaic structure of the French university system. They were protesting, vehemently, against the meagreness of their study conditions, the remoteness and high-handedness of their professors, the tedium of their academic routines, the lack of career outlets.

Cohn-Bendit and his friends lost *their* political revolution, at least for the short-term. But the milder students who followed the extremists seem to be winning *theirs*, or some of it. The revolt did succeed in cracking the foundations of the French temple of higher learning and in shocking the Government into rethinking the universities on an entirely new pattern. Edgar Faure soon set about applying radical reforms. The old centralized State system has been dismantled since 1968 and all universities have been created anew, from the bottom up, on a model closer to Anglo-Saxon ones. For the first time in post-Napoleonic history, they now have a fair measure of autonomy. Less stress is now set on

exams and formal lectures, more on human contacts, group work
and interpenetration of disciplines. The reforms have not
surprisingly encountered obstruction of all sorts, and the Government has had to make concessions. But by and large the new
system is working, and it is regarded as an improvement on the
old one even by many radicals normally anti-Gaullist. It will
appear in history as one of the most revolutionary innovations of
de Gaulle's eleven years in power. Before describing the new situation, let me trace the university *malaise* as it was before 1968.

Even before that year, students in France were frequently
militant in their discontent. They felt they had no means of
expressing grievances except by riots; this was due in no small
part to the lack of direct contact with the teaching staff. Students
found themselves the victims of a long-term crisis of growth and
mutation in higher education. The explosion in university
numbers was not matched adequately by the rise in funds or
changes in methods. Even today, though methods have improved,
funds are still short, and students live on pitiful grants or jostle
for places in overcrowded lecture-rooms and canteens. Plenty
of them should arguably not be at university at all.

Apart from a few private colleges, all higher education is the
responsibility of the State. And, under this State umbrella, there
has always been a sharp division between the dozen or so élite
Grandes Ecoles, each with some autonomy and strictly limited
entry, and the swollen, amorphous faculties of the universities
where anyone with the *bac* can enrol. The carefully chosen
polytechnicien considers himself in a different world from the
struggling, anonymous student in the university science departments. And so he is, in terms of prestige and training. Even
within the universities, there is a gulf between the utilitarian
degree-hunting of the new student proletariat, and the rarefied
academic *milieu* of professors and post-graduates. As in the
lycées but even more acutely, today's problem in higher education
is how to adapt the rigid élitist traditions of the past to modern
mass needs without too great a sacrifice of quality.

The over-all student population rose from 122,000 in 1839 to
247,000 in 1960, to 612,000 in 1968 and then to about 820,000 in
1976 – more than twice the British figure. Numbers at the Sor-

bonne were at least 160,000 by 1968; at Caen they have multiplied tenfold since 1939, and at Grenoble they have grown since 1952 from 3,800 to over 24,000. More and more middle-class people have come to want degrees, and there has been no legal means of denying any *bachelier* entry to a university. The teaching, always less individual than in Britain, is now a mass industry, and the universities, as someone put it, have become 'no more than student broiler-houses'.

By 1960 the shortage of staff and equipment was at its worst. After this the Gaullists made a big effort and just about managed to keep pace with the growth. The massive appointment of new staff reduced the student-teacher ratio, though it still stands at about fifteen to one, higher than in Britain. Seven new universities were opened before 1968, four of them within range of Paris (at Rouen, Amiens, Reims and Orléans) in an attempt to reduce pressure on the Sorbonne. Several of the older universities were virtually transplanted from their cramped buildings in the centre of towns to huge new American-style campuses on the outskirts. This has helped to ease conditions of work.

In Paris as well, new faculty centres appeared in the suburbs before 1968, at Orsay and the now notorious Nanterre; but the great bulk of the work at this elephantine university still went on within the charmed circle of the Latin Quarter, Mecca of so many young foreigners and provincials, and quintessence of the conflict in modern Paris between turbulent intellectual excitement and tedious physical congestion. A lecture-hall seating 500 is sometimes crammed with twice that number, even today, and some students will even sit through a lecture in a course outside their subject in order to be sure of a seat for the next one. Scientists often fail their exams because study laboratories are too over-crowded. Lodgings and hostels are in short supply, and even a meal in a cheap student canteen may involve a long wait in a queue. So Mecca's glory has been tarnished, and thousands of provincials have come to accept that it might be wiser to stay on their home ground, whatever the excitements of Paris.

The universities have also had to face the issue of whether they are providing the right kind of training and to the right people. More than 40 per cent of those enrolling withdraw without even taking the new short two-year degree; and no more full degrees are awarded than in Britain, for twice the number of students. This flagrant wastage of time and resources suggests that many who enrol should be going straight into jobs or some other kind of training. One reason for the high fall-out is that, although tuition fees are very low, many students are obliged to earn their keep. About 50 per cent get some help from parents, and 10 per cent draw a pre-salary from the Ministry if they are training to be teachers; but only 17 per cent have ordinary grants, and these average a mere 4,000 francs a year. This helps to explain why so many poorer families hesitate to launch their children into the *lycée* stream. Over 30 per cent of students have regular jobs, and mostly these are full-time, for part-time employment is hard to find in France. Some act as sales touts or even night-porters in the markets; many are *surveillants de lycée*, a job that is intellectually undemanding but a strain in other ways. Studies suffer severely.

Thousands of other students are not 'serious'; they enrol as a kind of status-symbol, or in order to be able to make use of the subsidized canteens and hostels, or (if their parents are well off) as a way of passing a pleasant, dilettante year or two before settling down to marriage or a post in the family firm. *Etudiants fantômes* they are called, and they infuriate their teachers. In some universities they account for up to 30 per cent of the student total. At Montpellier, where the problem is especially serious, a professor told me: 'Some 150 students signed up for my class, but I've no idea how many will seriously sit the exams. They drift casually in and out of lectures, as they feel like it. Go down to the beaches in summer, and you'll find them in hordes. It's a racket, a waste of our limited resources, and demoralizing for those who are trying to study properly.' Even among the more dedicated and responsible students, many simply feel out of their depth in a university course. After the close academic supervision of the *lycées*, they enter a world where, at least until 1968, there has been little personal contact between teacher and student; they feel isolated, adrift, bereft of real intellectual guidance in their studies. Many of them suffer breakdowns, or give up, or go on trying and failing the same examination.

Many professors, faced with the ever-swelling numbers in the faculties, have argued that university entrance should be made more difficult. Some would like the pass-mark of the *bac* raised, or a *numerus clausus* imposed with selective entry on the British model. They feel this would keep out many of those not really suited to university education and thus save much suffering and wastage. But not only are the students, jealous of their franchise, opposed to a *numerus clausus*; many progressive-minded professors too, anxious to improve the situation, have nevertheless felt that entry based on the *bac* is the only fair one, and that any other might lead to regional inequalities or the personal bias of selection boards. 'I know we get a lot of un-suitable students,' a young professor at Rennes told me, 'but at least the first year's work, and the weeding-out exam at the end of it, do give the student a chance to *prove to himself* that he shouldn't be there, rather than be told so in advance by some board.' It is an admirably liberal approach, if an expensive one. And this prescriptive right to higher education, for all who pass the same exam, is a rooted French tradition that neither the Fouchet reforms of 1966, nor even the more radical Faure ones, dared tamper with. The Fouchet reforms did, it is true, tighten the entry system a little: those passing the *bac* only at a second attempt could no longer enter automatically but had to face a board. But this did not stop numbers swelling ever more dangerously.

Fouchet also revised radically the cycle of studies and exams. He abolished the previous standard three-year degree course ending in a *licence* and established in its place a new and sharp distinction between 'short' and 'long' higher education. Every-one takes an initial two-year course ending in a diploma (today called the DEUG – *diplôme d'études universitaires générales*), and the aim is to persuade as many as possible to end their studies then. Other students continue, either into a one-year course ending in a *licence*, or into a two-year cycle culminating in a new exam, the *maîtrise*, which opens gates to research or post-graduate work. One aim has been to bring French degrees a little closer to those of other countries. But the principal motive of the reform has been to provide a short, easy course for weaker students and so reduce the wasted effort of those struggling beyond their abilities. At the same time some twenty colleges of an entirely new type have been created since 1966, University Institutes of Technology; they require only the new lower-grade 'pass' of the *bac*, and their purpose is to fill a much-needed gap just below Grande Ecole level by providing some kind of vocational higher education for future middle-rank technicians. Their growth has been slow and their total of students – now some 35,000 – has not been enough to relieve much pressure on the universities.

Basically these were utility reforms, to adapt university courses to the teaching of much larger numbers; inevitably they were criticized for 'trying to get graduates on the cheap' and for being applied incoherently. As with his secondary-school reforms, Fouchet made the mistake of pushing out his decrees piecemeal, with a typically Gaullist disregard for public relations and without consulting the teachers in advance. Had he consulted them, maybe the reforms would never have got through at all, for the university world as a whole, cliquish and suspicious of change, has tended to be a good deal less radical than planners in the Ministry. The reforms, though far from perfect, were a step in the right direction. But the Gaullists' failure to sugar the pill left the teachers angry and confused.

Many professors who accept the need to alter the ordinary degree courses have none the less been worried at the effect the changes might have on academic standards at a much higher level. The DEUG cycle is compulsory for all. Will this not hold back the more brilliant? What of the future of that most cherished of élite exams, the *agrégation*? This is a competitive *concours*, based on a thesis, prepared each year by a few hundred of the ablest post-graduates and corresponding roughly to a B.Litt. Most *agrégés* then make a career in the academic world, either as teachers in the senior classes of *lycées* or as university assistants and lecturers, and they develop a very special mentality. Once he starts preparing his *agrégation*, a student enters that élite academic stratum where values are so very different from those of the 'broiler-house' he has left behind. His contact with his professor at last becomes real, and he sits an exam where only a predetermined number each year are allowed to pass. And this is because the academics who control the exam, themselves all *agrégés*, do not want to devalue the exclusive prestige of their fraternity by widening the gates. Yet the demand for qualified *agrégés* in *lycées* and faculties has been growing fast; and since the number who wish to sit the exam has also been growing, it should be possible to grant more titles without a drop in standards. The professors pursue the argument that 'more means worse', but in reality many of them simply want to keep their own little academic world intact.

Many of those who pass the *agrégation* then try to move on to the next and most fearsome hurdle of all, the *doctorat d'Etat*, essential qualification for a university professor's chair. But whereas the thesis for an *agrégation* is a relatively slight affair, the *doctorat* involves up to ten or fifteen years' work preparing an exhaustive document of maybe 1,000 pages on a highly specialized subject. This usually has to be combined with a teaching job in a *lycée* or faculty, and many people emerge at thirty-five or forty quite worn out. But the final prize is great. A *docteur* who then manages to get elected to a professorship can do exactly what he likes for the rest of his life. He gets a pleasant salary, maybe 75,000 francs a year for what is in effect a part-time job, and need not write another word. All he has to do is give the odd lecture. Many professors still work hard, but others abuse their freedom. Today there is a growing movement, among younger *agrégés* and in the Ministry, in favour of lightening the *doctorat*. In science there may be a case for leaving things as they are, for here the *doctorat* is often a valuable piece of original research. But in the arts it can be absurdly academic and encyclopedic: what the examiners demand is often little more than an exhaustive bibliographical résumé of every published text on the subject, with little original thought involved. But the examiners, themselves *docteurs*, do not want to 'lower standards' or 'devalue the quality of research' by simplifying the thesis; that is, they want others to go through the same mill, and they don't want to share their privileges too widely.

There is much to admire about this high standard of scholarship. The *agrégés* are schooled to a formal clarity of thought and expression which has no equal, and which many of them later pass on in the *lycées* to other future *agrégés*, like monks on

Mount Athos handing down their secrets. Sometimes one of them leaves the monastery, like Jean-Paul Sartre, who began life as a *lycée* teacher. His implacable intellect bears the stamp of this training at its best, but also of its limitations; even he, with his belief in *engagement*, is marked by that divorce from everyday reality that typifies the French academic élite.* Whereas an Oxford don nowadays will readily appear on television, dabble in business or sit on commissions of inquiry, the average Parisian professor maintains a steady scorn for the world of industry, journalism or practical politics. Raymond Aron, who broadcasts, writes for *Le Figaro* and is something of a public figure, is an exception; but people are often surprised when they learn that he also happens to be a university professor. The same applies to Raymond Barre, appointed Prime Minister in August 1976, one of the very rare people whose career has moved to and fro between senior academic and political posts.

In general, though, academics are highly resentful of any intruder from outside, however distinguished: when Pierre Massé, a brilliant *polytechnicien*, gave up his job at the head of the Plan and broke all precedent by giving a course of lectures at the Paris law faculty, the reaction of many law professors was: 'But how *can* he? He's not a *professeur en droit*!' Everyone must abide by his *titre*, no one must poach on another's preserve. This attitude has also made it difficult for the Common Market to progress towards its ideal of harmonizing European degrees and diplomas. French professors are not the only ones at fault, but they are even less interested in equivalent foreign titles than their German or Italian colleagues. And the considerable lack of contact or sympathy between Europe's two greatest centres of learning, on Seine and Isis, is if anything more the fault of the French than the British.

It is true that a growing number of young professors and lecturers are coming to think differently and to form contacts more easily outside their own academic circle – with colleagues abroad, with non-university people in France, even with their own undergraduates. I quote the example of a lecturer in English at Rennes, Charles Lecotteley, who finds time also to be a muni-

* See pp. 544–51.

cipal councillor and the city's effective PRO, to pay frequent visits to its twin-town, Exeter, to play a large part in Anglo-Breton links, and even to stage an annual drama production in English with his students. Lecotteley of course has no ambitions for a doctorate; he would hardly have time. Undoubtedly research and scholarship would suffer if all behaved like Lecotteley; that is the excuse that many professors give for staying in their ivory towers. But the tragedy is that this deliberate abdication from the affairs of the rest of the nation, on the part of most university teachers, deprives French public life of some of the country's highest resources of talent.

The immediate victims of this self-seclusion have been the students. Before 1968 they had even less informal human contact with their teachers than in the *lycées*; and many a professor lecturing to the same class twice a week for a year might get to know the names of no more than a handful of them. A professor at Nancy once talked to me eagerly for an hour about the academic curriculum and its problems, and when at the end I asked: 'And your students – what do they feel about it all? What are they like?' he looked at me in surprise as if I were asking about Martians: 'Oh, *them*: I wouldn't know. You see, they're very secretive.' It is true that most students have tended to be individually secretive and corporately suspicious and aggressive in their attitude to their teachers – but whose fault was it largely? Students were thrown back on themselves: if they wanted to voice their feelings on any subject, instead of being able to stroll across the quad into the Dean's study for a chat over sherry (as at Oxbridge), they were forced into unionized protest action as if they were metal-workers wanting more pay. It was another of France's famous barriers.

Many of the younger university staff have long wanted to modify a system of which they, too, have been prisoners. A few have made real efforts to get to know their students or even to develop Oxbridge-type pastoral links. A sociology professor at Montpellier told me: 'I try to be a kind of moral tutor to some of them in my spare time. I feel they do need me. Sometimes my wife and I have them to dinner.' In some faculties, *groupes de travail* of about thirty to forty students were established even before 1968 under young assistant lecturers, who have a much better chance of making personal contact than the professors with their crowded *conférences*. But the rate of growth of the student population has made it impossible to develop any kind of tutorial system, as some would like; it is not until the *agrégation* that a student works under the close guidance of a professor.

Even in their leisure time, many feel a similar isolation, and this continues today. The paucity of clubs and organized social activity is another feature of French universities that marks them off from Redbrick, let alone Oxbridge. Each university has its student club centre, usually little more than two or three shabby rooms with a bar, a union bureau, a ping-pong table, a pick-up for *sauteries* (dances) on Saturday nights, and a notice-board covered with appeals for digs, part-time work or free lifts to Paris. Students tend to live private lives with their own little group of friends; few have the time, money or inclination for such a luxury as founding an arts or drama club. There are one or two striking exceptions to this pattern: at Nancy, notably, the students in the mid-1960s set up an ambitious cultural network of their own, with encouragement from the Rector. But in most places the authorities make little effort to help by providing premises or leadership. In the provinces, where most students are local and have family or friends close by, the sense of isolation is not always so acute, and the same applies in Paris for students whose homes are there or for a few in the friendlier hostels. But for tens of thousands of others who come to Paris, whether from the Côte d'Or or the Côte d'Ivoire, from Carcassonne or Casablanca, the obverse of the prize of freedom is to be anonymous in the lonely crowd, unable to find any congenial social context. Several of the more shy ones have told me of their acute difficulty in making friends or finding somewhere to belong to except, maybe, religious or politically activist circles. All this remains true today, despite 1968 and the Faure reforms.

The building of the big new provincial and suburban campuses is at least providing the challenge to create something different. These are the student equivalents of the Grands Ensembles, with some of the same social problems. Their inmates no longer live and work in town centres with cafés, shops and cinemas to hand;

they are out on their own in the more artificial setting of vast *cités résidentielles*, and the authorities have begun to accept that something must be done for them. Most of the newer campuses are at least equipped with facilities such as sports fields and club-rooms, even if by Anglo-Saxon standards they are rarely very impressive. Grenoble, in its usual pioneering role, is now the scene of a fascinating attempt to move towards the Anglo-American college system. The local branch of an official national body, the Oeuvres Universitaires, which has a general brief from the Ministry to look after the physical and moral welfare of all students, has persuaded a few younger professors to go out and live on the campus among them. This began in 1965. Men and girl students live in separate hostels, with strict rules about visiting; but they have a joint cultural and social centre, built with public money and well equipped with a theatre for films and plays, a record library, music and photograph rooms and so on. It is open day and night: the evening I called, the music room was packed with a cosmopolitan crowd listening to a Turkish student at the piano and a Canadian guitarist. Everyone seemed happy. The students are encouraged to run their own community life, under the friendly guidance of the resident professor. Already after six weeks they had founded a drama club, and arranged their own lecture society with visitors coming to talk about such extra-curricular but relevant topics as birth-control.

All this may seem stale and obvious to a British reader, but it marks the most revolutionary improvement in the social conditions and atmosphere of a French student's life. And clearly, once they are given some lead, they welcome it. One student at Grenoble, a Béarnais, told me: 'I was in the Cité Internationale at the Sorbonne before, and I was horribly lonely. You can't think what it means to have a young professor with us on the campus here, instead of the wardens they usually put in charge of hostels. We can actually *talk* to him.' Most of the older student hostels were, until the Faure reforms, controlled by the Ministry on a strict legalistic basis, and at one I was told: 'Paris would not allow us to hold dances on Saturday night, because the *statut* of our students' association had not been formally recognized as correct by the Ministry.'

This is just one example of the absurd centralization and bureaucracy that until 1968 plagued the universities as much as it did the schools. Though provincial faculties had some power to select their own staff, all their appointments had to be approved by the Ministry and were sometimes overridden; the same applied to any of their changes in routine and administration. A university's rector thus had a role quite different from that of an English vice-chancellor: he was a kind of *préfet*, appointed by Paris to administer not only the faculties but all the State education in his *académie* or region, down to and including the primary schools. And while some rectors were men of considerable presence and vision, others were little more than ciphers. A university had little corporate existence or distinctive personality of its own. It was often said: 'There is just one big university in France with groups of faculties scattered round the provinces, all following the same courses' – and if one university happened to outshine the others in a particular subject (as Lyon for medicine, or Grenoble or Toulouse for science) this was due usually to the heritage of some pre-Napoleonic tradition, to the prowess of some local personality, or to deliberate Government policy. Within each university the faculties had no organic connection with each other; they were each responsible via the rector to Paris, and there was hardly any of the inter-disciplinary penetration so much the rage in Britain. The rector's own freedom, too, was circumscribed, especially if he was known to be critical of Government policies: when Rector Martin of Caen, an outspoken critic of the Fouchet reforms, was about to set off to take part privately in a conference in Tokyo, the Ministry sent an official car to Orly airport and stopped him from boarding the plane under threat of dismissal. He was not considered a suitable ambassador for French education.

In the years before 1968 there was much deconcentration from Paris to the provinces, but not any derogation of power. The regional universities were encouraged to grow much faster than the Sorbonne, and were given most of the new funds. With their new equipment and their easier living conditions, they began to attract a growing share of the best teachers and students. No longer did a gifted professor at Lille or Dijon feel that his career had failed if it was not crowned with a chair at the Sorbonne; no longer did a bright *licencié* of Bordeaux or Besançon feel it so necessary to move to Paris to study for his *agrégation*. But this was not at all the same as decentralization. The tutelage prevented local initiatives and helped to inhibit relations between staff and students, thus adding to the frustrations that exploded in May 1968.

The 1968 revolt began not in the provinces but at Nanterre, a new overspill centre for Paris University in the drab north-west suburbs. Here in the winter of 1967–8 small action groups were formed by students, mainly those taking sociology, psychology and philosophy – subjects obviously more likely than, say, natural science or classics to attract and nurture radical political thinkers. These groups, led by Cohn-Bendit and others, began a little naïvely to plot proletarian revolution. Their discontent was aggravated by two factors. First, the bleakness and inhumanity of the Nanterre campus buildings, a desert of glass and steel. Second, the lack of job outlets in sociology and psychology, subjects popular with students but not yet widely accepted by French employers.

The story of their revolt, of how it spread to the Sorbonne and the rest of France and was brutally countered by the police, has been told so many times that I shall not tell it in detail again. For a few brief weeks France witnessed amazing scenes. Not to mention the barricades and the burning cars, there was the spectacle of the 'desanctified' Sorbonne like a cathedral in the hands of joyous pagans, with red flags and Maoist slogans stuck all over the venerable statues of the gods of French culture, Molière and others. In colleges and faculties throughout France the same thing happened. Professors and students who in the past had hardly exchanged a word sat around in groups in sunlit court-yards discussing their joint future, or created special assemblies to declare their universities 'autonomous' in defiance of the Ministry. After a few weeks the excitement subsided and it became possible to pick out the different strands in the revolt. It became clear that only a minority of French youth really shared the views of Cohn-Bendit and his friends. The small extremist element rallied wide sympathy for a while because of its daring and because of the stupid police repression against it; but in itself it contained some unpleasant and negative aspects of nihilism, violence and irresponsibility. In June, I met many serious students in Paris who at first were delighted by the seizure of the Sorbonne and the outburst of free debate, but later felt the whole thing had turned sour. Yet, if some revolutionaries spoilt their own cause, this does not invalidate the importance of the nation-wide upsurge. The student world appeared to have emerged decisively from its silence and reserve, to discover its own voice. Teachers and students, hitherto afraid and shy to make contact with each other, found that the contact was made for them by the force of events – and this has endured. The general public, and the Government especially, had their eyes opened as never before to the gravity of the university problem.

After consulting a wide range of professors and student leaders, Edgar Faure in the autumn put before Parliament a highly ambitious bill. The twenty-three universities and their hundred or so faculties would be abolished as such. Teachers and students would be invited as a first stage to group themselves as they thought best into some six or seven hundred '*unités d'enseignement et de recherche*' (UERs), each made up of a department or group of departments within a faculty. Each *unité* would then elect its own council by universal suffrage. Then the *unités* would group themselves together as they wished into new universities (smaller than the old ones), each with considerable autonomy over teaching and exam methods, and over how to use its budget. For France, all this was revolutionary. Faure was giving the university world a chance to *reform itself*, through a democratic process starting at grass-roots level. Only the broad framework was to be imposed: the rest each UER and new university could work out for itself, and the personality and constitution of each could differ widely. It was the reverse of the old centralized system where every new rule was decided at the top and passed down.

Faure pushed his bill through parliament with some skill, finally winning a 441–0 majority in the Assembly. The first stage of applying the reform, elections in the *unités*, took place early in 1969, and here Faure won another though more relative victory. His hope was to canalize the positive elements in the May movement by offering the students a sizeable role in preparing and managing the new structures. One third of the seats on the councils were reserved for student delegates. But it was feared that the students, not wanting to contaminate themselves by co-operating with the 'bourgeois' State, would reject this offer and boycott the elections. Indeed, the extreme Left did so: but the others voted in sufficient numbers for the councils to emerge as tolerably representative.

The new universities (using, of course, the existing buildings and campuses) gradually took shape in 1969–71. There are now 75 of them, made up of 684 UERs. Larger provincial universities have split into two or three new ones. Paris, where there are now 280,000 students, has thirteen: the seven central ones, carved out of what used to be known loosely as 'the Sorbonne', bear the down-to-earth names of 'Paris I', 'Paris II' and so on, while the other six are in the suburbs, one being Nanterre. There is no doubt that these new, smaller entities are a great deal more manageable and human than the old dinosaurs; and the Faure reforms, despite many difficulties, are working tolerably well. At least, there is more coherence and sense of purpose than in the case of the *lycées*.

The old rectors remain at their desks as the Ministry's pro-consuls in charge of each provincial *académie*. But their main job now is to administer school education; they have little more than a watching brief over the universities. Each of these elects its own governing council made up of one third students and two thirds teachers and other staff (even floor-sweepers are represented). The council can also co-opt delegates from the world outside – local personalities, or executives of local firms. The council elects its president, who has many of the powers formerly held by the rector. The Ministry does keep some strings, however. It decides on, and pays for, all major building and equipment projects. It allocates the annual budget of each university, which has no other means of raising funds. And it remains in charge of awarding the 'national' diplomas (e.g. *licence, maîtrise*). But a university can decide on its own teaching and exam methods leading up to these diplomas, and under more recent reforms it can even institute its own diplomas, which should then be submitted to the Ministry for approval. It can also vary the syllabus, so long as it satisfies the Ministry that a reasonable standard is being kept. Thus, some universities or UERs have virtually abolished exams and lectures while others have not. And the university has virtual autonomy over the spending of its working budget, and over internal administration. Gone are the days when even the holding of a dance in a student hostel needed permission from Paris. Moreover, the relationship between the UERs and the governing council can vary from place to place. Some universities allow their UERs to become virtually autonomous little colleges; some keep much tighter control.

The result of this whole process is that French universities are gradually developing separate and differing personalities, to a degree they never had before. Such traditions cannot be created in a day, but they will emerge. However, the reverse of this shining new democratic medal has been, as you might expect, a great deal of academic feuding and intrigue. When in 1969 the UERs came to negotiate with each other for grouping into universities, the atmosphere grew heavily political. Vast intrigues took place as to who should line up with whom. For example, disciplines in Leftist hands such as sociology were often reluctant to join with UERs of law or languages, where the professors were usually more conservative; similarly the science disciplines, relatively apolitical, fought shy of 'contamination' by the Leftists. The maths department of the old Sorbonne split into two *unités*, one in Right- and one in Left-wing hands, and each moved off to join a different new university. When huge Aix/Marseille with its 40,000 students divided into three universities, the split was made not on logical grounds of geography (the two towns being 20 miles apart) but on political ones. Such squabbles have led to an irrational wastage of resources in some places. Worse, they have in many cases hindered the cross-fertilization and multi-disciplinary teaching that was one of the prime aims of the Faure reforms. At Toulouse, for instance, the three universities are little more than the old faculties under a new name: law, letters, science. This is because the law professors, mostly Right-wing, refused to co-habit with their more Left-inclined colleagues in the other faculties, and vice versa: this thwarted Ministry proposals that each new university should be a microcosm of the old one, with opportunities for students to exchange courses and ideas across disciplines. Much the same has happened at Grenoble.

Matters have been further complicated by the fact that university politics always present a through-the-looking-glass picture of normal voting alignments; many of the professors most conservative on academic matters are politically on the Left (usually Communist rather than *gauchiste*) and very anti-Gaullist. The Left and Right have sometimes found themselves in unholy alliance to defend the *status quo*. And many professors, fearful of losing their chairs and their privileges under the new system, have fought either to block the reform or at least to ensure that the new bodies resemble as closely as possible the old faculties. The Ministry could have tried to step in to stop this happening and to impose its own solutions, but that would have been against the whole spirit of the reform, and Faure and his successors have understandably been against it. It is a familiar French dilemma: the price of democracy is inevitably a certain conflict.

Despite these difficulties, multi-disciplinarity has managed to make progress in some places. France hitherto lagged behind many countries in this; each discipline jealously preserved its own little world, and there was virtually no collaboration across these frontiers. But 'interpenetration', as it is often called, was one of the student demands in 1968; and as a first response Edgar Faure set up in the Paris region three new experimental inter-disciplinary centres for modern studies. The most *avant-garde* of them was housed in hurriedly built premises pleasantly sited in the forest of Vincennes – no repetition of the horrors of Nanterre! – and in an atmosphere of cheerful chaos and improvisation it set about teaching a mixed bag of contemporary subjects to some 9,000 students. Some teachers were drawn from the Sorbonne: one of them was Michel Foucault, the eminent structuralist. Others were invited from outside academic ranks and included Anthony Sampson, who came for a year to teach modern British politics and, as he put it, 'just be around'. This kind of innovation was revolutionary for France – what! a foreign journalist presuming to French academic wisdom? But the experiment at Vincennes has met with some success despite attempts by militant Leftist students to wreck it. It has now been extended elsewhere: at Nanterre the first year is interdisciplinary and you can study, say, English and sociology together. At Paris VII you can combine English and maths, or engineering and history.

The university teaching corps has emerged from the May crisis shaken and divided in much the same way as that in the *lycées*. Many conservatives have learned nothing and are trying to reassert their authority. But an increased number of others now recognize the need for change, and many are working along with the reform even if they judge it imperfect. As for the students, the problem has been how to prevent the ten per cent or so of dedicated 'revolutionaries' from sabotaging the reforms. These *gauchistes* have lost a good deal of influence since May; they are split into small groups and they fight against each other as well as against the orthodox Communist Left. Their policies have many contradictions and they seem to have overlooked many issues. They say they want to abolish exams but have not suggested what should be put in their place to ensure that merit and hard work are fairly assessed. They are indignant about lack of career outlets and of vocational training; but they also want the university to be '*une finalité culturelle*' that does not worry itself with practical ends. They want wide and easy entrance to the universities – and they expect the State's largesse to be infinite. One girl told a public meeting that if a thousand students each year felt like taking degrees in sociology, then the State had a duty to provide the corresponding number of suitable jobs for them. Even the most liberal-minded professors I talked to were often scathing about the extremists' sheer lack of sense. So far it has been possible to neutralize their influence to a large degree.

There has in fact, since the summer of 1968, been a good deal less violence and agitation in French universities than might have been feared. In the lecture-halls and study rooms the climate since the 1968 *rentrée* has been generally less chaotic than in the *lycées* and work has gone on despite the excitement of operating the new university structures. 'During lectures, my students are more argumentative than before,' said a young professor at Tours; 'they interrupt and want explanations – but that's no bad thing. At least they don't go to sleep.' A liberal professor at Nanterre, who wrote a stimulating book about the 1968 events under the pseudonym of Epistémon,* described how May had knocked professors off their sacred pedestals and turned them, in their students' eyes, into human beings whose ideas could now be taken seriously and discussed. In countless cases student–teacher relations are more direct and informal than before the crisis, and the appointment since 1969 of large numbers of new young *assistants* has brought the ratio of students to staff down from twenty to one to about fifteen to one and also made for easier contacts. 'A few students often stay behind with me now after lectures, and we chat for half-an-hour or so,' said a maths professor in Paris. And in one department of English I was told by the president of the *unité*, a senior professor, 'Here we *tutoie* as a matter of course now – we've gone beyond you British in informality!' This is still rare elsewhere, however. Many universities and UERs have now abolished the old, severe written examinations and replaced them with a system of 'continuous assessment' and credits for courses attended. This is inspired largely by American models, and by the work pioneered since 1957 at the Ecole des Mines in Nancy.† It means seminar work, and diplomas awarded on a record of regular exercises and orals rather than on big leaving exams. Most students prefer this new system, and, although it might seem to involve less intellectual slogging, in fact the students are said to be working harder than before, on average. Nearly everywhere there is now less emphasis, too, on *cours magistraux* and more on group work, helped by the improvement in the staff/student ratio.

One can therefore be cautiously optimistic about the legacy of the May crisis and the longer-term prospects of the new reforms. The situation is certainly brighter than in the *lycées*. So much new autonomy carries undoubted hazards – if some universities become too politically aligned, might not the Government withhold funds from those that displease it? Such risks have to be

* *Ces idées qui ont ébranlé la France* (Fayard, 1968).
† See p. 518.

faced. Today, in 1977, after seven or eight years of the new system, the UERs themselves are mostly operating quite smoothly. There is a greater degree of democracy and participation than before, while at the same time more work is being done, and not too much time is wasted in sterile political conflict. It is at the higher level, that of the new self-governing university councils, that things are still difficult. The Left-wing students and teachers have chosen these councils, rather than the UERs, as the terrain for their fight against the capitalist régime. Hence many of the councils are highly politicized, and sensible new projects are endlessly contested and blocked. A prominent journalist of liberal views told me: 'After 1969 I was elected from outside on to one of the Paris councils, and at first I was glad of the chance to help bridge the gulf between the university and the rest of the world, and to bring in new ideas. But all our meetings were wasted in such senseless wrangling that I got fed up and resigned.' This is a common experience, though matters do vary greatly from one university to another, often within the same town. Thus in Toulouse the mainly scientific university is very much calmer and less politicized than the mainly arts one. This typically French politicization is a disappointing but perhaps unsurprising legacy of the Faure reforms. Autonomy must pay its price. 'It's like adolescence,' one professor told me; 'it causes disruptions, but doesn't always last for ever.'

It seems there are three important further problems to solve, now that the new structures are established. First, ivory towers must be dismantled and universities brought into closer contact with the rest of French life. To bring in a few teachers from the non-academic world, as at Vincennes, is only a small first step. There is still too little contact between universities and industry in France, and much mutual suspicion. Many teachers do not want the 'purity' of their scholarship to be contaminated by the workaday world; and industrialists, in turn, fear that students sent to them from the UERs will be unruly, ill-taught *gauchistes*, so they prefer to collaborate with the Grandes Ecoles.

Secondly, the students' social and living amenities need to be improved. There has not been much change here since 1968. The students may be a little more relaxed through having better relations with their teachers; they may in some cases be a little less poor. But they still, most of them, lead lonely and difficult lives. It is partly their own fault; they will not group together to provide themselves with the social life that many Anglo-Saxon students enjoy. They expect to be catered for. Yet this needs massive funds which are hard to provide when student numbers are so high.

Thirdly, there is the notorious question of whether to establish selective entry, and how to avoid waste by directing students towards suitable courses. '*La sélection*' is still a hot political issue, highly contested. A limited kind of *numerus clausus* was finally imposed in medicine in 1971; first the students greeted it with a long strike, but now they have reluctantly accepted it. Even this does not operate at the moment of university entry; anyone with the right kind of *bac* can still enrol in a medical faculty, but at the end of his first year he must face a stiff competitive exam, which only about one student in six passes. The rest must transfer to another discipline, or leave university. This kind of *numerus clausus* has since been applied to pharmacy too, and is surreptitiously being adopted on a limited scale by one or two other faculties in some places. But in general the *bac* remains the universal passport. Faure himself rejected *sélection*, calling it 'cruel, unjust and dangerous', and no subsequent Government has had the courage to attempt to apply it. So the hardships of the overcrowded, under-funded 'student proletariat' remain, because of a system which they themselves insist on being retained. Meanwhile, over-all numbers continue to swell, though more slowly than before. In fact, the official 1976–7 figure of 820,000 in higher education may be misleading, for many students enrol in more than one UER or university in the same town, at least for their first year, and thus are counted twice. There is no official means of keeping a statistical check on this. And then there are the dilettante 'phantom' students. The total of serious students may not be more than 700,000.

After rejecting widespread selective entry, the two main solutions chosen by Faure and his successors have been to step up the building of the new technical colleges (*Instituts Universitaires de Technologie*), and to encourage more students in the faculties to leave after the short two-year course that ends with the DEUG. But neither has been very successful. The two-year IUT course has never acquired much prestige, with either employers or students, and the latter have generally preferred to try their luck in the faculties where there is always the chance of winning through to some more useful higher degree, such as the *maîtrise*. The IUTs have been regarded as something of a *cul-de-sac*, and their places are not always filled up – a waste of their new buildings. Similarly, not many students in the UERs are prepared to leave after the DEUG, since few employers will accept this as a valid diploma, even though its two-year inter-disciplinary course provides a good general higher education. Many teachers argue that the Government is at least partly to blame, for not setting a better lead. If more official bodies were to accept the DEUG as a qualification for certain grades of job, the private sector might follow suit, and the students would then have more incentive. But there has been the usual failure of liaison between Education and other Ministries. If they have not dropped out of their own accord after the first two or three terms, as a great many students do, the vast majority of the rest prefer to go on beyond the DEUG to try for the *licence* (a further year's course) or the *maîtrise* (a further two). And, under the liberal French system that is common to many countries, if you fail an exam, you generally have the right to sit it again the following year. About a third of students thus take three years rather than two over the DEUG, and the average time spent getting as far as the *maîtrise* is about 5·3 years instead of the scheduled four. Several professors have noted the tendency of students to try to prolong their studies – 'We're breeding protracted adolescents,' said one. All of this puts an added strain on resources.

Often they want to remain students because the alternative is real unemployment, without even the perks of a student meal-ticket. Graduate unemployment was growing fast even before the economic crisis, and since 1974 it has become an explosive problem – the inevitable result of having too many graduates, many of them ill-adapted to the job market. Since industry prefers to choose its brighter recruits from the Grandes Ecoles, even science graduates tend to drift into teaching as the best alternative. But this too has become harder to achieve, with the cut-back in teacher-training posts caused first by the drop in the birth-rate and then by crisis economies. It is the same in the arts: a girl studying German told me, 'What can I do but teach German? – maybe it's a vicious circle, but in order to be an interpreter, for instance, or work in an export firm, I'd need a specialized diploma, beyond my degree.' By 1975, when France's jobless total reached the million mark, about half of these were young people and an alarming number were graduates. Far more *maîtrises* were being awarded than the teaching profession could absorb; yet the *maîtrise* was not adequately geared towards other career outlets, such as business.

In 1975, faced with the prospect of a serious new student uprising, Giscard began to take action. The universities were hived off from the Ministry of Education into the charge of a new separate junior ministry under Jean-Pierre Soisson, and he was ordered to remodel the *maîtrise*. He came up with a highly sensible and – in its context – radical project, whereby each university was instructed to work out its own entirely new *maîtrise* courses in various disciplines, 'taking account of job possibilities on the local and national level', and to submit them for the Ministry's approval by the end of 1976. The *maîtrise* was now to be geared to the economy as much as to academia. Soisson then lost his job in a Government reshuffle early in 1976, to be replaced by the astonishing Alice Saunier-Séïte, hitherto *recteur* of Reims, a slinky, sexy, black-eyed widow of fifty with a taste for tight-fitting black trousers. The Press described her as 'a juicy autumnal fruit'. She had the job of applying the new reform, and soon ran into fearful trouble. First, many of the seventy-five universities objected to the manner in which the reform had been foisted on them without much consultation. Some of them threatened to apply their own *maîtrise* courses without seeking ministerial approval: this they had the right to do, under the Faure Act, but such diplomas would not have national validity. Secondly, the most controversial aspect of the new reform was that representatives of business and industry were to sit, alongside teachers and Ministry officials, on the

various commissions set up to approve the new courses. The
sensible aim was to seek the advice of the business world on the
kind of training needed. But for France this was a revolutionary
step, the first time that the world of the Patronat had ever been
invited to have a direct say in the doings of the ivory towers of
learning. Many teachers, especially on the Left, were furious; this
was unwarrantable capitalist intrusion. And the students, of all
political shades, were even more furious. In February large-scale
student strikes began, first in a few provincial universities such as
Amiens and Toulouse (arts), but spreading later to nearly
sixty others. Many teachers joined in, encouraging the protests.
By late April, some strikes had lasted ten weeks or more, and
little work was being done. In Paris and many other towns there
were large-scale riots and scuffles with the police, in much the
worst wave of student unrest since 1968. This time, however,
things were very different. This movement had started in the
provinces, not in Paris. It was not primarily ideological, and did
not have the aim of transforming society or joining up with the
workers. Though it was vaguely anti-capitalist, it was inspired as
much as anything by the fear of unemployment, and many of its
leaders were apolitical, very different from Cohn-Bendit and Co.
The students were striking for two very different reasons, which
became confused. Some were terrified that their particular
university would carry out its threat to boycott the reform, and
that therefore their *maîtrise* would not have national validity
and not be worth so much. This fear was very understandable.
Others, the more Leftish ones, were angry at being 'sold out to
the Patronat' and 'driven into industry by the boss class', as
they put it. But this was very paradoxical. The same students who
for years had been protesting at the lack of job outlets were now
up in arms against a reform that aimed to remedy just that.
'Better starve than be used to prop up a dying capitalism,' said
some of their leaders. In short, they were behaving as Left-wing
students can be expected to.

In face of the riots, black-jeaned Alice – who herself had been a
Left-wing supporter of the rebels back in 1968 – at first wavered
and offered concessions. 'She can't cope with all this, she's in
Wonderland,' said one commentator; another, after the smashing

of a number of shop-windows in one Left Bank riot, suggested she was in the other Alice book. Later, under orders from Giscard, she hardened again. And by early May the strikes had fizzled out through their own internal contradictions. The non-political majority, worried mainly about passing their exams, easily carried the day over the Leftist minorities. The universities were given a little more time, if they wished, in which to apply the reforms, and nearly all of them finally agreed to co-operate. By 1977–8 the various new *maîtrise* courses are expected to be in force, and a major step will have been taken to bring French higher education closer to the needs of modern life. At a cost to academic learning? – possibly, in a few cases. But does the reform mean that the universities will now exist merely to provide cannon-fodder for industry, or that the Patronat will dictate its will? 'Of course not,' a professor at the huge science university of Toulouse told me; 'the employers are associated with the new *maîtrises* only in an advisory capacity. We still call the tune. But we shall be grateful for their help – and for being forced at last to adapt our courses to outside reality.' It will be interesting to see whether, in a few years' time, some industries will at last be as ready to recruit their young executives and specialists from the universities as from the privileged Grandes Ecoles.

GRANDES ECOLES: EVEN THE 'POLYTECHNIQUE' IS CHANGING

The dozen or so great colleges known as the Grandes Ecoles, most of them devoted to engineering or applied science, have not suffered from State centralization or overcrowding to nearly the same degree as the sprawling monolith of the universities. Each has always been allowed a certain autonomy, and each keeps itself proudly apart for its own chosen élite. It is therefore not surprising that the Grandes Ecoles were left largely untouched by the storm of 1968. They account for no more than one in twenty of the numbers in higher education, but they turn out a high proportion of France's top administrators and engineers, and they enjoy a very special mystique. One or two are privately run; most belong to the State, but not all to the Ministry of

Education. The Ecole Polytechnique, for instance, comes under the Army Ministry. And one of their main differences from the universities is that each controls its numbers with its own fiercely competitive entrance exam, requiring two or three years' special study after the *bac*. Entry is thus a prize of the highest prestige.

There is much that is very fine about the Grandes Ecoles, that few reformers want to change. They have built up an *esprit de corps* that has served France well. The prestige they impart to their graduates has helped the technocrat or engineer to enjoy higher status and influence than he does in Britain, and this has played some part in France's economic recovery. There are some advantages to a modern nation for its key industrial executives to possess an engineering background; and although the old-boy network of some Ecoles is encrusted with favouritism and arrogance, it has created a unified and efficient élite, frequently able to join hands across the restricting barriers of French public life.*

All this is true, supremely, of the proudest of the schools, the Ecole Polytechnique, often known as 'X' for short because of its badge of two crossed cannon. By origin this is a military college, founded by Napoleon to train engineers for the armed forces. Today it is still run on the lines of an officer cadet school, with a serving general at its head: its pupils, *les X*, wear full-dress uniform with fantastic curly hats. They attend parades, and are allowed outside their gates for less than three hours each weekday, in contrast to the freedom of the ordinary student. But only a minority of *polytechniciens* today enter a military career; most go into the civil service or the big State industries. And neither Eton nor Balliol can equal the power of the freemasonry among the graduates of this mighty *alma mater*. Once an X always an X: in a land where informal contact between strangers is normally so difficult, all X high and low call each other *camarade* whether they have met before or not, and *tu* if they are fairly close in age, and the lowliest X can write out of the blue to a famous colleague and be sure of help and sympathy.

But is this arrogant apparatus substantiated by the actual quality of the teaching and training? By 1968 many people had

* See pp. 47–58.

come to feel that the structure of the 'X' and other Grandes Ecoles, their syllabus and selection methods, were in need of revision – despite the schools' qualities. If *les X* were still rising to so many of the top posts in the land, often it was due less to their training than to the school's prestige and their own innate brilliance, for there was no doubt of the quality of recruits. The same applied, to a lesser degree, to some other Ecoles. But attempts at reform tended to stumble on that most powerful political obstacle: nostalgia. Several leaders of the State have been ex-alumni (Pompidou was at the Normale Supérieure, next in prestige to the 'X') and their old-boy sentiments made them want to keep things unchanged.

After 1968, with the rest of the education world in turmoil, they were able to resist change no more. In 1969 some important reforms modernized the syllabus and administration at the Polytechnique. But methods of entry have not been changed, neither here nor in the other Grandes Ecoles, and it can still be argued that these are far too rigorous. The two- or three-year preparatory courses for the entry exams take place in special post-*bac* classes in *lycées*, known in slang as *khâgnes* (for the Normale) and *taupes* (for the other schools). So fierce is the competition that many students work a crippling seventy- or eighty-hour week over the whole period, turning into pale swots and driving themselves and their parents mad. 'Those who come out top for entry to the Polytechnique,' one professor used to tell his class, 'do not smoke, do not drink and are virgins.' The work in these *lycée* classes is of a far higher standard than in the average university faculty; in many ways, they represent the intellectual pinnacle of French education below *agrégé* level. But for all except the most brilliant it is an unnerving obstacle-race, with a large prospect of failure at the end. The Fouchet reforms, though they did not alter the *khâgnes* and *taupes* nor the methods of entrance, have at least equated them with the new initial two-year faculty cycle: anyone who fails Grande Ecole entrance but gets a reasonable mark can move straight on to the *licence* or *maîtrise*, instead of having to start again at the beginning in a faculty, as before. This saves some heartache and wastage of labour.

There is also a need for closer liaison between the Grandes Ecoles and the universities. However much the schools cherish their exclusiveness and restricted numbers, they have in fact suffered as much as the faculties from the rivalries and lack of contact between them. For instance, only the universities are empowered to grant *doctorats* and they are not keen to extend the privilege; therefore it is not easy to prepare to be a *docteur* on the staff of a Grande Ecole, and this is one reason why many schools are weak on higher research. Conversely, the universities cannot always make the best use of their handsome research funds because the calibre of their students is not high enough: the best ones are in the Ecoles. Each Ecole lives in its own little world and sets its own exams, unrelated to public degrees. Except at entry stage, they are not really competing with each other or with the universities, and so it is difficult to assess their calibre or results. Some are living on their reputation. At the 'X', the teaching of mathematics was, until 1968, so old-fashioned that it was reckoned that many students would have failed the maths *licence* if they sat for it, despite their brilliance.

Although there has been no general reform, some changes are now happening piecemeal: for instance, the Ecole Supérieure d'Electricité now shares some facilities and staff with Paris University's new science centre at Orsay. The Ecole Normale Supérieure, too, has been drawing closer to the Paris universities and encourages its students to sit for their exams. The Normale, concentrating on the humanities as much as on science, is rather different from the other Grandes Ecoles: its primary role is to prepare university and *lycée* teachers via the *agrégation*, although in practice nowadays, as with the 'X', many graduates prefer to buy themselves out of this obligation and go into administration or a literary career. The Normale is a superior kind of Balliol, the supreme citadel of French scholarship: Sartre was a *normalien*, and so were Blum, Jaurès, Herriot, Giraudoux, Soustelle, and many other famous figures beside Pompidou himself. Like the 'X' it is residential. But unlike the 'X' it is bohemian in spirit and largely free from discipline. Its students can wander about in jeans and are trusted to work as they choose. In the past few years it has even increased this freedom, and has modernized its curriculum, hugely improved its science research facilities, and generally brought itself up to date. Although its entry system (via the *khâgnes*) may still be open to criticism, in other respects it appears the very model of a great classical college that has managed to move with the times yet retain its old genius.

The Polytechnique is now moving along the same kind of path, under its 1969 reforms. First, it has become less military in its spirit and more democratic in its management. Though the students, because of their status as Army officers, are not allowed to join student unions, at least they now have seats on the school's governing boards. And though they must still wear uniforms and short hair, they are now allowed home for weekends – 'And if they get back late,' one teacher told me, 'well, they can always scramble over the wall after midnight.' Just like Oxford! – and like Oxford colleges, too, the 'X' has now gone co-ed: the first girl students, also with officer status, arrived in October 1972. 'So, military discipline will take another blow,' said one of the staff. And now that the college has moved, in 1976, to a new and more luxurious home at Palaiseau, in the suburbs, the parade-ground spirit will probably recede still further.

Secondly, since 1969 the syllabus has been modified and more research introduced, to encourage the training of scientists. Previously, *les X* had little incentive to develop originality: they received an encyclopedic general education at a high level, with plenty of thermodynamics, astrophysics, logic and economics, but their minutely detailed time-table was the same for everyone, leaving little scope for individual specialization or initiative. Pétain once said of a *polytechnicien*, 'That man knows everything but he knows nothing else.' The system produced fine administrators, but not great creative thinkers, and has sometimes been held responsible for the lack of top-level research scientists in modern France. Now, since 1969, though first-year studies are still the same for all, in the second year students can specialize and are encouraged to work on elaborate research projects on their own. Even so, when they leave the school, they still tend to gravitate to managerial desks rather than boffin jobs. 'But it's not the school's fault – it's that of French society,' I was told by Professor Laurent Schwartz, originator of the 1969 reforms;

'top executives have too much prestige in France, and scientists not enough. Many of our best brains leave us fully intending to work as researchers, and then get deflected by these snobbish pressures. They are judged by the number of telephones on their desk. No wonder France lags in research compared with Germany and Japan – it's not just a matter of low funds. Now we've reformed our teaching we really are turning out top-level people, but they're still not being properly used – it's a waste.'

M. Schwartz also admitted that too many students, once they had passed the enormous hurdle of entry, tended to rest on their laurels and not work hard enough at the school. They are not under great pressure to do so: the failure-rate for the passing-out exam is almost nil, and even with a low placing an 'X' is assured of a cushy job somewhere for the rest of his life, so great is the school's snob-appeal and old-boy solidarity. It still tends to breed an arrogant caste of *rentiers*, drawn almost entirely from the bourgeoisie – 'a bunch of spoilt, immature Minou Drouets', one law student told me, spewing out his sour grapes.

The traditions of the Polytechnique have come under challenge in recent years from several newer-style engineering schools. In Nancy, for instance, the Ecole Nationale Supérieure des Mines, one of the grandest of the Grandes Ecoles, was reformed on American-inspired lines in 1957 by the vigorous Bernard Schwartz (brother of Laurent), then its director. He did away with examinations and most lectures and divided the students into small study-groups, allowing them far closer contact with their teachers than was then usual in France. There are also close working links with local industry, with Lorraine industrialists taking part in seminars, and students going on practical courses in near-by firms. This is usual enough in the United States and even in Britain: in France it has marked something of a break with tradition. And Schwartz's pioneering has since had great influence on other schools and on some of the new universities.

An engineering school that opened in 1960, also at Nancy, the Institut des Sciences de l'Ingénieur, embarked on an even bolder and more unusual path, under its fanatical and messianic young director, Marcel Bonvalet. It is not a Grande Ecole at all, for it

takes students directly after the *bac*, and is really closer to the
IUTs. But this did not deter Bonvalet from the most startling
innovations, nor from aiming very high, perhaps too high. His
experiment has been open to many criticisms; but I have come
across few other ventures in modern France, of any kind, that
have impressed me more.

On a hill outside the town, it shines out into the night, floodlit,
with gay polychromatic glass façades of red, purple and gold.
Nothing could look less like the grey walls of the old 'X'. As I
arrived Bonvalet bounded up to me, sat down in his sleek office
with a bottle of malt whisky, and then excitedly propounded his
gospel at me non-stop for four hours, while three of his young
staff sat by as mute, admiring disciples. He is a *pied noir* born in
Bizerta in 1929, a short, tough-looking man with the *pied noir*'s
usual brash energy and contempt for red tape. After speeding
through his *doctorat-ès-sciences* at the Sorbonne he went back to
Tunisia in 1956 under a technical aid programme to help
Bourguiba set up crash-courses for technologists. There he
forged his basic methods of inductive, empirical teaching: later,
back in Paris, he persuaded some of the more progressive educo-
technocrats in the Ministry to let him try them out in France as
well. They built the new school in Nancy for him. There he
kicked nearly every French pedagogic precept out of his wide
windows, and especially the deductive method. Unlike Schwartz
at the Ecole des Mines, he claimed he was trying to produce
researchers, not men of action; but, like Schwartz, he started
from the belief that in an age of swift technological change you
need to teach not facts but principles and methods of inquiry.
His pupils were not told; they were made to find out for themselves. It was a blow in the face to the *cours magistral* of the
lycées, the faculties and the 'X'.

Bonvalet took nineteen-year-olds straight from their mathematics or technical *bac* and put them through an intensive and
imaginative four-year course. From their first day they were
encouraged to 'share the creative joy of the inventor' by exploring
inductively every channel of inquiry and knowledge. Second-
and third-year students acted partly as monitors and study-
leaders for the juniors in order, so Bonvalet told me, to help them

with their own revision and to provide a kind of leadership-training. Nearly all study was in small groups, with elaborate use of closed-circuit TV to link the many small classrooms with the central lecture hall, and, most important, in the senior years the accent was increasingly on operational research and experiment: students were given handsome funds for making their own equipment, with impressive results. I was shown several computers and other advanced gadgets they had built themselves. 'We've got two closed-circuit TV networks now,' said Bonvalet; 'the first, I admit, we bought, but the second the boys made – after all, it's so much cheaper.' The lighting, the panelled electric signs, the whole interior style of the building seemed more lavish and imaginative than in the average, fund-starved French college. 'Simple,' said Bonvalet; 'we made a lot of it ourselves. Saves money.'

Were his teaching methods, I asked, inspired by the United States, like Schwartz's? 'Christ no! *We* are inspiring *them*! Several American teachers and students are working here now to learn from us. All our methods we work out empirically.' It was clear that his arrogant enthusiasm carried the devotion of his staff and pupils – and he claimed to know personally all 300 of them. He reminded me of some hearty team-spirited English house-master, with technology in place of muscular Christianity – a refreshingly incongruous figure compared with the usual drily bureaucratic head of a French college. He said: 'The Sorbonne got my goat with its medieval, superficial academicism and lack of human contact. The "X" is just as bad, in its own way. Till now there's been a prejudice in France against inventive research. That's what we're trying to break down.'

An argument against Bonvalet was that in avoiding wide-ranging '*culture générale*' he swung too far to the opposite vocational extreme – the teaching of languages, economics and history he airily dismissed with, 'They've not the time for that – let them read books in the holidays.' But at least he is a man with fire in his belly, the kind of trouble-shooter that French official-dom can do with. As such he made enemies. After 1968 he departed from Nancy and for a while ran the university in Mada-gascar. But whatever happens to him personally, his influence has been enormous. Some of his methods have been taken up by Grandes Ecoles at Rouen, Toulouse and elsewhere – and of course by the Polytechnique itself.

There is much in the Grandes Ecoles' tradition of polyvalence and public service that it would be sad to lose. A swing too far to Bonvalet's opposite extreme might yield a narrower outlook, and prejudice the training of the kind of technocrat who has been one of France's greatest sources of strength. France may need more scientists, but she also still needs human beings. It ought to be possible to combine the positive elements of the Bonvalet and Schwartz reforms with the traditions and ideals of the present Grande Ecole framework. This is what the moderate reformers want. But amid the clamour of the diehards and the revolutionaries, it is not easy to achieve.

'LA JEUNESSE': REBELS OR CHUMS?

'*Mais que pensent les jeunes?*' ask the headlines in a constant stream of magazine articles: '*Nos jeunes, qui sont-ils?*' And few of them can find an easy answer. What are they like, this mysterious new generation, for whom all the educational crusades are being fought? Ostensibly, they are following much the same paths as modern youth in other Western countries, though less aggressively than in Britain. They have their own powerful new consumer market for music, clothes and cars; their own world of young singing idols; and their own fringe minorities of delinquents. All, or nearly all, have far more freedom from parents than cloistered French youth had before the war. They have more sexual licence; they have finally come under temptation from drugs, although later and less damagingly than in some other Western countries. Many are conscious of the gulf between their own morality and that of the older generation.

And that older generation in turn has become aware of youth as never before. *La Jeunesse* is now a slogan, a doctrine of faith in the future, a symbol of France's recovered vitality. For more than a century this used to be an adult-dominated country, where teenagers were treated as small-scale adults and were not expected to exist as a national group in their own right. Now the grown-up world has woken up, as it were, to the existence of a neglected minority in its midst, with its separate values and needs. Youth is solicited, analysed, indulged. But this parental lip-service to the new cult of youth is not always accompanied by actual understanding of individuals. And in some ways the youthful revolution *à l'anglaise* is more apparent than real in France; or at least, it has not yet found proper expression, despite the May uprising.

In the first decade or so after the war, many of the most important changes in France were due to a new generation rising against the standards of its elders – from the young farmers of the JAC to the cinema's *nouvelle vague*. And other phenomena (St-Tropez, Françoise Sagan, the early existentialists) gave the world a popular image of French youth in open revolt. By the late 1960s that image had become strangely deceptive. As often as not, older people would complain; 'But the young, they're so docile, so conformist.' While Britain's youth had leapt ahead in pre-cocious emancipation, the French remained, relatively, under the shadow of school and parent. Seduced by prosperity and placated by adult acceptance, many of them seemed to be tamed into a listless submissiveness, or else into a feeling of impotence. Then came May 1968, which revealed the frustrations lying beneath the surface of that conformism. Certainly, since that crisis French youth has become less docile in its dealings both with teachers and parents. But has May really made such a difference? The ring-leaders of the revolt, the student militants, were only a tiny minority. The succeeding generation, the vast army of French youth today, is not quite sure what to think.

The climate of 1945 was very different from today's: more austere, but also more open and adventurous. The upheavals of war-time had broken down some of the barriers that previously kept youth in its place, and an idealistic new generation was able gradually to make lasting inroads into the *positions acquises* of the age-hierarchy. It happened most strikingly in agriculture, and in the civil service and industry where some older men emerged discredited from the Occupation and young ones took their place. It is remarkable how youthful many of the post-war pioneers were at the outset: Leclerc was twenty-three when he began his cut-price campaign in Brittany, and Planchon founded his Villeurbanne theatre at twenty-one. Today the impetus of this generation is still driving forward, in nearly every field; and many of its leaders, now pushing fifty, are in key national positions. But their successors, now in their twenties or thirties, born into an age of greater ease and acceptance, have seldom shown the same innovating spirit (except in one brief spring of anarchic revolt). This has been even more apparent in the intellectual world. After the Liberation many young people flocked excitedly around Sartre and Camus at St-Germain-des-Prés, eager to revolt against their bourgeois background and help to forge a better world. This existentialist climate has since gradually dissipated.* The Sartrian disciples of those days have mostly settled down and become prosperous, and many are now leading the bourgeois lives they once denounced. Their young successors either find money-making, fast cars and hi-fi more appealing than philosophy; or else they are cynical and dispirited at the anti-bourgeois rebellion's failure to create a new society.

In the mid-1950s a few isolated and much-publicized events, vaguely influenced by existentialism, managed to sustain the impression of a generalized youthful revolt. In 1954 the eighteen-year-old Françoise Sagan, daughter of an industrialist, published her first novel, *Bonjour Tristesse*. Her sophisticated world of whisky and wealth was some steps away from the severe, intellectual *milieu* of the true existentialists; but her heroine's cool disillusion and rejection of social morality sounded a note that seemed to borrow something, however ill digested, from the ideas of Sartre. Two years later the young director Roger Vadim took a little-known actress to a modest Riviera fishing-port and there made on location *Et Dieu créa la femme*. And God-knows-who created Bardot and St-Tropez. Thousands from *une certaine jeunesse* rushed there at once. France and the world were amazed. Was this what French youth was like? Was Sagan's free-living heroine typical of French girls of eighteen? The next year, in 1958, the veteran director Marcel Carné made a film, *Les Tricheurs*, that seemed to confirm the picture. He described a *milieu* of young Parisians, bohemian 'intellectuals' and idle bourgeois students from good homes, united in the same anarchic

* See pp. 544–9.

dissipation, breaking up their parents' smart flats with wild
parties, stealing and cheating and casually fornicating. According to Carné, everyone in this *milieu* is a *tricheur* (cheat) and
honest feelings are taboo. Carné claimed that he knew this world
intimately and had drawn his portraits from life. The film caused
more of a stir than any other in France for years. Some people
thought that the film's portrait was out of date and related to a
St-Germain-des-Prés of the late 1940s, the phoney existentialists
who mistook liberty for licence. Others felt it was still true, of a
minority. There are still some *tricheurs*, even today, just as the
early Sagan novels were clearly based on experience and the
crowds around the bars and beaches of St-Tropez are patently no
fiction. The *tricheurs* borrowed from existentialism its permissiveness without its responsibility and took it as a cue to do
just what they liked; when the young bohemian Mephistopheles
of Carné's film goes into a shop to steal a record that he does not
want, he claims he is performing the perfect Gidean or Sartrian
acte gratuit. This muddled intellectual self-justification has under-
lain a good part of the fringe rebellions among post-war French
youth – though one can hardly claim that every St-Tropez lay-
about is motivated by such philosophical principles.

  The St-Tropez phenomenon has had plenty of post-war
counterparts, in Chelsea, California and elsewhere. What is
remarkable here has been its intensity in one small, picturesque
seaside location. The whole affair was hardly Vadim's fault, or
Bardot's: the publicists of *Paris-Match* and other such papers
pounced on them while they were filming in 1957, and somehow
managed to inspire a popular cult that answered a youthful need.
Bardot was built into a symbol of sensualist emancipation – and
the young crowds came, some innocently and some less so, to
find and to worship their goddess. Of course they simply drove
her away; she had bought a villa just outside St-Tropez, where she
still spends part of each year, but she was soon forced to build a
high wall round it, and neither she nor any other star today dares
to be seen in the streets or cafés of the town, through fear of being
mobbed by adoring fans. Yet the crowds still come, even today,
from every part of the world, impelled by the new religion of
glamour and stardom, or simply by curiosity. I met a Dominican

priest in St-Tropez who told me: 'This place is a kind of Lourdes. Young people feel a lack in their lives today, they want to be cured of their desolate yearnings, so they come here to be touched by magic and reborn. But they go away disappointed. All they find is each other.' Many of the most vicious elements in St-Tropez today are foreign, not French – the hordes of young German thugs and pederasts, the Chelseaites, the Swedes, the American beats. But the French are still also there in plenty; the girls of little more than sixteen who arrive from Paris without a penny and see how far their charms can carry them. Any summer night you can see them by the score, wide-eyed girls with gaudy jeans, bare midriffs and Bardot hair-styles, hanging around the modish bars like l'Escale, waiting for the next well-heeled pick-up who will let them sponge and stay a few more days.

Many of the boys and girls of this kind of *milieu*, in Paris or St-Tropez, come from cultured, conventional homes and have broken with their families. But they are not typical, totalling perhaps a few thousand. Many other young people today, especially students, seem to have managed to extricate themselves from old-style bourgeois morality in a less irresponsible manner; and if they are discreet, even while still living at home they can practise a good deal of Sartrian 'sincerity' in their private lives. As one Parisian student told me: 'It's not that we're trying to set up counter-conventions like the *tricheurs*. We're not against our parents' morality, we ignore it. The basis of our behaviour is rejection of constraint, and within this framework we are very moral.'

Among the less intellectual teenagers, the archetype in the 1960s was not a *tricheur* but a *copain* – the word means 'chum' or 'pal'. And in that decade it was the extraordinary pop movement of the *copains*, innocent and mildly charming but vapid, that gave a new brand-image to the whole of French youth and pushed the precocious cynicism of Sagan firmly on to the sidelines. A new generation, sipping its Coca-Colas, looked less to Bardot the sex-kitten than to Sylvie Vartan, chirpy little chum and elder sister, or to Françoise Hardy huskily leading all-the-boys-and-girls-of-her-age-hand-in-hand.

This movement began in 1959 when Daniel Filipacchi, a young disc-jockey and former *Paris-Match* photographer, launched a jazz programme on Europe Number One radio and borrowed the title of a song by Gilbert Bécaud to call it *Salut les Copains*. Instantly it was a smash-hit with teenagers, who were tired of sharing Brassens and Trenet with their elders and wanted something swinging and modern of their own, like the Americans had. Soon the programme was running for two hours nightly, using mainly American material.

Around the same period an obscure bar near the Opéra, the Golf Drouot, turned itself into a kind of teenagers' cabaret and so provided a breeding-ground for the first of France's own young pop singers. There a boy of sixteen with fair curly hair and an ugly mouth made his hesitant *début* under the name of Johnny Hallyday, singing American rock'n roll tunes in French. Filipacchi took him up – and a whole generation chose Johnny as their idol and self-image. French pop was born. He was followed by scores of others – besides Sylvie and Françoise (surnames are taboo among *copains*), the best known have been Richard Anthony, Claude Françoise, Adamo, Sheila, France Gall. And in 1962 Filipacchi astutely complemented his radio show with a glossy magazine also called *Salut les Copains*, which reached a sale of a million copies a month and got 10,000 fan letters a week. Its rather similar sister monthly for girls, *Mademoiselle Age Tendre*, sold 800,000 – both of them astoundingly high circulations for France.

At first the movement was highly derivative, much more so than its Liverpool equivalent. Not only did the stars borrow American tunes; many of them found it smart to adopt Anglo-Saxon names like Dick Rivers, and Eddy Mitchell; Hallyday's real name is Jean-Phillippe Smet. Gradually, however, the *copains* have acquired a certain French style of their own, less virile and inventive, more romantic and sentimental, than either Beatledom or American folk and rock. Some of them, including Johnny and Françoise, compose and write many of their own songs, and today probably about half the *copains*' material is home-grown and the rest imported and translated. The whole affair has been basically a shrewd commercial operation by

Filipacchi, who has become one of the richest men in France. But he and his stars can afford their mink and Ferraris just because they managed to provide millions with an outlet of self-identification they were looking for. The tradition of modern popular songs is much older and stronger in France than in Britain, but it has, therefore, belonged to an older generation, from Piaf through to Aznavour. Teenagers resented these as their parents' idols. But their own Johnny, singing ingenuously about being sixteen and its problems, was themselves and the boy next door. At his concerts, children would wave and shout hallo: 'He's young, he's jolly, he's just like us,' said one girl of fourteen, 'and not at all like a real music-hall star. So we love him.' Idols and fans are all equally *copains* together, and all are *tu*: this is the carefully fostered principle of their success, and if any idol breaks the code and behaves like an aloof Hollywood star, he is finished.

Parents at first were a little anxious, as gramophone-record sales shot into scores of millions and Hallyday became the most-photographed male in France after de Gaulle. Their concern reached its height after the night of 22 June 1963 when Filipacchi staged a 'live' open-air broadcast from the Place de la Nation in Paris, and 150,000 boys and girls, twisting and rocking, surged into the square and brushed aside the police. It was the first time in French history that teenagers had displayed their solidarity in public, on this scale. Some observers saw it as a political portent, comparing it with the mass-hysteria of the Nazi rallies. A few arrests were made and an inquiry was ordered. A little damage had been done to cars and windows, but this was due simply to the weight of the crowds, and to the presence among them of a handful of hooligans. Once the fuss had blown over, it became clear that the famous *Nuit de la Nation* was really quite innocent: the kids had simply wanted to dance, and to have a look at their heroes.

Parents soon came to see there was nothing much to worry about. Filipacchi, in fact, has always been shrewd enough to steer the *copains* away from rebellious paths that might have got him into trouble. Their revolt has been purely one of music and rhythm, not of morals. The very phrase *Salut les Copains* ('Hello, Chums!') gives some idea of the *Boy's Own Paper* or *True*

Romance spirit of the thing; and so harmless was the magazine that the Catholic Church felt safely able to copy it with its own rival monthly for the teenage faithful, *Formidable*, a bit more varied and a bit less artfully glossy but otherwise much the same. Filipacchi's editor-in-chief, Raymond Mouly, a young man in black leather jacket and side-whiskers, told me: 'I suppose we've simply created a new conformism, inevitably. But there's still something zippy and fresh about us – and we needed a change from Yves Montand. What we're really doing is to prolong the age of innocence, the *âge tendre*. Life is easier than in 1954, and people have more time to live their youth.'

This belongs to a typically French romantic tradition that seems to hark straight back to Gérard de Nerval and *Le Grand Meaulnes*: adolescents playing at love, sometimes touched by melancholy and *ennui* but not by cynicism or social indignation. Browse through the brilliantly edited pages of *Salut les Copains* and you will see what these idols were like, or at least how they were presented to be. Huge snazzy colour-photos in the manner of *Un Homme et une femme* would show the various stars wandering hand in hand through autumn woodlands or lazing on Mediterranean beaches. Photo-articles forty pages long would proclaim *Tout tout tout sur Sylvie* and *Tout tout tout sur Johnny*: that Sylvie dislikes celery and likes coloured candles, that Johnny likes hot-dogs and dislikes umbrellas. Johnny, philistine and petit-bourgeois, mad about cars and motor-bikes, was in reality much as he was made to seem; the perfect modern folk-hero, looking exactly like any French youth you see hanging around the streets with his *vélo* on a Sunday. Sylvie, Bulgarian by birth, was more intellectual: she used to read philosophy on the Métro before she became famous, and was known as *la collégienne du twist*. But with her tulip-mouth, her long ash-blonde curls and sturdy little figure, she projected the perfect image of the jolly bobby-soxer who'd become a star by mistake and when she bounced on to the stage of the Olympia music-hall as if it were an end-of-term concert, to trill *Ce soir, je serai la plus belle pour aller danser*, every *midinette* in the audience identified with her. In 1965, after a long engagement, Johnny and Sylvie became Mr and Mrs Smet: two hundred photographers were present, yet it seemed much closer in spirit to a typical middle-class wedding than, say, to aloof Bardot marrying some foreigner in Las Vegas.

Not all the *copains* have conformed quite so closely to this tame bourgeois ideal. Françoise Hardy, ex-student of German at the Sorbonne, tall and languid with a spoilt, sulky temperament, even brought a note of Grecoesque sorrow and self-doubt into some of her songs; there was more than a touch of Garbo about her, and she was one of the very few *copains* to have much following among maturer people as well as teenagers. But she kept roughly in line with the Filipacchi ethic, and her *mystère* did not simmer into actual revolt.

And now, in the late seventies, what has happened to the *copains*? After tiffs and reconciliations that filled all the headlines, the Smets are parents in their thirties, and have grown away from their teenage fans. '*Adieu les copains*!' wrote *l'Express* after their wedding; 'Johnny and Sylvie were *copains*. Mr and Mrs Smet will try to remain stars. And they will have lots more little Ferraris!' Johnny's golden reign is nearing its close: he has never really made the transition into a mature, adult star. Other younger singers, none of them very remarkable, are taking his and Sylvie's place, and Filipacchi is now making most of his money out of other concerns. The *copains*' appeal was always mainly to the less sophisticated middle teens; older or more alert ones tended to prefer a more robust nourishment such as Bob Dylan or English pop. A youth in Filipacchi's office who had spent some time in London once told me: 'I admit your young singers are more mature and original than ours; a group like The Animals, for instance, seem to have firm ideas about modern society.'

On its credit side, the *copain* cult may have fostered a kind of sweet romantic comradeship among French youth. Like British pop it certainly helped in the struggle against delinquency; and unlike British pop it was seldom crudely hostile to real culture. Its idols had undeniable puppy-charm; and, for all the commercial wire-pulling, there has been something spontaneous and infectious about their appeal to French youth in a voice it would recognize as its own. But that voice has not proved a very inspiring one: insipid, somewhat effeminate, content to idolize a safe world of glamour and niceness. Even the melodies were not very exciting. Parents, in fact, could safely look on the *copains* as a harmless way of keeping the children out of mischief. The young things were now being allowed to throw a party on their own; but Mummy and Daddy were on the *qui-vive* upstairs.

Under this discreet parental eye, France's six million teenagers have been elaborating their own semi-private world with its own crazes, conventions and slang – a world that is largely innocent but difficult for a non-initiate to grasp at first. Here are some examples of their slang. *Chouette, formidable* and *terrible* all mean 'super' or 'smashing'; *vachement* or *terriblement* mean 'very'; *ça chauffe* means 'things are getting hot'; *c'est du folklore*, 'it's stupid, out of date'; *dans le vent*, 'with it'; *moins de vingt dents*, a pun meaning 'the old'; *croulant* ('crumbling'), an 'adult', a word in vogue about fifteen years ago but now only used by *croulants* about themselves. The notorious term *yé-yé* more or less means 'pop', and derives from French attempts to pronounce 'yeah! yeah'! in their songs. Adults often apply it pejoratively to the whole *copain* generation; teenagers themselves use it rarely except to denote, also pejoratively, their own more *outré* elements.

When teenagers give parties on their own, they are usually informal *surprise-parties* which may sometimes develop into wilder *surboums* if *tricheurs* are around or parents well out of the way. Generally French bourgeois teenage parties are noticeably sedate by London standards, at least when given (as usually happens) in parents' homes. Outside the family foyer, however, things *chauffent terriblement*, notably at one or two new Paris night-spots catering for really switched-on youth. One of the early pace-setters in the mid-1960s was the fantastic Bus Palladium, near the Place Pigalle: this was a seedy old strip-joint for tourists which in 1965 decided to get with-it by importing an English pop group and appealing to a new clientèle. Its success was unprecedented. Smarties and beatniks, typists, students and celebrities, all flocked along to this one large darkened room where bodies swayed and jerked through the night to the strident music. The baroque church-like décor, with frescoes, aisles and Byzantine pillars, reinforced the impression of being present at some religious rite – and several of the pale-faced, long-haired acolytes could hardly have looked more biblical. Few reporters failed to comment on this: 'It's a midnight mass in full oecumenicism,' said the *Nouvel Observateur*. 'The priest sucks his micro, the communicants sip their Coca-Cola.' But reporters also noted how extraordinarily innocent and unerotic it all was.

One characteristic feature of French teenage society since the war has been the rise of the band or group. No longer expected to spend so much time with parents or relatives, young people nowadays often choose to go around in little groups of six or more, boys and girls together; frequently the relations remain platonic and fairly uncommitted, and there is less splitting into couples or 'dating' than in many Western countries. Of course, this trend provided fertile soil for the spreading of the *copains* cult.

As for adult-organized youth activities, teenagers mainly show no great enthusiasm for them, though boy-scouting is quite popular and some of the Church movements do well. The national chain of youth clubs (Maisons des Jeunes) might attract far greater numbers if they were better organized and had better amenities. Not that French youth moves to the opposite antisocial extreme: there is less delinquency than in many countries. Juvenile lawlessness appeared comparatively later in France, in 1959, with warring gangs of leather-jacketed youths known as *blousons noirs*. After they had swiped their bicycle chains at a number of innocent passers-by, they were severely repressed by the police, and today the gangs have largely split up and been succeeded by small groups of young professional thieves, or by sporadic hooliganism and pilfering.

Drugs too made their appearance on the youth scene much later than in many countries. It was not until 1969–70 that professional pedlars began any large-scale attempts to corrupt French teenagers, and that heroin, LSD and marijuana began to circulate in quantities. In Marseille and some other areas, pedlars now use the familiar trick of distributing free samples to schoolchildren, sometimes as young as twelve, in efforts to 'hook' them. The drug problem is still much less widespread than in the United States, but has been growing, and many *lycées* are affected: 76 per cent of addicts in France are said to be under twenty-four.

The education authorities at first reacted to this menace by pretending it did not exist. For years they felt confident that the sound moral upbringing of French youth would immunize them against this nasty American scourge. But now the problem has come into the open.

Whereas in post-war Britain youth has often channelled its energies into violent self-expression, destructive or creative, in France the dominant impression left by all the varying tendencies has been, at least until 1968, of a kind of docile listlessness. I do not wish to exaggerate this contrast, for the youth of the two nations also have much in common. But it does exist. The *copains* may have provided a generation with a new self-aware-ness, yet it has seemed unsure quite what to do with it. One answer to the puzzle lies in the influence of parents and school. It is true that French parents are less strict than they used to be, and are much readier to let sons and even daughters go out on their own; it is true they have grown more aware of their children's enthusi-asm and needs as *children*, instead of treating them as minor adults. Often they are indulgent with pocket-money. But their offspring have remained curiously under their sway.

In Parisian upper-class society parents in recent years have resorted to various ingenious devices to keep their teenage children in check. One of the most remarkable of these is the *rallye*, a kind of exclusive dancing-club for girls of fifteen to nineteen and their carefully chosen escorts. There are some dozens of these *rallyes* in Paris today; and a boy or girl who is entered for one by his or her mother must expect to spend from four to five years in a steady round of formal parties and dances, under close parental supervision. It helps to steer the young things towards suitable marriages, and to keep them out of mischief. And astonishingly, most of the young things appear to accept this discipline, as teenagers rarely would in London.

Another reason for the French teenager's submissiveness has been purely practical: the housing shortage. Emancipation from parents is not so easy when cheap furnished flats or rooms are still such a rarity: three in four of sixteen-to-twenty-four-year-olds live at home until marriage, including 54 per cent of young men of twenty-two to twenty-four. Yet even if there were no housing shortage, the picture might not change so radically. It is still considered the 'norm' to live with your parents; and very many young people, even when they do have the means to move away, prefer not to do so. This is changing, but not fast. A rich young girl I knew in Paris, who could easily have found and afforded a small flat of her own or with girl-friends, told me just before her wedding at twenty-six: 'Now at last I can get away from my mother.' In such cases children are suffering from parents' emotional blackmail; but in millions of other cases it is simply that young French, far more than young Anglo-Saxons or Nordics, seem to remain tied to their parents by psychological cords that they find hard to cut, even when there is no parental pressure. They are still often in the grip of the kind of obsessive child-parent relationships that are such a recurring theme of modern French literature.* Perhaps this is why, when they do revolt – against parents or against society more generally – the gesture is all the more extreme, just because it has cost them so much of their inner selves.

Young people will often profess unconventional or progressive ideas in abstract, but in practice when faced with concrete situations will defer to the lead and authority of their elders. I met a twenty-year-old Sorbonne philosophy student, living with his parents in Paris, who delighted me with his mature and profound ideas about modern society and his own destiny, then surprised me by saying: 'A few young friends of mine and I have formed a local dramatic club. Luckily, my father runs it for us. You see, without him, none of us would have the right authority, we'd just quarrel.' I refrained from replying that, in England, boys much younger and stupider than he were often in charge of the discipline of large schools. But it is plain as daylight that the French school system has a large influence here. It fails to provide any training in group initiative or responsibility, and so throws the child back on parental discipline. It presses him towards an intellectual precocity that is basically conformist. And the severe and formal approach of teachers outwardly inculcates docility, while inwardly producing a kind of frustrated resentment. Perhaps it is reaction against the severity of school, or against the shadow of

* See p. 372.

parents, that makes so many French teenagers behave so very badly when they escape to a different setting. In English towns such as Brighton, where they come *au pair* in the summer, they have a worse reputation for trouble-making than any other nationality, and it is often hard to decide whether they are spoilt or sadly deprived. It was this same reaction against discipline that caused the May uprising, when it came, to be so fierce in schools, colleges and homes.

Two opinion surveys of teenage attitudes in the early 1960s both gave a somewhat sobering picture. The first, carried out in 1961 among *lycéens* and apprentices by a psychologist, Yann Thireau, and an educationalist, Georges Teindas, showed them as 'interested above all in securing an easy life, with lots of money'. The heroes they admired most were scientists, sportsmen, world leaders – but they seemed to envy them less for their qualities than for their style of life: 'Prince Rainier, he's got money and he's happy', 'Churchill, he's rich', were two replies. The second inquiry was carried out in 1962 by the Institut Français d'Opinion Publique, among a wide range of boys and girls between sixteen and twenty-four. Asked what they valued most in life, the vast majority put health and money well ahead of love, freedom or religion. They laid immense stress on the home, mainly as a symbol of material security; they were anxious above all to secure good, well-paying jobs, and they were confident that they would be much more prosperous than their parents. They cared little about French politics – less than a third were able to cite the names of more than two Gaullist Ministers – but they showed even less concern for old-style patriotism and *la gloire*.

An inquiry carried out by IFOP and *l'Express* more recently, in February 1969, produced somewhat similar results, and lent weight to the impression that the May crisis had certainly not turned all French youth into revolutionaries. Sample interviews with the whole fifteen-to-twenty-nine age range gave a picture of a generation that was relatively contented, concerned with finding good jobs and securing more leisure and holidays, and ready to accept the social order, but also interested in world affairs and with some sense of public service. Discontent seemed to be greater among *lycéens* and students than among those in jobs, suggesting that youth's irritation may be more with the defects of the educational system than with society as a whole. Youth emerged as decidedly happier than at the time of a similar *IFOP/l'Express* survey in 1957, during the Algerian war, when 24 per cent declared themselves 'very happy' against 35 per cent in 1969. A more recent survey, by the magazine *Expansion* in 1975, found that 63 per cent of French youth (and as many as 88 per cent of those already in jobs) were confident about their future. Maybe surveys of this type should not be taken too literally (and it must be remembered that IFOP is Government-backed), but they cannot be ignored. Do they suggest that the May uprising had little effect on French youth, or that its catharsis has left them readier to face the future and has removed some of their sense of powerlessness and isolation? Perhaps a little of both. One certain legacy of May is that it has modified youth's relations not only with teachers but with parents. During and after May, family crises broke out 'on a scale the nation has not seen since Dreyfus', as one father put it. Schoolchildren disappeared from home for days on end, or hotly argued with their parents for the first time in their lives. Now that the dust has settled it is possible to see that, as in the classroom, certain barriers of reserve and indifference have been broken. Parents are now making a greater effort to understand their children, and there is more communication between them. Most families I talked to felt that the change had been for the better.

At the same time May seems to have sharpened the polarization between a small minority of truly 'revolutionary' youth and the rest. The former are mostly from bourgeois backgrounds. They may be naïve, but it is impossible to deny the warm-heartedness and sincerity of many of them. They might turn out to have great influence in a France of the future, but that will depend on the development of the world ideological struggle; for the moment, their role is limited. The cliché of *enragé* is as false as that of *tricheur* ten years ago if applied to French youth as a whole. Of the majority, some may be uneasy within a consumer society but they do not seek to overthrow it, and they frankly enjoy many aspects of it. I do think however that May has sharpened a great many young people's awareness of the problems of the world they live in. They have emerged as a little more serious, and a little more conscious than before that youth may have an active role to play in an adult society.

A significant minority of individuals do not fit easily into the pattern either of Left-wing activists, or mindless *copains*, or budding materialist technocrats. These are the more mature and thoughtful ones, mostly students or young graduates, many of them the kind of people who might have rallied to existentialism twenty years ago. I find their grave idealism and their integrity most impressive, and a little sad. These people *do* feel concern over such things as France's cultural decline; but often they feel also a kind of impotence, an alienation from the way modern materialist France has been moving and a sense of being unable to affect it. Some of them have been cowed by the failures and excess of the May revolt, or by the Gaullist climate of authoritarianism. They present an aura of solitariness and of reserve.

The Sorbonne student whose father ran his drama club seemed to typify their outlook: 'We don't feel we live in a coherent community, like you in Britain. In France, existentialism destroyed the illusion of community for us, and we've nothing to put in its place. A community is a fine idea, but it doesn't seem to work in practice: there are too many compromises and betrayals. *Enfin, on est toujours seul.* Many of my contemporaries seek an answer in Teilhardism – I prefer Kierkegaard, Nietzsche, Unamuno.' He said that he was studying philosophy and economics at the moment, and hankered to teach philosophy and go for a *doctorat*; but for practical financial reasons he would probably now concentrate on economics and go for an industrial career. He went on to criticize French parents for patronizing and indulging their children instead of providing constructive guidance: 'They give us lots of pocket-money because they've no ideas to give us. They just don't know what to say. It's a catastrophe.'

This serious-minded minority, whether Catholic or agnostic, literary or more scientific, share a kind of groping idealism that they may shrug off defensively when questioned. But the list of authors they care most about can be revealing. A large number, and not only the Christian believers, are drawn to Teilhard ↳ Chardin* and his fundamentalist vision that seems to reconcile God and the modern scientific world. Others are influenced by Camus and especially by *La Peste*, which has sold well over a million copies in France: its stoical humanism seems to offer something to many young agnostic liberals who cannot accept Teilhard's theism or Sartre's contorted Marxism. Others again turn to Malraux's early novels or his philosophical books on art (but not to Malraux the Gaullist), or they search for answers in the interior universe of Proust. Among younger and rather more naïve ones, at *lycée* age, the most popular author of all is still Antoine de Saint-Exupéry, idealist and man of action, prophet – in *Citadelle* and *Terre des hommes* – of heroic virtues that make good sense to a sixteen-year-old.

These diverse writers and others have in common the possession of some questing personal *Weltanschauung* that modern serious youth finds more rewarding than books of mere narrative or description. But it may be relevant that Teilhard, Saint-Exupéry and the young Malraux were also active men of science or adventure. Youth may have mostly turned its back on politics and political creeds, but many of them, except perhaps an aesthetic minority, do seek practical outlets for their idealism, rather than the ivory tower. Some take part in the neo-Catholic movements of social action; many come to terms later with State technocracy, and embark on public careers. Nearly all are attracted to some degree by the new interest of social or applied sciences. There has been a huge growth of awareness of social problems, both French and foreign; and an increasing interest in anthropology, geography, sociology and of course in film-making, the most practical and documentary of the arts. Many people seek outlets abroad for their ideals of social service. Thousands go out each year to developing countries, especially in ex-French Africa, as technicians, teachers or researchers. The Government-sponsored 'Volontaires du Progrès' scheme, equivalent of the Peace Corps or Voluntary Service Overseas, has had a good response and is often allowed as the equivalent of military service. Other young people turn to individual adventure, especially in a scientific

* See pp. 586–7.

spirit: men like Michel Siffre, who in 1963 stayed alone for thirty days at the foot of a 200-foot cave, to collect data about physical endurance; or Eric Tabarly, who won the trans-Atlantic solo-yachting race for the first time in 1964.

The decline of interest in politics after the end of the Algerian war was a self-evident phenomenon linked with Gaullism and the failures of the Fourth Republic. The ideological interest and the student politics that flared up suddenly in 1968 were fairly short-lived. However, since the Socialist Party's revival in the mid-1970s, many young people are now showing a renewed and active interest in politics by joining this much *à-la-mode* party. At the same time, since the early 1960s there has been a striking and, in my view, encouraging decline in old-style nationalism and patrio-tism* – except among a tiny Right-wing minority of younger people. De Gaulle's flag-waving left them cold; no longer do they stir to the sound of a military band on 14 July – *tout ça c'est du folklore*. They are less chauvinist than their elders, less insular than British youth; and most of them do believe in some ideal of a united Europe. Often I was told, in effect: 'We go to Frank-furt or Milan now as naturally as to Lyon or Bordeaux. We have no sense of frontiers any more. It's only the British whom we feel to be still "different", but we wish they weren't because we like them. And we wish that European universities and degrees were integrated, so that you could study for one year in Paris and the next in, say, Munich, just as you like.' These young people are most of them bored and cynical about the EEC in Brussels, where they see the nations haggling and defending their own interests just as before. But they believe in their own kind of Europe, which is nearer to the original post-war inspiration of Monnet and de Gasperi; and they are trying to build it, in their own way, almost despite the politicians.

Often I notice that when young French people talk generally about modern problems, they tend to set them in a European or world context, whereas English youth discussing the same things may relate them mainly to Britain. It suggests that the French are less insular, but also, I think, that they are less closely conscious of participating in a national community against which to set their

* See p. 699.

discussions. Despite their qualities as individuals, they have generally seemed shy of forming their own group initiatives, or – before 1968 – of translating their criticisms of the adult world into joint action. Even May 1968, though it gave the lie to many notions about youth's passivity, was in a sense the exception that proved the rule. Youth seemed unable to act except in one vast destructive movement of revolt against society. It must gird itself to storm a Bastille, or do nothing. It is not capable of more calm, regular and practical action. The exceptions are few enough to be especially striking – as when Alexis Gourvennec, aged only twenty-four, led the young Breton farmers in the 1961 artichoke wars and virtually reorganized North Finistère's agriculture. In the university world, I have already suggested the students' reticence at organizing anything for themselves beyond discussion and violent protest. It was therefore heartening to visit Nancy where in the 1960s the students built up their own ambitious cultural organization. There were three separate initiatives. First in 1958 a chemistry student, Jacques Laurent, founded the Centre Culturel Universitaire Lorrain, which soon reached a membership of 3,000 embracing fourteen arts clubs. Then a girl at the Letters Faculty, Nicole Granger, started the idea of an annual Nuit Culturelle, an intensive round-the-clock arts festival, embracing everything, music, poetry, drama, debate, in one ardent and sleepless week-end. It was hugely successful and drew many well-known guest stars from Paris: in 1965 all the films of Godard were shown one after the other almost non-stop for twenty-four hours! Thirdly an amateur drama group was founded in the late 1950s by a law student, Jack Lang, who then stayed on at Nancy as a junior lecturer, kept up his drama work, and in 1962 extended it by founding Nancy's annual international drama festival. The most unprecedented aspect of the whole situation is that this student-inspired movement has burst the bounds of the university and has revitalized the whole cultural life of the city of Nancy, previously staid and conventional. It shows what French youth can do, constructively, when they try.

It would not happen so easily in Paris. In the overcrowded and overwrought atmosphere of the capital, youth has generally found it harder to find a rallying-point or make an impact – except by resorting, as in 1968, to the most dramatic means. Take the case of two serious-minded brothers I met, living with their bourgeois parents in Montparnasse. The elder, aged twenty-five, had a boring but lucrative job in a building firm; the younger, twenty-one, was at the Sorbonne, studying psychology. Together they had founded a 'Centre pour la Diffusion des Moyens d'Expression', a pompous title for a real attempt to do something creative. On a modest scale, they were beginning to market their own highbrow records of unusual music, to edit a roneoed intellectual magazine and run a drama group. They had also taken over a little night-bar in a side-street and were planning to run it as *une boîte pour yé-yés sages*, a place where people like themselves could meet and talk, away from their parents and from too much *copains* music. It all seemed rather impressive, but they were pessimistic to me about their progress. One said: 'Whenever we've tried to get people of our age together in Montparnasse to do anything worth while, we've met passivity. People seem interested at first, but they expect us to do it all for them. They won't share responsibility. Or else they quarrel and form into splinter groups. It's happened already with our drama circle.'

Like others I've met of their type, the brothers expressed anxiety that the French vogue for technocracy and modernism was accentuating cultural decline. They saw their own Centre as a modest attempt to fight against this, and against pop. But they struck me with their sense of isolation. They seemed to have little feeling of unity or even contact with the scores of thousands of young French people who broadly share their ideas. They said: 'Whenever you try to do anything public in France you're up against adult vested interests – whether it's in publishing, or journalism, or even in the pop music world where, after all, the *copains* are a slick adult-run commercial operation. We've found few people ready to help our Centre with money, at all disinterestedly.' Another young man said: 'In every way, whether it's to form pop groups, or go on CND marches, or publish poetry, we don't feel that we have the same liberty of movement that youth seems to have in Britain.' Their little roneoed magazines, with articles criticizing the Press or literature or society, struck me as pathetic – paper-darts aimed at a world that took no notice. It is true that a few other young people, perhaps with more flair, are now succeeding as in Britain in breaking into the established commercial world: setting up their own fashion shops, pop music firms or other such businesses. Often they have parental capital behind them. This is new and unusual in France, but is still very limited. The 'underground' Press is much more restricted than in Britain. Of course it can be argued that this type of revolution in Britain has gone too far. A more serious danger is when men in their prime, at thirty-five or forty, find the way to the top blocked by stale and conservative elders in the key positions: this always used to be the problem in France, and this at least has improved radically since the war.

It is perilous to generalize about a world so elusive and constantly renewing itself as the youth of a nation, and there are plenty of human examples that may contradict everything I have written. Perhaps the central difficulty is to assess their attitude to technocracy and the modernization of France. Many of the more serious ones, as I have suggested, accept its necessity but are suspicious of the way it is happening; they fear that it masks a great deal of social injustice, materialism and neglect of cultural values. And so with the intensity of youth they reject modern France and all its works. They regard with horror the adult world they are about to enter: they detest the rat-race that forces them to compete for good jobs, now growing scarcer – 'A *lycée*, that's already sad; an office, that must be frightful,' said the sixteen-year-old daughter of a senior accountant. Later, at grips with making a career, they may come to terms with modern France and join in trying to influence it. This is probably easiest for people like the young neo-Catholic activists, who have a ready-made framework of idealism to belong to. Others have fewer such doubts and scruples even from the outset – such as the bright young technocrats-to-be of ENA and the Grandes Ecoles, who eagerly accept the challenge to help build a modern France, and the chance of combining it with a successful career. The earning of money, the getting of good and useful jobs, the acceptance of a competitive society that makes this possible: these are the primary concerns of all but a small part of French middle-class youth.

But among the important minority that does not think like this,

I am left with this impression of wasted potential, of an energy and idealism failing to find positive outlets. And whose fault is it? While the young feel a sense of frustration, older people complain: 'But it's not our fault. They're so secretive, so reluctant to come forward and take part in public life. They seem to know what they don't want, but to be unable to formulate what they do want.' This *malaise* of modern youth may not be unique to France. But in France it does seem linked to certain specific factors. I think that if the school system is now at last to be made more human, and if both teachers and parents become less paternalistic, youth may breathe more easily. And, although the old Gaullist authoritarianism may be on the way out, Giscard – for all his reformist intentions – maintains a régime that is still based on technocratic élitism. This, too, adds to the sense of impotence and isolation of many young people.

Chapter 11

INTELLECTUALS IN DISARRAY

NOTHING is more revealing of modern France than the contrast between the optimism and confidence of the average businessman, technician or senior civil servant, and the *malaise* among intellectuals. This is not solely because most intellectuals are on the Left and dislike a capitalist régime. It also goes deeper. Many of them feel an embittered frustration at the rise of a whole new way of progress that has brushed aside their own careful theories and precepts. After the war they rebelled, with success, against bourgeois conservatism – but now the fruits of that rebellion seem to have been snatched from them and exploited for other ends. Their dreams are drowned in the hubbub of technology. Scornful of pragmatic values, ignorant of economics and out of touch with ordinary working people, they might seem almost as out of place in a modern Socialist régime as they did under de Gaulle. It is the whole contemporary world that they fancy has betrayed them; or have *they* betrayed *it*, by burying their heads in the sand?

By 'intellectuals' I mean those writers, artists, academics and others, immersed in their own world of ideas and arguments, who have always formed a very special and recognizable caste in France, and especially in Paris. Often they have been highly vocal rather than directly influential; but always society has respected them as an honoured minority, like the holy men of India, and the word *intellectuel* has been simply a term of description like musician or sportsman, without pejorative overtones as in Britain. Today this is changing. Some of the prestige traditionally accorded to the writer or thinker is being transferred to the man of action or science; and many clever young people now shrink, as in Britain, from openly dubbing themselves as 'intellectuals'.

France no longer appears as the cultural champion of the West – and even Frenchmen will now often admit this. The economic and social resurgence of the nation has gone hand in hand with this ominous intellectual and artistic decline. The withering of the Sartrian movement in the early 1950s left Parisian intellectual life confused, fluid and with few ideological leaders: no wonder that so many of those serious young students feel bereft and sceptical, as they search for a living *maître à penser* with more spiritual nourishment to offer than the new technocratic ethos. Admittedly there are several bright spots of new and original activity in this generally bleak picture. One has been the rise of a dynamic Catholic humanism, extending far outside intellectual circles; another, the searching and stimulating new approach of the structuralists; the effervescence of young creative talent in the cinema during the 1960s; the growth of new theatre movements, especially in the provinces; and the new interest in contemporary music, poetry, television, journalism, radical political thinking, and the dearth of good young novelists and playwrights.

What are the reasons for the decline? There are French historical precedents to suggest that art and ideas flourish either under austerity (as in the 1945 period) or in settled prosperity (as in the time of Louis XIV or the *Belle Epoque*) but not in a period of rapid industrial transition when the nation's main energies are elsewhere. Maybe France's culture will re-emerge later, in a new guise, when it has shifted some of the weight of its inhibiting classical tradition. For the moment, the crisis seems due as much to a paralysis of outlook and expression, a stifling Parisian inbredness, as to sheer shortage of talent.

SLUMP IN SARTRE AND NO SUCCESSOR

Like so much else in modern France, the existentialist movement was generated during the war. It was in 1943 that Sartre brought out his key philosophical work, *L'Etre et le néant*, though he was already well known from his first novel, *La Nausée*, published in 1938 while he was a *lycée* teacher at Le Havre. The Occupation, with its disruption of bourgeois values, tempted many young thinkers besides Sartre towards a similar kind of disenchanted humanism, so that on the Liberation he found an immediate and sympathetic audience. For the next few years he and groups of disciples would sit in the St-Germain-des-Prés cafés and discuss problems of personal responsibility, especially in relation to political action. This was the real French existentialist movement, and it had much influence in academic and Left-wing circles. It was a time of high aspiration, when it seemed that social revolution might, after all, be possible in France; and these early post-war years were a period of intellectual fervour and originality, amid political chaos and economic gloom – the opposite of the situation in the 1960s.

Sartre also attracted, quite incidentally, a much larger group of rather less serious young people who rarely understood his ideas but relished a philosophy that seemed to preach complete licence. The more austere of his tenets they conveniently overlooked. This parasitic movement was also the product of war-time upheaval, but had little in common with Sartre save a revolt from established morality and a liking for the same cafés. They gave the world an entirely misleading image of the existentialist as a kind of indolent beatnik, whereas Sartre and his friends in their own way have always been ascetic, hard-working, even puritanical. Sartre publicly disclaimed these feckless adolescents – some of them boys from good Passy homes who would arrive each evening in their neat suits and hurry down to the café cloakrooms to don their local uniform of jeans, lumber-jackets and sandals.

This *milieu* is long dispersed now. Many of the rebels have made peace with their backgrounds, have gone back to the provinces or suburbs to become sober lawyers or teachers. Their St-Germain haunts are infected by a motley of tourists, some of them looking for Sartre and finding each other. Juliette Greco, who was the existentialists' idol, has long since made their bohemianism respectable by moving to the *boîtes* across the river; and today the Right Bank is getting its revenge by invading St-Germain with a Champs-Elysées *chic* of boutiques and drugstores. Neo-bourgeois values of affluent arti-smartness are triumphing in Sartre's very citadel – the maggots are at the Deux Magots. It is true that the *Quartier* still has its raffish habitués, but not its old cohesion and intensity. In 1957 I met an American couple there in search of advertised *soirées existentialistes* who, when I said they'd come a decade too late, asked me: 'But what about this new movement, the Poujadists? What are their literary cafés?'

The true existentialist movement has also withered, though it has left an indelible mark on French thinking. Its end was hastened by various external factors, notably by the disillusioning political failures of the Left under the Fourth Republic, and by the luring rise of a new climate of prosperity and technocratic reform. As so often in French history, the bourgeoisie has simply shifted its ground in face of internal revolt, and has re-formed its ranks. But the existentialist movement was destroyed also from within itself – by the failure of intellectuals to pass from mental *engagement* to any kind of effective action, and by the bewildering shifts and ambiguities in Sartre's own pronouncements, both philosophical and political, since about 1950.

Existentialism, at first seized on so hopefully as a light to live by, was soon felt by many intellectuals to lead to a moral *impasse*, at least in its atheistic Sartrian form. Developing the ideas of his German precursors, Heidegger and Husserl, Sartre taught that man creates himself by his actions, for which he has freedom of choice and total responsibility; each choice is 'absurd' because there is no norm of conduct or objective moral standard, but (and here Sartre has never made himself quite clear) in the act of choosing, a man confers value on what he chooses, for himself and all mankind. Many young French agnostics warmed to the courage and humanism of this austere philosophy, which at least seemed more hopeful than determinism. But to those who searched more closely among the contradictions of *L'Etre et le néant* and *L'Existentialisme est un humanisme* (1945), this humanism began to look suspiciously like solipsism; and not everyone felt able to share Sartre's gloomy view of the impossibility of human relationships – 'Hell,' he wrote in *Huis clos,* 'is other people.' Existentialism had brought freedom from the bonds of convention – but was it not an empty liberty? It is significant that even Simone de Beauvoir, closest and most loyal of all Sartre's followers, seems to echo some of this feeling of deception in the anguished closing pages of the last volume of her memoirs, *La Force des choses*.* 'What have I done with my liberty?' she cries: 'The only new and important thing that can happen to me now is unhappiness ... My acts of revolt are discouraged by the imminence of my death and the fatal approach of decay.' This, from a woman of only fifty-five. Her final astonishing sentence is, '*J'ai été flouée*': 'I've been had for a sucker!'

A more serious blow to Sartre's reputation has come, in the past twenty years, from his subordination of existentialism to his own political obsessions in apparent defiance of logic and consistency. His Marxism, and his hatred of Right-wing oppression, are in themselves perfectly respectable. But few people can accept the logic that led him from 'absurdity of choice' to doctrinaire commitment. If man has freedom of choice, by what existentialist right does Sartre then insist that Marxism is the only 'valid' choice? Sartre has never convincingly answered this question. Today he asserts that Marxism is the only great philosophy of this century, and that existentialism is merely its handmaiden, taking charge of a field of humanist ideas that it had neglected.

Sartre is by no means the only French bourgeois intellectual whose devotion to the Left goes hand in hand with a large ignorance of the actual working class. De Beauvoir, for instance, described in *La Force des choses* how, as late as 1949, she went to a meeting in Paris and 'was in contact with a popular *milieu* for the first time'. While Sartre espouses revolution in the name of the workers, that class itself is steadily emulating bourgeois habits and comforts – and how horrified he might be, if he ever met them.

In the 1950s Sartre quarrelled and broke with one after another of his former sympathizers; first he quarrelled with Camus in 1952, then with the Sorbonne's most brilliant existentialist, Maurice Merleau-Ponty. Sartre has always been harrowingly sincere and honest with himself, even when apparently distorting historical truth, and today aged over 70 he appears a somewhat lonely and tragic figure. As has often been said, it is the tragedy of a man with a deeply religious temperament who has killed God. And it is just because his early post-war influence was so great, and his intellectual magnetism so hypnotic, that he has left

* Gallimard, 1963.

such disarray among intellectuals throughout France. God has failed him; but he, too, is a god that failed. Serious eighteen-year-olds still eagerly discover his early books and find them relevant to their own problems; but they read them almost as classics, as if Sartre were as dead as Camus, Kafka or the pre-war Malraux. In May 1968, Sartre was quick to side publicly with the militant students, and even encouraged them to use violence and to boy-cott the ensuing reforms. This won him a certain sympathy with the *enragés*, but they did not look to him as a leader. It was *their* struggle, and he was simply on the sidelines. Since 1968 he has been taking an active part in certain Parisian political campaigns. He has campaigned in the streets against abuses such as racism; he has even risked imprisonment by sponsoring an extreme-Left magazine. This new activism has won him some respect; but it has little to do with his work as a philosopher or writer.

Existentialism has today merged into the air that a Frenchman breathes daily, like nineteenth-century rationalism. Few intellec-tuals any longer dub themselves existentialists, but all are marked by it. As a catalyst its influence has almost certainly been positive. It is easy to forget how stifling was the French pre-war bourgeois world, the world described by de Beauvoir in *Mémoires d'une jeune fille rangée*; and she and Sartre helped to open its windows a little. Nothing has been quite the same since – at least for any-one still under fifty with some intellectual leanings. Existentialism has helped to put the young on their guard against being duped: it has generated a climate of disenchantment, at its best sceptical and honest, at its worst cynical and apathetic.

In modern French sociology and criticism, in the *nouveau roman* and some of the films of the *nouvelle vague*, even in cabaret songs of the Brassens and Barbara type and in Sagan-style popular fiction, the continuing influence of existentialism has been clear. Inside the philosophical world it is still widely studied at uni-versities, mainly as a tool for re-assessing the older philosophies: it weakened the sterile hold of Kant and Descartes over the Sorbonne and forced a much-needed new approach to their ideas. And existentialism at least has the merit, compared with the Oxford positivist school, of appearing to be at grips with real moral problems, not merely with semantics.

But for some years existentialism left behind it a pregnant vacuum in French intellectual thought. Its fire had burned up the dead wood of bourgeois cant. Had it also killed the roots, or would new shoots break through? Throughout the 1950s and early 1960s the picture was mainly one of confusion: the flight continued from political idealism and the post-war ideal of *littérature engagée*, and new writers like Robbe-Grillet and Sollers took refuge in a private, asocial world of fantasy and stylistic experiment. Then in the later 1960s a new philosophical trend finally emerged, much more restricted in its appeal than existentialism, but of undoubted power. It is known as 'structuralism', and its leading exponents are Claude Lévi-Strauss, who teaches ethnology at the Collège de France, and Roland Barthes, literary critic. To an extent it has grown out of existentialism and shares with it an atheistic rejection of the bourgeois view of history and morality. But whereas Sartre's philosophy sees man as the free captain of his own conscience and destiny, the structuralists regard him as the prisoner of a determined system. Sartre springs from the humanist tradition, an old-fashioned moralist in a new guise: Lévi-Strauss and his friends use the language and methods of psychoanalysis, anthropology and linguistic philosophy. They believe that man's thought and actions have been determined, throughout history, by a network of structures, social and psychological, where free will plays a minimal part: and that history is like a series of geological layers, each created by the pressure of the preceding one. Lévi-Strauss has applied these ideas to the study of primitive societies, past and present; Jacques Lacan allies them to psychoanalysis; Roland Barthes, a Marxist, uses them in the field of semantics or 'semiology', the study of the set of signs and symbols which he believes shape our thoughts and actions; Jacques Derrida and Michel Foucault apply structuralism to philosophy proper, and in *Les Mots et les choses* the latter argued: 'Man with a capital M is an invention: if we study thought as an archaeologist studies buried cities, we can see that Man was born yesterday, and perhaps that he will soon die.' This book, published in 1966, sent tremors well outside academic circles: for months it was a best-seller, the smart topic of party conversation whether you had read it or (more probably) not, and it even prompted full-page articles in some of the weeklies with headlines like 'Man is Dead'. Around the same time Roland Barthes was publicly taken to task by the Sorbonne literary professor Raymond Picard, and their violent quarrel about structuralism also spilled on to the popular headlines. Two years later, an almost equally keen dispute broke out as to whether the 'spontaneous' and 'active' uprising of May 1968 had, or had not, disproved the whole determinist basis of structuralism. Anti-structuralists eagerly seized on the May explosion as a chance to refute a philosophy they hated. All this went to show that French intellectuals can still, even today, steal the public limelight now and again, as in very few other countries. It also showed something of the educated public's fascinated horror at a new philosophy that made even Sartre's ideas look humane and optimistic in comparison. Sartre had killed God; the structuralists were killing Man too. Their influence extends across a number of disciplines – sociology, psychology and literature as much as philosophy – and reaches far beyond France. In fact, the structuralists have made more impact on British intellectuals and academics than the Sartrians ever did. Their movement is a symptom of the belated French post-war discovery of anthropology and the other human sciences, which they have seized on with a typical French intellectual extremism, but also with creative imagination. Critics who are able to follow Barthes' thought usually find him, whether they share his views or not, immensely exciting and mentally elegant.

Structuralism marks the first incursion of scientific values into the traditional domains of French intellectual life. As such, it is no more than one facet of a much wider and more important development: today the febrile little ghetto of the Left Bank finds itself increasingly challenged and circumscribed by the rise outside its walls of a new modern society with very different ideals, intent on technology, technocracy and practical reform. And many *bona-fide* intellectuals have virtually defected to this camp, not necessarily by embracing structuralism, but simply by going to work with the reformers. Times have changed since the 1940s. The new bourgeoisie is more stable and prosperous than ever, and the bulk of the nation is absorbed in material and technical progress, or in trying to find concrete remedies for the black spots in housing, education, birth-control, environment and the rest. And in the 1960s many intellectuals deserted their ivory towers to hitch their energies to these mundane but urgent tasks, whether by joining the Gaullists or constructively opposing them.

So today there is a most striking divorce between those intellectuals who broadly accept modern France and are helping to build it and those – still probably the majority – who reject it, remaining attached to their old ideologies or retreating into a private world of experimentation. Each group charges the other with betrayal. The 'pragmatists' are accused of compromising with a bourgeois régime, and of abandoning the hopes and ideals of an eventual victory of the Left on its terms. They include a number of economists and social scientists – like the brilliant Michel Crozier, or Raymond Aron (who twenty-five years ago was on the editorial board of Sartre's review, *Les Temps Modernes*!). They, in turn, charge the 'diehards' with sticking their noses in the sand and refusing to accept that conditions have changed. It is a quarrel that goes deeper than party politics: the successful growth of a new progress-minded society has taken the old guard by surprise and left them barking in the wrong direction. Of course there are many ramifications between the two groups, and many famous figures who do not fit easily into either: Lévi-Strauss himself, for instance. But the prototypes are blatant enough: the contrast in the 1960s between Malraux building his cultural centres and Sartre crying woe in the wilderness.

This traditional type of French intellectual, whether committed to the Left or not so political, is usually an easily recognizable species, especially on the Left Bank. Many of them hold university or *lycée* posts, or write for Left-wing journals, or combine a living out of reading for publishers, writing low-selling novels, and giving talks on the hated State radio. They generally dress drably and live modestly, in shabby, low-rent flats around the *Quartier*; they are not flamboyantly bohemian or picturesque, and they do not even spend much time in cafés any more. Though nearly all of them are bourgeois by origin, they have few social contacts, except family ones, with the despised money-making, conventional bourgeoisie. And they cling together. Many have been through the precision-test of the *agrégation*, and share the Sorbonne's disdain for the rest of the world. Their capacity for semi-abstract rhetorical discussion, in a special *agrégés'* language of their own, seems inexhaustible. They have come in for a good deal of heavy criticism, from various quarters – and especially from a man who is really one of themselves, a philosophy teacher and journalist called Jean-François Revel, who has been moving from centre-Left to centre-Right.

In person Revel is a mild and affable man, short, rotund, fiftyish; in print, he is the wittiest and most unsparing Jeremiah. In four remarkable books* he lashed out at almost everything and everyone in modern France, and especially at the intellectual Left. The weakness of this kind of polemicist is that he overstates his case, he attacks too many things at once and cannot be taken quite seriously. Revel is no exception: but, inevitably, many of his shafts strike home. He has charged the intellectuals, first, with conformism:

> In the Left-wing reviews and weeklies, there is often a contrast between their political courage and their intellectual conformism. On page three, they risk police seizure,† on page seventeen they prostrate themselves before Claudel, Heidegger, or some other reactionary idol of thought or sensibility.

There is no need necessarily to share Revel's views on Claudel to agree with his main point, that most French intellectuals are scared of questioning their own basic assumptions or of getting too involved with others who share different ones. You see, they are still bourgeois beneath the skin. They live in a world of sacred cows, where the supremacy of certain accepted French authors and ideas must not be doubted – it stems back to the way they were taught Racine at the *lycée*. Revel also comments, acutely:

* *Pourquoi des Philosophes?* (Pauvert, 1957); *La Cabale des dévots* (the best of the four – Pauvert, 1962); *En France* (Julliard, 1965); *Contrecensures* (Pauvert, 1966).

† This was in 1962, during the FLN/OAS crisis.

Today's philosophy and literature have the function, in installing a *formalisation* of anxiety and revolt, of softening the reader's actual anxiety and revolt. By repeating every day to their placid and sated readers, 'you are very distressed', they succeed in tranquillizing them.

Or as a very bright *lycéenne* of eighteen told me, solemnly, 'We have a duty to be unhappy, Sartre tells us so.'

Revel castigates the notorious chauvinism* of French intellectuals – and what he calls their 'contempt for the authenticity of information' and 'great lack of interest in reality'. Several critics noted how, in *La Force des choses*, de Beauvoir repeatedly charged the Fifth Republic with 'fascism' but gave de Gaulle not one word of credit for decolonizing Africa or standing up to the Army and OAS. French intellectuals frequently give the impression that real life exists as grist to their own theories and not in its own right: they are afraid of peering outside the ghetto to look at the manifold changes in France, lest these do not fit in with their *idées reçues*.

Above all, Revel has attacked the hallowed notion of French 'clarity'. In this instance he found an ally in no less an organ than the *Times Literary Supplement*. In a special French number of the *TLS* in May 1962, a famous front-page article suggested that the French tradition of limpid thought and clear logic, from Descartes via Voltaire to today, was now little more than a myth, and that Parisian intellectuals were today among the most abstruse and muddle-headed on earth. 'Clarity is giving place to woolly subjectivism, private symbols are posing as proofs of profundity,' said the *TLS* with a passing swipe at *L'Année dernière à Marienbad*: among the morsels it quoted to make its point was this from a prize-winning poetic passage by Michel Deguy:†

L'homme *est* philosophique; c'est à dire qu'il est philosophé par le passage au travers de son être de ce jaillissement dont la trace va s'appeler tout de suite *philosophie*, trace oeuvre. La source se cache dans son propre flux; elle disparaît dans le fécondité de son sourdre. Penser c'est consentir à ce désir, qui nous constitue, de remémorer le sourdre indicible; c'est comme tenter de se convertir à la nuit d'où

* See pp. 706–7.

† One of the Tel Quel group of young aesthetes: see p. 566.

sort toute aube, et que les yeux, qui sont faits pour les lumineux, ne peuvent voir – tentative quasi suicidaire de gagner sur cette dérobade de l'originel pour le pressentir, recul de dos au plus près du foyer de notre être qui est abîme, perte d'être.

The *TLS* saw existentialism as one root of the trouble: 'a debased, haughty, and unscientific philosophy has invaded all thinking and all forms of expression'. Sartre himself, the article went on, was an original and courageous writer, but his imitators had abused his ideas and his language: 'He is largely responsible for the flourishing of a jargon that makes so much writing strictly unreadable, pretentious, precious and, above all, unclear.' The *TLS* called for a campaign against looseness (against vague words like *ontologie* and *dialectique* that were 'making France ridiculous') and it suggested that the linguistic purists should attack not *franglais* but highbrow obscurity as the most serious menace to pure French.

Revel, too, in *Pourquoi des Philosophes?* had been just as rude about 'clarity'. After attending a seminar on 'filmology' at the Sorbonne, he gave this summary of how the professor explained film projection:

On peut donc considérer comme définitivement démontré par la filmologie que le passage de la réalité pelliculaire à la réalité écranique par l'intermédiaire de la réalité lenticulaire constitue une authentique promotion anaphorique.

As the *TLS* pointed out, this epidemic is still largely confined to intellectuals. Talk to an engineer, salesman, clerk or schoolchild, and you will usually find him a model of orderly and precise expression – and the same is true of workers and peasants, within the limits of their vocabulary and knowledge. This is the splendid legacy of French education, whatever its other failings. But why do the intellectuals deliberately tie this lucid subtlety into knots, or obscure it with word-play? Some of them, maybe, want to prove their intellectual superiority by using a clever terminology that others can't follow. Passing the *agrégation* has so convinced them of their brilliance that they feel sure anything they write must be profound. Or else their style is a smoke-screen to hide their sheer lack of ideas. Or they are simply carried away by the Latin love of rhetoric and abstraction.

I must not imply that all intellectuals are like this. Many real and serious writers (such as Simone de Beauvoir) are impeccably clear. So, in their way, are the structuralists. Sartre may often be obscure, but he does leave the impression of struggling to express a genuine complexity of thought. Others have simply used this as an alibi for their own muddled vagueness, often allied to pomposity and lack of humour. 'French intellectuals are frequently terrified of humour,' said one critic; 'they think it's Right-wing.'

It is within a certain Parisian hard core that the various symptoms of intellectual *malaise* are most evident – at the Sorbonne, around the little reviews and a few *avant-garde* publishing houses. This *milieu* enjoys much less of the national limelight than it did twenty years ago: it has grown more esoteric, more specialized. But it still monopolizes a large part of organized intellectual society and has not lost its old arrogance and self-sufficiency. Scattered in isolation around the suburbs and provinces there are plenty of other writers, professors and thinkers, who are less pretentious and might even have something to say. But Paris seldom pays attention to them.

Outside this little Left Bank world a different climate is developing. The new participation of a number of intellectuals in reformist debate and action is throwing up new élites, closer to the British pattern. One sign of this is the growth of non-party economic and political study-groups; another, the displacement of old family business *patrons* by cultured and intellectually lively young technocrats: a third, the new keenness of students for the social sciences; and most important of all, the new Catholic ideal of militant social progress. As Michel Crozier has said:

Engagement is now more concrete, and philosophy and action have been growing closer together in the past ten years. All the new movements are marked by a need and a desire for contact across the barriers, a horror of *a priori* formulas, a passion for reforms and an ideology of participation.

This trend may not in every case be quite so disinterested and idealistic, however. Looked at from another angle, pragmatic realism may sometimes appear as an opportunistic switch to a now fashionable materialist ethos. There has been no sharper portent of the changing times than the change in the weekly *l'Express*. This used to be the very conscience of the intellectual Left, with long articles by Sartre and others on such matters as torture in Algeria. But after about 1964, though remaining supposedly anti-Gaullist, it jumped on to the bandwagon of technocracy and affluence, reshaped itself on the lines of *Time*, became very trend-conscious and modern-minded – and definitely lowered its intellectual quality, on its literary as well as its political side. Many of its older loyalists were dismayed, and switched to *Le Nouvel Observateur*; but clearly it appeals to a new, progress-minded, educated middle class. And the older intellectuals have only themselves to blame if they failed to provide any effective alternative to the new ethos. In a shrewd analysis of the situation, Crozier writes:

We have passed from the romantic period of the crisis, where the creative and irresponsible individual succeeded in partly breaking down the old structures [Sartre in the 1940s], to the period of routine and withdrawal where the structures regain their place. If we are now in the dead period of the cycle, it is natural that the traditional-style intellectual should no longer get a hearing; the weight of social constraints has re-appeared ... Such a period is naturally melancholy for the intellectual world. It easily gives an impression of retreat and decline. The illusions of the Liberation have been destroyed.

And Crozier goes on to speak of the rise of a new rationalism, and of the efforts of intellectuals to rethink their role and their attitudes, in face of a new, more fluid, more forward-looking climate. The crisis is likely to continue for some time. The old creative, turbulent, self-confident intellectual world, that made Paris the light and envy of the West, lies stricken, and is not likely to revive in its old form. It will re-emerge only by opening its eyes on a changing society, and accepting that change.

THE 'NEW NOVEL' AND AFTER; WHAT EXIT FROM ROBBE-GRILLET'S LABYRINTH?

Since Voltaire's day the novel in France has often been closely allied to philosophy, and therefore it is not strange to find that post-war French fiction has many affinities with the various intellectual currents and anxieties of recent years, from Sartre to the structuralists. In France, as in Britain, the novel has been going through a period of *malaise* and self-doubt, but the causes and the symptoms are quite different. Novelists in Britain, even the most highbrow, are in the main still loyal to a naturalist narrative tradition that in France over the past two decades it has been fashionable to consider outmoded; in France, the 'literary' novel (as opposed to the popular novel) is rife with metaphysical speculation and technical experiment with language and form – it is an intense, rarefied climate where every new work is potentially a poetic masterpiece but in practice more likely to be clever-clever and unreadable. You might say that the English novel has grown stale through remaining too conventional, the French 'new novel' has been boldly *avant-garde* but without the leaven of genius.

There is also a striking difference between the way novelists live in the two countries, and their attitudes to society. Most of the English ones exist placidly in the provinces or the suburbs, soberly reporting on the daily scene around them. French ones rarely have so much contact with the ordinary life of the nation: whether or not they live on the Left Bank itself, their orientation is still largely towards the specialized literary *milieu* of the capital. Their work is much more ambitious, but often less human. Like so many French intellectuals, they seem to be motivated by a kind of anti-bourgeois complex, a passionate rejection of the bourgeoisie to which by origin they belong. This motif of French literature is not new. Flaubert strongly criticized the bourgeoisie, though he used the ordinary narrative realism of his day: yet *Madame Bovary* caused as much of a shock then as Genet or Robbe-Grillet today, and narrowly escaped being banned. Today this kind of novel has become bourgeois, that is, the bourgeoisie read and accept it: so anti-bourgeois writers have been turning to other weapons, those of *avant-garde* style and sensibility rather than social criticism. Their trump card is to write novels that the ordinary bourgeois reader won't understand or enjoy.

In the past fifty years a great revolutionary movement has developed which stems back to Proust: though in his own social life he was a bourgeois reactionary, he still is venerated as having written 'the first and greatest anti-bourgeois novel'. This anti-bourgeois tradition has since been continued by others, such as Breton and Céline, and of course by Sartre himself. Early in his career he took up the novel as a vehicle for his philosophy, first in the metaphysical and allegorical *La Nausée* (1938), then in the more neo-realistic semi-documentary trilogy written in the 1940s, *Les Chemins de la liberté*. He was followed by Simone de Beauvoir in *L'Invitée* (1943) and *Les Mandarins*, and by a number of other writers (including Genet in his own unique *genre*) who just after the war formed a kind of school of existentialist novelists. Generally they did keep to the narrative form and – except for Genet – they innovated not so much in style or language as in their ferocious Marxist moralizing and their refusal to 'amuse' the reading public with what it expected – exciting plots, noble character-portrayal and other fictional devices. Induced by the rigours and verities of the Occupation, this was the era of *témoignages personnelles*. But the school fizzled out even faster than the other facets of the existentialist movement, and Sartre and de Beauvoir soon virtually gave up writing novels.

Albert Camus, like Sartre, brought a new questing philosophical intensity to the novel, and was much the finer stylist of the two. He was and still is more widely admired as a novelist than Sartre, and his vision of man struggling to give meaning and dignity to an 'absurd' existence – a vision more heroic and humane than Sartre's, if less intellectually rigorous – has influenced many younger writers. But Camus, too, appeared to lose faith in the novel as a form, and after *La Peste* (1947) he wrote only one more full-length novel (*La Chute*, 1956) before his death in a car accident in 1960, aged forty-six.

Parallel to Sartre and Camus, the first decade or so after the war was marked by a wide variety of different styles and approaches, showing that the traditional novel was and still is very far from dead. Younger novelists who emerged after the war frequently shared the existentialists' cynical hostility to bourgeois values, but without rallying to Sartrian *engagement*. There was even a reaction against it, into a kind of hedonist patrician egotism – witness a book like Roger Nimier's *Le Hussard bleu* (1950), or the early Sagan novels, or the work of Roger Vailland, a gifted and solitary Stendhalian figure, ex-Communist and eclectic adventurer, whose *La Loi* won the Prix Goncourt in 1957. And meanwhile, on the sidelines, largely ignored by the wider reading public, a number of other writers were pursuing some typically French aesthetic experimentations in the use of language and its inner links with reality: theorists like Maurice Blanchot, poetic surrealists like Queneau, Michel Leiris and Jean Douassot.

This is the background against which the writers known loosely as the 'New Novelists' emerged in the late 1950s. More journalistic ink has flowed over the so-called *nouveau roman* than over any other literary trend in Europe since the war, and probably more than it deserves, in terms of achievement. It is not really a 'school' at all, for its leading exponents – Alain Robbe-Grillet, Michel Butor, Nathalie Sarraute, Claude Simon and others – are rather different from each other and frequently quarrel and hold opposing views. They have been lumped together out of journalistic convenience, and through the smart public-relations work of their self-appointed prophet and president, Robbe-Grillet.

Yet they do have some things in common. In rejecting conventional character-portrayal and story-telling, they are in the broad line traced from Proust and Joyce via Céline, Queneau, Genet and others. Like Sartre they rebel against the Balzac tradition, but they go much farther than Sartre, and are even reacting against him too: Sarraute, for instance, has alleged that Sartre, Camus, Kafka and others were using the novel as a disguised form of diary-writing, to project their own subjective hopes and fears through the thoughts of an anonymous hero, whereas the true role of the modern writer should be to portray the actual perceptible world, that is, shorn of the author's moralizing. The most obvious common feature of all the new novelists' work is an obsession with minute physical description whether of objects or of sensations. Their semi-scientific approach to literature seems to have something in common with structuralism, and their rejection of much of the normal range of human values and interests is all too clear a symptom of the post-existentialist climate.

Robbe-Grillet is the one who has taken up the most extreme position and formulated his theories the most sharply. He is an enigmatic, unclassifiable creature, utterly untypical of one's stock picture of the French writer yet hard to imagine at work anywhere except in France. Though his novels are so very dehumanized, he himself is extremely human, jolly and relaxed; talking to him it is sometimes hard to avoid the conclusion that his whole operation might be partly a leg-pull at the expense of serious literature. 'Critics seem to have overlooked the humorous element in my books,' he once told me, 'but I laugh aloud when I read them to myself, as Kafka did at his. By far my favourite author is Lewis Carroll.' Precisely. Talking to him, or reading his books or seeing his films, one feels very much like Alice at the Mad Hatter's tea-party. '"Have some wine," the March Hare said in an encouraging tone. "I don't see any wine," remarked Alice. "There isn't any," said the March Hare.'

Now in his mid-fifties, Robbe-Grillet is dapper and quizzical with thick greyish hair and moustache. By training and early career he is an agricultural engineer and scientist, and he took up writing almost by chance in his late twenties after being impressed by Kafka, the French surrealists and *Brighton Rock*. He is anything but the usual Left Bank denizen, and he hates Paris literary society: he spends his time between a formal bourgeois flat in Neuilly and a country château near Caen, and his passionate hobbies are gardening, botany, carpentry and taking his pretty young wife on skiing holidays. He even has friends who are dons at Oxford and send him rare seeds and plants for his garden. It is not the way Sartre spends his time. I have said that Robbe-Grillet is hard to imagine except in France, though from this picture you might think him more like an English eccentric *manqué*. But his literary politicking is essentially French. From the moment that *Le Voyeur* won the Prix des Critiques in 1955 and made him famous, he set out to establish himself as *chef d'école* and to wage a vendetta against those who dared to write or admire any different kind of novel. This he does with *panache* but also with impish good humour. He enjoys flamboyant public arguments, press conferences and manifestoes, and sometimes his books and films appear as little more than weapons in a careful strategic campaign to prove certain theories about literature and perception.

His foremost dogma is that literature must rid itself of what

Ruskin called 'the pathetic fallacy', the tendency of novelists to describe objects emotively. According to Robbe-Grillet, mountains must not be allowed to loom 'majestically' or villages to 'nestle' in a valley, and it is better to write 'the glass is on the table' than 'reposes on the table'. He says, 'Around us, defying the onslaught of our animist adjectives, things *are there*,' and any attempt to endow the physical world with emotion is a step towards the illicit belief in God. This attitude, often known as *chosisme*, appears to have been influenced by the structuralist critic Roland Barthes, who has written warmly of Robbe-Grillet's novels and who similarly inveighs against the notion of 'the romantic heart of things'. These novels are rich in *chosisme* – especially in their long painstaking descriptions of such things as the shape and measurements of a window (in *Le Voyeur*) or of a tropical plantation (*La Jalousie*) or the physiognomy of centipedes.

But Robbe-Grillet, with apparent inconsistency, does not limit himself to *chosisme*. He denies that Man, despite appearances, has been banished from his pages in favour of Things. Although characterization, emotion, and action in the ordinary sense barely exist, he claims that Man still holds the centre of the stage and, as he told me, his detailed descriptions 'are *passionate*, an attempt to portray the world through the obsessed eyes of my heroes: if I describe a room with five chairs in it, what I am really describing is the obsession of the looker.' In all his novels and films the same scenes or incidents keep recurring in different guises, as if seen, remembered, or imagined by the same person in different ways. In *La Jalousie* – to my mind the best of his books – a kind of human situation does exist, a triangle of jealous husband, wife and suspected lover, and physical objects are seen with heightened awareness through the manic gaze of the unhappy husband. It is a technique in some ways better suited to the film than the novel, and this explains Robbe-Grillet's passion for the cinema. He said to me of his scenario for Resnais' *l'Année dernière à Marienbad*: 'What passes on the screen is the subjective struggle in the girl's mind, so the spectator can never be sure of the level of reality he is observing. The amount of furniture in the room varies according to how she is feeling.'

How are we to assess the artistic worth of all this? On the one hand Robbe-Grillet's great strength, in all his writing, is his sonorous and lyrical prose style that lends a dream-like fascination to many of his descriptions – and the same is true of his beautiful *mise-en-scène* in *L'Immortelle*, his first film as a director. But the effect, finally, is gratuitous and boring because there is no identifiable human impetus behind the images. Many critics have pointed out the basic contradiction in his work: on the one hand he proclaims his theory of the pre-eminence of the observable world, on the other he destroys it with a 'game of mirrors' that leaves us unable to discern what is real and what is not. 'Les choses' are not pre-eminent after all, they are the figments of human hallucination. And as John Weightman has suggested,* the very force of his dream-like descriptions creates a new 'pathetic fallacy' as potent as the one he campaigns against.

John Weightman has also analysed what he sees as Robbe-Grillet's 'religious fear of religion', his desire to purge the world of mysteries or symbols that could have any 'significance'. In all his work, and especially in his films, he first arouses our human interest and sympathy, then mockingly plants a booby-trap that snuffs it out and leaves us feeling cheated. Take *L'Immortelle*. The first half is a haunting and tender love-poem, stylized but discernibly human: a young Frenchman meets a mysterious and lovely woman in Istanbul, falls in love with her, woos her, loses her, searches for her wistfully through the eerie Turkish town-scape. Then the girl equivocally reappears and equivocally dies, and for the next half-hour Robbe-Grillet treats us to an assorted battery of trick-images which firmly ram home the message that we were suckers if we took the first half of the film at all seriously, for there is no reality. Filmgoers who seek in *L'Immortelle*, or *Marienbad*, for any deeper meaning beyond the surface beauties will seek in vain. Robbe-Grillet is at heart a scientist and an iconoclast, and he seems determined to prevent the rest of us from enjoying unscientific, literary or aesthetic pleasures of the old-fashioned sort: a curious vocation for an artist.

Robbe-Grillet has stolen much of the limelight because of his sheer novelty and shock-value, and because he is so articulate and

* *Encounter*, March 1962.

assertive, always ready to give interviews or dash across the world to attend a writers' congress. Other 'New Novelists' are less colourful, but some are worth taking just as seriously. A writer often classed together with Robbe-Grillet is Michel Butor, though in fact the two have little in common beyond having brought out experimental novels at about the same time. Butor is a mild and unassuming man of about fifty, formerly a *lycée* philosophy teacher. He has publicly attacked Robbe-Grillet's theories, and his own books are much less far removed from the traditional novel. He is a dedicated Proustian and his books, like Proust's, are concerned with time: they even have coherent characters and plots, of a sort, though often these are turned upside-down through Butor's obsession with the relativity of time and the time-space relationship. His best-known novel, *La Modification* (1957), takes place entirely in the mind of one character on a train-journey from Paris to Rome, with appropriate mental flashbacks. I myself prefer his earlier book, *L'Emploi du temps* (1956), with its nightmarish descriptions of Manchester where Butor had spent a year as a grammar-school teacher. The book opens with a young Frenchman beginning to write an account of his arrival in Manchester six months previously: but soon his present life becomes so fascinating to him that a second, more up-to-date thread of narrative interweaves with the first in his journal, and as life leaps ahead faster than his pen, soon there are several different accounts running parallel, and past and present are jumbled ever more closely together. The attempt to step into a new dimension of time is ingenious, and an English reader is intrigued by the horrified French-eye view of Manchester as a Kafkaesque city from which there is no escape: but, as in all Butor's books, the characters and events are a good deal less graphic than the time-theories. He is now moving away from fiction towards experimental prose that tries to explore the new time-space ratio in an age of supersonic travel. Clocks, timetables, airports, fascinate him. I do not think Butor is a great writer, but I find his conundrums more stimulating, if less finely written, than Robbe-Grillet's.

Nathalie Sarraute is different again. She is much older: a White Russian Jewish *émigré* to Paris, now in her seventies, who has changed her style little since her first novel over forty years ago. She was relatively unknown until Robbe-Grillet's breakthrough gave notoriety to the experimental *chosiste* novel – and she has admitted that she owes some of her public success to Robbe-Grillet, though she objects to the way he patronizes her, quite unjustifiably, as his pupil. Like Robbe-Grillet she has openly and frequently condemned the moralistic novel of explicit narrative or social comment, and this has led them to be bracketed together. But her themes and subject-matter are very different from his: she is concerned not with appearance and memory, but with the living tissue of tiny, subtle sensations that she believes to make up the fabric of our lives. She admires Proust and Virginia Woolf, and uses a stream-of-consciousness technique not so very different from theirs to depict minutely a world of psychological flickerings (*tropismes*, she calls them) which for her are the real substance of human contact and sensibility. Her novels are difficult to read, and not rich in outward plot or character, but within her self-imposed range she is manifestly a psychological realist, and a true poet.

Another gifted woman writer who is sometimes lumped with the 'New Novelists' is Marguerite Duras. Her elliptical techniques of dialogue and narrative possibly entitle her to be classed as experimental: but at heart she is less close to Robbe-Grillet than to the *engagé* Sartrian school. Witness the difference between the two Resnais films: *Hiroshima mon amour* with her script, and the never-never-land of *Marienbad*. But she is not a pamphleteer: she is a warm-blooded writer with a feeling for real people and predicaments, and that is something to welcome in the French novel today. In the best of her stories – *Le Square*, *10.30 d'un soir d'été*, *Les Petits Chevaux de Tarquinia* – she portrays a rare sensitivity to atmosphere and place, the delicacy of relationships and the difficulty of communication. My only criticism is that, like many women intellectuals of her type, she is not above lapsing into women's-magazine emotionalism.

The most powerful of all the 'New Novelists', though not the best known outside France, is Claude Simon, who is now in his sixties. Even more than Butor and Sarraute, his books recall Proust – and also Faulkner, whose influence he freely admits.

Like Faulkner he writes about violence: *La Route des Flandres* (1961) deals with the events of 1940, and *Le Palace* (1962) recalls his own memories of Barcelona at the outbreak of the Spanish War. Like Proust he struggles obsessively to recapture on paper the colour and smell of his youth; his giant sentences, sprawling like pages of baroque metaphor, are like a very parody of Proust's. His obscurity, and his disregard for narrative, earn him a place of honour in the *nouveau roman*: but he writes passionately, from the heart, not with chilly calculation.

There are other 'New Novelists' too: among the best known are Robert Pinget, Claude Ollier and Claude Mauriac (son of François). All, or nearly all, see it as the writer's task to experiment with the links between language and consciousness rather than to depict society or tell a story; all, or nearly all, are Left-wing in their personal sympathies, and several including Robbe-Grillet signed the manifestoes against the war in Algeria; but not often does any hint of such views or of any topical social concern enter their pages. Sometimes they appear to be chiefly preoccupied with writing novels about the problems of writing novels, especially Mauriac and Philippe Sollers. Needless to say, this inward-looking and rarefied school of literature has not found any great success with a wider public: few of their books have sold more than 3,000 or 4,000 copies, except for some of the *succès d'estime* of Robbe-Grillet and Butor, which have reached 60,000 or so in pocket editions. Today the phenomenon of the *nouveau roman* is fast fading out. It no longer has many imitators among young novelists; and its leaders have virtually ceased writing novels. Students and *lycéens* rarely turn early to these writers as they do, still, to Camus, Sartre and Malraux.

What then has the 'new novel' achieved? Many critics, including some of those who are not its greatest admirers, see it as essentially a catalyst, paving the way for the future. One well-known critic, Robert Escarpit, told me: 'I see the *nouveau roman* as a language laboratory or testing ground: Butor, Pinget, and company are doing for us what Joyce did for English. These books will have a permanent influence, but they won't last in themselves. Their role is to open a new door.'

Nearly all the 'New Novelists' are now over fifty. Among the younger writers following through the door they are said to have opened, two main trends became discernible in the 1960s. The first was the emergence of an arrogant and vocal coterie of young aesthetes, led by the experimental writer Philippe Sollers. They have their own monthly review, *Tel Quel*, which champions the ideal of formal literary beauty. Their style owes something to Robbe-Grillet, whom they salute as a *maître-à-penser*, but they also claim affinities back to Valéry, Artaud and others, and they have links with the structuralists. Their concern is for exquisiteness of language, irrespective of content; one of their number is Michel Deguy, whose prize work I quoted from the *Times Literary Supplement* article, and he is typical of them. They have been compared to Mallarmé and his school, and they seem to have much in common with his ingrown preciosity and disregard for ideas or coarse reality. They are not especially numerous but they are typical of the kind of current Left Bank intellectual obscurantism that Revel and others have attacked. And in literary circles their dogmatic influence has amounted to a kind of tyranny – 'We have created a new theology,' Sollers admitted proudly in 1971.

Another trend, which is not linked to any Parisian coterie like the *Tel Quel* group but is the product of two or three isolated talents, is for the kind of novel that gives vent to an aggressive personal disgust at the universe, in language often ferocious. These writers owe something to the *nouveau roman* in their techniques, and you can trace affinities too with Genet, Beckett or the American beats. But more directly they are giving personal expression to the kind of *malaise* that exists among serious youth in some student and other circles. Claude Néron, a Belgian living in France, is one name; another was Albertine Sarrazin, a kind of female Jean Genet who wrote at first hand about an underworld of prisons, pimps and prostitutes, and who died in 1967 at the age of thirty. These writers hold no literary theories; it may be too schematic to regard them as a trend. The most distinguished of them is a handsome, blond Adonis in his middle thirties who looks like a clean-living rugger captain and writes like Dante in Hell. Jean-Marie-Gustave le Clézio is actually of British nationality. He comes from Mauritius and now lives in Nice. He is reserved and laconic, and tends to give anti-interviews expressing his disgust at himself and the interviewer – the opposite of Robbe-Grillet. His first novel, *Le Procès-verbal*, won the Prix Renaudot and narrowly missed the Goncourt in 1963, and was described by François Erval in *l'Express* as 'the most remarkable début in French literature since the war'. It is on the familiar theme of a young man's search for meaning and identity, but expressed in an unusual heightened style of tormented ingenuity, with realistic settings drawn from his own experience. Then came in 1966 his much-praised *Le Déluge*. This takes up the theme of his first book and lifts it on to a cosmic level while retaining the everyday settings. It is the story of a young man's nightmare odyssey through the streets of a modern city, haunted by death and decay, leading to a final expiation where, alone by the sea after days of storm, he turns his eyes to the force of the sun and blinds himself. Le Clézio marries this epic allegory of man's destiny not with the semi-abstract world of Samuel Beckett but with the ordinary details that he finds revolting about life today, in an overcrowded city of noise, greed and alienation. His personal hell makes the work of many of the other 'New Novelists' look like contrived doodlings. But since *Le Déluge* he has tended to repeat himself in later books. He does not after all seem to be a writer capable of great development.

If the 'New Novel' has stolen much of the critical limelight in the past decade, this does not mean that public taste follows suit or that the traditional novel is dead. Conventional writers like Henri Troyat, Jean Lartéguy, Maurice Druon and Gilbert Cesbron easily top the best-seller lists, with sales maybe ten or fifty times that of the average *nouveau roman*. And even among 'literary' novels, very few today are classifiable as *nouveaux romans*. There are still plenty of serious or ambitious new novels of narrative that deal with cherished French themes of family life and conflict, or with off-beat amorous adventures in exotic lands, or with high society. Robert Sabatier has won immense success in the past few years with his sensitive studies of pre-war middle-class childhood: *Les Allumettes suédoises* sold 300,000. This genre is, you might say, the French equivalent of L. P. Hartley.

And the leading annual literary prizes which make so much difference to sales – the Goncourt, the Renaudot, the Fémina, and others – are much more often given to this kind of book than to an experimental one. When Butor's *La Modification* won the Renaudot in 1957, and then sold 100,000 copies, it was an exception.

Even the traditional novel, almost as much as the 'New Novel', shows a curious reluctance to deal squarely with the themes of modern France. Serious writers, whatever their approach to the novel, prefer to set their books in the past, or abroad, or around private subjects of love, fantasy or childhood, rather than to analyse what it is like to live in this country today. This is true, for instance, of Michel Tournier's brilliant Gothic fantasy, *Le Roi des Aulnes*, which won the Goncourt in 1971; or of Pierre-Jean Remy's ambitious and fascinating study of Europeans in modern and last-century Peking, *Le Sac du Palais d'Eté*, Prix Renaudot winner also in 1971. At a time when French society is in a fascinating period of transition, the novel has virtually abdicated its classic role as chronicler of that society – and in France, even the modern inheritors of that role, cinema and television, are not doing this particular job very well. True, there are some exceptions: sharp little studies of bourgeois cupidity continue to appear, such as de Beauvoir's *nouvelle*, *Les Belles Images*, but one has the feeling that it's all been said before, with the same *parti pris*. The French novel remains essentially bourgeois, especially when it is trying not to be: there is virtually no equivalent of the new English school of working-class fiction (for what *that* is worth). And although a few bourgeois intellectuals have made brave attempts to penetrate the mysteries of modern working-class life (as Christiane Rochefort has in *Les Petits Enfants du siècle*) these usually lack conviction.

Sometimes I ingenuously ask a writer or publisher: 'France today needs her Balzac, her Flaubert, as much as ever: why is no one filling this gap?' The 'New Novelists' just laugh. Robbe-Grillet said to me: 'Flaubert and Balzac were great writers in their day, but you can't write like that now, and those who try to are bad writers. The role of the novelist today isn't to explore social values, for these already exist: it is to discover *new* values.'

Some authors, including Butor, claim that they *are* writing about real modern life but simply using new techniques. But what really seems to have happened is that, in trying to escape from the tyranny of Balzac, these writers have imposed a new tyranny, a new conformism, which is just as strong. Young writers often complain: 'After what Robbe-Grillet's done to the novel, we don't feel able to write in the traditional manner any more.' Many intellectuals, too, feel it a point of honour *not* to write the kind of readable novel which the bourgeoisie can enjoy and which therefore might encourage bourgeois complacency. Hence much of the self-conscious difficulty of modern writing.

There is therefore this gap in France between bourgeois and experimental fiction, with few writers, say, of the Iris Murdoch or Angus Wilson type in a middle position. It is true that, with the waning of the influence of the *nouveau roman*, a trend back to the serious novel of narrative or of contemporary social manners has begun to emerge in the 1970s – books such as Jean Carrière's *L'Epervier de Maheux*, 1972 Goncourt winner, a stark study of rural life in the Cévennes; or Jean d'Ormesson's *Au plaisir de Dieu*, a witty analysis of upper-class society since 1900; or Victor Pilhes' 1974 Prix Fémina winner, *L'Imprécateur*, which actually does tackle a contemporary social theme, for it is a kind of satire on the Paris international business world. It will be fascinating to see whether these three excellent books are harbingers of a major new shift in French fiction. For the moment, they are still the exception. Escarpit said to me: 'If the kind of book you're wanting rarely appears, I think it's the fault of publishers, critics and public as much as of writers. If anyone today wrote, say, an uncompromising realistic satire on provincial life, it would fall between two stools. The highbrows would deride it as old-hat and not what the novel is for: and bourgeois publishers and booksellers would be frightened it would offend their readers.' Many younger writers feel that the influence of structuralism and of the Robbe-Grillet and Sollers schools severely inhibits them from producing a good traditional novel. François Nourissier, a serious realistic novelist, said in 1975: 'The past 20 years have seen a growth of critical forms to the detriment of creative forms; a takeover by pedagogues, linguists, psycho-analysts and philosophers of the literary heritage . . . and this has stifled the literary spirit of adventure, the ambition and taste for imaginative writing. The quest for the "new novel", and the experimentation of the *Tel Quel* school, while unquestionably legitimate, have wrought such terrorism as to cause a collective mental block among young writers.'

This state of affairs derives partly from the special position of the writer in French society. He is publicly esteemed, his views are quoted in the newspapers much more often than in England: but generally he lives in less close contact with ordinary society than English writers from Hardy to John Braine. French novelists have tended to mix with each other in a rarefied Parisian *milieu*, scorning the provinces – 'I was born in Amiens, but you can't *live* there,' one told me – and in extreme cases they make it almost a point of faith not to know what ordinary philistines are like. Their raw material of life is generally drawn from their own childhood memories of family crises, or from their current intrigues and *amours*. It is a world centring round the great Parisian publishing houses and the monthly and quarterly reviews, such as Sartre's *Temps Modernes* and the *Nouvelle Revue Française*. These reviews are less powerful and numerous than they used to be, but occupy a far larger place in French literary life than their English equivalents such as *Encounter*. It is a world dominated by gossip and politicking over who is going to review whom, and how the writers' juries will vote for the annual prizes; a world where the caprice of fashion plays almost as large a role, in its own highbrow way, as in the London pop scene. And there is far less *va-et-vient* and easy communication than in London between this strictly literary world and the wider, less high-powered one of TV, radio and journalism.

In the great days, until the 1930s, there was an aristocratic flavour to this literary *milieu*, centring round the *salons* of the great cultured families. In this way writers (for example Proust) were in touch with at least one section of true French social life. Since the war the *salons* have been dying, and many intellectuals have retreated from their influence to within their own closed ranks. But today, since the 1960s, a new phase is becoming apparent which might have great influence. The intellectual cliques are beginning to disperse under the impact of economic change and the new modern style of living. Some of the more successful writers, seduced by affluence, are indulging in fast cars, week-end cottages and regular foreign travel, and are becoming less dependent on the Parisian ghetto; or else they move out from their old Left Bank flats to new homes in the suburbs, just like other bourgeois. A few other writers have decided, like a growing number of Parisians, that the provinces might be the best place to live in after all. Le Clézio has placed on record his hatred of Paris: admittedly, Nice where he lives is not the most typical of French towns nor is he likely to be its Balzac, but I fancy that he and others are more likely to be able to realize themselves in the provinces than amid the pressures of Paris. And if there is to be a French creative revival in the arts, my guess is that it will come not from Paris but from the new intellectual life that is burgeoning in provincial towns. And against this kind of background, a French writer is much less likely to be isolated from the rest of society.

The French novel still shows a certain vitality, even if one may not always admire the expression it takes. I wish I could say the same of French poetry, which has gone into near-eclipse since the death of Eluard in 1952. The few notable French poets still alive (figures as diverse as Francis Ponge, Henri Michaux and René Char) are all over sixty. Saint-John Perse died in 1975, aged eighty-eight. Hardly a single younger poet has made any impact and publishers seem even more scared of marketing poetry than in England.

FRANCE'S NEW DYNAMIC: MILITANT LAY CATHOLICISM

While intellectuals like Barthes and Lévi-Strauss have become in a sense the anti-Christian theologians of the age, the Catholics in France have been turning from theology and ritual to social action. Look closely at any of the grass-roots movements of social reform since the war, and in nearly every case you will find that some nucleus of Catholic militants has played a central part: the farming revolution led by the Jeunesse Agricole Chrétienne is the obvious example, but there are many others too, in business, industry and trade-unionism, in the student world or among animators of the Grands Ensembles and even in the campaign for birth-control. In a country where the Church has tended in the past to be reactionary and integrist, this neo-Catholicism, as it is called, marks a striking change.

And so one hears talk in France of a 'post-war Catholic revival'. But the term can be misleading: the revival is one of quality, not quantity. Regular church-going is still at a low ebb, the traditional influence of the parish priest has been everywhere declining, and most people in practice are quite pagan. But among those who do believe there has been a re-examining and a sharpening of faith, and a major shift of emphasis towards Christian witness and away from old-style piety and ritual. This began partly as a lay-inspired movement; but today it embraces many of the clergy too, especially the younger ones, and it has won the qualified support of many bishops. The French hierarchy has been moving to the Left since the war; and France has played as large a part as almost any country in helping to influence the new policies of the Vatican.

To anyone who knows the pre-1939 history of the Church in France all this may seem extraordinary. Although since 1905 the State has been secular and the Church disestablished, until much more recently the hierarchy identified itself closely in practice with the ruling upper-bourgeois class, and protected its own interest by defending the social *status quo*. In rural areas priest and gentry were natural allies. The Church was ultra-clerical, allowing little scope for lay action, and expecting its priests to be obeyed; and it inspired the bitterest anti-clericalism. The Church was also anti-temporal, concerned exclusively with spiritual, not social, welfare. And often it was nationalistic almost to the point of fascism. Many of its leaders supported Maurras's extreme Right-wing *Action Française* movement in the 1930s. Many bishops even collaborated under the Occupation, or at least lifted no finger to help the Resistance. So the Catholic element in the Resistance passed into the hands of lay leaders, notably Georges

Bidault, and from this there emerged after the war the new liberal Catholic political movement, the MRP.

But even in the 1930s the Church was not entirely monolithic in its Right-wing stance. From early in the century several forces had been at work to 'rechristianize' the urban masses and carry the fight against Communism on to the enemy's ground. Before the war the Christian trade union (CFTC) was formed, and young workers' movements were started, the Jeunesse Ouvrière Chrétienne and the JAC itself. Then in 1943 a simple Paris priest, the Abbé Godin, published an epoch-making book, *France, pays de mission*, which for the first time openly faced up to the truth that France was no longer a Christian but a pagan country, and that the Church must alter its ways radically to meet this situation. Soon a new *Mission de France* was active, whose priests took an oath to 'devote their life to the christianization of the working class'. Then in 1944 the collaborationist bishops and priests emerged discredited from the Occupation – there were even demands for them to be shot as traitors. Old-style clericalism received the heaviest blow to its prestige since Dreyfus. The way was open for the rise in influence of other bishops, the liberals. Cardinal Feltin, Archbishop of Paris, was a liberal; so were Cardinals Gerlier at Lyon and Liénart at Lille. In this new climate, the *Mission de France* embarked on one of the most dramatic Christian experiments in the world since the war: the worker-priests. About a hundred priests turned themselves into factory-workers, sharing their lives, their dress. The aim was partly to preach Christian example, partly to discover what the downtrodden pagan working class was really like, and so to bridge the gulf of ignorance that separated it from the bourgeois Church. And so profoundly disturbed were the priests by the sufferings of this class that many of them became influenced by Marxism and began to militate in the Communist trade union. The Vatican (under Pius XII) grew worried. In vain Feltin and Liénart pleaded for the experiment to continue; the priests, they said, had *not* lost their faith, they were simply coming to terms with working-class reality. In 1954, on the orders of Rome, the movement was virtually suspended. But about half of the priests felt so strongly that they refused to obey. They remained in their factories, some of them losing their faith and joining the Communist Party, others endeavouring in painful solitude to reconcile the Kingdom of God with the class struggle.

For several years after 1954 the intellectual leadership of the neo-Catholic movement was left in disquiet by the collapse of the worker-priest movement. Many felt that the Church had betrayed them. But the worker-priests, so it now seems, were really no more than a storm-troop spearhead that had advanced too far ahead of its supporting army and been mown down. The rest of that army has since continued to move forward; and today the worker-priest movement has been superseded by all sorts of new kinds of militant social Christian action.

The dechristianization of France is a process that was taking place gradually, as in many Western countries, for nearly a century. Although a high percentage of people still pay lip-service to Christianity through social convention (nearly 90 per cent are still baptized) most of them neglect it entirely except at the crucial moments of christening, marriage and burial. In the middle classes weekly church-going as a family status-symbol has fallen off considerably, though much more in Paris and other big cities than in small towns. At the same time the traditional role of the priest has declined, both as moral and social leader in rural parishes, and as intimate friend and counsellor to bourgeois families. Figures for attendance at Mass, after declining for several decades, now seem to have levelled off: in Paris about 14 per cent of people go to Mass each week, while in traditional Catholic rural areas like the Vendée the figure may reach 80 per cent, or fall to well below 10 per cent in industrial centres. The over-all picture is clear: old-style, pious Catholicism is still slowly retreating in areas where it is strongest, while in the most heavily pagan areas a new-style Catholicism is beginning to make some progress.

This weakening of clericalism has inevitably been followed by a softening of anti-clericalism too. And so the sharpest of all the feuds that have torn France in the past century is fading away into history. In some country districts it may linger on, where villages are still ranged into two camps, behind the *curé* and the teacher; this is true especially of an area like the Brittany hinterland where the Church was most closely associated with the feudal gentry. But in many other regions the old quarrels between Rouges and Blancs are coming to seem as much a part of folklore as horse-drawn carriages or country-dancing. The younger generation aren't worried any more. And so the issue of State aid for Church schools, over which so many Third and Fourth Republic parliaments fought and bled, is dying too. Although the Gaullist régime, being loyally Catholic, increased the level of aid to these schools after 1958, the non-Catholic Left no longer get so worked up about it all. For them this was one of the least of the régime's faults. Under the new laws, the State pays virtually the whole of a Church school's staff salaries, and some other expenses too, depending on how much freedom each school may wish to retain. But despite the increased aid, the percentage of children in Church schools declined during the 1960s, especially at primary level – it moved from 20 per cent in 1959 to 17 in 1967, though it has since picked up slightly as parents are put off by the post-1968 troubles in the State *lycées*. However, despite 1968, the two systems, Church and State, are moving closer together. An increasing number of teachers in Church schools are non-Christians; many Catholic families send their children to State schools, while many State *lycées* have Catholic almoners attached to their staff. A liberal *curé* in Rodez, a typical Massif Central country town, told me: 'A parent today chooses his school for practical reasons more than confessional ones. Or at least, he wants to be able to make the choice privately and freely, without social pressure, and without the whole thing being made into a public issue. The only people still interested in the *école laïque* debate are little pressure-groups made up of the anti-clerical teachers and old-guard priests themselves. But the general public couldn't care less.'

The same priest also told me: 'Younger Catholics round here have been trying to widen their faith by asking what God expects of them in their daily life and work. They are more concerned with concrete charity than with spiritual studies. They feel it's more important to aid the community than not to eat meat on Friday.'

The JAC has been typical of this trend, but it is noticeable elsewhere too, and most priests now support it. Retreats, rosaries and theological dogmas now count for less; and the new emphasis is more on economic or social sins in relation to society than on private sexual ones. In fact the opinion polls suggest that younger Catholics' attitudes to pre-marital sex and contraception are not widely different from those of non-believers. Nearly every Catholic leader I met emphasized these changes in one way or another. Jean-Marie Domenach, editor of the intellectual review *Esprit*, said: 'A young man's faith is no longer nearly so "protected" by the environment of family and parish. It has to pass through the ordeal of contact with atheism, and if it survives, it may be more real than in the old days.'

And so in this new climate the Catholics have been moving to action-stations everywhere. They have been influenced by Teilhard and his optimistic world-loving, and possibly even more by Emmanuel Mounier, founder of *Esprit* and one of the most courageous early advocates of the need for the Church and all Christians to engage in improving the world. The immediate post-1945 generation – that of Debatisse and Leclerc – were especially successful in pushing up into positions of influence. As well as in the JAC, neo-Catholics have also been influential since the war in the Centre des Jeunes Patrons; in the CFDT (formerly CFTC), the most progressive of the trade unions; and in the political discussion-groups such as the former Club Jean Moulin. 'We animate a large part of the upper civil service,' Domenach told me triumphantly, as if announcing the success of some bloodless *Putsch*. And according to one estimate, over 50 per cent of the mayors of France are now ex-JACists or ex-JOCists.

A senior Jewish technocrat told me, not unsympathetically: 'These Catholics, they're everywhere. One secret of their strength is that they've got a *réseau*, a sort of underground network, even if it's not a very unified one. And they've got such energy – they're always devoting whole evenings to their work.' The Catholic Church, which though disestablished used to be a major establishment in France, defending its own clearly defined positions, has now taken on the colouring almost of an occult lay freemasonry, a minority pressure-group that is on the offensive because it has more to gain than to lose.

The dynamic has come initially from the laity, and their relations with the Episcopate are equivocal and not easy to define. The whole movement is made up of scores of different organizations, some of them completely secular and autonomous of the Church (like the CJP and the CFDT), others formally under its ecclesiastical authority and often running into conflict with it. Equally hard to pinpoint have been the attitudes of the new militants towards State technocracy. Some of them support or at least accept the régime and they work within its ranks to build a more humane and efficient society; others strongly oppose it and are on the Left in the classic sense, angrily aware of how little the Gaullists have done to cure social injustices. The worker-priests and their successors belong here, and so do several student movements. But all the militants, whatever their political views, have their activism in common; they are working, as someone said, 'to build the Kingdom of God on earth – something that the Church never used to care much about'.

The reactions of the clergy to the new trends are equally variable. Some of the older ones feel lost and *dépassés* and are struggling to preserve the old order of things. There is a certain confusion among the older rank-and-file clergy, many of whom feel unforceful and under-educated beside the clever lay militants, and are unsure what the role of the priesthood should be under the changed conditions. But an increasing number of younger priests are actively leading the new Catholicism – and this is true especially of the Dominicans, who are fewer in number than the Jesuits in France, but more progressive. Père Cardonnel told me: 'We are trying to deconfessionalize and declericalize the faith. Lots of unbelievers come to my Mass, because I adapt Christ's teaching to modern life, in their own language.'

This tendency increased after the crisis of May 1968. Some priests, influenced by the militant students and workers, began to form little groups describing themselves as '*les prêtres contestataires*', saying that they wanted to form a kind of Left-wing opposition within the Church. These priests felt that the traditional role of the priesthood was now out of date: a priest must

be more than a 'purveyor of sacraments', he could no longer
regard himself as part of a special caste or hide behind the mystic
authority of his calling, but must go out and mix with ordinary
people on equal terms. Many priests began to refuse to play the
Church's traditional bourgeois social game: some refused to
marry their parishioners in church, or baptize their children,
unless they were sure they were sincere believers. In November
1968, priests wrote an open letter to the Episcopate demanding
that the role of the priesthood be re-examined and hinting that
the celibacy rule should be abolished.

This letter caused a horrified raising of hands among many
older or more conservative clergy. But the Episcopate received it
tolerantly and promised to treat it seriously. An important fact is
that the Episcopate itself, after some years of hesitation, has in the
past decade increasingly swung its weight behind the liberal
Catholic movement in France and has clearly been influenced by
it. Though the bishops are not so *avant-garde* as the militants, they
are in advance of the older rank-and-file clergy and of the older
pious masses. This is not such a new development: as I said,
cardinals like Feltin and Gerlier were in favour of worker-
priests twenty years ago, and even back in the 1930s Cardinal
Liénart was being denounced by the Lille Patronat as 'the Red
bishop' because of his support for the working class. But such
men used to be in a minority within the Episcopate; now they are
not. During the Algerian war a number of bishops denounced
Army brutalities; this is something that could never have
happened in *Action Française* days. More recently they have come
out against the Government in support of workers' strikes, and in
1966 they even published an official manifesto criticizing the
Patronat's credo of profit. As tacticians they are now aware of the
crucial need for the Church to come to terms with the challenge
of Communism; as Christian humanists they now accept that the
Church must lend its weight in the fight for social justice. But their
position on many matters is still *nuancé*, and many bishops are
trying to steer a delicate course between two sides. After all, the
Church still gains much strength from its traditional alliance with
the ruling bourgeoisie, and there are plenty of senior clergy who
point out the dangers of the Church, as it were, changing sides in

the French class struggle. Within the Episcopate there are forces pulling in both directions. The hierarchy has also become worried at the crisis of recruitment to the priesthood. As the old distinctions between clergy and laity become blurred, as more priests indulge in social action and more laymen in militant evangelism, so the career of priest comes to appear, to an eager young Christian, as not so much less attractive as less essential. He can carry out Christ's work without feeling he need don the cassock for life. The number of priests in France has fallen from 45,000 in 1960 to 32,000 today; new recruits to the seminaries were 155 in 1975, against 917 in 1963. The average age of priests is rising, and soon there will be a serious shortage. Many bishops in France state in private that ending the celibacy rule is an essential step; but they will not sanction it themselves until Rome gives the word.

And how has the French working class reacted to the Catholics' new interest in them? It is a vital question to ask, but not easy to answer. Hitherto the working class has identified Christianity so firmly with the bourgeoisie that in some industrial areas for a worker to admit to being a Christian was like claiming to vote on the Right, a kind of betrayal. And the figures for Mass bore this out: in the middle classes, church-going was up to ten times as common as among workers. It is doubtful whether these figures have yet altered more than marginally. But several trade unionists report signs of a thaw in attitudes: workers now much more easily admit to being Christian, or to being friends with Christians.

There are several Leftish Catholic organizations that stress the need for closer links between Christians and the pagan working *milieu*. One is the magazine *Témoignage Chrétien*, very *progressiste*, which was upbraided by the hierarchy for publishing an article by a Communist leader. Another body is *Vie Nouvelle*, inter-ideological rather than purely Christian, a sort of intellectual boy-scout movement linking Catholics, Protestants, Marxists, rationalists and others. In Montpellier one of its leaders is Père Cardonnel, who told me how he enjoyed holding public debates with prominent local atheists and touring the village on joint preaching missions with a Protestant colleague. 'Young people welcome us,' he told me, 'but many of the older bourgeois are shocked. You see, normally in Montpellier the *haute société catholique* and *haute société protestante* just don't mix.' Oecumenical links with France's 3 per cent Protestant minority are much in vogue among the neo-Catholics; there are numerous joint youth movements and church services, all over France, and the Protestants have been playing their own willing part in the *rapprochement*, especially through the influence of their famous oecumenical centre at Taizé.

A much more remarkable new dialogue is that between Catholics and Marxists. These are the two most dynamic ideological groups in France, and they have a weird respect and fascination for each other. I am not referring to the old Stalinist diehards within the Party, nor to Sartre and his immediate circle, but to some of the thousands of other active Marxists in France, doctors, teachers, trade unionists and the like, many of them relatively open-minded and pragmatic, some Communist, some Socialist, some without party label. Like the neo-Catholics they are frequently notable for their energy, their dedication, their urge towards practical social action. And when the two of them meet, they often feel much more common ground with each other than either has, respectively, with old-style Catholics or with Stalinists, Sartrians or vague liberals. Their strange flirtation offers many striking examples in France today, both in ideological debate and in joint welfare activity.

J.-M. Domenach said to me: 'This kind of field collaboration began in the Resistance, and with a few lapses it's gone on since. You see, it's the old-style liberals with Alain-type ideals who just haven't been able to stay the course – they've lacked the right spiritual force. But we notice that the Marxists, like us, do have that kind of force – for good or ill.' Not all neo-Catholics would generalize as arrogantly as this, but many say much the same thing. Domenach went on: 'Whenever at grass-roots level you find disinterested individuals actually doing voluntary social work in France, they are nearly always Catholics or Marxists. Recently, for instance, *Esprit* ran an inquiry into handicapped children, and we found that nearly all the people helping in this field were militants of one group or the other.' In the other camp Professor Raymond Dugrand of Montpellier University told me: 'I left the

Party after Hungary, but I'm still a Marxist. Today I feel more at ease with the new Catholic Left than with most CP members. Last year, for instance, some local priests and I ran a fund-raising campaign for World Famine Relief; and often Cardonnel and the CFDT invite me to join in their discussions.' In a poor district of Paris, I found Catholic and Marxist doctors working in harmony in a campaign to combat mental disease and alcoholism. In local government the new alliance in Grenoble between the Catholic mayor, Hubert Dubedout, and the Marxist Left, offers another example.

When it comes to the exchange of ideas, it is less easy to see what has been achieved. At least, both sides are ready to talk. The Communist Party has copied the Catholics' Semaines de la Pensée Catholique with its own similar study-conferences, Semaines de la Pensée Marxiste, held through the year in various towns. Each side invites the other to take part in these debates. This dialogue became rather more circumscribed for a time, after the Prague and Paris crises of 1968. Before then, it was the unorthodox Communist philosopher Roger Garaudy, admirer of Teilhard de Chardin, who played the leading part in trying to explore common ground between Christians and Marxists in these debates. But he was later expelled from the Party, partly for his condemnation of Soviet action against the Czechs. Moreover, the Marxists in France so sharply split into two factions after 1968, Party loyalists and *gauchistes*, that the Catholics found it much harder to talk to them. A Catholic who associated with the *gauchistes* was thereby *persona non grata* with the Party; and conversely, if he associated with the Party. But in the 1970s, after the decline in influence of the *gauchistes*, the Communist Party again began to woo the Catholics as part of its new campaign for a more open-minded and liberal image. So the dialogue has been actively resumed. However, many outsiders remain sceptical as to the sense of Catholic-Marxist links. Barbara Bray in a BBC talk on France said, 'These people are making a false synthesis of the two ideologies, based on sloppy, wishful thinking.' In strict rationalist terms she may be right. But practical field contacts between Catholic and Marxist individuals are going ahead as strongly as ever. Such individuals are often able to see each other's point of view and to find some common cause in the service of mankind. If these two dynamic forces are able to unite some of their energies for the common good, surely the woolly thinking does not matter quite so much.

From a strictly Christian point of view the most obvious danger is that, amid all this new secular zeal for social progress, Christ himself may be overlooked. 'Some of the faithful complain,' a Dominican told me, 'that we priests don't talk about God any more, we talk about the housing crisis.' Many Catholics and Church leaders are aware of this dilemma. 'We have gained a great deal in rejecting integrism,' said one liberal priest, 'but are we not losing the virtues of contemplation and the sense of sin?' The Episcopate, too, are worried. They are frightened, obviously, of Marxist contagion, and of the danger that the flight from orthodox piety and ritual may go too far.

The French Episcopate and the Vatican are also concerned at the decline of their own authority and discipline, caused by the multifarious upsurge of lay militancy. Many of the new movements, even those directly under the formal tutelage of the Church like the Jeunesse Etudiante Chrétienne, have frequently been taking policies and even doctrines into their own hands. And although the Episcopate today has come willingly to accept what the French call *pluralisme* – that is, the possibility for various differing tendencies to exist within the Church – it does not want to lose its over-all control of what is happening.

So in the mid-1960s the Church began a careful campaign to re-assert its authority. On the orders of Rome, a ruthless and enigmatic new figure appeared on the scene: Mgr Pierre Veuillot. He was first appointed Coadjutor of Paris in 1961, then in 1966 at the age of only fifty-three he succeeded Feltin as Archbishop of Paris and president of the French Episcopate, and a year later was made a Cardinal. By 1965 he was making his presence felt almost as much as de Gaulle. In tones of awed irony, *Le Nouvel Observateur* described this potentate as 'a technocrat of divine right, less a pastor than a prefect, a man who believes that the Church must be efficient like a business, and must be served like the State under Stalin or the Pentagon under McNamara'. This brilliant and chilly paternalist was in many ways a liberal.

He was anti-integrist and clearly did not intend to undo the great work of the past twenty years; he even played a decisive role in securing the return of the worker-priests in 1965. Another of his acts was to suppress the scandalous class-distinctions in the marriage and burial services, which used to be graded according to how much you could pay for them; this did not win him friends among the older bourgeoisie. But he was also an authoritarian liberal. And in 1965, his hand fell heavily on the unruly Jeunesse Etudiante Chrétienne. This student body had taken up an extreme Left-wing position, declaring it to be the duty of Christians to collaborate with Communists and others in helping the poor and in supporting Spanish students against Franco. Veuillot then issued an ultimatum to the JEC. He said that the Church accepted that individuals *as lay Christians* had a right to take part in this kind of temporal action; but he added that the JEC, being a corporate part of the Church, had no such right to implicate the Church in politics. He forced the dismissal of the JEC leaders and their replacement by others more submissive. In February 1968 Veuillot died. He was succeeded by Cardinal Marty, a man of a very different stamp, a simple and affable person, neither intellectual nor authoritarian.

Veuillot had not been hitting out only at the Left, however. The neo-Catholic movement provoked a virulent Right-wing reaction to it within certain Christian circles, and this too worried the hierarchy. The tradition of integrism is dying in France, but not without a last-ditch fight: as recently as 1967 a Catholic paper like *Le Monde et la Vie* was still selling 200,000 copies a month, and its pages were horrifying – long eulogies of Pétain and wartime Catholic fascists, savage attacks on Teilhard de Chardin, on worker-priest ideals, or any form of dialogue with non-believers. This purist minority is particularly angry at recent changes in the liturgy. Mass is now celebrated in French, not in Latin, the priest faces the congregation when officiating, and often there is hymn-singing. In some conservative areas, the pious have marked their displeasure at all this by pointedly continuing to make their responses in Latin. These unreconciled integrists represent only a small proportion of practising Catholics; they are far fewer in number than those who can be classed as neo-Catholics. But they are vocal and well organized, and have even threatened to secede from the body of the Church, just as the small Left-wing minority nearly seceded before the war. It is an indication of how far the tide has turned.

In the summer of 1976, an international scandal broke out when France's most notorious integrist priest, seventy-year-old Mgr Marcel Lefebvre, former Archbishop of Dakar, openly challenged the Pope. Five years earlier Lefebvre had set up his own 'traditionalist' seminary at Ecône, in Switzerland, where he set about training young men on integrist lines. In June 1976, against the express orders of the Pope, he ordained thirteen of them as priests. The Pope replied by suspending the archbishop, thus forbidding him to say Mass or administer the sacraments. Lefebvre then lashed out, as he had several times before, claiming that the liberal reforms since Vatican Council II were 'a huge enterprise of self-destruction . . . of tradition, religious teaching, the liturgy, the priesthood'. He planned to continue saying the Mass in Latin. In August, he held a rally in a sports stadium in Lille, attended by 7,000 integrists from all over Europe. He gave a speech that was as much political as religious, and made his extreme-Right sympathies fully clear; the Church, he said, was flirting dangerously with Communism.

The Vatican was clearly embarrassed, and it seemed that the Pope might have no alternative but to excommunicate the rebel – who would then establish his 'parallel' Church and thus provoke the first major schism in the Church for fifty years. Lefebvre had already gone fund-raising across North America, and with the money he had bought five châteaux in France in which to establish priories. According to one survey, as many as twenty-eight per cent of French Catholics sympathized with the rebel bishop. However, the French hierarchy and the clergy as a whole came out firmly against him. Although Lefebvre's has been the most violent integrist backlash so far, it would appear to be doomed in the long term. He may succeed for a while in carrying on an outlawed 'parallel' church, but finally it will die away.

Since 1968 the various conflicts within the Church have become more highly politicized, as in so many spheres of French life. Today the liberal Catholic movements born of the post-war years, the JAC and so on, are keeping their influence: but they are being challenged and made to seem almost conservative by new, much more radical groups, inspired either by the ideals of May 1968 or by Christian commando action in some other countries. Some of these groups have political aims: the '*Echanges et Dialogues*' movement includes nearly a thousand Left-wing priests dedicated to 'the liberation of Christianity from the Church' which they regard as a tool of the bourgeoisie. Many of them have factory jobs like the old worker-priests, and never wear clerical clothes; some are militants within the CFDT or PSU. There are now some 750 worker-priests in France, that is, Catholic priests who also have ordinary full-time jobs in factories or offices, most of them men with Leftish views. And opinion surveys since 1974 show that over 50 per cent of priests under forty are pro-Socialist; that six times as many priests of all ages find the Socialist Party closer to their evangelical ideals than the UDR; that 84 per cent of priests never wear the cassock; and that 86 per cent are against compulsory celibacy for the clergy. These figures are a startling indication of how far the French priesthood has evolved in the past two decades.

Some of the new groups are not directly political, but more concerned with trying to forge a new community style of Christian life and worship. Some of their leaders are priests who have married, in defiance of Rome. They are not very interested in liturgy or ritual, but are setting up free-thinking experimental '*communautés de base*' where a simple life is lived intensely in common. The best known is at Boquen, in Brittany.

The hierarchy, as you might expect, has reacted warily to all this activity. Cardinal Marty and his successor since 1975 as president of the French Episcopate, Mgr Etchegaray, Archbishop of Marseille, are both mild men of liberal sympathies and have shown little inclination to reimpose the Church's authority as sharply as Veuillot did. Perhaps they could not, today – the Left has grown too strong, even within the priesthood. Marty and a number of his bishops were even said to have annoyed Pompidou with their social sympathies – notably when Chaban-Delmas visited the Lille area in 1972 and the radical Bishop of Arras tolled bells against him in protest against Government policies.

More recently, Marty has spoken out strongly against Giscard's policy of arms sales abroad. For Marty and many of his fellow-bishops, these are sincere matters of conscience. It may also be true that the hierarchy in France is aware – perhaps more aware than the Vatican – that the future hopes of Christianity lie more with the new militant groups and with the working class than with the old pious bourgeoisie. So they do not want to identify too closely with the régime – nor with the Leftists. It is not an easy balancing-act.

It is possibly symptomatic of intellectual decline in France that the post-war Catholic revival has not been accompanied by the appearance of any outstanding new writers or thinkers. The earlier generation of great Catholic novelists and poets like Claudel, Péguy, Bernanos and Mauriac has had little contemporary sequel. A number of priests (Fathers Congar, Chenu and de Lubac) have written doctrinal or philosophical works of some value; but almost all the post-war French novelists are agnostics. Domenach told me: 'I find it hard to get really good young Catholic writers for *Esprit*. We seem to be in a barren patch, intellectually. Everyone's energies have gone into activism.'

The neo-Catholic movement does have its two great *maîtres-à-penser*, but both are dead – Mounier, who died in 1950, and the towering figure of Teilhard de Chardin, who died in 1955 aged seventy-four. In France and throughout the world, the Teilhard cult is still of phenomenal proportions. There are those who claim that he has had more posthumous influence than any other world thinker since Marx; and Louis Armand, in an unguarded moment, even declared: 'Teilhard is certainly France's greatest gift to the world since the beginning of this century, perhaps even her sole serious contribution.' In France alone, nearly two million copies have been sold since 1955 of the difficult, labyrinthine, abstract books of this Jesuit heretic whom the Jesuits first denounced, then eulogically reinstated. His appeal to the ordinary lay Christian, and to many non-Christians too, is self-evident: an immensely generous and optimistic vision of the immanence of God in the modern world around us, in science, in nature, in art, and a belief in a time-conquering life-force that is built on the unity of his religious faith and his scientific convictions as a palaeontologist. An agnostic can drink at the Teilhardian fountain without having to accept the mumo-jumbo of Christian ritual; a Christian can drink there, too, and find a spiritual justification for the modern world of science and progress that the Church itself does not really know how to give him. There is a certain Teilhard snobbism: in some circles, he is the *one* author you just cannot admit to not having read. And there is an anti-Teilhard snobbism, too. Many scientists object to his scientific vagueness, and many Christians to his theological woolliness; and rationalists like J. F. Revel grow purple in the face at what they see as the sloppy wishful-thinking of young idealists eager to embrace Teilhard's portmanteau solution of life's mysteries.

And so the debate goes on. Some neo-Catholics find in Teilhardism a kind of theological justification for their actions; but the rationalists allege that materialist technocracy is simply using Teilhard's ideas as a cover and a spiritual alibi. This seems to me unfair. Technocracy is necessary and inevitable; and if it carries inherent dangers, then the religious or humanist idealism of many of the technocrats is likely to be the best safeguard against them. Teilhard can give technocracy a soul. I think it is for these kinds of reasons that the neo-Catholic movement is one of the most encouraging developments in France since the war; it is the spiritual leaven in a materialist economic revolution. While structuralists, existentialists and others are paralysed by their honest doubts about the meaning of life, those with some kind of religious faith are able to free their energies for helping mankind.

Chapter 12

ALL THE ARTS LANGUISH – SAVE ONE?

Is France still '*mère des arts*' and Paris still the cultural capital of the West? Some of the symptoms of sclerosis I have already traced among French philosophers and novelists can be seen also in French painting and music, and even in the theatre, at least in terms of new plays if not of production. It is principally in the cinema that France has still in my view been leading the world, at least in the years after the astonishing arrival of the so-called '*nouvelle vague*' directors in the late 1950s. But today even the French cinema is in relative decline: many new-wave directors are developing middle-aged spread, few new ones have appeared. This may be temporary; the world of the cinema is often volatile. At any rate, in this chapter I first trace the rise of the *nouvelle vague* and its current crisis, then consider its work in terms of artistic achievement.

CINEMA IN BLOOM, CINEMA IN CRISIS

Françoise Sagan once told Kenneth Tynan, when asked about the new plays in Paris: 'But my generation doesn't go to the theatre any more – we go to the cinema.' It was not meant as a philistine remark, quite the reverse. The cinema has for long been intellectually respectable in France, and since the war the passion for it among younger educated people has been stronger than in any other country. Throughout Paris and the provinces, nearly ten thousand new 'cine-clubs' have sprung up, where young people gather in a hired hall or flea-pit to watch anything from the latest Truffaut to an old scratched copy of *Potemkin*, and then eagerly discuss it. In Paris before the war there were only two or three art-house cinemas; today there are several score, and in one of them a recent revival of Renoir's *La Grande Illusion* drew more people than had seen it in all Paris on its original run in 1938.

The French intellectual devotion to films dates back almost to Méliès himself. The cinema has never had to struggle, as in England, to win acceptance beside painting or music as a major art form. In the 1920s Cocteau was turning to film as readily as to verse, as the medium for his poetry. And writers like Sartre, Malraux and Robbe-Grillet have readily collaborated in film-making, or even directed films themselves. The French believe that cinema, given the right conditions, can be used just as powerfully or subtly as any other art to express a personal artistic vision, despite the pressures of a mass-entertainment industry.

This was the cinematic background from which the hundred or more young directors of the *nouvelle vague* emerged with such clamour in the late 1950s – less by accident than through an explosive necessity of self-expression. A new generation had arrived that had taught itself cinema in its teens, in the ciné-clubs, *cinémathèques* and art-houses, and grew up 'speaking cinema' as its elders spoke literature or an earlier age had lived in the language of religion. Jean de Baroncelli, film critic of *Le Monde*, wrote in 1959: 'Young creative people today have a cinematic instinct and the cinema is their first choice. Fifty years ago a young man with something to say would compose poetry, twenty years ago he would write a novel, today he dreams of making a film. Perhaps, in the eyes of some, it is the only means of expression really adapted to our epoch.' But why? The difficulties of writing a humanist novel in the literary climate of recent years, the drawbacks of working for conformist State television – these are two obvious factors that have drawn talent towards the cinema. The cinema also combines lyricism with documentary, to a higher degree than any other art, and this duality appeals deeply to the French. As I suggested earlier, the flight from ideologies has taken the French down two distinct paths, towards the aesthetic and towards the concrete and practical; the cinema unites the two. Location-shooting fascinates by its actuality, and the camera does not lie; but the camera is also a tool of fantasy, the perfect poetic liar.

The 1930s had been a golden age, that of the great films of Clair, Carné and Renoir. Then, after the hiatus of war-time, it seemed at first that the great days were beginning anew. Carné made one of his best films, *Les Enfants du paradis*, in 1945. Several newer talents emerged, too; and the first post-war years were at least a luminous silver age for the French cinema, with such films as Autant-Lara's *Le Diable au corps*, Becker's *Casque d'or* and Clément's *Jeux interdits*. But as the 1950s wore on a creeping paralysis appeared. The established directors, mostly by now in their forties or over, grew steadily bankrupt of ideas and inspiration – save for one or two rare figures like Robert Bresson and the ageing Renoir. Subjects became safe and stereotyped: *policiers,* sex dramas or costume pieces, carrying with them the stale air of the studios. Producers were scared of trusting to new talent or new themes. But meanwhile France itself was changing, a new mood and style of life were emerging that the cinema seemed to ignore, and a new generation began to lose patience with the artificialities offered it on the screen. Television, too, was just making its impact. Several safe-formula films unexpectedly flopped around 1957. Producers wondered whether to turn to epic spectaculars (which few of them could afford) or to try some novelty.

The new generation then proceeded to force their hand, in the most remarkable revolution in the cinema's seventy-year history. Scattered groups of young would-be feature directors were waiting their chance, working either in 'shorts', or as critics, or even essaying their own self-financed low-budget features. In the mid-1950s one or two unusual films began to appear, unnoticed at first except by a select public: Astruc's *Les Mauvaises Rencontres*, for instance, and Agnès Varda's *La Pointe courte*. Then in 1956 a youngish producer, Raoul Lévy, engaged a very young *Paris-Match* journalist, Roger Vadim, to try his hand at a realistic but rarely attempted theme, the amorality of modern pleasure-loving youth, to be set on location in St-Tropez. Today, when the rest of the new wave has thundered on far beyond it, *Et Dieu créa la femme*, gaudy, slick and cynical, looks old hat; but in the prevailing climate of Fernandel comedies and studio rehashes of Colette it was startling. It was not a great film, but it broke new ground. For almost the first time in the French cinema since the war, here was youth looking at itself with a raw directness; and instead of the traditional coquette in a man's world, *à la* Martine Carol, here was a new type of young heroine, wild, sensual and emancipated, much closer to contemporary youth. More to the point, the film won an immediate and fantastic commercial success, in France and throughout the world. And this at once incited other producers to look for other new talent and new real-life subjects. They did not need to look far.

A number of directors, no longer so young, had already been working for some years in documentary, helped by a generous system of Government grants and commissions. These men gladly seized the chance to make their first features, and so in 1958–9 Georges Franju, aged forty-six, directed *La Tête contre les murs,* and Alain Resnais, aged thirty-six, made *Hiroshima mon amour.* A second source of talent was the very young group of critics on the magazine *Cahiers du Cinéma*: Godard, Chabrol, Truffaut and others. Several of them were from moneyed backgrounds, and in their passion to get started they did not wait to be invited but sank their own capital into modest features. Thus Chabrol made *Le Beau Serge* in 1958 for 480,000 francs with a legacy inherited by his wife, and thus Truffaut himself partly financed *Les Quatre-Cent Coups* (1959).

It was an exciting time to be in Paris. I remember early in 1959 attending previews of Chabrol's first two films (*Le Beau Serge* and *Les Cousins*) without having heard of him before, and enjoying the shock of a new cinema language, rather as Londoners had done in the theatre three years earlier with Osborne's *Look Back in Anger.* French cinema was back in touch with real life. Resnais and Truffaut took leading prizes at Cannes that spring, and Truffaut arrogantly declared war on the establishment directors and the whole commercial system. The gates were open. *L'Express* invented the label '*nouvelle vague*', and journalists applied it indiscriminately to any new name, conveniently ignoring the wide differences between the *Cahiers* group and Resnais and his friends, or between either of them and loneriders like Franju and Malle. Some of the new directors were genuine innovators and revolutionaries; others were simply applying an up-to-date personal style to conventional themes and subjects. But like all generalizations the label had some validity; in several ways, the new directors differed from the immediate post-war generation.

The first and most important difference lay in their devotion to what is called the '*film d'auteur*', the concept of a film as a unique personal creation like a novel. This is not a new idea in France, though the new directors have carried it farther than before. The French have always attached more importance than Anglo-Saxons to the director's role, and even in publicity for an ordinary commercial film, the director's name is often given as much prominence as the stars' – an honour reserved in Britain for a rare figure like Hitchcock. *Un film de Basil Dearden* or *le chef-d'œuvre de Robert Hamer* you can see in blazing neon outside French cinemas, announcing names largely unknown to their own British public. It is a custom much fairer to the man who actually *makes* the film, even if it leads to some French critics' absurd *penchant* for endowing routine foreign directors with artistic qualities they don't possess.

Astruc as early as 1948 wrote a famous article, 'Le Caméra-Stylo', that came to be treated as a manifesto: 'The cinema . . . becomes bit by bit a language . . . the form through which an artist can express his thoughts, just as in an essay or novel.' In other words, first, the director should write his own script; next, the script itself will fade in importance, for the camera will do the 'writing' as the film is made. Many of the new directors have been using just these techniques. Many of them approached their early films just as if they were first novels – the semi-autobiographical *Les Quatre-Cent Coups* is a good example. Even when they adapt from books (as Truffaut with *Jules et Jim*) they are usually careful to take little-known or banal ones which they transform completely, rather than be inhibited by scruples of fidelity like so many British films. A film must be itself, an original creation and not a copy of something else. And even those like Resnais, who do not write their own scripts, are usually at pains to use original material and to work in close imaginative harmony with their writer.

Finally, these new directors have in common the fact that they came straight into features at the top. Several had studied at the official French film school,* but very few had worked their way up through the usual slow, dispiriting channels of technical apprenticeship in big studios. What this lost them in experience, it added in freshness. And most of them were in their twenties, at a time when the French cinema wore a heavily middle-aged look. They arrived with anti-industry ideas on how to make films: no big stars or lavish sets, and therefore less need for concessions to alleged popular tastes. And for a while they got what they wanted, helped by three favourable circumstances that they would not have found so easily in the British film world.

The first of these was the French system of aid for the cinema. A select number of serious shorts and documentaries receive State grants known as *primes à la qualité*: these helped to sustain the early careers of Resnais and others, and thus did much to prepare the way for the new wave. For feature films there are no outright grants but a number of State advances, given also on a basis of quality: a jury, made up partly of leading cultural figures, allots the loans to films of likely artistic merit, irrespective of their commercial prospects. Of course politics enters into it too, and several worthy projects have been turned down because of their subject-matter, or because the director is *mal vu*. But on the whole the loans have gone to the good films; and in this way Resnais, Bresson, Varda, Chabrol and others were able in the late 1950s to take risks with commercially difficult subjects.

Next, the trade unions are much more easy-going than in Britain. There are not the same obstinate requirements about set working-hours and large minimum crews, and this makes it much easier to shoot on a low budget or to avoid having to down tools in mid-inspiration because it's time for tea. Thirdly, production and distribution have been relatively haphazard in France, at least until recently, and in the early years of the new wave a producer or backer would trust to hunch as much as to routine assessment. Though this has rendered the French industry more vulnerable in time of crisis, it greatly helped independent production once the stalemate of the 1950s was broken. Peter Brook, who tried in vain to make films in his own country in the

* The Institut des Hautes Etudes Cinématographiques (IDHEC).

1950s, easily found a backer in France to make *Moderato Cantabile* there in 1960, and in 1962 he told me: 'The star was Moreau, the script was by Duras from her own novel. The backers simply trusted our talents, they never demanded to see a written script in advance as they nearly always do in Britain. That's what I like about filming in France. We were able to improvise as we went along, and the crews were artists who shared our own creative enthusiasm, not time-serving technicians.' Matters have changed for the worse in France since then; but there is no doubt that the climate of those years enabled the new wave to make its breakthrough.

Several of the first films (*Les Cousins*, for instance) were big box-office successes and easily recouped their slender costs. Producers suddenly were convinced that the public wanted novelty, and they switched from a policy of few and expensive films to one of many and cheap ones. For a while, any young hopeful with a new idea found a camera thrust in his hands. In 1959–63 more than 170 French directors made a first film, a gold-rush phenomenon without parallel in cinema history. But the boom did not last. Inevitably, few of the new directors proved to have the talent of Truffaut or Resnais. Encouraged by producers to be as 'personal' as they liked – since this was the apparent formula for success – many of the newcomers went outrageously too far. They simply made frivolous cult-films about themselves and their friends. Before long, an image formed in the public's mind of a typical new-wave film – featuring the easy-going love-lives of some group of idle, well-to-do young Parisians, full of arty camera shots and in-jokes about other films – imitations, in fact, of *Les Cousins*. The mass public soon wearied of a realism that had declined into gossip, and returned to its de Funès comedies and Christian-Jacques period pieces. Most of the new films lost money.

In fact, apart from a few successes, the new wave has never proved a great money-spinner inside France. Several of its finest films (including *Lola* and Resnais' *Muriel*) lost money because they were over the heads of a general public, while even *Jules et Jim* had to rely mainly on exports to recover its costs. Despite the cinemania of students and intellectuals, the ordinary France of farm and suburb is not a great film-loving nation: the French go to the cinema even less often than the British do, and there is little reason to suppose that ordinary public taste is much higher than anywhere else.

Thus it is not surprising that the French film industry in the past ten years or so has been suffering from the same economic squeezes as in other countries. Television belatedly made its impact in the 1960s, and so did the motor-car and other rival attractions; between 1957 and 1971 1,500 cinemas closed, and annual cinema attendances fell from 411 to 175 million. They have since picked up slightly, and in 1957 audiences were back at 181 million, but high inflation has brought new problems, and the French industry is ill-suited to cope with this kind of crisis. There are few big organized cinema circuits and too many small independent producers. Although in confident times this liberal fluidity is ideal for low-budget personal films, it leads to high costs and inefficiencies that can ill be supported in time of recession. And so, in the early 1970s French backers again became reluctant to take gambles. Mag Bodard, producer for Bresson, Demy and Varda, told me in 1972; 'The conditions under which Brook filmed here no longer exist. Backers have become terrified of the experimental. They insist on seeing a script first. It's as bad as in Britain, and that's not the way to make a *film d'amateur*.'

But the French cinema is a resilient beast, and one that manages to thrive on misfortune. In the mid-1970s, when the British cinema was almost defunct and the economic crisis was at its worst, the French cinema turned out more full-length feature films than ever before: 234 in 1974, 222 in 1975. Of those made in 1975, only 62 were co-productions; the rest were genuine French films, including no less than 37 first features by new directors. Most were made on small budgets and few were of high quality; in fact, rather too many were the 'soft porn' quickies then in vogue, in the wake of *Emmanuelle*.* But at least a young director with the right perseverance *is* still able to find some kind of backing for a difficult subject and his untried talent.

*See pp. 653–4.

Matters are far brighter than in Britain. It may be symptomatic that when Roman Polanski left his native Poland for the West in 1960, he first tried and failed to get backing in France, then found it in Britain of all places, and after several years in Hollywood then finally settled in France in 1975, where he made *The Tenant*.

Yet the cinema still lives from crisis to crisis, and nearly every director talks to you as if he believes his present film will be his last. A few years ago the older commercial directors were blaming the new wave for alienating the public from the cinema, with their plotless, obscure and facetious films. The younger directors in turn, and their producers, laid the blame on the Government – with some reason – for its heavy taxes and for changes in the aid system which favoured routine domestic production rather than quality films for export. But one remedy open to film-makers became obvious: they turned abroad for help, and especially to America. For many years, co-productions had been common with other European countries, chiefly Italy, and this certainly helped to widen the markets for French films; but it did not solve the industry's basic problems, nor has the Common Market yet succeeded in creating a European film pool. Meanwhile, the giant American companies have been showing themselves only too eager, as elsewhere, to increase their hold on French production and distribution by offering the backing that the French could find in their own country. And so, in films, as in so much else, the French have been belatedly following the common European trend.

Some examples are notorious. For years, Truffaut looked in vain for French backing for *Fahrenheit 451*, then found it from Universal and made the film at Pinewood in 1966 with English dialogue and non-French stars. United Artists financed Malle's *Viva Maria!* Demy's *Les Demoiselles de Rochefort* became a hybrid Franco-American spectacular. The effects of this kind of American backing are double-edged. There is no doubt that for some low-budget films it has its advantages, so long as the director maintains his integrity. Both Godard and Varda have been financed by Columbia, and both of them were left entirely free to make their own modest films in their own way. But when it comes to paying for Julie Christie, or for Malle's Bardot–Moreau caper in Mexico, matters may be different. There seems to be a certain cleavage at the moment between those directors like Rivette who continue to make films on their own rigorous terms, and those like Malle and Chabrol who have compromised with a commercial system they once denounced. The artistic dangers of internationalized cinema are too well known to need repeating: by all means let nations see each other's films as much as possible, but this does not mean we want bogus international casts and denationalized themes carefully geared to the tastes of a worldwide audience.

The *nouvelle vague* has thus come a very long way in the space of twenty years. Some directors have forsaken the old ideals or seem to have nothing new to say; others – artists as different as Rohmer and Truffaut – are continuing to develop, and a satisfying number of the original 'new wave' are still making interesting films. If at present, in the mid-1970s, there are fewer good new French films than fifteen years ago, by next year that may no longer be so. I have dwelt on the economic problems simply in order to explain the whole; the real issue is to assess, in cultural terms, what the new directors have achieved.

THE NEW CINÉ-POETS: FRIVOLITY AND GENIUS

At the time of *Jules et Jim* and *Saturday Night and Sunday Morning*, I once imagined (*pace* G. B. Shaw and Isadora Duncan) a snatch of repartee between the two nations' young cinemas: 'Ah, François (or Claude, or Agnès), with my social-realist conscience and your lyrical camera style, what a film we could make together!' 'Yes, Karel (or Lindsay or Tony), but what if it had my social realism and your lyricism?' Since then, things have changed a little, and the British cinema has taken a few steps away from realism towards its own brand of leaden fantasy. In France, the young directors' gaze at the world around them is often so oblique that it seems they're not noticing it at all. And for this they have been criticized. Why so very few films on the housing shortage, the new working class, the farmers' revolt, the effects of the Algerian war? Why so many films set in the past, or abroad, or inside the director's dreamworld?

There are reasons for this neglect, among them (at least under de Gaulle) being censorship and self-censorship; or sheer frivolity and fear of involvement. But in fairness it needs to be said that the French cinema has other preoccupations, too, which the British cinema rarely shares. Some of the new directors are, in a sense, poets, who in earlier times might have expressed themselves through lyric poetry – and it might be as irrelevant to rebuke them for ignoring social themes as to complain that Keats never wrote about the Napoleonic wars or that Matisse painted no *Guernica*. The realism of Resnais, or of Demy's *Lola*, may not be surface social realism, but on a deeper level it is psychological realism. And though many of the new films are childishly frivolous and escapist, others in their oblique and sometimes baffling way *are* a kind of analysis of France today, at a more subtle and disturbing level than the explicit social comment of many British films. This is true of Godard, and, say, of Resnais' *Muriel* or Varda's *Le Bonheur*. But just as Robbe-Grillet revolted against Balzac, so the new French cinema has been reacting against the *films à thèse* of people like Cayatte, or the cosy middle-class realism of so many Gabin films.

The new directors are so diverse that this kind of generalization is not easy, and it is best to look at the work of each in turn. First, then, the *Cahiers* group, led by Chabrol, Truffaut, Rohmer and Godard. Working together in their twenties on this magazine, they proclaimed not only their hatred of the established commercial 'system' but also their view that brave humanist content was irrelevant to a film's greatness, just as abstract or cubist art could be as great as realistic landscape painting. Godard has since changed his views radically. But at the time this stance led some of the *Cahiers* group to weird critical excesses. *Bicycle Thieves* and the Gorky triology were ignored, and American 'B' pictures lauded; idolatry was heaped on directors like Hitchcock, Hawks and Preminger, whose smooth commercial products you would have thought to be at the opposite pole from *Cahiers*' own art-for-art's-sake approach. Hidden virtues were found in the most unlikely films. 'The art of Hitchcock,' wrote Chabrol in a book on his Master, 'is to show us the profundity of a moral idea . . . and this leaves us with the feeling of a Unity which is the very

Unity of the world, an original light which reflects on the sombre facets of Evil some of its most beautiful rays.' Fortunately, once they got a camera between their hands, these young men generally ignored their own fanciful abstractions and came up with work that in its own way was strongly humanist.

Claude Chabrol, the first of the group to make a full-length film, is the archetype of *nouvelle vague* flair-plus-perversity. He shot *Le Beau Serge* in 1958, on location in his childhood village of Sardent, near Limoges. At a time when the only peasants on French screens were harmlessly comic and Pagnolesque, here was a film that seemed near to the truth. It told a story of alcoholism and brutish decadence in one of the poorest parts of France, and for all its naïvety and sententiousness, it was clearly drawing on felt personal experience. Its raw intensity excited the critics. Next Chabrol made *Les Cousins*, about a gentle provincial student's corruption by a cynical *milieu* of young Parisian sophisticates. Again there was the nervously urgent camerawork, the rawness of style that when I first saw it reminded me of D. H. Lawrence. The mood was cool and modern. It would be common enough today, but was still rare on the screen in 1959. Chabrol seemed to be quoting the actual voice of modern French youth, and the crowds flocked to *Les Cousins*. Then in 1960 came *Les Bonnes Femmes*, which I stubbornly admire though many critics have called it 'irresponsible' and 'neo-fascist'. This was a savage little study of Parisian shopgirls, their naïve dreams. their cruel defeat by life – symbolized in the closing sequence where the most sympathetic of the girls falls for a maniac who strangles her in a wood. Granted, Chabrol's picture of the girls was stylized rather than acutely realistic; yet behind his sardonic misanthropy there did seem to lurk a kind of despairing tenderness, a typically French awareness of human isolation and the tragic wastage of life. After a period of semi-eclipse in the earlier sixties, Chabrol has strongly re-emerged since about 1967 with a series of stylish psychological thrillers, notably *Les Biches*, *Que la bête meure*, *Les Noces rouges* and *Nada*. These films have not only been good box-office; they have won high praise from serious critics. Chabrol is prolific, turning out one or two films every year. Not all are good, but all are polished and visually subtle, and some make lyrical use of provincial settings – witness the Dordogne village in *Le Boucher*. But personally I do not find them as fascinating as his earlier, clumsier but more humanistic ones. Instead of saying something about society (as in *Les Bonnes Femmes*), he has become a smooth entertainer – like his idol, Hitchcock.

François Truffaut, like Chabrol, began his career in a blaze of humanism based on personal experience: *Les Quatre-Cent Coups*, the story of a boy driven to delinquency by loneliness and unhappiness, was drawn partly from Truffaut's own childhood and his experiences in a remand home. Not only was the *mise-en-scène* masterly, but the film was a model of implied social criticism (of school, police, parental responsibility) without preaching any sermons. But since then Truffaut too has usually avoided themes that relate either to his own life or directly to society. He says he is not interested in dealing with 'the political and social problems of our time' and that 'the best of the permanent subjects is love'. He is no great innovator, either in techniques or ideas, and his colossal reputation rests largely on his lyrical gifts and his gentle humanism, seen at their best in the dazzling first half of *Jules et Jim* and in *La Nuit américaine*. As Penelope Houston has put it: 'He has the gift of making film-making look wonderfully easy, like a man running down a long, sunlit road with a camera in his hand.' But his more recent films have been uneven. *L'Enfant sauvage* (1970), based on a true story of a doctor's attempts to 'civilize' a boy brought up like a wild animal in the forests, showed Truffaut's courageous preparedness to tackle non-commercial subjects and in its way was a remarkable film. So in its different way was *Baisers volés* (1968), a tender and inventive comedy of bourgeois manners. But some of his later comedies have been less effective. Truffaut is settling down as a gentle humanist in the tradition of Renoir. By far the best of his more recent films has been *La Nuit américaine* (*Day for Night*), a witty and tender story about people making a film, with Truffaut cast as himself, the director. The film was made to express Truffaut's own passion for the movie world, and is as autobiographical as *Les Quatre-Cent Coups*.

While Truffaut, Chabrol and Godard have rarely lived up to

their brilliant debuts, Eric Rohmer, their contemporary in the *Cahiers* group, has proved the opposite. Though he got off to a slow start and won no success till *La Collectionneuse* in 1967, he is now in the prime of artistic maturity and on current form is arguably France's finest director. For my money, *Le Genou de Claire* is one of the two best French films of the past ten years (along with *La Nuit américaine*). Like Truffaut, Rohmer is concerned not with social or topical problems but with private relationships. But his vision is more profound and consistent than Truffaut's. The films he has made since 1967 are a series of what he calls '*contes moraux*', analysing the moral dilemmas of relations between men and women. In *Ma nuit chez Maud*, a serious-minded engineer, a good Catholic, re-examines his life and his principles in the light of his encounter with two very different women; in *Le Genou de Claire*, a diplomat on holiday by the lake of Annecy finds himself disturbingly attracted by two teenage girls. There is not much plot in Rohmer's films; people talk a great deal and very intelligently about their thoughts and feelings, attitudes are illumined from within, a spell is cast. It is a very literary kind of cinema, and Rohmer's best films have the density and subtlety of a good novel, without resorting to tricks of camera style or to clever-clever use of confusing flashbacks. In *Le Genou de Claire*, he creates the most exquisite poetry out of minor incidents – young girls by a lakeside in summer, wistful encounters between middle age and adolescence. His most recent work, *Die Marquise von O* (1975), a romantic period story filmed in Germany, and in German, is also a masterpiece. Rohmer's films are sometimes called 'reactionary' or 'bourgeois' by the Leftists, in that his characters are all middle class, entirely wrapped up in their private worlds. But these worlds are what happen to interest him, and so he is being entirely sincere and true to himself as an artist. He has not been corrupted by big budgets or slick commercial subjects like some of his colleagues. And his very elegant and serious films appeal only to a minority – the kind of people who read Proust.

Jean-Luc Godard could not be more different from Rohmer in his outlook, style, and subject-matter. But like Rohmer he has remained true to himself and makes films that nowadays have only an off-beat minority appeal. This distinguishes these two artists from many of the more 'commercial' new-wave directors. It hardly needs repeating that Godard is one of the most remarkable phenomena in European film-making since the war. Like many people, I do not care for his more recent, highly political, semi-documentary films. Sadly, since a serious road accident in 1971 his talent seems to have deserted him, but his earlier work, up to and including *Weekend* (1968), is amongst the most original and fascinating ever produced in the cinema. Therefore I give a good deal of space to a director who, for all his quirkiness, has had a great deal to say about the kind of place France is today. Those who have heard all this before from *Sight and Sound*, or who can't stand Godard's films, may (as he might say) rejoin me six pages later.

Son of a Protestant French doctor, Godard was born in Paris in 1930 and brought up near Lausanne. While at the Sorbonne he began to write film-reviews, and so became involved with the *Cahiers* crowd and started to make cheap 16mm shorts. His first feature, *A bout de souffle* (1959), was filmed in streets and flats with a hand-held camera for 400,000 francs, less than a thousandth the budget of *Cleopatra*. Not everyone found the subject or the main characters especially rewarding (Belmondo's posturing beatnik hero, Seberg's bewildered American girl); but no one was in doubt that the wry, semi-improvised, *ciné-vérité* style marked a debut more truly original than even Chabrol's. Godard blithely broke all the cinema's textbook rules, simply by not noticing them.

Over the next few years his work steadily matured and strengthened. By keeping to tiny budgets he has been able to choose his own terms of style and subject, without concession. And so he went on till 1968 making as many as two or three films a year; in 1966, he was shooting two simultaneously! It is more the way a painter or poet works, erratically and compulsively by flair or mood, than according to studio routine. Several of the films are very slight, barely more than notes for a film, but that is not the point: he has built up an *œuvre*, and the films in a sense all relate to each other, and add up to more than the sum of their parts.

By 1968 he had made fourteen features and nine shorts. Among the best, to my mind, are *Vivre sa vie* (1962), *Alphaville* (1965) and *Pierrot le fou* (1965). The films grew steadily more way-out and individual, the prototype of *films d'auteur*. And he became steadily more talked about – and fought over – in France. His admirers (they include Malraux and Aragon) more and more readily used the word 'genius' in print; his detractors (and there are many, including writers like Marguerite Duras) more and more loudly called him childish, woolly-minded and facile. For *Le Nouvel Observateur*, *Pierrot le fou* was 'the finest French film ever'; for *Paris-Match* it was 'made just for a handful of fanatics'.

Many people have objected to the casual disregard for plot and sequence, to the flippant private jokes and the audience-teasing. Others have found this endearing – as when, in *Bande à part*, after the first ten minutes a narrator's voice (Godard's) mockingly résumés the action so far 'for the benefit of late arrivals'. Many critics have remarked on the fragmented, pop-art surface of Godard's films, with their sign-symbols and slogans, and he has even been called 'the Rauschenberg of cinema'; some critics dislike this style and find his films too expendable, but others think it is just this quality in his work that makes it so expressive of the modern world. It is true that he can be childishly frivolous. But though he was taken up by the highbrows and modishly exploited as one of today's cult-figures, it would be quite false to assume that he personally is in any way a modish or assertive kind of person.

In company he is genuinely shy, even meditative, and he is not an easy person for a journalist to interview. The first time I talked to him at length was just after I had seen *Pierrot le fou* in 1965, and at first it was hard to believe that this picaresque firework of a film, all corpses and poetry, was really the work of this taciturn little man who looked like a small-town clerk. We had a café lunch of beer and salami sandwiches (his choice). No one seemed to recognize him. He chain-smoked fat yellow cigarettes and looked at me critically behind his dark glasses. He was dressed drably in a dark check suit. He had wispy hair, thin on top, and a complexion swarthy but sallow. It was hard to make him smile. I got the impression of a solitary, rather sad sort of person, utterly without 'side' or the desire to be thought fashionable or clever.

And thus he has kept a kind of purity, in the often corrupting world of the cinema. Each new Godard film before 1968, for all the private jokes and visual high spirits, struck me as an ever sharper personal statement of horror at the way he felt modern life was going. Violence and terrorism, loneliness, confusion, the dehumanizing effects of science and affluence haunt him, and out they come, Goya-like, in his anarchic yet strangely topical films, with their almost prophetic grasp of psychological changes beneath the contemporary surface. Life, like a bright light, seems to hurt and bewilder him. When someone asked his ex-wife, Anna Karina, why he always wore dark glasses, she said: 'It's not that his eyes are too weak. His universe is too strong.'

He has always seen himself as a documentarist. 'When I first started making films,' he told me, 'I knew little of life, I just copied it from other films I'd seen. Now my films are moving closer to life, I think.' It is not hard to trace this evolution. For all their *ciné-vérité* techniques, there was nothing very documentary in the ordinary sense about his first films, the anarchic *A bout de souffle*, or the amorous intrigues of *Une Femme est une femme* (1961). But his later films moved away from fiction towards a kind of film essay-writing, which is how he himself regards them; *Masculin-Féminin* (1966) is little more than a series of whimsical vignettes of modern French youth, and *Deux ou trois choses que je sais d'elle* (1967) is intended as a report on life in the Grands Ensembles – '*elle*' is Paris. *Weekend* (1968), the most ferocious and misanthropic of all his films, shows French society disintegrating into brigandry and cannibalism under the pressures of so-called civilization. The motor car, with its ritual mass murders on French main roads every week-end, is the principal villain of this extraordinary film. Godard said recently: 'A country can rarely have offered such a range of exciting subjects as France today. The choice is bewildering. I want to cover everything – sport, politics, even groceries – look at Edouard Leclerc, a fantastic man whom I'd love to do a film about or with. You can put anything and everything into a film, you *must* put in everything.'* And he added, teasingly: 'My secret ambition is to be put in charge of French newsreels. Each of my films constitutes a report on the state of the nation: they are news *reportages*, treated in a quirkish way, perhaps, but rooted in actuality. *Vivre sa vie* (about prostitution) ought to have been subsidized by the Ministry of Health and *Le Petit Soldat* by the Ministry of Information.' This film about FLN–OAS terrorism was banned in France from 1960 to 1963!

Those who disliked Godard's quirks, or took him too literally, were often annoyed that he wasn't more directly *engagé* about public themes. *Le Petit Soldat* was a sympathetic portrait of a young man who happened to be working for the OAS in Switzerland; and it drove some on the Left to accuse Godard of crypto-fascism. But he told me: 'The film was simply trying to mirror the confusion and traumas caused by torture and terrorism, on either side. Maybe it was expressing a kind of regret that I can't feel strongly about causes, that I wasn't twenty at the time of Spain.' But since 1968 he *has* felt strongly; it is ironic that this has made him a less good film-maker.

It was in *Alphaville* (1965) that his then attitudes emerged most explicitly. This film used a tongue-in-cheek science-fiction plot to point a *1984*-ish moral about the destruction of the soul by computers and planners. 'I set it in the future,' he said, 'but it's really about the present – the menace is already with us.' One of the *trouvailles* behind this brilliant film is that the portrait of Alphaville, soulless city of machines, was edited almost entirely from Paris location shots, filmed in modern buildings and computer centres. Lemmy Caution, secret agent and reporter for *Le Figaro-Pravda*, 'left Alphaville that night by the Boulevard Extérieur' says the narrator – and there are Eddie Constantine and Anna Karina driving along just that Paris street. At another point, the grim technocrats who rule the city are shown brain-washing their enemies '*dans des HLMs, c'est-à-dire, les Hôpitaux de la Longue Maladie*', and the camera pans up a Sarcelles skyscraper. To a Paris audience, these typical Godard jokes were both funny and

* Reprinted from *Le Nouvel Observateur* in *Sight and Sound*, Winter 1966/7.

frightening. 'Alphaville,' he told me, 'is Paris or any other modern city. The job of artists like me is to set ambushes for the planners. We can't hope to win – but we can delay things.'

In this film and others Godard remains detached from his characters, like a reporter. *Pierrot le fou*, however, stands out from this period as much the most personal and anguished of all his work and, I think, the greatest. It was ten years ahead of its time, and it was not very well understood in Britain – but Godard saw it as a turning-point in his career. A melancholy young writer (Belmondo) escapes from Paris with the girl he adores (Karina, of course) to a desperate idyll of perfection on an empty beach near Toulon. But their flight is counterpointed with menacing scenes of anarchic violence, gangsterish murders, bloody car accidents and reminders of Vietnam. Finally the girl betrays him, and in a climax of fierce beauty Belmondo shoots her, paints his face blue, wraps sticks of dynamite round his head, and blows himself into the clear Mediterranean sky where the film fades on an image of sun and space and voices whispering, '*Nous enfin réunis pour l'éternité.*' Godard has described it as 'a film gay and sad both at once, bound up with the violence and loneliness that lie so close to happiness today. It's very much a film about France.'

It's also very much a film about Godard. In nearly all his work he is expressing an alarm at a transformation of the modern world that eludes his emotional grasp – or else he is haunted by a vision of some other, purer life of the past. And Pierrot is Godard with his quest, his fears, his sense of betrayal. I asked him, 'I suppose at heart you're just an old-fashioned romantic?' 'Yes, in a way. Or at least I've a nostalgia for a simple, natural life, for Rousseau's idea of *l'homme bon*, or for the kind of spontaneous gaiety and simplicity that comes into some of my films like the dance in the café in *Bande à part*.' 'Are you solitary?' 'Yes, but aren't we all, today? Or rather, we no longer like solitude when we get it, as Rousseau did. It makes us anxious.'

The most personal element in *Pierrot le fou* is the role played by Karina. Godard met and married this high-spirited, unintellectual Danish girl soon after making *A bout de souffle*. He created her, like Pygmalion – and she has starred in seven of his films. Several sequences in them are virtually poems about her. But soon before he made *Pierrot le fou*, she left him for the actor Maurice Ronet. It is not hard to guess what Godard felt; although they got divorced, he made her the star of three of his subsequent films, and *Pierrot* appeared as an almost embarrassing hymn of love to her. The hero is very serious, immersed in poetry and philosophy; the heroine, gay, frivolous and bewitching, soon gets bored and can't live up to his level. It was this tug-of-war between Karina's temperament and Godard's that added tension to many of his films.

He has managed to stick to his own path by rejecting big studio sets and expensive stars (with occasional exceptions), so that his films do not need to reach a wide public to pay their way. *Une Femme mariée* cost 500,000 francs, one-fiftieth the budget of an average Hollywood star vehicle. He generally films only on location, and often with a tiny crew and hand-held camera. On the set, in contrast to the nonchalance of some directors, he is usually tense and absorbed – for a scene for *Pierrot le fou*, shot in a bowling-alley south of Hyères, I watched him drive his two stars over the same snatch of dialogue for fifteen separate takes in seventy-five minutes, and no one turned a hair. And unlike nearly all other directors, he does not prepare a complete scenario in advance but writes the script daily as the film goes along; the dialogue is not exactly improvised, as is sometimes supposed, but the actors do not know until each morning's filming what lines they are to speak. In this way, he will often change the story half-way through (he films chronologically, which again is unusual); or he will work out new ideas in the middle of a shot, or down tools completely for a day if he's not in the mood. This behaviour helps to lend his films their fresh and impromptu look and it effectively removes the temptation of Hollywood contracts. He isn't even invited.

I do not claim that all his pre-1968 films were successful. Some were too slight, or over self-indulgent. But none were dull. And I would defend to the last his methods and approach to filming, as being the most likely to produce valuable work. Intellectually his work has sometimes been facile and muddled; but his films have their own logic, and were a true and sensitive picture of the world he saw around him, France's world. As Françoise Giroud said in her *l'Express* review of *Pierrot le fou*: 'Godard too is mad. He knows how to talk about happiness and the pain of loving. He uses spontaneously a language where words, images and colour are integrated. Godard's films, I like them, even the ones I don't like.'

Even before 1968 he was turning towards more political subjects, though still with a certain detachment: witness *la Chinoise* (1967), which elliptically criticized a group of young Maoists. But since May 1968 (when he openly sided with the *gauchistes*) he seems to have got caught up in the Maoists' own un-Godard-like solemnity; he has become more committed to the ideological struggle and much less interested in making films about anything else. He has directed a series of baffling, rather incoherent semi-documentaries, on such subjects as fascism in Italy, the fall of Dubček, and the May crisis itself. In 1972, recovered from a serious motor-bike crash the year before, he re-emerged with his first more-or-less normal feature film for some time, *Tout va bien*: it had big stars (his fellow-Leftists, Yves Montand and Jane Fonda) and told the story, more or less, of a workers' revolt in a factory. It preached various *gauchiste* sermons rather pompously, and seemed much influenced by Godard's new co-author and inspirer, the Leftist theoretician J.-P. Gorin. What has happened to him? Where is the poetry of his earlier films, the lyricism, the concern with 'happiness and the pain of loving', even the cheeky humour? – it is even suggested that Godard the new austere Leftist considers lyrical effects and purely personal themes like loneliness as decadent and bourgeois. He has now left Paris, and is running a video workshop in Grenoble. Perhaps he will never make another good film – but that would not invalidate his past achievements. And there are still those who think he is ahead of his time, pioneering a cinema of the future which the rest of us are too blind to see.

Of the two most influential figures among the original *nouvelle vague* directors, the other is Alain Resnais, as important an innovator as Godard and a much more controlled and dignified stylist. The two men are totally different. Resnais is usually linked with his close friends Chris Marker, Agnès Varda and Henri Colpi, as a group who are somewhat older and less insolent than the *Cahiers* team, more professional in the strict sense, and more closely involved with current *avant-garde* literature.

Born in 1922, Resnais had made several outstanding documentaries before he stupefied the 1959 Cannes Festival with his Hiroshima love-story, sometimes regarded by critics as one of the three landmarks of world cinema, along with *Citizen Kane* and *The Battleship Potemkin*. He is a withdrawn, elusive person, even harder to interview than Godard and much more reticent about articulating his views. And this same enigmatic quality is apparent in his films. Although every one of them is marked with his own highly personal style, he prefers not to write his own scripts, and in each case has collaborated with some well-known novelist; thus it is not always easy to tell how much in these strange films really belongs to Resnais. He confesses that he has no gift for dialogue or narrative and therefore needs the help of writers. Some of his critics go farther and suggest that he is not really very concerned about subject-matter at all. But except for *Marienbad* (a very special case) all his films have humanist themes, and in every case he has taken an original idea, not an adaptation, and worked on it closely with a writer. Politics and ordinary social realism are clearly not his concern; but certain other themes recur, whoever his collaborator, and these are time and memory, the difficulties of identity, the erosion of love and loyalties by the chaos of modern living and the sheer passing of the years.

Hiroshima mon amour annoyed some people because it began as a film about atomic war and then turned into something quite else, a love story, or rather two love-stories linked in the mind of the heroine. They found this trivial, even in bad taste; a minor private tragedy was being exalted and a major public one ignored. Others replied that Resnais and his writer, Marguerite Duras, were suggesting that no public tragedy can be any more than a sum of private ones and were therefore deliberately contrasting the two. What is clear is that the film's story and theme are of minor importance compared with its style. By marvellous editing and camera-work, by the imaginative integration of image, music and language, Resnais transmuted an unremarkable script into a work of great power and subtlety. It was the mature expression of a technique he had elaborated through the course of his documentaries and was to repeat in most of his later films; the elegiac travelling-shots, the incantatory repetition of images and phrases that has often been likened to grand opera, and the use of stream-of-consciousness flashbacks to convey, as in Proust, the actual texture and feel of memory.

Some of the same themes recurred in his next film, *L'Année dernière à Marienbad*, but this time the script, by Alain Robbe-Grillet, was beyond redemption. Duras' scenario may not have been inspired but at least it was warm and real; Robbe-Grillet's was neither. In a baroque luxury hotel, a man meets a girl and tries to persuade her that they had a love-affair the year before; the images on the screen reflect her state of mind. Whether they *did* have the affair is immaterial – Resnais and Robbe-Grillet have given significantly different accounts of what the film is supposed to mean. For the first twenty minutes Resnais' mesmeric *mise-en-scène* gives promise of a masterpiece; but soon, devoid of any human interest, the film lapses into repetitive and chilly boredom. It showed the dangers of Resnais' reliance on writers with a strong individuality of their own.

Muriel (1963), scripted by Jean Cayrol, returned to a much more recognizable, everyday world, and its characters were patently real – but the mood was still baffling, this time in a different way. In modern Boulogne-sur-Mer a woman of forty meets her former lover, and a young man is haunted by memories of war service in Algeria – everything is clear, ordinary, real, yet everything is shifting, fragmentary, elliptical. Resnais in this film abandoned his usual fluid 'travelling' style for a more staccato one with short shots, broken sequences, deliberately bewildering jump cuts. The aim, so he has stated himself, was to express a certain *malaise* current in France in 1962, at the time of the OAS crisis, a sense of personal insecurity, of loss of identity. It was a fascinating film, hard to take in at first viewing, and probably the most personal that Resnais has made. *La Guerre est finie* (1966) was much more straightforward: again the theme was time's corrosive influence, this time not on love but on political idealism, and it showed a Spanish Left-wing agent in France in the mid-

1960s, weary and self-doubting in a world that was fast forgetting Guernica. Again Resnais left us guessing, just a bit. He beat no political drum, beyond obvious republican sympathies. Was he saying, here and in *Hiroshima*, that the age of clear-cut causes is past, and that what matters now is private tenderness? *Je t'aime, je t'aime* (1969) was another investigation into time and memory, less connected to topical themes than any of the earlier films save *Marienbad*. In *Stavisky* (1974) he took a more straightforward and commercial subject, the story of the famous swindler of the 1930s, but made of it a film of great visual beauty that touched subtly on his usual obsessions. Like the pre-1968 Godard, Resnais appears preoccupied by the bewilderment and impermanence of modern life, and this explains their fragmented styles; but where Godard expressed his unease by a kind of instinct, Resnais would seem to be more calculating. Yet to search amid his ambiguities for any kind of 'message' is to get lost in an endless jungle.

Agnès Varda, like Resnais, began her film career in documentary. One of the best of her early films was *Du côté de la Côte*, a highly satirical look at the Riviera made, oddly enough, as propaganda for the national tourist office. She is a slight, dark, squirrel-like woman of Greek origin, born in 1928, and in a profession dominated by men she is one of the world's very few distinguished female directors. Like Resnais, she is known to hold strong Left-wing views in private, while in her films she is more concerned with non-political themes. *Cléo de 5 à 7* (1962) was a tender and moving study of two hours in the life of a young Parisienne singer, with sensitive evocation of the modern daily life of Paris. Love, solitude, fear of death, the fragility of life, were beautifully woven together in a lyrical whole.

Then came *Le Bonheur* (1965), one of the strangest and most interesting of all the new-wave films. It was an intellectual attempt, so Varda admits, to analyse the concept of happiness. To explore her theme, she chose what she saw as a modern prototype of the happy simpleton: a young carpenter living joyously in a suburban villa with his pretty blonde wife and lovely babies. When he starts an even more joyous affair with another girl, his bliss is multiplied by two, until his wife (whom he still loves) goes off and drowns herself. But this proves to be no more than a passing cloud on the surface of his ecstatic amorality; the film ends, three months later, with his domestic idyll going on exactly as before, save for a new blonde wife in place of the old one. It was a shocking film in the truest sense, and was meant to be so. On the surface the style was all sweetness, with bright colours, soft smiles and Mozart clarinet music, but this made the irony all the sharper. The result was far more disturbing than many a conventional exposé of violence or perversion.

Some audiences were outraged. Ordinary satires on bourgeois adulteries were two a penny and perfectly acceptable, but here was a film that purported to be serenading all the solid lower-class family virtues only to stick out its tongue at them. What was Varda really getting at? Some critics objected that the characters and their behaviour were so unreal that the film lost its point. But as Varda has said, realism was not her aim; it was a stylized film, and in a stylized way it conveyed brilliantly the ruthlessness of a certain kind of mindless happiness. It was also expressing Varda's own ambivalent attitude to a suburban *milieu* utterly remote from her own Left-Bank world. She envied these simple people, and she despised them. The screen pullulates with images of fecundity and happy domesticity – chortling toddlers, pregnant women, breasts giving suck, street-signs like 'la Route Dorée', Renoir-like shots of girls amid flowers, all backed by the Mozart score. In its odd way, *Le Bonheur* seems very much a criticism of certain contemporary values. It is a pity that Varda has done no work of the same quality since – *Les Créatures* and *Lion's Love* were severe disappointments.

The other new directors are a diverse lot. Louis Malle, though younger than Godard, is a director who harks back to an older generation. He is an Edwardian figure, dapper and well bred, who lives and moves in upper-class formal Parisian society – rare for a film-maker. Despite the stylistic modishness of many of his films – *Zazie dans le Métro*, *Viva Maria!* – he is confessedly not interested in contemporary subjects and prefers to set his films in the past or adapt them from classic novels. He is a superb master of technique, and thus was able to keep *Viva Maria!* above the level of a fatuous romp; but he lacks a defined personal style of his own, and his films are so diverse that it is not easy to see that they were made by the same man. Unlike Godard, he seems to have little to 'say' – save in two solitary masterpieces where the inner Malle showed through, films totally different from each other and from all the rest. The first of these two, *Le Feu follet* (1963), was adapted from a novel of the 1920s by Drieu la Rochelle, about a young alcoholic's vain search for a meaning in life, ending in suicide. Malle transposed it to his own modern Parisian *milieu*, and, helped by a fine performance from Maurice Ronet, made it into an exceptionally restrained and sympathetic film, Bresson-like in its concentration on the hero's inner suffering. But he depressed himself so much in the process that, Malle-like, he next hopped off gaily to Mexico to film Moreau and Bardot in their underpants. This was followed by a 'period' thriller and then, inexplicably, by the second of his personal, ultra-serious films, *Calcutta* (1968), a harrowing documentary about poverty in India. Then came *Le Souffle au cœur* (1970), a beautifully shot but rather insipid story of adolescence set in the 1950s, with an up-to-date plot about incest tacked on. Malle says he regards *Le Feu follet* as a kind of expiation. The most interesting of his recent films is *Lacombe, Lucien* (1974), the story of a dim-witted teenage peasant in the Massif Central during the war, who by accident came to work for the Germans. The film had superb period detail, but as a study of Fascist collaboration it was too elliptical and never came to grips with its subject. Malle has since made a futurist fantasy, *Black Moon*, a difficult film that has not had much commercial success. He seems to be retreating again from the big-star box-office formula, and remains as unpredictable as ever.

Very different from Malle are the *cinéma-vérité* exponents, Chris Marker, Jean Rouch and Mario Ruspoli, who have all chosen to remain in documentary. Most of their best work has been done abroad (in Africa or Asia) but Marker in *Le Joli Mai* (1963) and Rouch in *Chronique d'un été* (1961) have both made attempts, not entirely convincing, to apply their candid-camera techniques to life in Paris itself. Contemporary themes of a different kind can be found in the work of Alain Jessua, whose *La Vie à l'envers* (1964) dealt imaginatively with a young man's schizophrenic retreat into nihilism before the pressures of living. The splendid Jean-Pierre Mocky specializes in high-spirited satires on bourgeois hypocrisy, tinged with his own brand of comic surrealism: *Les Snobs* (1962) was an ingenious burlesque at the expense of provincial society, and *Les Vierges* (1966) a witty and subtle analysis of current French taboos about virginity.

Finally, there is what I call the charm school, a number of directors whose world is one of innocence and goodness. All villains are cardboard ones; all tragedies happen safely off-stage. In truth, they form no school as such; but their kind of filming was strongly in vogue in the 1960s. Pierre Etaix belongs here in a way, though his more direct affinities are back with Keaton, Tati and the early Fellini. He followed his comedy *Le Soupirant* (1962) with *Yoyo* (1965), the dream-like tale of a rich man who becomes a circus clown. *Tant qu'on aura la santé* (1967) was a charming satire on the inconveniences of modern living, funnier than most of Tati.

The true pioneer of the charm school was Agnès Varda's husband, Jacques Demy. His first feature, *Lola* (1960), was a wistful poetic reverie about a group of people in Nantes, their yearnings, their loves lost and found, their memories. It was an entirely unpretentious film, made just to please himself, and it beautifully created a private imaginative world. I think it is one of the very best of French post-war films. But after this, Demy was seemingly seduced by the discovery that his personal brand of make-believe had commercial possibilities. *Les Parapluies de Cherbourg* (1964) took up the same themes as *Lola*, but the humanist and poetic qualities were somewhat obscured by the gimmicks of arty colour-tones and chanted dialogue. Still haunting his beloved seaports of western France (he was brought up in Nantes), Demy next made *Les Demoiselles de Rochefort* (1966), and by now the rot had set in: big stars, big sets, and the result a disastrous aping of Kelly-Donen musicals with the true Demy love-themes beginning to look mechanical. Like Varda, he has made nothing of any interest for some years.

In fact Demy was briefly replaced as *chef de file* of the charm school by Claude Lelouch, who at the age of twenty-eight won the 1966 Cannes Grand Prix with *Un Homme et une femme*, the biggest box-office hit the new wave has ever made. It is hard to know how best to assess this very romantic, very Parisian film, about a racing-driver and a young widow who meet in chic Deauville in winter. It can easily be dismissed – and has been – as a middlebrow *Sound of Music*, a banal little love-story dressed up with colour-mag trimmings and loaded with cosy schmaltz. Yet it can also be regarded as the complete *film d'auteur*, for Lelouch not only invented and wrote the story himself but was his own cameraman; and his patent joy in film-making communicates itself to the audience through the stunning photography and *mise-en-scène*. Thus what might have been just a contrived and plushy package turns out to be a kind of work of art. I also find the film very revealing of a certain France at a certain point in time. Its French world of fast cars and smart resorts is recognizably that towards which the new-rich glamour-dazzled middle class are aspiring. The film caught a mood. But in Lelouch's career it has proved something of a flash in the pan. He has produced nothing else of distinction either before or since.

This lyricism – seen too in the work of better directors than Lelouch – is one of the *nouvelle vague*'s strongest virtues. Twenty years after they first broke on to the scene, what are we to make today of this very disparate generation of directors? It is clear that – with few exceptions – they have not been very concerned to deal realistically with modern French problems. They have other interests. One thing they have achieved is to renew the great lyrical traditions of the French cinema, which spring from Cocteau, Clair, Vigo and Renoir. Here they have been helped by some brilliant cameramen who deserve almost equal credit: Sacha Vierny working with Resnais, Henri Decaë with Chabrol and Malle, Raoul Coutard with Godard, Truffaut and Demy, as well as Nestor Almendros and others. At its best the poetry that results from this work is very personal and cannot be called escapist. The new directors have not banished Man from their work in the manner of the more extreme 'New Novelists': love, solitude, responsibility, these are the human themes of most of their best films. Though the approach may often be oblique, the French *are* trying to mirror a reality and express a contemporary mood in their films; the questions they pose are more metaphysical and spiritual than those of the British cinema, but none the less real, and I think they go deeper. They are less obsessed than we are by the problems of community; but they are obsessed by individual solitude within a community, by romantic love as a way out of solitude, by the chaos on the fringes of modern life, by the struggle for self-identity. French films today are about love, and British ones about sex; French films are about despair, and British ones about social climbing and social situations. Compare, for instance, *Muriel* with a British film that admits its influence, *Accident* (admittedly, directed by an expatriate American). The British film, one of Losey's best, meant no more than it said, its style lacked mystery; Resnais' film cast shadows longer than itself, which the British cinema very rarely does. Or take the fascinating double-bill that ran for many months recently in a London cinema, *Sunday, Bloody Sunday* and *Le Genou de Claire* – an instructive contrast in national styles of film-making. Rohmer was articulate and profound about some very minor relationships; Schlesinger took much more serious relationships but treated them laconically and superficially, so that the main interest of his film was not his characters' emotions but their social setting.

Yet despite these virtues I do think that French directors' relative lack of interest in social issues is a limitation in the French cinema. Some directors claim that they would like to tackle social themes but are dissuaded by producers and backers, who believe that the public are not interested in this kind of realism; though the French are fascinated by themselves as individuals, they are frightened of looking too closely at themselves as a society. There may be some truth in this. There is also the danger of censorship or other official pressures,* if a film deals too directly with a topic involving Government policies; this may have lessened under Giscard, but it can still sometimes lead producers to practise a cautious self-censorship, rather than risk wasting their money. But sometimes such considerations are simply an alibi for the directors' own lack of interest. Many of

* See pp. 649–54.

them admit they would rather stick to what they know and care about – and it is a facet of French class rigidities that most of the new-wave directors are bourgeois living in Paris. However beautifully the French cinema depicts individuals, it rarely tries to explore their full social and working context, as the Italian and Anglo-Saxon cinemas so often do. Truffaut's recent Parisian comedies skate over the surface of life there. Rohmer's characters live, however intensely, in a world of their own. Chabrol's Dordogne village in *Le Boucher*, though perfectly realistic, was no more than pretty wallpaper for a horror-story. Even a more Left-inclined director such as Resnais tends to set his films in the past or to deal with foreign themes (cf. *Hiroshima mon amour*, *Stavisky*).

It is true that since 1968 there have been signs of change, though – always excepting Godard – this has not come from the *nouvelle vague*. A few other directors have begun to make rather more political films, about the Algerian war, for instance, or the Occupation. Ever since the death of de Gaulle, and the success of the documentary *Le Chagrin et la pitié* in 1971, there has been a spate of films dealing more or less frankly with themes of collaboration and resistance under the Germans. A Gaullist taboo has been lifted. It is partly that the Government under Giscard is more liberal; or it may be that some producers are aware that new youthful audiences have an appetite for such subjects. And on the fringe of the commercial cinema, a kind of semi-'underground' has grown up since 1968: low-budget co-operative films on Left-wing themes, many of them never reaching the commercial circuits. Nearly all of Godard's post-1968 films belong to this category; so does a remarkable film, *Coup pour coup*, by Marin Karmitz, which took precisely the same theme as Godard's *Tout va bien* (a workers' revolt in a factory) and handled it a great deal better. But the films of Karmitz, Godard and others are polemics, regarded by their authors as weapons in the revolutionary struggle. Where is the director taking a more detached, Balzacian look at French society today, its suburban snobberies and solitude, its dying villages, its consumer greed, its holiday mania, its scholastic turmoil, all its other joys and frustrations?

The situation has in some ways returned to what it was in the mid-1950s, before the new wave arrived. The public wants – or is

supposed to want – laughter, thrills and sex, and producers are
wary of offering much else. The biggest box-office hits are nearly
always French low comedies, gangster films, or banal love-stories.
And while backers lack daring, directors mostly lack new ideas.
When a good film does come along – like *La Nuit américaine* –
it may still be very good indeed, with all the old French magic.
But they have become fewer. Many of the best of the *nouvelle
vague* directors seem either to be running out of inspiration (as
Varda, and maybe Chabrol) or making films more rarely (as
Resnais). Scores of newcomers have emerged in the past ten
years, but few show a really exciting talent. Probably the best is
Bertrand Tavernier, who makes powerful and provocative films
about problems of guilt and social morality, most of them set in
the past. After seeing *Le Juge et l'assassin* (1976), Joseph Losey
said, 'Tavernier will become one of the great directors. He is
possibly the most interesting of the new French film-makers.'
Other new directors with talent include Jean Eustache (whose
Godardian study of permissive Parisian youth, *La Maman et la
putain*, was followed by the very different *Mes petites amoureuses*,
an austere portrait of a provincial childhood); André Téchiné
(whose much-praised Brechtian family saga, *Souvenirs d'en
France*, I found rather too contrived); Jean-Charles Tacchella,
whose *Cousin Cousine* is a charming, if too indulgent, study of
suburban manners; and Pascal Thomas (*Les Zozos*, *Pleure pas la
bouche pleine*) who is leading a new trend in off-beat comedies of
provincial adolescence, vaguely reminiscent of the early Truffaut.
And there are the new young Belgians and Swiss making films in
French (Delvaux, Tanner, Goretta), although properly speaking
they belong to France's cinema no more than do the talented new
Quebécois school. All in all, a number of the new French film-
makers show charm and freshness, but except for Tavernier's
their films are mostly light-weight, and they seem little more
ready than the *nouvelle vague* to mirror contemporary France
with any seriousness. This is no longer a golden age, but a minor
silver one. 'The French cinema has lost its international class,'
wrote *l'Exprèss* recently; 'It is artistically decadent,' added a
writer in *Le Monde*. But critics were saying much the same under
the Fourth Republic, just before the new wave. The cinema

changes fast. Who ever would have guessed, ten years ago, that by 1975 the West German cinema would have knocked both France and Italy off their pedestals, to become currently the most exciting and creative in Europe? It may be France's turn again soon. At least, over the past twenty years, the cinema has shown more vitality in France than almost any of the other arts.

SIX THOUSAND ACTORS IN SEARCH OF A PLAYWRIGHT

'What marvellous actors! What terrible new plays!' wrote *l'Express* of the 1963 Paris theatre, and it is a phrase that could apply equally to almost any of the past twenty seasons. As in Britain, the French theatre has changed considerably since the war, but not with quite the same fecundity. As in Britain, the bourgeois commercial theatre has declined since the 1950s at the expense of new State-subsidized repertory companies, which are attracting new younger audiences and can afford to experiment with new kinds of drama. And as in Britain and the United States, new styles of 'fringe' and 'underground' theatre have appeared since the late 1960s, often political and provocative. But the theatre movement has been less widely creative than in Britain, partly because of the shortage of new playwrights. In fact, making what might seem a virtue of necessity, many *avant-garde* directors are now creating a new kind of theatre which does not depend on fidelity to formal written texts. They improvise their own, during rehearsals.

The post-war *malaise* of the Parisian *théâtre du boulevard* is by now common gossip. These forty or so private theatres until not so long ago did a handsome trade by providing the bourgeoisie with their staple entertainment. A 'boulevard comedy' was a clearly defined *genre*, a safe play that would amuse and gently shock, but without being too *avant-garde* – André Roussin, for instance. This kind of audience has now shown signs of disaffection: ticket prices have risen sharply, television, cinema and travel are presenting rival claims, and the boulevard play itself has grown bankrupt in ideas and wit. A very few of these plays still manage to sustain long runs – *Fleur de Cactus*, for instance, or the comedies written jointly by a popular new team, Barillet and Grédy – thus proving that the potential theatre audience is as large as ever. But they are balanced by an increasing number of flops, and the public is clearly growing more selective. A play usually needs star names in its cast to have a chance of success. I find that today there is something fusty and dispiriting about the average Paris boulevard theatre with its rickety seating, faded décor and sour, underpaid staff.

The four or five national or municipal theatres in Paris present a very different picture. Helped by their subsidies, they grew steadily more prosperous and successful during the first two decades or so after the war. Each of the national theatres is responsible to the Ministry of Culture, but its State-appointed director is allowed a free artistic hand. The Théâtre National Populaire had a brilliant post-war career first under its founder, the great Jean Vilar, from 1951 to 1963, and then for a while under his successor, Georges Wilson, who continued Vilar's policy. The auditorium of the theatre it used at the Palais de Chaillot is huge, seating 2,700, and thanks to this and to a subsidy that by 1968 was 2·6m francs a year, it was able to carry out a policy of low prices and so play to full houses. It built up an audience quite different from the boulevard theatres' and closer to that of the ciné-clubs: students, young intellectuals, and even some working-class people who would never dream of rubbing shoulders with Passy at an Achard comedy. The TNP broke with the Comédie Française tradition of insistence on French classical comedy; it did indeed play the French classics, but placed a larger emphasis on foreign ones, and on serious modern plays. One of its greatest post-war successes was Alfred Jarry's satire on bourgeois stupidity, *Ubu Roi*, written in 1896, but hitherto little known even in France itself. The TNP also introduced wide new Parisian audiences to Shakespeare, Brecht, Chekhov, Osborne and others. Every summer the company would decamp with its repertoire to the Palais des Papes in Avignon, and built this into one of the foremost annual drama festivals in Europe. Gérard Philipe, greatest of post-war French actors, worked regularly with the TNP before his death in 1960, and his performance in Corneille's *Le Cid* at Avignon will be long remembered as a supreme moment of French post-war theatre. In productions of this kind the TNP was able to remain faithful to the best in the French classical tradition, while extending the theatre to new popular audiences.

In 1960 André Malraux took the inspired step of inviting Jean-Louis Barrault to run a new company at the Théâtre de France, formerly the Odéon. With an annual subsidy of 2.4m francs, Barrault carried out a policy not very different from that of Olivier in London. His public was more fashionable than that of the TNP and his *mise-en-scène* more lavish, but his choice of plays was often as adventurous. You might find Shakespeare's *Henry VI* in the repertoire alongside new French plays by Duras or Billetdoux; and the outstanding production was Genet's provocative *Les Paravents* in 1967. In May 1968, when militant students seized the Odéon theatre and used it as a kind of open parliament, Barrault at first wavered, then dramatically sided with the revolutionaries, crying: 'I am completely on your side. Barrault is no longer the director of the theatre ... Barrault is dead!' For this Malraux punished him by dismissing him. All in all, it was a sour and undignified ending to one of the few bright chapters in the French post-war theatre.

At the Comédie Française, the artistic picture has been more variable since the war. This State company was founded in the seventeenth century and has barely yet emerged into the twentieth. It considers itself the trustee of French classical drama, and of a certain rhetorical, stylized tradition of acting which is ill-suited to modern plays. It performs the classical comedies well, in its own way, but is rarely successful with tragedies. It enjoys a huge State subsidy (38·8 million francs in 1976) but misuses it through archaic administration. And its attitude to the public can be arrogant and insulting; you are liable to be shouted at rudely as you go to buy a ticket or claim your seat. Sometimes its productions are so superb that criticism is disarmed; I shall never forget the colours and cadences of its *Cyrano de Bergerac* in 1964. And the theatre has even begun cautiously to essay modern drama; in 1966 it staged the French première of Ionesco's *La Soif et la faim*, and (to the delight of the Left) managed to shock its traditional dinner-jacket audiences with the scene that parodies Christian conversion. But there is still much that needs changing at the Comédie Française, and it is not the kind of French institution that lends itself readily to reform.

The policy of the TNP at the Palais de Chaillot in the fifties and sixties had a number of spontaneous counterparts in the provinces* in the remarkable post-war crop of regional repertory theatres. The movement has even spread to the Paris working-class suburbs, where several little theatres have opened in the past few years at Aubervilliers, Nanterre, St-Denis, and elsewhere, as well as at Ménilmontant where the Théâtre de l'Est Parisien has the status of Maison de la Culture. Most of these provincial and suburban theatres are municipally supported; many have State subsidies too. Their standard of acting is not always so very high, for most leading actors prefer to live in Paris where the range of work is more varied and film and TV studios are close by. But the new provincial theatres do attract the good directors, and much of the best new experimental production is now taking place outside Paris.

The advantages to cultural life in France of this colonizing movement are obvious enough. The dangers are that it might render even harder a revival of the Paris theatre, especially in terms of discovering new plays. At present the Parisian climate is not such as to encourage young writers to try their hand at new plays, or producers to risk unusual productions, except in tiny 'fringe' theatres or in the national, subsidized ones where outlets are obviously limited. In fact, the provinces and suburbs are now playing their part in discovering or importing new plays – Gombrowicz, Obaldia, Weiss and Pinget have all been given French premières outside Paris, and *Oh! What a Lovely War* was first performed in France by the modest little company in Nanterre. This is heroic, and a victory for decentralization; but inevitably it deprives some new plays of a chance to make a national impact.

Since 1968 or so, some striking changes in State policy – partly but not entirely prompted by the May events – have added fresh laurels to the provinces. First, the mighty TNP began to falter. Audiences fell off, deficits piled up, several productions fell foul of the critics. Wilson, though a fine actor, was not proving a good

* See pp. 261–3.

administrator or leader; and his choice of plays began to seem too off-beat and experimental to have hopes of filling so large an auditorium. Nor was he helped by May; the *gauchistes* who had formed a large part of his regular audience now regarded all commercial or State-backed theatres – even if they put on radical plays – as 'bourgeois institutions' and therefore to be boycotted. Finally in 1972 the Ministry and Wilson parted company, and the Minister took the dramatic step of abolishing the TNP as such in Paris and transferring its title, its attributes and its subsidy to the provinces – to Planchon* at Villeurbanne! So Planchon and his company, in their fine new theatre, are now rewarded with the official status of France's leading modern drama company; they are 'le TNP' and they have the duty of mounting their own productions at home and then sending them on tour to the rest of France, to Paris, and abroad. Planchon has working with him the man who is regarded as France's most brilliant young experimental director, Patrice Chéreau. And the Ministry has converted the TNP's old home at the Palais de Chaillot into a kind of informal Maison de la Culture, a bit like London's Roundhouse only larger. At first, in 1972, the inspired Jack Lang† of Nancy was invited to come and run it; but despite his fertile creative ideas he proved a terrible administrator, and after a personal quarrel with the new Minister of Culture, Michel Guy, he left in 1975. His successor, André-Louis Perinetti, has invited several leading directors, both French and foreign, to mount special experimental productions at the Chaillot. But the results so far have been disappointing, and much of the blame is put on the stark and uncomfortable auditorium and inadequate stage machinery devised by Lang.

Meanwhile, the old Théâtre de l'Odéon, shorn of Barrault, has become a kind of annexe to the Comédie Française, used by a national youth theatre company and by various touring companies, both provincial and foreign. The policy is to present a varied repertoire of interesting plays, modern and classical. This in fact is where Planchon's TNP performs when in Paris. And in 1976 Michel Guy brought off what was regarded as a great coup

* See pp. 261–2.
† See p. 539.

in persuading Giorgio Strehler, director of the Piccolo Teatro di Milano, to come with his famous company for a two- or three-month season of plays *in Italian* at the Odéon every year. It was a way of helping Strehler to overcome his well-known difficulties in Milan. And it fitted in well with Guy's new prestige policy of trying to attract the finest world talent to Paris, in theatre as in music and art, and so make the city once more the undisputed cultural capital of Europe.

Another new venture in subsidized theatre is run not by the State but by the Paris city council, which has taken over the enormous Sarah Bernhardt, renamed it Théâtre de la Ville, redesigned it in an original modern style, and put it in the charge of Jean Mercure who is offering a safe, respectable repertory of plays on the Giraudoux or Chekhov level. As for Barrault, he has made an exciting come-back: he has taken over part of a derelict railway station, the Gare d'Orsay, turned it into an exciting open-stage theatre, almost a kind of circus, and is drawing enthusiastic crowds mainly of young people for his productions, as well as concerts and happenings. A recent success was Duras' *Des journées entières dans les arbres*, with his wife, Madeleine Renaud, in the main role. Barrault at sixty-six is more buoyant than ever. He collaborates closely with his friend, Peter Brook, who runs an international drama research centre in Paris, also subsidized by Michel Guy.

These varied new ventures, however uneven in their results, show that there is plenty of sparkle left in the Paris theatre. In fact there has been a kind of revival; the theatre is now on the whole as lively as in London, and that certainly was not so ten years ago, before London's decline. However, one problem in Paris is still the dearth of good new French playwrights, as compared with earlier days. Take a step farther back into time, and the situation was brilliant: Genet, Ionesco, Beckett, Adamov, Sartre, Camus, de Montherlant, Audiberti, Anouilh – not all of these are French, but all have written in French and lived in France, and their contribution to European theatre in the past forty years has been colossal. But Camus and de Montherlant are dead, none of the others are under sixty, and few are still writing for the theatre. When their work gets presented in

London, it arrives 'like light from a burnt-out star,' as Irving Wardle wrote in *New Society*, and has little relevance to the Paris theatre today. In more recent years what new French plays has Paris seen? In 1966 there was a new Ionesco, *La Soif et la faim*, originally staged in Düsseldorf, and the superb Théâtre de France production of Genet's *Les Paravents*, which was written in 1961 and had already been seen in several countries abroad. Marguerite Duras, now in her sixties, has made an interesting jump from fiction to theatre, and several of her short plays – *La Musica, Le Square*, and others – have been well received. But of younger playwrights one of the very few with real promise is François Billetdoux, who claims to be making a much-needed bid to bridge the gulf between the bourgeois theatre of entertainment and the Beckett–Ionesco–Genet theatre of despair and the absurd. Billetdoux's *Il faut passer par les nuages*, about a woman's drift away from daily life and love into a kind of saintliness, was the triumph of Barrault's company in 1965. But there is virtually no one else – no one in his thirties or forties to correspond to the younger British playwrights – for what *they* are worth. On the boulevards, nearly all the worthwhile plays are revivals or foreign imports, like Albee and Schisgal, Osborne and Pinter. Young talent wanting to express itself in dramatic form has turned more readily to the cinema.

However, *natura abhorret vacuum* . . . and now a new kind of theatre is beginning to appear in Paris which relies much less on written texts by playwrights. Instead, producer and cast take a theme and collectively improvise a play around it as they rehearse. Or they take a literary text, and build it into a kind of dramatized recital. One of the pioneers of this genre is Antoine Vitez, a leading *guru* of the *avant-garde* Paris theatre. He will take, for instance, a novel by Aragon, *Les Clochers de Bâle*, and with five or six other actors will turn it into an improvised play, with much jumping about and declamation. Some critics find Vitez' work brilliant, others consider it tediously gimmicky. He has even been invited to the Comédie Française, where, in 1975, his new interpretation of that consecrated modern classic, *Partage du Midi*, was regarded by some as a massacre of Claudel's poetry, by others as a splendid rediscovery of it.

The most distinguished new venture of textual improvisation in recent years has been that of the Théâtre du Soleil. This is a young, idealistic *troupe* that grew up impromptu without its own theatre and with no State help. It also reminds one of Joan Littlewood's Theatre Workshop – it, too, has a woman (Ariane Mnouchkine) as its animating genius; it, too, is militantly Left-wing; it, too, as in *Oh, What a Lovely War!*, pastes up history into a collage of superb dramatic effect. This is what Mnouchkine and her troupe did with the French Revolution, relating it to the events of 1968 in their brilliantly original *1789*, which has caused more stir than any play in Paris for years. At first it failed to find any theatre in Paris, and finally in 1971 was performed in a former cartridge factory at Vincennes, a suitably explosive setting. The company has since taken it abroad – it came to the Roundhouse in 1971 – and has followed it at Vincennes with an almost equally effective sequel, *1793*. 'We use drama as a tool with which to fight bourgeois society,' says Mlle Mnouchkine. But over and above politics, in theatre terms the question is how far this kind of improvisation renders the traditional playwright obsolete. Certainly it may place him in a different role: even a writer like Billetdoux is today presenting producers with notes for plays rather than studied dialogue to be followed word for word.

The Théâtre du Soleil is the best known and most talented of scores of little companies that have sprung up in the past few years. Vitez has his little theatre too, in the working-class suburbs. Usually these groups base themselves in Paris and tour round France, performing where they can, in ill-lit halls or sumptuous Maisons de la Culture. Some improvise, some use written plays. It is all very haphazard, often not very brilliant; but it is alive. At the same time, another important new vogue in Paris is that of the *café-théâtre*. There are now some dozen of these, tiny late-night theatres with cafés or bistros attached, where you watch either a kind of revue or one-man show, or else a modern playlet, usually foreign – there was a fine production of *Under Milk Wood* in 1971. These little theatres are *à la mode* with the bourgeoisie and do not necessarily share the same Leftist ideals and audiences as Ariane Mnouchkine. Even so, they are all part of the new diversified challenge not only to the old boulevard theatres but also to the officialized TNP or Comédie Française formula. The French theatre world, despite its lack of playwrights, is thus in an exciting and effervescent phase of transition. But it is having to fight ever harder for its audiences. The problem is partly one of quality. A really outstanding production, whatever its politics, will always draw audiences – whether it is *1789* or Terry Hands's *Richard III* at the Comédie Française. But this kind of quality is rare. The plethora of new activity in the French theatre, both traditional and experimental, does not often rise above the mediocre.

About modern French painting and sculpture I do not feel competent to speak. But it seems to be a truism that Paris is no longer the world's unrivalled capital of art. The world's great painters no longer flock to live there; and New York and even London have become more important as markets for dealers and galleries. Few young French painters have made any wide impact. Only in tapestry-making has there been a flourishing revival, led by the late Jean Lurçat and encouraged by State patronage.

France's musical life is at last undergoing a revival, after being in a moribund state virtually since the war. André Malraux in 1965 admitted, 'France is not a musical nation', and he showed few signs of being personally interested in music or of attempting to cure the malaise; his Ministry, as all musicians complained, treated this as the poor relation of the arts. In his day, the official musical life of the country remained extraordinarily formal and conservative, and so great was the prejudice of the establishment against modern music that France's greatest composer-conductor, the serialist Pierre Boulez, was for many years spurned in his own country. French serialism has played an important world role in modern music; but to study it, you have had to go abroad! And in 1966 Boulez, furious with Malraux's policy, declared he would no longer work in France. He spent the next few years as conductor of leading orchestras in London and New York, where he won the highest distinction. But the Government then grew a little remorseful at having lost such a genius, and in 1972 Pompidou personally persuaded Boulez, with some difficulty, to come back and run an ambitious new research centre for modern music, to form part of the new Beaubourg arts complex.* This centre, the Institut de Recherche et de Co-ordination Acoustique/ Musique, was due to open early in 1977. Boulez is already spending a great deal of his time back in Paris; his concerts with the Orchestre de Paris have been a great success, and in 1976 he formed a new chamber orchestra in Paris. The prophet is no longer without honour in his own land. In fact, for many years there *has* existed a small but devoted audience in France for modern music of various kinds; it is simply that until now it has never won official support. Messaien and Xenakis live in Paris, and their concerts have an enthusiastic following of mainly young people. If in its classical concerts Paris lags far behind the quality of London or some German cities, in contemporary music it is ahead. This may seem odd, in view of the uninspired formalism of most music teaching in France, but this paradox itself provides the clue: the dull infrastructure inhibits good classical music, while modern music is an open revolt against it. Young music-lovers will thus not always answer 'yes' to Sagan's question. Many prefer Stockhausen.

In the world of opera, matters were especially grave – until 1973. The two national opera-houses in Paris have always had some fine singers and musicians, but suffered from terrible administration and poor artistic direction. Their public began to desert them: by 1967 the Opéra Comique was playing to 41 per cent capacity and the Opéra to 69 per cent, compared with 90 to 100 in Milan, Hamburg and London. The fusty Opéra, once so glorious, had become a laughing-stock in the musical world. Then in the early 1970s the Opéra Comique, considered unviable, was closed down as a theatre, to become a musical training school; this venture has not proved very successful. The Opéra itself, the splendid Palais Garnier, was expensively renovated at a cost of 15 million francs, and in 1972 the Government scored a magnificent *coup* in persuading the great Swiss, Rolf Liebermann, formerly in charge of the Hamburg Opera, to turn down similar offers from the New York 'Met' and from Berlin, and become artistic manager in Paris. Since 1973 Liebermann has pursued a policy of engaging the world's finest singers, directors and conductors,

* See pp. 309–10.

usually at very high prices. Mostly it has paid off, and some independent critics now consider that the Paris Opera is once again the equal of La Scala, the Garden or the Met – a stunning recovery. Some productions – for instance, Strehler directing *Figaro* under Solti's baton, or Dexter's *Forza del Destino* – have been magnificent. Liebermann may not have been so successful in his choice of directors from outside the world of opera: René Clair's *Orphée et Eurydice* was a failure, and Ustinov did little better. Nor has the quality of the staging of most productions lived up to that of the music. But at least the public has returned; box-office is up to 98 per cent capacity, and most performances are sold out. However, despite Liebermann's artistic triumphs, he has not been able to solve, indeed he was not given the means or the brief to solve, the grave financial and administrative problems of the Opéra. It lumbers under an archaic bureaucratic system whereby the spending of every franc, even on a new set of blotting-paper, has to be accounted for to the Ministry of Finance. And the tyranny of the Left-wing unions among the staff has aggravated this. They have insisted on work schedules that make any flexibility of rehearsal extremely difficult, and they have perpetuated an absurd level of over-staffing on the non-creative side; with 1,100 permanent and 1,000 temporary employees, the Opéra is the largest State-run opera/ballet complex in the West. Thus its huge subsidy (98 million francs in 1976) is badly mis-spent. Only 13 per cent of revenue comes from the box-office, and 60 per cent of the budget goes on salaries of non-artistic personnel. In May 1976, when France was faced with economy cuts in so many fields, Jacques Chirac, the Prime Minister, told Liebermann that he would tolerate the situation no longer. The Opéra must put its financial house in order, or it would lose its subsidy altogether and be forced to close. There was a great crisis for several weeks, with ballet-dancers and others going on strike, and finally a compromise was hammered out with the unions, who made certain concessions. The Opéra will now make some cut-backs in staff, and will try to supplement its revenue by doing more provincial tours, and more recording and broadcasting work. And its subsidy will remain. But so will many of the basic administrative problems.

Liebermann has often been accused of hiring too many top foreign singers, and not giving enough chance to French singers. His answer is that good French singers are few – not because they lack the voice, but because the standard of teaching in France is so poor, for singers and also for instrumentalists. The thirty regional conservatoires that form the backbone of French music are run on stuffy, pedagogic lines and shut their doors to any spirit of free enjoyment. A number of young people have tried to revolt against this tradition, and to meet their needs an organization called Jeunesse Musicale de France has grown up which puts on local concerts, usually well patronized. Opera has also continued to survive in the provinces, far better at least than in Britain. The permanent companies in Marseille and Lyon are especially flourishing, and there has been a recent revival in Toulouse too, city of the *bel canto*. Summer festivals for music and opera in Provence – Aix, Arles, Orange – and elsewhere are also extremely successful. In short, Malraux was wrong: there is a big potential for all kinds of music today in the land of Berlioz and Debussy. But if music continues to be so much neglected in schools,* and so poorly taught in the conservatoires, this potential cannot express itself at the level of performance. Officialdom realizes this. But, while the Ministry of Culture now gives a high priority to music, this cannot be said of the Ministry of Education. Will Françoise Giroud, appointed Minister of Culture under Raymond Barre, be able to sing a siren song to any effect?

TELEVISION: FROM CAPTIVITY TO MEDIOCRITY

Television was slower to make its impact in France than in many countries: in 1959 there were still only a million sets, and no more than three million in 1963 compared with twelve million by then in Britain. But today the French are catching up at least numerically: they now have over thirteen million sets (in Britain there are fifteen million) and three State networks. A nation always conservative about changing its social and cultural habits has finally caught the craze of *la télé* along with other symptoms of modernism. Until recently a cultured family would admit to

* See pp. 478–9.

having TV only '*pour les bonnes*' or '*pour les gosses*'; today the set will often be taken out of hiding and put in the *salon*.

But if France has been slow to follow this path, it has not been due solely to public tastes, nor to the inability of poorer families to afford sets. Government policy, especially in the Gaullist era, played a large part. Only since 1975 has the State sanctioned the kind of competition that has galvanized British television ever since 1955, and for many years before this it gave a low priority to developing the network coverage. The Second Network began transmission only in 1964, and only in 1973 did France acquire a third network, many years later than Britain or Germany. Much more important than this: if French television today is less excitingly creative than French cinema, and less varied and dynamic than TV in Britain, the causes lie in its many years of political subservience to the Government, and its consequent failure to develop much personality or quality of its own. Only since Giscard came to power has television been allowed a relative degree of liberty, but by courtesy rather than by right. The State monopoly remains. And the legacy of so much State control may well explain the mediocrity of nearly all television today. Throughout this book I have stressed that Gaullist autocracy has had benefits for France in some fields; broadcasting has not been one of them.

It is a legacy that dates back long before the Gaullist era. The Office de la Radio et Télévision Française (as it was called until the 1974 reforms) began life before the war as a branch of the Postal Ministry, and after 1939 depended directly either on the Ministry of Information or on the Prime Minister's office. It is this basic flaw, as much as the Gaullists' later exploitation of it, that caused the trouble. After the war a number of liberals made worthy efforts in Parliament to have the ORTF provided with a genuine autonomy like the BBC – but no Government dared part with so valuable a weapon. Ministers often alleged that the State needed the ORTF in order to balance the anti-authority tendencies of the Press. Frequently, under premiers like Guy Mollet, there was suppression of anti-Government views in broadcasts or measures against hostile staff journalists. When the Gaullists arrived, matters grew even worse. Tolerance of free discussion was never their forte, and in the early 1960s, they began to place their own trusted militants in the key posts of the ORTF.

In political debate and news coverage there had never been much pretence at what BBC and ITA know as parity. Now there was less than ever. A head of TV News once sought to justify this to me: 'How can you have parity in a land with so many parties? If we had a debate, say, between a Minister and the opposition, and we chose a Communist, we'd have the Socialists and radicals up in arms for being left out.' Fortunately for the Gaullists, de Gaulle himself was a brilliant TV performer and for a while carried all before him: 'I have two political weapons,' he was once quoted as saying: 'TV and TV: TV, because I am so good at it; and TV, because my opponents are so bad.' But in the 1965 election campaign, viewers found his rivals – François Mitterrand and especially Jean Lecanuet – rather persuasive on the screen too. This was thought to be a reason for the big slump in his vote. After the elections it set off a policy struggle between leading Gaullists. The 'Liberals' argued that too much State control was defeating its own ends, and unless democracy itself was to be scrapped, there would have to be all-the-year-round political TV exchanges, as in Britain. The diehards, led by Pompidou, thought the campaign had shown the dangers of *any* relaxation, of letting the opposition leaders on to the screen even at election times. The liberals won a qualified victory, and in 1966 one or two regular programmes were introduced, in which politicians of all shades were interviewed.

This kind of ding-dong battle between liberals and conservatives continued until May 1968, when the general strike gave the ORTF staff their cue for a showdown with the régime. For years their resentment had been building up. Now many of them were eager to join the students and workers in 'contesting their structures'. At first the Government's inept handling of TV coverage of the Sorbonne riots played into their hands. It refused to let the ORTF screen any account of the first days of the riots, although the Press and commercial radio stations mentioned little else. This so angered the staff that on 14 May they forced an ultimatum on their management and won: they were allowed to put out a special programme including an interview with Cohn-Bendit. Soon after, when Gaullist power appeared to be crumbling, the staff staged a virtual *putsch* and for a few glorious days found themselves able to say what they liked on their screens. It did not last long. The Gaullists, even in their enfeebled state, would not permit the TV centres to be 'occupied' like the Sorbonne or the Renault works. TV was too crucial; the police or army would soon have been moved in. Rather than risk this and so lose all, the staff chose to strike, and for a month there was virtually no television in France. At first the Government gave signs it might yield, but from mid-June it toughened its attitude and began to take reprisals against the strikers, dismissing some of them and suspending their programmes. Its vague promises for a revision of the statute were not followed up. The strike was a heroic bid for liberty, but in the short run at least it failed.

More than sixty journalists on radio and TV were dismissed; thirty others were 'exiled' from Paris to ORTF offices in the regions or abroad. Several of the best programmes, including *Face à face* and *Caméra Trois*, were axed and replaced by others less outspoken. A few of the expelled journalists and producers were later allowed to return, but generally in subordinate positions with less power than before. Thus Léon Zitrone, a commentator with a big popular following, found himself relegated to sports reporting as repayment for his role in the strike. It was evidently part of the new policy to purge the ORTF of many of its 'star' personalities (who might try to exploit their popularity with viewers in order to combat the régime) and to install permanently a safe mediocrity. It was a policy of trying to depersonalize TV programmes by easing out the arty, original creators – as someone put it, 'an attempt to make TV like another State body, the Régie Renault – smooth production belts and no irregularities'.

News programmes however did not show a greater semblance of parity and fair play than they had in the earlier sixties; for instance, more screen time than before was devoted to speeches by opposition leaders. This was because the ORTF had come under such criticism that it now employed a certain subtlety and avoided needling the opposition unnecessarily – when I myself took part in a French TV programme, I was *not allowed* by my

producer to criticize the Communists! But in a way all this
remained a façade. The Government still closely controlled all
programming. News material was edited to show it in a good light;
bulletins would carefully spotlight official ceremonies and statements, especially those involving the Head of State. Documentary programmes would criticize the United States, or glorify
French achievements. Frequently such things were not the
individual producer's fault; many of them were radicals, like most
creative people, but they had to toe the line or else . . . And official
pressure affected almost every kind of programme. One producer filmed an objective report on the shortage of nurses; the
ORTF showed it to the Ministry of Health, then banned it.
Another producer filmed a sympathetic account of a priest's
difficulties in a Communist district; the ORTF refused to screen
it, although the Church leaders to whom it was shown approved
of it. Almost every programme on a social or economic subject had
to be vetted in advance by the relevant Ministry. This frequently
led to self-censorship.

Kowtowing to Ministers could sometimes reach comic proportions. On one occasion the ORTF hired an aircraft to fly
back a special recording of a France *v.* Ireland rugby match in
Dublin, because they happened to hear that Pompidou was a
rugby fan and was hoping to watch it the same night. Equally, the
ORTF lived in fear of the Quai d'Orsay and frequently sup-
pressed items or programmes which it was told might not suit
France's foreign interests. Therefore it was not surprising that the
ORTF was reluctant to take part in any multi-national TV
venture that might involve a loss of French sovereignty or a slap
to French prestige. The *cause célèbre* in this domain is the history
of *European Journal*. This six-nation quarterly magazine programme was first pioneered by an ORTF producer in 1963: each
nation would film a report on one of its neighbours and then all
six would screen the results – a fine idea. The French thought they
could dominate the project nicely. But then the BBC belatedly
agreed to join in, and the French found themselves no longer
dominant. And when early in 1965 the German ZDF network
made a sympathetic but entirely objective film about de Gaulle's
opponent, Gaston Defferre, the ORTF refused to screen it and

thus broke the spirit of the whole venture. Soon afterwards the ORTF walked out of *European Journal* and left the BBC virtually to run it.

Pompidou's election as President in 1969 marked yet another change in Government policy – and this time, at last, a real change for the better in the objectivity of news programmes. The liberal-minded Premier, Jacques Chaban-Delmas, sympathetic to the malaise among TV journalists, persuaded a reluctant Pompidou to let him try an experiment. On each of the two networks, news and current affairs were hived off from the rest to form a separate unit under a director who was to have a high degree of autonomy. As an earnest of its good faith, the Government also abolished the Ministry of Information with its crypto-fascist aura. Chaban-Delmas chose for the more widely viewed First Network a distinguished TV journalist known for his radical views, Pierre Desgraupes, who had played a large part in the 1968 strikes. For the next three years Desgraupes managed to inject a degree of critical comment and impartiality into his bulletins and documentaries. He was not required to submit his material in advance for higher approval: he was responsible only to the ORTF's governing board, who often held angry post-mortems but had no power to intervene save to urge his dismissal if they felt he had gone too far. It is true that, partly out of caution, partly through lack of resources, the critical views he presented tended to be those of the safely 'established' opposition (i.e. the Communist Party and others) and very rarely did he conduct BBC-style searching inquiries of his own into the Government's real nightmares, the grass-roots of discontent among, for example, students and *lycéens*, or Maoists in factories. Perhaps he knew the tacit limits of his freedom. But some step forward had been made.

Alas, however, all the other programmes on both networks – variety, drama, culture, sport and the rest – remained subordinate to the old ORTF hierarchies and were strictly forbidden to include any political material, however indirectly. They suffered from ORTF bureaucracy at its worst, and their mediocrity grew more marked than before. For one of the dangers of the Gaullist approach to television had always been not only that it curbed freedom but also that it created a bureaucracy unsuited to a creative medium. Unlike their BBC opposite numbers, most of the top ORTF administrators were not broadcasters at all but men brought in from the civil service or industry – one of them had worked at Simca – and few of them had experience or much understanding of programme production. A constant war raged between them and the producers, and the *malaise* was felt right round the office, with Desgraupes' 'ghetto' offering (in 1969–72) the only escape from it. The top-heavy bureaucratic organization of the ORTF, in the worst French tradition, intensified over the years as TV and radio expanded. There were 12,000 administrative and clerical members of the staff, and 250 creators; the place was still run like a sub-department of the Post Office, which is what it once was, with endless paperwork and petty regulations.* Even the BBC seemed by contrast a model of flexibility. One extraordinary rule was that when an ORTF film team went abroad it had to check in at the nearest French embassy to collect its living expenses! And even for his own budget the Director-General was frequently at the mercy of Ministry of Finance auditing and interference.

Anyone visiting the ORTF's TV headquarters in the Rue Cognac-Jay, near the Eiffel Tower, was struck by the difference in ambiance from the BBC or ITV. It was like a third-rank Ministry: sad *huissiers* in shabby uniforms, drab offices and make-shift studios, a general air of grumpiness. Above all, the whole set-up discouraged good new recruits. The ORTF never bothered much with a recruiting or training policy like the BBC's, and it was not surprising that the brightest talent preferred to stay away. The creative ones would rather freelance in films or journalism, the executives go into the prestige branches of the civil service or into industry. It was precisely the opposite of the British situation, where the BBC carries high prestige and where probably too high a proportion of the country's best young brains are going into TV or journalism, at the expense of industry and public administration. A happy medium might be best. Certainly there were always some good creative directors at the ORTF, but on the planning and executive side the level was pretty

* See p. 686.

dismal – and few of France's brilliant young *cinéastes* showed much readiness to work for television even on a freelance basis.

Until the 1969 reshuffle that followed de Gaulle's and Malraux's retirement, French TV at least tried to keep up a certain cultural and moral tone, however uninspired the results. State monopoly did seem to carry one advantage: there was no need to compete with commercial TV for audiences (save in parts of eastern France) and therefore the proportion of serious or cultural material could be kept fairly high. So long as de Gaulle and Malraux remained in charge of the spiritual well-being of the French, the ORTF bought little of the American pulp material so common on British screens – and though French quizzes and variety shows can be as banal as any, at least before 1969 they were balanced by twenty to thirty hours a week (excluding schools TV) devoted to the arts, history, travel and so on. The approach was often dull and conformist, and the editing sloppy by British standards, but no one could deny the high cultural tone. Television was didactic in the true French pedagogic manner, and took relatively little account of audience reactions. Some of the regular serious programmes were in fact good: an historical series such as *Le Caméra explore le temps* regularly secured high viewing figures.

But as the ownership of TV sets spread among the urban working classes in the later 1960s, dissatisfaction with this kind of programming began to grow. The huge new urban audiences tended to feel that the ORTF was not for them, it was 'Parisian' and un-entertaining. So they watched with reluctance, or in frontier zones they switched to other networks. Even before 1969, the Government began to woo this audience with a policy of *panem et circenses*, partly for electoral reasons, partly to sugar the pill of screen propaganda. The cultural items were not ousted, but supplemented – as someone said, 'We have two TVs, that of Audiberti and that of Fernandel.' Then in 1969 this new policy was greatly strengthened: when news and current affairs were granted their independence, everything else on the two networks – variety, drama, culture, sport and so on – was placed under two network controllers closely responsible to the Director-General of the ORTF and his board; hence, to the Government. And the

Government's tacit order-of-the-day was: 'You must lull and placate the public with light entertainment, don't show them anything controversial or disturbing.' So, American pulp material began to flood into French screens, as did old commercial films, more than 200 a year. A number of more worthwhile programmes did survive – historical documentaries, arts magazines and so on – but they were inhibited by an absurd edict banning all topical and political content, for this was judged to be exclusively the preserve of the current affairs units. The ludicrous result was that many modern plays, films or cultural subjects fell between the two stools and could find no slot on French screens. One producer made some films on modern art in Cuba; they were never shown because, inevitably, they touched on Cuban politics. Another producer wanted to build a variety show round Joan Baez; but the dangerous ideology of her songs was not allowed in variety shows, so she too was banned. And so on. As a result, viewers received a most curiously blinkered picture of the modern cultural world; Franco's TV, or Husák's, could hardly have managed it better. And liberal producers, writers and others were more reluctant than ever to work for television, save for the news 'ghettoes'.

It is true that, despite all this, provided they avoided controversy and did not overspend their budgets, ORTF producers did often have rather more *artistic* freedom than they might find on the BBC. That is, given a safe subject, the producer was left to get on with it in his own way, even at editing stage. Though budgets were usually tight, at least there were far fewer union restrictions than in British TV, and as in the cinema, the cameraman (often ex-IDHEC) was eager to share his producer's creative joy. Sometimes too eager: 'I wish they wouldn't all fancy they're a lot of bloody Eisensteins,' said one British producer who had worked with French crews. But at least this meant that French TV, when it tried, could pull off remarkable technical feats, especially in Outside Broadcasts – witness the astonishing 'live' coverage of an ascent of Mont Blanc, back in 1959.

But French TV in the ORTF days never established the same organic connection with daily life as the BBC and ITV have in Britain. It would rarely use *vox pop* street interviews (at least not on topical subjects, for aforesaid reasons) and did not try to give the man-in-the-street that sense that he, too, was a TV performer. And yet, despite these and other limitations, the small screen *has* of course influenced modern French life, as it has in any Western country. It has played a definite role in the reanimation of the provinces, and in breaking down the old barriers between Paris and the 'French desert'. Thanks partly to TV, teenage girls in the remotest country towns now quickly pick up the latest Parisian hair-styles, while peasants have had their horizons widened far beyond the nearest parish-pump and market. But television has inevitably had its disruptive social effects too. There are plenty of complaints that TV has been destroying the French art of conversation; in cafés, people sit in the dark in front of the screen, instead of arguing. It may be a cause, too, of the decline of gastronomy. One reason why the French resisted TV for so long is that they traditionally prefer to spend their evenings talking and eating; but now *le télé-snack* is beginning to make its fateful appearance even at the French dinner table. No time to *mijoter* the casserole; *Les Dossiers de l'écran* starts at 8.30 p.m.!

It soon became clear that the Pompidou Government was not after all going to relax its hold on French broadcasting. But what of the world outside? Could France remain insulated against the way that global TV was moving? The early 1970s saw the advent of an age of satellites and of 'live' round-the-world TV, where frontiers would have no more meaning than in radio. Soon a Parisian with the right kind of set would be able to twiddle a knob and pick up maybe a dozen foreign networks as easily as the ORTF. Already the Gaullist Government had been forced to face the challenge of what are known as the 'peripheral' broadcasting stations, notably in radio but also in TV.

For a number of years the ORTF's three radio networks enjoyed little more than 20 per cent of the French listening audience. Most people then, as today, tuned in to Radio Luxembourg, Radio Monte-Carlo, the two stations in Andorra, or the powerful and popular Europe Number One with its transmitters in the Saar. These are all commercial stations, largely French-owned and backed by French advertising, and neatly dodging the

State monopoly by broadcasting from just outside French soil. They are not pirates, but legally registered in their respective countries. Their forte is popular music and entertainment (e.g. Europe Number One's former *Salut les copains*), which the Saar station has generally combined with news-bulletins far more objective than those of the ORTF. No wonder it draws the audiences.

The same pattern has also been shaping in television, though limited by the much shorter range of TV transmission. Télé-Luxembourg (an adjunct of the radio company) has a viewership of one million in Lorraine, at least three times as many as in Luxembourg itself; in Nancy, 98 per cent of sets are adapted to receive it. In Provence, Télé Monte-Carlo (separately owned from RMC) claims a regular viewership of a million or more, from Menton to Marseille. Both these TV companies put their emphasis on variety, quiz-games and popular films; there is virtually no culture, and within their reception zones they have attracted more viewers than the State networks, notably among the working class. Foreign-based TV reaches roughly one French home in five. In Alsace 90 per cent of sets are adapted to one or other German *Rundfunk*. And even ITV and BBC in the Channel Islands attract a small audience in the Cotentin, around St-Malo, and as far inland as Rennes. A holiday hotel in Carteret altered its dinner-hour so that its British summer guests could watch *Coronation Street*!

In the 1960s, the Government reacted to this whole situation, most astutely, by surreptitiously acquiring financial control over most of the main French peripheral stations. A Government-owned holding firm known as Sofirad (Société Financière de Radiodiffusion) has for some years owned 80 per cent of the shares of Radio Monte-Carlo and 97 per cent of those of the Radio des Vallées d'Andorre. Since 1962 Sofirad has extended its hold over Europe Number One too, through a series of intrigues, and controls 46·8 per cent. The Luxembourg company is freest from State control, and in 1966 the Luxembourg Government rejected an attempt by Sofirad to acquire a holding. Nevertheless, every one of these stations is dependent on official French goodwill in other ways: they need to keep studios and offices in Paris, and the cables between these and their transmitters belong to the French Post Office, while TMC's transmitter above Monaco is actually on French soil. It is in the interests of none of these stations to offend Paris. Therefore their programmes are seldom outspoken; TMC screens virtually no news or political material. The peripheral stations' freedom is relative, and they are not such a menace to the State networks as might appear. Moreover the Government does not altogether object to their existence, or no doubt it would have found ways of suppressing some of them completely; although they detract from the State networks' audiences, they are also a useful source of revenue to the Treasury via Sofirad.

Commercial broadcasting had therefore already entered France by the back door when, in 1968, the front door too was finally set ajar for it and State TV began to take just a few advertisements. The ORTF had continually faced a deficit which was only partially removed in 1966 when the annual TV-cum-radio-set licence was put up from 90 to 100 francs. Already for some years there had been a measure of semi-disguised publicity on TV: little films 'of national interest' exhorted the public to drink more fruit juice, or eat more pasta, without mentioning brand-names, and this was paid for by the industry concerned. Then powerful commercial interests began lobbying the Government to introduce ordinary brand advertising; and the Press lobbied back, fearing that this would cut their revenue. But they lost their battle, and the reasons were basically Treasury ones. Rather than sanction independent commercial TV on British or American lines, the Government followed the Italian model, allowing advertisements on its own channels at certain periods. This was introduced, by decree, in October 1968.

Advertising had been going along merrily for three years when, in the winter of 1971–2, there erupted the worst of all the ORTF's scandals, the so-called affair of '*la publicité clandestine*'. A senator from Roubaix, aptly named André Diligent, produced a wealth of carefully researched and irrefutable evidence that a number of TV producers had been receiving bribes from commercial firms to plug their products discreetly in ordinary programmes. Innocent-seeming shots of the UTA airline and of Levi jeans in a travel film about Corfu; other shots, in other films, of people drinking Russian vodka or Nicolas wines. In these and many other cases it was proven that feature producers and commentators had accepted large sums for this kind of clandestine publicity. Worse, some of the bribes were given for plugging charity appeals that neatly tied in with commercial interests – an appeal to the public to buy rice for starving Laotians was in fact subsidized by the Camargue rice-growing firm that sold the supplies! One producer, whose salary was barely 7,300 francs a month, had been able, thanks to his bribes, to buy himself not only a smart flat in Paris but two country houses.

A National Assembly inquiry in the spring of 1972 corroborated the Senate's findings, and drew the wise conclusion that the bribery affair was no more than a symptom of a deeper problem. The ORTF itself was rotten – and it seemed significant that nearly every case of bribery had occurred in the 'entertainment' departments, and not in the current affairs units where morale was higher. Every newspaper printed long articles pointing out what was wrong – the weak men at the top, the frequent changes of senior staff and of policy, the crippling bureaucracy, all this leading inevitably to abuses and corruption that no one was in a position to control. As an example of the bureaucracy, *l'Express* quoted the story of a producer who wanted to borrow fourteen smoking-jackets from the wardrobe department for a variety show. 'Impossible,' he was told, 'we hire only by the dozen.' 'Give me two dozen then.' 'No – that is not authorized in your budget.' So two of the dancers had to appear in jerseys and tights.

The Government, embarrassed, at first tried to play down the whole ORTF affair. It allowed sanctions to be taken discreetly against some eighteen guilty producers, but it made out that the 'bribery' affair was an isolated one and not part of a general *malaise*. However, this happened also to be the moment when the Government was stirring itself to prepare for the 1973 elections. What better, then, than to couple a few face-saving reforms at the ORTF with a discreet recovery of control over the news media? Michel Debré, whom I saw at the time, told me without batting an eyelid, 'Yes, of course I agree with you that the ORTF lacks objectivity – it's far too Leftist and critical. It's up to us, the Government, to get a firm grip on it again, so as to ensure its objectivity.' So, in the summer of 1972, a new statute for the ORTF was hurried through Parliament. The current-affairs units were re-integrated with the other programme departments – whereupon Desgraupes resigned. The various networks and one or two other services were each at last given a certain administrative autonomy, in a seemingly genuine effort to break up the monolithic and clumsy bureaucracy. The two main TV networks (a third, regionally based, joined them in 1973) now had separate programme staffs, even separate correspondents abroad, and began to compete with each other for the best talent and for audiences. Yet there was something more than a little spurious about this competition – as compared, for example, with BBC versus ITV – for the ORTF remained a single unit. Its governing body was now granted a slightly more democratic basis, although it still had a working majority of Government representatives and was still largely a cipher. In short, though the new reforms did reduce some of the ills of bureaucracy, in terms of freedom they were less a step forward than a return to the *status quo ante* 1969. The man put in to apply them, as the ORTF's new chairman and Director-General, Arthur Conte, was a Gaullist deputy, but as a former Socialist and a journalist of radical views, he began promising various liberal measures. However, he soon fell foul of his Gaullist masters, and left. By the time Pompidou died, in April 1974, it was clear that nothing very much had changed at the Office.

Pompidou was a traditionalist, whose unfortunate phrase, 'French Television is the Voice of France', was often quoted against him. In fact, an ORTF correspondent in London once complained to me that he felt too much like a diplomat, at the beck and call of the Embassy. Pompidou was against ending the ORTF's monopoly, or yielding to the growing lobby for a rival commercial network. So, when Giscard came to power, with a different outlook on this, as on so many matters, how would he resolve the problems? There are many people in France whose dream has always been that one day the ORTF should have a truly autonomous statute 'like the BBC's' – but what does this really mean? Autonomy is a matter of will and tradition, not just of texts. When, after May 1968, certain radicals began drawing up a project for a 'liberalized' ORTF, they got hold of a copy of the BBC's charter and found to their amazement that on paper it actually provided for *less* autonomy than the ORTF's statute. The BBC's board is designated by the Government and approved by the Queen. It is the British style of public life – *le fair play*, so envied and inimitable – that gives the BBC the freedom it in practice enjoys. Autonomy for the ORTF would mean, presumably, a board independently elected and sovereign – but what Government could easily grant that, so long as French political polarization remains what it is? Given the temperament of the French, their tendency to resist authority hotly or else side with it too easily, is 'objective' TV feasible? Many Left-wing producers and reporters, when given the chance, are at least as guilty of non-objectivity as the Gaullists, and it is this which makes any Government wary of granting full freedom. As one producer said to me in 1972, 'What the Government fears is a TV service in the hands of people who would contest the basic structure of society. In Britain and the USA, the main parties fundamentally agree about society; in France, the Communists and others fundamentally contest it, and they have many partisans who work within the ORTF. That is the difference. It is not easy to delegate freedom and responsibility to those you do not basically trust.' Another TV pundit, Max-Pol Fouchet, told me he shared these qualms but felt the answer was for French TV to become deliberately '*multi-passionnelle*', with some of the staff being 'objective' and others spontaneously reflecting a variety of different views. This happens, more or less, on the BBC – but then the British are rather less *passionnés*.

Giscard was fully aware of these dilemmas. When he came to power he pledged an immediate new deal for French broadcasting, although he knew what the limits would have to be. He rejected any idea of a rival commercial TV network, even though his brother Olivier was a leader of the lobby for it. Giscard knew the political outcry such a project would provoke, not only from his Gaullist allies but also, for obvious reasons, from the anti-capitalist Left. The Left-wing unions were powerfully entrenched in the

ORTF, at all staff levels, and while resenting Gaullist control of the medium they were also strongly opposed, ironically enough, to any break-up of the Office, fearing this might lead to an even more pernicious capitalist system and also endanger their members' jobs and privileges. Better, they felt, the devil that you know. Giscard, however, had the courage to override this obstacle. His new statute, which came into force in January 1975, took the 1972 decentralizing reforms a stage further by totally abolishing the ORTF and putting in its place seven entirely separate bodies. Three are television programme companies, one for each network. A fourth administers all the radio networks, including the external services (which, oddly for a country as concerned with its world influence as France, have been greatly cut back). A fifth produces TV plays and filmed dramas, which it sells to the networks. A sixth looks after transmitters and all fixed technical equipment. The seventh is an audio-visual institute, dealing with archives and research.

This is not after all such a radical reform, for no private interests are involved and the State retains ultimate control as before. Each TV company is a mini-ORTF: its governing board has a majority of State appointees plus one or two union and parliamentary delegates, and its elected chairman and senior executive staff must in practice be approved by the Elysée. Its revenue comes, as before, partly from advertising and partly from a State grant derived from the set licence fees. And, with a few exceptions, the same old people are in the top executive posts, having merely played a certain amount of musical chairs. Jacqueline Baudrier, the chairman of the radio company, Jean-Louis Guillaud, director of the first TV network (TF1), Claude Contamine, chairman of the third network (FR3), and several others, all held senior though different posts in the old ORTF. Yet there are two important innovations, which at least have led to an improvement. The first is that Giscard himself has publicly guaranteed the impartiality and freedom of the new services, and has placed them under his personal *tutelle*. This sounds like a contradiction in terms – autonomy and *tutelle* – but, in practice, Giscard's aim was the liberal one of protecting the networks against Gaullist or other such pressures, and of being able to act as arbiter. This has more or less worked. He has allowed the networks to go their own way, and instances of political censorship or even of self-censorship are much fewer than under the old régime. The weakness is that all depends on Giscard's good will; and under a less liberal President, or indeed under Giscard himself in time of political upheaval, the old abuses could easily return. French TV has won a kind of freedom on parole, sanctioned neither by law, nor yet – as in Britain – by tradition.

The second change for the better is that the break-up of the old monolith has led to a much lighter and more flexible administration within each company. Each can manage its own budget in its own way, and is no longer subject to Ministry of Finance interference as in the days up until 1975 when the O R T F was still administered virtually like a Government sub-department. The new programme companies are run like private firms; they are smallish, and do not have to bother with technical problems of studio equipment, which are dealt with by a separate service. A senior producer at TF1 told me: 'This makes our life much easier. We have a small, efficient team of top people, and I can get a decision from them within 24 hours which in the old days might have taken three months. Frankly, the BBC could learn something from us now!' On the rival channel, Antenne 2, things work less smoothly, but largely for personality reasons.

The senior posts are now all held by people with long experience of broadcasting or allied fields; the practice of bringing in civil servants or politicians no longer exists. True, Giscard's watching brief means that he or Poniatowski are usually consulted over senior staff changes, even, for example, the replacement of the head of current affairs at Antenne 2. But the percentage of Gaullists in such posts is now greatly reduced, and a number of top journalists and producers are Socialists. With its new relative freedom, television is at last raising its prestige as a career, and a number of liberal journalists have drifted into the new companies from the Press and the peripheral radio stations. There is not yet much attempt at systematic training or career-structuring on the BBC model; but this is alien to the French tradition in the media. Instead there is a fluidity, as in newspapers or the entertainment world, with people coming and going and much depending on who knows whom; and this has certain advantages.

The news bulletins have become livelier, interviews with Ministers are now more critical and less obsequious, and the Opposition gets more exposure. An event such as the Communist Party congress gets huge coverage, more or less objective; and lengthy 'live' face-to-face debates, for example between Fourcade and Mitterrand, are common. But, alas, there is another side to this new and brighter picture, and it is that the new competition between networks, allied to much tighter budgeting, has led to a trivialization and lowering of cultural level, or so most critics assert. French TV is moving closer to the British or even the American pattern, and is finding that greater freedom, political and also financial, can lead to greater vulgarity. TF1 gets 70 per cent of its revenue from advertising and A2 45 per cent (there is no advertising on FR3), and these sums are topped up by State grants awarded supposedly on the basis of merit, but taking popularity into account as well as quality. The networks are thus engaged in exactly the same ratings battle as BBC and ITV, with some of the sad results that advocates of the old, single, State-run monopoly, such as de Gaulle, foresaw. News bulletins are livelier than before, yes; they are also more sensational, more personalized, with 'star' newscasters trying to ape Ed Murrow in a bid to pull in the audiences – all very different from the plodding old ORTF days.

The companies are under-financed, and have been under pressure to make even greater economies during recent hard times. As a result they have found it cheaper to show old cinema films and American soap-operas (always popular with audiences) than spend a lot of money on new productions, of whatever kind. At least twelve feature films are shown a week, some of them, it is true, the great classics – Visconti, Buñuel, Bergman, etc. – but arguably this is not the prime function of television. The networks, having no dramatic facilities of their own, do buy a certain number of specially made French serials, TV plays and films from a separate State company that has inherited the ORTF's old drama studios in eastern Paris, but this arrangement is due to be phased out. In the meantime, there are fewer long documentaries, fewer cultural programmes and fewer new TV plays than under the old ORTF, or than on British TV. Only in its literary programmes, and its live political debates, does French TV have the edge over BBC and ITV. Its dramatic output is especially weak; and current affairs documentaries tend too often to take the form of long studio debates, so much cheaper and easier to produce than filmed location work. A Sunday afternoon satire show on TF1, *Le Petit Rapporteur*, has been one of the few creative innovations of the new companies and is also a huge popular success, watched by over 50 per cent of viewers. It some-times takes the mickey out of Giscard or other politicians, but in a good-humoured, not-too-sharp, and semi-surrealistic way; it is nearer to *Monty Python* or *The Two Ronnies* than to *TW3*. And French TV as a whole remains slapdash in its presentation. Despite the qualities of the film-work, its studio continuity and editing often appear old-fashioned and untidy. Captions may come up in the wrong place or upside-down, compères practise a Gallic verbosity, and the damsels known as *speakerines* still seem to have strayed out of some Hollywood glamour film of the 1930s. It is all oddly unaesthetic for a nation so artistic, and I think it relates to that typical French insistence on form rather than detail which I referred to *à propos* of new architecture.

Yet despite all these failings the over-all record of the new régime seems to me positive. It must be given more time to settle down. Already the networks have succeeded in developing widely differing personalities, as they never did under the 1972 reforms: TF1 solid, reliable, and official-seeming, a bit like BBC1; Antenne 2 more adventurous and creative, readier to stick its neck out, but also more chaotic and uneven – traits which stem from the nature of the team assembled round A2's mercurial and pugnacious chairman, Marcel Jullian, a former publisher. He signed up Brigitte Bardot to play journalist and do some hard-hitting interviews, but after one or two sizzling appearances she slunk away; he engaged Sartre to do a historical film series which was then quietly shelved, perhaps under secret pressure from on high; he openly accused the Minister of Defence of lying; and in a bitter debate in Parliament, in November 1975, Jullian had the honour of hearing his network condemned by the Gaullists as a hotbed of Leftism and by the Left as a State tool. In short, he is not exactly the old ORTF type. This you find more readily on FR3, run by a Gaullist, Claude Contamine, and rather too timidly pro-establishment in its regional news bulletins, but excellent in some of its non-political, regionally made documentaries. If only Giscard or someone like him can stay in power, and if only it can find ways of increasing its budget, then French television may finally improve to the point of being *both* free and outspoken *and* creatively exciting. But they remain, as ever, big 'if's.

CENSORSHIP BLOWS HOT AND COLD

While in Britain all forms of censorship of the arts grew much more liberal during the 1960s, in Gaullist France it tightened up, and not only in television. Cinema felt the pinch, and so did literature, traditionally so free in France. Not that one could speak of any reign of terror: France in some ways remained more free than Britain, even under de Gaulle, and some of the new curbs were insignificant though denounced as 'scandals' by the Left. Yet there was a perceptible new climate of creeping official puritanism, uncharacteristic of France. With it went, more expectedly, a certain political censorship. Under Giscard, the political censorship has been almost entirely removed, and so has the official puritanism, save for a very recent and justifiable clamp-down on the excesses of the new pornographic cinema.

Political censorship is nothing new. It has flourished from Napoleon to Guy Mollet and beyond. It was worst during the Algerian war, both before and after de Gaulle's return to power, although since then it has eased. But alongside it there came a new kind of moral censorship, deriving not only from the nature of the Gaullist régime but from the loosening of French society, which brought bourgeois values into open collision with traditionally free bohemian ones. Frequently the new puritanism had religious undertones, but less at the dictates of the Church hierarchy than of the old-style Catholic rearguard; and the pious and straitlaced Madame de Gaulle herself was said to have been an *éminence grise* behind many of the official measures.

In the cinema, formal censorship is carried out not as in Britain by the industry itself, but by the Minister of Culture (before 1969, by the Minister of Information), who has the power to ban any film without giving reasons. In practice he usually lets himself be guided by a permanent Government committee of civil servants and moral leaders, who besides vetting completed films also practise a kind of pre-censorship – that is, they see each film at script stage so as to advise the producer whether it will later get a visa. This could be a convenient way of nipping undesirable subjects in the bud. Some directors claim they have desks full of scripts they dared not film in the Gaullist era – say, on Communists or the police. Some films, such as Godard's *Le Petit Soldat*, were first completed, then banned for straight political reasons – but this kind of censorship eased after the end of the Algerian war. And it certainly was no worse under de Gaulle than in earlier days; Kubrick's *Paths of Glory* was banned entry into France in 1957 because it criticized the French Army in the Great War. The new puritanism never led to visually erotic cuts on the British model – the shots of masturbation in Bergman's *The Silence* went by unscathed – but it did indulge in coy morality, as when Godard's *La Femme mariée* (1964) had its title changed to *Une Femme mariée* to avoid the implied slur on *all* French wives.

Political censorship in the cinema eased considerably after de Gaulle's departure. The four-year ban on the Italian-made *La Bataille d'Alger*, which gives a harsh picture of French Army methods in the Casbah in 1957, was lifted in 1971; in the same year *Le Chagrin et la Pitié*, though banned by the ORTF, was freely shown in cinemas, as it probably would not have been five years previously. Under Pompidou, films about factory riots (Godard's *Tout va bien*, Karmitz's *Coup pour coup*) could be shown – as could a film satirizing the police (Mocky's *Chut*) so long as the satire was not too realistic! But though outright bans were very few, pressure was still sometimes exercised more subtly at earlier stages; thus when, in 1972, Yves Boisset was preparing to film *l'Attentat*, based on the Ben Barka affair, he found Orly Airport, Air France and the police refusing him their co-operation for the filming of certain key location sequences.

In the theatre there is virtually no censorship of any kind. Scripts do not have to be vetted in advance. If a play provokes riots or disorders, the police have the power to close the theatre, but this virtually never happens. Right-wing Catholics staged riots during *The Representative*, to induce the police to take it off; but they failed. As in Britain, plays critical of foreign heads of State are liable to be banned; thus in 1969 the Government would not let the TNP perform Gatti's anti-Franco play, *Passion en violet, jaune et rouge*. But this kind of political censorship is rare. Plenty of controversial plays can always be found in French theatres – not on the boulevards, of course, but in *café-théâtres*, and even in the subsidized theatres, especially those in the provinces run by people like Planchon.

Yet literature, totally immune for more than a century, began under de Gaulle to feel an official squeeze. In 1949 the Fourth Republic passed a sane and effective law aiming to protect youth against trashy pornography. In 1958 the Fifth Republic suddenly intensified this law, and extended it to cover all literature, under a decree that sidestepped Parliament. An anonymous tribunal in the Ministry of the Interior then had the power to declare any book pornographic, and there was no defence or trial. The usual penalty was *interdiction à l'affichage* – that is, the book could not be displayed in shops, or put in a catalogue, or advertised. This could seriously affect sales. A publisher or bookseller who disobeyed was liable to fines or imprisonment. And a publisher who had three books penalized in a year then had to submit all his works to the Ministry in advance of publication, and risk their seizure. Even the august house of Gallimard came near to this fate, with two books penalized in one year, one of them its translation of *The Naked Lunch*.

Why was a law aimed to protect the young distorted like this to give the Ministry power to ban any book it disliked? According to reports, it began when Yvonne de Gaulle found an illustrated erotic work on a bookshop counter. Her outrage gave the cue to a latent clique of puritan officials. But the law was illogical; it concerned only new books or new editions. Genet, Céline and others equally provocative went unmolested. It is fair to say that very few new books of any value have suffered; but a law as fascist and arbitrary as this could easily lead to political abuses. Publishers were angry, and wanted to be allowed to stand fair trial for their books.

The situation was all confusion. Some officials in the Ministry were liberal, and they sabotaged and countermanded the work of the puritans, so that it was a question of having the right contacts. 'That's France for you,' said one publisher who after having three books penalized had ignored the injunction to present the rest of his list and apparently got away with it. Some publishers have been victimized, others left alone. Jérôme Lindon, owner of the Leftish *avant-garde* Editions du Minuit, who had eleven of his books seized by the police during the Algerian war, stated in 1965 that he felt the régime had become liberal towards literature since the end of that war and he was therefore voting for de Gaulle. Yet his friend Maurice Girodias has been savagely prosecuted, under an old law of 1881 that prescribes seizure and imprisonment for publishing books 'dangerous to public order and morals'. Girodias and his father made their name by publishing in English, in Paris, books by Henry Miller, Nabokov and others, that in those days were not permitted in Britain or the United States. It is an odd logic of justice that Girodias should later be penalized for books that now come out freely in London and New York, and can even be published in Paris *in French*! Genet is on sale in Paris in French, but Girodias' English translation of *Notre-Dame des Fleurs* was banned under the 1881 law. And in 1966 Girodias was sentenced to imprisonment for publishing, in English, a harmless novel by Aubrey Beardsley.

Sometimes political censorship has been a matter of de Gaulle's personal honour. Although the old-established satirical weekly *Canard Enchaîné* was allowed, as a kind of licensed jester, to lampoon Mongénéral, at the same time an old law was brought out of the cupboard that holds it a crime to insult the head of State. In 1959–66 there were more than 300 convictions under this law – from the writer Jacques Laurent who criticized Mauriac's idolatry of de Gaulle, to a merchant seaman who was caught drawing a rude picture of de Gaulle on a café table. Editors protested that, now the head of State was also head of Government, he should not be immune from criticism or even lampoon. But the

French Press as a whole is too weak and timid for its protests to be often effective.

The law on books has not been repealed, although under Giscard it has fallen into abeyance. He declared after coming to power that all forms of censorship were to be henceforth abolished. And this was clearly his intention. But during 1975 the wave of cinema pornography developed alarmingly in France, a little later than in some other countries but at least as severely. A relatively harmless French 'soft porn' film, *Emmanuelle*, broke all box-office records, with 1,800,000 tickets sold on its first Paris run alone. More serious, though, was the American 'hard porn' now slipping past the new liberal censors. It was reckoned that the French sex-film market multiplied sixfold from 1968 to 1974, in terms of numbers of spectators and of showings of films. Advertising was particularly brazen: you could walk down a quiet provincial street and see garish full-frontal drawings outside cinemas, or over-explicit slogans – '*Venez voir le sexe le plus raide . . .*' Most pernicious was the fact that in some smallish towns all three cinemas, say, might be showing sex-films simultaneously, leaving the public no choice. Catholics and Communists alike began raising cries of alarm; and opinion polls showed that 59 per cent of Frenchmen now wanted a tightening of censorship, whereas a previous poll under Pompidou in 1973, before the 'porn' wave became serious, showed an almost identical majority in favour of a loosening of censorship. Liberals were in a dilemma, for, though they disliked censorship on principle, it was hard to justify these new films on any artistic grounds. Occasionally a new work by Borowczyk or Bertolucci might arrive that allied pornography to artistry or serious purpose. But the vast mass of the new product was mindless, crude and stacked with perversion, sado-masochism and violence.

Giscard felt obliged to act, for electoral reasons if nothing else. He ordered Michel Guy to prepare a Bill, which was discussed with the cinema trade and then hurried through Parliament late in 1975. It instituted a new 'X' classification of films banned to under-eighteen-year-olds, either because of their sex content or because of their 'incitation to violence'. These films can be screened only in certain 'specialized' cinemas, totalling 109, and there can be no external visual advertising, merely a showing of the title of the film and a note of its 'X' category. The films are taxed at a special VAT rating of 33 per cent of the box-office, double the normal VAT on cinema receipts; and they are deprived of the tax rebate normally allowed as a form of aid to the industry – in other words, they are doubly taxed. One aim is to use the extra revenue from this for helping to finance 'serious' films. The cinema trade expressed great indignation at the new law, and claimed that 400 to 500 cinemas might have to close. They also found the new 'X' classification too arbitrary, and at least a hundred appeals were launched against it, on behalf of individual films.The producers of *Emmanuelle II*, successor to the previous hit, said they found the law so unfair and so crippling that they would not show the film in France, but keep it for export only.

The public and critics were generally satisfied with the law, but there were some fears among liberals that its interpretation could be arbitrary. Would it be retroactive?–and if so, would the ban and the tax now apply to certain 'serious' erotic or violent films (including Bergman's *The Silence* and Kubrick's *A Clockwork Orange*) that have always been justifiably banned to eighteen-year-olds but have never been penalized financially? Will the new law not cause a renewal of self-censorship among serious film-makers who genuinely want to tackle bold subjects? Above all, might not a less liberal future régime use the phrase 'incitation to violence' as an alibi for re-introducing political censorship? These were questions being asked in Paris intellectual circles in the summer of 1976. At least the Minister of Culture appointed in August, Françoise Giroud, is a far greater lover of the modern cinema than Michel Guy (I quoted earlier her praise for Godard) as well as a well-known opponent of censorship. She will probably interpret the new law sensibly, knowing that some limits must be set to curb the 'hard porn' wave.

I have suggested that unfair censorship under a régime such as de Gaulle's might have been combated more effectively if France possessed a stronger Press. Today the weakness of that Press is going from bad to worse. The combined sales of the Paris daily papers four years ago was little more than four million, and today is not much above three million. *France-Soir* has fallen from a peak of 1·4 million to a mere 600,000, and has recently been threatened with closure, as has even such a stalwart as *Le Figaro*. Rising costs, a clumsy and expensive distribution system, a fall in revenue due to competition from TV advertising – these and other factors have thrown Parisian newspapers into an even greater state of crisis than those of London or New York in the past few years. Journalists have been dismissed by the score, dailies have closed or merged. And as the French Press with its high costs relies on more than 300m francs' worth of assorted annual State subsidies to keep alive at all, it is often careful not to offend the Government too openly. Of course there are exceptions, such as the Communist *L'Humanité*, and indeed *Le Monde* which has been moving steadily Leftwards in the last few years and is now openly pro-Socialist and very indulgent, some would say much too indulgent, towards the Communists. The highly serious and supposedly fair-minded *Le Monde* has come in for a lot of criticism recently, for allegedly slanted and dishonest reporting, notably of overseas events; for example, its welcoming of the new régime in Cambodia as a great victory for freedom and democracy. Whether or not these criticisms are valid, at least it remains true that *Le Monde* is one of the few genuinely independent dailies in Paris, and its steady rise in circulation (now 580,000 after almost tripling in fifteen years) is encouraging as a sign that more and more people have the appetite and education to read such a serious and analytical paper. Yet even *Le Monde* is not always fearless or straightforward in tackling French domestic problems. There may therefore be direct economic and political causes for the relative weakness of the Parisian Press. The provincial Press* is financially sound, but editorially mediocre; and there is no French paper with a truly national circulation as in Britain, save *Le Monde* on a limited scale.

Since 1975, a possible saviour of the French Press, though of a dubious kind, has loomed large on the horizon. Robert Hersant, centre-party deputy, alleged war-time collaborator, man of power and mystery, has for some years been quietly building up a

* See pp. 265–6.

Press empire of provincial dailies and weeklies and of successful specialized magazines such as *l'Auto-journal*. In 1975, Hersant launched out more ambitiously by buying the ailing *Le Figaro* and, in 1976, a half-share in the also ailing *France-Soir*. And his plans began to leak out for making *Le Figaro* into a mass national paper by printing local editions of it in various towns, notably places like Toulouse and Lille where the existing local paper is Left-wing. Government or big-business interests might be behind him, it was rumoured, in this apparent bid to counter the Leftish tendencies of many provincial papers. Hersant's own Right-wing views are well-known, and so is his brilliance as a businessman. France, then, seems to be in the process of acquiring her first modern Press tycoon, to replace the retiring generation of in-effectual ones, led by Jean Prouvost, a man whose interests were mainly in textiles anyway. Hersant may be able to inject into the French Press the capital, the dynamism and the managerial ability that it sorely needs – but at what price to democracy? He does not appear to be the type to let the politics of his news-papers go their own way, like the late Lord Thomson. He seems closer to a Beaverbrook or Randolph Hearst. Already, *Le Figaro* has been showing a trend towards the Right-wing. Yet the lack of an independent and reasonably objective Press on any scale is as serious a handicap for French society as the weaknesses of its television. While France modernizes so fast in so many other ways, the backwardness of her information media is a serious cause for concern.

Chapter 13

CONCLUSION

CAN GISCARD'S 'LIBERAL SOCIETY' HEAL THE WOUNDS OF MAY 1968?

IN the years immediately before 1968 the various uneven and complex transformations described in this book were taking place in a context of political stability and outward calm. Since then a series of paradoxical and dramatic events have set French affairs in a new light. A violent uprising all but destroyed the Gaullist régime, which a month later secured the greatest electoral victory in recent French history; the next year, de Gaulle's defeat in a referendum led directly to a victory for his dauphin and closest protégé, Georges Pompidou. So the Gaullists lost and then won, and again, lost and then won. Then in 1974, after five years of comparative calm, a new President, Valéry Giscard d'Estaing, began to face a far more long-drawn-out and intractable crisis than that of 1968: economic recession coupled with the rise of a united Left, these two factors together provoking a far keener political polarization than France had known since the thirties and forties. What has been the effect of these changes on the erratic but ineluctable process of social and economic change that has been the theme of this book? Have the sequels of the May uprising and the economic crisis accelerated progress, or have they marked the sharpening of a reaction?

The May uprising was an important event, but its heroics and fireworks dazzled many people at the time into over-emphasizing its importance. There was *not* any sudden revolution, in the ordinary sense of the term – save, to a degree, in the world of education. A new capitalist régime has remained in power, not differing so greatly from its predecessor except in style, and many of the old faces are still behind their ministerial desks. Most French experts agree that today's basic national problems, described in this book – the adaptation of archaic structures to modern conditions – are the same as existed before May. That crisis complicated some of these problems and made their solution more urgent; it also gave a new impetus towards solving them. Frenchmen's eyes were opened as never before. The crisis dragged out into the limelight all that was still wrong with France, behind the façade of undoubted growing prosperity under de Gaulle. It forced the French to requestion the society they were living in. Above all, it has intensified the manifold conflicts between old and new described in this book. This could be positive, for though it has led to a good deal of short-term confusion, it may – as many people believe – give a better chance than before of finding solutions.

There were various separate strands in the May uprising – euphoric, revolutionary, materialist and constructively reformist, to put them in that approximate order of ascending importance. First, there was the element of national carnival. '*La France s'ennuie*' was the title of a much-quoted article by Pierre Viansson-Ponté in *Le Monde* a few weeks before the crisis broke – and there is little doubt that the French were growing bored with years of papa-knows-best government and were ripe for a break from routine. The barricades, the waving flags, the hitch-hiking across a strike-bound Paris, the jolly workers' picnics in the occupied factories – it is not to belittle the more serious motives of the uprising to say that all this appealed to the theatrically minded French, especially the younger ones. Revolution retains a special and romantic appeal in France, and many a Frenchman's instinct was to rally emotionally to the challenge of Cohn-Bendit without necessarily sharing his views or aims. Many students and *lycéens*, however much in earnest about their frustrations, would not have been human had they not also relished this ideological excuse to play truant on a grand scale. Some French observers, including Raymond Aron, indeed dismissed the whole affair as little more than this kind of euphoric irresponsible holiday – 'the Club Méditerranée run riot on a nation-wide scale', said an American writer. This has an element of truth, but is far from the whole truth.

There were also the revolutionaries – Maoists, Trotskyists, Guevarists, dedicated anarchists and other *groupuscules*. They were in earnest; for them, this was no carnival. Most were students, but a few were young workers, and even before May there had been a few examples of student–worker joint action – at Caen and Nantes, principally – previously unheard of in France. These revolutionaries were few in number – maybe 5 to 10 per cent of the student total – but vigorous, and so able to lead the revolt. Although some of their leaders (including Cohn-Bendit) used provocative tactics of violence as hard to admire as those used against them by the police, and although most of them showed a naïvety of thinking and a vagueness about the kind of ideal new society they wanted, yet in most cases their sincerity and generosity of heart were patent. 'Our society is rotten – I'm devoting my life to creating workers' communes,' the educated young daughter of a rich Parisian told me, a girl who could easily, had she wished, while away her youth on a round of smart Paris social events and trips to the Côte d'Azur. Most of the other revolutionaries, like her, were from bourgeois homes. They came from a *milieu* that put its stress on money values, on status symbols, on competitive careerism and holding on to class privileges, and many of them revolted against this and proclaimed their hostility to the boredom and greed of a consumer society.

Alas for them, this hostility was shared by few of the industrial workers whom they tried so hard to rally to their cause. Although a few skilled workers and *cadres* were also involved in a kind of outburst against some aspects of the affluent society, the rank and file went on strike because they wanted a larger share in that society, not because they were sated with it. This was a main cause of the revolution's failure. Had students and workers united *en masse* for a new society, the Communist and other union leaders could not have held them back. Most workers went on strike for the usual classic reasons: better pay and conditions, linked on this occasion with a vaguely formulated desire for more humane and respectful treatment from employers, but stopping short of revolution.

The most original and far-reaching aspect of the uprising was that these two groups, student idealists and wage-demanding workers, were joined by large sections of the French artistic, scientific and executive intelligentsia, protesting against many of the real and most important obstacles to the modernization of French life. Their revolt was against over-centralization, excessive authority and failure to delegate power, cumbersome bureaucracy and entrenched privileges – in nearly all the professions as well as in industrial and office life. Doctors set up 'soviets' in hospitals and proclaimed the abolition of the old, strict hierarchies. Architects demanded of Malraux the liquidation of their 'evil' guild, while even chemists began contesting their own privileges* – a sign that the fires were licking into the most surprising corners of the edifice of French vested interests. Cinema directors and technicians held a month-long special assembly to replan their industry, and much the same happened in the worlds of music and art. As for the much more important and widespread movements in television, in education and in the factories, these I have discussed in earlier chapters. Once the great national debate had started, no group wanted to miss the chance of speaking out – even footballers occupied the HQ of the French Football Federation, hoisted the red flag above it and hung out a banner, 'Le football aux footballeurs!' Maybe there was an element of carnival in all this too, and a desire to protest out of solidarity – no profession felt it could afford to be left off the bandwagon at such a moment. But what is significant is that nearly all the protests were similar in character, they marked a bid for a more human and tolerant system, for more democracy and flexibility. Poujadist-type grievances were in second place. This was a revolt *inside* each profession, a revolt of the rank and file against the established structure and not, as has always been more usual in France, a corporatist revolt of whole professions against Government policy or economic conditions. This was the movement's originality.

And nine years later, what have been the results of all this fine enthusiasm? What are the lasting gains, if any?

During the first year, up until the departure of de Gaulle, the results were disappointing for many of those who had struck out

* See pp. 180–81.

for a new deal – and this not only because the massive Gaullist election victory in June 1968 seemed like an endorsement of the *status quo*. In Paris that July spirits were still quite high, and the excitement and passionate arguments kindled by the May events had not yet subsided. Conservatives were relieved that the country had been saved from anarchy, while radicals, though mostly disappointed by the elections, felt nevertheless that something *must* now happen, that the Gaullists could not just sit and do nothing to answer the grievances expressed in May. But over the following six or nine months the atmosphere changed gradually to one of disquiet. Hopes steadily faded that the régime would prove to have been shocked by the May uprising into recovering its earlier dynamism or finding a more democratic style. Only in the university field did its promised reforms pack much punch. And de Gaulle himself withdrew increasingly into isolation, blocking most of the proposals put to him by his Ministers. By the early spring of 1969, in the weeks before the referendum, there was a mood of melancholy which infected the Gaullists almost as much as their opponents – though it must be stressed that this mood was stronger in the neurotic and politically sensitive capital than in the French provinces, habitually more serene.

After de Gaulle's resignation in April 1969, the election of Pompidou as President two months later marked the return of a certain confidence, at least in some quarters. And the first months of his régime were encouraging. He immediately embarked on a more realistic policy than de Gaulle's. He devalued the franc; he lifted the embargo on British entry into the EEC; he modified de Gaulle's costly prestige policies, especially in nuclear energy and electronics; and he appointed a man of decided liberal intentions as his Prime Minister, Jacques Chaban-Delmas. Chaban in turn chose two brilliant and radical civil servants for the top posts on his staff: Simon Nora, who had once worked with Mendès-France, and Jacques Delors, a young progressive Catholic from a modest background. Together they launched a Kennedyesque programme under the slogan '*la nouvelle société*', and pledged themselves to unblock France's '*société bloquée*' with its rigidities and deep divisions. This was no mere window-dressing; they believed sincerely in what they were doing. And in

the next three years, they did have some success in putting certain
national industries and public services on to a more rational basis,
and in giving workers a better deal, especially in the big public
industries.* But at the same time it became steadily more apparent that Pompidou's own radicalism had the severest limits.
Many of the more fundamental reforms that Chaban and his
team were proposing to carry through – in regionalism and local
government, in the State administration, in education, and
elsewhere – were either vetoed by Pompidou personally or subtly
killed in the bud by more conservative Ministers such as the
powerful Raymond Marcellin at the Interior. Delors told me in
1971, 'I'm continually being sniped at by the diehard wing of the
UDR, who call me "*un PSU dangereux*" – it makes my job very
hard.'

Pompidou believed that the overriding priority for France was
for her to become more wealthy and her industries more efficient
and competitive; if this could be achieved, so he thought, then
most social problems would gradually solve themselves, for they
spring from poverty and economic backwardness. And he wanted
to stage-manage this transition so gently that it would avoid
provoking undue disorder and unrest. Thus he supported Nora's
plans for rationalizing public industries† because these were in
line with economic realism; and he allowed Delors' *contrats du
progrès* to go through, because these were clearly a way of
keeping the unions quiet, of preventing major strikes, and
encouraging productivity. But when it came to the kind of radical
structural reforms that concern people's deep-ingrained habits
and vested interests, and thus are sure to rouse violent sectional
opposition, he generally said 'no' – in the sacred interests of
public calm. He allowed very little to be changed in the *lycées*; he
sanctioned only the timidest of regional reforms; he proved no
bolder than de Gaulle at dealing with land ownership and
speculation; he placated the small shopkeepers at the cost of the
hypermarkets; and, above all, he in most cases forbade the kind
of badly needed shake-up that Chaban and his team wanted to
make in the work routines and hierarchic systems of the bureau-

* The *contrats du progrès* – see pp. 87–8.

† See p. 90.

cratic State administration. This, he felt, would have turned the *petits fonctionnaires* against him.

It would be wrong to overlook the positive aspects of Pompidou's policies. He was right in setting a high store by economic progress, so that there would be more wealth for the nation to share. But his policies were incomplete and short-sighted. He was wrong in thinking that France could cure all her ills simply through getting richer. Crozier told me in 1972, 'I've been helping Delors with some of his reforms, but now I'm fed up with this régime. Pompidou may be more of a realist than de Gaulle in foreign and economic affairs, but he's less of a true reformer.'

Pompidou was a former banker, and his natural associates were the big businessmen and financiers – men whom de Gaulle disliked or ignored. Pompidou's approach to social problems was very different from de Gaulle's. After 1969 he quietly interred de Gaulle's romantic plans for worker participation – not only because they were clearly impracticable, but because they were a blow at capitalism and detested by the Patronat. Pompidou showed himself more indulgent than de Gaulle towards the world of financiers and speculators – witness the Paris town-planning scandals. He allowed a number of shady property deals and other corrupt practices in high places to go virtually unchecked. As one liberal said to me recently, 'De Gaulle's foreign policy was outrageous and his manner intolerable, but at least he had a high level of integrity and we felt that in his day the régime had a basic morality, even to the point of puritanism. Under Pompidou, we're not quite so sure.'

One thing was clear: Pompidou had not learned the lessons of May. In 1972 he suddenly dismissed the excellent Chaban and replaced him with the colourless Pierre Messmer. The next year Pompidou fell ill, and there was a general stalemate in affairs until his death in April 1974. There was then elected a new, younger President with a far bolder vision of liberal reform than Pompidou. So, how has Giscard fared? First, let us look a little more generally at the influence of May on French society.

In itself the May movement was manifestly a positive one, despite its excesses; it was not a Poujadist attempt to set the clock back. But the success of the various professions and *cadres* in securing the new structures they clamoured for has inevitably been chequered and limited. In some cases there has been no change at all, and after all the shouting and the brave resolutions the soviets have dispersed and the old mandarins have re-established their authority. Among chemists, for instance, who represent one of France's most archaic closed-shops, there has been no sequel to the demands of certain younger members of the profession in May for a relaxation of their absurd privileges. On the other hand, in the teaching hospitals May has provoked an official shake-up which is allowing more freedom and influence for younger doctors and students. The uneven and fluctuating situation today that I described in the chapters on industry and education applies, broadly speaking, throughout French insti-tutions. Perhaps the most positive element is that there *is* now a little more human contact and discussion between the different strata of the hierarchy, and Monsieur le Directeur or Monsieur le Secrétaire-Général is a little more ready than before to listen to the views of his juniors. But a new and more democratic organization of command and decision is slow to emerge – except in universities where, amid great difficulties, it is being imposed officially. And, as Crozier observed to me recently, the decline since May in the prestige of established authority has led in some institutions to a kind of power vacuum, where people are unable to work properly because there is no one to lead them and they have no training in organizing their own group leadership. A characteristically French problem. But I think that, all in all, the positive influences of May are outweighing the reactionary swing-back against it. The easier climate between unions and employers, described in an earlier chapter, is one symptom. The French desire for change, and acceptance of the need for change, has been strengthened.

The young revolutionary *gauchistes*, however, have not yet had much success in promoting *their* ideals. Their violent tactics, and the vagueness and wildness of many of their public statements, lost them a good deal of national sympathy in the months after May, and so did their decision to boycott the Faure reforms. Even within student *milieux*, their successors today appear somewhat isolated. They see that the bourgeois society they tried to destroy is still entrenched, and that the French may want reform but not revolution. Some of the veterans of the May movement, now aged around thirty, have gone off to form self-sufficient 'communes' in the American style; others have moved into industry and are helping the workers to form militant cells; others, as is so often the way of ex-revolutionaries, have quietly capitulated and settled down with bourgeois jobs and families.

The May uprising, then, caused no revolution, nor did it immediately alter the pattern of French politics. After the 1969 presidential election the non-Communist Left at first emerged more divided and ineffectual than ever. The May uprising was in itself a crisis outside conventional politics, and at least for the next three or four years – until the elections of 1973 and 1974 – the main political struggles in France were to take place outside the framework of the parties. But is this not to say that real political interest, in a wider sense, was ever dead. The May crisis did help to revive an interest in public affairs, especially among the young. *Lycéens* previously wrapped up in the arts or sport or pop suddenly found themselves debating every public issue from Che Guevara to the new birth-control laws. Adults too came to take a new and more critical look at the society they were living in.

This legacy of May was a healthy one. But unfortunately there was another side to the coin. The passions aroused by the crisis were so strong that they tended to reopen a number of old French wounds which had seemed to be healing. I am speaking of the French tendency to fly to extremes and refuse all compromise with anyone of a different political viewpoint. Strikers' fury at the Government, bourgeois' fury at the anarchist students, these and other tensions served to repolarize French public life in the months after May, just when it had seemed in recent years that a more tolerant and co-operative spirit was emerging. The better climate between unions and Patronat maybe marked an exception to this trend; but in schools and colleges personal relations between diehard and progressive teachers grew noticeably worse after May, and many staff common rooms split into two camps barely on speaking terms. Even in the arts, the new political tensions sometimes wrecked the basis of former co-operation. It is symptomatic that the Maison de la Culture at Bourges ran quite smoothly until May 1968, when the Right-wing mayor quarrelled with the Left-wing director's indulgence towards militant students and secured his removal. Malraux's vindictive dismissal of Barrault was a similar case and so, conversely, was Vilar's refusal to collaborate with Malraux over the State opera houses.

In the first years of the Gaullist régime a number of non-Gaullists of good faith collaborated with the Government and useful practical work was done. But one by one they began to drop away, even before 1968. In local affairs Dubedout at Grenoble, who came to power in 1965 without party ambitions or views, found it increasingly hard to avoid taking sides – with the opposition. This kind of polarization increased after 1968, and I am not sure which I have found the more disquieting spectacle, the anaesthetized apolitical France of the decade 1958–68, or the sharpening of knives that followed. It is depressing, because often there is a remarkable unity of views between the two sides on what needs to be done – as between Malraux and Vilar over opera – but intransigence over collaboration in doing it. Both the Gaullists and the non-Gaullists have been to blame, the former very often for their high-handedness and autocratic manner, the latter for their doctrinaire suspicion of other people's motives.

Today these wounds are still far from healed, and I would say that France remains more polarized than she was before 1968. Of all the legacies of May, this is the most negative – and the rise of the Left since 1974 has simply added to it. It is true that, on the positive side, there is the new, more open dialogue in trade union relations and the more open attitude of the Communist Party; but this, paradoxically, goes hand in hand with a sharpening of ideological conflicts in many areas. This is partly because May has opened people's eyes, thus making them more frightened and aggressive in defence of their interests: a cathartic process. What is more, a whole body of opinion, on the extreme Left, has rejected French established society more forcibly than in the past; and any Leftist who collaborates with that society in trying to improve it is regarded by them as a cowardly traitor – '*un récupéré*', as the saying goes, someone whom bourgeois society has managed to salvage and rehabilitate for its own ends. This Leftist rejection has taken many forms: when in 1972 a Government-backed commission under Louis Joxe began to work out some interesting and radical proposals for *lycée* reform, the main Leftist teachers' union stated in advance that it would reject all the proposals on principle, whatever they were! It is a sad cutting-off-your-nose-to-spite-your-own-face kind of approach, and it has been seen in labour relations too. When in 1969 Jacques Delors proposed a new scheme whereby workers would partake in decisions on employment and training policies, the Patronat accepted it but the unions themselves turned it down – and Delors commented, in an article in *Preuves*, 'It's easy to see *la société bloquée* at work here: one partner demands participation because he knows he won't get it; but once it's offered to him, he becomes afraid of the change and the upset this will cause in his comfortable role of opposition, and so he reacts with the ideological argument: "we must avoid being *récupérés*".' Delors told me in 1971 how isolated he felt – 'I'm publicly rejected by the social forces I'm trying to help – the unions tell me in private what a good job I'm doing, but they won't say so, or act accordingly, in public.'

This is a recrudescence of the familiar French refusal to compromise, or to accept the good faith of one's political opponents. To quote Delors again: 'The French love a situation that permits the most violent ideological quarrels while side-stepping the real problems that need to be tackled. That's what the "blocked society" means.' It is all discouraging, after the progress that seemed to have been made in the 1960s towards more pragmatism and consensus. But this apparent step backwards may be a necessary phase on the road forward. May 1968 opened Frenchmen's eyes to a great number of injustices, archaisms, barriers, that hitherto had been carefully concealed by the protective cotton-woolling of society; it forced them to think and to talk about these things, as an essential step towards remedying them, and of course in the process many people feel threatened or angry, and act accordingly. May has brought hidden antagonisms into the open: but that is the only way to cure them, and so the new conflicts and tensions may not be so negative after all.

In many respects the May crisis and its sequels have simply provoked the conservative forces in France into a last-ditch stand against change. The battle to defend vested interests is now in its most crucial phase. It is a situation full of paradoxes, for this defence movement tends to be aimed equally against the radical Left, against certain of Giscard's reforms, and in some cases against the rising tide of modernization in commerce and industry. The conservatives are striking out wherever they see themselves menaced, and this applies to Left-wing professors trying to cling to their university privileges, to neo-Poujadists fighting against supermarkets and taxation, or to *patrons* wielding a heavy stick against strikers. Briefly, the position today is this: whereas the pace of post-war change was fairly leisurely up until 1968, May marked an attempt to speed up the pace dramatically, thus provoking a vehement reaction of which the Gaullist land-slide vote in 1968 was one symptom. If you try to push convalesc-ence too fast, you risk a relapse. Now the conflict between reform and reaction, the theme of so much of this book, is being intensi-fied – and conservative forces are still immensely strong in France, as they have shown recently in many ways. The next few years will be crucial. The May crisis has brought these issues into the open, and has made the French more aware that changing structures means changing human attitudes which cannot be done by a technocrat waving a slide-rule. But the Pompidou régime never took enough account of this. 'Liberal' in the economic sense, and avowedly capitalist, it was pushing France further towards an American style of prosperity, within the framework of an EEC scarcely less capitalist in colouring. But it was clear when Giscard came to power that this economic ideal needed to be reconciled with social justice and a social policy – as in Sweden, maybe – and if this did not happen, if capitalism went ahead with little regard to any social philosophy, then the barricades and the red flags might come out again one day.

Valéry Giscard d'Estaing, when he came to power, saw all this very clearly. He is an enigmatic figure. By background he is more élitist and patrician than Pompidou or even de Gaulle, and his private social life is that of smart dinners and country château week-ends with the rich and titled. He is an intellectual, a snob, a super-technocrat, and his contacts with ordinary people have been nil or at best feudal. But he is also a 'modernist' with an international outlook; and even before 1974 he was pondering how France could be transformed into a more open and egalitarian society, closer to the Anglo-Saxon or Scandinavian model. Once installed at the Elysée, he pronounced his ideal of wide-ranging humanistic reforms leading to his *société liberale avancée*. He believes sincerely that this alone can answer the real aspirations of the French, make them happy, and avert violent upheavals or the election of a grey collectivist régime of the Left.

Some of his earliest measures were matters of personal style, to prove that he was capable of moving closer to the people. He tried to break through the old stiff ceremonial that habitually surrounds the President; he entered the Elysée in shirt-sleeves, phoned journalists himself in their offices, gave breakfast to his dustmen, invited himself to dinner in ordinary homes, and so on. It was easy to scoff at this as a P R gimmick; but on the whole it went down well with the public. Maybe one or two eyebrows were raised late in 1974 at indications that some dinners were with *citoyennes*, extending beyond dinner-time; but the discreet French were simply concerned at the effect this might have on his work capacity, for unlike the British they regard a public man's private life as his own business.

In his first months Giscard also reduced the age of majority and franchise from 21 to 18 (a brave move, seeing that the young allegedly vote Left); he made divorce easier; and pushed through the much-needed Bill legalizing abortion, in face of hostility from most of his own supporters in Parliament. This is a striking example of how his reformism can be closer to public sentiment than to that of his own politicians; polls showed seventy-three per cent of the people favouring the reform, while most *majorité* deputies were against! He also gave a new and much more liberal deal to State television and radio, and set in train some radical reforms in education. All this I have described in earlier chapters. It was quite a formidable record for a first year in power, far more than Pompidou or even de Gaulle had ever managed in a similar length of time. Giscard also hinted at plans for rather more difficult structural reforms in other fields – in labour relations, regional government, the legal and taxation systems, and so on.

But his reform plans were soon to fall foul of a concurrence of circumstances not altogether his fault. The first was the economic recession, which distracted attention from some of his plans, limited the funds available for them, and forced him to give priority to quite other, unpopular measures in the fight against inflation. Thus, with workers and employers so scared about jobs and profits, this was hardly the best climate in which to introduce radical new co-management schemes.

The second and more serious circumstance was the rise of the Left. The narrowness of François Mitterrand's defeat in the 1974 Presidential election (he polled 49·2 per cent, to Giscard's 50·7), far from discouraging the Left, made most of their leaders feel that victory next time was firmly within their grasp. The Communists and Socialists, though still quarrelling in public on some issues, now had at last formed a Joint Programme, and this held. The Socialists modernized their party and benefited from a huge influx of recruits – which was partly a normal anti-Government mid-term swing to be expected when the economy is going badly, and partly the result of sheer popular frustration and desire for change after more than sixteen years of much the same régime. The old wild revolutionary fervour of 1968 had died away, and many of the youngish ex-rebels were now joining the Socialists as the party of moderate, sensible reform. Violent revolt was out of fashion, and reform was in. And many radicals did not trust Giscard's brand of reformism, however sincerely he meant it, for they knew that behind him lay capitalist interests and the diehards of the UDR.

By the time of the Left-wing gains in the local elections of March 1976, French political circles had been pushed into a damaging pre-electoral frenzy a full two years before the next general election was due. And politics were more sharply polarized than for many years. You could say this was a legacy of 1968. But it was also the fault of the Constitution. The election of the President by universal suffrage had been invented by de Gaulle in 1958 with the aim of providing a strong leader with a large majority, able to unite the country, as he himself did for some years. But when the majority is tiny, as it was in 1974, the effect, far from encouraging consensus, has been to polarize the nation more dramatically than was ever the case in the fluid, multi-party days of the Fourth Republic. And so Giscard has found himself the latest sad victim of that ugly French polarization that always rears its head in time of crisis. The sharpening of knives in both camps is making it increasingly hard to hold to that middle ground of consensus that Giscard has been trying to mark out. Yet, as he and others realized, the absurdity is that this polarization is the product of political structures – including flaws in the Constitution – and does *not* fully correspond to grassroots opinion, a large part of which, as in Britain, does not want to be polarized and is thoroughly fed up with the political feuds. All the opinion polls suggest this. One leading sociologist, Alain de Vulpian, told me in 1976 of the results of a major inquiry he had made: 'We have found that the French, on the whole, feel that all the political parties misunderstood their real needs. They are getting fed up with politics, bureaucracy, institutions, bosses, social conventions; they want a return to a far more private, personal life, forming their own groups of friends and associations. They also want better "quality of life" and environment. And they care far more about reforming the legal system than about the nuclear deterrent. They feel politics are divorced from the real life of the country, and they hate being polarized by the political power game.'

Giscard has therefore felt justified, rightly in my view, in trying to seek a new consensus via reform and thus woo floating voters from the Left. But Jacques Chirac and his principal adviser, Pierre Juillet, and many other Gaullists, have never agreed with this strategy. They felt, as did some of the Patronat, that Giscard's 'woolly crypto-Socialism' was playing into the hands of the Left, and that electoral victory could be achieved only by a strong conservative law-and-order government, based on old-style moral virtues. This was the basis of the conflict between Giscard and Chirac which led to the latter's resignation as Prime Minister in August 1976. So Giscard is now going ahead with the reform policy. He is a man with personal weaknesses; he has often vacillated and made errors of judgement. But he is right to stick to his guns, and to assert that to backtrack on his liberal promises would be damaging. The French, in their muddled way, *want* change; if Giscard does not give it, they will vote Socialist all the more. In their hearts many of them actually welcome his reforms, but often contest them out of political perversity. Jean Sérisé, one of Giscard's senior advisers at the Elysée, told me in 1976; 'This reform dilemma is nothing new. I know, from visits to my little home town, that people's attitudes are most contradictory. *A priori* they are frightened; they've a phrase – "reforms, to hell". Yet they feel a desire for change. And when I ask them to analyse their dislike of specific projects, they give confused, irrational answers. If presented tactfully, reforms *can* be accepted, though I do admit we've made some errors of presentation. Remember, governments since the war have pushed through a simply vast number of reforms, mostly contested hotly at first by pressure groups, then accepted.' How true – this book has been full of such instances.

Giscard has been moving ahead with some controversial reforms in education, and with measures to protect the environment – his record is especially strong here – and to help the family. But under pressure either from Patronat and unions, or from his Gaullist allies, he has backtracked on some other major proposals. In 1975 he postponed indefinitely the plan for directly elected regional assemblies, anathema to the Gaullists. And his labour charter based on the Sudreau report is finally a watered-down affair which is not being promoted with any haste or zeal. Giscard does not always have the political courage of his convictions. And there are two other major areas where he has not done nearly enough to cure major French discontents. The first is inequality of wealth and privilege. The second is over-bureaucracy and the gulf separating the ruling technocrats from the people. These are areas where reform is in any case peculiarly difficult, and where Giscard himself would be obliged to strike blows at his own personal milieux – the milieux of wealth and State power. But if he fails to act effectively, it could prove his undoing.

In 1976, in the face of Gaullist opposition, Giscard managed to get a small, very mild capital gains tax pushed through Parliament. It was not much more than a gesture, as the income it will provide for the Treasury is minimal. But the furore it caused on the Right – when most other western countries have for years had much more extensive taxes of this kind – shows how savagely the French wealthy classes will fight to defend their last yacht or tiara. Now Raymond Barre is vaguely promising a rather more important measure: a reform of the tax system that will attack that most sacred of French sports, tax-evasion. This is practised mainly by the self-employed, and is believed to deprive the exchequer of up to 50,000m francs a year, almost as much as the 66,000m that comes from direct income tax on wages. It remains to be seen whether anything will really come of this before the elections. Yet French workers are well aware that their income inequalities are the highest in north-west Europe and not much less than in Italy or Spain. Thanks to increases at the bottom end of the scale, average differentials in firms have been reduced from 10:1 to about 7:1 in recent years. But this is still much higher than in Britain or Germany. Moreover, it does not take account of the self-employed, whose incomes cannot be controlled like those of business managers or other senior employees. Lawyers, architects, private doctors, owners of businesses, even some journalists, are able to make huge sums and pay little tax on them, and their average standard of living today is probably about twice that of their British counterparts. Raymond Barre's plan of September 1976 made a small first step towards limiting the incomes of the rich; but Left-wing voters will hardly consider it adequate.

The issue of technocracy is a more complex one. According to Michel Crozier and other sociological experts, one of the strongest legacies of May is a lingering resentment that 'they' – the rulers, the technocrats, the bosses, the authorities of all sorts – are out of touch with the needs of the people, and that ordinary Frenchmen do not have enough control of their own destiny. Some progress has been made here in education, and also in some factories; but not in terms of regional government, and certainly not where it matters most, in relations between State administrations and the public. I heard a typical story of a young man in the Dordogne who tried to form a private association for the defence of the environment and protection of historic sites: he won the support of local farmers and other citizens, but came up against the opposition of the Prefect and other local State officials who were quite simply jealous that his schemes might rival their own, or else feared that he might turn into some kind of Left-wing trouble-maker. Again and again one hears stories of this kind, of the State opposing private initiatives for fear that they might become politicized. Or one hears of the resentment aroused by the clever young *énarques* from the Inspection des Finances or other State bodies who go round France taking their arrogant decisions, thinking they know all the answers, yet never in their lives having been in contact with ordinary people facing ordinary problems. This is the other side of the coin of effective central planning. I analysed it earlier in the economic chapter, and quoted Simon Nora's view on how the élitist system was a great asset in the days when France was modernizing and her politics were still unstable, but is an obstacle now to the emergence of a more open society where people want to participate. Yet a remedy is extremely hard to devise. Maybe the Government could set some kind of lead. But Giscard, despite his ideal of a 'liberal society', seems curiously closed to this problem – maybe himself being the supreme product of the élitist system. Of the 43 members of his Government, 31 have come from the civil service, and the style of his régime is more technocratic than ever, well-meaning, but out of touch with ordinary people. Stanley Hoffmann, the American expert on France, has put his finger on this.* 'Reduction of inequalities of wealth is important, yes. But by far the biggest problem facing France is to reform the structures of authority, that is, to give the ordinary citizen the chance to have something to do in this new French society. There are lots of private associations of all kinds in France, but they remain on the sidelines, and this can only lead them into resistance or opposition ... Giscard lacks an over-all reformist plan. On the one hand, he's a modernist, with an Anglo-Saxon style of discourse; yet he also thinks like a man brought up in the Ministry of Finance, for whom France is governed by four or five people who come, if possible, from that Ministry. The idea that change consists essentially in creating institutions lively enough themselves to generate change is one that completely escapes him. French

* *Le Point*, 26 July 1976.

society has changed fantastically, but is still up against this problem of authority.'

To this must be added Giscard's other shortcomings: his secretiveness, dislike of discussion and confrontation, fondness for making arbitrary decisions, erratic choice of colleagues, and tendency to make generous promises and not carry them out – not out of deceit or demagogy, but simply through imprudence or lack of foresight. These, quite apart from the policy differences, were some of the character traits that Chirac could not cope with. Now the more calm, reassuring and down-to-earth Barre has been brought in to try to give greater cohesion and fulfilment to Giscard's flighty idealism. But the situation before the elections remains horrifyingly uncertain. There are those who argue that Giscard and Barre should now make use of the crisis to apply the scalpel much more ruthlessly; that is, they should say clearly to the French people: 'Economic ills will not be cured by tinkering with finance; it is now or never that we must apply the structural remedies' – and according to this argument, the French middle classes *are* now ready for such sacrifices. But it is not sure. Meanwhile, more and more middle-class people are joining the Socialist ranks, especially *cadres* and civil servants. According to some polls, about half the civil service is now pro-Mitterrand. Either they are fed up with the effect of the crisis on their living standards; or else, thinking of their future careers, they are jumping on the bandwagon in time. Giscard does not have much time in which to reverse this trend. Above all, he must find some way, as de Gaulle did, of appealing directly to the people over the heads of the politicoes, and of breathing credibility into his genuinely generous liberalism. Otherwise, in the next elections, a flick of the national whim could set France's most enlightened President of this century up against a Left-wing Parliament, and bring the proud, successful new France crashing towards crisis and maybe disaster.

STRUCTURAL REFORM: DANGERS OF
THE STATE AS NANNY

'France is becoming, has already become, *another country*,' says Jean-François Revel. 'The mutations are gigantic, everything is stirring before our eyes,' says Jean-Luc Godard. 'The contrast is startling between the France of the late 1940s and the new France of the 1960s and 1970s,' says Michel Crozier. The French, in short, believe they are living in a period of revolution. And peasants and provincials believe it, as well as Parisian intellectuals. The familiar France of the past is losing its power to protect them; it crumbles at their touch, and a new, unknown landscape is opening out. But what kind of France will there be, in twenty or thirty years' time? How great a price will the old France, with all her genius, have to pay to the new?

As I see it, there are four main question-marks over the future. One, what happens if the Left win the parliamentary elections and Giscard is still there as President? – how can the constitutional crisis be resolved, and will the Left be capable of governing without plunging France either into chaos or into totalitarianism? This vast political question is deliberately outside the scope of this book. The other three questions I must try to answer. Two, will the current process of modernizing the economy and administration be carried through, and will prosperity continue to increase? Three, will a more open and flexible society emerge at the same time, and will the old barriers of mistrust give way to a greater community spirit and fairer sharing of wealth and privilege? Four, can France modernize without losing her style and originality, or is much of the uniqueness of French civilization doomed to disappear with the old France? On the second point, I am reasonably optimistic. On the third I am not too pessimistic for the long term, though the process is manifestly slow and painful. On the fourth there is more doubt.

Short of a world war or other global disaster, or a major upheaval in France far worse than that of 1968, and despite the economic setbacks of the past three years, there is reason to hope that the transformation of the French economy will go forward, however unevenly. The French will continue to grow more prosperous, and there is now every hope that they will do so as independent Europeans in unity with the rest of the EEC, rather than as satellites of the big American corporations.

So much progress has been made in the past twenty years that it is hard to imagine a return to the old days of protectionism and commercial apathy, even under a less stable Government than the present one. Lüthy's Sisyphean rock is over the crest: the major industries, after a difficult period of adaptation and gathering of speed, have now built up a solid and durable rhythm. And on a wider psychological level, too, changes have taken place which would appear to be definitive, at least for the next decades: protectionism, fear of mechanization, deliberate limitation of production, these characteristic French attitudes of the past have been steadily disappearing from industry, commerce and farming, and a new spirit is spreading. Therefore, by a natural momentum, the firms, shops and farms will continue to group together and modernize, or face extinction. The process will continue to cause hardship and bitterness to the older generation, and will still be hotly resisted for many years; but it is unthinkable that their sons should return to the old ways. A new, very modern France is gradually imposing itself on the old France, which is dying away.

Yet there are many practical obstacles still in the way of modernization – outdated laws and regulations, restrictive privileges, official rules and practices that inhibit expansion or give an alibi to sloth or inefficiency. These obstacles are not so great as to block over-all national progress, but they are enough to slow it down and to distort it; and there might be dangers in allowing a technically advanced economy to grow up over outmoded structures, like putting too powerful an engine in a rickety car. Only the Government can impel the necessary reforms, and thus ensure that modernization goes forward smoothly rather than chaotically. De Gaulle's régime did in fact reform quite a lot, as this book has shown. But towards the end it veered in the direction of conservatism, and its handling of the economy betrayed three areas of failure: failure to back up its reforms with adequate funds; lack of the courage to carry out other, more contentious, reforms which are urgently needed; and failure to delegate power. Giscard, for all his good intentions, has been guilty of some of the same failures.

Despite increases in the budgets for education and public works, State spending under de Gaulle was heavily slanted towards prestige operations, especially the nuclear policy. This impeded the Government from doing more to remedy France's social injustices – grave shortage of low-cost housing, inadequate grants for students, poor hospital conditions, and old-age pensions which remained disgracefully low, though higher than in pre-Gaullist days. For all its passion for efficiency and social progress, the Gaullist régime did not display an over-large social conscience, and made little effort to ensure that the nation's new prosperity was fairly spread. Moreover, the restrictions in public spending led, in many cases, not only to injustice but to actual inefficiency; time and again the ship of reform was spoiled for a ha'p'orth of tar, and an otherwise admirable new measure went off at half-cock through lack of funds for implementing it. This was true of the SAFERs in agriculture, the ZUPs and ZADs for housing, and the Maisons de la Culture.

Pompidou after 1969 timidly began to redress this balance. Though he cut down on prestige spending, and on subsidies to declining industries, his main budgetary effort went towards boosting France's industrial and financial power rather than on making it a pleasanter and easier country to live in. Only since about 1971 were there signs of a real effort to increase public service spending. Until now, individual wealth had been allowed to outstrip the growth of public amenities in a way that simply frustrated the full enjoyment of that wealth; the shortage of telephones, of sports fields, of modern roads in crowded areas, were obvious examples. In France, much more than in Britain, you still need to be rich in order to insulate yourself against the sheer daily inconveniences of public life. If the nuclear policy – which Pompidou and Giscard have continued – has been partly to blame for these shortages, so has the Government's fear of causing an outcry by increasing taxes. And this, in turn, is the public's fault, for if there is one national character trait that has barely changed yet, it is the Frenchman's rooted conviction that his neighbour, not himself, should pay the cost of public services. Giscard since 1974 has put a much greater accent than Pompidou on environmental and social measures; but his style has been severely cramped by the crisis and the inevitable cut-back in public spending.

The next problem is that of the structural reforms still pending. It would not be fair to minimize the efforts that the Gaullists made. They had more success than any previous Government in battering a breach in the network of *positions acquises* that has strait-jacketed France for so long, and they carried through a number of vital reforms in face of determined sectional opposition. I would list especially the Pisani agricultural measures, the extension of the TVA to commerce, the prefectoral changes, the Schéma Directeur for Paris, the repeal of the 1920 anti-contraception law, the Fouchet and Faure educational reforms, the labour reforms since 1968, and several more specialized measures such as the removal of the *bouilleurs de cru*'s hereditary privileges and the transfer of Les Halles. But in a number of cases – and education and regional development provide examples – the Gaullists' high-handed approach to their public, whether teachers or local councillors, lost them much of the co-operation that reforms need if they are to be fully effective. What is more, other important projects have lain on the shelf because of the Government's fear of challenging the *droits acquis* of this or that section of the community. Land and property ownership has provided the most flagrant instance. Here, more than anywhere, social progress was held up by archaic structures: here, more than anywhere, the Pompidou Government was afraid of provoking hostility – in this case, that of its own business allies. Giscard in 1975 embarked on modest reforms to deal with some of the abuses, but other vested privileges still to be challenged include those of middlemen, chemists, lawyers, Paris taxi-drivers and a variety of small trades.

And within the civil service and public administration itself, efficiency is held up by the dead weight of petty bureaucracy and outdated rules and routines, which cannot easily be reformed because of wary opposition from the *petits fonctionnaires* themselves. In many Ministries, prefectures or other public offices, one is struck again and again by the gulf between the small élite at the top, vigorous and efficient, and the junior employees whose muddle or lethargy simply sabotages the technocratic effort. This is a common problem anywhere, but especially in France. One answer would be to improve the quality of civil service training at below-ENA level; while ENA turns out its brilliant élite, not enough is done to train the middle and lower ranks. These junior officials are mostly badly paid, and another answer would be to raise their salaries, reduce their numbers, and bring in modern methods and machinery – an operation whose initial investment might soon be recovered in improved 'productivity'. Albin Chalandon, Minister of Equipment in 1969–72, did manage to enforce some modernization of routines in the highly traditional Ponts et Chaussées department, despite fierce opposition from its *cadres*. But this is one of the few cases where Pompidou or Giscard have sanctioned this kind of shake-up; it always meets such resistance, even from those likely to benefit from it, that Governments tend to consider it politically more trouble than it's worth.

The French economy is opening out so fast, and is becoming so vulnerable to world competition, that, as each year goes by, France can less and less afford the luxury of her quaint old weaknesses. And the implanting of modern techniques of production, planning and marketing on top of unsuitable structures simply leads to wastage of investment and unbalance. The new *marchés-gares* are fitted with teleprinters, but the middlemen's mafia is still in place. The efforts to build new flats, offices and roads are frustrated by the nightmare of ancient laws and permits.

Some of the many problems of this kind are righting themselves, little by little, for they simply require new techniques and outlook: others are more organic and institutional, and therefore demand concrete official action. In the past few years, the initiative for such action has come as often from the European Commission in Brussels as from the French Government – indeed, many people have seen European integration as the most likely long-term hope for solving France's structural problems. The Commission has made some progress, though slowly, in its efforts to persuade Governments to harmonize transport, taxation, company law, and so on. There are other areas where the process has hardly begun – equivalence of diplomas, for instance, and common standards for licensing of drugs – for the French and other member Governments often reject the Commission's proposals for integration. But yet, if it is so hard to reform

France's structures from within, it might well prove that a shock from outside through European integration could provide the necessary spur and incentive. The adoption of the Value-Added Tax, of the Common Agricultural Policy, and of some other EEC measures, has shown that the French will accept pills sugared in Brussels more readily than those sugared by their own Government. But the twilight that has descended on the EEC – since the wet blanket of British entry, and since the monetary disruption of the economic crisis – seems to have put an end to further hopes of integration for the time being.

The third and last problem rests on a paradox: the State has failed to make the most effective use of its power, yet it enjoys too much power. As has often been pointed out, structural reform is peculiarly difficult in France because the State represents the toughest vested interest of all and suffers from the most insidious of structural defects, over-centralization. This ubiquitous role of the State in France has its roots deep in royalist history and was reinforced by Napoleon. It has frequently carried advantages in the promotion of effective government and some of these it retains today, notably through the prefectoral system and centralized bodies such as the Plan. Obviously France's post-war economic recovery owes much to the lead given by a powerful body of State technocrats, while in certain public services such as railways and electricity France is a model of what intelligent centralized control can achieve. But in many sectors of national life the system is open to abuse, notably under an authoritarian régime like de Gaulle's or a technocratic one such as Giscard's. And even its practical assets are today becoming more questionable.

Even in certain public services it is arguable that the State is taking upon itself more than it can properly handle; there are plenty of economists who have long argued that the way to solve the shortages of telephones, motorways and low-cost housing is to take these things away from restrictive Ministerial budgeting, raise loans for them on the open market, and let private enterprise do the job. But the State has been the victim of its own *étatiste* tradition and has proved reluctant to delegate. However, it has recently begun to sanction motorway construction by private firms, and there is talk of this experiment being extended to telephone installation. And very recent reforms have freed the railways, the Paris transport authority, and some other public bodies, from a measure of State *tutelle*: they remain in State hands, but are now freer to take their own commercial and administrative decisions, as in the State-owned manufacturing concerns such as Renault and Aérospatiale. This improves their flexibility and efficiency, especially in handling labour relations. So the State is tentatively shifting its policy – in the face of strong resistance from the doctrinaire centralists.

In the sphere of relations between the State and private industry, the problem remains more controversial. When so much power and decision is in the hands of the State, private initiatives are inhibited or driven into opposition and talents and resources are under-used. This book has been full of instances, both in economic and in political or cultural affairs. The State's control of banking and finance curbs the development of Paris as a free capital market. State supervision of private firms may often restrict their spirit of enterprise and their dynamism – and during the 1974–6 economic crisis firms became increasingly irritated at what they saw as increasing State interference, preventing them from carrying out profitable policies. In other fields, democratic activity in the communes and in the new regions is stunted by the power of the prefects, however go-ahead they may be; the bureaucracy of State education has inhibited human contact between teacher and pupil; and the running of broadcasting under State *tutelle* had notorious drawbacks in the old ORTF days which have been only partially cured under the new system.

The real dilemma is that, in a great many cases, the State technocrats and planners appear to be *more* vigorous, liberal and far-sighted than private or local bodies might be. Malraux had a larger vision of civic cultural needs than the mayor of Caen; Delouvrier saw the problems of Greater Paris more clearly than a man like Berrurier; the Education Ministry's reformers are more progressive than the teachers. And if progress were left, as so often in Britain, to the groundswell of local opinion and initiative, the *esprit de clocher* might win the day. But this is a vicious circle. So long as *étatisme* remains so strong it is bound to drive much local initiative into the role of opposition, as happens in the communes; or else it simply stunts local roots. Often I have been struck by the French citizen's sense of impotence at embarking on any co-operative public project unless it has official origin or sanction. And this is not essentially because their action would be against the law; but they would be trying to walk without Nanny. Only when the State agrees to delegate some of its own power, and to invite a more authentic local participation, will a more vigorous sense of community arise; this is especially true in regional government.

Napoleonic centralization is a waning asset under modern conditions. The Gaullist régime made a bold step in this direction with the new university system, and lesser steps in the case of some public services; but its regional reforms were timid. Giscard today has an ideal of a more open and participatory society, and at least has shown a desire to bring this about, in education, in labour relations and regional reform. But he is too much a prisoner of his own technocratic, élitist background; he *believes* in the efficiency of the central machine of State, and it would never occur to him to dismantle it. There is a certain contradiction in his thinking here. And under his style of government, the technocrats and the administrators are more cut off from the people than ever – just at a time when the people are getting more and more fed up with this. No wonder the Left is gaining ground.

BIRTH-PANGS OF A NEW CIVIC SPIRIT

The acceptance of *étatisme* and the tenacity of vested interests are two French traits that have their roots deep in the social character of the nation, with its bias towards clearly defined authority, routine and hierarchy. Many Frenchmen recognize that this formal society, for all its historic virtues, is no longer ideally adapted to the more flexible conditions of today. In private conversation they will often regret the relative lack of continuous public debate or of the Anglo-Saxon sense of private involvement in public issues. And they know that Gaullism, though it may have aggravated this state of affairs, was also a symptom of it. Yet a new leaven has been at work in society, behind the façade of Gaullist autocracy, and it is not impossible that one day the old pattern of social harmony, built on the protective balancing of rival interests, will give place to a new pattern, more open, flexible and trustful.

Over the centuries the French created a framework where each class, each group, each interest had its own position and privileges, many of them defined by written rules and laws, or at least by accepted custom. In a nation prone to violence and disorder, this was found to be the best way of avoiding conflict or the oppression of one group by another or by the central government. And it brought a degree of harmony and stability, although its defensive rigidity made change and progress more difficult. The role of the State was to guarantee and defend the interests of each group, even if this meant the propping up of obsolescence; hence the importance of the supreme legal body of State, the conservative Conseil d'Etat. Throughout public life extreme importance was laid on juridical texts and defined prerogatives, so that everyone knew what was expected of him; the Code Napoléon, for instance, laid down rules even for the details of family life. It was a system that gave the individual a certain security; and, paradoxically, it left him with a good deal of freedom, so long as he kept to the basic rules. Society had found how to steer French creative individualism away from anarchy, without having to draw the reins too tight.

But the system was based also on the mutual mistrust of one group of individuals for another. A Frenchman grew up to look on his neighbour as potentially a selfish and hostile rival who might try to do him down, and laws and privileges existed to protect him against this. Those he could really rely on were limited to his family: 'In a crisis, friends don't help you but family do,' a small-town mayor once told me, and this attitude persists. Though the Frenchman would also join vigorously in association with fellow-members of his own trade or social group, this was more for mutual self-defence than out of real sentiment or civic duty. There were few organic loyalty-groupings between the unit of the family and that of the State. And even his attitude to the State was ambivalent. Though he respected its impartiality as legal arbiter, and though *la patrie* would evoke in him a feeling of patriotic duty in time of foreign menace, this sense of duty did not extend towards the State's democratic incarnation, the Government of the day. This was not to be trusted: it was elected by *les autres*, that is, other Frenchmen, and its agents, the public authorities, were to be evaded, suborned or hoodwinked. The Frenchman's rational fear of the hostility of other sections of society was extended, rather less rationally, to the assumption that the public administration, too, was some kind of malignant rival force, operating on behalf of *les autres*.

This framework and these attitudes remain, though their force is weakening. They have been encouraged over the years by an educational system that has offered the child little practical training in leadership or sense of community, matters which were hardly considered relevant.

Today, however, a modern way of life is beginning to make nonsense of the old barriers and formalities. On the farms, on the housing estates, in the universities, new conditions are demanding a new spirit of co-operation and therefore of trust. The new economy is irked by the old practices and regulations, and by the rigid patterns of hierarchy within firms and offices which frustrate so much talent. Now a new generation is arising, more pragmatic, more tolerant, less legalistic; and new élites are trying to crack breaches in the old framework. As Crozier has pointed out, the breaking-point has been reached in a familiar French cycle, where society first resists change with all its force and allows an intolerably archaic situation to build up, then, under the impulse of a few dynamic individuals, it accepts complete change on every front, all at once, only to re-close its ranks when the revolution is over. This was the kind of situation that was building up to crisis-point before 1968.

In this book I have not attempted to describe the arch-complex French legal system, nor the current attempts to reform it; these are matters for a specialist. But also in a more general sense, the attachment to legalism and to formal routine pervades almost every aspect of French public life and thought, as anyone knows who has lived in France. It is not simply that the laws and regulations themselves are ubiquitous and often abstruse; the

French are also conditioned to thinking in terms of them, even when it is not strictly necessary. For instance, there is a law of 1901 which sanctions privately formed clubs and associations as being *de l'utilité publique* – and if he wants to start up a *crèche*, a sports centre or a youth club, a Frenchman will not feel easy until it has been institutionalized under this law. As if to open a private *crèche* were an act of dangerous subversion. *Etatisme*, once again.

This spirit is now gently on the wane, in official minds and in private ones, as the new pragmatic values of technocracy gain ground. The lawyer, whose prestige in France used to be paramount, is losing position to the planner and technician; and it is significant that the Ecole Nationale d'Administration today puts the emphasis on economics rather than law, whereas the older generation of public executives received an essentially law-based training. But the *actual* texts and regulations that govern daily French life have not, except in a few cases, been altered, and this is a large part of the problem. If these were reformed, public reflexes would have some incentive to follow suit. Almost any transaction involves a maddening amount of paperwork, based on ancient regulations that have grown more complex, not less, with the accretion of the years. The lawyers grow fat on the work this brings them, and so tight is their closed shop that they are able to obstruct any moves that would reduce their profiteering; try buying a house in France, or starting a business, or getting divorced.

Even a simple matter like collecting expenses from the old ORTF for a TV assignment once drove me into one of those brief fits of violent francophobia which afflict every francophile. I was told that I could not have more than the regulation 132 francs Paris daily living allowance, yet I was booked in a hotel-room that cost almost that amount. When I protested, I was made to fill in several long forms with such details as my mother's maiden name and my father's place of birth, then I was obliged to stand in queues at cash-desks and go half across Paris to another office, and only when a tolerant official deftly fiddled the rigid rules for me was I able to collect the money at all. Peter Forster in the *Sunday Times* magazine (9 April 1967) has described a similar experience:

If you go to buy a consignment of wine at my local Co-op Vinicole in the Midi, you take your wicker bottle to the cellarman; the office girl fills in a form which you take across town to the tax-collector, who fills in another form, to establish such details as the number of your car, estimated time of arrival and departure, amount and price; then he snips it out with scissors; you sign, pay a few francs tax; go back to the Co-op, another form is filled in, you pay for the wine, you collect it. And by this time you need it.

Thousands of man-hours are wasted in France each hour on this kind of activity. The French have their own ways of cutting certain corners and circumventing some of the bureaucratic absurdities, and this is known as *le système D*. That is, everyone, even including officials, accepts that red tape can be tacitly ignored from time to time when no one is looking, especially when it is done between pals or after a friendly *verre*. An English friend of mine with a summer villa in the South of France applied for electricity to be installed: he was told this would take years of delay and form-filling, 'but,' added the village mayor with a shrug, 'there's some old wiring stacked in the vaults of the *mairie* and the local electrician might fix you up if you ask, but keep it quiet.' *Système D* brings human proportion into inhuman official procedures, and helps to make life workable. But it may not be the way to run a large nation's economy in a nuclear age.

The planners and technocrats are well aware of this problem, and would like to revise and simplify the official machinery. The Rueff-Armand report in 1960 proposed just this; and some improvements have since been made in the complex French system of indirect taxation. But as juridical changes tend to involve the consent of the lawyers and the Conseil d'Etat, they easily become tied down in wrangling and obstruction. In their attempts to simplify bureaucratic procedures the reformers are inhibited too, by the hostility of the *petits fonctionnaires* themselves. In a number of Ministries or public offices, bold technocratic initiative has foundered on the inability or refusal of junior staff to adapt to the changes. In a nation deeply addicted to habit, some of this is simply a failure of the older or duller ones to comprehend new routines. But it springs also from mistrust. In any office, every post or grade has its clearly defined duties and rights; and every individual fears that *he* will be the one to suffer from changes, and so he digs his heels in. Better the devil that you know.

This climate of mistrust extends also to French petty official-dom's relations with the public. A *petit fonctionnaire* will rarely give public honesty or good faith the benefit of the doubt; and a private individual will rarely believe that a public servant is on his side and trying to help him. The mask of anonymous authority stands between them, and only when, by rare effort or good luck, they make informal human contact are matters improved. A young Frenchman once told me with admiration of an incident at Dover on his first visit to Britain. He needed to make an urgent telephone-call to Paris, but had no small change and his train for London was about to leave. 'That's all right,' said the GPO operator, 'I'll put you straight through, and later, when you've got change, just put six shillings and threepence in any phone-box and press the button.' He told me: 'It would never happen in France.' Every visitor to France has had some experience, converse to this, of French official bloody-mindedness and refusal to help in difficulty if it means the smallest departure from routine: 'Ça! – ça ne me concerne pas,' they snap scornfully from behind their *guichet*. But what the tourist does not always realize is that this is not just the French being rude again. It arises from a vicious circle of impersonal authoritarianism which pervades all official life and of which the individual in a sense is prisoner. A *fonctionnaire*, as a private person, might be friendly and helpful if approached in the right way. The same spirit colours relations between public and police. Since the end of the Algerian crisis the police *have* grown rather less officious and brutal, and have even been making official-inspired efforts to improve their image with the public. But that image is still one of the least happy in Europe. Towards the ordinary public they are often all smiles and courtesy, especially outside Paris; but if there is any kind of riot or disturbance (as in May 1968), or if they are questioning a suspect, they can still turn very nasty. It derives partly from the Napoleonic conception of a suspect as guilty until proved inno-cent – the root of many French troubles.

The Rueff-Armand committee saw the damage caused by this

malaise of impersonality and mistrust between public and officials: not only was it unpleasant, it also led to wasteful conflicts that impeded efficiency and progress. Their report urged that public bodies should try to personalize their employees' relations with the public – for instance, by putting namecards on the desks and *guichets*, as in the United States. Since then a number of public offices have tried to follow this kind of path. Uniformed young *hôtesses* with quick smiles have begun to replace the old shuffling *huissiers*. Helped by this turnover of generations there certainly has been some improvement, mainly in the larger and more modern-minded offices; it has by no means yet spread everywhere, and I would not pretend that every post-office worker is as charming and obliging as the young heroine of *Le Bonheur*.

The real issue is the French concept of authority as something absolute, monarchic and anonymous, and this colours relations within organizations as much as it does those with the public. In almost any office or firm clearly defined areas of responsibility are laid down for the different grades, and the links between them are strictly formal. Michel Crozier suggests that one of the most characteristic of French traits is the fear of informal relations between subordinates and superiors; work routines and chains of command are therefore codified and formalized, in order to avoid favouritism and conflict. And so it becomes difficult for anyone in a junior position to act officially on his own initiative, for this means breaking the codes. Crozier points out that the desire to avoid awkward face-to-face confrontations is a common facet of French society, noticeable in all work relations. He thinks that this hierarchic pattern of bureaucracy may have served France well in the past, in order to ensure smoothness and to protect the individual, but that in a period like the present it can lead to waste and strain, making it difficult to introduce modern office methods or new directives, or to put young men of initiative where they are needed, at NCO or subaltern level. It is one reason why the bold technocratic zeal of post-war years has not always achieved its aims.

Is any new spirit of social trust and civic co-operation emerging in France? Again, one is struck by the contrast between the dynamic idealism of certain new élites and the reticence of the many – and it makes the question hard to answer. Certainly, some of the signs are positive: first, the decline in the ferocity of the old sectarian rivalries. Catholics and anti-clericals are no longer at each others' throats. Peasants are losing their suspicion of townsfolk. Poujadist opposition to big business has become less of a militant force in industry. Even working-class hatred of the bourgeoisie is being drained of some of its old bitterness as the workers steadily *s'embourgeoisent*. The disputes of local politics are today less doctrinaire than they used to be, and more concerned with practicalities; they may still be heated, but the sides are now more likely to find a common language. It is easier to convince your opponent of the wisdom of building a new road or factory than to change his views on God or Marx. The French seemed to have tired of ideologies after a succession of *débâcles* that showed up their futility – the ideals of the Right were eroded by the Second World War and Algeria, and those of the Left by the failures of the Fourth Republic. And in this context, though the old rival groupings are still largely in place, they have lost much of their power. It is true that intransigence has flared up again in a new guise since 1968, especially among younger people; this proves how deeply rooted in the French character this trait must be. But the new-style extremism is at least rather more forward-looking; it is for change rather than against it.

At the same time, élites and leaders of an entirely new kind have been emerging outside the framework of party politics. Unlike the old groups, they are essentially concerned with helping the community as a whole, rather than with defending this or that interest against the rest. And this is a striking change. The neo-Catholics provide many of the most noticeable of these new élites, but not the only ones. They include men and women of all shades of belief, working in industry, education, social service or public affairs. Many of them have been in State service, men like Lamour, or Pisani, or Jacques Delors who pioneered the *contrats du progrès*; or they are individuals like Leclerc or Dubedout; or leaders of the birth-control movement or animators of the Grands Ensembles; or pioneers of education or popular culture, like Marcel Bonvalet in Nancy or Jo Tréhard in

Caen. These are the heroes of my book, and I am not alone in thinking that on pioneers of this kind much of France's future depends. If a new civic spirit is emerging in France, this is it. For all the diversity of their specialized activities, they are working to help *everyone* to a better future, whether it is by developing the Languedoc, cutting retail prices, legalizing contraceptives, training scientists or bringing lively culture to a dull town.

But the men and women of these élites, though they number many thousands, are only a small minority in France; and they give the impression of fighting against great odds. Indeed, in some cases their work has suffered a setback through the polarization that has set in since May 1968. Several people remarked to me, in effect: 'Everywhere in France you find these little nuclei of dedicated people of *bonne volonté*. They are making progress, but why do they fail to have more impact? Why do they find it so hard to carry others with them?' Or as Peter Forster wrote in the *Sunday Times*: 'I often think France today is a land where a few people living in the twenty-first century are trying to pull the rest out of the nineteenth.'

In many an organization the dynamism seems to end abruptly below a certain level – and with it much of the civic idealism, for the two go hand in hand. For instance, when Pisani was Minister of Agriculture, I was struck by the brilliance of the young team on his personal staff (*cabinet*), and the gap between them and the bored bureaucrats at lower echelons who tended to mismanage or even to obstruct the Minister's new measures. In Britain, whether at official or unofficial level, one has the impression that the load of effort and initiative is more evenly shared; the pioneers are usually much less talented, ambitious and energetic than in France, but the gulf dividing them from the rest is smaller, too. And although, in industry in Britain, trade-union practices are probably a bigger obstacle to progress than any problem is in France, yet in civic affairs there is no doubt which country has the more developed sense of democracy.

Part of the explanation may be that French social and civic loyalties are today in a curious period of hiatus and possibly of transition. Family ties are weakening, and so are the old aggressive sectarian rivalries; and frequently the individual finds no new alternative focus for his loyalties, save that of a technocracy imposed from outside, which he may consider cold and arbitrary and which frequently does not consult his views. So, *le français moyen se replie sur lui-même*: hugging his new prosperity, he lurks behind the privacy of his new flat and new car, neither hurling brickbats at his neighbour nor joining forces with him, and warily waiting for someone else to meet the community's collective requirements. It is the drama of the Grands Ensembles. De Caumont in Caen, Dubedout in Grenoble, and others elsewhere, have found how hard it is to arouse civic interest on any scale. This is true, at least, in the towns. In the countryside, where the social revolution has been more dramatic, not only are resistances stronger (e.g. over *remembrement*, or *arrachement des vignes*) but a new spirit of co-operation is developing more widely too. And even on the Grands Ensembles we have seen signs of a thaw.

It may be unwise to be too sanguine, but I think that various economic and social trends now in progress are likely in the long term to favour the growth of a new sense of community. The inter-penetration of classes, the decline of ties of kinship and, above all, the shift to a less rigorous and probably more humane educational ethos – these movements will continue, and will have their influence. More and more firms will be forced, by sheer economic pressure, to adapt their hierarchic routines to new methods; more and more people will travel abroad, and will pick up the outlook of more easy-going societies. The influence and spirit of the new élites will continue to spread more widely, as it has been doing. The French may come to realize that their mistrust is a defence they do not need any more and co-operation a virtue they can no longer do without. This at least is a possibility. But there is also a danger, as Crozier has pointed out, that an old pattern may repeat itself, and that society, once it has absorbed dramatic change, will simply put up new protective barriers on different ground.

On the level of national rather than local affairs, the development of a keener sense of community and democracy will depend, clearly, on the political future of France. Under de Gaulle, there was the same kind of transitional hiatus as in local affairs, and even more obviously so: the old warring politics of the Fourth Republic gave way to a muzzled Gaullist calm. But behind the façade of Gaullist autocracy, a new spirit was at work; new alignments were taking place and new élites preparing for the future. They were exemplified by some of the new non-party politico-economic clubs and discussion groups that sprang up, of which the best known was the Club Jean Moulin. Named after the greatest hero of the Resistance, this club united an important number of senior civil servants, politicians, businessmen, trade-unionists, academics and others, who held study conferences on modern problems in a non-party spirit. Though the club's centre of gravity was mildly Leftish, de Gaulle did not prevent his own loyalists and civil servants from taking part. He is even said to have remarked: 'It's the best way I know of getting my *hauts fonctionnaires* to work overtime.' Thus the club helped informally to aliment the Gaullist administration with new ideas from outside, even from the opposition. But even before the May crisis, this club was running into typically French difficulties: the Socialists tried to take it over, and this led the Gaullists and the civil servants to walk out, so that the club lost much of its *raison d'être* and today has ceased to exist. Yet though this particular venture has failed, the interchange of ideas goes on, through the new contacts with the unions, and elsewhere.

Within these circles, and within the committees of the Plan and the higher ranks of the civil service, there is considerable free discussion and criticism. The Plan in particular has helped to build up a new kind of élite public opinion in France, with continual contact between technocrats and others in public and private service. But the essential difference from Britain is that this kind of discussion *is* confined to an informed élite in semi-private: there is not the same nation-wide forum of open public opinion. Though Gaullism intensified this, in a sense it has always been so and derives clearly enough from the nature of French society and ordinary French attitudes to authority.

People do not have the same sense of personal responsibility for public events as in Britain, or the same feeling that the pressure of grass-roots opinion *can* influence events. And therefore they often do not even try. For instance, there has been little public

CND-type campaigning in France, though hordes of people, especially young ones, object to the *force de frappe*. Social injustices – such as low old-age pensions, or bad housing, or police treatment of suspects – will evoke the odd article or formal protest, and not the kind of national outcry caused, say, by the *Cathy Come Home* film or the mildest of police excesses in Britain. Many people in France feel strongly about such things, but they also feel powerless; it is up to *les autres*, the authorities, to do something about it. Hence there is little public-inspired consumer protection on the lines of the Consumers' Association; the initiative for this has had to come from the Government. An exception to this pattern has been the progress made by the campaign for birth-control; but the process was slow, was essentially due to the work of a few pioneers, and manifestly had difficulty in rallying grass-roots public support, not through opposition so much as reticence. Another exception, in a sense, was the student outburst of 1968; but its violence and excess was in contrast to the way in which grievances are aired in Britain or some other countries.

Open public discussion is naturally more difficult in a country divided by the tensions of rival groups, where debate rapidly becomes conflict. Therefore the French prefer to conduct debate through communiqués and *prises de position* (formal statements of view by bodies or individuals) rather than by chatting things over in public. The loosening-up of society might be expected to have modified this pattern; but the Gaullist régime had if anything the opposite effect. The mediocrity of broadcasting, and the tameness of the provincial Press and weakness of the Paris Press, all aggravate the situation. But these are symptoms as much as causes of the relative lack of frank public discussion; a more truly democratic nation would not tolerate the kind of broadcasting system it has.

FRIENDLINESS, FORMALITIES AND FOREIGNERS

The French are not everyone's favourite people. And the British especially, whose own values and qualities are so different, often find it hard to like them. They have wit and *finesse*, and charm when they choose to display it. But, so it is alleged, they can also be rude, grasping, indifferent and cruel. The French do not even like themselves very much; they can be as beastly to each other as to foreigners. Many of their personal traits are bound up inevitably with the nature of their society, and if this society is now becoming a little more open and relaxed, does it mean that the French as individuals are becoming any nicer? First, a subjective reaction. They have become nicer to *me*, I find, largely because after more than twenty years of patient effort I have finally learned how to get along with them. With exceptions, I now find them stimulating, responsive and loyal. But it has not been easy. You have to learn to accept the French on *their* terms, which means speaking good French and overcoming that English awkwardness towards foreigners that is often taken for arrogance. You have to remember that at first encounter a stranger is very often prickly, until you take the trouble to chat him up and show him you are his friend. Personally, French brusqueness has ceased to irritate me; I find it in many ways more dignified than the indiscriminate bonhomie or obsequiousness of some races. A Frenchman is charming only when he really means to be, or as a way of showing that he likes you; in his personal dealings he is frequently less hypocritical than the English. Above all, I like the French because they present a challenge. I like their alertness, their quick, cynical humour, their refusal to suffer fools gladly, and their articulateness, which makes it possible to establish immediate intellectual contact with almost anyone. But any challenge demands effort, and sometimes the French wear me out and I sigh for more easy-going company. Especially among Parisians, I grow irked by their competitive restlessness, their lack of consideration, their relentless search for individual self-fulfilment, and often by their social formality.

If there is any generalization to be made about French niceness, it is that provincials have more of it than Parisians. So different are the two temperaments that it is usually necessary to specify this distinction; and today's complaints by foreign visitors about French rudeness and aggressiveness can mostly be found to refer in practice to Parisians, or to crypto-Parisians on the

Côte d'Azur. Paris has always been mercurial, anonymous, indifferent towards the weak or lonely, and today she has more than her share of modern big-city neurosis; the sheer physical problems of living there, and the *malaise* of past political crises and present cultural staleness, have all served to set Parisian tempers on edge. In the provinces, on the other hand, life goes at a speed the nerves can stand, and there is a new exciting feeling of living in a time of growth and renewal, which makes people more relaxed as well as more confident and cheerful.

It is Parisians who are the least inclined to be neighbourly or civic-minded. It is in Paris that motorists will most ruthlessly steal the parking-space you are just manoeuvring to back into, or will tersely refuse to move their own car two feet forward to give you room to park; it is in Paris that a man can collapse groaning in the street and no one will do more than look on curiously. In 1957 Françoise Sagan had an accident on a main road just south of Paris; she was trapped beneath her overturned car, and it was many minutes before her companion could get a passing motorist (most of them Parisians) to stop and help him lift it off. As a result she nearly died. So a day or two later a Paris paper staged a dramatic-looking 'accident' near the same spot. In fifty minutes, fifty cars passed without stopping, most of them with Paris number-plates; the fifty-first, who did stop, was a farmer from a nearby village. No one, to my knowledge, has tried a similar test in the provinces, but I doubt if the results would be so horrific. Of course, excuses can be made. Police procedures, as much as anything, inhibit samaritanism in France; if you help or bear witness in an accident, you are often held for hours for questioning and even treated as a suspect.

It is also fair to say that the Sagan incident was twenty years ago; and, since then, I think the climate has improved. Tensions have relaxed and morale has lifted, especially since the end of the Algerian crisis. Today people are a little more prepared to be civil and helpful to each other, even in Paris and notably in its new suburbs. In Massy I was even stopped twice within two minutes and asked if I wanted help in finding my way. And younger people, those under forty or so, are markedly more courteous and willing in France than the older ones, who sometimes still seem to be marked by the strains and humiliations of the preceding forty or so years. Worst of all are those middle-aged, middle-class Parisiennes who treat the world as their enemy. This is the opposite of the situation in Britain, where the very young are so often boorish and aggressive, and placid matrons are the readiest to help strangers with advice.

There has also been some relaxation of the social formality and ceremonial that has always been as much a feature of daily human contact as it is of the basic patterns of society. At its best, and on smart occasions, this formality can lend French social life an attractive elegance and subtlety, as in the great *salons* of the past. But ordinary daily life is not a smart occasion, and I can't help feeling that much of the time the formality induces strain and a kind of stiltedness, so that people are not making real contact with each other. It is these aspects of French civilization that I personally find the least attractive – the endless calling of each other by titles ('*Oui, Madame l'Inspectrice-Générale!*'), the insistence on etiquette, the long stylized endings to even the simplest of letters, the respect for a person's position and diplomas more than for what he is ('*Ah, Monsieur est polytechnicien!*'), and those grim social gatherings where everyone sits in starched clothes on uncomfortably elegant chairs. Though the French can be as outspoken and unconventional as anyone in the voicing of opinions and in conversation, they can also be oddly conventional about manners and behaving '*comme il faut*' and the need to '*sauver les apparences*'. A young American told *Le Nouvel Observateur*:

A French family once asked me to dinner. The hostess wanted to 'montrer ce qu'est la France'. She got out what remained of her wedding gifts, put the little plates in the big ones, three glasses in front of each plate. They called me 'Monsieur' and, helped by heavy reinforcements of silver and of *cuisine française*, they gave me a lesson in good manners. I'd have rather had three slices of salami and been called Pat.

A younger generation is now rapidly showing impatience with this approach and is setting less store by titles and decorum. Today there are fewer ceremonial banquets with speeches, and more informal home entertaining. Among the new *cadres*, especially in a town like Grenoble, a new American-style openness and casualness is emerging which can be traced also in the Club Méditerranée and some other new leisure and holiday habits. Among younger, modern-minded people the trend, just as in Britain, is towards casual clothes, casual décor and entertainments, and what the smart advertisements call *une élégance vraiment relax*. But though they try hard, the French don't always find it easy to be spontaneously relaxed; sometimes it makes them self-conscious and they lapse back guiltily into their more traditional guise of formality.

The use of christian names likewise is on the increase among younger people, though still far more restricted than in Britain or America, where the coinage has been debased virtually into meaninglessness. In France, *tu* provides an alternative step towards friendliness; and men will often call each other *tu* but stick to surnames even when they are quite close friends, and especially if they have been at school or in the Army together. *Tutoiement* has now become almost universal among students and teenagers, though elsewhere it is still largely restricted to family life and male camaraderie. And though a man is today much more likely than twenty years ago to know the wife of a friend or colleague by her christian name, to call her *tu* in public would still give quite the wrong impression. Women are usually much more formal than men, even with each other. I know two professional-class married couples aged about forty where the men are firm friends and use surnames and *tu* with each other, while the wives, though they know each other quite well, say *Madame* and *vous*.

Although the French will easily strike up conversation on acquaintance with strangers, they do not make real friends lightly, and most true friendships are formed in youth or only very slowly over the years among professional colleagues. Once made, friendships between men tend to be enduring and loyal; but the reserve against breaking the ice with new friends can often lead to a chilly atmosphere, especially in office life. This follows, inevitably, from rigid hierarchization of French working relations. Except at senior executive level, office colleagues seldom try to meet each other socially, and casual friendship is rare between staff of differing grades. Thus the social *ambiance* of the average French office is noticeably less bright and relaxed than in Britain or America, and this can make life lonelier for anyone who arrives to work in a new town, especially Paris, without existing friends. The most one can say is that this pattern is changing in a number of newer-style offices (those influenced by American methods or devoted to such things as PR or films) and among younger employees.

These slow mutations in the French social character are not easy to define or pin down; but a much more clear-cut change has been the decline in French insularity and old-style nationalism. This may sound an odd thing to say – it was not always the impression that France gave to the world in the 1960s, at least in her foreign policies. But de Gaulle was untypical. It is true that the French *are* mostly proud of what he achieved in the late 1950s and early 1960s to haul France back into the front rank of nations – how could they not be? And it is true that they shared, to a degree, his resentful jealousy of Americo-British dominance. But few of them approved the intransigence of his nationalism; and only a very few, older people or diehard Right-wingers, went along with his own particular definition of French glory and grandeur. The French may still be touchy about themselves, and prickly towards foreigners; but the old ideal of *la gloire française* today means almost nothing to them. The Algerian *débâcle* banished that dream for ever; and today the Army has crept away humbly on to the sidelines of national life, shorn of its old prestige. When the bugles sound and the flags wave on the *Quatorze Juillet*, the nation may still, out of old habit, stand to attention with a tear in its eye; but these rituals are losing their meaning. Older people perhaps will feel nostalgic, or bitter, but few still have any illusions; and the vast majority of the young are completely opposed to this form of nationalism, whatever they may still be taught in their schoolbooks.

Instead, there is a new and genuine feeling for Europe. Opinions may vary on how far European integration ought to go, and on whether or not the EEC is too capitalist; but hardly anyone, except a very few on the far Right or extreme Left, today challenges the basic idea of the European Community or the need for France and her neighbours to draw together. Even the Communists are no longer opposed to the principle of the EEC, though they would like to reform it. Young people especially are losing their old sense of frontiers, and many of them feel today towards Italians or Germans as forty years ago, say, a Burgundian felt towards a Provençal or a Norman – rivalry maybe, and strangeness, but also a sense of belonging to the same community. Among a few, the most dedicated 'Europeans', there is a kind of anti-nationalism, springing from self-disgust at past French failures – a desire to merge their Frenchness in a new wider identity. But the average Frenchman does not go as far as this; his Europeanism is based on the reasoned conviction, which has spread widely since the war, that France on her own is powerless and doomed, and the only way to preserve and extend French influence is to collaborate more closely with others.

This is different from the spirit in Britain, where I would say there is less *chauvinism* than in France today but a great deal more *insularity*. The French feel sharply competitive towards other countries, sometimes jealous of them, sometimes scornful, but at least vividly aware of their existence; the British still hardly notice them. In UNESCO for instance, or a number of other international activities, unofficial as well as governmental, the British tend not to be interested and the French tend to exploit the situation for the spreading of their own influence. International sporting or cultural events tend to be under-reported in the British Press; in the French Press they get fuller coverage, but with huge emphasis on the French role. All this marks a change from pre-war days when the French, too, were enclosed behind their frontiers, or at best regarded other countries as reflections of French civilization. Today the French are culturally on the defensive; they are aware that their culture has lost some of its old dominance and universality, and it makes them prickly, difficult, sometimes arrogant. But, in the world today, their competitive attitude may be healthier than the British one. A Frenchman may remain convinced of the virtues of his own way of life, but at least he regards, say, a Swede's or an Italian's as offering some comparison. A Frenchman may feel superior to other peoples, but not fundamentally *different*, so, when he wishes to, he can easily make contact with them.

French public interest in the rest of the world has increased hugely since the war, and a nation that rarely used to venture abroad is now a nation of travellers – not only as tourists, but as explorers, exporters, students, or technicians in backward countries. In the smallest country towns, lectures or film-shows on *l'Iran d'aujourd'hui* or *J'ai vu vivre les Brésiliens* will draw ready audiences. I think that the educated Frenchman today – a few intellectuals apart – has a more realistic conception of his country's position in the world than the Englishman has of Britain's role. For all their latent chauvinism, the French do seem to think of themselves in terms of a wider community, not as a special case, and in ordinary conversation on social or other problems will talk about 'We in the West' or 'We in Europe' where an Englishman would speak of 'Britain'.

There has also been a striking change, within the past five years, in French attitudes towards speaking other languages, notably English. Seeing that theirs was formerly the leading world language of diplomacy, culture and other exchanges, the French are naturally resentful at the way it has been overtaken by English, and at least until very recently French public servants were officially forbidden to speak in any other language at international meetings. But now the French have more or less decided, 'If you can't lick 'em, join 'em.' They recognize, regretfully, that in the interests of promoting their foreign trade and their position in the world, they have no choice but to use the world's leading language of today, as everyone else is doing. A turning-point came in May 1974, when Giscard on the night of his Presidential-election victory made a little speech for the foreign TV networks in his fluent English. Some French diehards were shocked, and de Gaulle must have turned in his grave. But it was official recognition of the fact that to speak English was now not merely allowed, it was encouraged. For several years now, foreign language classes have been compulsory in most schools and universities, and a majority of people choose English; at the same time, the introduction since 1971 of in-service training schemes into all factories and offices has brought many thousands of young executives and secretaries into the languages labs for crash courses. As a result, the average young educated Frenchman today speaks good English, as he would not have done ten years ago. I have no statistics, but the number of Frenchmen with fluent English must have at least doubled in the past five years. Often, of course, they will prefer to speak French when they can, especially on their own soil; but faced with a foreigner who can only mumble a few words of bad French, they will no longer pretend not to speak any English, as many once did.

Another great change is of course in French attitudes to Germany. Here the ferment began immediately after the war, in shocked reaction against the futility of three Franco-German tragedies in eighty years, and it was greatly encouraged by an even sharper change of mood on the German side. Today only among a proportion of older French people and French Jews is there much residue of the old hatreds. When German NATO troops began to be stationed in Lorraine and Champagne in the 1950s there was rarely any kind of incident; and today patriotic Nancy, despite its heritage of war memories, is happily twinned with Karlsrühe. Several hundred thousand young French and Germans visit each others' countries annually under the auspices of the Franco-German Youth Office. Of course it is among the new post-Hitler generation that the *rapprochement* goes furthest – and there are older Frenchmen who are worried that the French are once again being incautious and forgetting too easily the lessons of the past. But this can be argued either way. I would not say that the French today always *like* the Germans as individuals (they usually prefer the English), but they feel respect, a kind of involvement and understanding, and a desire to work along with the better elements in Germany to build a new future. A French Jew told me: 'You can't expect me to like the Germans, but, rationally, I'm in favour of the *rapprochement*. Germany and France are like man and wife: Germany raped her in 1940, but then did the honest thing and married her. It's an uneasy marriage, but it works.'

Relations with Germany are in many ways closer than with Britain, and I am not speaking merely of the economic links built up during twenty years of the EEC. The British may be preferred as individuals, but they remain a mystery. A girl *agrégée* in Normandy told me: 'The British have more *finesse* and humour than the Germans, but I don't feel I understand them in the same way. All those yachting types who come to Cherbourg where I live are so aloof, they make me uneasy. Though England is so near, I don't feel much urge to go there. Yet I often visit countries like Italy.' A young Parisian told me: '*L'Allemand est un con, mais un bon con. Les Anglais, ils sont trop différents de nous.*' There is thus an odd paradox about attitudes to Britain today. On the one hand there is a fantastic vogue for things English, especially among the young – dress, dances, pop music, slang, films, royalty. This anglo-mania is not entirely new. On a much narrower scale it has long existed among the upper classes, who have considered it *de bon ton* to import their Savile Row suits, whiskies and nursemaids from across the Channel, and to cultivate English *milords*. But even today when the craze is so much more widespread it remains curiously superficial; seldom does it relate to any deeper curiosity about what British society is really like, or how it has changed, or how it might be relevant to France. Some Socialists and liberals may still cherish a wistful admiration for British justice and democracy, but even this is now tempered by a growing contempt for the British over their economic plight, their new political and social difficulties, and their sharply waning influence in the world. French clichés and misconceived ideas about British life remain stronger than British ones about France. There is the Major Thompson rolled-umbrellas-fog-and-crumpets image, which persists, and there is the newer Beatles image, but between the two there is a void. And the French aren't really interested in filling the void. Britain is quaint and colourful but not 'real' to them in the way that Italy, China, America, Africa are real. Jean-Luc Godard said to me: 'British films aren't really *creative*; maybe it's because British life just isn't very interesting. A British worker seems less sympathetic than, say, an Italian worker, and I like London less than most big cities. The British are quite nice, but they're closed up, they're a special case. They've chosen to be that way.' It is a familiar French viewpoint. Britain is one of the countries with least appeal for the French at a serious level – largely, I think, because it *is* such a special case that even its best features have little validity as a model to be copied or rivalled. You can try to imitate German punctuality, or American cost-accounting, but not English self-mockery or a constitution that has nothing written down.

Yet there are other societies that fascinate the French as valid challenges to their own: the whole Communist world, Scandinavia, Israel, even Germany and Italy, and above all the United States. Here again there is a paradox. Though America's economic dominance is feared, her policies criticized (especially during the Vietnam war), and her naïve tourists and brash uncultured commercialism held in contempt, the French are blindly copying many of those aspects of America they affect to despise. They are mesmerized by American society as a pre-figuration of what they yearn to be and dread becoming. On the more frivolous level, the copycatting of gadgets and habits is not always very different from the cult of things English; but at the most serious level, planners and technocrats are aware that France has a great deal to learn from America, if only she can avoid copying the faults too. In short, the French want to wear American trousers but with a different colour, while British trousers simply don't fit.

Attitudes towards Russia and Eastern Europe evolved rapidly in the years before 1968, perhaps more so in France than in most Western countries. (And on this occasion, by '1968' I am referring to the great cataclysm of *August*, not the relatively minor French one in *May*.) De Gaulle took the lead in the West in *rapprochement* with the Soviet bloc; and most liberal Frenchmen responded quite gladly to his policy – up until the moment of the Prague tragedy – because of the new social and cultural opportunities it offered. The French have always felt affinities with a part of Europe traditionally under France's cultural influence (notably Poland and Rumania); and they readily began forming new contacts with the more civilized elements in the people's democracies. Frenchmen began to feel that Eastern Europe, like the Common Market, was part of the territory on their doorstep. A Parisian friend of mine thought nothing of motoring to Moscow for his summer holiday in 1966; student groups from such places as Wroclaw attended the Nancy drama festival as a matter of course; the Club Méditerranée hired a Russian ship for the first of its summer cruises; and *Salut les Copains* has regularly printed fan-letters from young Czechs or Hungarians, as if the unity of the European teenage world were beyond dispute. It goes without saying that, after 21 August 1968, the Russian crime in Czechoslovakia threw this whole policy of *rapprochement* into the same confusion for the French as for other Western peoples, and they are only now recovering from it.

As for attitudes to the *tiers monde*, it is worth noting that France spends nearly twice as much money as Britain on overseas aid (admittedly, not without strong Gaullist *arrière-pensées* of prestige). The policy has sometimes been sharply criticized by Right-wing isolationists, but is supported by most informed opinion; and I would say that individually the French are as ready as any Western people to play their part in giving help to developing countries. Many thousands of teachers and technicians are working abroad on official aid schemes, and usually there is no shortage of candidates for such posts. Many young people look on it with a sense of vocation.

Within France coloured immigrants are accounted for largely by 800,000 Algerian workers, 220,000 Moroccans, and 120,000 Tunisians, plus a mere 45,000 Negroes and Asians. Considering these numbers, which are greater than Britain's coloured population, it is remarkable that there is relatively so little tension. Recently there has been some trouble with immigrants in Marseille. But in general the Algerians come for shortish periods without their families, and do not even attempt to integrate, so they are not seen as a threat. Moreover, for all their habitual social mistrust and latent chauvinism, the French are not especially colour-conscious, less so than Anglo-Saxons. There are no official bars at all; a recent President of the Senate, Gaston de Monnerville, was a Negro from Martinique. And even at the height of the Algerian crisis, when there was widespread FLN terrorism in France, daily and personal relations between the French and the 400,000 Algerian immigrant workers remained largely free from unpleasantness. It would not be true to claim that today there is no colour bar at all; there are always a few landlords who prefer not to take North Africans, or social circles that will not readily accept them. But the problem, in so far as it exists, is essentially an economic one. The immigrants tend to herd together in unhealthy shanty towns, often rejecting better homes even when these are offered.

The French have always shown tolerance towards immigrant minorities, and there is a long and honourable tradition of granting political asylum to refugee groups. The strangers are usually left peacefully alone to lead their own lives; this is the reverse side of the coin of French indifference to neighbours. There are still some large White Russian, Polish and Spanish exile communities in France, mostly less closely integrated into their new homeland than similar groups in America or even in Britain. Newer foreign minorities have more recently come to join them, arriving not for political refuge but to find work. There are 570,000 Italians in France, over 700,000 Portuguese, and others, living and working beside the French with virtually no friction. If there *is* any discriminatory feeling, it is directed more towards the country's half-million Jews, who in the mass are not foreign but French! Anti-semitism in France has a long history – witness Dreyfus. A number of Frenchmen took advantage of the Occupation to carry out their own private pogroms; and more recently, Mendès-France's repeated post-war setbacks can be traced in part to anti-semitic bias against him. A recent IFOP survey found that 10 per cent of French were avowedly anti-semitic, and less than 25 per cent thought the Jews people 'like anyone else'. But then the Jews, being French, are not to be ignored in quite the same way as Algerians or Portuguese; rather they form one of the most assertive of France's rival group interests. I would not say that anti-semitism was at all flagrant in France, and probably it is no worse than in Britain; but it exists.

If there is any last stronghold today of old-style French insularity and disregard for other nations, it is to be found among the hard-core Left Bank intelligentsia. They were brought up in the belief that French culture alone is complete and universal, and many of them stick to this belief. Just as the Sorbonne pays little attention to non-French universities and degrees, so its professors, as Revel has noted, sometimes defer as long as possible the translation into French of key works of scholarship or the scrutiny of foreign philosophies. Even French novelists and critics, passionately absorbed in their own Parisian literary rivalries, tend to turn a blinkered and bored eye on foreign writing. Invite them in a group to a party with their foreign colleagues, and they will make a few polite noises, then relapse into their own chatter. Many of them can accept foreign culture only on French terms; and the modern authors they accept most fully are the few they have managed to transmute into a French cultural context, like Faulkner and Joyce. British and French insularities are in fact at cross-purposes. In Britain the intellectuals admire French traditional culture while the philistine upper classes are mildly anti-French; in France it is the reverse. There are plenty of exceptions to this pattern, but it is broadly true.

Today French culture has been losing its universality and self-sufficiency: it is a fortress buffeted from without and partly starved within, and it no longer represents the full measure of man within its own harmonious whole. Many intellectuals refuse to admit this. To do so would require the humility of starting to accept another culture's terms of reference, to recognize other values as equally valid. And so they simply strengthen the barricades and narrow their front. Others, a growing number, do admit change and try to adapt to it; but it hurts their pride. Almost against their will, Parisians find themselves applauding brilliant imported plays, paintings, books and opera. It adds to their prickly defensiveness and sometimes they take it out on the tourist, whom they suspect of patronizing them. And they are forced to ask themselves the biggest question of all: What is happening to the French genius? Is Frenchness itself on the wane?

A DECLINE OF FRENCHNESS?

Modernism wears similar trappings in any part of the Western world today, as nations grow closer together and lose some of their old idiosyncrasies. And whether or not you call this process 'Americanization', it means inevitably that much of the old picturesque Frenchness will disappear. In the old days the

French had berets and bidets and the English did not, the English had pubs and the French had *bistros*, the French had *l'amour* and the English had sport, or so it was supposed. Today it's no longer at all clear who has what, as nations copy each other fast and even the British convert to the decimal system. But this kind of change is superficial; nostalgically sad in a way, but not catastrophic. The real question to ask is whether a nation's essential genius will be lost in the process of unification. What is to be the future of this Gallic civilization that has shed its light over Europe for so many centuries? What of the real French virtues, will these be able to adapt and survive? – a flair for style and care for quality; the honouring of individual prowess, the ethos of individual fulfilment; lucidity of thought, a passion for ideas, a certain concept of liberty, of human proportion, of harmony amid diversity; the enrichment of the present through the past. Can these last?

France is passing through a more difficult period of transition than almost any other Western country, and this demands tolerance and patience from those who love her. Not all the present symptoms are happy ones, and they have been driving many francophiles to despair. The *Corriere della Sera*, for instance, wrote in a recent supplement on French affairs, 'France is no longer the world's mirror of freedom or democracy, nor of intelligence, art, good taste and literature.' One common lament was of course for the decline of freedom under de Gaulle – the growth of censorship and official puritanism, the various encroachments of the State, the apparent endorsement by the French people of an autocratic régime. But is worth remembering that France has passed through similar periods before, under the two Napoleons for example, and her genius survived. The French seem to find that they need these periodic bouts of authoritarian rule, and are sufficiently mature to be able to digest them. Gaullism can now be looked back on as no more than a phase, and today under Giscard there is already a more liberal and humanistic spirit in public affairs.

The *malaise* of *la culture* and *la pensée* however seems more sinister and more enduring. It has brought with it a kind of self-curtailment of freedom and a most un-French conformism of thought; the saddest aspect of the Parisian intellectual world today is its air of conventionality. Though little of this is due directly to State censorship, in a more general sense I think it *has* been influenced by the political climate. Benevolent autocracy is rarely the happiest background for the arts and ideas; it was the same under Bonaparte. The creative spirit is usually most vigorous either in times of oppression or austerity, or else in a secure age of freedom and wealth; and France today lies between the two.

But other causes of the cultural crisis lie deeper than Gaullism. This nation today is so absorbed in its exciting new economic revolution that its energies and aspirations are no longer so focused on the arts or literature as they were in harder or more static times. In theory, there should be enough talent available for both; there is no reason why, say, Lamour's dedication to the Languedoc development should preclude Sartre's writing a great novel. But civilization does not work like that. France's cultural staleness is part of the staleness of the West in this age of technology and mass media, but it appears especially severe in France in contrast to her past brilliance. It is an age that favours the disseminating of culture to new mass audiences, via theatre, TV and education (and this is happening in France, as elsewhere). But it does not so easily favour original creative power.

The French may therefore have to wait for their socio-economic mutation to move nearer completion before there can be a creative revival. They will also need, I think, to escape a little further from the weight of their own cultural tradition, which is at once their glory and their burden. They are living on cultural capital, and it is partly because the conventional notion of culture is still so strong in France that spontaneous creativity has grown stale. It makes the educated Frenchman a civilized and erudite person, but may make it harder for him to be original. The education system has remained static and conformist far too long in its curriculum and its methods; this, as much as anything, has led to the clouding of limpid creative thought among intellectuals. The current shake-up of education may, in the long run, help to bring in a new spirit. Other factors will also help: the revival of the provinces, the slow interpenetration of classes, the growth of foreign influences. I suspect that the Parisian cultural world will gradually become less of an intense, enclosed hothouse; some of its one-time style and brilliance may be sacrificed for ever, but it might eventually regain a sanity and fertility it has lost today.

Craftsmanship and good taste are aspects of French civilization that have been prized alongside the arts, and these too are under assault. This is true of *cuisine* and high fashion, as of certain prestige industries like porcelain. What will happen to the French tradition of quality, in a mass-consumer age? In certain specific fields standards are clearly being kept up, and I have confidence that some industries will continue to survive as enclaves, catering at high prices for specialized markets: a few good individual restaurants, the perfumes of Grasse and the tapestries of Aubusson, the great vintage wines, and the *haute couture* of a few Paris firms. But the issue is whether French taste and concern for quality can transplant themselves to the new mass-production world that will soon cover all but 1 per cent of the field. Twenty years ago Lüthy saw the ideal of craft perfection as a major obstacle to modern efficiency. Today this problem is righting itself, but an inverse one is taking its place. So far French factory-made consumer goods, like furniture and textiles, do not often show a very happy sense of style, though the car industry provides an exception. Style is still largely the preserve of individualism; when it comes to decorating a private villa, or renovating an old country *auberge*, or floodlighting a public building, French taste will assert itself splendidly, soaring above British taste. Yet they have not learned to apply the same flair to industrial design. It is one aspect of the French maladjustment to their hastily espoused modernism.

Another aspect of hasty, ill-digested modernism is the ubiquitous new portent of 'Americanization', one of today's great talking-points. In the 1950s Italy and Britain seemed much more Americanized than France, which appeared to be holding out. In the 1960s France overtook her neighbours. It is this glossy, restless, hedonistic new surface of French life, much of it American-inspired, that as much as anything differentiates the mood since the mid-1960s from the struggling, cautious, riven France of the 1950s. Many thinking Frenchmen are acutely aware of the problem, and hardly a month goes by without some newspaper article on the theme, 'Are we becoming Americans?' How has it happened that the French, although so chauvinistic and superior, have suddenly begun to acquire foreign habits so fast? Does it mean they have lost their own originality?

Many of the features of the American craze are banal in the extreme – the barbecues and drugstores, the pop stars with rock 'n' roll names, the vogue for American thrillers and Westerns. In the seaside resort of Royan, there is a mock Wild West town with a railroad train that is attacked twice weekly by mock Indians, and a sheriff who greets holiday-makers with 'Hi ya, pardners, *comment ça va*?' There is the weird new Anglo-American language, '*franglais*', that has invaded all the advertisements and is now battering at the gates of daily speech.* French purists are furious at these abuses of French. Their rage is understandable, but I think it is partly misplaced. The French language, like the whole French way of life, needs some renewal and invigoration; and if this is not to come in a civilized manner via an élite – as French culture and language were once exported to England and Russia – then it will have to come in this vulgarian way, and be properly assimilated later. Secondly, though the *franglais*, the cowboys and the barbecues may be fatuous and undignified, much of the more serious Americanization that is taking place seems to me positive and necessary. If a nation is to modernize, it cannot *help* copying the Americans to some extent; they got there first, and not to take advantage of this would mean a wasteful duplication of effort. Therefore I think that such ventures as the Libby's experiment in the Gard, the introduction of Trujillo's discount methods or of American cost-accounting, and even the new American-style student campuses and public-relations techniques, are all steps in the right direction.

The French at least are aware of how much is at stake, in face of the American challenge. Late in 1967 the owner of *l'Express*, Jean-Jacques Servan-Schreiber, published a notable book with just that title, *Le Défi Américain*, which sold more than 400,000 copies in its first three months – the highest sale ever recorded in France in that space of time! The author warned powerfully that the 'technological gap' between the United States and Europe

* See pp. 406–8.

was increasing, and that unless France and her European partners, including Britain, pooled their resources and federated immediately in order to compete, Europe would either become an outright American colony or would slip into the status of a 'backward' region like South America. It was not an *anti*-American book; in fact, Servan-Schreiber wrote with sympathetic admiration of American methods and dynamism. If anything, it was anti-Gaullist and laid the blame on Gaullist policy for Europe's failure of co-operation. The author thought that although France was making stronger efforts than any other nation to meet the American challenge, these efforts were vitiated because they were too national and self-centred. The point I wish to make is not whether Servan-Schreiber was right or wrong – and time has since shown that he exaggerated the menace – but that his particular topics should have yielded the number-one best-seller and should have become *the* French talking-point in the winter of 1967–8. The French are excitedly aware, far more than the sleepy British, of the real issues facing modern technological society. Like Servan-Schreiber they realize that the answer is to copy the best from America but to adapt it to French, and European, needs and traditions. From the computers down to Coca-Cola, the issue is the same.

For the moment there does seem to be too much blind copying, at least on the more superficial levels. But it should not lead us to overlook the fact that the French *are* making their own contributions to modernism as well. I am thinking not only of the serious economic achievements – the Plan for instance, where Jean Monnet was originally inspired by the challenge of American efficiency, but has built out of it something uniquely and characteristically French. I am thinking also of the flavour of ordinary modern life in France: inspired by America maybe, but with French dressing added. Just as Godard and Truffaut have borrowed the plots and conventions of cheap American gangster films and made of them something as artistically and unmistakably French as a canvas by Delacroix, so the new social institutions like the student campus, the smart housing estate or the drugstore are often less American than they appear on the surface. Take *le drug store*: the French have borrowed an American term, and an American formula of late-closing, multi-purpose *boutiques*, and have turned it into a new conception whose zippiness, half vulgar and half chic, owes much more to Paris than to any Main Street chemist's. Or take the film *Un Homme et une femme*: a hero who pilots cars for an American firm, a heroine who makes Wild West films, an ethos of glossy romance that seems perilously close to the new American-inspired ideals of affluence; yet the sensibility of the film, and its exhilarating elegance, are products made-in-France that neither Hollywood nor the British cinema could ever rival. In short the French, despite their imitativeness, despite their immature lack of certainty about the way modern life is going, still manage to bring to life certain qualities of their own that I can only call taste and sense of proportion. There is still relatively little of the public vulgarity and brash commercialism that are so evident in America and, increasingly, in Britain. I fear these may develop in France, and I think very frankly that their absence is allied to the extreme slowness of the social revolution. The price of a just democracy is often a certain measure of vulgarity.

I have referred to French sensibility and sense of proportion. One reason why they find adjustment to the onrush of modernity so traumatic is, I think, this imaginativeness. They, or at least the more thoughtful ones, are more aware than most peoples of the spiritual dangers involved, and it is a constant theme of their literature and films. While the British adapt steadily and phlegmatically to modern life, soberly concerned about practical moral issues and whether everyone is getting a fair deal, the French reaction is perhaps less mature but more sensitive. They are frenetic, dazzled, half unable to cope, and their anxieties are more personal and metaphysical, less social, than British ones. Talk to a serious-minded young Frenchman, someone like Godard, and he will tell you of his worry about the impact of advertising and publicity on the individual, about the dangers of alienation and the essential solitude of modern life. A horror of the new, mass-consumer world of noise, publicity gimmicks, and frustrated privacy has been the theme of several films, from Tati's *Playtime* to Etaix's *Tant qu'on aura la santé*. Georges Perec's *nouvelle, Les Choses,* aroused wide discussion for its portrait of an archetypal young modern Parisian couple adrift on a sea of meaningless material aspirations. The solitude of the individual, too, has been a constant preoccupation of modern French thinking from Sartre and Camus to the present. It recurs today in the *nouvelle vague* films, notably Godard's; in the work of le Clézio; in conversations with young people; even in pop songs like Hallyday's *Idole d'or* or Françoise Hardy contrasting her own loneliness with the comradeship of *Tous les garçons et les filles de mon âge.* This concern with solitude is more than cant culled from existentialism or Marxism, though undoubtedly Sartre and others have influenced this mood. It is the way that many of the French sincerely see life, in a land where the individual counts for more than the community, and where the decline of the old ties is leaving him with a sense of isolation and of vulnerability to the new forces of science and mass persuasion.

To be aware of these manifold problems is the first step towards solving them. But can the French succeed? Pierre Massé, when head of the Plan, told me that he thought the most crucial problem facing the French was how to borrow the good things from American civilization without the bad, and his own Fourth Plan warned France of the dangers of copying America's *civilisation des gadgets* too thoughtlessly. A young technocrat at Lacq once told me with horror of his meeting with one of America's foremost engineers: 'He knew everything about engineering, but he knew nothing else; he was the most uncultured and incurious man I've ever met.' The French, perhaps more than any other nation in Europe, bring a vast heritage of wisdom and taste and humanism to the difficult task of preserving the best of the past in order to marry it with the future. The greater the heritage, the more difficult that process, and inevitably some things will be lost.

A while ago, France seemed to be preparing to bury her talents in a napkin; to build a bulwark around her traditions and protect them *against* the future. That policy would have spelt decay, and it has now been averted; the French have opened their eyes to the future. They now know that France *must* modernize, or go the way of the Aztecs. If some of the things we hold most precious about France appear to be lost in the process, that is sad but inevitable. Some of them may be lost for ever, some may appear in a new guise. The present transformation in France – call it peaceful revolution, if you like – is causing changes on such a scale that it is not possible to tell what sort of a nation France will be when it is over, or whether she will have the same qualities we have known. The French genius, as we know it, is going into partial eclipse and may remain there for some time. I have faith it will finally reappear – as it has done, repeatedly, ever since Charlemagne.

BIBLIOGRAPHY

GENERAL

Jacques Delors: *Changer* (Stock, 1975)

J.-B. Duroselle, François Goguel, Stanley Hoffmann, Charles Kindleberger, Jesse Pitts, Laurence Wylie: *France: Change and Tradition* (Harvard University Press and Gollancz, 1963)

Janet Flanner: *Paris Journal, 1944–65* (Gollancz, 1966)

Herbert Lüthy: *The State of France* (Martin Secker & Warburg, 1955)

François Nourissier: *Les Français* (Rencontres, 1967)

J.-F. Revel: *En France* (Julliard, 1965)

Raymond Rudorff: *The Myth of France* (Hamish Hamilton, 1970)

Alfred Sauvy: *La Montée des jeunes* (Calmann-Lévy, 1960)

Anthony Sampson: *The New Europeans* (Hodder & Stoughton, 1968)

J.-J. Servan-Schreiber: *The American Challenge* (Hamish Hamilton, 1968; Penguin, 1969)

Pierre Viansson-Ponté: *Histoire de la République Gaullienne* (2 vols: Fayard, 1970–71)

Philip M. Williams and Martin Harrison: *Politics and Society in de Gaulle's Republic* (Longmans, 1971)

1985: la France face au choc du futur (produced by the Commissariat Général au Plan; Armand Colin, 1972)

MAY 1968 CRISIS

Raymond Aron: *La Révolution introuvable* (Fayard, 1968)

'Epistémon': *Ces Idées qui ont ébranlé la France* (Fayard, 1968)

Philippe Labro: *Ce n'est qu'un début* (Edition Spéciale, 1968)

Patrick Seale and Maureen McConville: *French Revolution 1968* (Heinemann and Penguin, 1968)

Alain Touraine: *Le Mouvement de Mai ou le communisme utopique* (Le Seuil, 1968)

ECONOMY AND INDUSTRY

François Bloch-Lainé: *Pour une Réforme de l'entreprise* (Editions du Seuil, 1963)

J.-J. Carré, P. Dubois, E. Malinvaud: *La Croissance française* (Le Seuil, 1972)

Gilles Guérithault: *Guide pratique de l'automobile* (Arthaud, annual)

Jacques Guyard: *Le Miracle français* (Editions du Seuil, 1965)

Jacques A. Kosciusko-Morizet: *La 'Mafia' polytechnicienne* (Seuil, 1973)

Jean-Claude Thoenig: *L'Ere des technocrates* (Editions d'Organisation, 1973)

French Planning: Some Lessons for Britain (PEP, 1963)

AGRICULTURE

Michel Debatisse: *La Révolution silencieuse* (Calmann-Lévy, 1963)

Michel Gervais, Claude Servolin, Jean Weil: *Une France sans paysans* (Editions du Seuil, 1965)

Serge Mallet: *Les Paysans contre le passé* (Editions du Seuil, 1962)

Henri Mendras: *Sociologie de la campagne française* (Presses Universitaires de France, 1965)

Henri Mendras: *La Fin des paysans* (SEDEIS, 1967)

François de Virieu: *La Fin d'une agriculture* (Calmann-Lévy, 1967)

Gordon Wright: *Rural Revolution in France* (Oxford University Press, 1964)

COMMERCE

Etienne Thil: *Combat pour la distribution* (Arthaud, 1964)

PROVINCES

Pierre Bonte: *Bonjour, Monsieur le Maire* (La Table Ronde, 1965)

Christian Beringuier, André Boudou, Guy Jalabert: *Toulouse – Midi Pyrénées* (Stock, 1972)

J.-F. Gravier: *Paris et le désert français en 1972* (Flammarion, 1972)

Olivier Guichard: *Aménager en France* (Laffont, 1965)

Jérôme Monod and P. de Castelbajac: *l'Aménagement du Territoire* (PUF, 1971)

Jérôme Monod: *Transformation d'un pays* (Fayard, 1974)

Michel Philipponneau: *Debout Bretagne!* (Presses Universitaires de Bretagne, 1970)

Philippe Saint Marc: *La Socialisation de la nature* (Stock, 1972)

Paul and Germain Veyret: *Grenoble et ses Alpes* (Arthaud, 1962)

PARIS

Alain Griotteray: *L'Etat contre Paris* (Hachette, 1962)
Peter Hall: *World Cities* (Weidenfeld & Nicolson, 1966)

HOUSING

Gilles Anouil: *Les Secrets du logement* (Editions Modernes, 1961)
Marc Bernard: *Sarcellopolis* (Flammarion, 1964)
Gilbert Mathieu: *Peut-on loger les français?* (Editions du Seuil, 1965)
Christiane Rochefort: *Les Petits Enfants du siècle* (Grasset, 1961)

SOCIETY

Michel Crozier: *The Bureaucratic Phenomenon* (Tavistock Press, 1964)
Michel Crozier: *La Société bloquée* (Le Seuil, 1970)
Pierre Daninos: *Snobissimo* (Hachette, 1964)
Simone de Beauvoir: *The Second Sex* (Cape, 1953)
Paul-Marie de la Gorce: *La France pauvre* (Grasset, 1965)
Joffre Dumazedier: *Vers une Civilisation du loisir?* (Editions du Seuil, 1962)
Etiemble: *Parlez-vouz franglais?* (Gallimard, 1964)
Ménie Grégoire: *Le Métier de femme* (Plon, 1965)
Serge Mallet: *La Nouvelle Classe ouvrière* (Editions du Seuil, 1963)
Edgar Morin: *Plodémet* (Allen Lane, The Penguin Press, 1971)
Georges Perec: *Les Choses* (Julliard, 1965)
Pierre Simon: *Le Contrôle des naissances* (Payot, 1967)
Laurence Wylie: *Village in the Vaucluse* (Harrap, 1961)

EDUCATION, YOUTH

W. D. Halls: *Society, Schools and Progress in France* (Pergamon, 1965)
Martin Mayer: *The Schools* (Bodley Head, 1962)
André Rouède: *Le Lycée impossible* (Editions du Seuil, 1967)
Françoise Sagan: *Bonjour Tristesse* (Julliard, 1956)
John Weightman: *The Sorbonne* (article in *Encounter*, June 1961)

INTELLECTUALS, LITERATURE, RELIGION

Roland Barthes: *Critique et vérité* (Editions du Seuil, 1966)
Maurice Cranston: *Jean-Paul Sartre* (article in *Encounter*, April 1962)
Michel Crozier: *La Révolution culturelle* (pamphlet, 1964)
Adrien Dansette: *Le Destin du Catholicisme Français* (Flammarion, 1965)

Michel de Saint-Pierre: *Les Nouveaux Prêtres* (La Table Ronde, 1964)

Michel Foucault: *Les Mots et les choses* (Gallimard, 1966)

Bruce Morrisette: *Les Romans de Robbe-Grillet* (Editions du Minuit, 1963)

Maurice Nadeau: *Le Roman français depuis la guerre* (Gallimard, 1963)

J.-F. Revel: *Pourquoi des philosophes?* (Julliard, 1957)

J.-F. Revel: *La Cabale des dévots* (Julliard, 1962)

Georges Suffert: *Les Intellectuels en chaise longue* (Plon, 1974)

John Weightman: *Alain Robbe-Grillet* (Article in *Encounter*, March 1962)

Réflexion chrétienne et monde moderne, 1945–65 (published by le Centre Catholique des Intellectuels Français, 1966)

ARTS

Roy Armes: *French Cinema since 1946* (2 vols., Zwemmer, 1966)

Jean Collet: *Jean-Luc Godard* (Seghers, 1963)

Penelope Houston: *The Contemporary Cinema* (Penguin, 1963)

Georges Sadoul: *Histoire du cinéma mondial* (Flammarion, 1959)

Situation du cinéma français (*Esprit*, June 1960)

I should like to acknowledge my debt to *Le Monde* and *Le Point* and their staff correspondents. Without the help of their regular coverage of French problems, I should have found this book difficult to write. I am indebted also to the Editor of *New Society* for permission to draw on an article I wrote in that paper, for my section on the Grand Corps (pp. 49–58).

INDEX

Principal page references are in **bold type**. Book, play and film titles are not indexed: see under name of author or director. Some general themes are indexed – e.g. 'decentralization' – but not where the location of the subject is evident from the Contents list on pages 7–9.